ᴖᴗrary+

Financial Accounting Theory

Second European Edition

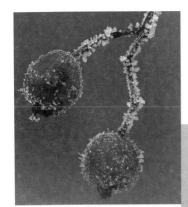

Second European
Edition

Financial
Accounting
Theory

Craig Deegan,
Jeffrey Unerman

The **McGraw·Hill** Companies

London Boston Burr Ridge, IL Dubuque, IA Madison, WI New York San Francisco
St. Louis Bangkok Bogotá Caracas Kuala Lumpur Lisbon Madrid Mexico City
Milan Montreal New Delhi Santiago Seoul Singapore Sydney Taipei Toronto

Financial Accounting Theory, Second European Edition
Craig Deegan and Jeffrey Unerman
ISBN-13 978-0-07-712673-5
ISBN-10 0-07-712673-4

Published by McGraw-Hill Education
Shoppenhangers Road
Maidenhead
Berkshire
SL6 2QL
Telephone: 44 (0) 1628 502 500
Fax: 44 (0) 1628 770 224
Website: www.mcgraw-hill.co.uk

British Library Cataloguing in Publication Data
A catalogue record for this book is available from the British Library

Library of Congress Cataloguing in Publication Data
The Library of Congress data for this book has been applied for from the Library of Congress

Acquisitions Editor: Leiah Batchelor
Development Editor: Karen Harlow
Production Editor: James Bishop
Marketing Manager: Alexis Thomas

Cover design by Adam Renvoize
Printed and bound in Great Britain by Bell and Bain Ltd, Glasgow
Page Layout: S R Nova Pvt Ltd., Bangalore, India

ISBN-13 978-0-07-712673-5
ISBN-10 0-07-712673-4

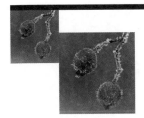

Dedication

My efforts are dedicated to my daughter and best friend Cassandra
Joy Deegan for all the love and support she gives.

– Craig Deegan

This book is dedicated to France Zappettini for his enduring support and inspiration.

– Jeffrey Unerman

Brief table of contents

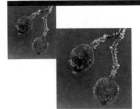

Detailed table of contents

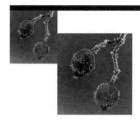

Preface

This book has been written to provide readers with a balanced discussion of different theories of financial accounting. Various theories for and against the regulation of financial accounting are critically discussed and a variety of theoretical perspectives, such as those provided by positive accounting theory, political economy theory, stakeholder theory, institutional theory and legitimacy theory, are introduced to explain different types of voluntary reporting decisions. The book also analyses and evaluates the development of several significant normative theories of accounting. These cover approaches that have been proposed to account for changing prices, including recent developments in the use of fair values, different perspectives about the accountability of business entities, and developments in various conceptual framework projects such as the current IASB/FASB conceptual framework project. The book also emphasizes the role of a number of factors in explaining both international differences in accounting and recent institutional efforts towards international harmonizing of accounting, including theoretically informed insights from the IASB/FASB convergence project.

In addition to providing explanations for why or how organizations should disclose particular items of financial information, the book investigates research that explores how or whether people at an aggregate and individual level demand or react to particular disclosures. Reflecting the growing relevance of social and environmental (or sustainability) reporting issues to students, government, industry and the accounting profession, sustainability accounting and reporting issues are discussed in depth. The book also provides insights into the role of financial accounting from the perspective of a group of researchers who are often described as working from a critical perspective.

Divided into 12 chapters sequenced in a logical order, this book can provide the entire core material required for a course on financial accounting theory. Alternatively, the book can be used as a key text for more general courses which include coverage of aspects of financial accounting theory. All of the material within the book could realistically be covered in the average 10- to 12-week university term or semester.

Because it offers a balanced perspective of alternative and sometimes conflicting theories of financial accounting and reporting, this book also provides a sound basis for readers contemplating further research in different areas of financial accounting. In writing this book, a style has been adopted that enables students at both the undergraduate and postgraduate level to gain a sound understanding of financial accounting theory. As each chapter incorporates research from throughout the world, the book is of relevance to financial accounting theory students internationally.

Much of the explanatory material has been drawn from European practical examples – thus making the text even more accessible and relevant to students in Europe. To assist in the learning process, each chapter provides learning objectives, chapter summaries and end-of-chapter discussion questions. Throughout the book readers are encouraged to critically evaluate and challenge the views presented. To give the various perspectives a 'real world' feel, many chapters use recent articles from different newspapers directly relating to the issues under consideration.

In the five years since the first European edition of this book was published, it has proved very popular among both students and lecturers throughout Europe and more widely. In addition to appreciating the academic coverage of the book, readers have praised the accessible and engaging style in which it is written. This new European edition retains the features of the earlier edition that students and lecturers found so appealing and distinctive, such as the use of straightforward explanations, frequent practical examples and illustrations using newspaper articles. However these have now been updated in this new edition to reflect the sometimes significant developments in accounting theory in the past five years. With many illustrations drawn from European business and accounting situations, we believe this European edition will continue to be just as appealing, accessible and relevant to readers as the previous edition.

Craig Deegan and Jeffrey Unerman
February 2011

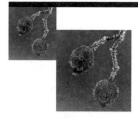

Guided tour

Learning objectives

Each chapter opens with a set of learning objectives, summarizing what knowledge, skills or understanding students should acquire from each chapter.

Opening issues

This section introduces the chapter by providing a topical debate issue for students to consider while they progress through the chapter.

Accounting Headlines

To give various perspectives covered a 'real-world' feel, many chapters include topical articles from a variety of newspapers, directly relating to issues under consideration.

Chapter summary

This briefly reviews and reinforces the main topics students will have covered in each chapter to ensure they have acquired a solid understanding of the key topics.

Questions

This end-of-chapter feature is the perfect way to practise the techniques students have been taught and apply the methodology to real-world situations.

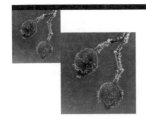

Technology to enhance learning and teaching

*Visit **www.mcgraw-hill.co.uk/textbooks/deegan** today*

Online Learning Centre (OLC)

After completing each chapter, log on to the supporting Online Learning Centre website. Take advantage of the study tools offered to reinforce the material you have read in the text, and to develop your knowledge of financial accounting in a fun and effective way.

Resources for students include:

- Weblinks
- Multiple choice questions
- Short answer questions

Also available for lecturers:

- PowerPoint Slides
- Tutorial Exercises
- Solutions Manual
- Essay questions

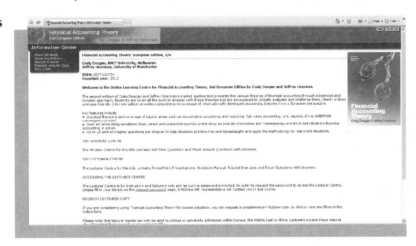

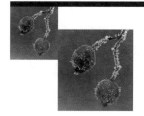

Custom Publishing Solutions: Let us help make our content your solution

At McGraw-Hill Education our aim is to help lecturers to find the most suitable content for their needs delivered to their students in the most appropriate way. Our **custom publishing solutions** offer the ideal combination of content delivered in the way which best suits lecturer and students.

Our custom publishing programme offers lecturers the opportunity to select just the chapters or sections of material they wish to deliver to their students from a database called CREATE™ at **www.mcgrawhillcreate.com**

CREATE™ contains over two million pages of content from:

- Textbooks
- Professional books
- Case books - Harvard Articles, Insead, Ivey, Darden, Thunderbird and BusinessWeek
- Taking Sides - debate materials

across the following imprints:

- McGraw-Hill Education
- Open University Press
- Harvard Business Publishing
- US and European material

There is also the option to include additional material authored by lecturers in the custom product – this does not necessarily have to be in English.

We will take care of everything from start to finish in the process of developing and delivering a custom product to ensure that lecturers and students receive exactly the material needed in the most suitable way.

With a Custom Publishing Solution, students enjoy the best selection of material deemed to be the most suitable for learning everything they need for their courses – something of real value to support their learning. Teachers are able to use exactly the material they want, in the way they want, to support their teaching on the course.

Please contact your local McGraw-Hill representative with any questions or alternatively contact Warren Eels **e:** warren_eels@mcgraw-hill.com.

Make the grade

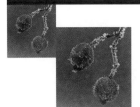

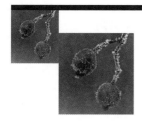

Acknowledgements

Authors' Acknowledgements

Many people must be thanked for helping us write this book. Professor Rob Gray from the University of St. Andrews is to be thanked for very useful and insightful advice provided in the initial development of earlier editions of this book and, through his Centre for Social and Environmental Accounting Research, for generously providing a great deal of useful research material. We also thank Professor David Owen from the University of Nottingham for his incisive advice and encouragement throughout the writing of both editions of this book. Dr Julie Cotter from the University of Southern Queensland is also to be thanked for her views about how the book should be structured and for her assistance in the writing of Chapter 10. In relation to development of the original Australian edition, we also thank Professor Reg Mathews (Charles Sturt University), Brian Millanta (Macquarie University), Colin Dolley (Edith Cowan University), Dean Ardern (La Trobe University) and Natalie Gallery (University of Sydney), for providing critical comments in relation to a number of the chapters, and Tanya Ziebell (University of Queensland) for unearthing some difficult-to-find research papers.

In developing this European edition, we are very grateful for the helpful, perceptive and constructive comments – and for their strong encouragement – provided by Professor Brendan O'Dwyer (University of Amsterdam), Professor Richard Laughlin (King's College, University of London), Professor Brendan McSweeney (Royal Holloway, University of London), Dr Alan Murray (University of York), Professor Christopher Napier (Royal Holloway, University of London) and, as noted above, Professor David Owen (University of Nottingham).We are also especially grateful to our colleagues at Manchester Business School and RMIT for their ongoing support. Lastly, we thank the staff at McGraw-Hill for supporting this project. Particular thanks go to Mark Kavanagh, Leiah Batchelor, Tom Hill, James Bishop, Alexis Thomas and Karen Harlow in the UK and to Luisa Cecotti and Valerie Reed in Australia.

We hope readers continue to find this European edition interesting, informative and enjoyable to read, and we welcome constructive feedback.

Publisher's Acknowledgements

Our thanks go to the following reviewers for their comments at various stages in the text's development:

Carolyn Isaac, Nottingham Trent University
Teye Marra, University of Groningen
Alan Murray, University of York
Dr Othata, University of Botswana
Javed Siddiqui, University of Manchester

Chris Soan, Newcastle University
Trina Small, Dublin City University
Mahbub Zaman, University of Manchester

We would also like to extend our thanks to Firoozeh Ghaffari (University of Middlesex) and Prajakta Desai for their contribution to the supporting web resources which accompany the textbook.

Every effort has been made to trace and acknowledge ownership of copyright and to clear permission for material reproduced in this book. The publishers will be pleased to make suitable arrangements to clear permission with any copyright holders whom it has not been possible to contact.

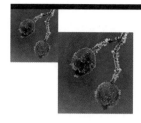

About the Authors

Craig Deegan

Craig Deegan BCom (University of NSW), MCom (Hons) (University of NSW), PhD (University of Queensland) is Professor of Accounting within the School of Accounting at RMIT University, Melbourne, Australia. Craig has taught at both undergraduate and postgraduate levels at universities in Australia for more than two decades and has presented lectures internationally, including within the United Kingdom, United States, South Africa, France, China, Singapore, Hong Kong, Malaysia, South Korea, Taiwan and New Zealand. Prior to working within the university sector Craig worked as a chartered accountant in practice. He is a Fellow of the Institute of Chartered Accountants in Australia.

Craig's research has tended to focus on various social and environmental accountability and financial accounting issues and has been published in a number of leading international accounting journals, including: *Accounting, Organizations and Society*; *Accounting and Business Research*; *Accounting, Auditing and Accountability Journal*; *British Accounting Review* and *The International Journal of Accounting*. He is on the editorial board of a number of leading international journals and is a long-standing member of the judging committee of the ACCA Australia and New Zealand Sustainability Reporting Awards.

Jeffrey Unerman

Jeffrey Unerman BA (CNAA), MSc (London), PhD (Sheffield), ACA, FCCA, FCPA, FHEA is Professor of Accounting and Accountability at Manchester Business School, University of Manchester. He has extensive teaching experience at both undergraduate and postgraduate level and has also presented lectures and key note addresses in many countries. Before joining the academic sector, he qualified as a chartered accountant (he is currently a member of both the Institute of Chartered Accountants in England and Wales [ICAEW] and the Association of Chartered Certified Accountants [ACCA], and is an honorary member of CPA Australia) and worked both in practice and commerce.

His research, which has been published in a range of books and international academic journals – including *Accounting, Organizations and Society*; *Accounting, Auditing and Accountability Journal*; *Critical Perspectives on Accounting*; *Accounting and Business Research*; *The European Accounting Review*; *British Accounting Review* and *Accounting Forum* – has focused on issues of accountability both for social and environmental performance and for the management of intellectual capital. He serves on the editorial boards of a number of journals, is an associate editor of *Accounting, Auditing and Accountability Journal* and is joint editor of *Social and Environmental Accountability Journal*. He is also Vice-Chair of the British Accounting and Finance Association and a member of the ACCA Research Committee.

01

Introduction to Financial Accounting Theory

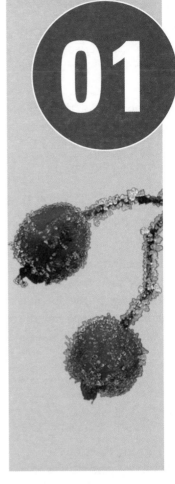

Upon completing this chapter readers should:

- ❖ understand that there are many theories of financial accounting;
- ❖ appreciate how knowledge of different accounting theories increases our ability to understand and evaluate various alternative financial accounting practices;
- ❖ understand that the different theories of financial accounting are often developed to perform different functions, such as to describe accounting practice or to prescribe particular accounting practices;

- ❖ understand that theories, including theories of accounting, are developed as a result of applying various value judgements and that acceptance of one theory, in preference to others, will in part be tied to one's own value judgements;
- ❖ be aware that we should critically evaluate theories (in terms of such things as the underlying logic, assumptions made, and evidence produced) before accepting them;
- ❖ understand why students of accounting should study accounting theories as part of their broader accounting education.

Opening issues

At the beginning of each chapter in this book a number of issues or problems are raised that relate to the material covered. On completion of the chapter you should be able to supply answers to these problems. In this introductory chapter, some of the issues that we can initially consider are as follows:

1 Why do students of financial accounting need to bother with the study of 'theories'? Why not just study some more of the numerous accounting standards (and there are certainly plenty of them!) or other pronouncements of the accounting profession?

2 Why would (or perhaps 'should') accounting practitioners and accounting regulators consider various theories of accounting?

3 Do all 'theories of accounting' seek to fulfil the same role, and if there are alternative theories to explain or guide particular practice, how does somebody select one theory in preference to another?

No specific answers are provided for each chapter's opening issues. Rather, as a result of reading the respective chapters, readers should be able to provide their own answers to the particular issues. You might like to consider providing an answer to the opening issues before reading the material provided in the chapters, and then, on completing the chapter, revisit the opening issues and see whether you might change your opinions as a result of being exposed to particular points of view.

1.1 What is a theory?

In this book we consider various theories of financial accounting. Perhaps, therefore, we should start by considering what we mean by a 'theory'. There are various perspectives of what constitutes a theory. The *Oxford English Dictionary* provides various definitions, including:

> A scheme or system of ideas or statements held as an explanation or account of a group of facts or phenomena; a hypothesis that has been confirmed or established by observation or experiment, and is propounded or accepted as accounting for the known facts; a statement of what are held to be the general laws, principles, or causes of something known or observed.

The accounting researcher Hendriksen (1970, p. 1) defines a theory as:

> A coherent set of hypothetical, conceptual and pragmatic principles forming the general framework of reference for a field of inquiry.

The definition provided by Hendriksen is very similar to the US Financial Accounting Standards Board's definition of their Conceptual Framework Project (which in itself is deemed to be a *normative* theory of accounting), which is defined as:

> A coherent system of interrelated objectives and fundamentals that can lead to consistent standards. (FASB, 1976)

The use of the word 'coherent' in two of the above three definitions of theory is interesting and reflects a view that the components of a theory (perhaps including assumptions about human behaviour) should logically combine together to provide explanation or guidance in respect of certain phenomena.

The definitions are consistent with a perspective that theories are not *ad hoc* in nature and should be based on logical (systematic and coherent) reasoning. Therefore, when we talk about a 'theory' we are talking about much more than simply an idea or a 'hunch', which we acknowledge is different to how the term 'theory' is used in some contexts (for instance, we often hear people say they have a 'theory' about why something might have occurred when they really mean they have a 'hunch').

As we will see in this book, some accounting theories are developed on the basis of past observations (empirically based), of which some are further developed to make predictions about likely occurrences (and sometimes also to provide explanations of why the events occur). That is, particular theories may be generated and subsequently supported by undertaking numerous observations of the actual phenomena in question. Such empirically based theories are said to be based on inductive reasoning and are often labelled 'scientific' as, like many theories in the 'sciences', they are based on observation. Alternatively, other accounting theories which we also consider in this book do not seek to provide explanations or predictions of particular phenomena but, rather, *prescribe* what *should* be done (as opposed to describing or predicting what *is* done) in particular circumstances.

Llewelyn (2003) points out that the term 'theory' in accounting not only applies to 'grand theories' which seek to tell us about broad generalizable issues (like the theory of gravity in physics), but also applies to any framework which helps us make sense of aspects of the (social) world in which we live, and which helps provide a structure to understand our (social) experiences. We stress that different theories of accounting often have different objectives. Llewelyn provides some interesting views about what constitutes theory. She states (2003, p. 665) that:

> Theories impose cohesion and stability (Czarniawska, 1997, p. 71). So that whenever 'life' is ambiguous (which is most of the time!) people will work at confronting this ambiguity through 'theorizing'. Also, because 'life' and situations commonly have multiple meanings and give rise to different assessments of significance, everyone has a need for 'theory' to go about their everyday affairs. 'Theories' do not just reside in libraries, waiting for academics to 'dust them down'; they are used whenever people address ambiguity, contradiction or paradox so that they can decide what to do (and think) next. Theories generate expectations about the world.

Because accounting is a human activity (you cannot have 'accounting' without accountants), theories of financial accounting (and there are many) will consider such things as people's behaviour and/or people's needs as regards financial accounting information, or the reasons why people within organizations might elect to supply particular information to particular stakeholder groups. For example, in this book we will consider, among others, theories which:

- *prescribe* how, based upon a particular perspective of the role of accounting, assets *should* be valued for external reporting purposes (we consider such prescriptive or normative theories in Chapters 5 and 6);
- *predict* that managers paid bonuses on the basis of measures such as profits will seek to adopt those accounting methods that lead to an increase in reported profits (we consider such descriptive or positive theories in Chapter 7);

- seek to *explain* how an individual's cultural background will impact on the types of accounting information that the individual seeks to provide to people outside the organization (we consider such a theory in Chapter 4);
- *prescribe* the accounting information that should be provided to particular classes of stakeholders on the basis of their perceived information needs (such theories are often referred to as decision usefulness theories, and we discuss them in Chapter 5);
- *predict* that the relative power of a particular stakeholder group (with 'power' often being defined in terms of the group's control over scarce resources) will determine whether that group receives the accounting information it desires (which derives from a branch of stakeholder theory, which is discussed in Chapter 8);
- *predict* that organizations seek to be perceived by the community as *legitimate* and that accounting information can be used as a means of gaining, maintaining or regaining the legitimacy of the organization (which derives from legitimacy theory, considered in Chapter 8).

1.2 Why it is important for accounting students to study accounting theory

As a student of financial accounting you will be required to learn how to construct and read financial statements prepared in conformity with various accounting standards and other professional and statutory requirements. In your working life (whether or not you choose to specialize in accounting) you could be involved in such activities as analysing financial statements for the purposes of making particular decisions, compiling financial statements for others to read, or generating accounting guidance or rules for others to follow. The better you understand the accounting practices underlying these various activities, the more effective you are likely to be in performing these activities – and therefore the better equipped you are likely to be to succeed in your chosen career.

Given that accounting theories aim to provide a coherent and systematic framework for investigating, understanding and/or developing various accounting practices, the evaluation of individual accounting practices is likely to be much more effective where the person evaluating these practices has a thorough grasp of accounting theory. Although we believe that all students of accounting (like students in any subject) should always have been interested in critically evaluating the phenomena they have studied, we recognize that, in the past, many students have been content with simply learning how to apply various accounting practices without questioning the basis of these practices.

However, in the wake of the sub-prime banking crisis of 2007 to 2009, where it has been claimed by many that the financial accounts of several financial institutions did not adequately communicate information about underlying financial assets, liabilities and risks, it has arguably never been more important for accountants to understand thoroughly and be able to critique the accounting practices which they use. These criticisms of the role of accounting in the sub-prime crisis (an issue we will return to when we discuss pressures for accounting regulation in Chapter 2 and fair value accounting in Chapter 5) followed a number of high-profile accounting failures (such as Enron and WorldCom in the USA, Ahold in the Netherlands, Parmalat in Italy, Shell in the Netherlands and the UK, and Addeco in Switzerland), that also pointed to the need for a thorough, theoretically informed understanding of accounting practices. Without such a theoretically informed understanding, it is difficult to evaluate the suitability of current accounting practices, to develop improved accounting practices where current practices are unsuitable for changed business situations, and to defend the reputation of accounting where accounting practices are wrongly blamed for causing companies to fail. This is a key reason why it is important for you to study and understand accounting theories.

As a result of studying various theories of financial accounting in this book, you will be exposed to various issues including:

- how the various elements of accounting should be measured;
- what motivates managers to provide certain types of accounting information;
- what motivates managers to select particular accounting methods in preference to others;
- what motivates individuals to support and perhaps lobby regulators for some accounting methods in preference to others;
- what the implications for particular types of organizations and their stakeholders are if one method of accounting is chosen or mandated in preference to other methods;
- how and why the capital markets react to particular accounting information;
- whether there is a 'true measure' of income.

Accounting plays a very important and pervasive role within society. Simply to learn the various rules of financial accounting (as embodied within accounting standards, conceptual frameworks and the like) without considering the implications that accounting information can have would seem illogical and, following alleged accounting failures in the sub-prime banking crisis and previously at Enron and other organizations, potentially dangerous.

Many significant decisions are made on the basis of information that accountants provide (or, in some circumstances, elect not to provide), so accountants are often regarded as being very powerful and influential people. The information generated by accountants enables others to make important decisions. For example: should they support the organization? Is the organization earning sufficient 'profits'? Is it earning excessive 'profits'? Is the organization fulfilling its social responsibilities by investing in community support programmes and recycling initiatives and if so, how much? In considering profits, is profitability a valid measure of organizational success? Further, if the accountant/ accounting profession emphasizes particular attributes of organizational performance (for example, profitability) does this in turn impact on what society perceives as being the legitimate goals of business?[1] As a result of considering various theories of financial accounting, we provide some answers to the above important issues.

At a broader level, an understanding of accounting theories can be crucial to the reputation and future of the accounting profession. Unerman and O'Dwyer (2004) have argued that a rise in high-profile accounting failures raised the level of awareness among

---

[1] In Chapters 2 and 3 we consider some research (for example, Hines, 1988) which suggests that accountants and accounting do not necessarily provide an unbiased account of reality, but rather, create reality. If the accounting profession emphasizes a measure (such as profitability) as being a measure of success and legitimacy then, in turn, profitable companies will be considered successful and legitimate. If something other than profitability had been supported as a valid measure, then this may not have been the case.

non-accountants of some of the significant impacts that accounting has on their lives. These events also may have led to a substantial reduction in the level of trust which many non-accountants place in financial accounts and in accountants. If we are to rebuild this trust, and the reputation of accountants, it is now more crucial than ever that we develop the capacity to critically evaluate accounting practices and to refine these practices as the business environment rapidly changes. The insights from a varied range of accounting theories are essential to this process of continual improvement in financial accounting practices.

1.3 A brief overview of theories of accounting

There are many theories of financial accounting. That is, there is no universally accepted theory of financial accounting, or indeed, any universally agreed perspective of how accounting theories should be developed. In part this is because different researchers have different perspectives of the role of accounting theory and/or what the central objective, role and scope of financial accounting should be. For example, some researchers believe that the principal role of accounting theory should be to *explain* and *predict* particular accounting-related phenomena, such as to explain why some accountants adopt one particular accounting method while others elect to adopt an alternative approach. Meanwhile, other researchers believe that the role of accounting theory is to *prescribe* (as opposed to *describe*) particular approaches to accounting, for example, based on a particular perspective of the role of accounting, there is a theory that prescribes that assets *should* be valued on the basis of market values rather than historical costs.

Inductive accounting theories

Early development of accounting theory relied on the process of induction, that is, the development of ideas or theories through observation. According to Chalmers (1982, p. 4) the general conditions which would ideally exist before theory can be developed through observation are:

- the number of observations forming the basis of a generalization must be large;
- the observations must be repeated under a wide variety of conditions;
- no accepted observation should conflict with the derived universal law.

From approximately the 1920s to the 1960s, theories of accounting were predominantly developed on the basis of observation of what accountants actually did in practice. That is, they were developed by the process referred to as 'induction'. This can be contrasted with a process wherein theories are developed by deductive reasoning, which is based more upon the use of logic rather than observation.[2]

---

[2] In Chapter 5 we will consider various theories of accounting that were developed to deal with problems that arise in times of rising prices – for example, when there is inflation. Such theories include one developed by a famous accounting researcher named Raymond Chambers. His theory of accounting, known as continuously contemporary accounting, was developed based on a number of logical assumptions about what types of information the readers of financial accounting reports needed. His theory was not based on observing what accountants do (which would be inductive reasoning) – rather, his theory was based on what he thought they *should* do, and utilizing various key assumptions about people's information needs, he derived his theory through deductive (logical) reasoning. His proposals for accounting represented radical departures from what accountants were actually doing in practice.

Returning to the use of observation to develop generalizable theories (inductive reasoning), after observing what accountants did in practice, common practices were then codified in the form of doctrines or conventions of accounting (for example, the doctrine of conservatism). Notable theorists at this time included Canning (1929), Hatfield (1927), Paton (1922) and Paton and Littleton (1940). Henderson *et al.* (2004, p. 54) describe the approaches adopted by these theorists as follows:

> Careful observation of accounting practice revealed patterns of consistent behaviour. For example, it could be observed that accountants tended to be very prudent in measuring both revenues and expenses. Where judgement was necessary it was observed that accountants usually underestimated revenues and overstated expenses. The result was a conservative measure of profit. Similarly, it could be observed that accountants behaved as if the value of money, which was the unit of account, remained constant. These observations of accounting practice led to the formulation of a number of hypotheses such as 'that where judgement is needed, a conservative procedure is adopted' and 'that it is assumed that the value of money remains constant'. These hypotheses were confirmed by many observations of the behaviour of accountants.

While there was a general shift towards prescriptive research in the 1960s, some research of an inductive nature still occurs. Research based on the inductive approach (that is, research based on observing particular phenomena) has been subject to many criticisms. For example, Gray *et al.* (1987, p. 66) state:

> Studying extant practice is a study of 'what is' and, by definition does not study 'what is not' or 'what should be'. It therefore concentrates on the status quo, is reactionary in attitude, and cannot provide a basis upon which current practice may be evaluated or from which future improvements may be deduced.

In generating theories of accounting based upon what accountants actually do, it is assumed (often implicitly) that what is done by the majority of accountants is the most appropriate practice. In adopting such a perspective there is, in a sense, a perspective of *accounting Darwinism* – a view that accounting practice has evolved, and the fittest, or perhaps 'best', practices have survived. Prescriptions or advice are provided to others on the basis of what most accountants do – the 'logic' being that the majority of accountants must be doing the most appropriate thing. What do you think of the logic of such an argument?

As a specific example of this inductive approach to theory development we can consider the work of Grady (1965). His research was commissioned by the American Institute of Certified Public Accountants (AICPA) and was undertaken at a time when there was a great deal of prescriptive (as opposed to descriptive) research being undertaken. Interestingly, in 1961 and 1962 the Accounting Research Division of the AICPA had already commissioned prescriptive studies by Moonitz (1961) and Sprouse and Moonitz (1962) which proposed that accounting measurement systems be changed from historical cost to a system based on current values. However, before the release of these research works, the AICPA released a statement saying that 'while these studies are a valuable contribution to accounting principles, they are too radically different from generally accepted principles for acceptance at this time' (Statement by the Accounting Principles Board, AICPA, April 1962).

History shows that rarely have regulatory bodies accepted suggestions (or, as some people call them, prescriptions) for significant changes to accounting practice. This is an interesting issue considered more fully in Chapter 6 when we discuss conceptual framework projects. However, it is useful to consider at this point a statement made in the United States by Miller and Redding (1986, p. 64):

> The mere discovery of a problem is not sufficient to assure that the FASB will undertake its solution … There must be a suitably high likelihood that the Board can resolve the issues in a manner that will be acceptable to the constituency – without some prior sense of the likelihood that the Board members will be able to reach a consensus, it is generally not advisable to undertake a formal project.

Grady's (1965) work formed the basis of APB Statement No. 4, 'Basic Concepts and Accounting Principles Underlying the Financial Statements of Business Enterprises'. In effect, APB Statement No. 4 simply reflected the generally accepted accounting principles of the time. That is, the research was inductive in nature (as it was based on observation) and did not seek to evaluate the logic or merit of the accounting practices being used. It was therefore not controversial and had a high probability of being acceptable to the AICPA's constituency (Miller and Redding, 1986).

While some accounting researchers continued to adopt an inductive approach, a different approach became popular in the 1960s and 1970s. This approach sought to *prescribe* particular accounting procedures, and as such was not driven by existing practices. The 1960s and 1970s period is commonly referred to as the 'normative period' of accounting research. That is, in this period the financial accounting theories were not developed by observing what accountants were doing – by contrast many of the theories being developed at this time were based on development of arguments about what the researchers considered accountants *should* do. Rather than being developed on the basis of inductive reasoning, these theories were being developed on the basis of deductive reasoning. At this time there tended to be widespread inflation throughout various countries of the world and much of the research and the related theories sought to explain the limitations of historical cost accounting and to provide improved approaches (based upon particular value judgements held by the researchers) for asset measurement in times of rapidly rising prices. However, while a number of highly respected researchers were arguing that measuring assets on the basis of historical cost was inappropriate and tended to provided misleading information, particularly in times of rising prices, there was a lack of agreement between the various researchers about what particular asset measurement basis should be used. For example, some argued that assets should be valued at replacement costs, some argued that assets should be valued at net realizable value, whereas other researchers argued for measurements based on present values. Throughout this debate there was no clear choice in terms of which approach was best, and perhaps because it was difficult to resolve the differences in opinions provided by the various normative researchers, the historical cost approach to accounting continued to be used.

Predictive accounting theories

In the mid- to late-1970s there were further changes in the focus of accounting research and theory development. At this time a great deal of accounting research had the major aim of *explaining* and *predicting* accounting practice, rather than *prescribing* particular approaches. This was another movement by many accounting researchers away from descriptive research – this time towards predictive research. Nevertheless, there are many researchers who still undertake descriptive research. What is being emphasized is that a variety of accounting theories have been developed across time – for example, some are descriptive in nature, some attempt to explain and predict particular aspects of financial accounting practice, and other financial accounting theories generate guidance about what accountants should do. Different theories serve different purposes.

In reading accounting research you will see that much research is labelled either *positive research* or *normative research*. Research that seeks to predict and explain particular phenomena (as opposed to prescribing particular activity) is classified as *positive research* and the associated theories are referred to as *positive theories*. Henderson *et al.* (2004, p. 414) provide a useful description of positive theories. They state:

> A positive theory begins with some assumption(s) and, through logical deduction, enables some prediction(s) to be made about the way things will be. If the prediction is sufficiently accurate when tested against observations of reality, then the story is regarded as having provided an explanation of why things are as they are. For example, in climatology, a positive theory of rainfall may yield a prediction that, if certain conditions are met, then heavy rainfall will be observed. In economics, a positive theory of prices may yield a prediction that, if certain conditions are met, then rapidly rising prices will be observed. Similarly, a positive theory of accounting may yield a prediction that, if certain conditions are met, then particular accounting practices will be observed.

As noted above, positive theories can initially be developed through some form of deductive (logical) reasoning. Their success in explaining or predicting particular phenomena will then typically be assessed based on observation – that is, observing how the theory's predictions corresponded with the observed facts.[3] Empirically (observation) based theories can continue to be tested and perhaps refined through further observation, perhaps in different institutional or geographical settings, and a great deal of published research is undertaken to see if particular results can be replicated in different settings, thereby increasing the generalizability of the theory in question. Apart from providing the basis for predicting future actions or effects, positive accounting research often goes to the next step of attempting to provide explanations for the phenomena in question.

In Chapter 7 we consider a positive theory of accounting principally developed by Watts and Zimmerman (relying upon the works of other researchers, such as Jensen and Meckling, 1976, and Gordon, 1964). Their positive theory of accounting, which they called *Positive Accounting Theory*, seeks to predict and explain why managers (and/or accountants) elect to adopt particular accounting methods in preference to others.[4]

---

[3] Again, it is stressed that not all theories will be assessed in terms of how the theory's predictions match actual behaviour. Normative theories, for example, might provide prescription about how accounting should be undertaken, and such prescription might represent significant departures from current practice. These theories, which may be developed through logical deduction, should not be evaluated by observing the theories' correspondence with current behaviours of accountants.

[4] It should be noted at this point that Positive Accounting Theory is one of several positive theories of accounting (other positive theories that relate to accounting would include legitimacy theory and certain branches of stakeholder theory). We will refer to the general class of theories that attempt to explain and predict accounting practice in lower case (that is, as positive theories of accounting) and we will refer to Watts and Zimmerman's positive theory of accounting as Positive Accounting Theory (that is, in upper case).

Chapter 7 demonstrates that the development of Positive Accounting Theory relied in great part on work undertaken in the field of economics, and central to the development of Positive Accounting Theory was the acceptance of the economics-based 'rational economic person assumption'. That is, an assumption was made that accountants (and, in fact, all individuals) are primarily motivated by self-interest (tied to wealth maximization), and that the particular accounting method selected (where alternatives are available) will be dependent upon certain considerations, such as:

- whether the person supporting the use of a particular accounting method, for example a manager or an accountant, is rewarded in terms of accounting-based bonus systems (for example, whether they receive a bonus tied to reported profits);
- whether the organization they work for is close to breaching negotiated accounting-based debt covenants (such as a debt-to-asset constraint);
- whether the organization that employs them is subject to political scrutiny from various external groups, such as government, employee groups or environmental groups (with that scrutiny being focused on the organization's reported profits).

The assumption of self-interest, as embraced by researchers that utilize Positive Accounting Theory, challenges the view that accountants will predominantly be objective when determining which accounting methods should be used to record particular transactions and events (objectivity is a qualitative characteristic promoted within various conceptual frameworks of accounting, as we see in Chapter 6).[5]

Positive theories of accounting do not seek to tell us that what is being done in practice is the most efficient or equitable process. For example, while we have a (positive) theory of accounting, developed to predict which accounting methods most accountants will use in particular circumstances (Positive Accounting Theory), this theory will not tell us what we should do (it is not a 'prescriptive' theory), nor will it tell us anything about the efficiency of what is being done. As Watts and Zimmerman (1986, p. 7) state:

> It [Positive Accounting Theory] is concerned with explaining [accounting] practice. It is designed to explain and predict which firms will and which firms will not use a particular [accounting method] … but it says nothing as to which method a firm should use.

As we will see shortly, the practice of electing not to advise others as to what should be done in particular circumstances has been the subject of criticism of positive accounting research.

Prescriptive (normative) accounting theories

While positive theories tend to be based on empirical observation, there are other theories based not upon observation but rather on what the researcher believes *should* occur in particular circumstances. For example, in Chapter 5 we discuss a theory of accounting

---

[5] As we emphasize throughout this book, researchers make a choice between the theories they will apply in particular circumstances. In part, the choice of theory will be influenced by the researchers' own beliefs and values. For example, many accounting researchers will not use Positive Accounting Theory to explain particular phenomena because they reject the central assumption made within the theory that all individual action is best described on the basis that individuals are driven by self-interest. For example, Gray *et al.* (1996, p. 75) reject Positive Accounting Theory because it portrays 'a morally bankrupt view of the world'. We will return to Gray *et al.'s* dismissal of Positive Accounting Theory later in this chapter.

developed by Raymond Chambers. His theory of accounting, called *continuously contemporary accounting*, describes how financial accounting *should* be undertaken. That is, his theory is prescriptive. Central to his theory is a view that the most useful information about an organization's assets for the purposes of economic decision-making is information about their 'current cash equivalents' – a measure tied to their current net market values. As such, it prescribes that assets *should* be valued on the basis of their net market values. Theories that prescribe (as opposed to describe) particular actions are called normative theories as they are based on the norms (or values or beliefs) held by the researchers proposing the theories (they are also often referred to as prescriptive theories). The dichotomy of positive and normative theories is one often used to categorize accounting theories and this dichotomy is adopted throughout this book.

As noted above, normative theories of accounting are not necessarily based on observation and therefore cannot (or should not) be evaluated on the basis of whether the theories reflect actual accounting practice. In fact they may suggest radical changes to current practice. For example, for a number of decades Chambers had been advocating the valuation of assets on a basis related to their net market values – a prescription that challenged the widespread use of historical cost accounting (it is interesting to note, however, that in recent years the use of market values for asset valuation has gained popularity with the International Accounting Standards Board, an issue we will examine further in Chapter 5 when we look at fair values in accounting). Other researchers concerned about the social and environmental implications of business (see, for example, Gray and Bebbington, 2001; Gray *et al.*, 1996; Mathews, 1993) have developed theories that prescribe significant changes to traditional financial accounting practice (Chapters 8 and 9 of this book consider such theories). The conceptual framework of accounting that we discuss in Chapter 6 is an example of a normative theory of accounting. Relying upon various assumptions about the types or attributes of information useful for decision-making, the conceptual framework of accounting provides guidance on how assets, liabilities, expenses, income and equity should be defined, when they should be recognized, and ultimately how they should be measured. As we see in later chapters, normative theories can be further subdivided. For example, we can classify some normative theories as 'true income theories' and other theories as 'decision usefulness theories'. The true income theories make certain assumptions about the role of accounting and then seek to provide a single 'best measure' of profits (for example, see Lee, 1974).[6]

Decision usefulness theories ascribe a particular type of information for particular classes of users on the basis of assumed decision-making needs. According to Bebbington *et al.* (2001, p. 418) the decision usefulness approach can be considered to have two branches, the *decision-makers emphasis* and the *decision-models emphasis*. The *decision-makers emphasis* relies on undertaking research that seeks to ask the users of the information what information they want.[7] Once that is determined, this knowledge is used to prescribe what information should be supplied to the users of financial statements. Much

---

[6] Much of the work undertaken in developing 'true income theories' relies upon the work of Hicks (1946). Hicks defined 'income' as the maximum amount that can be consumed by a person or an organization in a particular period without depleting the wealth that existed for that person or organization at the start of the period.

[7] For example, in recent years a number of research studies have asked a number of different stakeholder groups what types of social and environmental performance information the stakeholders considered to be useful to their various decision-making processes.

of this research is questionnaire based. This branch of research tends to be fairly disjointed as different studies typically address different types of information, with limited linkages between them.

Another variant of the decision-makers emphasis, which we explore in Chapter 10, is security price research. Briefly, security price research works on the assumption that if the capital market responds to information (as evidenced through share price changes that occur around the time of the release of particular information) the information must be useful.[8] This forms the basis for subsequent prescriptions about the types of information that should be provided to users of financial statements. It also has been used to determine whether particular mandatory reporting requirements (such as the introduction of new accounting standards) were necessary or effective, the rationale being that if a new accounting standard does not evoke a market reaction, then it is questionable whether the new requirement is useful or necessary in providing information to the stock market or investors. Research that evaluates information on the basis of whether it evokes a market reaction, or whether stakeholders indicate that it is useful to them, ignores the possibility that there could be information that is 'better' than that provided or sought. There is also a broader philosophical issue of whether the information they 'want' is actually what they 'need'. These broader issues are explored throughout this book.

On the other hand, proponents of the *decision-models emphasis* develop models based upon the researchers' perceptions of what is necessary for efficient decision-making. Information prescriptions follow (for example, that information should be provided about the market value of the reporting entity's assets). This branch of research typically assumes that classes of stakeholders have identical information needs. Unlike the decision-makers emphasis, the decision-models emphasis does not ask the decision-makers what information they want but, instead, concentrates on the types of information considered useful for decision-making. As Wolk and Tearney (1997, p. 39) indicate, a premise underlying this research is that decision-makers may need to be taught how to use this information if they are unfamiliar with it.

1.4 Evaluating theories of accounting

In the process of studying accounting, you will typically be exposed to numerous theories of accounting, and accompanying research and argument which attempts either to support or reject the particular theories in question. In undertaking this study you should consider the merit of the argument and the research methods employed by respective researchers. What many students find interesting is that many researchers seem to adopt one theory of accounting and thereafter adopt various strategies (including overt condemnation of alternative theories) in an endeavour to support their own research and theoretical perspective. In some respects, the attitudes of some researchers are akin to those of the disciples of particular religions. (In fact, Chambers, 1993, refers to advocates of Positive Accounting Theory as belonging to the 'PA Cult'.) In Deegan (1997), a series of

---

[8] Based on the efficient markets hypothesis which predicts that the stock market instantaneously reacts, through price adjustments (changes), to all relevant publicly available information.

quotes are provided from the works of various high-profile researchers who are opposed to Watts and Zimmerman's Positive Accounting Theory. In providing arguments against the validity of Positive Accounting Theory, the opponents have used such terms and descriptions as:

- it is a dead philosophical movement (Christenson, 1983, p. 7);
- it has provided no accomplishments (Sterling, 1990, p. 97);
- it is marred by oversights, inconsistencies and paradoxes (Chambers, 1993, p. 1);
- it is imperiously dictatorial (Sterling, 1990, p. 121);
- it is empty and commonplace (Sterling, 1990, p. 130);
- it is akin to a cottage industry (Sterling, 1990, p. 132);
- it is responsible for turning back the clock of research 1000 years (Chambers, 1993, p. 22);
- it suffers from logical incoherence (Williams, 1989, p. 459); and
- it is a wasted effort (Sterling, 1990, p. 132).

The quoted criticisms clearly indicate the degree of emotion that a particular theory (Positive Accounting Theory) has stimulated among its critics, particularly those accounting researchers who see the role of accounting theory as providing prescription, rather than description. As a student of financial accounting theory, you may find it interesting to ponder why some people are so angered by such a theory – after all, it is just a theory (isn't it?). Many proponents of Positive Accounting Theory have also tended to be very critical of normative theorists.

The Positive Accounting Theorists and the normative theorists would be considered to be working from different 'paradigms' – paradigms which provided greatly different perspectives about the role of accounting research. According to Hussey and Hussey (1997, p. 47):

> The term paradigm refers to the progress of scientific practice based on people's philosophies and assumptions about the world and the nature of knowledge; in this context, about how research should be conducted. Paradigms are universally recognised scientific achievements that for a time provide model problems and solutions to a community of practitioners. They offer a framework comprising an accepted set of theories, methods and ways of defining data … Your basic beliefs about the world will be reflected in the way you design your research, how you collect and analyse your data, and even the way in which you write your thesis.

The above discussion of a 'paradigm' is consistent with Kuhn (1962), who states that a paradigm can be defined as an approach to knowledge advancement that adopts particular theoretical assumptions, research goals and research methods.[9]

In explaining or describing why a certain 'camp' of researchers might try to denigrate the credibility of alternative research paradigms it is relevant to consider one of the various views about how knowledge advances. Kuhn (1962) explained how knowledge, or science,

---

[9] A similar definition of a paradigm is provided by Wolk and Tearney (1997, p. 47). They define a paradigm as a shared problem-solving view among members of a science or discipline.

develops: scientific progress is not evolutionary, but rather, revolutionary. His view is that knowledge advances when one theory is replaced by another as particular researchers attack the credibility of an existing paradigm and advance an alternative, promoted as being superior, thereby potentially bringing the existing paradigm into 'crisis'. As knowledge develops, the new paradigm may be replaced by a further research perspective, or a prior paradigm may be resurrected. In discussing the process of how researchers switch from one research perspective (or paradigm) to another, Kuhn likens it to one of 'religious conversion'.[10] While the perspective provided by Kuhn does appear to have some relevance to explaining developments in the advancement of accounting theory, so far no accounting theory has ever been successful in overthrowing all other alternatives. There have been, and apparently will continue to be, advocates of various alternative theories of accounting – many of which are discussed in this book.

Returning to our brief review of financial accounting theories, we have stated previously that positive theories of accounting do not seek to prescribe particular accounting practices (that is, they do not tell us which accounting practices we should adopt). Some critics of this positive theoretical perspective have argued that the decision not to prescribe could alienate academic accountants from their counterparts within the profession. As Howieson (1996, p. 31) states:

> an unwillingness to tackle policy issues is arguably an abrogation of academics' duty to serve the community which supports them. Among other activities, practitioners are concerned on a day-to-day basis with the question of which accounting policies they should choose. Traditionally, academics have acted as commentators and reformers on such normative issues. By concentrating on positive questions, they risk neglecting one of their important roles in the community.

Counter to this view, many proponents of Positive Accounting Theory have, at different times, tried to undermine normative research because it was not based on observation (observation-based research was deemed by them to be 'scientific', and 'scientific research' was considered to be akin to 'good research'), but rather was based on personal opinion about what should happen. Positive Accounting Theorists often argue that in undertaking research they do not want to impose their own views on others as this is 'unscientific', but rather they prefer to provide information about the expected implications of particular actions (for example, the selection of a particular accounting method) and thereafter let people decide for themselves what they should do (for example, they may provide evidence to support a prediction that organizations that are close to breaching accounting-based debt covenants will adopt accounting methods that increase the firm's reported profits and assets thereby 'loosening' the effects of the accounting-based debt covenants).

However, as a number of accounting academics have quite rightly pointed out, and as we should remember when reading this book, selecting a theory to adopt for research (such as public interest theory, capture theory, legitimacy theory, stakeholder theory or Positive Accounting Theory) is based on a value judgement; what to research is based on a value

---

[10] Kuhn's 'revolutionary' perspective about the development of knowledge is in itself a theory and, as with financial accounting theories, there are alternative views of how knowledge develops and advances. Although a review of the various perspectives of the development of science is beyond the scope of this book, interested readers are referred to Chalmers (1982), Feyerabend (1975), Lakatos and Musgrove (1974), and Popper (1959).

judgement; believing that all individual action is driven by self-interest as the Positive Accounting Theorists do is a value judgement; and so on. Hence, no research, whether utilizing Positive Accounting Theory or otherwise, is value free and it would arguably be quite wrong to assert that it is value free. As Gray *et al.* (1987, p. 66) state:

> In common with all forms of empirical investigation we must recognise that all perception is theory-laden. That is, our preconceptions about the world significantly colour what we observe and which aspects of particular events we focus upon. Thus accountants are more likely to view the world through accounting frameworks and conventions.

Watts and Zimmerman (1990, p. 146) did modify their original stance in relation to the objectivity of their research and conceded that value judgements do play a part in positive research just as they do in normative research. As they stated:

> Positive theories are value laden. Tinker et al. (1982, p. 167) argue that all research is value laden and not socially neutral. Specifically, 'Realism operating in the clothes of positive theory claims theoretical supremacy because it is born of fact, not values' (p. 172). We concede the importance of values in determining research: both the researcher's and user's preferences affect the process.
>
> Competition among theories to meet users' demand constrains the extent to which researcher values influence research design. Positive theories are 'If … then' propositions that are both predictive and explanatory. Researchers choose the topics to investigate, the methods to use, and the assumptions to make. Researchers' preferences and expected pay-offs (publications and citations) affect the choice of topics, methods and assumptions. In this sense, all research, including positive research, is 'value laden'.

The position taken in this book is that theories of accounting, of necessity, are abstractions of reality, and the choice of one theory in preference to another is based on particular value judgements. Some of us may prefer particular theories in preference to others because they more closely reflect how we believe people do, or should, act. We cannot really expect to provide perfect explanations or predictions of human behaviour, nor can we expect to assess perfectly what types of information the users of financial statements actually need – our perceptions of information needs will most probably be different from your views about information needs. There is a role for prescription if it is based on logical argument and there is a role for research that provides predictions if the research methods employed to provide the predictions are assessed as valid.

1.5 Can we prove a theory?

While this book does not intend to provide an in-depth insight into the development of scientific thought, one interesting issue that often arises with students is whether a theory can actually be 'proved'. In this book we consider various theories – a number of which provide alternative explanations for the same events. In the next section of this chapter we will consider how to evaluate a theory in terms of logic and evidence, but before we consider such evaluation we should perhaps consider the issue of whether we can prove a theory.

One's view about whether we can prove a theory as correct depends upon how one views the development of scientific thought. When it comes to accounting theories – which might, for example, consider how people react to particular accounting numbers, or might consider why accountants would choose particular accounting methods in preference to others – we need to appreciate again that financial accounting is a human activity (we cannot have accounting without accountants) and that common sense would dictate that not all people will react in a similar way to accounting numbers. Hence, logic might indicate that a theory of financial accounting (and therefore a theory that describes human behaviour in relation to accounting numbers) would not provide perfect predictions of behaviour in all cases (and in this explanation we are talking about positive theories – theories that seek to explain and predict particular phenomena).

If the theories of financial accounting were developed to explain and predict peoples' actions and reactions to financial accounting information (that is, they are positive theories), then we might consider that if a theory provides sound predictions the majority of the time then the theory is still of use, albeit that its predictions are not 'perfect'. That is, we would evaluate it on the basis of the correspondence between the prediction of behaviours provided by the theory and the subsequent behaviour, and we might accept that a theory is useful although it does not provide accurate predictions in all cases. That is, an 'acceptable' theory might nevertheless admit exceptions.[11] It should also be appreciated that while we might use observations to 'support' a theory, it would generally be inadvisable to state that we have proved a theory on the basis of observations. There is always the possibility that one further observation might be made that is inconsistent with our theory's predictions.

In relation to the issue of whether we can 'prove' a theory (or not) it is useful to refer to insights provided by a group of theorists known as 'falsificationists' – the major leader of which is considered to be Karl Popper.[12]

Popper, and the falsificationists, considers that knowledge develops through trial and error. For example, a researcher might develop hypotheses from a theory.[13] To develop scientific knowledge, the falsificationists believe that these hypotheses must be of a form that allows them to be rejected if the evidence is not supportive of the hypotheses. For example, a hypothesis of the following form would be deemed to be falsifiable:

> *Hypothesis 1: Managers that receive bonuses based on accounting profits will adopt income-increasing accounting methods.*

According to Popper and other falsificationists, knowledge develops as a result of continual refinement of a theory. When particular hypotheses are deemed to be false through lack of empirical support, the pre-existing theories will be refined (or abandoned). The refined

---

[11] The degree to which we might consider a theory to be acceptable will perhaps depend upon the costs or implications associated with the theory 'getting it wrong' in a particular circumstance. For example, if the theory related to medicine and the theory was wrong only 10 per cent of the time – thereby causing deaths in 10 per cent of the patients – then such a theory might not be acceptable. In accounting we might tolerate higher levels of inconsistency between theory predictions and related outcomes.

[12] One of the first detailed descriptions of falsificationism appeared in Popper (1968).

[13] Simply stated, a hypothesis can be defined as a proposition typically derived from theory which can be tested for causality or association using empirical data. For example, a hypothesis might be: the greater the negative media attention given to a particular social issue the greater the amount of annual report disclosures addressing the issue.

theories will be accepted until a related hypothesis is deemed to be false (falsified) at which time the theory will be further refined. Chalmers (1982, p. 38) provides a useful overview of falsificationism. He states:

> The falsificationist freely admits that observation is guided by and presupposes theory. He is also happy to abandon any claims implying that theories can be established as true or probably true in the light of observational evidence. Theories are construed as speculative and tentative conjectures or guesses freely created by the human intellect in an attempt to overcome problems encountered by previous theories and to give an adequate account of the behaviour of some aspects of the world or universe. Once proposed, speculative theories are to be rigorously and ruthlessly tested by observation and experiment. Theories that fail to stand up to observational and experimental tests must be eliminated and replaced by further speculative conjectures. Science progresses by trial and error, by conjectures and refutations. Only the fittest theories survive. While it can never be legitimately said of a theory that it is true, it can hopefully be said that it is the best available, that it is better than anything that has come before.

We can contrast Popper's view regarding how theories are developed with the views adopted by the inductivists considered earlier in this chapter. The inductivists construct theories based on typically long periods of careful observation. We will not pursue this discussion any further in terms of how theories develop, but consistent with some of the above discussion we would caution readers about making any claims to 'proving' a theory. It is always safer to say that our evidence 'supports' a theory but that it is also possible that we might embrace an alternative theoretical perspective at a future time should better explanations for a particular phenomenon become available.

1.6 Evaluating theories – considerations of logic and evidence

Throughout this book we discuss various theories of financial accounting. Where appropriate, we also undertake an evaluation of the theories. We consider such issues as whether the argument supporting the theories is (or at least appears to be) logical and/or plausible in terms of the central assumptions (if any) that are being made. If possible the argument or theory should be broken down into its main premises to see if the argument, in simplified form, appears logical. What we emphasize is that we/you must question the theories that we/you are exposed to – not simply accept them. Acceptance of a theory and its associated hypotheses (as indicated previously, hypotheses can be described as predictions typically expressed in the form of a relationship between one or more variables) must be tied to whether we accept the logic of the argument, the underlying assumptions and any supporting evidence provided.

Evaluating logical deduction

As an example of logical deduction, consider the following simplistic non-accounting related argument (reflecting the biases of one of the authors – it refers to surfing). It shows that although the argument may be logical (if we accept the premises), if it can be shown that one of the premises is untrue or in doubt, then the conclusions or predictions may be rejected. Where we have a number of premises and a conclusion we often refer to this as a syllogism.

- All surfers over the age of 35 ride longboards.
- Jack is a surfer over the age of 35.
- Jack therefore rides a longboard.

If we accept the above premises, we might accept the conclusion. It is logical. To determine the logic of the argument we do not need to understand what is a 'surfer' or what is a 'longboard'. That is, we do not need to refer to 'real-world' observations. We could have deconstructed the argument to the form:

- All As ride a B.
- C is an A.
- Therefore C rides a B.

An argument is logical to the extent that *if* the premises on which it is based are true, *then* the conclusion will be true. That is, the argument (even if logical) will only provide a true account of the real world if the premises on which it is based are true. Referring to the above syllogism, evidence gathered through observation will show that the first premise does not always hold. There are surfers over 35 who do not ride longboards. Hence we reject the conclusion on the basis of observation, not on the basis of logic. Therefore we had two considerations. If the argument seeks to provide an account of real-world phenomena we must consider the logic of the premises and the correspondence between the premises and actual observation. This simplistic example can be extended to a review of theories. We might try to break the theory down into a series of premises. When the central premises are considered do they lead to a logical conclusion? Further, if the premises are based on 'real world' observation, do they seem to be true? However, it should be remembered that not all theories or arguments seek to correspond with real-world phenomena – for example, some normative theories of accounting promote radical changes to existing practices. For many normative theories we might consider only the logic of the argument and whether we are prepared to accept the premises on which the argument is based.

Returning to the subject of the syllogism provided above, we could have argued alternatively that:

- A lot of surfers over 35 ride longboards.
- Jack is a surfer over 35.
- Therefore Jack rides a longboard.

The above is not a logical argument. The first premise has admitted alternatives and hence the conclusion, which does not admit alternatives, does not follow. We can dismiss the argument on the basis of a logical flaw without actually seeking any evidence to support the premises.

Evaluating underlying assumptions

In Chapter 7 we review in greater depth Positive Accounting Theory as developed by such researchers as Jensen and Meckling (1976) and Watts and Zimmerman (1978). As noted earlier, their positive theory of accounting has a number of central assumptions, including an assumption that all people are *opportunistic* and will adopt particular strategies to the extent that such strategies lead to an increase in the personal wealth of those parties making the decisions. That is, self-interest is a core belief about what motivates individual action. Wealth accumulation is assumed to be at the centre of all decisions. The theory does not incorporate considerations of morality, loyalty, social responsibility and the like.

If we were to accept the economics-based assumption or premise of researchers such as Watts and Zimmerman that:

■ self-interest tied to wealth maximization motivates *all* decisions by individuals,

plus *if* we accept the following premises (which we might confirm through direct observation or through research undertaken by others) that:

■ manager X is paid on the basis of reported profits (for example, he/she is given a bonus of 5 per cent of accounting profits); and

■ accounting method Y is an available method of accounting that will increase reported profits relative to other methods,

then we might accept a prediction that, all other things being equal:

■ manager X will adopt accounting method Y.

The above argument appears logical. Whether manager X is paid on the basis of reported profits and whether accounting method Y will increase reported profits are matters that can be confirmed though observation. But if the premises are both logical and true then the conclusion will be true.

The above argument may be logical but we might only accept it if we accept the critical assumption that the actions of individuals are motivated by the desire to maximize personal wealth. If we do not accept the central assumption, then we may reject the prediction. What is being emphasized here is that you need to consider whether you are prepared to accept the logic and the assumptions upon which the arguments are based. If not, then we may reject the theory and the associated predictions. For example, in Gray *et al.* (1996) the authors explicitly state that they reject the central assumptions of Positive Accounting Theory (although by their own admission it has 'some useful insights') and that they will not use it as a means of explaining or describing the practice of corporate social responsibility reporting. (Corporate social reporting is a topic covered in Chapter 9 of this book.) As they state (p. 75):

> There is little doubt that these theories have provided some useful insights into the way in which they model the world. There is equally little doubt that some company management and many gambling investors may act in line with these theories. It is also the case that some authors have found the form of analysis employed in these theories useful for explaining corporate social reporting; but apart from the limitations which must arise from a pristine liberal economic perspective on the world and the profound philosophical limitations of the approach, the approach cannot offer any justification why we might accept the description of the world as a desirable one. It is a morally bankrupt view of the world in general and accounting in particular. Its (usual) exclusion of corporate social reporting is therefore actually attractive as an argument for corporate social reporting.

In Chapter 6 we discuss the conceptual framework project, which is considered to be a normative theory of accounting (applying a decision-usefulness perspective). This framework provides a view about the objective of general purpose financial reporting (to provide information that is useful for economics-based decisions) and the qualitative characteristics that financial information should possess. It also provides definitions of the elements of accounting (assets, liabilities, income, expenses, equity) and prescribes recognition criteria for each of the elements. As we will discuss in Chapter 6, in recent years the US Financial Accounting Standards Board (FASB) and the International Accounting Standards Board (IASB) have been undertaking an initiative to develop, on a joint basis, an improved conceptual framework for financial reporting. In May 2008 the FASB and the IASB jointly released an Exposure Draft entitled: *Exposure Draft of an Improved Conceptual Framework for Financial Reporting* and in relation to providing a definition of the revised conceptual framework, it defined it as:

> a coherent system of concepts that flow from an objective. The objective of financial reporting is the foundation of the framework. The other concepts provide guidance on identifying the boundaries of financial reporting; selecting the transactions, other events and circumstances to be represented; how they should be recognised and measured (or disclosed); and how they should be summarised and communicated in financial reports.

Hence, if we were to decide whether we agreed with the guidance provided within the revised conceptual framework, which is an example of a normative theory (as we have already indicated, a normative theory prescribes how we should undertake a particular activity – in this case, how we should do financial accounting) then we clearly would need to evaluate the assumed objective identified in the framework. As everything else is constructed around this objective (as the quote above shows, it is deemed to be the 'foundation of the framework'), if we disagree with the stated objective then logically we would have to disagree with the balance of the prescriptions provided in the revised conceptual framework. The Exposure Draft states that:

> The objective of general purpose financial reporting is to provide financial information about the reporting entity that is useful to present and potential equity investors, lenders and other creditors in making decisions in their capacity as capital providers.

Therefore, if we believed the central objective of financial accounting was to provide information to a broad cross-section of stakeholders, inclusive of employees, local communities, and other groups who are not directly involved as capital providers then we would reject the conceptual framework being developed by the IASB and FASB – despite the fact that it might be considered to be logically structured.

While the in-depth study of logic and a critique of argument are beyond the scope of this book, interested readers should consider studying books or articles that concentrate on the development of logical argument.[14] Thouless (1974) describes various approaches to identifying logical flaws in arguments and he also identifies 38 'dishonest tricks in argument' that some writers use to support their arguments. Some of the 'tricks' he refers

---

[14] A good book in this regard is entitled *Straight and Crooked Thinking*, written by Robert H. Thouless (1974). Sterling (1970) is also useful.

to, and which are often used to distract readers from limitations in the logic of an argument or theory are:

- the use of emotionally toned words;
- making a statement in which 'all' is implied but 'some' is true;
- evasion of a sound refutation of an argument by use of a sophisticated formula;
- diversion to another question, to a side issue, or by irrelevant objection;
- the use of an argument of logically unsound form;
- change in the meaning of a term during the course of an argument;
- suggestion by repeated affirmation;
- prestige by false credentials;
- the appeal to mere authority; and
- argument by mere analogy.

When reading documents written to support particular ideas or theories, we must also be vigilant to ensure that our acceptance of a theory has not, in a sense, been coerced through the use of colourful or emotive language, or an incorrect appeal to authority. We referred to some earlier quotes from critics of Positive Accounting Theory – some of which were very emotive. Quite often (but not always) emotive or colourful language is introduced to support an otherwise weak argument. Where emotive or colourful language has been used, we should perhaps consider whether we would take the same position in terms of accepting the author's arguments if that author had used relatively neutral language. Thouless (1974, p. 24) provides some advice in this regard. He suggests:

> The practical exercise which I recommend is one that I have already performed on some passages in which truth seemed to be obscured by emotional thinking. I suggest that readers should copy out controversial passages from newspapers, books, or speeches which contain emotionally coloured words. They should then underline all the emotional words, afterwards rewriting the passages with the emotional words replaced by neutral ones. Examine the passage then in its new form in which it merely states facts without indicating the writer's emotional attitude towards them, and see whether it is still good evidence for the proposition it is trying to prove. If it is, the passage is a piece of straight thinking in which emotionally coloured words have been introduced merely as an ornament. If not, it is crooked thinking, because the conclusion depends not on the factual meaning of the passage but on the emotions roused by the words.

Universal applicability of theories

While we must always consider the logic of an argument and the various assumptions that have been made, what we also must remember is that theories – particularly those in the social sciences – are, by nature, abstractions of reality. We cannot really expect particular theories about human behaviour to apply all the time. People (thankfully) are different and to expect theories or models of human behaviour (and remember, accounting theories relate to the action of accountants and the users of accounting information) to have perfect predictive ability would be naive. If a number of theories are available to describe a particular phenomenon, then considering more than one theory may provide a more rounded perspective. Difficulties will arise if the theories provide diametrically opposite predictions or explanations – in such cases a choice of theory must generally be made.

For those theories that attempt to predict and explain accounting practice (positive theories of accounting) it is common practice to test the theories empirically in various settings and across various types of decisions – but what if the particular theories do not seem to hold in all settings? Should the theories be abandoned? Returning to an issue we considered previously in this chapter, can we accept a theory that admits exceptions? Certainly, readings of various accounting research journals will show that many studies that adopt Positive Accounting Theory as the theoretical basis of the argument fail to generate findings consistent with the theory (however, many do). According to Christenson (1983, p. 18), an outspoken critic of Positive Accounting Theory:

> We are told, for example, that 'we can only expect a positive theory to hold on average' (Watts and Zimmerman, 1978, p. 127, n. 37). We are also advised 'to remember that as in all empirical theories we are concerned with general trends' (Watts and Zimmerman, 1979, pp. 288–289), where 'general' is used in the weak sense of 'true or applicable in most instances but not all' rather than in the strong sense of 'relating to, concerned with, or applicable to every member of a class' (American Heritage Dictionary, 1969, p. 548) … A law that admits exceptions has no significance, and knowledge of it is not of the slightest use. By arguing that their theories admit exceptions, Watts and Zimmerman condemn them as insignificant and useless.

Christenson uses the fact that Positive Accounting Theory is not always supported in practice to reject it.[15] However, as stressed previously, as a study of people (accountants, not 'accounting'), it is very hard to see how any model or theory could ever fully explain human action. In fact, ability to do so would constitute a very dehumanizing view of people. Hence, the failure of a particular study to support a theory might not in itself provide a basis for rejecting a theory as 'useless and insignificant'. From another perspective, the failure to support the theory may have been due to the data being inappropriately collected or the data not providing a sound correspondence with the theoretical variables involved. However, if the theory in question continuously fails to be supported, then its acceptance will obviously be threatened. At this point we could speculate whether in fact there are any theories pertaining to human activities that always hold.

Generalizing theories from the testing of samples

In developing and testing accounting theories many accounting researchers use methods borrowed from the pure sciences (such as physics and chemistry) which assume that the phenomena being studied will behave in the same way in all similar situations. As we will see when reading accounting (and other) research, these researchers believe that it is possible to develop generalizable accounting theories and therefore that the results they derive from particular samples of observations can be generalized to the

---

[15] Where a proposition is not supported in a particular instance, many of us have probably heard the phrase 'the exception proves the rule' being applied. Such a statement implies that we cannot accept a rule or proposition unless we find some evidence that appears to refute it. This clearly is an illogical argument. As emphasized above, we must always guard against accepting arguments that are not logically sound.

broader population of the phenomenon in question. Other researchers hold the opposite view – that it is not possible to make any valid generalizations in social sciences as we are dealing with human activity, and human behaviour varies from person to person. These researchers will develop theories of a fundamentally different nature to those developed by researchers who believe that it is possible to generalize in accounting theory, and these theories will tend to deal with specific localized situations. Between these two extremes, there are other researchers (such as Laughlin, 1995, 2004) who believe that it is possible to make some very broad generalizations in developing social science theories, but the way these broad generalizations apply to specific situations will vary according to the specific individual factors applicable to each situation. Researchers holding this view regarding the way the world works may use some very broad theories to help understand some aspects of the phenomena they are studying, but are ready to amend and adapt these broad generalizations in light of specific evidence from each individual study.

While a comprehensive review of research methods is beyond the scope of this book, if researchers are attempting to generalize the findings of their studies (based on particular samples) to a larger population, we need to consider the data on which the generalization is based.[16] For example, if we are going to generalize our findings from a sample (we typically cannot test the whole population), then we must consider how the original sample was chosen. For instance, if we have a prediction that all companies will adopt a particular accounting method in times of inflation and we test this prediction against the 10 largest companies listed on the stock exchange in a period of inflation, then common sense should dictate that the findings really should not be considered generalizable. Can we really be confident about what small companies will do given that our sample only included large listed companies? Hence, throughout your readings of various research studies you should consider not only how the argument is developed, but also how it is tested. If there are flaws in how the testing has been done, we may question or reject the significance of the findings. We must evaluate whether the data collected really represent valid measures of the theoretical variables in question.

As noted previously, for normative theories it is usually not appropriate to test them empirically. If researchers are arguing that accountants should provide particular types of accounting information, or if other researchers are providing a view that organizations have a social responsibility to consider the needs of all stakeholders, then this does not mean that what they are prescribing actually exists in practice. For example, if Chambers' model of accounting prescribes that all assets should be valued at their net market value, and we go out and find that accountants predominantly value their assets on the basis of historical cost, we should not reject Chambers' theory as he was *prescribing*, not *predicting* or *describing*. We should always keep in mind what the researchers are attempting to achieve. Our acceptance of Chambers' theory is dependent upon whether we accept the logic of the argument as well as the assumptions made by Chambers, including the assumption that the central role of accounting should be to provide information about an entity's ability to adapt to changing circumstances (which he argues is best reflected by measures of assets that are tied to their net market values), and the assumption that firms should exist primarily to increase the wealth of the owners.

---

[16] Entire books are dedicated to research methods. Interested readers may refer to Bryman (2004), Collis and Hussey (2003), Ghauri and Gronhaug (2002) and Humphrey and Lee (2004).

1.7 Outline of this book

In a book of this size we cannot expect to cover all the theories of financial accounting. We nevertheless cover those theories that have tended to gain widespread acceptance by various sectors of the accounting community.

In Chapter 2 we provide an overview of various financial reporting decisions that entities typically face, emphasizing that some reporting pertaining to particular transactions and events is regulated, while some is unregulated. We emphasize that financial accountants typically make many professional judgements throughout the accounting process and we discuss the qualitative attribute of objectivity, but emphasize that considerations (other than the pursuit of objectivity) may sometimes influence accounting method selection and disclosure practices.

Chapter 3 provides an overview of various arguments for and against the regulation of financial reporting, with an outline of various perspectives on the *costs* and *benefits* of regulating financial reporting. The chapter explores why some accounting approaches and/or methods are adopted by regulators and/or the profession, while others are not. The political process involved in the setting of accounting standards is highlighted.

Chapter 4 explores the international harmonization of accounting requirements. Recently, moves have been made to standardize accounting practices internationally. The European Union has been at the forefront of such moves. This chapter considers some potential costs and benefits of this process. Consideration is also given to issues of *culture* and how *cultural differences* have typically been proposed as a reason to explain international differences in accounting requirements. International standardization ignores this research and assumes that all countries (with different cultures) can and should simply adopt the same accounting practices.

Chapter 5 gives an overview of various normative (or prescriptive) theories of accounting that have been advanced to deal with the valuation of assets and liabilities in financial accounts, and consequently the measurement of income. The chapter provides an explanation of several normative (or prescriptive) theories of accounting that have been advanced to deal with various accounting issues associated with periods of rising prices (inflation) and explores theoretical arguments that have been developed in relation to the controversial topic of fair value accounting (that was implicated by some as a factor exacerbating the recent 'sub-prime' banking crisis).

Conceptual frameworks as normative theories of accounting are considered in Chapter 6. Applying material covered in Chapter 3, Chapters 5 and 6 also consider why various normative theories of accounting did not gain favour with the accounting profession or the accounting standard-setters.

Chapters 7 and 8 show that while much financial reporting is regulated, organizations still have some scope for voluntarily selecting between alternative accounting methods for particular types of transactions. The treatment of many transactions and the disclosure of many/most issues associated with various social and environmental events relating to an organization is unregulated. Chapters 7 and 8 consider some theoretical perspectives (including Positive Accounting Theory, legitimacy theory, stakeholder theory, political economy theory and institutional theory) that explain what drives the various unregulated/voluntary reporting decisions.

Chapter 9 considers the development and use of new systems of accounting that incorporate the economic, social and environmental performance of an organization.

The relationship between accounting and sustainable development is explored. This chapter includes a consideration of the limitations of traditional financial accounting, with particular focus on its inability to incorporate significant social and environmental issues.

Chapters 10 and 11 consider how individuals and capital markets react to various corporate disclosures. These chapters consider the various theories that have been used to test whether the market is actually using particular types of disclosures, as well as theories that indicate how individuals use accounting information. The chapters also consider who should be deemed to be the users of various types of disclosures. Issues associated with stakeholder *rights to know* are also explored.

The concluding chapter, Chapter 12, provides an overview of various critical perspectives of accounting – perspectives that tend to criticize the entire system of accounting as it stands (accounting practice is anthropocentric, masculine and so on) – arguing that accounting tends to support current social systems, which favour those with economic power, but marginalize the interests of parties who lack control of necessary resources.

In summary, the balance of this book can be presented diagrammatically, as in Figure 1.1.

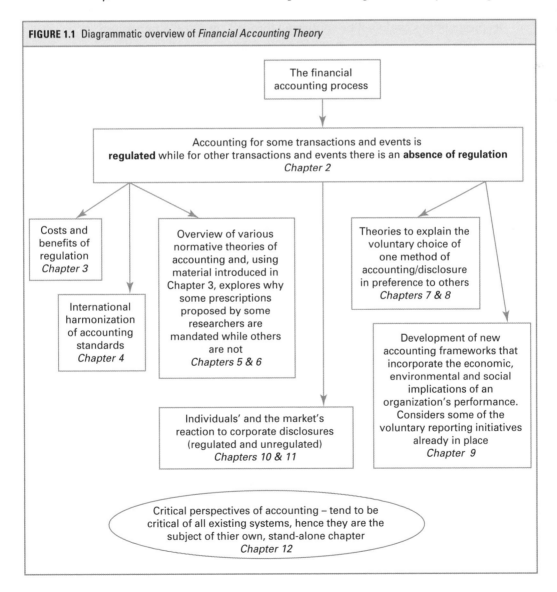

FIGURE 1.1 Diagrammatic overview of *Financial Accounting Theory*

Questions

1.1   What is the difference between a positive theory of accounting and a normative theory of accounting?

1.2   If you developed a theory to explain how a person's cultural background influences how they prepare financial statements, would you have developed a positive theory or a normative theory?

1.3   In an article that appeared in the *Guardian* ('Why are Barcelona so annoying?', 22 May 2010) Barney Ronay commenting on the style of football played by Barcelona writes: 'Above all I dislike their non-contact tippy-tappy style of play, often deemed, like Barcelona themselves, to be intrinsically "good". I have a theory the popularity of this style owes a lot to the fact that it looks good on TV: a televisual style, suited to the armchair rhythms of possession-foul-replay-pundit-blather.' Do you believe he really has a 'theory' in terms of the way we defined a 'theory' in this chapter?

1.4   Why would it not be appropriate to reject a normative theory of accounting because its prescriptions could not be confirmed through empirical observation?

1.5   The IASB and the FASB are currently developing a revised conceptual framework of financial reporting. If you had been asked to review the framework – which is an example of a normative theory of accounting – why would it be important for you to pay particular attention to how the objective of financial reporting is defined within the framework?

1.6   What is the difference between developing a theory by induction and developing a theory by deduction?

1.7   Is the study of financial accounting theory a waste of time for accounting students? Explain your answer.

1.8   Gray, *et al.* (1987, p. 66) make the following statement in relation to research based on the inductive approach (that is, research based on observing particular phenomena):

> Studying extant practice is a study of 'what is' and, by definition does not study 'what is not' or 'what should be'. It therefore concentrates on the status quo, is reactionary in attitude, and cannot provide a basis upon which current practice may be evaluated or from which future improvements may be deduced.

With the above comment in mind, do you consider that research based on induction is useful for improving the practice of financial accounting?

1.9   Explain the meaning of the following paragraph and evaluate the logic of the perspective described:

> In generating theories of accounting that are based upon what accountants actually do, it is assumed (often implicitly) that what is done by the majority of accountants is the most appropriate practice. In adopting such a perspective there is, in a sense, a perspective of accounting Darwinism – a view that accounting practice has evolved, and the fittest, or perhaps 'best', practices have survived. Prescriptions or advice are provided to others on the basis of what most accountants do – the logic being that the majority of accountants must be doing the most appropriate thing.

1.10 This chapter explains that in 1961 and 1962 the Accounting Research Division of the American Institute of Certified Public Accountants commissioned studies by Moonitz, and by Sprouse and Moonitz, respectively. These studies proposed that accounting measurement systems be changed from historical cost to a system based on current values. However, before the release of these studies, the AICPA released a statement saying that 'while these studies are a valuable contribution to accounting principles, they are too radically different from generally accepted principles for acceptance at this time' (Statement by the Accounting Principles Board, AICPA, April 1962). Explain why, if something is 'radically different' (though it might be logically sound), this difference in itself might be enough to stop regulators embracing a particular approach to accounting.

1.11 Read the following quotation from Miller and Redding (1986). If constituency support is necessary before particular accounting approaches become embodied in accounting standards, does this have implications for the 'neutrality' and 'representational faithfulness' (qualitative characteristics that exist in various Conceptual Framework Projects around the world) of reports generated in accordance with accounting standards?

> The mere discovery of a problem is not sufficient to assure that the FASB will undertake its solution … There must be a suitably high likelihood that the Board can resolve the issues in a manner that will be acceptable to the constituency – without some prior sense of the likelihood that the Board members will be able to reach a consensus, it is generally not advisable to undertake a formal project (Miller and Redding, 1986, p. 64).

1.12 As Watts and Zimmerman (1986, p. 7) state, Positive Accounting Theory is concerned with explaining accounting practice. It is designed to explain and predict which firms will, and which firms will not, use a particular accounting method, but says nothing as to which method a firm should use. Do you think that this represents an 'abrogation of the academics' duty to serve the community that supports them'?

1.13 This chapter describes two branches of 'decision usefulness' theories. Briefly identify and explain what they are.

1.14 Briefly explain the *revolutionary perspective* of knowledge advancement proposed by Kuhn (1962).

1.15 What is a 'paradigm' and would you expect accounting researchers to embrace more than one paradigm when undertaking research? Explain your answer.

1.16 In your opinion, can accounting research be 'value free'? Explain your answer.

1.17 If an accounting researcher adopts a particular accounting theory to predict which firms will make particular accounting disclosures, how much supporting evidence must the researcher gather before he or she can claim that the theory is 'proved'? Explain your answer.

1.18 Assume that you have been asked to evaluate a particular theory of accounting. What factors would you consider before making a judgement that the theory appears 'sound'?

1.19 If you were trying to convince another party to support your theory about a particular facet of financial accounting, would you be inclined to use emotive or colourful language? Why, or why not?

1.20 What do we mean when we say that 'theories are abstractions of reality'? Do you agree that theories of accounting are necessarily abstractions of reality?

1.21 What is a 'hypothesis' and do you consider that accounting research should necessarily involve the development of empirically testable hypotheses?

1.22 Would you reject as 'insignificant and useless' a positive theory of accounting on the basis that in a particular research study the results derived failed to support the hypotheses and the related theory? Explain your answer.

References

Bebbington, J., Gray, R. & Laughlin, R. (2001) *Financial Accounting: Practice and Principles*, London: International Thomson Business Press.

Bryman, A. (2004) *Social Research Methods*, Oxford: Oxford University Press.

Canning, J.B. (1929) *The Economics of Accountancy: A Critical Analysis of Accounting Theory*, New York: Ronald Press.

Chalmers, A.F. (1982) *What Is this Thing Called Science?*, Brisbane, Australia: University of Queensland Press.

Chambers, R.J. (1993) 'Positive accounting theory and the PA cult', *ABACUS*, **29** (1), 1–26.

Christenson, C. (1983) 'The methodology of positive accounting', *The Accounting Review*, **58** (January), 1–22.

Collis, J. & Hussey, R. (2003) *Business Research*, London: Palgrave Macmillan.

Czarniawska, B. (1997) *Narrating the Organization*, Chicago, IL: University of Chicago Press.

Deegan, C. (1997) 'Varied perceptions of positive accounting theory: A useful tool for explanation and prediction, or a body of vacuous, insidious and discredited thoughts?', *Accounting Forum*, **20** (5), 63–73.

FASB (1976) 'Scope and implications of the conceptual framework project', Financial Accounting Standards Board.

Feyerabend, P. (1975) *Against Method: Outline of an Anarchic Theory of Knowledge*, London: New Left Books.

Ghauri, P. & Gronhaug, K. (2002) *Research Methods in Business Studies: A Practical Guide*, Harlow: FT Prentice Hall.

Gordon, M.J. (1964) 'Postulates, principles, and research in accounting', *The Accounting Review*, **39** (April), 251–63.

Grady, P. (1965) 'An inventory of generally accepted accounting principles for business enterprises', *Accounting Research Study No. 7*, New York: AICPA.

Gray, R. & Bebbington, J. (2001) *Accounting for the Environment*, London: Sage Publications.

Gray, R., Owen, D. & Adams, C. (1996) *Accounting and Accountability: Changes and Challenges in Corporate Social and Environmental Reporting*, London: Prentice-Hall.

Gray, R., Owen, D. & Maunders, K.T. (1987) *Corporate Social Reporting: Accounting and Accountability*, Hemel Hempstead: Prentice-Hall.

Hatfield, H.R. (1927) *Accounting, its Principles and Problems*, New York: D. Appleton & Co.

Henderson, S., Peirson, G. & Harris, K. (2004) *Financial Accounting Theory*, Sydney: Pearson Education Australia.

Hendriksen, E. (1970) *Accounting Theory*, Homewood, IL: Richard D. Irwin.

Hicks, J.R. (1946) *Value and Capital*, Oxford: Oxford University Press.

Hines, R. (1988) 'Financial accounting: In communicating reality, we construct reality', *Accounting Organizations and Society*, **13** (3), 251–62.

Howieson, B. (1996) 'Whither financial accounting research: A modern-day bo-peep?', *Australian Accounting Review*, **6** (1), 29–36.

Humphrey, C. & Lee, B. (eds.) (2004) *The Real Life Guide to Accounting Research: A Behind-the-scenes View of Using Qualitative Research Methods*, Oxford: Elsevier.

Hussey, J. & Hussey, R. (1997) *Business Research: A Practical Guide for Undergraduate and Postgraduate Students*, London: Macmillan Business.

Jensen, M.C. & Meckling, W.H. (1976) 'Theory of the firm: Managerial behavior, agency costs and ownership structure', *Journal of Financial Economics*, **3** (October), 305–60.

Kuhn, T.S. (1962) *The Structure of Scientific Revolutions*, Chicago, IL: University of Chicago Press.

Lakatos, I. & Musgrove, A. (1974) *Criticism and the Growth of Knowledge*, Cambridge: Cambridge University Press.

Laughlin, R. (1995) 'Empirical research in accounting: Alternative approaches and a case for "middle-range" thinking', *Accounting, Auditing & Accountability Journal*, **8** (1), 63–87.

Laughlin, R. (2004) 'Putting the record straight: A critique of "methodology choices and the construction of facts: Some implications from the sociology of knowledge"', *Critical Perspectives on Accounting*, **15** (2), 261–77.

Lee, T.A. (1974) 'Enterprise income-survival or decline and fall', *Accounting and Business Research*, **15**, 178–92.

Llewelyn, S. (2003) 'What counts as "theory" in qualitative management and accounting research?', *Accounting, Auditing & Accountability Journal*, **16** (4), 662–708.

Mathews, M.R. (1993) *Socially Responsible Accounting*, London: Chapman and Hall.

Miller, P.B.W. & Redding, R. (1986) *The FASB: The People, the Process, and the Politics*, Homewood, IL: Irwin.

Moonitz, M. (1961) 'The basic postulates of accounting', *Accounting Research Study No. 1*, New York: AICPA.

Paton, W.A. (1922) *Accounting Theory*, Lawrence, KS: Scholars Book Co., reprinted 1973.

Paton, W.A. & Littleton, A.C. (1940) *An Introduction to Corporate Accounting Standards*, Evanston, IL: American Accounting Association.

Popper, K.R. (1959) *The Logic of Scientific Discovery*, London: Hutchinson.

Popper, K. (1968) *The Logic of Scientific Discovery*, 2nd edn, London: Hutchinson.

Sprouse, R. & Moonitz, M. (1962) 'A tentative set of broad accounting principles for business enterprises', *Accounting Research Study No. 3*, New York: AICPA.

Sterling, R.R. (1970) *Theory of the Measurement of Enterprise Income*, Lawrence, KS: University Press of Kansas.

Sterling, R.R. (1990) 'Positive accounting: An assessment', *ABACUS*, **26** (2), 97–135.

Thouless, R.H. (1974) *Straight and Crooked Thinking*, London: Pan Books.

Tinker, A.M., Merino, B.D. & Neimark, M.D. (1982) 'The normative origins of positive theories: Ideology and accounting thought', *Accounting Organizations and Society*, **7** (2), 167–200.

Unerman, J. & O'Dwyer, B. (2004) 'Enron, WorldCom, Andersen *et al*: A challenge to modernity', *Critical Perspectives on Accounting*, **15** (6–7), 971–93.

Watts, R.L. & Zimmerman, J.L. (1978) 'Towards a positive theory of the determination of accounting standards', *The Accounting Review*, **53** (1), 112–34.

Watts, R.L. & Zimmerman, J.L. (1979) 'The demand for and supply of accounting theories: The market for excuses', *The Accounting Review*, **54** (2), 273–305.

Watts, R.L. & Zimmerman, J.L. (1986) *Positive Accounting Theory*, Englewood Cliffs, NJ: Prentice-Hall.

Watts, R.L. & Zimmerman, J.L. (1990) 'Positive accounting theory: A ten year perspective', *The Accounting Review*, **65** (1), 131–56.

Williams, P.F. (1989) 'The logic of positive accounting research', *Accounting Organizations and Society*, **14** (5/6), 455–68.

Wolk, H.I. & Tearney, M.G. (1997) *Accounting Theory: A Conceptual and Institutional Approach*, Cincinnati, OH: International Thomson Publishing.

02

The Financial Reporting Environment

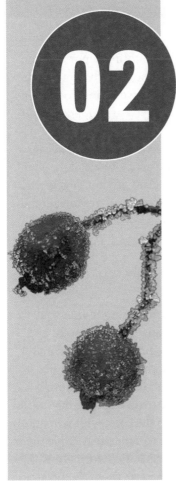

❖ LEARNING OBJECTIVES

Upon completing this chapter readers should:

❖ have a broad understanding of the history of the accounting profession and of accounting regulation;

❖ be aware of some of the arguments for and against the existence of accounting regulation;

❖ be aware of some of the theoretical perspectives used to explain the existence of regulation;

❖ be aware of how and why various groups within society try to influence

the accounting standard-setting process;

❖ acknowledge that many accounting decisions are based on professional opinions and have an awareness of some of the theories used to explain what influences the accountant to choose one accounting method in preference to another;

❖ be aware of some of the arguments advanced to support a view that the accountant can be considered to be a powerful member of society.

Opening issues

Through such mechanisms as conceptual framework programmes, accounting professions throughout the world promote a view that accounting reports, when prepared properly, will be objective and will faithfully represent the underlying transactions and events of the reporting entity. Is it in the interests of the accounting profession to promote this view of objectivity and neutrality, and if so, why? Further, because of the economic and social impacts of many accounting decisions (for example, decisions that involve choosing one method of accounting in preference to another), and because accounting standard-setters take such economic and social impacts into account when developing new accounting standards, standard-setters themselves are not developing accounting standards that can subsequently enable a reliable account of organizational performance to be provided. Do you agree or disagree with this view, and why?

2.1 Introduction

Financial accounting is a process involving the collection and processing of financial information to assist in the making of various decisions by many parties internal and external to the organization. These parties are diverse and include present and potential investors, lenders, suppliers, employees, customers, governments, the local community, parties performing a review or oversight function, and the media. Financial accounting deals with the provision of information to parties not necessarily involved in the day-to-day running of the organization. As there are many parties external to the firm, with potentially vastly different information demands and needs, it is not possible to generate a single report that will satisfy the specific needs of all parties (reports that meet specific information needs are often referred to as special purpose reports). As such, the process of financial accounting leads to the generation of reports deemed to be general purpose financial statements.[1]

Financial accounting tends to be heavily regulated in most countries, with many accounting standards and other regulations governing how particular transactions and events are to be recognized, measured and presented. The reports generated, such as the

---

[1] In its 'Preface to International Financial Reporting Standards', the International Accounting Standards Board (IASB) defines 'general purpose financial statements' as reports 'directed towards the common information needs of a wide range of users' (IASB, 2008, paragraph 10). Paragraph 6 of the IASB's current *Framework for the Preparation and Presentation of Financial Statements* (IASC, 1989) states that the framework 'is concerned with general purpose financial statements ... including consolidated financial statements. Such financial statements are prepared and presented at least annually and are directed toward the common information needs of a wide range of users. Some of these users may require, and have the power to obtain, information in addition to that contained in the financial statements. Many users, however, have to rely on the financial statements as their major source of financial information and such financial statements should, therefore, be prepared and presented with their needs in view'. However, in the most recent draft (as at the time of writing this chapter) of the proposed new FASB/IASB conceptual framework (FASB, 2008, paragraph OB2), which we will discuss further in Chapter 6, the role of general purpose financial reporting is defined more narrowly as being: 'to provide financial information about the reporting entity that is useful to present and potential equity investors, lenders, and other creditors in making decisions in their capacity as capital providers. Information that is decision useful to capital providers may also be useful to other users of financial reporting who are not capital providers.'

statement of financial position, the income statement, the statement of comprehensive income, the statement of cash flows, the statement of changes in equity, and supporting notes, are directly affected by the various accounting regulations in place.[2] When existing accounting regulations change, or new accounting regulations are implemented, this will typically have an impact on the various accounting numbers (such as particular revenues, expenses, assets and liabilities) included in the reports provided to the public.

Ideally, users of financial reports should have a sound working knowledge of the various accounting standards and other regulations because, arguably, without such a knowledge it can be difficult (or perhaps near impossible) to interpret what the reports are actually reflecting. For example, 'profit' is the outcome of applying particular accounting rules and conventions, many of which are contained within accounting standards. As these rules change (as they frequently do), the same series of transactions will lead to different measures of 'profits' and net assets. Such a situation leads to an obvious question: should readers of financial reports be expected to understand financial accounting? The answer is yes, even though many users of financial statements (including many company directors and financial analysts) have a very poor working knowledge of accounting.

Throughout the world, various professional accounting bodies have stated specifically that users of financial reports do need to have some level of knowledge of financial accounting if they are to understand financial reports properly. For example, the IASB's conceptual framework (IASC, 1989, paragraph 25) states that:

> users are assumed to have a reasonable knowledge of business and economic activities and accounting and a willingness to study the information with reasonable diligence.[3]

If we are to review an annual report of a company listed on a stock exchange, we will soon realize just how confusing such a document would be to readers with a limited knowledge of accounting (and, as became clear in the aftermath of the sub-prime banking crisis and the earlier collapse of Enron, many people with formal qualifications in accounting also have trouble interpreting the accounting reports of companies which have more complex financial structures and engage in more complex financial transactions). Unfortunately, many readers of financial statements have tended to consider figures such as 'profits'

---

[2] As a result of the release of the revised IAS 1 'Presentation of Financial Statements' in September 2007, which became effective from 1 January 2009, important terminology changed. For example, we now refer to a balance sheet as a 'statement of financial position', and rather than having a profit and loss account, we now have a 'statement of comprehensive income'. This latter statement may be split and presented in two parts: an 'income statement' (showing all items down to the profit or loss for the period) and a 'statement of comprehensive income' (showing other items that are not part of the profit or loss). There is no clear theory to explain how changing the names or formats of these financial statements will provide positive benefits for users or preparers of financial statements.

[3] Within the United States Conceptual Framework Project, reference is made to the 'informed reader' who should have sufficient knowledge of accounting to be able to appropriately interpret financial statements compiled in accordance with generally accepted accounting principles. As will be indicated in Chapter 6, there is currently a joint project being undertaken between the IASB and the Financial Accounting Standards Board (US) to develop a revised conceptual project. In the latest Exposure Draft for this new conceptual framework (FASB, 2008, paragraph BC2.31) it was noted that users 'should have a reasonable degree of financial knowledge and a willingness to study the information with reasonable diligence'.

or 'assets' as being 'hard' objective numbers that are not subject to various professional judgements. Hence, although such users may not understand some of the descriptions of accounting methods used, they may believe that they understand what 'profits' and 'net assets' mean. As we know, however, the accounting results (or numbers) will be heavily dependent upon the particular accounting methods chosen, as well as upon various professional judgements made. Depending upon who compiles the accounting reports, measures of profits and net assets can vary greatly.[4]

A review of annual reports will indicate that many companies provide summary 'highlight' statements at the beginning of the reports. Often, multi-year summaries are given of such figures as profits, return on assets, earnings per share, dividend yield, and net asset backing per share. By highlighting particular information, management could be deemed to be helping the less accounting-literate readers to focus on the important results. However, a downside of this is that management itself is selecting the information to be highlighted (that is, such disclosures are voluntary) and, as a result, a large amount of otherwise important information may be overlooked.

Financial accounting can be contrasted with management accounting. Management accounting focuses on providing information for decision-making by parties who work within an organization (that is, for internal as opposed to external users) and it is largely unregulated. While we will find that most countries have a multitude of financial accounting standards which are often given the force of law, the same cannot be said for management accounting. Because management accounting relates to the provision of information for parties within the organization, the view taken is that there is no need to protect their information needs or rights. It is the information rights of outsiders who are not involved in the day-to-day management of an entity that must be protected. Because financial reports are often used as a source of information for parties contemplating transferring resources to an organization, it is arguably important that certain rules be put in place to govern how the information should be compiled. That is (adopting a pro-regulation perspective), to protect the interests of parties external to a firm, some regulation relating to financial accounting information is required. We now briefly consider the history of accounting practice and its associated regulation.[5]

2.2 An overview of the development and regulation of accounting practice

This section examines the development of accounting regulations in jurisdictions where the primary role of financial accounts has been to aid investment decisions made by external investors in developed capital markets. As we will see in Chapter 4, the primary

---

[4] Yet all the various financial statements prepared by the various teams of accountants for the same organization may be deemed to be *true and fair* despite the differences in net assets or reported profits – which implies that different teams of accountants are able to provide different versions of the 'truth'.

[5] Although we are focusing on financial accounting in this text, a similar argument can be made in favour of the regulation of social and environmental reporting. Corporations generate many social and environmental impacts that can affect a variety of stakeholders. Such stakeholders arguably have a right-to-know about the social and environmental implications of an organization's operations. Such information could then provide the basis for decisions about whether the stakeholders will support the organization's operations in the future.

role of financial accounting in many European countries has historically been different to this capital market based role. However, with increasing globalization of business and capital markets, the role of financial accounting by large companies in all European countries is now primarily focused on the provision of information to capital markets, and regulations developed over a long period of time in economies dominated by capital markets (with large numbers of external shareholders) now apply to most large European Union (EU) companies.

While the practice of financial accounting can be traced back many hundreds of years, the regulation of financial accounting in most economies dominated by capital markets (such as the USA, UK, Ireland, Australia, Canada) generally commenced in the twentieth century. In part, this lack of regulation in the early days may have been due to the fact that until recent centuries there was a limited separation between the ownership and management of business entities, and, as such, most systems of accounting were designed to provide information to the owner/manager. In the last century there was an increase in the degree of separation between ownership and management in many countries, and with this increased separation came an increased tendency to regulate accounting disclosures.

Reliance on double-entry accounting

Early systems of double-entry bookkeeping and accounting, similar to the system we use today, have been traced back to thirteenth- and fourteenth-century Northern Italy. One of the earliest surviving descriptions of a system of double-entry accounting is by the Franciscan monk Luca Pacioli as part of his most famous work entitled *Summa de Arithmetica, Geometrica, Proportioni et Proportionalita*, published in Venice in 1494. A review of this work (there are translated versions) indicates that our current system of double-entry accounting is very similar to that developed many hundreds of years ago. Even in the days of Pacioli there were debits and credits, with debits going on the left, credits on the right.[6] There were also journals and ledgers. Reflecting on the origins of double-entry accounting, Hendriksen and Van Breda (1992, p. 36) state:

> Debits, credits, journal entries, ledgers, accounts, trial balances, balance sheets and income statements all date back to the Renaissance. Accounting, there-fore, can claim as noble a lineage as many of the liberal arts.[7] Accounting students can take pride in their heritage. Part of this heritage is a rich vocabulary, almost all of which dates back to this period and much of which is fascinating in its origin.

Debits and credits, which as we now know originated a number of centuries ago, have, over the ages, proved to be the bane of many an accounting student. So, did we really need them? Why couldn't we have simply used positive and negative numbers? For example, if we were to pay wages, why couldn't we have simply put a positive number under the wages column

---

[6] According to Hendriksen and Van Breda (1992, p. 36), our use of the word debit can be traced back to the word *debere* (which is shortened to dr). This is the Latin word for an obligation, and can be interpreted as meaning *to owe*. The word credit (abbreviated to cr) can be linked to the Latin word *credere* which means to believe or trust in someone.

[7] Hatfield (1924) points out that Luca Pacioli (who was a prominent academic of his day) was a close friend of Leonardo da Vinci, and that da Vinci was one of the first people to buy a copy of *Summa de Arithmetica* and drew the illustrations for one of Pacioli's later books.

and a negative number under the cash column? The simple answer to this question appears to be that negative numbers were not really used in mathematics until the seventeenth century. Hence, the t-account was devised to solve this problem with increases being on one side, and decreases on the other. But why keep the t-account, now that we accept the existence of negative numbers? Pondering this issue, Hendriksen and Van Breda (1992, p. 51) comment:

> Textbook writers still explain how debits are found on the left and credits on the right and teach students the subtraction-by-opposition technique that was made obsolete in arithmetic three centuries ago. Programmers then faithfully seek to reflect these medieval ideas on the modern computer screen.

As we will see in subsequent chapters, there are many criticisms of our financial accounting systems. For example, there is an increasing trend towards the view that financial accounting should reflect the various social and environmental consequences of a reporting entity's existence. Unfortunately, however, our 'dated' double-entry system has a general inability to take such consequences into account – but we will cover more of this in later chapters, particularly in Chapter 9.

Early development of professional accounting bodies

While accounting and accountants have existed for hundreds of years, it was not until the nineteenth century that accountants within the United Kingdom and the United States banded together to form professional associations. According to Goldberg (1949), a Society of Accountants was formed in Edinburgh in 1854, later to be followed by a number of other bodies, including the Institute of Chartered Accountants in England and Wales (ICAEW), which was established in 1880. According to Mathews and Perera (1996, p. 16), from the early years the ICAEW was very concerned about the reputation of its members and as a result set conditions for admission, including general education examinations, five years of articles served with a member of the institute, and intermediate and final examinations in a range of subjects.

Within the United States the American Association of Public Accountants was formed in 1887 (Goldberg, 1949). This association went on to form the basis of the American Institute of Certified Public Accountants (AICPA). While members of these bodies were often called upon to perform audits in particular circumstances, and while companies were generally required to prepare accounting reports subject to various company laws and stock exchange requirements,[8] there was a general absence of regulation about what the reports should disclose or how the accounting numbers should be compiled (that is, there was effectively a 'free-market' approach to accounting regulation).[9]

---

[8] For example, within the United Kingdom the Joint Stock Companies Act of 1844 required that companies produce a balance sheet and an auditor's report thereon for distribution to shareholders before its annual meeting. This requirement was removed in an 1862 Act, but reinstated in a 1900 Act. In 1929 a requirement to produce a profit and loss account was introduced.

[9] In 1900 the New York Stock Exchange required companies applying for listing to prepare financial statements showing the results of their operations as well as details about their financial position. In 1926 the exchange further required that all listed companies provide their shareholders with an annual financial report in advance of the companies' annual general meetings. The report did not have to be audited.

Early codification of accounting rules

In the early part of the twentieth century there was limited work undertaken to codify particular accounting principles or rules. Basically, accountants used those rules of which they were aware and which they (hopefully) believed were most appropriate to the particular circumstances. There was very limited uniformity between the accounting methods adopted by different organizations, thereby creating obvious comparability problems. Around the 1920s a number of people undertook research that sought to observe practice and to identify commonly accepted accounting conventions. That is, they sought to describe 'what was', rather than assuming a normative position with regards to 'what should be'. By simply describing current practice, the researchers gave themselves limited possibility for actually improving accounting procedures. As Mathews and Perera (1996, p. 20) state:

> This led to a practice-theory-practice cycle and tended to retard the progress of accounting, because there was no value judgement exercised in respect of the practices which were observed. In other words, there was no opportunity to examine critically what was being practised before the next generation of accountants were prepared in the same manner.

Early researchers who provided detailed descriptions of existing conventions of accounting included Gilman (1939), Paton (1922), Paton and Littleton (1940) and Sanders *et al.* (1938). These studies described such things as the doctrines of conservatism, concepts of materiality, consistency, the entity assumption and the matching principle.

A great deal of the early work undertaken to establish particular accounting rules and doctrines was undertaken in the United States. In 1930 the accounting profession within the United States cooperated with the New York Stock Exchange (NYSE) to develop a list of broadly used accounting principles. According to Zeff (1972), this publication is one of the most important documents in the history of accounting regulation and set the foundation for the codification and acceptance of generally accepted accounting principles. The NYSE requested the accounting profession to compile the document as it was concerned that many companies were using a variety of (typically undisclosed) accounting methods.[10]

Development of disclosure regulations

Within the United States it was not until 1934 that specific disclosures of financial information were required by organizations seeking to trade their securities. The Securities Exchange Act of 1934, as administered by the Securities Exchange Commission (SEC), stipulated the disclosure of specific financial information. The SEC was given authority to stipulate accounting principles and reporting practices. However, it allowed the accounting profession to take charge of this activity as long as it could clearly indicate that it would perform such duties diligently. In an effort to convince the SEC that it could identify acceptable accounting practices, the American Institute of Accountants (one of the predecessors of the AICPA) released a study by Sanders *et al.* (1938) entitled *A Statement of Accounting Principles*.

---

[10] Five of the identified principles subsequently formed the basis of Chapter 1 of *Accounting Research Bulletin* No. 43, as issued by the Committee on Accounting Procedure.

In 1938 the SEC stated (within Accounting Series Release No. 4) that it would only accept financial statements prepared in accordance with the generally accepted accounting principles of the accounting profession – thereby giving a great deal of power to the profession. In part, ASR No. 4 stated:

> In cases where financial statements filed with the Commission ... are prepared in accordance with accounting principles for which there is no substantial authoritative support, such financial statements will be presumed to be misleading or inaccurate despite disclosures contained in the certificate of the accountant or in footnotes to the statements provided the matters are material. In cases where there is a difference of opinion between the Commission and the registrant as to proper principles of accounting to be followed, disclosure will be accepted in lieu of correction of the financial statements themselves, only if the points involved are such that there is substantial authoritative support for the practices followed by the registrant and the position of the Commission has not previously been expressed in rules, regulations, or other releases of the Commission, including the published opinion of its chief accountant.

While the above statement does indicate that the SEC was to allow the accounting profession to determine acceptable practice, many considered that the SEC was also warning the accounting profession that it must take an authoritative lead in developing accounting standards, otherwise the SEC would take over the role (Zeff, 1972). From 1939 the Committee on Accounting Procedure, a committee of the accounting profession, began issuing statements on accounting principles, and between 1938 and 1939 it released 12 *Accounting Research Bulletins* (Zeff, 1972).

Development by the accounting profession of mandatory accounting standards is a relatively recent phenomenon. In the United Kingdom it was not until 1970, when the Accounting Standards Steering Committee was established (later to become the Accounting Standards Committee and then the Accounting Standards Board), that UK accountants had to conform with professionally developed mandatory accounting standards. Prior to this time the ICAEW had released a series of 'recommendations' to members. In the United States, although there had been Accounting Research Bulletins (released by the Committee on Accounting Procedure, formed in 1938), and Opinions (released by the Accounting Principles Board (APB), formed in 1959), these Bulletins and Opinions were not mandatory. Rather they indicated perceived best practice. There tended to be many corporate departures from these Bulletins and Opinions and, as a result, in 1965 a rule (Rule 203 of the AICPA) was introduced that required departures from principles published in APB Opinions to be disclosed in footnotes to financial statements. From 1 July 1973 the APB was replaced by the Financial Accounting Standards Board (FASB), which has subsequently released many accounting standards that are mandatory.

As noted at the beginning of this section, and as will be explored in greater depth in Chapter 4, historically financial accounting practices (and therefore the regulation of financial accounts) in many European Countries was not primarily focused on the provision of information to aid investment decisions by external shareholders in capital markets. Regulation of accounting through professionally developed standards is therefore an even more recent phenomenon in large parts of Europe than it is, for example, in the UK, Ireland or the Netherlands. However, regulation through accounting standards (specifically through International Financial Reporting Standards) of the consolidated financial statements of all companies whose shares are traded on any stock exchange in the EU became compulsory from 1 January 2005.

Twenty-first century political pressure on financial accounting regulation

Political pressures arising after several high-profile accounting and audit failures in the United States in 2001 and 2002 (such as Enron and WorldCom) led to a significant change in the accounting regulatory frameworks of many countries. Although, as Unerman and O'Dwyer (2004) point out, these were not the first large-scale accounting failures to occur since the inception of regulation through professional accounting standards, they were much larger than previous failures and occurred at a time of sharply falling stock markets. Private investors who were already losing confidence in stock markets due to their financial losses from falling share prices now perceived accounting failures as contributing to even larger losses. In this climate, politicians came under pressure to make accounting and related corporate governance regulation more rigorous, and they passed legislation (such as the US Sarbanes–Oxley Act of 2002) to give greater legal force to many existing and new regulations.

Significant political pressure for changes in accounting regulations and regulatory regimes was again exerted for a period following the sub-prime banking crisis and ensuing global financial crisis from 2007/8 onwards. The sub-prime banking crisis saw several banks fail, including the major financial institution of Lehman Brothers, and others need very large amounts of state support. These failures exacerbated a loss of confidence within the global banking system – with such confidence being an essential element in the smooth running of the banking system, which in turn is essential for economic stability and growth. Among the many practices that have been implicated in causing the sub-prime banking crisis and ensuing credit crunch and global financial crisis, the effectiveness of financial accounting and its regulation has been called into question (for a variety of theoretical perspectives on the role of accounting and accountants in the sub-prime crisis and credit crunch see, for example, Arnold, 2009; Hopwood, 2009; Laux and Leuz, 2009; Roberts and Jones 2009; Sikka, 2009). Politicians questioned why the financial statements of failed banks had not given adequate warning of the significant risks and problems faced by the banks. This political questioning of the role of accounting, and pressure to take action to ensure that financial statements helped to provide greater transparency in the future, reached the highest level when it was placed on the agenda of the G-20 leaders' summit meetings from their inception in 2008.[11] At the first of these summit meetings, in November 2008, the first of the five policy areas in the area of reforming financial markets was *Transparency and Accountability*:

> **Strengthening Transparency and Accountability:** We will strengthen financial market transparency, including by enhancing required disclosure on complex

---

[11] The G-20 is a forum for the finance ministers and central bank governors from 19 of the world's largest economies plus the European Union. In responding to the global financial crisis, the G-20 convened a series of semi-annual summits of the leaders of the G-20 countries, starting in November 2008 in Washington, DC, and followed by London in April 2009, Pittsburgh in September 2009, Toronto in June 2010 and Seoul in November 2010.

financial products and ensuring complete and accurate disclosure by firms of their financial conditions. Incentives should be aligned to avoid excessive risk-taking. (G-20, 2008a, paragraph 9)

In detailing how they were to achieve the desired reforms in this area, the G-20 leaders agreed a series of short-term and medium-term actions, most of which required changes in specific accounting regulations or in the manner in which accounting is regulated (G-20, 2008b, p. 1):

Immediate Actions by March 31, 2009

- The key global accounting standards bodies should work to enhance guidance for valuation of securities, also taking into account the valuation of complex, illiquid products, especially during times of stress.

- Accounting standard setters should significantly advance their work to address weaknesses in accounting and disclosure standards for off-balance sheet vehicles.

- Regulators and accounting standard setters should enhance the required disclosure of complex financial instruments by firms to market participants.

- With a view toward promoting financial stability, the governance of the international accounting standard setting body should be further enhanced, including by undertaking a review of its membership, in particular in order to ensure transparency, accountability, and an appropriate relationship between this independent body and the relevant authorities.

- Private sector bodies that have already developed best practices for private pools of capital and/or hedge funds should bring forward proposals for a set of unified best practices. Finance Ministers should assess the adequacy of these proposals, drawing upon the analysis of regulators, the expanded FSF [Financial Stability Forum], and other relevant bodies.

Medium-term actions

- The key global accounting standards bodies should work intensively toward the objective of creating a single high-quality global standard.

- Regulators, supervisors, and accounting standard setters, as appropriate, should work with each other and the private sector on an ongoing basis to ensure consistent application and enforcement of high-quality accounting standards.

- Financial institutions should provide enhanced risk disclosures in their reporting and disclose all losses on an ongoing basis, consistent with international best practice, as appropriate. Regulators should work to ensure that a financial institution's financial statements include a complete, accurate, and timely picture of the firm's activities (including off-balance sheet activities) and are reported on a consistent and regular basis.

At the G-20 summit in September 2009, the G-20 called for further strengthening of accounting standards in the form of an early completion by June 2011 of the FASB/IASB convergence project, aiming to produce a single set of accounting standards for use internationally. By the time of the June 2010 summit, this timetable had slipped slightly with a revised target to achieve convergence by the end of 2011:

> We re-emphasized the importance we place on achieving a single set of high quality improved global accounting standards. We urged the International Accounting Standards Board and the Financial Accounting Standards Board to increase their efforts to complete their convergence project by the end of 2011 (G-20, 2010, p. 20, paragraph 30).

We will return to issues of international convergence in accounting standards in Chapter 4.

2.3 The rationale for regulating financial accounting practice

As indicated above, even though financial reports have been in existence for hundreds of years, the regulation of accounting in economies dominated by capital markets (with large numbers of external investors) is a fairly recent phenomenon. Early moves for regulation of accounting were introduced in the United States around the 1930s and followed events such as the Wall Street stock market crash of 1929. Rightly or wrongly it was argued that problems inherent to accounting led to many poor and uninformed investment decisions (Boer, 1994; Ray, 1960), and this fuelled the public desire for information generated by companies to be subject to greater regulation.

In most countries with developed capital markets and large numbers of external investors, there is a multitude of accounting regulations covering a broad cross-section of issues – but do we really need all this regulation? As we will see in the next chapter, there are two broad schools of thought on this issue. There are parties who argue that regulation is necessary, with reasons including:

- markets for information are not efficient and without regulation a sub-optimal amount of information will be produced;
- while proponents of the 'free-market' (or 'anti-regulation') approach may argue that the capital market *on average* is efficient, such *on average* arguments ignore the rights of individual investors, some of whom can lose their savings as a result of relying upon unregulated disclosures;
- some parties who demand information about an organization can often obtain their desired information due to the power they possess as a result of their control over scarce resources required by the organization. Conversely, parties with limited power (limited resources) will generally be unable to secure information about an organization, even though that organization may impact on their existence;
- investors need protection from fraudulent organizations that may produce misleading information, which, due to information asymmetries, cannot be known to be fraudulent when used; (such as apparently occurred at WorldCom in the USA and Parmalat in Italy in the early 2000s);
- regulation leads to uniform methods being adopted by different entities, thus enhancing comparability.

Others argue that regulation is not necessary, particularly to the extent that it currently exists. Some of the reasons cited against accounting regulation include:

■ accounting information is like any other good, and people (financial statement users) will be prepared to pay for it to the extent that it has use. This will lead to an optimal supply of information by entities;[12, 13]

■ capital markets require information, and any organization that fails to provide information will be punished by the market – an absence of information will be deemed to imply bad news;[14]

■ because users of financial information typically do not bear its cost of production, regulation will lead to over-supply of information (at cost to the producing firms) as users will tend to overstate the need for the information;

■ regulation typically restricts the accounting methods that may be used. This means that some organizations will be prohibited from using accounting methods which they believe most efficiently reflects their particular performance and position. This is considered to impact on the efficiency with which the firm can inform the markets about its operations.[15]

When regulation is introduced, there are various theories available to describe who benefits from such regulation. There is the *public interest theory* of regulation which proposes that regulation be introduced to protect the public. This protection may be required as a result of inefficient markets. Public interest theory assumes that the regulatory body (usually government) is a neutral arbiter of the 'public interest' and does not let its own self-interest impact on its rule-making processes. According to Scott (2003, p. 448), following public interest theory, the regulator 'does its best to regulate so as to maximise social welfare. Consequently, regulation is thought of as a trade-off between the costs of regulation and its social benefits in the form of improved operation of markets'.

A contrary perspective of regulation is provided by *capture theory*, which argues that although regulation is often introduced to protect the public, the regulatory mechanisms are often subsequently controlled (captured) so as to protect the interests of particular self-interested groups within society, typically those whose activities are most affected by the regulation. That is, the 'regulated' tend to capture the 'regulator'. Posner (1974, p. 342)

---

[12] Advocates of a regulated approach would argue, however, that accounting information is a public good and as a result, many individuals will obtain the information for free (this is often referred to as the 'free-rider' problem). Once this occurs, reliance on market-mechanism arguments tends to be flawed and the usual pricing mechanisms of a market cannot be expected to operate (Cooper and Keim, 1983).

[13] This 'free-market' perspective is adopted by researchers who work within the agency theory paradigm. This paradigm is discussed in Chapter 7.

[14] Accepting this perspective, and consistent with Akerlof (1970), companies that fail to produce necessary information, particularly if the information is being produced by other entities, will be viewed as 'lemons' (a lemon is something of inferior quality), and these 'lemons' will find it more costly to attract funds than other ('non-lemon') entities.

[15] For example, pursuant to IAS 38 'Intangibles', all expenditure on research has to be expensed as incurred. This means that all companies have to adopt the same 'one-size-fits-all' approach, even though some entities may have undertaken very valuable research that will lead to significant future economic benefits. On the basis of efficiency this regulation is deemed to be inappropriate as it does not allow annual report readers to differentiate between companies with, or without, valuable research.

argues that 'the original purposes of the regulatory program are later thwarted through the efforts of the interest group'. Empirical evidence of a regulator making individual decisions which favour the groups that it regulates is not sufficient to demonstrate regulatory capture (as each of these decisions might be regarded as the most appropriate in the circumstances). Rather, most of the regulator's whole programme of regulation needs to work in the interests of the regulated, and usually against the interests of those who the regulator is intended to protect. This implies that accounting regulations can have a different impact on different people or groups, and there is evidence (discussed in the next chapter) showing that specific accounting regulations do have social and/or economic consequences that vary between different groups.

Both public interest theories and capture theories of regulation assert that initially regulation is put in place to protect the public (capture theory simply asserts that the regulated will then subsequently attempt to control the regulatory process). Another view, which is often referred to as *private interest theory* (or *economic interest group theory*), is proposed by researchers such as Stigler (1971) and Peltzman (1976). This theory relaxes the assumption that regulations are initially put in place to protect the public interest, as well as the assumption that government regulators are neutral arbiters not driven by self-interest. Stigler (1971) proposes that governments are made up of individuals who are self-interested and will introduce regulations more likely to lead to their re-election. In deciding upon particular regulation they will consider the impacts on key voters, as well as on election campaign finances. Individuals with an interest in particular legislation are deemed more likely to get their preferred legislation if they can form themselves into large organized groups with strong cohesive voting power. These theories of regulation (public interest theory, capture theory and private interest theory), as well as others, are further considered in Chapter 3.

If we are to accept the need for accounting regulation, a further issue to consider is who should be responsible for the regulation – should it be in the hands of the private sector (such as the accounting profession), or in the hands of the public (government) sector?[16] Can private sector regulators be expected to put in place regulations that are always in the public interest, or will they seek to put in place rules that favour their own constituency? Obviously, answering such a question will be dependent upon our particular view of the world (and our own view of the world will in turn influence which particular theory of regulation we are more likely to embrace). Advocates of private sector accounting standard-setting would argue that the accounting profession is best able to develop accounting standards because of its superior knowledge of accounting, and because of the greater likelihood that its rules and regulations would be accepted by the business community. Proponents of public sector accounting standard-setting argue that government has greater enforcement powers, hence the rules of government are more likely to be followed. It might also be less responsive to pressures exerted by business, and more likely to consider overall public interest.

---

[16] In some countries, accounting regulation is in the hands of both private sector and public sector entities. As an example, within the EU, accounting regulations are developed by the International Accounting Standards Board (private sector) but have to be endorsed by the Accounting Regulatory Committee (public sector) before they are enforced for EU companies. In the United States, both the Financial Accounting Standards Board (private sector) and the SEC (public sector) have released accounting standards.

What we demonstrate in subsequent chapters is that the regulation of accounting (or indeed an absence of regulation) can have many economic and social consequences. As such, the accounting standard-setting process is typically considered to be a very political process, with various interested parties lobbying the standard-setters.

2.4 The role of professional judgement in financial accounting

As we know from studying accounting, the process involved in generating accounts depends upon many professional judgements. While the accounting treatment of many transactions and events is regulated, a great deal of accounting treatment pertaining to other transactions and events is unregulated. Even when particular regulations are in place, for example that buildings must be depreciated, there is still scope to select the useful life of the building and the residual value. Many such judgements must be made – should an item be capitalized or expensed? This in turn will depend upon crucial assessments as to whether the expenditure is likely to generate future economic benefits.

At the core of the accounting process is an expectation that accountants should be objective and free from bias when performing their duties. The information being generated should *represent faithfully* the underlying transactions and events and it should be *neutral* and *complete* (IASC, 1989, paragraphs 33, 36 and 38).[17] However, can we really accept that accounting can be 'neutral' or objective? Throughout the world, several national accounting standard-setters have explicitly considered the economic and social implications of possible accounting standards prior to their introduction (the consideration of economic and social consequences prior to the release of an accounting standard is specifically referred to in conceptual framework projects such as the IASB's *Framework for the Preparation and Presentation of Financial Statements*). In these countries, if the economic or social implications of a particular accounting standard have been deemed to be significantly negative, then it is likely that the introduction of the standard would have been abandoned – even though the particular standard may have been deemed to reflect more accurately particular transactions or events. While it is difficult to criticize a process that considers potential impacts on others, it is nevertheless difficult to accept that accounting standards are neutral or unbiased. In a sense the acceptance of the need to consider economic and social consequences as part of the standard-setting process has created a dilemma for standard-setters. According to Zeff (1978, p. 62):

> The board (FASB) is thus faced with a dilemma which requires a delicate balancing of accounting and non-accounting variables. Although its decisions should rest – and be seen to rest – chiefly on accounting considerations, it must also study – and be seen to study – the possible adverse economic and social consequences of its proposed actions ... What is abundantly clear is that we have entered an era in which economic and social consequences may no longer be ignored as a substantive issue in the setting of accounting standards. The

---

[17] According to Hines (1991, p. 330) it is in the accounting profession's interest to publicly promote a perspective of objectivity. As she states, 'the very talk, predicated on an assumption of an objective world to which accountants have privileged access via their "measurement expertise", serves to construct a perceived legitimacy for the profession's power and autonomy'.

profession must respond to the changing tenor of the times while continuing to perform its essential role in the areas in which it possesses undoubted expertise.

However, this willingness to take into account the possible wider social and economic consequences in developing accounting standards has reduced in several countries in recent years. For example, in the United Kingdom in 2001 and 2002, many large companies blamed (possibly unfairly) the rules in a controversial new accounting standard on pension costs for their decisions to withdraw elements of their pension schemes from many employees. This can be considered to have been a significant negative social consequence from the new accounting standard for these employees, but the UK accounting regulator refused to change the accounting standard (despite considerable political pressure).

In Chapters 7 and 8 we consider various theoretical perspectives proposed as explanations for why particular accounting methods may be implemented by a reporting entity (remember, the accounting treatment of many transactions and events is not subject to accounting standards). Consistent with a perspective of objectivity is a view that organizations are best served by selecting accounting methods that best reflect their underlying performance. This is referred to as an 'efficiency perspective' (derived from Positive Accounting Theory which is explained in Chapter 7). The efficiency perspective asserts that different organizational characteristics explain why different firms adopt different accounting methods (Jensen and Meckling, 1976). For example, firms that have different patterns of use in relation to a particular type of asset will be predicted to adopt different amortization policies. Advocates of the efficiency perspective argue that firms should be allowed to choose those accounting methods that best reflect their performance, and that accounting regulations that restrict the set of available accounting techniques will be costly. For example, if a new accounting standard is released that bans a particular accounting method being used by a reporting entity, then this will lead to inefficiencies as the resulting financial statements may no longer provide the best reflection of the performance of the organization. It would be argued that management is best able to select which accounting methods are appropriate in given circumstances, and government or other bodies should not intervene in the standard-setting process. This perspective, however, does not consider that some financial statement preparers may be less than objective (that is, like Lehman Brothers, Enron, WorldCom or Parmalat are all alleged to have been, they may be *creative*) when preparing the financial reports. The efficiency perspective also dismisses the comparability benefits that may arise if standard-setters reduce the available set of accounting methods.

An alternative perspective to explain why particular accounting methods are selected (and which is also derived from Positive Accounting Theory) is the 'opportunistic perspective'. This perspective does not assume that those responsible for selecting accounting methods will be objective. Rather, it assumes that they will be driven by self-interest (Watts and Zimmerman, 1978). This perspective provides an explanation of the practice of *creative accounting*, which is defined as an approach to accounting wherein objectivity is not employed, but rather, refers to a situation where those responsible for the preparation of accounts select accounting methods that provide the result desired by the preparers. As an example, an organization might, like Lehman Brothers or Enron, opportunistically elect to structure certain transactions in a manner designed to remove specific assets and related liabilities from its balance sheet (a technique known as *off balance sheet funding*). This is not because these assets and liabilities do not 'belong' to the organization, but perhaps may be because this off balance sheet funding has the effect of reducing the reported debt to equity (capital gearing or leverage) ratio. This may be regarded as useful by managers at a time when the organization is close to breaching particular accounting-based agreements negotiated with external parties, such as loan agreements that have a stipulated minimum allowable debt to equity ratio, below which particular assets of the reporting entity may be seized. Accounting Headline 2.1 provides an example from the collapse of Lehman Brothers that illustrates how financial statements were allegedly manipulated to portray a misleading picture of the bank's financial position.

Apart from the efficiency and opportunistic perspectives, there are a number of other theoretical perspectives proposed to explain why an entity may select particular accounting and disclosure policies (other perspectives include legitimacy theory, political economy theory, and stakeholder theory). Chapter 8 further explores some of the alternative theoretical perspectives. However, what is being emphasized at this point is that although there is much accounting regulation in place (and there are various theories to explain the existence of regulation), there are also many accounting decisions that are unregulated (giving rise to various theories to explain the choice of particular accounting methods from the set of available alternatives).

Accounting Headline 2.1 _____

Example of alleged misleading creative accounting at Lehman Brothers

Lehman Brothers bosses could face court over accounting 'gimmicks'

By Andrew Clark

A court-appointed US bankruptcy examiner has concluded that there are grounds for legal claims against top Lehman Brothers bosses and auditor Ernst & Young for signing off misleading accounting statements in the run-up to the collapse of the Wall Street bank in 2008 which sparked the worst financial crisis since the Great Depression.

A judge last night unsealed a 2,200-page forensic report by expert Anton Valukas into Lehman's collapse, which includes scathing criticism of accounting 'gimmicks' used by the failing bank to buy itself time. These included a contentious technique known as 'repo 105', which temporarily boosted the bank's balance sheet by as much as $50bn (£33bn).

The exhaustive account reveals that Barclays, which bought Lehman's US businesses out of bankruptcy, got certain equipment and assets it was not entitled to. And it reveals that during Lehman's final few hours, chief executive Dick Fuld tried to get Gordon Brown involved to overrule Britain's Financial Services Authority when it refused to fast-track a rescue by Barclays.

With Wall Street shaken by the demise of Bear Stearns in March 2008, Valukas said confidence in Lehman eroded: 'To buy itself more time, to maintain that critical confidence, Lehman painted a misleading picture of its financial condition.'

The examiner's report found evidence to support 'colorable claims', meaning plausible claims, against Fuld and three successive chief financial officers – Chris O'Meara, Erin Callan and Ian Lowitt.

Valukas said the bank tried to lower its leverage ratio, a key measure for credit rating agencies, through a device dubbed 'repo 105', through which it temporarily sold assets with an obligation to repurchase them days later, at the end of financial quarters, in order to get a temporary influx of cash. Lehman's own financial staff described this as an 'accounting gimmick' and a 'lazy way' to meet balance sheet targets.

A senior Lehman vice-president, Matthew Lee, tried to blow the whistle by alerting top management and Ernst & Young. But the auditing firm 'took virtually no action to investigate'. ...

A lawyer for Fuld last night rejected the examiner's findings. Patricia Hynes of Allen & Overy said Fuld did not structure or negotiate the repo 105 transactions, nor was he aware of their accounting treatment. She added that Fuld 'throughout his career faithfully and diligently worked in the interests of Lehman and its stakeholders'.

A spokesman for Ernst & Young, which is headquartered in London, told Reuters the firm had no immediate comment because it was yet to review the findings.

Source: *Guardian*, 12 March 2010, p. 25
©Guardian News and Media Limited 2010

2.5 How powerful is the accountant?

The idea of accountants being very powerful individuals within society is probably not an idea that is shared by many people. Indeed, many people might unfairly see accountants as rather boring, unimaginative and methodical individuals. Certainly this is the stereotype that many people attribute to accountants.[18] According to Bougen (1994), such a view is, in large part, driven by the interdependency between accounting and bookkeeping. Reflecting on the work of Bougen, Dimnik and Felton (2006, p. 133) state:

> Although much accounting work requires judgment, imagination and creativity, bookkeeping is boring and routine. Bougen suggests that historically, accountants may have been willing to accept a personally disparaging, often laughable image because it was in their professional interest to do so. Since bookkeeping is also identified with positive characteristics such as objectivity, accuracy and conservatism, the stereotype of the unimaginative, harmless, methodical number cruncher may have actually heightened the accountant's reputation for dependability, giving the profession more credibility with the public.

Following from the above quote, it could be argued that accountants might actually have decided to embrace an unimaginative and harmless persona because of the financial benefits associated with being seen as 'dependable' and 'credible'. How clever! Nevertheless,

---

[18] According to Dimnik and Felton (2006, p. 131), a stereotype may be defined as a collection of attributes believed to describe the members of a social group.

accountants are frequently the subject of many a cruel joke. They are often portrayed as small, weak individuals with poor social skills. For example, consider the depictions of accountants in various films and television programmes. In the (in)famous *Monty Python* Lion Tamer sketch, in which John Cleese is cast as a recruitment consultant who interviews Michael Palin (who plays Mr Anchovy, the accountant and aspiring lion tamer), Cleese describes the accountant as:

> An extremely dull fellow, unimaginative, timid, lacking in initiative, spineless, easily dominated ... Whereas in most professions these would be considerable drawbacks, in accountancy they are a positive boon.[19]

Some of us might also remember such characters as Louis Tully, the 'nerd' accountant in *Ghostbusters* (1984) who invites business associates to a party rather than friends so as to make the party tax-deductible, and Leo Getz, the bumbling accountant who constantly annoys two police officers in *Lethal Weapon 2* (1989) and *Lethal Weapon 3* (1992). These are only two of many poor depictions that films make of accountants. While accountants may be the subject of such (poorly informed and unpleasant) depictions and taunts, we can rest in the knowledge that we accountants are indeed very powerful individuals.[20] The assertion that accountants are *powerful* (which is obviously more flattering than being seen as dull and unimaginative) is based on a number of perspectives, as follows:

- The output of the accounting process (for example, *profits* or *net asset backing per share*) impacts on many decisions such as whether to invest in or lend funds to an entity, whether to lobby for increased wages based on profitability, whether to place an entity into technical default for failure to comply with previously agreed accounting-based restrictions, whether to lobby government for intervention because of excessive *profits*, and so on. That is, many transfers of funds (and therefore wealth) arise as a result of reports generated by accountants through the accounting process. For example, many extremely large companies throughout the world have had to cease operations because they have breached various borrowing agreements – borrowing agreements that are directly tied to numbers generated by the accountant (for example, organizations might have entered an agreement that restricts the amount of debt they can borrow relative to their total assets). Because accounting is heavily reliant on professional judgement, the judgement of the accountant can directly impact on various parties' wealth.

- There is also a perspective that accountants, in providing objective information to interested parties, can, in a sense, provide or transfer to them a source of 'power' to drive changes to corporations' behaviour. That is, accounting information informs people about certain aspects of an organization's performance and this information – compiled by accountants – might motivate the people to take various actions that

---

[19] Smith and Briggs (1999) provide a more thorough overview of how accountants have been portrayed in films and on television. Other research to consider how accountants are depicted in films includes Cory (1992), Beard (1994) and Holt (1994).

[20] In further research, Dimnik and Felton (2006) undertook a review of 121 films and while many accountants are depicted as 'plodders' (having low-level jobs with little status) or 'dreamers' (who are deemed to be out of touch with reality), a number of films actually portray the accountant as a hero.

might be advantageous or disadvantageous to the organization. Such actions might not be initiated in the absence of the accounting information. As Gray (1992, p. 404) states:

> power can be exercised in some degree by all … external parties. For that power to be exercised there is a basic need for information (as an essential element of the participatory democratic process …) and this information will be an extension of that currently available. That is, the widest possible range of participants must be emancipated and enabled through the manifestation of existing but unfulfilled rights to information.

Accountants generate information that is used to guide the actions of many people throughout society. Indeed, much of the 'language' used in business is directly tied to the work undertaken by the accountant.

■ By emphasizing particular performance attributes (such as profits), accountants can tend to give legitimacy to organizations that otherwise may not be deemed to be legitimate. The financial press often praises companies because of their reported profits. That is, profitability might tend to be a 'proxy' for legitimacy. However, profitability is also often used as a basis for criticizing a company. For example, consumer groups or employee groups might use the reported profits of a company as a justification for demanding that the company reduce the costs of its goods or services, or pay higher salaries to its workforce. What is being emphasized here is that the output of the accounting system is used in many different ways throughout society – further evidence of the influence of accounting and, therefore, of accountants.

Further reflecting on the above points, we can consider the work of Hines (1988, 1991). Hines (1991, p. 313) stresses a perspective that 'financial accounting practices are implicated in the construction and reproduction of the social world'. What she is arguing is that by emphasizing measures such as profits (which ignores many negative social and environmental impacts) accounting can cause people to support organizations that may not otherwise be supported. By holding profitability out as some sort of ideal in terms of performance, profitable companies are often considered to be *good* companies despite the fact that such organizations might generate various negative social and environmental impacts.

Consider Accounting Headline 2.2. The newspaper report emphasizes the profits (and cost reduction measures) of the Anglo-Dutch oil company Royal Dutch Shell (commonly known simply as Shell). If profits increase from one period to the next (or if the profits are larger than other organizations within the industry), this is typically portrayed as a sign of sound management. The earning of profits tends to be seen as consistent with a notion of legitimacy – profits are reported and emphasized as some form of objective measure of performance. But as we know, and what the media typically neglects to note, the measure of profits really depends on the assumptions and judgements made by the particular team of accountants involved. As can be seen from Accounting Headline 2.2, no mention is made of the accounting methods employed by Shell. This is typical of media coverage given to corporate performance, with accounting results (for example, profits) being apparently promoted as hard, objective calculations. Financial accounting can engender such views because it is promoted (through such media as conceptual frameworks) as being objective

Accounting Headline 2.2

Example of how profitability is emphasized as a sign of good management

Shell profits surge 60% as oil prices rise

By Dan Milmo

The Anglo-Dutch oil group reported earnings of $4.9bn (£3.2bn) for the first three months of the year – a day after BP posted a figure of $5.6bn.

A recovering global economy helped Shell post a 60% rise in first quarter profits today as the rising oil price and increased production from new projects produced figures that exceeded analysts' expectations.

The Anglo-Dutch oil company said earnings rose to $4.8bn (£3.2bn) in the first three months of 2010, compared with $3bn for the same period last year.

Shell attributed some of the gain to the resurgent oil price, which has climbed from $44 per barrel of Brent crude last year to an average of $76 at the beginning of 2010. Analysts were also surprised by a stronger-than-expected boost in oil and gas production, which rose 6% as the company's Sakhalin II project in Russia and its deepwater Parque das Conchas fields off Brazil were ramped up.

However, Shell's chief executive, Peter Voser, was keen to ascribe the profits increase to the company's own actions as well as the strong oil price, pointing to cost-cutting measures and the rise in output as major contributors to its first-quarter performance.

"I am pleased with the results in the first quarter 2010, which were largely driven by our own actions," he said. "The priorities are for a more competitive performance, for growth, and for sharper delivery of strategy. There is more to come from Shell."

Shell's profits statement beat analysts' forecasts. "The first-quarter results reflect the beginning of a more encouraging trend," said Tony Shephard, a Charles Stanley analyst. However, several experts believed that the main factor in Shell's improved earnings was the rise in the average oil price.

Analysts also praised Shell's new initiatives, which include a joint gas project with the state-owned China National Petroleum Corporation in Sichuan province. Another new project has attracted controversy in recent weeks, however, resulting in Shell having to defeat a call by environment groups and investors at its annual meeting for a review of oil sands operations in Canada.

Shell is the latest oil company to report improved figures over the past week. BP reported a 135% increase in net profits on Tuesday and Italy's Eni posted a 3.6% rise in net profits last week. Major US oil companies ExxonMobil and Chevron also due to publish results this week.

Fears over Greece's sovereign debt crisis have dragged down the crude oil price in recent days, but increased demand in China, India and the Middle East is expected to sustain the upward trend, prompting Barclays Capital to forecast that the price for a barrel of crude could pass $100 this year.

Source: *Guardian,* 29 April 2010, p. 31
©Guardian News and Media Limited 2010

and reliable and having the capacity to accurately reflect underlying facts.[21] As Hines (1991, p. 315) states in relation to conceptual framework (CF) projects:

> It appears that the ontological assumption underpinning the CF is that the relationship between financial accounting and economic reality is a unidirectional, reflecting or faithfully reproducing relationship: economic reality exists objectively, inter-subjectively, concretely and independently of financial accounting practices; financial accounting reflects, mirrors, represents or measures this pre-existent reality.

What also should be appreciated is that the measures of profit calculated for Shell (and also other organizations) ignore many social and environmental externalities caused by the reporting entity. While the products of an oil company such as Shell are an essential element of the way we live our lives today, and therefore of economic development and growth in the immediate future, they also lead to many negative social and environmental consequences. The way that companies are managed, and the strategic and operational decisions they take, can have a major impact on the nature and extent of these social and environmental externalities – both in the short and long term. Accounting, however, ignores these externalities.

A counter view to the above perspective (that accounting is *objective* and provides an accurate reflection of a pre-existent reality) is the view adopted by Hines that accountants can, in a sense, create different realities, depending upon the particular judgements taken, the accounting standards available, and so on. That is, accounting does not objectively reflect a particular reality – it creates it. This view is also supported by Handel (1982, p. 36) who states:

> Things may exist independently of our accounts, but they have no human existence until they become accountable. Things may not exist, but they may take on human significance by becoming accountable … Accounts define reality and at the same time they are that reality … The processes by which accounts are offered and accepted are the fundamental social process … Accounts do not more or less accurately describe things. Instead they establish what is accountable in the setting in which they occur. Whether they are accurate or inaccurate by some other standards, accounts define reality for a situation in the sense that people act on the basis of what is accountable in the situation of their action. The account provides a basis for action, a definition of what is real, and it is acted on so long as it remains accountable.

While one team of accountants may make various accounting assumptions and judgements which lead to a profit being reported, it is possible that another team of accountants may make different assumptions and judgements which lead to the same organization (with the same transactions and events) reporting a loss. Recording a loss may generate many negative reactions from various stakeholder groups (for example, from shareholders, media and analysts) and may cause real negative cash-flow consequences for

---

[21] Authors such as Molotch and Boden (1985) provide a view that a form of social power is attributed to those people and professions able to 'trade on the objectivity assumption' (p. 281).

the reporting entity. Hines (1991, p. 20) further reflects on the power of the accounting profession. She states:

> If, say, auditors qualify their report with respect to the going-concern assumption, and/or insist that a corporation's financial statements be prepared on the basis of liquidation values, this in itself may precipitate the failure of a company which may otherwise have traded out of its difficulties.

Another point to be made (which is related to the above point), and one which we consider further in Chapter 3, is that few, if any, accounting standards are introduced without some form of economic and social impact (which, as we know from previous discussion in this chapter, is considered by many accounting standard-setters). As an example, we can consider the various arguments that were raised a few years ago over the implementation of International Accounting Standard (IAS) 39 (Financial Instruments: Recognition and Measurement) by several EU countries. Many European banks argued that implementation of IAS 39 would require them to value certain financial assets and liabilities in a manner which would not reflect the underlying economic reality of many financial transactions, and this would result in unrepresentative and highly volatile profit or loss figures, and substantially weakened balance sheets. It was further argued that these weakened balance sheets and highly volatile reported profits would impact on market perceptions of banks' creditworthiness, thus increasing their cost of capital. Banks in some European countries successfully lobbied their own governments to actively support the banks in seeking to change certain requirements of IAS 39. As we will see in Chapter 4, as part of the EU regulatory process the EU established the Accounting Regulatory Committee (ARC) whose task is to scrutinize all international accounting standards and recommend whether they should be enforced in the EU. Successful lobbying by banks in Italy, Spain, Belgium and France led to these countries' members of the ARC voting against EU adoption of IAS 39 in July 2004, apparently because of its potential negative economic impact. Further lobbying also delayed EU recognition in 2009 of the new International Financial Reporting Standard (IFRS) 9 that replaced IAS 39.

Because of the wider social and economic impacts that are potentially created by new accounting standards, perspectives of accounting as being neutral in its effects are now widely dismissed (Zeff, 1978). Many national standard-setting bodies throughout the world explicitly state in their various documents (which often form part of their respective conceptual frameworks) that economic and social implications of particular pronouncements must be considered prior to the introduction of new accounting rules. As Zeff (1978, p. 60) states:

> The issue of economic consequences has, therefore, changed from one having only procedural implications for the standard-setting process to one which is now firmly a part of the standard-setters' substantive policy framework.

The IASB, which has effectively now taken over the accounting standard-setting process of many countries (including all members of the EU), does not have such a formal requirement to consider the broader social and economic implications of its accounting rules – although members of the IASB do have to agree to 'act in the public interest' and the trustees of the IASB's supervisory body (the International Financial Reporting Standards Foundation) do have formal duties of accountability to a range of public authorities from a variety of countries (IASCF, 2010). However, members of the IASB must be aware that, in practice, if they develop too many accounting standards which have widespread negative social and/or economic impacts in many nations, the governments of these nations are likely to reduce or withdraw their support for continued use of International Financial Reporting Standards in their nations. An example of this awareness, and how the IASB in practice responds to some such pressures, is how the IASB has sought to respond to and address the accounting regulatory reforms called for by the G-20 summits from 2008 onwards, as discussed earlier in this chapter.

Hence we are left with a view that while the notion of objectivity and neutrality is promoted within various conceptual frameworks (perhaps, as Hines suggests, as a means of constructing a perceived legitimacy for the accounting profession), various factors such as the possible economic and social implications, and the potential influences of management self-interest (culminating in some form of *creative accounting*) can lead us to question such claims of objectivity. This chapter has also promoted a view that despite various stereotypes that are often attributed to accountants, accountants are actually a very powerful group of individuals. Many decisions with real economic and social implications are made on the basis of accounting information. Whether the supply of accounting information – which we now should appreciate has many implications throughout society – should be left to market forces, or whether accounting should be subject to regulation, is an issue that we investigate further in the next chapter.

Chapter summary

In this chapter we explored how parties both within, and outside, an organization use the output of the financial accounting process in many different decisions. Because the financial accounting process provides information to parties external to the organization who otherwise would not have information, and because this information is often used as the basis for many decisions, it is generally accepted that it is necessary to regulate the practice of financial accounting.

Financial accounting practices are heavily regulated. However, in countries dominated by strong capital markets (with large numbers of external investors), the history of financial accounting regulation is relatively recent and there was a general absence of such regulation prior to the twentieth century. In the early parts of the twentieth century, accounting research often involved documenting commonly used accounting practices. This research led to the development and acceptance of broad principles of accounting that all accountants were expected to follow. Over time, broad principles gave way to the development of specific accounting standards. Accounting standards began to be released by various accounting professional bodies throughout the world around the 1970s, and standard-setting activity has tended to increase since then. Financial accounting practices throughout the world today are generally regulated by a large number of accounting standards.

The act of regulating accounting practices through the continual release of new and revised accounting standards has led to various arguments for and against regulation. The arguments range from the belief that there is no need to regulate accounting practices (the 'free-market' approach) to a view that regulation is necessary to protect the interests of those parties with a stake in a reporting entity. Arguments against regulation often rely upon the view that the output of the financial accounting system should be treated like any other good, and if the market is left to operate freely, optimal amounts of accounting information will be produced. Introducing regulation leads to an oversupply of accounting information and can cause organizations to use accounting methods that do not efficiently reflect their actual operations, financial position and financial performance. As we see in subsequent chapters, such 'free-market' arguments are challenged by many people.

This chapter has also briefly considered various theories about who is likely to benefit from regulation once it is introduced (Chapter 3 extends much of this discussion). We considered public interest theory, which proposes that regulation is introduced to protect the public and, when putting regulation in place, regulators seek to maximize the overall welfare of the community (which obviously requires trade-offs between particular costs and benefits). Another theory that we considered was capture theory, which proposes that, while regulation might initially be introduced for the public's benefit, ultimately the group that is regulated will gain control of the regulation process. That is, they will eventually 'capture' the regulatory process. We also considered private interest theories of regulation, which propose that the regulators introduce regulation that best serves the regulators' own private interest. That is, regulators are motivated not by the public interest, but by their own self-interest. For example, politicians will introduce regulation likely to generate enough support to ensure their re-election.

We also considered issues associated with the 'power' of accountants. Arguments were advanced to support a view that accountants hold a very powerful position within society (which stands in contrast to how they are often portrayed in the media). Accountants provide information that is used in many decisions and they are able to highlight or downplay particular facets of an organization's performance.

Questions

2.1 What expectations do accounting standard-setters have about the accounting knowledge of financial statement readers?

2.2 Do you consider that users of financial reports should have a sound working knowledge of the various accounting standards in use? Explain your answer.

2.3 Do you believe that the media portray accounting numbers, such as profits, as some sort of 'hard' and objective performance indicator? Why do you think they might do this, and if they do, what are some of the implications that might arise as a result of this approach?

2.4 Briefly outline some arguments in favour of regulating the practice of financial accounting.

2.5 Briefly outline some arguments in favour of eliminating the regulation pertaining to financial accounting.

2.6 Do you think that a general increase in the extent of separation between the ownership and management of organizations leads to a greater or lesser amount of accounting regulation? Why?

2.7 Pursuant to capture theory: how, by whom, and why would a regulator be captured?

2.8 As this chapter indicates, Stigler (1971) proposes a theory (*private interest theory*) in which it is proposed that regulatory bodies (including accounting standard-setters) are made up of individuals who are self-interested, and these individuals will introduce regulation that best serves their own self-interest. Under this perspective, the view that regulators act in the public interest is rejected. From your experience, do you think that this is an acceptable assumption? Assuming that you reject this central assumption, would this have implications for whether you would be prepared to accept any predictions generated by the private interest theory?

2.9 If regulators acted in accordance with predictions provided by the private interests theory of regulation, which assumes that all individuals (including politicians and regulators) are motivated by their own economic self-interest, then what likelihood do we think there would be for the introduction of regulations aimed at reducing the problems associated with climate change – particularly if business corporations opposed such regulations?

2.10 If you believed that regulators acted in accordance with either capture theory, or the private interests theory of regulation, would you believe that accounting standard-setters will develop accounting standards that most fairly present information about the financial position or performance of a reporting entity?

2.11 Because accounting standard-setters throughout the world typically consider the potential economic and social consequences of potential accounting standards when developing accounting standards, it has been argued that reports developed in accordance with the accounting standards cannot be considered neutral or unbiased. Do you agree with this perspective? Is this perspective consistent with the qualitative attributes typically promoted in accounting conceptual framework projects?

2.12 Why would 'free-market' advocates argue that the regulation of financial reporting will lead to an oversupply of accounting rules and standards?

2.13 What is the basis of an argument that states that accounting regulation can act to undermine the efficiency with which the reporting entities present information about their financial performance and position?

2.14 Hines (1991) promotes a view that it is in the interest of the accounting profession to publicly promote a view that the information they generate is 'objective'. Why do you think this is the case?

2.15 Solomons (1978, p. 69) quotes the American Accounting Association: 'Every policy choice represents a trade-off among differing individual preferences, and possibly among alternative consequences, regardless of whether the policy-makers see it that way or not. In this sense, accounting policy choices can never be neutral. There is someone who is granted his preference, and someone who is not.'

Required:

Evaluate the above statement.

2.16 While it is difficult to criticize a process that considers potential impacts on others, at the same time it is difficult to accept that accounting standards are neutral or unbiased.

Required:

Evaluate the above statement.

2.17 Hines (1991, p. 313) stresses a view that 'financial accounting practices are implicated in the construction and reproduction of the social world'.

Required:

What does Hines mean in the above statement? Do you agree or disagree with her, and why?

2.18 Why might accountants be construed as being powerful individuals?

2.19 Explain what the following statement by Handel (1982, p. 36) means and provide an argument to either support or oppose the contention:

> Things may exist independently of our accounts, but they have no human existence until they become accountable. Things may not exist, but they may take on human significance by becoming accountable ... Accounts define reality and at the same time they are that reality ... The processes by which accounts are offered and accepted are the fundamental social process.

References

Akerlof, G.A. (1970) 'The market for "lemons": Quality uncertainty and the market mechanism', *Quarterly Journal of Economics*, **84**, 488–500.

Arnold, P.J. (2009) 'Global financial crisis: The challenge to accounting research', *Accounting, Organizations and Society*, **34** (6–7), 803–809.

Beard, V. (1994) 'Popular culture and professional identity: Accountants in the movies', *Accounting, Organizations and Society*, **19** (3), 308–18.

Boer, G. (1994) 'Five modern management accounting myths', *Management Accounting*, (January), 22–27.

Bougen, P.D. (1994) 'Joking apart: The serious side to the accountant stereotype', *Accounting, Organizations and Society*, **19** (3), 319–35.

Cooper, K. & Keim, G. (1983) 'The economic rationale for the nature and extent of corporate financial disclosure regulation: A critical assessment', *Journal of Accounting and Public Policy*, **2** (3), 189–205.

Cory, S.N. (1992) 'Quality and quantity of accounting students and the stereotypical accountant: Is there a relationship?', *Journal of Accounting Education*, **10**, 1–24.

Dimnik, T. & Felton, S. (2006) 'Accountant stereotypes in movies distributed in North America in the twentieth century', *Accounting, Organizations and Society*, **31** (2), 129–155.

FASB (2008) 'Exposure Draft: Conceptual Framework for Financial Reporting: The Objective of Financial Reporting and Qualitative Characteristics and Constraints of Decision-Useful Financial Reporting Information', Norwalk, CT: Financial Accounting Standards Board.

G-20 (2008a) *Declaration: Summit on Financial Markets and World Economy*, Washington: G-20.

G-20 (2008b) *Washington Summit: Action Plan to Implement Principles for Reform*, Washington: G-20.

G-20 (2010) 'Annex II (Financial Sector Reporm) to the G-20 Toronto Summit Declaration', Toronto: G-20.

Gilman, S. (1939) *Accounting Concepts of Profits*, New York: Ronald Press.

Goldberg, L. (1949) 'The development of accounting', in: Gibson, C.J., Meredith, G.G. & Peterson, R. (eds.) *Accounting Concepts: Readings*, Melbourne: Cassell.

Gray, R. (1992) 'Accounting and environmentalism: An exploration of the challenge of gently accounting for accountability, transparency and sustainability', *Accounting Organizations and Society*, **17** (5), 399–426.

Handel, W. (1982) *Ethnomethodology: How People Make Sense*, Hemel Hempstead: Prentice-Hall.

Hatfield, H.R. (1924) 'An historical defense of bookkeeping', *The Journal of Accountancy*, **37** (4), 241–53.

Hendriksen, E.S. & Van Breda, M.F. (1992) *Accounting Theory*, Homewood, IL: Irwin.

Hines, R. (1988) 'Financial accounting: In communicating reality, we construct reality', *Accounting Organizations and Society*, **13** (3), 251–62.

Hines, R. (1991) 'The FASBs conceptual framework, financial accounting and the maintenance of the social world', *Accounting Organizations and Society*, **16** (4), 313–51.

Holt, P.E. (1994) 'Stereotypes of the accounting professional as reflected in popular movies, accounting students and society', *New Accountant*, 24–25.

Hopwood, A.G. (2009) 'The economic crisis and accounting: Implications for the research community', *Accounting, Organizations and Society*, **34** (6–7), 797–802.

IASB (2008) *Preface to International Financial Reporting Standards*, London: International Accounting Standards Board.

IASC (1989) *Framework for the Preparation and Presentation of Financial Statements*, London: International Accounting Standards Committee.

IASCF (2010) *IASC Foundation Constitution*, London: IASC Foundation.

Jensen, M.C. & Meckling, W.H. (1976) 'Theory of the firm: Managerial behavior, agency costs and ownership structure', *Journal of Financial Economics*, **3** (October), 305–60.

Laux, C. & Leuz, C. (2009) 'The crisis of fair-value accounting: Making sense of the recent debate', *Accounting, Organizations and Society*, **34** (6–7), 826–34.

Mathews, M.R. & Perera, M.H.B. (1996) *Accounting Theory and Development*, 3rd edn, Melbourne: Thomas Nelson Australia.

Molotch, H.L. & Boden, D. (1985) 'Talking social structure: Discourse, domination and the Watergate hearings', *American Sociological Review*, 477–86.

Paton, W.A. (1922) *Accounting Theory*, Lawrence, KS: Scholars Book Co., reprinted 1973.

Paton, W.A. & Littleton, A.C. (1940) *An Introduction to Corporate Accounting Standards*, Evanston, IL: American Accounting Association.

Peltzman, S. (1976) 'Towards a more general theory of regulation', *Journal of Law and Economics* (August), 211–40.

Posner, R.A. (1974) 'Theories of economic regulation', *Bell Journal of Economics and Management Science*, 5 (Autumn), 335–58.

Ray, D.D. (1960) *Accounting and Business Fluctuations*, Gainesille, FL: University of Florida Press.

Roberts, J. & Jones, M. (2009) 'Accounting for self interest in the credit crisis', *Accounting, Organizations and Society*, 34 (6–7), 856–67.

Sanders, T.H., Hatfield, H.R. & Moore, U. (1938) *A Statement of Accounting Principles*, New York: American Institute of Accountants.

Scott, W.R. (2003) *Financial Accounting Theory*, Toronto: Pearson Education Canada Inc.

Sikka, P. (2009) 'Financial crisis and the silence of the auditors', *Accounting, Organizations and Society*, 34 (6–7), 868–73.

Smith, M. & Briggs, S. (1999) 'From beancounter to action hero', *Charter*, 70 (1), 36–39.

Solomons, D. (1978) 'The politicization of accounting', *Journal of Accountancy*, 146 (5), 65–72.

Stigler, G.J. (1971) 'The theory of economic regulation', *Bell Journal of Economics and Management Science*, (Spring), 2–21.

Unerman, J. & O'Dwyer, B. (2004) 'Enron, WorldCom, Andersen *et al*: A challenge to modernity', *Critical Perspectives on Accounting*, 15 (6–7), 971–93.

Watts, R.L. & Zimmerman, J.L. (1978) 'Towards a positive theory of the determination of accounting standards', *The Accounting Review*, 53 (1), 112–34.

Zeff, S.A. (1972) *Forging Accounting Principles in Five Countries*, Champaign, IL: Stipes Publishing Co.

Zeff, S.A. (1978) 'The rise of economic consequences', *Journal of Accountancy*, 146 (6), 56–63.

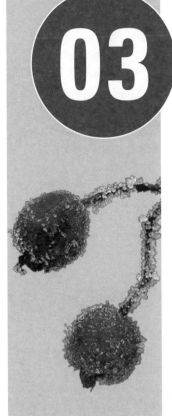

03

The Regulation of Financial Accounting

❖ LEARNING OBJECTIVES

Upon completing this chapter readers should:

❖ understand some of the various theoretical arguments that have been proposed in favour of reducing the extent of regulation of financial accounting;

❖ understand some of the various theoretical arguments for regulating the practice of financial accounting;

❖ understand various theoretical perspectives that describe the parties who are likely to gain the greatest advantage from the implementation of accounting regulation;

❖ understand that accounting standard-setting is a very political process which seeks the views of a broad cross-section of financial report users;

❖ understand the relevance to the accounting standard-setting process of potential economic and social impacts arising from accounting regulations.

Opening issues

1 Throughout the world in recent years a number of industries have been deregulated, for example the banking industry, the telecommunications industry and the airline industry. There were numerous similar calls for a reduction in accounting regulations prior to the widely publicized accounting 'scandals' at Lehman Brothers, Enron and other large companies in recent years (these calls used such terminology as *accounting standard overload*) – but what could some of the implications have been if financial accounting was deregulated?

2 If financial accounting were to be deregulated, what incentives or mechanisms might operate to cause an organization to produce publicly available financial reports? Would these mechanisms operate to ensure that an optimal amount of reliable information is produced? What is the 'optimal' amount of information?

3.1 Introduction

In Chapter 2 we briefly considered a number of theories to explain the existence of accounting regulation. This chapter extends that discussion. While financial accounting is quite heavily regulated in many countries, with this level of regulation generally increasing in the aftermath of the recent sub-prime banking crisis and high-profile alleged accounting failures at Lehman Brothers, Enron, WorldCom, Parmalat and other companies, it is nevertheless interesting to consider arguments for and against the continued existence of, and general growth in, regulation. It is also interesting to consider various theories that explain what drives the imposition of regulation. By considering such theories we will be better placed to understand why some of the various accounting prescriptions become formal regulations while others do not. Perhaps some proposed accounting regulations did not have the support of parties that have influence (or power) over the regulatory process. At issue here is whether issues of 'power' could or should be allowed to impact on the implementation of regulations, including accounting regulations. Is it realistic to expect that the interests of various affected parties will not impact on the final regulations? We will see that the accounting standard-setting process is a very political process. While some proposed requirements might appear technically sound and logical, we will see that this is not sufficient for them to be mandated. What often seems to be important is whether various parts of the constituency, who might be affected either socially or economically by the regulations, are in favour of them.

In considering accounting regulations, we examine arguments for reducing or eliminating regulation, many of which propose that accounting information should be treated like any other good and that forces of *demand* and *supply* should be allowed to determine the optimal amount of information to be produced. Proponents of this 'free-market' approach (that is, proponents of the view that the provision of accounting information should be based on the laws of supply and demand rather than on regulation) have at times relied on the work of the famous eighteenth-century economist Adam Smith, and his much cited notion of the 'invisible hand'. However, we will see that what he actually proposed was the need for some regulation to support the interests of those individuals who would otherwise be disadvantaged by the functioning of unregulated market systems.

We also consider a number of perspectives that explain why regulation might be necessary. We review the *public interest theory of regulation*. While public interest theory provides an explanation of why regulation is necessary to protect the rights of the public, there are other theories which we will consider (for example, *capture theory* and *economic interest theory of regulation*) that provide explanations of why regulations might be put in place that actually serve the interests of some groups at the expense of others (rather than serving the 'public interest'). This chapter considers how perceptions about the economic and social consequences of potential accounting requirements affect the decisions of standard-setters. It also considers whether, in the light of regulators considering economic and social consequences, it is possible for financial accounting ever to be expected to have qualitative characteristics such as *neutrality* and *representational faithfulness* (as proposed in conceptual frameworks of accounting, such as the IASB *Framework for the Preparation and Presentation of Financial Statements*).

3.2 What is regulation?

As this chapter will consider various theories of regulation, and various arguments for and against regulation, it is useful to first define what we actually mean by 'regulation' and 'regulator'. The *Oxford English Dictionary* defines a regulation as:

> A rule or principle governing behaviour or practice; *esp.* such a directive established and maintained by an authority.

The *Oxford English Dictionary* further defines a regulator as:

> An official or agency responsible for the control and supervision of a particular industry, business activity, area of public interest, etc.

Therefore, on the basis of these definitions, we can say that regulation is designed to control or govern conduct. Hence when we are discussing regulations relating to financial accounting, we are discussing rules that have been developed by an independent authoritative body that has been given the power to govern how we are to prepare financial statements, and the actions of the authoritative body will have the effect of restricting the accounting options that would otherwise be available to an organization.[1] The regulation would also be expected to incorporate a basis for monitoring and enforcing compliance with the specific regulatory requirements.

---

[1] While our definition of reporting refers to an independent authoritative body, capture theory (to be discussed shortly) would question whether, in the longer run, regulators will be able to maintain their independence from those individuals or groups that are subject to the regulations.

3.3 The 'free-market' perspective

As indicated in Chapter 2, a fundamental assumption underlying a 'free-market' perspective to accounting regulation is that accounting information should be treated like other goods, and demand and supply forces should be allowed to freely operate so as to generate an optimal supply of information about an entity. A number of arguments have been used in support of this perspective. One such argument, based on the work of authors such as Jensen and Meckling (1976), Watts and Zimmerman (1978), Smith and Warner (1979), and Smith and Watts (1982) is that, even in the absence of regulation, there are private economics-based incentives for the organization to provide credible information about its operations and performance to certain parties outside the organization, otherwise the costs of the organization's operations will rise. The basis of this view is that, in the absence of information about the organization's operations, other parties, including the owners of the firm (shareholders) who are not involved in the management of the organization, will assume that the managers might be operating the business for their own personal benefit.[2] That is, the managers will be assumed to operate the business for their own personal gain, rather than with the aim of maximizing the value of the organization (there is assumed to be a lack of alignment of goals between the external owners and the managers).[3] It is further assumed that potential 'external' shareholders will expect the managers to be opportunistic, and in the absence of safeguards will reduce the amount they will pay for the shares. Likewise, under this economics-based perspective of 'rationality' (self-interest), potential lenders (such as banks and bondholders) are assumed to expect managers – like everybody else – to undertake opportunistic actions with the funds the lenders might advance, and therefore in the absence of safeguards the lenders will charge the organization a higher price for their funds.[4] That is, the lenders will 'price-protect' – such that the higher the perceived risk, the higher is the demanded return.

The expectations noted above (which are based on the rather pessimistic assumption that all parties will assume that others will work in their own self-interest unless constrained to do otherwise) will have the effect of increasing the operating costs of

---

[2] The costs that arise from the perspective of the owner when the owner (or principal) appoints a manager (the agent) would include costs associated with the agent shirking (being idle) or consuming excessive perquisites (using the organization's funds for the manager's private purposes). These are called agency costs. Agency costs can be defined as costs that arise as a result of the delegation of decision-making from one party, for example the owner, to another party, for example the manager (representing an agency relationship). Agency costs are more fully considered in Chapter 7, where we consider agency theory. Another agency cost that might arise when decision-making is delegated to the agent could include the costs associated with the manager using information that is not available to the owners for the manager's personal gain. Smith and Watts (1982) provide an overview of the various conflicts of interest that arise between managers and owners.

[3] What should be appreciated at this point is that these arguments are based on a central assumption that individuals will act in their own self-interest, which, in itself, is a cornerstone of many economic theories. If an individual acts with self-interest with the intention of maximizing personal wealth, this is typically referred to as being 'economically rational'. 'Economic rationality' is a theoretical assumption, and, as might be expected, it is an assumption that is challenged by advocates of alternative views about what drives or motivates human behaviour.

[4] In considering the relationship between managers and lenders, actions that would be detrimental to the interests of lenders would include managers paying excessive dividends; taking on additional and possibly excessive levels of debt; and using the advanced funds for risky ventures, thereby reducing the probability of repayment. Smith and Warner (1979) provide an overview of some of the conflicts of interest that arise between managers and lenders.

the organization – the cost of attracting capital will increase and this will have negative implications for the value of the organization.[5] In situations where managers have large investments in their organization's shares (that is, where they are a type of 'internal' shareholder), it will be in the interests of the managers to maximize the value of the firm – as they will often gain more economically from an increase in the value of their investment than they would gain in direct 'spoils' from opportunistic behaviour. To achieve this maximization of share value managers will voluntarily enter into contracts with shareholders and lenders which make a clear commitment that certain management strategies, such as those that might be against the interests of the shareholders and lenders, will not be undertaken. For example, management might make an agreement with debtholders that they will keep future debt levels below a certain percentage of total assets (the view being that, all things being equal, the lower the ratio of debt to assets, the lower is the risk that the organization will default on paying the debtholders). To safeguard the debtholders' assets further, the organization might agree to ensure that profits will cover interest expense by a specified number of times (referred to as an interest coverage clause). In relation to concerns that the manager might 'shirk' (which might be of particular concern to shareholders, given that shareholders will share in any profits generated by the actions of the managers), the organization might require managers to be rewarded on the basis of a bonus tied to profits, so the higher the profit (which is in the interests of shareholders and lenders), the higher will be the rewards paid to managers. Most private corporations will give their managers (particularly the more senior managers) some form of profit share (Deegan, 1997) as well as being involved in negotiated agreements with lenders (such as debt to asset constraints and interest coverage requirements).

What should be obvious from the brief discussion above is that such contractual arrangements are tied to accounting numbers (for example, paying the manager a bonus based upon a percentage of profits). Hence the argument by some advocates of the 'free-market' perspective is that in the absence of regulation there will be private incentives to produce accounting information. That is, proponents of this view (based on agency theory which is more fully discussed in Chapter 7) assert that there will (naturally) be conflicts between external owners and internal managers, and the costs of these potential conflicts will be mitigated through the process of private contracting and associated financial reporting.[6] Organizations that do not produce information will, according to proponents of this view, be penalized by higher costs associated with attracting capital, and this will damage the financial interests of those managers who own shares in their organization. Further, depending upon the parties involved and the types of assets in place, it is argued that the organization will be best placed to determine what information should be produced to increase the confidence of external stakeholders (thereby decreasing the organization's cost of attracting capital). Imposing regulation that restricts the available set of accounting methods (for example, banning a particular method of depreciation or amortization which has previously been used by some organizations) will decrease the efficiency with which

---

[5] This is based on the assumption that the value of an organization is the present value of its expected future net cash flows. A higher cost of capital will result in a decreased net present value of future cash flows.

[6] This is consistent with the usual notion of 'stewardship' wherein management is expected to provide an account of how it has utilized the funds that have been provided.

negotiated contracts will reduce agency costs.[7] Given the theoretical economics-based assumption that managers will act in their own self-interest, according to this theoretical perspective there will also be a contractual demand to have the accounting reports audited by an external party. Such an activity will increase the perceived reliability of the data, and this in turn is expected to reduce the perceived risk of the external stakeholders, thus further decreasing the organization's cost of capital (Francis and Wilson, 1988; Watts, 1977; Watts and Zimmerman, 1983). That is, financial statement audits can also be expected to be undertaken, even in the absence of regulation, and evidence indicates that many organizations did have their financial statements audited prior to any legislative requirements to do so (Morris, 1984).[8]

Hence, if we accept the above arguments, we can propose that in the presence of a limited number of contracting parties then, perhaps, reducing regulation might seem reasonable given the view that various items of financial information (as negotiated between the various parties) will be provided. Further, such information will be expected to be subject, where deemed necessary by the contracting parties, to an audit by an independent third party. However, in the presence of a multitude of different parties, this argument that private incentives will lead to optimal amounts of accounting information (and a reduced need for regulation) seems to break down. As Scott (2003, p. 416) states:

> Unfortunately, while direct contracting for information production may be fine in principle, it will not always work in practice ... In many cases there are simply too many parties for contracts to be feasible. If the firm manager were to attempt to negotiate a contract for information production with every potential investor, the negotiation costs alone would be prohibitive. In addition, to the extent that different investors want different information, the firm's cost of information production would also be prohibitive. If, as an alternative, the manager attempted to negotiate a single contract with all investors, these investors would have to agree on what information they wanted. Again, given the disparate information needs of different investors, this process would be extremely time-consuming and costly, if indeed, it was possible at all. Hence, the contracting approach only seems feasible when there are few parties involved.

Market-related incentives

While the above 'free-market' (or anti-regulation) arguments are based on a private contracting perspective, there are further arguments for reducing or eliminating accounting regulation that are based on various market-related incentives, principally tied to the 'market for managers' and the 'market for corporate takeovers'. The 'market for managers' argument (see Fama, 1980) relies upon an assumption of an efficient market for managers

---

[7] It has also been argued that certain mandated disclosures will be costly to the organization if they enable competitors to take advantage of certain proprietary information. Hakansson (1977) used this argument to explain costs that would be imposed as a result of mandating segmental disclosures.

[8] As Cooper and Keim (1983, p. 199) indicate, to be an effective strategy, 'the auditor must be perceived to be truly independent and the accounting methods employed and the statements' prescribed content must be sufficiently well-defined'. Public perceptions of auditor independence were damaged as a results of revelations in 2002 of Andersen's role in both designing and auditing complex accounting transactions at Enron (Unerman and O'Dwyer, 2004).

and that managers' previous performance will impact upon how much remuneration (payment for services) they command in future periods, either from their current employer or elsewhere. In adopting this perspective it is assumed that, even in the absence of regulations controlling management behaviour and in the absence of other contractual requirements, managers will be encouraged to adopt strategies to maximize the value of their organization (which provides a favourable view of their own performance) and these strategies would include providing an optimal amount of financial accounting information. However, arguments such as this are based on assumptions that the managerial labour market operates efficiently and that information about past managerial performance will not only be known by other prospective employers, but will also be fully impounded in future salaries. It also assumes that the capital market is efficient when determining the value of the organization and that effective managerial strategies will be reflected in positive share price movements. In reality, these assumptions will clearly not always be met. Markets will not always be efficient. The arguments can also break down if the managers involved are approaching retirement, in which case future market prices for their services in the 'market for managers' may be irrelevant.

The 'market for corporate takeovers' argument works on the assumption that an under-performing organization will be taken over by another entity that will subsequently replace the existing management team. With such a perceived threat, managers would be motivated to maximize firm value to minimize the likelihood that outsiders could seize control of the organization at low cost. The 'market for corporate takeovers' and the 'market for managers' arguments assume that information will be produced to minimize the organization's cost of capital and thereby increase the value of the organization. Therefore, the arguments assume that management will know the *marginal costs* and *marginal benefits* involved in providing information and, in accordance with economic theories about the production of other goods, management will provide information to the point where the marginal cost equals the marginal benefit. While the disclosure of accounting information will be in the interests of shareholders, it will also be in the interests of managers – there will be an alignment of interests. However, working out the marginal costs and marginal benefits of information production will be difficult, and to assume that the majority of corporate managers have the expertise to determine such costs and benefits is, again, perhaps somewhat unrealistic.

There is also a perspective that, even in the absence of regulation, organizations would still be motivated to disclose both good and bad news about their financial position and performance. Such a perspective is often referred to as the 'market for lemons' perspective (Akerlof, 1970), the view being that in the absence of disclosure the capital market will assume that the organization is a 'lemon'.[9] That is, the failure to provide information is viewed in the same light as providing bad information. Hence, even though the firm may be worried about disclosing bad news, the market may make an assessment that silence implies that the organization has very bad news to disclose (otherwise they would disclose it). This 'market for lemons' perspective provides an incentive for managers to release information in the absence of regulation, as failure to do so will have implications for the manager's

---

[9] Something is a 'lemon' if it initially appears or is assumed (due to insufficient information) to be of a quality comparable to other products, but later turns out to be inferior. Acquiring the 'lemon' will be the result of information asymmetry in favour of the seller.

wealth (perhaps in the form of current lower remuneration and a decreased value in the market for managers). That is, 'non-lemon owners or managers have an incentive to communicate' (Spence, 1974, p. 93).

Drawing upon arguments such as those adopted in the 'lemons' argument above and applying them to preliminary profit announcements, Skinner (1994, p. 39) states:

> Managers may incur reputational costs if they fail to disclose bad news in a timely manner. Money managers, stockholders, security analysts, and other investors dislike adverse earnings surprises, and may impose costs on firms whose managers are less than candid about potential earnings problems. For example, money managers may choose not to hold the stocks of firms whose managers have a reputation for withholding bad news and analysts may choose not to follow these firms' stocks … Articles in the financial press suggest that professional money managers, security analysts, and other investors impose costs on firms when their managers appear to delay bad news disclosures. These articles claim that firms whose managers acquire a reputation for failing to disclose bad news are less likely to be followed by analysts and money managers, thus reducing the price and/or liquidity of their firms' stocks.

Reviewing previous studies, Skinner (1994, p. 44) notes that there is evidence that managers disclose both good and bad news forecasts voluntarily. These findings are supported by his own empirical research which shows that when firms are performing well managers make 'good news disclosures' to distinguish their firms from those doing less well, and when firms are not doing so well managers make pre-emptive bad news disclosures consistent with 'reputational-effects' arguments (p. 58).

Evidence provided by Barton and Waymire (2004) showed that shareholders of US firms that made higher quality disclosures preceding the stock market crash of 1929 experienced significantly smaller losses during the major stock market crash. Prior to the crash there was a general absence of disclosure regulation. In an argument that supports a 'free-market' (anti-regulation) approach to accounting regulation they state (p. 69):

> Viewed collectively, our evidence suggests that managers respond to investor demand for information and that managers' voluntary financial reporting choices can promote investor protection. That is, economic forces in advanced markets provide managers with incentives for beneficial financial reporting even in the absence of regulatory mandate.

The argument above provides the view that economic forces operate to motivate managers to provide information to investors even in the absence of regulation.

Arguments that the market will penalize organizations for failure to disclose information (which may or may not be bad) of course assume that the market knows that the manager has particular information to disclose. As has been seen with the many apparently unforeseen accounting failures in recent years (such as Lehman Brothers, Enron, WorldCom and Parmalat), this expectation might not always be so realistic, as the market will not always know that there is information available to disclose. That is, in the presence of information asymmetry (unequal distribution of information) the manager might know of some bad news, but the market might not expect any information disclosures at that time. However, if it does subsequently come to light that news was available that was not disclosed, then we could perhaps expect the market to react (and in the presence of regulation, we could expect regulators to react as failure to disclose information in a timely manner may be in contravention of particular laws in that jurisdiction). Also, at certain times, withholding information (particularly of a proprietary nature) could be in the interests of the organization. For example, the organization may not want to disclose information about certain market opportunities for fear of competitors utilizing such information.

So, in summary to this point, there are various arguments or mechanisms in favour of reducing accounting regulation (including private contracting, markets for managers, markets for corporate takeovers and the 'market for lemons'), as even in the absence of regulation firms will have incentives to make disclosures. We now consider some arguments in favour of the alternative of regulating financial accounting practice.

3.4 The 'pro-regulation' perspective

In the above discussion we have considered a number of reasons proffered in favour of reducing or eliminating regulation. One of the most simple of arguments is that if somebody really desired information about an organization they would be prepared to pay for it (perhaps in the form of reducing their required rate of return), and the forces of supply and demand should operate to ensure an optimal amount of information is produced. Another perspective was that if information is not produced there will be greater uncertainty about the performance of the entity and this will translate into increased costs for the organization (for example, in the absence of sufficient information about an organization then such an organization will be considered to be of higher risk, and riskier organizations find it relatively more expensive to attract capital). With this in mind, organizations would, it is argued, elect to produce information to reduce costs. However, arguments in favour of a 'free market' rely upon users paying for the goods or services that are being produced and consumed. Such arguments can break down when we consider the consumption of 'free' or 'public' goods.

Accounting information is a public good – once available, people can use it without paying and can pass it on to others. Parties who use goods or services without incurring some of the associated production costs are referred to as 'free riders'. In the presence of free riders, true demand is understated because people know they can obtain the goods or services without paying for them. Few people will then have an incentive to pay for the goods or services, as they know that they themselves might be able to act as free riders. This dilemma in turn is argued to provide a lack of incentive for producers of the particular good or service, which in turn leads to an underproduction of information. As Cooper and Keim (1983, p. 190) state:

> Market failure occurs in the case of a public good because, since other individuals (without paying) can receive the good, the price system cannot function. Public goods lack the exclusion attribute, i.e., the price system cannot function properly if it is not possible to exclude nonpurchasers (those who will not pay the asked price) from consuming the good in question.

To alleviate this underproduction, regulation is argued to be necessary to reduce the impacts of market failure.[10] In specific relation to the production of information, Demski and Feltham (1976, p. 209) state:

> Unlike pretzels and automobiles, [information] is not necessarily destroyed or even altered through private consumption by one individual … This characteristic may induce market failure. In particular, if those who do not pay for information cannot be excluded from using it and if the information is valuable to these 'free riders', then information is a public good. That is, under these circumstances, production of information by any single individuals or firm will costlessly make that information available to all … Hence, a more collective approach to production may be desirable.

However, as we often come to expect, there are counter-arguments to the perspective that the supply of 'free goods' should be regulated. Some economists argue that free goods are often overproduced as a result of regulation. The argument is that segments of the public (the users of the good or service), knowing that they do not have to pay for the free good, will overstate their need for the good or service. This argument could perhaps be applied to investment analysts. Investment analysts will typically be a main user of accounting information. If they lobby for additional regulation that requires further disclosure, they will tend to receive a disproportionate amount of the benefits relative to the costs of producing this further information. When considering the consumption of free goods it is argued by some that non-users effectively subsidize the consumers of the public good as, like other parties, the non-users pay towards the production of the good without benefiting from its consumption. The result of concerted lobbying by particular parties, such as analysts, could in turn lead to the existence of what has been termed an accounting standards overload, which creates a cost for companies in terms of compliance. However, if we do not regulate, then in the presence of the 'free riders' we could arguably have an underproduction of accounting information. Clearly, this is not an easy thing to balance and we can start to understand the difficult position in which regulators find themselves.

Regulators often use the 'level playing field' argument to justify putting regulations in place. From a financial accounting perspective, this means that everybody should (on the basis of fairness) have access to the same information. This is the basis of laws that prohibit insider trading, which rely upon an acceptance of the view that there will not be, or perhaps should not be, transfers of wealth between parties simply because one party has access to information which others do not.[11] Putting in place greater disclosure regulations will increase the confidence of external stakeholders that they are playing on a 'level playing field'. If this helps build or sustain confidence in the capital markets, then it is often deemed to be in 'the public interest'. However, we will always be left with the issue as to what is the socially 'right' level of information. Arguably, such a question cannot be answered with any level of certainty.

---

[10] In relation to the supply of information, Scott (1997, p. 329) defines market failure as 'an inability of market forces to produce a socially "right" amount of information, that is, to produce information to the point where its marginal cost to society equals its marginal benefit'.

[11] There is also the view (Ronen, 1977) that extensive insider trading will erode investor confidence such that market efficiency will be impaired.

Many theories which argue in favour of free-market approaches to accounting regulation rely upon the work of the famous eighteenth-century economist Adam Smith (originally published in 1776 but republished in 1937), as a basis for supporting their free-market approach. Adam Smith has become famous for his notion of the 'invisible hand'. The 'invisible hand', which was mentioned only once in his five-book treatise, appears in Book Four of the *Wealth of Nations*, referring to the distribution of capital in society: 'the annual revenue … is always equal to the whole product of its industry … as every individual attempts to employ his [her] capital … every individual necessarily endeavors the capital as great as he can … he intends only his own industry … his own gain … led by an invisible hand by it.'[12]

Subsequent free-market exponents have drawn on the notion of the 'invisible hand' to promote a belief in 'market omnipotence', arguing against state involvement because it 'disturbs the spontaneous order and the spontaneous society' (Lehman, 1991, p. xi). That is, without regulatory involvement there is a view that somehow, as if by an 'invisible hand', productive resources will, as a result of individuals pursuing their own self-interests, find their way to their most productive uses. Some writers actually went to the next step by arguing that leaving activities to be controlled by market mechanisms will actually protect market participants. For example, Milton Friedman (1962, p. 82) states:

> The central feature of the market organisation of economic activity is that it prevents one person from interfering with another in respect of most of its activities. The consumer is protected from coercion by the seller because of the presence of other sellers with whom he can deal. The seller is protected from coercion by the consumer because of other consumers to whom he can sell.

These views ignore market failures (such as unequal access to information) and uneven distributions of power. Adam Smith was concerned with particular problems that occur in monopolistic situations where suppliers might drive up prices for needed goods. According to Collison (2003, p. 864):

> Smith … was against legislation that protected the strong and the privileged either by conferring monopoly powers over consumers, or by worsening the already weak position of employees. He did not counsel against steps taken to protect the weak and was not against regulation *per se*.

Therefore Smith did not advocate that there should be no regulatory intervention. He was aware of the problems that might arise in an unregulated free market and, while it is rarely mentioned by the advocates of the 'free market', Smith actually wrote of the need for the government to be involved in the 'public interest' to protect the more vulnerable. As Lehman (1991, p. x) states:

> Among the passages revealing Smith's concern for harmful unintended consequences [of the free-market approach] are those appearing in Book V, Chapter 1, where Smith writes that in the progress of the division of labour, the progress of the great body of people will be the man [or woman] who spends much time doing a few simple operations, with no invention, with no tender

---

[12] This quote is reproduced from Lehman (1991).

> sentiment, incapable of judging, incapable of defending the country in war. In every society, the great body of people will fall this way, 'unless the government takes some pains to prevent it'.

This view is also supported by Collison (2003, p. 863) who states:

> Adam Smith himself was well aware that conditions in the world he inhabited did not conform to the competitive ideal: he was not opposed to government action in pursuit of general welfare; indeed he favoured it, and was acutely conscious of the danger of undue power in the hands of the capitalist class.

So if we accept that Smith's work has been misrepresented as a treatise in favour of the 'free market' (as a number of authors suggest), why has it been misrepresented? Collison (2003) argues that it is in the interests of many businesses that regulatory interference (such as the introduction of minimum wage controls, or disclosure requirements) be reduced. As such, he provides a view that many businesses used the work of acclaimed economists (such as Adam Smith and Milton Friedman) as a form of 'propaganda' to support their arguments for reduced regulation.[13,14]

According to Collison, arguments such as those presented by famous economists such as Smith or Friedman, and 'the corporate propaganda which is used to sell it to the public', were anticipated by Adam Smith who warned of the negative impacts that could be caused by economically powerful interests, particularly when they are unrestrained due to an absence of adequate regulation or competition. According to Smith (as quoted in Collison, 2003):

> The clamour and sophistry of merchants and manufacturers easily persuade ... that the private interest of a part, and of a subordinate part of the society is the general interest of the whole. (Smith, 1776/1880, Bk. I, Ch. X, Pt. II, p. 101)

In other words, as far back as 1776 Adam Smith argued that it is predictable that business managers will argue that what is in the interests of the business organizations will actually be in the interests of the society as a whole – an argument that is still heard today over 235 years later. That is, it is the interest of managers to argue that if business prospers, then society shall also prosper. This perspective is consistent with the economic interest theory of regulation, which we consider later in this chapter.

While we have provided only a fairly brief overview of the free-market versus regulation arguments, it should be stressed that this is an argument that is ongoing in respect of many activities and industries, with various vested interests putting forward many different and often conflicting arguments for or against regulation. It is an argument that is often the subject of heated debate within many university economics and accounting departments

---

[13] Other authors (such as Carey, 1997) have argued that many larger businesses were able to influence academics (through the provision of funding) to support particular views. The results of the academic research studies, which often supported the views held by the groups that provided the research funding, were then provided to government to substantiate or support particular positions.

[14] Collison also argues that the works of other well-respected economists have been misrepresented by vested interests. For example, the works of Berle and Means (1932) have 'become identified with conflicts of interest between owners and controllers of wealth when they explicitly argued that both should be subservient to wider interests ... They commended public policy rather than self interest as the proper mechanism for allocating corporate income streams. As with Adam Smith, their names have arguably become misleadingly linked with a particular agenda'.

throughout the world. What do you think? Should financial accounting be regulated, and if so, how much regulation should be put in place?

As an example of another, post-Enron, perspective on the 'regulate or not to regulate' debate, consider Accounting Headline 3.1, which argues that regulation can introduce inefficiencies into the market. It questions whether an increasing amount of accounting regulation has been effective in protecting investors.

Having discussed arguments for and against regulation, we will now consider a number of theories that describe why regulation is put in place, as well as describing which stakeholders are expected to benefit from regulation. The following theories might assist our understanding of why, in particular situations, decisions were made for legislative reform. For example, according to Barton and Waymire (2004, p. 67):

> The October 1929 market crash is seen as among the most significant financial crises in US history (Galbraith, 1972) and was followed within five years by the most extensive changes in financial reporting requirements in US history.

Accounting Headline 3.1

Perspectives about the regulation of accounting

Future Enrons will result from over regulation of accountancy, says IEA Study

Referring to the recent Enron and World-Com scandals, David Myddelton, Professor of Finance and Accounting at Cranfield Business School, says that such events are more likely, not less likely, to occur in the future as a result of increased regulation of accounting. The UK and EU are increasingly following the failed approach of the US in prescribing in detail how companies produce accounts.

'In nine years the volume of accounting regulation has increased by 150%, from an already high level, at a huge cost to companies, without any corresponding benefit', says Myddelton in [his book] *Unshackling Accountants*. Sometimes regulators impose standards that are wrong and even dangerous.

Myddelton is highly critical of new regulations, such as the International Standards, being imposed by professional bodies, by international organizations and by government regulators. He suggests that radical new approaches to accounting are not generally accepted by the profession and are likely to lead to greater risk of financial and accounting scandals.

At the very least, increasingly prescriptive approaches to accounting lull users into a false sense of security and prevent auditors and accountants from using their judgement to ensure that accounts provide a reasonable picture of a company's financial situation. Users of accounts should understand that they come with 'health warnings' attached and interpret accounts with caution. Increasing the regulation of accounting shifts responsibility away from users and gives them a false sense of security. It also prevents the evolution of new and better accounting practices to deal with a changing world.

Source: *Press release from the Institute of Economic Affairs, London, 25 June 2004. (This article is available free from www.iea. org.uk)*

But why would there be such reform? Barton and Waymire further state (2004, p. 69) that:

> Regulators often cite investor protection as a basis for more stringent financial reporting requirements enacted after financial crises. The investor protection justification has a long history dating back at least to British legislation passed in the wake of corporate bankruptcies in the 19th century (Littleton, 1933, pp. 272–287). Investor protection arguments surfaced in the US after the 1929 stock market crash as justification for the financial reporting requirements embodied in the Securities Act of 1933 and the Securities Exchange Act of 1934 (Parrish, 1970, Pecora, 1939). The intent of the Securities Acts was to protect investors from exploitation by informed traders in the large-scale securities markets that developed to support financing of enterprises with diffuse ownership structures (Berle and Means, 1932). More recently, the US Congress and Securities and Exchange Commission (SEC) have cited investor protection as the basis for recent reporting rules following the market decline of the past few years (US House, 2002). Implicit in the investor protection justification for financial reporting regulation is that higher quality reporting would have lessened investor losses during the recent crisis and that managers lacked incentives to supply higher quality financial information voluntarily.[15,16]

However, just because legislators have justified the introduction of new legislation in terms of an effort to protect investors, does this mean that investor protection was their real motivation – or did they have other private incentives? The following theories will provide different perspectives on why the above 'extensive changes' were made. For example, public interest theory of regulation would propose that such regulatory changes were brought about in the interest of the public – which would be consistent with an 'investor protection' style of argument. By contrast, economic interest theories of regulation would suggest that the regulations might have been put in place so that regulators themselves, who would have been under pressure due to the large losses that had been suffered, look like they are doing something and this may help them retain their positions as regulators (and therefore help them retain their related income stream). In such an explanation the introduction of the legislation is not so much about public interests, but more about the private interests of those in change of introducing the legislation. Again, as we emphasize throughout this book, there are different ways of looking at the same phenomenon, such that while some researchers may view the introduction of legislation as being in the public interest (a view embodied within public interest theory), other researchers may consider that the same actions were taken because they best served the private interests of those in control of introducing the legislation (economic interest group theory of regulation).

---

[15] Consistent with a free-market approach to accounting information, Barton and Waymire (2004, p. 70) note: 'of course, mandatory disclosure requirements need not be the sole source of investor protection – self-interested managers supply information voluntarily to reduce agency costs (Jensen and Meckling, 1976; Watts and Zimmerman, 1986) and information costs in securities markets (Dye, 2001; Verrecchia, 2001)'.

[16] The US Securities Exchange mission 'is to protect investors, maintain fair, orderly, and efficient markets, and facilitate capital formation' (SEC, 2009, p. 3). It is interesting that the mission of the SEC does not embrace a responsibility to stakeholders other than just investors – such as local communities, employees, and so forth. Perhaps there is a view that if 'investors' are protected then the rest of society will benefit? We will explore this issue more fully in Chapter 9.

3.5 Public interest theory

According to Posner (1974, p. 335) public interest theory 'holds that regulation is supplied in response to the demand of the public for the correction of inefficient or inequitable market practices'. That is, regulation is initially put in place to benefit society as a whole, rather than particular vested interests, and the regulatory body is considered to be a neutral arbiter that represents the interests of the society in which it operates, rather that the private interests of the regulators.[17] The enactment of legislation is considered a balancing act between the social benefits and the social costs of the regulation. Applying this argument to financial accounting, and accepting the existence of a capitalist economy, society needs confidence that capital markets efficiently direct (or allocate) resources to productive assets. Regulation is deemed to be an instrument to create such confidence.

Many people are critical of this fairly simplistic perspective of why regulation is introduced (for example, Peltzman, 1976; Posner, 1974; Stigler, 1971). Posner (1974) questions the 'assumptions that economic markets are extremely fragile and apt to operate very inefficiently (or inequitably) if left alone; the other that government regulation is virtually costless' (p. 336). Posner also criticizes arguments that legislation is typically initially put in place for 'the public good' but only fails to achieve its aims due to government ineptitude, mismanagement or lack of funds. As he states (p. 337):

> [There is] a good deal of evidence that the socially undesirable results of regulation are frequently desired by groups influential in the enactment of the legislation setting up the regulatory scheme … Sometimes the regulatory statute itself reveals an unmistakable purpose of altering the operation of markets in directions inexplicable on public interest grounds … The evidence that has been offered to show mismanagement by the regulatory body is surprisingly weak. Much of it is consistent with the rival theory that the typical regulatory agency operates with reasonable efficiency to attain deliberately inefficient or inequitable goals set by the legislature that created it.

Proponents of the economics-based assumption of 'self-interest' would argue against accepting that any legislation was put in place by particular parties because they genuinely believed that it was in the public interest. Rather, they consider that legislators will only put in place legislation because it might increase their own wealth (perhaps through increasing their likelihood of being re-elected), and people will only lobby for particular legislation if it is in their own self-interest. Obviously, as with most theoretical assumptions, this self-interest assumption is one that (hopefully!) does not always hold. We consider the private interest group theory of regulation later in this chapter. In the following discussion we consider the regulatory capture theory of regulation. Unlike the private interest group theory of regulation, capture theory admits the possibility that regulation might initially be put in place for the public interest. However, it argues that the regulation will ultimately become controlled by those parties who it was supposed to control.

---

[17] This perspective would not be accepted by advocates of the 'rational economic person' assumption as they would argue that all activities, including the activities of regulators and politicians, are primarily motivated by a desire to maximize personal wealth rather than any notion of acting in the *public interest*.

3.6 Capture theory

Researchers who embrace capture theory (capture theorists) would typically argue that although regulation might be introduced with the aim of protecting the 'public interest' (as argued in public interest theory briefly described above), this laudable aim of protecting the public interest will not ultimately be achieved because in the process of introducing regulation, the organizations that are subject to the regulation will ultimately come to control the regulator. The regulated industries will seek to gain control of the regulatory body because they will know that the decisions made by the regulator will potentially have significant impacts on their industry. The regulated parties or industries will seek to take charge of (capture) the regulator with the intention of ensuring that the regulations subsequently released by the regulator (post-capture) will be advantageous to their industry. As an example of possible regulatory capture we can consider the contents of a recent newspaper article entitled 'Banking split essential to avoid new financial crisis, warns OECD adviser' (*Guardian*, 28 May 2010, p. 32) in which it was stated:

> The global economy will be plunged into a second and even more serious crisis unless banks are split into separate retail and speculative arms, a senior policymaker from the west's leading thinktank said today … Blundell-Wignall, speaking in a personal capacity at the OECD's annual forum in Paris, said one of the big obstacles to better global governance was 'institutional capture' of policymakers by the leading global financial institutions.

As another illustration of the phenomena of regulatory capture, consider Accounting Headline 3.2 which claims evidence of regulatory capture in both the banking and oil industries in the USA – which the article argues has contributed to negative outcomes for society.

Obviously there are economic benefits to an industry (such as banking or the oil industry discussed overleaf) if it is able to 'capture' the body that regulates it. According to Mitnick (1980), there are at least five ways in which a regulated entity or industry will be able to capture a regulatory body, these being (Mitnick, 1980, p. 95, as reproduced in Walker, 1987, p. 281):

1 Capture is said to occur if the regulated interest controls the regulation and the regulated agency;

2 or if the regulated parties succeed in coordinating the regulatory body's activities with their activities so that their private interest is satisfied;

3 or if the regulated party somehow manages to neutralise or ensure non-performance (or mediocre performance) by the regulating body;

4 or if in a subtle process of interaction with the regulators the regulated party succeeds (perhaps not even deliberately) in co-opting the regulators into seeing things from their own perspective and thus giving them the regulation they want;

5 or if, quite independently of the formal or conscious desires of either the regulators or the regulated parties, the basic structure of the reward system leads neither venal nor incompetent regulators inevitably to a community of interests with the regulated party.

Accounting Headline 3.2

Evidence of regulatory capture in the banking and oil industries

Oil spill is just latest US disaster caused by regulatory failures

By Lara Marlowe

AMERICA: Regulatory capture – the domination of US regulatory agencies by industries – is at the heart of banking and oil spill crises.

The proper role of government is a debate as old as America. It marks the most profound division between Republicans and Democrats, and perhaps the biggest difference between the US and Europe.

President Barack Obama relaunched that debate at a graduation ceremony on May 1st last: 'Government is what ensures that mines adhere to safety standards and that oil spills are cleaned up by the companies that caused them,' he said. 'We know that too much government can stifle competition and deprive us of choice and burden us with debt. But we've also seen clearly the dangers of too little government – like when a lack of accountability on Wall Street nearly leads to the collapse of our entire economy.'

The BP oil spill – now officially the worst in US history – is the most recent in a string of disasters caused by the failure of regulatory authorities ... Richard Posner, an economist and lawyer at the University of Chicago, defined the notion of regulatory capture. 'Regulation is not about the public interest at all, but is a process by which interest groups seek to promote their private interest,' Posner wrote. 'Over time, regulatory agencies come to be dominated by the industries regulated.'...

'What's also been made clear from this disaster is that for years the oil and gas industry has leveraged such power that they have effectively been allowed to regulate themselves,' Obama lamented, reminding us George W Bush and Dick Cheney were oil men.

Source: *The Irish Times*, 29 May 2010 (online edition) Courtesy of The Irish Times

Therefore, while the introduction of regulation can, in many cases, be explained in terms of protecting the 'public interest', it is argued that inevitably it will be difficult for a regulator to remain independent of those parties or industries being regulated, as the survival of the regulatory body over a period of time often depends on satisfying the expectations of those parties or groups being regulated. Further, the greater the industry's total resources relative to those of the regulator, the greater will be the chance that the regulator will ultimately be unable to remain independent.

Accounting Headline 3.3 provides commentary on how it appears that one industry – involved in the production of asbestos – was able to continue operating when evidence suggested that it was in the public interest for regulation to be introduced that curtailed the use of asbestos. The evidence suggests that industry was able to 'capture' the regulatory process and thereby allow asbestos use to be continued – to the advantage of the industry, but to the detriment of society.

Accounting Headline 3.3

A possible case of regulatory capture

Asbestos: key question hasn't been answered

By Alan Mitchell

The dangers of asbestos emerged in the 1920s. Why did successive governments fail to protect us, asks economics editor Alan Mitchell.

There's one question that the inquiry into James Hardie will not answer. Why did successive federal and state governments sit back and allow thousands of Australians to be poisoned by exposure to asbestos? We must answer that question if we are to have any hope of avoiding similar disasters in the future.

On the face it, the history of asbestos in Australia, the US and Europe looks like a monumental example of 'regulatory capture'. Regulatory capture is a common phenomenon in which regulators, governments, regulatory authorities and professional bodies come to identify more with the interests of the people they are supposed to be regulating than with the interests of the people they are supposed to protect.

On the question of asbestos, Australian governments appear to have taken their lead from the US and Europe. The failure of US federal and state governments to protect their citizens against asbestos is outlined by Michelle White, professor of economics at the University of California at San Diego, in the spring edition of the *Journal of Economic Perspectives*. According to White, physicians recognized that exposure to asbestos caused disease, and asbestosis was named and described in British medical journals, in the 1920s. About the same time insurance companies in the US and Canada stopped selling life insurance to asbestos workers. Safer substitutes for many uses were known as early as the 1930s, yet US consumption of asbestos did not peak until 1974.

Workers' compensation became available in the US from the 1930s, but asbestos producers successfully lobbied state governments for low levels of compensation and restrictive eligibility rules.

In the 1970s, the newly established US Occupational Health and Safety Administration (OSHA) began regulating the exposure of workers to asbestos. But when studies showed that the new regulation was too lax, the OSHA was slow to respond, allegedly because of industry concerns. In the late 1970s the Consumer Product Safety Commission pressured manufacturers to remove asbestos voluntarily from products such as hairdryers, but these efforts were halted under the Reagan administration. In late 1980s the Environmental Protection Agency proposed a ban on asbestos use, but the ban was overturned by the federal court on technical grounds in 1991 and the agency never appealed.

White concludes that US governments were slow to limit asbestos exposure because asbestos producers were able to capture the regulators.

And yet, despite this failure, the US appears to have done considerably better than Europe. Levels of asbestos exposure were higher in Europe and consumption of asbestos products declined more slowly. European death rates from mesothelioma are almost twice those in the US, and while the US rate appears to have peaked, death rates in the major European countries are expected to double over the next 20 years.

As in the US, the problem appears to have been regulatory capture. But in the US court-awarded damages appear to have curbed the use of asbestos.

What about Australia? Until 1966, Australia was a major producer of crocidolite, the type of asbestos fibre most strongly associated with mesothelioma. During the 1960s, Australia was one of the highest consumers of chrysotile asbestos per head of population. The Productivity Commission notes in its 2004 report on workers' compensation that 'asbestos exemplifies the delayed response of government authorities to the incidence of disease'.

'Although there was reasonable scientific knowledge about the risks of exposing workers to asbestos by the 1950s, it was not until much later that governments in Australia introduced legislation to control the use of asbestos.' Participants in the commission's inquiry complained that governments were still slow to implement controls of chemical hazards in the workplace.

What are the lessons from the asbestos saga?

The most important lesson is that we should never completely trust governments and their regulatory authorities. We should think carefully when we clip the wings of the courts and opportunistic lawyers. For years they appear to have been more effective than politicians at curbing the use of asbestos in the US.

Perhaps we also should be wary of the repeated attempts by our politicians to concentrate the ownership of Australia's media in the hands of a few friendly industrialists.

Source: *The Australian Financial Review*, 9 August 2004

As with various industries, at various times and in various jurisdictions it has been argued that large accounting firms have captured the accounting standard-setting process. This was of such concern in the United States that in 1977 the United States Congress investigated whether the (then) Big Eight accounting firms had 'captured' the standard-setting process (Metcalf Inquiry). Walker (1987) argued that the Australian Accounting Standards Review Board (ASRB) (which was subsequently replaced by the Australian Accounting Standards Board) was apparently 'captured' by the accounting profession.[18] He cites a variety of evidence in support of this argument, concluding that within two years of its formation:

> the profession had managed to influence the procedures, the priorities and the output of the Board. It was controlling both the regulations and the regulatory agency; it had managed to achieve coordination of [its] activities; and it appears to have influenced new appointments so that virtually all members of the Board might reasonably be expected to have some community of interests with the professional associations. (Walker, 1987, p. 282)

As we know, proponents of capture theory typically argue that regulation is usually introduced, or regulatory bodies are established, to protect the public interest. For

---

[18] Walker was a member of the ASRB from 1984 to 1985. In commenting on his motivation for documenting the case study of the ASRB, Walker states (p. 285) that: 'The main concern was to highlight the way that a set of standard setting arrangements designed to permit widespread consultation and participation were subverted by some likeable, well-meaning individuals who were trying to promote the interests of their fellow accountants'.

example, from an accounting perspective new regulatory systems and regimes are often established in response to high-profile accounting failures where members of the public are perceived to have suffered a financial loss, and where it is argued that new regulations will help prevent a repeat of the accounting failures. This happened with the establishment of the Securities Exchange Commission in the United States in the early 1930s, which was formed in response to the Wall Street Crash of 1929; with the establishment of the UK Accounting Standards Steering Committee in the early 1970s following negative publicity over accounting failures at some large UK companies in the late 1960s; with the establishment of the Accounting Standards Board in the United Kingdom in 1990 following further large-scale accounting failures in the late 1980s; with many tighter accounting and corporate governance regulations being imposed in many countries following the accounting failures at Enron, WorldCom, Parmalat and other companies in the early 2000s; and with recent high-level political pressures for global convergence on a single set of high quality accounting standards following the sub-prime banking crisis and ensuring global financial crisis. While the resultant regulatory bodies are often portrayed as 'objective' and 'independent', in the past their members have often predominantly been professional accountants and finance directors (the preparers of accounts who these regulatory bodies are meant to be regulating!), which Walker (1987) argues is an important component of regulatory capture.

However, in recent years there has been a movement towards ensuring greater independence of accounting regulators. For example, the International Accounting Standards Board (IASB) has 16 members,[19] of whom all but three have to work full-time and exclusively for the Board, and are required to sever their ties with previous employers. They are also appointed by the board of 22 Trustees of the International Financial Reporting Standards (IFRS) Foundation who have all agreed that they will act in the public (not their own private) interest and whose appointments must in turn be approved by a 'Monitoring Board' that represents a broad cross-section of interests. While this may help in giving an image of detached and impartial objectivity to the IASB standard-setting process (which is discussed in the next chapter), it should be remembered that the members of the IASB are still mostly professionally qualified accountants whose views are bound to be conditioned to a certain extent by their previous experiences and training. Furthermore, the constitution of the IFRS Foundation, whose Trustees appoint IASB members, stipulates that 'The mix of Trustees shall broadly reflect the world's capital markets and diversity of geographical and professional backgrounds' (IASCF, 2010, paragraph 6). In these circumstances, it is reasonable to question how independent and impartial the accounting standard-setting process can be. Accounting Headline 3.4 shows some concerns over this issue. It is an extract from an opinion article in a leading UK newspaper.

Accounting Headline 3.5 provides information about another possible example of regulatory capture. It refers to the alleged capture of the regulation relating to the alcohol industry within the United Kingdom. Consistent with regulatory capture, the methods proposed by the alcohol industry to address problems associated with the excess consumption of alcohol were embraced by government with the government

---

[19] Before the adoption of the new IFRS Foundation constitution in 2010, there were 14 full-time members of the IASB. The new constitution increased this number to 16 members to be in place by a deadline of 1 July 2012. The new constitution also changed the name of the body from the IASC Foundation to the IFRS Foundation.

Accounting Headline 3.4

Questioning the public interest remit of the IASB

Make accountants accountable

By David Cronin

... [The French] finance minister, Christine Lagarde, is perturbed by a new blueprint for changing the way that assets held by banks are valued that has been drafted with the Pittsburgh summit in mind. Her anger would perhaps be better directed not at the detail of the proposal but at the body behind it: the International Accounting Standards Board. The IASB is a private firm dominated by the accounting industry, banks and multinational companies. Although it was only established in 2001, it sets the standards that listed companies in more than 100 countries must follow. Its activities may sound arcane, yet without clear accounting standards none of us can have any idea what major firms, some of which are more powerful than governments, are up to.

Lagarde's reservations notwithstanding, the EU has been generally supportive of the IASB. Am I the only one struggling to explain why such an untrustworthy and unaccountable group is treated with respect not only by governments but also by some anti-poverty campaigners? Christian Aid and a few like-minded organizations are calling for the G20 to demand that the IASB co-operates in efforts to secure a new system whereby large companies have to report how much tax they pay in each country where they operate.

I fully support the principle of country-by-country reporting and applaud the fight against tax swindling, which, according to Christian Aid, could be depriving poor countries of $160bn per year. But how can we have any confidence in a body like the IASB, stuffed with men (its 15-member board has only one woman) with a deep-rooted aversion to regulation?

In December last year, Prem Sikka, an accounting professor at the University of Essex, wrote: 'Accounting has done grievous harm to too many innocent citizens and is central to the current financial crisis. Rather than allowing private interests to make public policies, accounting rules should be made by an independent body representing a plurality of interests.'

If the standards of the IASB have been central to causing the crisis, why on earth is it still operating?

Source: *Guardian,* 15 September 2009 (online edition)
©Guardian News and Media Limited 2010

not supporting policies which appeared to be more likely to be effective in reducing 'problem drinking'.

As we appreciate from reading previous chapters in this book, while a particular theory, such as capture theory, may be embraced by some researchers, there will be others who oppose such theories. Posner (1974), an advocate of the economic (private interest) theory of regulation (which we will look at next), argues against a regular sequence wherein the original purposes of a regulatory programme are subsequently thwarted through the efforts of the regulated group. He states:

> No reason is suggested as to why the regulated industry should be the only interest group to influence an agency. Customers of the regulated firm have

an obvious interest in the outcome of the regulatory process – why may they not be able to 'capture' the agency as effectively as the regulated firms, or more so? No reason is suggested as to why industries are able to capture only existing agencies – never to procure the creation of an agency that will promote their interests – or why an industry strong enough to capture an agency set up to tame it could not prevent the creation of the agency in the first place (p. 340).

A key component underlying all the above perspectives on regulatory capture is that different groups will have different interests, and that accounting regulations will have an impact on these social and/or economic interests. If particular groups did not perceive a potential threat (or opportunity) from a regulator to their specific social or economic interests, why would they devote resources to attempting to capture their regulator? The remainder of this chapter discusses perspectives on the impact of these private interests on the regulatory process.

Accounting Headline 3.5

A further possible example of regulatory capture

Government 'too close to alcohol industry': medical journal attacks plans for 24-hour pub licensing

By Sarah Boseley, Health editor

The government is too close to the drinks industry to deal with growing alcohol-related problems, an article in the *British Medical Journal* says.

Wayne Hall, a professor in Queensland University's office of public policy and ethics, offers a savage critique of policies for dealing with excessive drinking that leads to violence and deaths. He says Australia has brought alcohol consumption down over the past two decades, while it has soared in the UK.

'The UK government's new alcohol policy, which includes "partnership" with the alcohol industry, shows all the hallmarks of regulatory capture in that it embraces the industry's diagnosis and preferred remedies for the alcohol problem,' he writes.

'The problem, in the industry's view, is a "minority" of drinkers who engage in antisocial behaviour and put their health at risk; the preferred remedies are public education about safe drinking, improved policing, better treatment for alcohol problems and self regulation by the alcohol industry – the policies which evidence suggests are the least likely to reduce problem drinking.'

The government, he says, has failed to introduce the most effective measure – imposing higher taxes on higher strength alcoholic drinks.

'It justifies this decision by saying that increased price has not been shown definitely to reduce harm due to alcohol, an assertion at odds with the views of the world's leading researchers on alcohol.'

Instead of reducing access to alcohol, the government 'embraces the paradoxical idea that allowing drinking for up to 24 hours a day will reduce binge drinking and public disorder,' he writes.

He points to the different approach taken in Australia. Although the Australian government also adopted liberalisation policies, it imposed lower taxes on low-alcohol beer, those with less than 3.8%. It also set a tougher drink-driving level of 0.05% alcohol in the blood instead of 0.08% as in the UK, and introduced random breath tests.

The rise of alcohol sales in Britain is probably the result of lowering the cost while increasing its availability, coupled to heavy promotion by the industry, he says.

Alcohol abuse is thought to cost the economy £30bn a year and alcohol dependency rates in the UK are among the highest in Europe, at 7.5% of men and 2.1% of women.

'If the UK government remains deaf to the arguments of its critics, it should honour its promise to evaluate the effects of its policies,' he writes.

'Then it would have the necessary evidence to drop policies that have failed and replace them with policies that have a chance of reducing (rather than merely preventing further rises in) alcohol-related harm.' He believes the UK should also invest in treatment for those with problems.

The BMJ also features papers by researchers who claim two psychosocial interventions would save society five times as much as they cost.

The two interventions – social behaviour and network therapy and motivational enhancement therapy – both give counselling and social support to heavy drinkers without them having to 'dry out' in a residential clinic.

Alcohol Concern called on the government to spend money to save money. 'We welcome the publication of such comprehensive research backing up what we have known for years: treatment works,' said Geethika Jayatilaka, its director of policy and public affairs.

'Every year thousands of people access help and support from specialist alcohol services and are able to turn their lives around. But without adequate funding agencies are struggling to survive and there are still too many people who cannot access the treatment.'

Almost three times more people die from alcohol than from drugs, she said, and yet alcohol services receive only a fifth of the funding.

Source: *Guardian,* 2 September 2005 (online edition)
©Guardian News and Media Limited 2010

3.7 Economic and social impacts of accounting regulation

Before examining various theories which address the influence of private interests on the accounting regulatory process, it is necessary to establish whether accounting regulations can and do have a social and/or economic impact on the interests of preparers or users of accounts. Although many people might argue that accounting regulations just affect how underlying economic transactions and events are reflected in the financial reports, without any impact on the nature or shape of this underlying economic reality, there is a considerable body of evidence which demonstrates that accounting regulations have real social and economic consequences for many organizations and people.

For example, one of the first new accounting standards issued by the IASB dealt with the accounting treatment of share options (IFRS 2). Although many companies use large numbers of share options as part of their management remuneration and incentive plans, prior to the release of IFRS 2 in 2004 most companies simply ignored costs associated with issuing share options to employees when calculating their annual profit. The justification for this former practice was that when executives exercised the share options, and the company issued new shares to these executives at below market value, this did not apparently cost the company itself anything – despite it diluting the value of existing shareholders' investments. However, the IASB view was that by granting valuable share options to employees, companies were able to pay these employees a lower salary than if they had not been granted share options. As the company receives valuable services from employees in exchange for these options, which would have been recorded as an expense if they had been paid for in cash (as part of salary or a cash bonus), under IFRS 2 the fair value of share options now has to be recognized as an expense in the income statement. This new accounting treatment did not have any direct impact on cash flows, as companies that continue to offer the same employee share option and remuneration packages as before will still pay their employees the same amount of money as they did before. All that IFRS 2 requires is recognition in the financial statements of an expense that exists but was previously not recognized. Although implementation of IFRS 2 should have had no direct impact on underlying cash flows, during the development of IFRS 2 it was extensively argued that it would have many indirect negative economic and social consequences for a multitude of people. As some companies would be required to recognize a potentially large share option expense each year, some people maintained that these companies would be less likely to use share options as part of their pay and rewards packages. If valuable share options are an effective way to motivate managers, and help align their self-interests with those of shareholders, a reduction in use of this form of incentive could lead to less motivated executives (or a less motivated workforce overall if share options were granted to many employees). This could lead to a reduction in underlying company performance, simply because IFRS 2 changed the manner in which a specific item was reflected in the financial statements. Therefore, while it was argued that IFRS 2 (in common with most, if not all, other accounting standards) should not lead to any direct changes in underlying business performance or cash flows, its indirect economic consequences could be potentially large and negative.

A more extensive indirect impact of new accounting regulations on employees' social and economic interests seems to have occurred with the implementation of a new UK accounting standard on pension liabilities in the early 2000s. This new standard introduced considerable volatility into the accounting measurement of pension fund assets and liabilities for a type of company pension scheme know as a defined benefit, or final salary, scheme. Many investment experts maintain that this type of pension is usually more generous, and less risky, to employees than the common alternative forms of pension provision. As briefly mentioned in Chapter 2, many companies claimed that the increased volatility in accounting numbers (but not in the underlying economic performance of a pension fund) arising from the introduction of this new accounting standard contributed to their decisions to close their final salary pension schemes, and switch new (and sometimes existing) employees to less advantageous pension schemes. This clearly had a negative impact on the social and economic interests of many employees, who are now likely to receive reduced pensions when they retire. However, it is possible that these companies might have closed their final salary schemes in any event (as they were becoming ever more expensive to fund), and just used the new accounting standard as a convenient excuse to hide the real motives for closure of these schemes.

There are many other examples of accounting standards that have potential indirect economic and social impacts. Indeed, some might argue that all accounting regulations will have an impact on managerial decisions (as managers will seek to manage their business so as to optimize their reported accounting numbers), and the resulting changes in managerial decisions will have a social and/or economic impact on those affected by the decisions. Several academic studies, which are discussed in the next section, have illustrated how the potential economic consequences of proposed accounting standards motivated particular organizations to lobby regulators either in opposition to particular accounting standards, or in support. This lobbying attempts to shape the regulations in a manner that will maximize the expected positive, or minimize the expected negative, economic consequences from the new accounting regulations for the lobbying organizations.

3.8 Lobbying and the economic interest group theory of regulation

The economic interest group theory of regulation (or, as it is sometimes called, the private interest theory of regulation) assumes that groups will form to protect particular economic interests. Different groups, with incompatible or mutually exclusive interests and objectives, are viewed as often being in conflict with each other and each will lobby government or other regulators to put in place legislation that economically benefits them (at the expense of the others). As an example, consumers might lobby government for price protection, or producers lobby government for tariff protection. This theoretical perspective adopts no notion of *public interest* – rather, private interests are considered to dominate the legislative process.[20]

In relation to financial accounting, particular industry groups may lobby the regulator (the accounting standard-setter) to accept or reject a particular accounting standard. For example, Hope and Gray (1982) show how a small number of aerospace companies were successful, during a consultation process, in changing the detailed requirements of a UK accounting standard on research and development in favour of their (private) interests. This was despite the overwhelming majority of participants in the consultation process not sharing the objections that had been made to the original proposals by the aerospace companies. These original proposals required all research and development expenditure to be charged as an expense in the year in which it had been incurred. The aerospace companies successfully argued that in certain circumstances they should be allowed to treat development expenditure as a form of capital expenditure, and charge it as an expense in future years by matching it against the income which it eventually generated. Although the impact on reported profits over the life of a project would be nil (the accounting treatment simply allowed a deferral of the expenditure between years), this accounting treatment resulted in higher net assets being reported in the balance sheet each year during a project

---

[20] As Posner (1974) states, 'the economic theory of regulation is committed to the strong assumptions of economic theory generally, notably that people seek to advance their self-interest and do so rationally'.

than would have been the case if the development expenditure had been charged against profits in the year it was incurred. At the time, the prices which these aerospace companies could charge the UK government for large defence contracts were based upon a percentage return on net assets. Clearly, the higher the reported net assets in any particular year, the more a company could charge the government for a contract, so it was in the private interests of these aerospace companies that the accounting standard permitted deferral of development expenditure.

A more recent example of successful lobbying of an accounting regulator by an industry group, apparently seeking outcomes which were in the industry's own interests, was lobbying by some European banks against revised provisions in International Accounting Standard (IAS) 39. As discussed briefly in Chapter 2, banks in several European countries argued that some of the provisions of IAS 39 (which has now been superseded by IFRS 9) would result in their accounts showing significant volatility which did not reflect the underlying economic reality, and that this could be damaging to a bank's perceived financial stability. The IASB made some limited changes in response to the banks' concerns, but refused to change IAS 39 substantially. As we will see in the next chapter, from 1 January 2005 accounting standards issued by the IASB became the accounting regulations that had to be followed by all companies which have their shares traded on any stock exchange in the European Union (EU). However, as part of the EU accounting regulatory process, for any accounting regulation to be mandated for use by EU companies it has first to be endorsed by the European Commission. The endorsement of each IAS/IFRS follows advice from the EU's Accounting Regulatory Committee (ARC), which has one member from each of the EU member states. At a meeting of the ARC in July 2004, four member states (out of the 25 that were then members) voted against full EU endorsement of IAS 39 and a further six states abstained, principally objecting to the elements of IAS 39 that banks in their countries had lobbied against. The 15 states that voted in favour of full endorsement of IAS 39 were insufficient to form the two-thirds majority of the ARC required for approval by the EU of an IAS/IFRS.[21]

Subsequently, from 2009 the IASB replaced IAS 39 with IFRS 9 *Financial Instruments*.[22] The implementation of changes that IFRS 9 made to the provisions of IAS 39 were accelerated in response to pressure from the G-20 following the sub-prime banking crisis and ensuing global financial crisis. However, in response again to lobbying from interests in certain EU members states, the EU delayed recognition of IFRS 9 so companies listed on stock exchanges within the EU could not initially use it in preparing their financial statements. Accounting Headline 3.6 shows that while some companies in EU countries were opposed to the provisions of IFRS 9, others supported them and were not happy with the EU's actions.

---

[21] In recent years, environmental groups have also lobbied government to introduce a requirement for companies to report various items of social and environmental information. Such submissions could perhaps prove a problem for advocates of the view that lobbying behaviour will be dictated by private concerns about wealth maximization (the rational economic person assumption). Perhaps (and we are clutching at straws here!) to maintain support for their 'self-interest' view of the world, proponents of the economic interest theory of regulation might argue that the submissions are made by officers of the environmental lobby group in an endeavour to increase their probability of reappointment.

[22] The first phase of IFRS 9 was published in 2009, replacing some parts of IAS 39. The remainder of IFRS 9 was scheduled to be published by the end of 2010, replacing the whole of IAS 39. The latest date for companies to implement the first phase of IFRS 9 is for accounting periods beginning on or after 1 January 2013.

Accounting Headline 3.6

Lobbying in the EU against recognition of provisions in IFRS 9

Companies set to defy accounting rule delay

By Rachel Sanderson, Peter Smith and Nikki Tait

Some of Europe's biggest multinational companies are preparing to defy moves by Brussels to delay the introduction of new global accountancy rules within the European Union.

Four companies contacted by the *Financial Times* say that they are looking to use the so-called IFRS 9 rules as 'proforma' accounts for 2010 and may begin to prepare the numbers for internal use for this year end.

Other big companies might prepare accounts as if the new rules were in place in parallel with official financial statements, say accounting firms.

Brussels shocked the accountancy community this month when it delayed introduction of the International Accounting Standards Board's radical overhaul of the way financial institutions value assets. The delay came just as the new rules were introduced in most of the rest of the world outside the US.

The EU decision means that European companies officially cannot use the rules while companies in more than 80 countries outside the US can. This has angered many multinationals, particularly in the UK, which believe they will be put at a competitive disadvantage.

Those companies say that the new rules are an improvement for companies and investors.

European Commission officials say they want more time to look into whether the rethink would cause European companies to report more of their assets at current market prices. Critics of this system say this can lead to greater volatility of accounts.

Under the overhaul, loans, or securities similar to loans, will be held at the price banks paid for them, provided the part of the firm that owns them is not engaged in trading. Everything else will be held at fair value. Bank analysts believe that this will cut the proportion of assets held at market prices, which is about 50 per cent for big European firms.

Pauline Wallace, a partner in regulation at PwC, the accounting firm, says that for some companies IFRS 9 produces 'more meaningful numbers' than the current IAS 39 system.

Brussels' decision, which followed calls by the Group of 20 nations for clearer rules in response to the financial crisis, revealed a deep split among European financial institutions.

UK banks and insurers, ING, Deutsche Bank and Italian insurer Generali were among those in favour of early adoption of IFRS 9 for use this year end, according to minutes from a committee meeting.

However, French and Italian banks, German insurers and European regulators such as the European Central Bank were in favour of postponing a decision until next year.

Douglas Flint, HSBC chief financial officer, believes that Brussels' decision puts European companies at a disadvantage. Companies in favour of IFRS 9 also see it as a vital step to a single set of global accounting standards, including convergence of the rules of the Federal Accounting Standards Board in the US with the IASB.

Source: *Financial Times*, 26 November 2009, p. 13
©The Financial Times Limited 2010

In considering an early study on lobbying of accounting regulators, Watts and Zimmerman (1978) reviewed the lobbying behaviour of US corporations in relation to a proposal for the introduction of general price level accounting – a method of accounting that, in periods of inflation, would lead to a reduction in reported profits. They demonstrated that large politically sensitive firms favoured the proposed method of accounting, which led to reduced profits. This was counter to normal expectations that companies generally would prefer to show higher rather than lower earnings. It was explained on the (self-interest) basis that it was the larger firms which could be subject to negative public sentiment (and pressures for regulation of their prices) if their profits were widely seen to be abnormally high, and they might therefore be seen more favourably if they reported lower profits. Hence, by reporting lower profits, there were less likely to be negative wealth implications for the organizations (perhaps in the forms of government intervention, consumer boycotts or claims for higher wages).

Accounting firms also make submissions as part of the accounting standard-setting process. If we are to embrace the economic interest group theory of regulation, we would argue that these submissions can be explained as efforts to protect the interests of professional accountants. Perhaps auditors favour rules that reduce the risk involved in an audit, as more standardization and less judgement reduces the risk of an audit, and therefore the potential for costly law suits. Evidence in Deegan *et al.* (1990) also supports the view that audit firms are relatively more likely to lobby in favour of particular accounting methods if those methods are already in use by a number of their clients. Analysts also frequently lobby regulators for increased disclosure, perhaps because they can use the information in their job, but pay only a very small amount for it (other non-users will effectively subsidize the costs of the information – part of the free-rider issue discussed earlier in this chapter).

Under the economic interest group theory of regulation, the regulator itself is an interest group – a group that is motivated to embrace strategies to ensure re-election, or to ensure the maintenance of its position of power or privilege within the community. For example, Broadbent and Laughlin (2002) argue that in the UK lobbying surrounding the development of accounting regulations applicable to governmental accounting for projects involving private sector provision of public services (known as Private Finance Initiative projects, or Public Private Partnerships), various regulatory bodies adopted positions which could be interpreted as seeking to defend or enhance their standing with the groups who appoint them and give them legitimacy. We should remember that regulatory bodies can be very powerful.

The regulatory body, typically government controlled or influenced, has a resource (potential regulation) that can increase or decrease the wealth of various sectors of the constituency. As Stigler (1971, p. 3) states:

> The state – the machinery and power of the state – is a potential resource or threat to every industry in society … Regulation may be actively sought by an industry, or it may be thrust upon it. … as a rule, regulation is acquired by the industry and is designed and operated primarily for its benefit … We propose the general hypothesis: every industry or occupation that has enough political power to utilize the state will seek to control entry.

Under this 'economic interest' perspective of regulation, rather than regulation initially being put in place for the *public interest* (as is initially assumed within capture theory and also in public interest theory), it is proposed that regulation is put in place to serve the *private interests* of particular parties, including politicians who seek re-election. According to Posner (1974, p. 343), economic interest theories of regulation insist that economic regulation serves the private interests of politically effective groups. Further, Stigler (1971, p. 12) states:

> The industry which seeks regulation must be prepared to pay with the two things a party needs: votes and resources. The resources may be provided by campaign contributions, contributed services (the businessman heads a fund-raising committee), and more indirect methods such as the employment of party workers. The votes in support of the measure are rallied, and the votes in opposition are dispersed, by expensive programs to educate (or uneducate) members of the industry and other concerned industries ... The smallest industries are therefore effectively precluded from the political process unless they have some special advantage such as geographical concentration in a sparsely settled political subdivision.[23]

Under the economic interest theory of regulation, the regulation itself is considered to be a *commodity* subject to the economic principles of supply and demand. According to Posner (1974, p. 344):

> Since the coercive power of government can be used to give valuable benefits to particular individuals or groups, economic regulation – the expression of that power in the economic sphere – can be viewed as a product whose allocation is governed by laws of supply and demand ... There are a fair number of case studies – of trucking, airlines, railroads, and many other industries – that support the view that economic regulation is better explained as a product supplied to interest groups than as an expression of the social interest in efficiency or justice.

The above position is consistent with that adopted by Peltzman (1976). He states (p. 212):

> The essential commodity being transacted in the political market is a transfer of wealth, with constituents on the demand side and their political representatives on the supply side. Viewed in this way, the market here, as elsewhere, will distribute more of the good to those whose effective demand is the highest ... I begin with the assumption that what is basically at stake in the regulatory process is a transfer of wealth.

The idea being promoted by the advocates of economic interest group theories of regulation is that if a particular group (perhaps a minority) does not have sufficient power (which might be reflected by the numbers of controlled votes, or by the potential funds available to support an election campaign) then that group will not be able to effectively lobby for regulation that might protect its various interests. This view is compatible with some

---

[23] As an example, Stigler (1971, p. 8) refers to the railroad industry. 'The railroad industry took early cognizance of this emerging competitor, and one of the methods by which trucking was combated was state regulation. By the early 1930s all states regulated the dimensions and weights of trucks.'

of the arguments used by a number of critical theorists (discussed in Chapter 12), who often contend that the legislation supporting our social system (including corporation law and accounting standards) acts to protect and maintain the position of those with power (capital) and suppresses the ability of others (those without financial wealth) to exert a great deal of influence within society. Consistent with this view, advocates of the economics interest group theory of regulation would also argue that regulators will utilize their power to regulate to transfer wealth from those people with low levels of political power (who have a limited ability to influence the appointment of the regulator) to those parties with greater levels of political power. Reflective of this possibility, in a review of the United States Securities Acts of 1933 and 1934, Merino and Neimark (1982, p. 49) conclude that:

> The security acts were designed to maintain the ideological, social and economic status quo while restoring confidence in the existing system and its institutions.

They further state (p. 51) that the establishment of the Securities Acts:

> may have further contributed to the virtual absence of any serious attempts to ensure corporate accountability by broadening the set of transactions for which corporations are to be held accountable.

We consider the works of some critical theorists in greater depth in Chapter 12.

3.9 Accounting regulation as an output of a political process

If we accept that accounting standard-setting is a political process, then the view that financial accounting should be *objective*, *neutral* and *apolitical* (as espoused internationally within various conceptual framework projects such as the IASB's *Framework for the Preparation and Presentation of Financial Statements*) is something that can be easily challenged. As we saw in the previous section, because financial accounting affects the distribution of wealth within society it consequently will be political.[24]

Standard-setting bodies typically encourage various affected parties to make submissions on draft versions of proposed accounting standards. This is deemed to be part of the normal 'due process'.[25] If the views of various parts of the constituency are not considered, the implication might be that the very existence of the regulatory body could be challenged. As Gerboth (1973, p. 497) states:

> When a decision making process depends for its success on the public confidence, the critical issues are not technical; they are political … In the face of conflict between competing interests, rationality as well as prudence lies not in seeking final answers, but rather in compromise – essentially a political process.

---

[24] For example, whether dividends are paid to shareholders will be dependent upon whether there are reported profits. Further, whether a company incurs the costs associated with defaulting on an accounting-based debt agreement (such as a debt to asset constraint, or an interest coverage requirement) may be dependent upon the accounting methods it is permitted to apply.

[25] Due process can be defined as a process wherein the regulator involves those parties likely to be affected by the proposed regulation in the discussions leading to the regulation – it provides an opportunity to 'be heard'.

In the earlier example of objections made by banks in some EU countries to certain detailed provisions of IAS 39, the failure of the IASB to compromise or concede to the wishes of these banks, and the willingness of certain EU governments to fight the banks' case, led to a confrontation between two regulators – the EU and the IASB. At the time, this confrontation was seen as potentially highly damaging to both regulators. If the EU endorsed a revised EU regulation on accounting for financial instruments which had important (although possibly only small) differences from IAS 39, then rules underlying the accounts of EU companies would be different from the rules underlying the accounts of non-EU companies, and this would frustrate the objectives of international accounting standardization (which we discuss in the next chapter). A common accounting regulation required both sides to compromise.

An obstacle to reaching compromise between two powerful (and sometimes apparently intransigent) international regulatory bodies is that, as we discussed earlier in this chapter, accounting standards (and therefore financial accounting reports themselves) are the result of various social and economic considerations.[26] Hence, they are very much tied to the values, norms and expectations of the society in which the standards are developed. Therefore, it is arguably very questionable whether financial accounting can ever claim to be *neutral* or *objective* (Hines, 1988, 1991). While it is frequently argued within conceptual frameworks that proposed disclosures should be useful for decision-making, this in itself is not enough. The proposed requirements must be acceptable to various parts of the constituency, and the benefits to be derived from the proposals must, it is argued, exceed the costs that might arise. Obviously, determining these costs and benefits is very problematic and this is an area where academic advice and academic research is often used. According to Beaver (1973, p. 56):

> without a knowledge of consequences … it is inconceivable that a policy-making body … will be able to select optimal accounting standards.

May and Sundem (1976) take the argument further. They argue that:

> If the social welfare impact of accounting policy decisions were ignored, the basis for the existence of a regulatory body would disappear (p. 750).

As noted above, while in principle accounting standard-setters need to consider the potential costs and benefits of particular accounting requirements before they are put in place, this is not a very straightforward exercise. As the IASB stated in an Exposure Draft released in 2008 (released as part of a joint process between the IASB and the US Financial Accounting Standards Board to develop a new conceptual framework of financial reporting, an issue to which we will return in Chapter 6):

> The boards (IASB and FASB) observed that the major problem for standard-setters in conducting rigorous cost-benefit analyses in financial reporting is the inability to quantify the benefits of a particular reporting requirement, or even to identify all of them. However, obtaining complete, objective quantitative

---

[26] At this point we will not pursue the perspective adopted by the economic interest group theory of regulation. If we had persisted with this perspective we would argue that the standard-setters would support those submissions which best served the standard-setters' self-interest.

information about the initial and ongoing costs of a requirement, or the failure to impose that requirement, would also be extremely difficult. Regardless of the difficulty, standard-setters should endeavour to take into account both the benefits and the costs of proposed financial reporting requirements (IASB, 2008, p. 61, paragraph BC2.63).

Any consideration of possible economic consequences (the costs and the benefits) necessarily involves a trade-off between the various consequences. For example, if neutrality/representational faithfulness is sacrificed to reduce potential negative impacts on some parties (for example, preparers who might have otherwise been required to disclose proprietary information, or to amend their accounting policies with the implication that they will default on existing debt contracts) this may have negative consequences for users seeking to make decisions on the basis of information provided.

While it is accepted that accounting standards are developed having regard to social and economic consequences, it is also a requirement in many jurisdictions – including all EU member states – that corporate financial statements be 'true and fair'. But can we really say they are *true* when the standards are determined depending upon various economic and social consequences? Perhaps it is easier to say they are *fair* in the sense that they are drawn up in accordance with the rules incorporated in accounting standards. 'Truth' itself is obviously a difficult concept to define and this might explain why in some jurisdictions it was decided that *true and fair* was achieved if financial reports simply complied with relevant accounting regulations and generally accepted accounting practice.

As another issue to consider, would it be reasonable to assume that users of financial reports generally know that accounting reports are the outcome of various political pressures, or would they expect that the reports are objective and accurate reflections of an organization's performance and financial position? There could in fact be an accounting report *expectations gap* in this regard, although there is limited evidence of this.[27] According to Solomons (1978, p. 71), 'It is perfectly proper for measurements to be selected with particular political ends if it is made clear to users of the measurement what is being done.' However, is it realistic or practical to assume that users of financial statements would be able or prepared to accept that financial accounting necessarily needs to accommodate political considerations? Further, could or would users rely upon financial statements if they had such knowledge? Would there be a reduction of confidence in capital markets?

The argument that economic consequences need to be taken into account before new rules are introduced (or existing rules are changed) also assumes that in the first instance (before any amendments are to be made) there was some sort of equity that did not need addressing or rebalancing. As Collett (1995, p. 27) states:

> The claim that all affected parties such as the preparers of reports are entitled to have their interest taken into account in deciding on a standard, and not only dependent users, assumes that the position immediately prior to implementing the standard was equitable. If, however, users were being misled prior to the

---

[27] Liggio (1974) and Deegan and Rankin (1999) provide definitions of the expectations ga p. An expectations gap is considered to exist when there is a difference between the expectations users have with regard to particular attributes of information and the expectations preparers believe users have in regard to that information.

standard – for example, because certain liabilities were being kept off the balance sheet – then the argument that the interests of preparers of reports were being neglected in the standard-setting process would lose its force.

This appears to have been the case both at Lehman Brothers and earlier at Enron, where substantial liabilities were 'hidden' from users of the financial accounts through complex financial arrangements that resulted in these liabilities 'being kept off the balance sheet'. As Unerman and O'Dwyer (2004) explain, the false image portrayed by Enron's financial reports led many people, including Enron's employees, to lose money which they would probably not have invested if they had been aware of the true extent of Enron's liabilities. The senior executives ultimately responsible for preparing Lehman Brothers' financial statements, and those responsible a few years earlier for preparing Enron's financial reports, appear to have provided misleading information which resulted in the economic resources of external parties being allocated in a highly inefficient manner – but a manner which might have been perceived at the time by Lehman Brothers' or Enron's senior executives as being in their own personal interests. Perhaps the absence of adequate regulation had very real and significant economic consequences in these cases, which potentially demonstrates that regulation might be needed in some instances to protect the interests of less powerful stakeholders.

As a further related issue for readers to consider, is it appropriate for regulators to consider the views of financial statement preparers when developing accounting standards, given that accounting standards are put in place to limit what preparers are allowed to do, that is, to regulate their behaviour in the *public interest*? As we can hopefully see, regulating accounting practice requires many difficult assessments.

Chapter summary

In this chapter we considered various arguments that either supported or opposed the regulation of financial accounting. We saw that advocates of the 'free-market' (anti-regulation) approach argue that there are private economic incentives for organizations to produce accounting information voluntarily, and imposing accounting regulation leads to costly inefficiencies. To support their argument for a reduction in financial accounting regulation, the 'free-market' advocates rely upon such mechanisms as private contracting (to reduce agency costs), the market for managers and the market for corporate takeovers.

Advocates of the 'pro-regulation' perspective argue that accounting information should not be treated like other goods. As it is a 'public good' it is unrealistic to rely upon the forces of supply and demand. Because users of financial information can obtain the information at zero cost (they can be 'free riders'), producers will tend to produce a lower amount of information than might be socially optimal (which in itself is obviously difficult to determine). Further, there is a view that the stakeholders of an organization have a right to various items of information about an entity, and regulation is typically needed to ensure that this obligation is adhered to by all reporting entities. Regulation itself is often introduced on the basis that it is in the 'public interest' to do so – the view being that regulators balance the costs of the regulation against the economic and social benefits that the legislation will bring. Clearly, assessments of costs and benefits are difficult to undertake and will almost always be subject to critical comment.

There are alternative views as to why regulation is introduced in the first place. There is one perspective (referred to above) that legislation is put in place for the *public interest* by regulators who are working for the interests of the constituency (public interest theory). Public interest theory does not assume that individuals are primarily driven by their own self-interest (hence public interest theory makes assumptions that are not in accordance with many economic theories which have as their core assumption that all individuals are driven by self-interest, with this self-interest being tied to efforts to maximize personal wealth). However, an assumption of self-interest is made by other researchers who argue in favour of an economic interest theory of regulation. They argue that *all* action by *all* individuals can be traced back to self-interest in which all people will be seeking to increase their own economic wealth.[28] Under this perspective, regulators will be seeking votes and election funding/support, and through embracing self-interest will tend to provide the legislation to groups who can pay for it either in terms of providing votes or providing funds or other resources to support the regulators' re-election.

Capture theory provides another perspective of the development of regulation. It argues that while regulation might initially be put in place for well-intentioned reasons (for example, in the 'public interest'), the regulated party will, over time, tend to gain control of (or capture) the regulator so that the regulation will ultimately favour those parties that the regulation was initially intended to control.

In this chapter we have also considered how perceptions about potential economic and social consequences impact on the development of accounting standards. In the light of this we have questioned whether financial accounting reports can really be considered as neutral, objective and representationally faithful – as the IASB *Framework for the Preparation and Presentation of Financial Statements* would suggest.

Questions

3.1 As this chapter indicates, some people argue that the extent of regulation relating to financial accounting is excessive and should be reduced.

    a What arguments do these people use to support this view?

    b How would you rate the arguments in terms of their logic?

3.2 What is the basis of the 'market for lemons' argument?

3.3 Given the process involved in developing accounting standards, do you believe that accounting standards can be considered as 'neutral' (that is, not serving the interests of some constituents over others)?

---

[28] There are, of course, many researchers who oppose this (rather cynical) view of human behaviour. Authors such as Gray *et al.* (1996) refer to this perspective as being 'morally bankrupt' and providing very little hope for efforts to address pressing global problems such as ongoing global environmental deterioration We consider some of these alternative perspectives in Chapters 8 and 9.

3.4   What is meant by saying that financial accounting information is a 'public good'?

3.5   Why would an 'accounting standards overload' occur?

3.6   Can regulatory intervention be explained on fairness or equity grounds? If so, what is the basis of this argument?

3.7   It is argued by some researchers that even in the absence of information organizations have an incentive to provide credible information about their operations and performance to certain parties outside the organization, otherwise the costs of the organization's operations will rise. What is the basis of this belief?

3.8   In this chapter there was an argument provided by some companies that introducing mandatory reporting requirements will tend to stifle innovation in relation to reporting. Do you believe that the introduction of mandatory reporting requirements in relation to a particular area of reporting (for example, social and environmental reporting) will act to stifle innovation in reporting? Explain your view.

3.9   Read and evaluate the following paragraph extracted from Cooper and Keim (1983, p. 202):

> It should also be noted that the nature and degree of the effect of disclosure requirements (and other aspects of security regulation) on public confidence in the financial markets is unknown. Investors who have never read a prospectus or even thumbed through a 10-K report may have a great deal more confidence in the capital markets because the SEC and its regulations are an integral aspect of the financial system. The salutary effect of such enhancement of the perceived integrity and credibility of the investment process is to reduce the cost of capital for all firms, and the magnitude of this effect may be quite significant.

3.10   Private contractual incentives will assist in ensuring that, even in the absence of regulation, organizations will provide such information as is demanded by its respective stakeholders. Evaluate this argument.

3.11   What is the 'market for corporate takeovers' and how would its existence encourage organizations to make accounting disclosures even in the absence of regulation?

3.12   In this chapter, market failure has been defined as the inability of market forces to produce a socially 'right' amount of information, that is, to produce information to the point where its marginal cost to society equals its marginal benefit. While in theory this calculation may be possible, in reality what are some of the problems with applying such a definition of market failure?

3.13   What assumptions are made about the motivations of the regulators in:

    a   the public interest theory of regulation?

    b   the capture theory of regulation?

    c   the economic interest theory of regulation?

3.14   Is it realistic to assume, in accordance with 'public interest theory', that regulators will not be driven by their own self-interest when designing regulations?

3.15   Identify and evaluate the key negative economic and social consequences which might potentially arise following the introduction of an accounting standard with which you are familiar.

3.16 Under the economic interest theory of regulation, what factors will determine whether a particular interest group is able to secure legislation that directly favours that group above all others?

3.17 What do we mean when we say that financial accounting standards are the outcome of a political process? Why is the process 'political'?

3.18 If an accounting standard-setter deems that a particular accounting standard is likely to adversely impact some preparers of financial statements, what do you think it should do? Justify your view.

3.19 Let us assume that a government regulator makes a decision that all companies with a Head Office in South Africa must separately disclose, within their annual financial report, the amount of expense incurred in relation to the training of employees. The companies must also spend at least 5 per cent of their reported profits on training employees. You are required to:

a explain the decision made by the regulator in terms of *public interest theory*;

b explain the decision made by the regulator in terms of the *economic interest group theory of regulation.*

3.20 One of the most pressing problems confronting the world is global warming. Arguably, to effectively address this issue, governments across the world will be required to introduce regulations to mitigate the impacts of business activities on the environment. These regulations would necessarily require corporations to make significant changes to how they operate and this predictably will have negative implications for the profitability of many organizations (however, in the long run no organizations and hence no profits will exist if action is not taken). You are required to explain whether the various theories discussed in this chapter provide hope, or otherwise, that regulations will be introduced which ultimately will benefit future generations, but which will require corporations to change how they do business.

3.21 Let us assume that the government has become concerned that existing disclosure regulation tends to fixate on the financial performance of organizations but fails to address other aspects of corporate performance, including a failure to provide information about corporate social and environmental impacts as well as information about various initiatives and investments an organization has undertaken to improve its social and environmental performance. As such, the government has decided to introduce legislation that will require business corporations to provide information about the social and environmental impacts of their operations, as well as the social and environmental initiatives undertaken by the corporations. You are required to:

a explain from a public interest theory perspective the rationale for the government introducing the legislation and how the government will ultimately assess whether any proposed legislation should actually be introduced;

b predict from a capture theory perspective the types of constituents who will benefit in the long run from any social and environmental disclosure legislation;

c predict from an economic interest group theory perspective of regulation whether any potential legislation to be introduced will lead to an increase in the accountability of corporations in relation to their social and environmental performance despite any implications this increased corporate accountability might have for the maintained financial success of large but heavily polluting organizations.

References

Akerlof, G.A. (1970) 'The market for "lemons": Quality uncertainty and the market mechanism', *Quarterly Journal of Economics*, **84**, 488–500.

Barton, J. & Waymire, G. (2004) 'Investor protection under unregulated financial reporting', *Journal of Accounting and Economics*, **38**, 65–116.

Beaver, W.H. (1973) 'What should be the FASBs objectives?', *The Journal of Accountancy*, **136**, 49–56.

Berle, A.A. & Means, G.C. (1932) *The Modern Corporation and Private Property*, New York: Macmillan.

Broadbent, J. & Laughlin, R. (2002) 'Accounting choices: Technical and political trade-offs and the UK's private finance initiative', *Accounting, Auditing & Accountability Journal*, **15** (5), 622–54.

Carey, A. (1997) *Taking the Risk Out of Democracy: Corporate Propaganda versus Freedom and Liberty*, Urbana, IL: University of Illinois Press.

Collett, P. (1995) 'Standard setting and economic consequences: An ethical issue', *ABACUS*, **31** (1), 18–30.

Collison, D.J. (2003) 'Corporate propaganda: Its implications for accounting and accountability', *Accounting, Auditing & Accountability Journal*, **16** (5), 853–86.

Cooper, K. & Keim, G. (1983) 'The economic rationale for the nature and extent of corporate financial disclosure regulation: A critical assessment'. *Journal of Accounting and Public Policy*, **2** (3), 189–205.

Deegan, C. (1997) 'The design of efficient management remuneration contracts: A consideration of specific human capital investments', *Accounting and Finance*, **37** (1), 1–40.

Deegan, C., Morris, R. & Stokes, D. (1990) 'Audit firm lobbying on proposed accounting disclosure requirements', *Australian Journal of Management*, **15** (2), 261–80.

Deegan, C. & Rankin, M. (1999) 'The environmental reporting expectations gap: Australian evidence', *British Accounting Review*, **31** (3), 313–46.

Demski, J. & Feltham, G. (1976) *Cost Determination: A Conceptual Approach*, Ames, IA: Iowa State University Press.

Dye, R.A. (2001) 'An evaluation of "essays on disclosure" and the disclosure literature in accounting', *Journal of Accounting and Economics*, **32**, 181–235.

Fama, E. (1980) 'Agency problems and the theory of the firm', *Journal of Political Economy*, **88**, 288–307.

Francis, J.R. & Wilson, E.R. (1988) 'Auditor changes: A joint test of theories relating to agency costs and auditor differentiation', *The Accounting Review*, **63** (4), 663–82.

Friedman, M. (1962) *Capitalism and Freedom*, Chicago: University of Chicago Press.

Galbraith, J.K. (1972) *The Great Crash: 1929*, 3rd edn, Boston: Houghton Mifflin.

Gerboth, D.L. (1973) 'Research, intuition, and politics in accounting inquiry', *The Accounting Review*, 48 (3), 475–82.

Gray, R., Owen, D. & Adams, C. (1996) *Accounting and Accountability: Changes and Challenges in Corporate Social and Environmental Reporting*: London: Prentice-Hall.

Hakansson, N.H. (1977) 'Interim disclosure and public forecasts: An economic analysis and framework for choice', *The Accounting Review* (April), 396–416.

Hines, R. (1988) 'Financial accounting: In communicating reality, we construct reality', *Accounting Organizations and Society*, **13** (3), 251–62.

Hines, R. (1991) 'The FASBs conceptual framework, financial accounting and the maintenance of the social world', *Accounting Organizations and Society*, **16** (4), 313–51.

Hope, T. & Gray, R. (1982) 'Power and policy making: The development of an R & D standard'. *Journal of Business Finance and Accounting*, **9** (4), 531–58.

IASB (2008) 'Exposure draft of An Improved Conceptual Framework for Financial Reporting: Chapter 2 Qualitative characteristics and constraints of decision-useful financial reporting information'. London: International Accounting Standards Board.

IASCF (2010) *IASC Foundation Constitution*, London: IASC Foundation.

Jensen, M.C. & Meckling, W.H. (1976) 'Theory of the firm: Managerial behavior, agency costs and ownership structure', *Journal of Financial Economics*, **3** (October), 305–60.

Lehman, C. (1991) 'Editorial: The invisible Adam Smith', *Advances in Public Interest Accounting*, **4**, ix–xiv.

Liggio, C.D. (1974) 'The expectations gap: The accountant's Waterloo', *Journal of Contemporary Business*, **3** (3), 27–44.

Littleton, A.C. (1933) *Accounting Evolution to 1900*, New York: American Institute Publishing.

May, R.G. & Sundem, G. L. (1976) 'Research for accounting policy: An overview', *The Accounting Review*, **51** (4), 747–63.

Merino, B. & Neimark, M. (1982) 'Disclosure regulation and public policy: A socio-historical appraisal', *Journal of Accounting and Public Policy*, **1**, 33–57.

Mitnick, B.M. (1980) *The Political Economy of Regulation*, New York: Columbia University Press.

Morris, R. (1984) 'Corporate disclosure in a substantially unregulated environment', *ABACUS* (June), 52–86.

Parrish, M.E. (1970) *Securities Regulation and the New Deal*, New Haven: Yale University Press.

Pecora, F. (1939) *Wall Street under Oath: The Story of our Modern Money Changers*, New York: Simon and Schuster.

Peltzman, S. (1976) 'Towards a more general theory of regulation', *Journal of Law and Economics* (August), 211–40.

Posner, R.A. (1974) 'Theories of economic regulation', *Bell Journal of Economics and Management Science*, **5** (Autumn), 335–58.

Ronen, J. (1977) 'The effect of insider trading rules on information generation and disclosure by corporations', *The Accounting Review*, **52**, 438–49.

Scott, W.R. (1997) *Financial Accounting Theory*, Upper Saddle River, NJ: Prentice-Hall.

Scott, W.R. (2003) *Financial Accounting Theory*, Toronto: Pearson Education Canada Inc.

SEC (2009) 'U.S. Securities and Exchange Commission Draft Strategic Plan for fiscal years 2010–2015', Washington, DC: Securities and Exchange Commission.

Skinner, D.J. (1994) 'Why firms voluntarily disclose bad news', *Journal of Accounting Research*, **32** (1), 38–60.

Smith, A. (1937) *The Wealth of Nations*, New York: Modern Library.

Smith, C.W. & Warner, J.B. (1979) 'On financial contracting: An analysis of bond covenants', *Journal of Financial Economics* (June), 117–61.

Smith, C.W. & Watts, R. (1982) 'Incentive and tax effects of executive compensation plans', *Australian Journal of Management* (December), 139–57.

Solomons, D. (1978) 'The politicization of accounting', *Journal of Accountancy*, **146** (5), 65–72.

Spence, A. (1974) *Market Signalling: Information Transfer in Hiring and Related Screening Processes*, Cambridge, MA: Harvard University Press.

Stigler, G.J. (1971) 'The theory of economic regulation', *Bell Journal of Economics and Management Science* (Spring), 2–21.

US House (2002) 'Sarbanes-Oxley Act of 2002', 107th Congress, 2d Session, House Report 107–610.

Unerman, J. & O'Dwyer, B. (2004) 'Enron, WorldCom, Andersen *et al*: A challenge to modernity', *Critical Perspectives on Accounting*, **15** (6–7), 971–93.

Verrecchia, R.E. (2001) 'Essays on disclosure', *Journal of Accounting and Economics*, **32**, 97–180.

Walker, R.G. (1987) 'Australia's ASRB: A case study of political activity and regulatory capture', *Accounting and Business Research*, **17** (67), 269–86.

Watts, R.L. (1977) 'Corporate financial statements: A product of the market and political processes', *Australian Journal of Management* (April), 53–75.

Watts, R.L. & Zimmerman, J.L. (1978) 'Towards a positive theory of the determination of accounting standards', *The Accounting Review*, **53** (1), 112–34.

Watts, R.L. & Zimmerman, J.L. (1983) 'Agency problems: Auditing and the theory of the firm: Some evidence', *Journal of Law and Economics*, **26** (October), 613–34.

Watts, R.L. & Zimmerman, J.L. (1986) *Positive Accounting Theory*, Englewood Cliffs, NJ: Prentice-Hall.

International Accounting

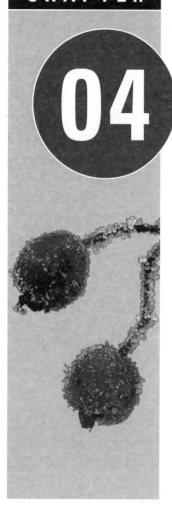

04

❖ LEARNING OBJECTIVES

Upon completing this chapter readers should:

❖ understand the background to recent actions by the International Accounting Standards Board (IASB) and other standard-setting bodies to implement the adoption of a uniform set of accounting standards for worldwide use (this set of accounting standards being known as International Financial Reporting

Standards or, in abbreviated form, IFRSs);

❖ understand some of the perceived advantages and disadvantages for countries that adopt IFRSs;

❖ appreciate that prior to many countries recently adopting IFRSs there were a number of important differences between the accounting policies and practices adopted within various countries. Such differences are decreasing across time as various countries elect to adopt accounting standards released by the IASB;

❖ understand various theoretical explanations about why countries might adopt particular accounting practices in preference to others and be able to evaluate whether, in light of the various theories, it is appropriate to have one globally standardized set of accounting standards;

❖ be able to explain what is meant by the term harmonization (or standardization) of accounting;

❖ be able to identify and explain some of the perceived benefits of, and obstacles to, harmonizing or standardizing accounting practices on an international scale;

❖ understand the key factors that are leading to greater international harmonization of accounting – especially within the European Union.

Opening issues

Since the start of 2005, accounting standards issued by the International Accounting Standards Board (IASB) have become the accounting standards which are to be followed in many countries throughout the world, including all member states of the European Union (EU). Do you believe that different countries should adopt the same accounting standards – that is, that a one-size-fits-all approach to financial accounting is appropriate despite differences in cultures, legal systems and financial systems? Do you believe that this is the best avenue for EU accounting regulation to follow (rather than having different rules in each member state, or a common set of accounting rules developed specifically by EU regulators separate from the accounting rules in other parts of the world)? What are some of the advantages and disadvantages that arise as a result of a country (or group of countries such as the EU) adopting the accounting standards issued by the IASB?

4.1 Introduction

In the previous chapters we considered how regulation can shape the practice of financial reporting. We learned that various factors can influence the actions of regulators (for example, the regulators' perceptions about what is in the 'public interest' or about what the economic implications of a newly proposed accounting standard might be), and that various theoretical perspectives can be applied when making a judgement about the factors that will be more likely to impact on a regulator's ultimate decision to support, or oppose, particular financial accounting requirements. We saw how differences in, or changes to, accounting regulations can result in different accounting 'numbers' being reported for a given underlying transaction or event, and how these differences in reported accounting results can lead to both positive and negative social and economic consequences. Clearly, therefore, any differences in accounting regulations between different countries are likely to result in the accounting outcomes reported from a specific set of transactions and/or events varying from country to country.

In this chapter we consider theoretical explanations regarding why, in the absence of efforts to globally harmonize or standardize accounting practices, we might expect accounting regulations and practices to vary between different countries. In doing so we can explain why there was a large degree of variation in accounting practices internationally prior to recent decisions by many countries to adopt the accounting standards issued by the IASB. These previous differences are explained by such factors as the differences in national cultures and institutional practices. In light of previous research that indicates that people in different countries, or from different cultures, will have different information demands and expectations, we will explore the logic of recent global efforts to establish one set of accounting standards for worldwide use. We will address the question of whether it really makes sense that organizations in diverse countries all adopt the same accounting standards in an apparent acceptance of a 'one-size-fits-all' approach to financial reporting.

Within the chapter we provide a discussion of recent initiatives undertaken, principally driven by the IASB, to establish a uniform set of accounting standards for global use. We will see that over 100 countries have now adopted the accounting standards issued by the IASB, even though these standards often represented a significant change to the accounting standards that had previously been developed domestically within the respective countries. We will also see that a significant exception to this general trend has been the United States which has, unlike most other countries, decided against adopting the accounting standards released by the IASB. To date the US continues to use its own domestic standards, being those standards issued by the Financial Accounting Standards Board (FASB), although we will see that in 2008 the US Securities Exchange Commission (SEC) did pass a ruling allowing foreign listed entities that are also listed on the stock exchange in the US to lodge their reports drawn up in accordance with IFRSs without the necessity to provide a reconciliation to US Generally Accepted Accounting Procedures. We will learn that the FASB and the IASB have entered into an arrangement whereby they are trying to eliminate major differences between their respective standards (converge their standards) and once this is achieved then the SEC has indicated a possibility that domestic companies will thereafter be required to also follow IFRSs, as is the case in most other countries. However, despite recent pressure from political leaders for faster convergence (particularly in the wake of the sub-prime banking crisis and global financial crisis) the timing of any move by the US to adopt IFRSs is still far from certain.

We commence the chapter with a brief discussion of the international differences that existed between the accounting practices of various countries prior to many countries recently adopting IFRSs.

4.2 Evidence of international differences in accounting prior to recent standardization initiatives

As we will discuss in this chapter, in recent years many countries have elected to adopt the accounting standards issued by the IASB, with such implementation typically being effective in such countries (such as members of the EU) from 2005. However, to understand how the accounting rules of different nations had led to vastly different accounting results prior to recent standardization efforts (and hence to put into context some of the arguments for standardization) it is useful to consider some actual examples of how a particular company's results varied dramatically depending upon which particular nation's accounting standards were being utilized to account for its various transactions. To this end we can consider research undertaken by Nobes and Parker (2004) – research undertaken prior to the recent widespread adoption of IFRSs.

Nobes and Parker (2004, p. 4) undertook a comparison of the results of a small number of European-based multinationals each of which reported their results in accordance with both their home nation's accounting rules and US accounting rules. Their comparative analysis shows, for example, that the underlying economic transactions and events of the Anglo-Swedish drug company AstraZeneca in the year 2000 produced a profit of £9,521 million when reported in conformity with UK accounting rules, but the same set of transactions produced a reported profit of £29,707 million when prepared pursuant to US accounting rules – a difference of 212 per cent in reported profits from an identical set of underlying transactions and events! Extending this analysis to a more recent period, the 2006 annual report of AstraZeneca (the final year that companies with a dual home country and US listing had been required to provide a reconciliation between their results using IFRSs and using US accounting rules) shows that net income derived from applying IFRS accounting rules of $6,043 million became a net income of $4,392 million when calculated in accordance with US accounting rules – this time a difference of 27 per cent lower than under the IFRS rules. In its balance sheet (or as it is now known, its statement of financial position), AstraZeneca's shareholders' equity at 31 December 2006 was $15,304 million when reported in accordance with IFRS accounting rules, but this became $32,467 million when determined in accordance with US accounting rules, a difference of 112 per cent. Although percentage differences of this size might be unusual, examination of the financial reports of almost any company that reported its results in accordance with more than one nation's set of accounting regulations will have shown differences between the profits reported under each set of regulations and between the financial position reported under each set of regulations.

A further dramatic example of the existence of differences between the accounting rules of different countries was provided by Enron. As Unerman and O'Dwyer (2004) explain, in the aftermath of the collapse of Enron many accounting regulators, practitioners and politicians in European countries claimed that the accounting practices which enabled Enron to 'hide' vast liabilities by keeping them off their US balance sheet would not have been effective in Europe. In the United Kingdom this explanation highlighted the differences between the UK and US approaches to accounting regulation. It was argued that under UK accounting regulations these liabilities would not have been treated as off balance sheet, thus potentially producing significant differences between Enron's balance sheet under UK and US accounting practices.

Having considered how different countries' accounting rules can generate significantly different profits or losses, we can consider whether such differences are a justification for the decision by many countries to adopt accounting standards issued by the IASB. Obviously if various countries adopt the same accounting rules then the differences between the results that would be reported in different countries will disappear. What do you think? Is removing international differences in accounting results sufficient justification for standardizing international accounting? Certainly, this justification has been used by the IASB and regulators within the EU and in other countries to justify the use of IFRSs.

The following section of this chapter will highlight some of the advantages that have been identified to justify efforts to standardize accounting internationally. However, it should be appreciated that there are many accounting researchers who argue that there are very good reasons that accounting rules should be different in different countries (due to such factors as underlying national differences in culture, legal systems, finance systems, and so forth). The theoretical reasons given to explain why international differences are expected to exist, and perhaps should still exist, can in turn be used as possible arguments against the international standardization of accounting – something that nevertheless has been actively pursued by the IASB. Towards the end of this chapter we will consider the various theoretical arguments that have been proposed in opposition to standardizing international accounting.

4.3 Does it really matter if different countries use different accounting methods?

Before considering some of the perceived advantages associated with having a standardized system of accounting it is useful to first clarify some important terminology. Nobes and Parker (2010, p. 80) distinguish between 'harmonization' and 'standardization' of accounting. They define 'harmonization' as:

> a process of increasing the compatibility of accounting practices by setting bounds to their degree of variation.

'Standardization' of accounting is explained as a term which 'appears to imply the imposition of a more rigid and narrow set of rules [than harmonization]' (p. 80). Therefore, harmonization appears to allow more flexibility than standardization, but as Nobes and Parker (2010) point out, the two terms have more recently been used almost synonymously in international accounting. Nevertheless, what appears to be happening through the efforts of the IASB is a process of standardization.

Nobes and Parker (2010) explain that the reasons for the recent efforts to increase international *standardization* of financial accounting are similar to the reasons previously used to justify standardizing financial accounting within an individual country. If investors are increasingly investing in companies from diverse countries, and these investors use financial reports as an important source of information upon which to base their investment decisions, then there is a view held by many people (but not all people), that standardization is important to enable them to understand the financial reports, and to have a reasonable basis to compare the financial accounting numbers of companies from different countries. Just as is the case domestically (see the arguments in Chapters 2 and 3), both *understandability* and *interpretation* of financial accounting information should be more effective if all accounts are compiled using the same set of underlying assumptions and accounting rules. If an international investor has to understand numerous different sets of accounting assumptions, rules and regulations, then the task of making efficient and effective international investments decisions is considered to be complicated considerably.

Further, if the long-term finance needs of a multinational company are too great for the providers of finance in a single country, then it may need to raise finance by listing its securities on the stock exchanges of more than one country. For reasons of domestic investor protection, the stock exchange regulators in a particular country might be reluctant to permit a company's shares to be traded on its exchange if that company does not produce financial reports which are readily comparable with the financial reports of all other companies whose shares are traded on that exchange – that is, reports which have been prepared using comparable assumptions (or rules). Also, where a company has to produce financial accounting reports in accordance with the accounting rules of each of the stock exchanges where its shares are traded, its accounting procedures would be considerably simplified if there was a single set of internationally recognized accounting rules which were acceptable to all the stock exchanges where its shares are traded. It arguably makes sense to utilize a single set of international accounting rules and regulations for all companies listed on any stock exchange.

A further reason for international standardization of accounting provided by Nobes and Parker (2010) is that it will facilitate greater flexibility and efficiency in the use of experienced staff by multinational firms of accountants and auditors. Otherwise, different accounting regulations in different countries would act as a barrier to the transfer of staff between counties. However, whether such a factor provides real benefits to parties other than accounting firms and multinational companies is not clear.

Ball (2006, p. 11) identifies a number of other advantages that are often advanced to support the case for the global standardization of financial reporting. Some of the additional advantages include the following: first, the adoption of IFRSs might be done on the premise that the decision will lead to more accurate, comprehensive and timely financial statement information, relative to the information that would have been generated from the national accounting standards they replaced. To the extent that the resulting financial information would not be available from other sources, this should lead to more-informed valuations in the equity markets, and hence lower the risks faced by investors. Another perceived benefit of adopting IFRSs relates to the increased financial information that would be available to small and large investors alike. Small investors might be less likely than larger investment professionals to be able to access or anticipate particular financial statement information from other sources. Improving financial reporting quality will allow smaller investors to compete more fully with professional (larger) investors, and hence will reduce the risk that smaller investors are trading with better-informed professional investors (such a risk is known as 'adverse selection').[1]

---

[1] Adverse selection is an economics term which represents a situation in a market where buyers cannot accurately gauge the quality of the product that they are buying, but where sellers have knowledge about the quality of the product they are selling.

While many perceived advantages, including those provided above, can be listed in relation to standardizing international accounting, it is obviously very difficult to quantify such benefits or advantages. Ball (2006, p. 9) states:

> There is very little empirical research or theory that actually provides evidence of the advantages or disadvantages of uniform accounting rules nationally, or internationally.

Hence, it is not at all clear from an empirical perspective whether the decision made by the EU, that EU member states would adopt IFRSs from 2005 for all listed companies, was the 'right' one. Also, whether the benefits of adopting IFRSs are shared by a majority of corporations within a country, or whether the benefits are confined to larger multinational corporations, is a matter of conjecture. If it is only the larger organizations that benefit then perhaps we may need to question the equity associated with any process that required all companies within a country to switch from domestic standards to IFRSs. In this regard Chand and White (2007) question the relevance of IFRSs to a smaller, less developed country such as Fiji which has a relatively small capital market. They ask (p. 607):

> Why would a developing country such as Fiji that does not have a well established capital market adopt the IFRSs? Questions concerning the effects of harmonized accounting standards on domestic users and local communities have largely been left unanswered.

Having identified some of the perceived advantages relating to standardization (and we will discuss some perceived disadvantages later in this chapter) it is useful now to consider the main organization involved in standardizing accounting on an international basis – this body being the IASB.

4.4 A brief overview of the IASB and its globalization activities

In the following pages of this chapter we will describe recent initiatives that have been implemented to standardize financial accounting on a global basis. In doing so we will provide a brief description and history of the IASB – the organization at the centre of the global standardization of accounting. We will also provide a brief description of the standardization efforts in the EU.

In understanding the history of the IASB we perhaps need to go back over 50 years and make reference to a former president of the Institute of Chartered Accountants of England and Wales (ICAEW), namely Henry Benson. Benson was elected as president of the ICAEW in 1966 and was the grandson of one of the four brothers who, in 1854, founded the accounting firm, Coopers (which through various mergers and so forth has become part of PricewaterhouseCoopers). In relation to Benson's influence on international accounting, Veron (2007, p. 10) states:

> When elected (in 1966), Benson gave a short address to the Institute's Council, in which he mentioned invitations he had received to visit his counterparts at the Canadian Institute of Chartered Accountants and the American Institute of Certified Public Accountants. He then added: '*I have had the feeling for a long time that our relations with those Institutes were very friendly but somewhat*

remote and, with the Council's approval, I shall see whether I can perhaps get them on to a more intimate basis'.

These characteristically understated words marked the beginning of international accounting standard-setting. Benson recalls the moment in his autobiography, published in 1989 under the title *Accounting for Life*: '*My private but unstated ambition at that stage was to make it, as I think it turned to be, a turning point in the history of the accountancy profession. The United Kingdom, America and Canada were the three most important countries at that time in the world of accountancy, but there was very little dialogue between them. No attempt had been made to make them closer together to advance the interests of the profession as a whole or to get a common approach to accountancy and audit problems. The Canadian institute was closer to the American institute than we were because of their geographical position but each of the three pursued its own policies without reference or collaboration with the other two. I hoped to change this.'*

Following Benson's visits, the three bodies jointly established an Accountants' International Study Group in February 1967, which soon published papers on accounting topics and gradually developed its own doctrinal framework. This then formed the basis for the creation in 1973 of the International Accounting Standards Committee (IASC) by an extended array of accounting bodies from Australia, France, Germany, Japan, Mexico and the Netherlands, in addition to Canada, the United Kingdom (plus Ireland associated with it), and the United States. The IASC's stated aim was to issue international standards of reference which would guide the convergence of national standards over time. Benson was duly elected the IASC's first chairman, and opened its offices in London.

When the IASC was established in 1973 it had the stated objectives of:

> formulating and publishing in the public interest accounting standards to be observed in the presentation of financial statements and promoting their worldwide acceptance and observance; and working generally for the improvement and harmonisation of regulations, accounting standards and procedures relating to the presentation of financial statements. (IASC, 1998, p. 6)

Veron provides a description of the work performed by the IASC in the years following its formation in 1973. He states (2007, p. 11):

> In the ensuing years, the IASC prepared and published a growing number of documents constituting an increasingly comprehensive body of rules, eventually completed in 1998 as a set of 39 so-called 'core' International Accounting Standards (IAS). Simultaneously, its governance evolved constantly to accommodate a growing and increasingly diverse stakeholder base. Belgium, India, Israel, New Zealand, Pakistan and Zimbabwe joined as associate members as early as 1974, and many other countries later followed suit. In 1981, the IASC's Consultative Group was formed with representatives of the World Bank, United Nations, OECD, and various market participants. This group was joined in 1987 by the International Organisation of Securities Commissions (IOSCO, which brings together the SEC and its national counterparts around the world), and

in 1990 by the European Commission and FASB, the US standard-setting body, as these two organisations joined IASC meetings as observers. In 2000, IOSCO recommended the use of IAS for cross-border offerings or listings. By the same time, a number of developing countries had taken the habit of using them as the reference for drafting their own national standards. Some, like Lebanon and Zimbabwe, had even made their use a requirement for banks or publicly-listed companies. Several developed countries, such as Belgium, France, Italy and Germany, had also adopted laws allowing large listed companies to publish consolidated accounts using IAS or standards very similar to them, without having to 'reconcile' them with national standards. Following the Asian crisis of the late 1990s, international accounting standards were also endorsed by the G7 Group of industrialised countries and by the Financial Stability Forum, a group of financial regulators hosted by the Bank for International Settlements in Basel.

The IASC's approach to accounting regulation essentially followed the Anglo-American model (which we explain later in this chapter), but initially many of the International Accounting Standards (IASs) it published permitted a wide range of accounting options. As such, they were not particularly effective at standardizing accounting practices internationally, as different companies (or countries) could use substantially different accounting policies while all being able to state that they complied with the single set of IAS regulations. Therefore compliance with IASs did not ensure or enhance the comparability or understandability of financial accounts – a key purpose of accounting regulation – and was not accepted by stock exchanges as a basis of the preparation of financial reports to support a listing on their exchange.[2]

In the late 1980s the International Organization of Securities Commissions (IOSCO), a body representing government securities regulators worldwide, recognized that to foster a greater number of multinational companies raising funding from stock exchanges in more than one country it would be useful to have a single set of rigorous international accounting standards – compliance with which would be acceptable to any stock exchange regulated by an IOSCO member. This would then reduce the costs of companies that had to produce a different set of financial accounting results for each of the countries in which their shares were listed. However, for IASs to be acceptable for this purpose, they would have to be much more effective at standardizing accounting practice, and would therefore need to permit a much narrower set of accounting practices or options.

Accordingly, the IASC then embarked on a comparability and improvements project to reduce the range of permitted options in IASs, and thereby make them acceptable to IOSCO (Purvis et al., 1991). This project culminated in the publication of a revised core set of IASs by 1999, which was then accepted by IOSCO members – with the important exception of the US Securities Exchange Commission. After this endorsement by IOSCO, any company which drew up its accounts in accordance with the revised IASs could use this single set of IAS-based accounts to support its listing on any stock exchange regulated by any IOSCO member anywhere in the world – again, with the exception of the United States.

---

[2] The IASB's *Framework for the Preparation and Presentation of Financial Statements* identifies comparability and understandability as two primary qualitative characteristics of financial information (the other two primary qualitative characteristics being relevance and reliability).

After completion of the core of this comparability and improvements project, the IASC was replaced in 2001 by the IASB, which adopted all existing IASs and from 2001 has published new regulations in the form of International Financial Reporting Standards (IFRSs).[3] The IASB has a structure which is seen to be considerably more independent and rigorous than the former IASC (although there are still some concerns about the independence of the IASB as we will discuss later in this chapter).

The replacement of the IASC with the IASB was one key element of significant changes made in the late 1990s to how the IASC conducted its operations. The IASC Foundation was created and this body, through a group of trustees, was established to supervise the operations of the newly created International Accounting Standards Board.[4] Subsequently, between February 2008 and January 2010 the IASC Foundation reviewed its constitution, and introduced an amended constitution from 1 March 2010. As part of this revised constitution, the IASC Foundation was renamed the International Financial Reporting Standards Foundation (or the IFRS Foundation), and it has the following objectives (IASCF, 2010, p. 5):

a to develop, in the public interest, a single set of high quality, understandable, enforceable and globally accepted financial reporting standards based upon clearly articulated principles. These standards should require high quality, transparent and comparable information in financial statements and other financial reporting to help investors, other participants in the world's capital markets and other users of financial information make economic decisions.

b to promote the use and rigorous application of those standards.

c in fulfilling the objectives associated with (a) and (b), to take account of, as appropriate, the needs of a range of sizes and types of entities in diverse economic settings.

d to promote and facilitate adoption of International Financial Reporting Standards (IFRSs), being the standards and interpretations issued by the IASB, through the convergence of national accounting standards and IFRSs.

The 2010 IFRS Foundation constitution established a new 'Monitoring Board' whose purpose is to 'provide a formal link between the Trustees and … those public authorities that have generally overseen standard-setters' (IASCF, 2010, p. 10). In addition, the Monitoring Board is required to approve the appointment of all IFRS Foundation Trustees.

The 22 Trustees of the IFRS Foundation are responsible for the IASB's governance and oversight, including funding (IASCF, 2010). However, the Trustees are not to be involved in any technical matters relating to the standards. The responsibility for technical matters

---

[3] When the IASC issued accounting standards they were referred to as International Accounting Standards (IASs). When the IASB now issues accounting standards they are referred to as International Financial Reporting Standards (IFRSs). Many of the IASC standards are still in existence, although many have been modified or updated by the IASB. These modified standards are still referred to as IASs and retain the same title and number, rather than becoming an IFRS, such that at the international level there are many IASs as well as numerous newly released IFRSs. A list of the currently applicable accounting standards can be found on the IASB's website, which is located at www.iasb.org.

[4] The IFRS Foundation has 22 Trustees of which six Trustees are appointed from North America, six from Europe, six from the Asia/Oceania region, one from Africa, one from South America and two 'from any area, subject to establishing overall geographical balance'.

associated with accounting standards rests solely with the IASB. The Trustees of the IASC Foundation also appoint the members of the IASB, the IFRS Interpretations Committee and the IFRS Advisory Council.

The IFRS Interpretations Committee is the interpretative body of the IFRS Foundation and its mandate is to 'interpret the application of IFRSs and provide timely guidance on financial reporting issues not specifically addressed in IFRSs' (IASCF, 2010, p. 16). The Interpretations Committee comprises 14 voting members who are drawn from a variety of countries and between them have a balance of technical expertise. Its interpretations and guidance are subject to IASB approval and have the same authority as a standard issued by the IASB.

The IFRS Advisory Council is a forum for the International Accounting Standards Board (IASB) to consult a wide range of representatives 'with an interest in international financial reporting, having diverse geographical and functional backgrounds' (IASCF, 2010, p. 16).

At the time of the 2010 revision to the IFRS Foundation constitution, the IASB had 14 members. The revised constitution specified that this was to rise to 16 members by 2012. At least 13 of the 16 IASB members have to work full-time for the IASB, and the remainder must devote 'most of their time in paid employment' (IASCF, 2010, p. 11) to the IASB. Together, IASB members must:

> comprise a group of people representing, within that group, the best available combination of technical skills and background experience of relevant international business and market conditions in order to contribute to the development of high quality, global accounting standards. (IASCF, 2010, pp. 11–12)

To approve an IFRS (or an Interpretation), at least 10 of the 16 members of the IASB need to vote in favour of the relevant requirements. It should be noted, however, that while the IASB develops standards, it does not have any power of enforcement of their use in particular jurisdictions. As we will see later in this chapter, the IASB's lack of ability to enforce accounting standards has meant that there is a potential that different countries will enforce the requirements of various IFRSs in a less than uniform manner.

Despite the reforms to the IASB and the IFRS Foundation discussed above, IFRSs/IASs have still not been accepted by the US Securities Exchange Commission as an adequate basis for the preparation by US companies of accounts to support a listing on a US stock exchange.[5] However, the IASB and the US standard-setter (the Financial Accounting Standards Board – or FASB) have been working to reduce the differences between international standards and US accounting standards in what is referred to as its convergence project (Nobes and Parker, 2010). We will return to a discussion of this project shortly.

Role of the EU

A very significant participant in the process of standardizing accounting practices internationally was the EU. A key reason why the EU became involved in accounting

---

[5] As noted elsewhere in this chapter, foreign listed companies are allowed to lodge their financial statements within the US in accordance with IFRSs. This concession, however, is not extended to US companies.

regulation at the EU level (rather than leaving this entirely to individual member states) is that a founding principle of the EU is freedom of movement within the EU of people, goods and capital. As we saw earlier in this chapter, differing accounting principles in different countries have been considered to act as an impediment to investors understanding and comparing the financial accounts of companies in these different countries, and thereby act as an impediment to them freely investing their capital in companies from different EU member states (an inhibition to the free movement of capital). The approach towards harmonization of accounting in the EU has historically differed from the IASC/IASB approach. This should be of little surprise, given that most countries in the EU, by definition, follow a continental European system of accounting (to be discussed shortly) rather than the Anglo-American model of the IASC/IASB, so the EU approach to accounting harmonization has historically been through legislation. This EU legislation has primarily been in the form of EU directives on company law, which have to be agreed on by the EU and then implemented in the domestic legislation of each EU member state. This is a very lengthy process, and during the 1990s the EU recognized that it was far too inflexible to respond to the requirements of a dynamic business environment where financial accounting practices needed to adapt quickly to rapidly changing business practices – especially for companies that rely on 'outsider' forms of finance (which include an increasing number of the largest companies in many continental European nations. 'Outsider forms of finance' refers to finance received from parties, such as shareholders, that do not get involved in the management of the organization).

Following proposals made in 2000, the EU agreed in 2002 that from 1 January 2005 all companies whose shares were traded on any stock exchange in the EU would have to compile their consolidated accounts in accordance with IASs/IFRSs.[6] This was seen as a method of both ensuring accounting rules were flexible enough to suit the needs of a dynamic business environment, and ensuring that the financial accounts of EU-listed companies maintained international credibility. Further details regarding the EU adoption of IASs/IFRSs are shown in Accounting Headline 4.1, which reproduces a press release issued by the European Commission when this route for accounting regulation was formally adopted in 2002.

Having read Accounting Headline 4.1, it appears that the views being embraced in favour of the adoption of IASs/IFRSs are based on various beliefs about the information people need in making various decisions (which can be tied back to decision usefulness theories – some of which we consider in Chapters 5 and 6); beliefs about how individuals and capital markets react to accounting information (which can be tied back into behavioural and capital markets research – the topics of Chapters 10 and 11); and a view that the adoption of IASs/IFRSs is in the public interest, rather than being driven by the private interests of particular constituents (and we considered public interest theories and private interest theories in Chapter 3). There also appears to be a view that new accounting methods will be embraced in a similar manner across various countries (which perhaps disregards some of the literature discussed in this chapter – for example, that religion, culture or taxation systems influence the usefulness of various alternative accounting approaches).

---

[6] For a small number of companies, the deadline was 2007 instead of 2005.

Accounting Headline 4.1

EU adoption of IASs/IFRSs

Agreement on International Accounting Standards will help investors and boost business in EU

The European Commission has welcomed the Council's adoption, in a single reading, of the Regulation requiring listed companies, including banks and insurance companies, to prepare their consolidated accounts in accordance with International Accounting Standards (IAS) from 2005 onwards (see IP/01/200 and MEMO/01/40). The Regulation will help eliminate barriers to cross-border trading in securities by ensuring that company accounts throughout the EU are more reliable and transparent and that they can be more easily compared. This will in turn increase market efficiency and reduce the cost of raising capital for companies, ultimately improving competitiveness and helping boost growth. The IAS Regulation was proposed by the Commission in February 2001. It is a key measure in the Financial Services Action Plan, on which significant progress has been made in the last few weeks (see IP/02/796). Unlike Directives, EU Regulations have the force of law without requiring transposition into national legislation. Member States have the option of extending the requirements of this Regulation to unlisted companies and to the production of individual accounts. Although the Commission put forward the IAS proposal long before the Enron affair, this is one of a series of measures which will help to protect the EU from such problems. Others include the Commission's recent Recommendation on Auditor Independence (see IP/02/723) and its proposal to amend the Accounting Directives (see IP/02/799).

Internal Market Commissioner Frits Bolkestein said: 'I am delighted that the IAS Regulation has been adopted in a single reading and am grateful for the positive attitude of both the Parliament and the Council. I believe IAS are the best standards that exist. Applying them throughout the EU will put an end to the current Tower of Babel in financial reporting. It will help protect us against malpractice. It will mean investors and other stakeholders will be able to compare like with like. It will help European firms to compete on equal terms when raising capital on world markets. What is more, during my recent visit to the US, I saw hopeful signs that the US will now work with us towards full convergence of our accounting standards.'

To ensure appropriate political oversight, the Regulation establishes a new EU mechanism to assess IAS adopted by the International Accounting Standards Board (IASB), the international accounting standard-setting organisation based in London, to give them legal endorsement for use within the EU. The Accounting Regulatory Committee chaired by the Commission and composed of representatives of the Member States, will decide whether to endorse IAS on the basis of Commission proposals.

In its task, the Commission will be helped by EFRAG, the European Financial Reporting Advisory Group; a group composed of accounting experts from the private sector in several Member States.

EFRAG provides technical expertise concerning the use of IAS within the European legal environment and participates actively in the international accounting standard setting process. The Commission invites all parties interested in financial reporting to contribute actively to the

▶ work of EFRAG. The Commission recently proposed amendments to the Accounting Directives which would complement the IAS Regulation by allowing Member States which do not apply IAS to all companies to move towards similar, high quality financial reporting (see IP/02/799).

Source: European Commission Press Release, IP/02/827, 7 June 2002

Despite the European Commission's enthusiasm for the adoption of IASs/IFRSs, there were concerns that, for both legal and political reasons, the EU could not be seen to endorse in advance regulations which could be developed at any time in the future by an international body not under control of the EU (Nobes and Parker, 2010). That is, the EU was unwilling to give a blanket approval covering all future IFRSs (which would apply to many EU companies) without considering the details of these IFRSs. Therefore, as can be seen in Accounting Headline 4.1, the EU established a mechanism whereby each IAS/IFRS would have to be endorsed separately by the EU before becoming mandatory for listed companies in the EU. This endorsement process involves an eleven-member committee entitled the European Financial Reporting Advisory Group (EFRAG), with members drawn from preparers and users of accounts, commenting on each IAS/IFRS to the EU's Accounting Regulatory Committee (ARC). The ARC has a member from each EU state, and votes on whether to recommend approval of the IAS/IFRS to the EU Commission, with a two-thirds majority of the 27 members of the ARC required to recommend approval of any IAS/IFRS. This mechanism was used in 2004 to block recommendation of full EU endorsement of IAS 39 (on financial instruments) by governments who argued that aspects of IAS 39 were unrealistic and would have potentially significant negative economic consequences on banks in their nations. As shown in Accounting Headline 3.4 (in Chapter 3), similar concerns in 2009 led the ARC to defer recognition of provisions within the new IFRS 9, which was replacing provisions in IAS 39. It will be interesting to see whether these actions by the EU will damage the long-term movement towards international harmonization and standardization of accounting, as was argued by some commentators at the time.

4.5 The United States' role in the international standardization of financial accounting

Despite the above issues, the major event that is seen to have triggered over 100 countries adopting IFRS was the decision taken by the EU to adopt IFRSs as the accounting standards to be used for preparing the consolidated financial statements of publicly listed companies from 2005.[7] Prior to the adoption of IFRSs, these countries used accounting standards that were typically developed on a domestic basis.

---

[7] The proposal to adopt IFRSs was confirmed in a Regulation of the European Parliament and European Council released on 19 July 2002. IFRS and IFRIC Interpretations, once adopted by the IASB, need to be specifically acknowledged (and translated into various languages) by the European Commission to become part of EU law. National standards are still commonly used in European countries for individual (non-consolidated) financial statements.

One notable exception to the global adoption of IFRSs is the United States. But before considering the US position on global standardization, it is useful to briefly consider the two main bodies responsible for accounting regulation within the United States, these being the Securities and Exchange Commission, and the Financial Accounting Standards Board. Briefly, in relation to their history, following the US Stock Market crash of 1929, the newly established US securities legislation of 1933 and 1934 led to the creation of the Securities and Exchange Commission (SEC). The SEC was given the authority to develop accounting regulation; however, it decided to rely upon the expertise of the US accounting profession to develop accounting standards. Over the following decades the US accounting profession developed various documents that became known as constituting Generally Accepted Accounting Principles (GAAP). In 1973 the SEC entrusted the task for developing accounting standards to the newly formed Financial Accounting Standards Board (FASB).[8] The FASB is a private sector body that was established to act in the 'public interest'. While the FASB was established to be independent, the SEC has the power to over-ride the accounting standards issued by the FASB should it see fit to do so.[9]

In the US, reliance is still placed on accounting standards issued by the FASB, rather than on the standards issued by the IASB. That is, unlike many other countries the US has not yet adopted IFRSs. Given that the US represents the world's major capital market, the non-involvement of the US represents a significant limitation in the global acceptance of IFRSs. The US appeared very strong in its resolve not to adopt IFRSs believing that its 'rules-based' standards were superior to the more 'principles-based' standards of the IASB.[10] However, this resolve to retain their own standards (and to reject IFRSs) appeared to diminish around 2001/2002 with various 'accounting scandals' involving organizations such as Enron.[11] As Veron (2007, p. 23) states:

> The context was profoundly modified by the Enron bankruptcy in December 2001 and other accounting scandals that erupted in 2002, following the bursting

---

[8] Prior to this time the Accounting Principles Board (a committee of the American Institute of Certified Practicing Accountants) was responsible for developing US GAAP.

[9] See the following websites for further information about the SEC and FASB respectively: www.sec.gov and www.fasb.org.

[10] In basic terms, rules-based accounting standards tend to be relatively lengthier and provide explicit guidelines on how to account for specific attributes of different transactions and events. By contrast, principles-based accounting standards tend to be less detailed and more concise. Rather than providing detailed rules for particular transactions and events, in principles-based standards reference is made to general principles that should be followed. These principles might be incorporated within a conceptual framework of accounting. Principles-based accounting standards require the exercise of greater levels of professional judgement relative to rules-based accounting standards. As an example of the difference, a rules-based accounting standard might say that a particular type of intangible asset shall be amortized over 20 years whereas a principles-based standard might require that the intangible assets be amortized to the extent that the economic value of the asset has declined since the beginning of the accounting period. Accounting standards released by the FASB are generally considered to be more rules-based than accounting standards issued by the IASB (which are considered to be principles based).

[11] Enron was an energy company that was based in Texas. Prior to its bankruptcy in late 2001 it employed approximately 22,000 people and was one of the world's leading electricity, natural gas, pulp and paper, and communications companies, with reported revenues of $111 billion in 2000. At the end of 2001 it became apparent that the company's financial position was generated through extensive accounting fraud. Enron represented one of the biggest and most complex bankruptcy cases in US history.

of the late-1990s stock market bubble. Before this wave of controversy, specific US GAAP standards had been occasionally criticised but overall it was widely considered, in the US and elsewhere, that US GAAP as a whole were the best available set of accounting standards … But Enron's collapse shattered the perception of high quality. It exposed the shortcomings of some detailed US GAAP rules, most notably those on consolidation which gave Enron enough leeway to hide its now famous 'special-purpose entities' (with their funny names such as Chewco, Raptor, Jedi, or Big Doe) off its balance sheet, packing them with real debts backed by flimsy assets … In February 2002, a Senate Committee investigating the Enron debacle heard the testimony of IASB Chairman David Tweedie who explicitly criticised the rules-based approach which is prevalent in US GAAP, contrasting it with the more principles-based stance adopted by the IASB. Shortly thereafter, the Sarbanes–Oxley Act specifically mandated the SEC to study how a more principles-based system (such as IFRS) could be introduced in the United States.

With the perceived limitations of some US accounting requirements in mind, the FASB and the IASB entered a joint agreement in 2002 to converge and improve the standards of both the IASB and the FASB. The ultimate consequence of the Convergence Project would be that the US would ultimately adopt revised and improved IFRS regulations agreed between the IASB and FASB. As Veron (2007, p. 24) states:

> Since the early 2000s the FASB has been working with the IASB to narrow the differences between US GAAP and IFRS – a process they call 'convergence', but which in fact is very different from the unilateral convergence of, say, Australian or South Korean accounting standards towards IFRS. The premise, enshrined in the so-called Norwalk Agreement of September 2002[12] and renewed by a FASB-IASB Memorandum of Understanding in February 2006, is that both the FASB and the IASB would need to move some way towards each other. In this process, on some issues FASB adopts standards identical or near-identical to existing IFRS (e.g. for stock option expensing); on other issues the IASB adopts standards identical or near-identical to existing US GAAP rules, as with the IFRS 8 standard on 'operating segments'; and on yet other issues the two bodies jointly develop entirely new projects.

As we noted in Chapter 2, the sub-prime banking crisis from 2007 and the ensuing credit crunch and global financial crisis led to further questioning of the adequacy of existing accounting rules and practices. As part of the response to the concerns raised, the G-20 called in 2009 for further strengthening of accounting standards through completion by June 2011 of the FASB/IASB convergence project. By the time of the G-20 June 2010 summit it was apparent that the June 2011 deadline was unlikely to be met, so a revised target was called for to achieve convergence in accounting standards by the end of 2011:

> We re-emphasized the importance we place on achieving a single set of high quality improved global accounting standards. We urged the International

---

[12] It was signed in FASB's home city of Norwalk, Connecticut, hence becoming known as the Norwalk Agreement.

Accounting Standards Board and the Financial Accounting Standards Board to increase their efforts to complete their convergence project by the end of 2011. (G-20, 2010, p. 20, paragraph 30)

Revelations of accounting practices at the failed Wall Street bank Lehman Brothers further indicated the need for global convergence in accounting regulations. Accounting Headline 4.2 explains how Lehman Brothers used loopholes in accounting regulations to present an unrealistically healthy picture of its financial position, while Accounting Headline 4.3 highlights some tensions between key European and US stakeholders in the FASB/IASB convergence project.

Accounting Headline 4.2

Role of international differences in accounting in misleading accounting at Lehman Brothers

The Repo men must be stopped

By John Lanchester

Here's a name we haven't been hearing much about in the aftermath of the credit crunch: Sarbanes–Oxley. That was the US Congress's response to the collapse of Enron, a piece of legislation that was intended to be the biggest crackdown ever on dodgy corporate accounting. The law was enacted in 2002, was loudly complained about by Wall Street and, as we can clearly see from the crash, did nothing of value except making institutions pay formal obeisance to rules they thought a waste of time. When it came to protecting the public, the world's biggest crackdown on lax accounting had exactly zero effect.

The scandals keep coming. It is more than 18 months since Lehman Brothers, the US investment bank, imploded, almost taking down the global financial system with it. You might think there wouldn't be much

more bad news that could come out of the bank.

You would be wrong.

The broad outline of what happened to Lehman has been in the public domain for more than a year. The bank, under the leadership of Wall Street's longest serving boss, Richard Fuld, borrowed too much – it was, in the jargon, 'overleveraged' – and made huge bets on the US property market. When that market started collapsing, Lehman needed to borrow to meet its obligations – but credit had tightened up, and the bank went under.

But the report by Andrew Valukas, a senior lawyer appointed by the US government to examine Lehman's bankruptcy, has nonetheless astonished the world of money because of the detail it reveals about what was going on inside

▶

the bank. The Valukas team has produced a hugely comprehensive report that shows the lengths to which Lehmans went to hide its problems – and the way in which its actions turn out, disturbingly, to have a British dimension.

Going into the crunch, Lehman's staff needed to muddy the waters about how much money they had borrowed. They did this by hiding assets from the balance sheet. Imagine if you wanted to conceal from your creditors just how much you'd borrowed. So you'd lend some assets – say, £100,000 worth – to a neighbour in return for the equivalent amount of cash, with a promise to take them back days after your creditors had finished looking over your books. Your books, pumped with all that cash, would look a lot healthier.

The loaned stuff would still belong to you, and still appear on your accounts as assets. This is called a "repo" deal, short for "repurchase". But wait! What if you lent your assets for slightly less than they were worth – say £105,000 of assets in return for £100,000 cash. Oh, well that's completely different. That's a Repo 105, named after the 105% assets swapped for 100% cash. You could now book the deal as a 'true sale', and make the assets disappear from your books. Then you could take them back a few days later, and everything is peachy. That is what Lehman's bankers did to make $50bn disappear into thin air.

Does that sound like a good idea? No? That's what some American law firms thought. So Lehman came to Britain, and got a favourable opinion from Linklaters, one of the City's biggest and most respected law firms. Linklaters' response to this news being made public was this: 'The examiner [that is, Valukas] does not criticise those opinions or suggest they were wrong or improper. We have reviewed the opinions and are not aware of any facts or circumstances which would justify any criticism.'

The scandalous and unforgivable thing is that that's true. Lehman's accountants, Ernst & Young, also signed off on the deal. There is nothing wrong with what happened, by prevailing City standards. It was all within the rules.

This fresh Lehman scandal sums up two of the biggest problems that we, the voting, taxpaying public, still have with the banks a year and a half after we bailed them out. First, the operation of capital markets is international but the legislative regimes that control it are local. Financial institutions are constantly on the alert for ways in which they can exploit differences between jurisdictions – Repo 105 is merely a publicly revealed example of what happens all the time. Even Sarbanes–Oxley, the monster crackdown on tricky accounting by the US government, turned out to be wholly ineffective. Any action has to be co-ordinated and international, or it is worthless. And that co-ordination is easier to call for than achieve. This is one of the reasons why we have had 18 months of talk, and little action to actually restrain the banks.

The second thing we can learn from Repo 105 is that the culture of investment banking is out of control.

Source: *Guardian*, 20 March 2010, p. 31
©Guardian News and Media Limited 2010

Accounting Headline 4.3

European versus US tensions in IASB/FASB convergence project

The long and winding roadmap

By Mario Christodoulou

Convergence has become the major goal for the Financial Accounting Standards Board (FASB) ... By 2011, both the International Accounting Standards Board (IASB) and FASB need to find common ground on each and every accounting standard. The goal is to create a truly global financial language. ...

The world looked so rosy in August 2008 for proponents of convergence in the US. Lehman Brothers had not collapsed, the world was struggling through an emerging credit crunch, but banks had stood strong. It was in this climate that Christopher Cox, the US Securities and Exchanges Commission (SEC) chairman, announced a tentative convergence roadmap.

It was a significant step. The SEC is the lynch pin to international convergence plans. The pair might agree on the standards, but without SEC approval, the final book will be little more than a paperweight for US-only listed companies.

Cox's roadmap envisioned all US companies switching to International Financial Reporting Standards (IFRS) by 2014. At that moment, US accounting codes would be dropped and the migration to international standards would begin.

'The increasing world-wide acceptance and US investors' increasing ownership of foreign companies make it plain that, if we do nothing and simply let these trends develop, comparability and transparency will decrease for US investors and issuers,' he said at the time. It was a high-point in the convergence story.

In September, Lehman Brothers collapsed. In November, the Democrats won the race to the White House.

Christopher Cox chose Barack Obama's inauguration day to step down. No announcement or statement preceded his departure, only an email to staff. His replacement, Mary Schapiro, was welcomed. Floyd Norris, the *New York Times'* chief financial correspondent, named her as 'perhaps the most experienced regulator in Washington'.

But her attitude to accounting convergence, at first, seemed a long way from Cox's. During her confirmation hearings, she controversially said she would 'not be prepared to delegate standard-setting or oversight responsibility to the IASB'. ...

Perhaps the most significant event of the post-Cox era came in September when the G20 group of nations, with the backing of the US administration, also committed to global standards.

But, if the landscape in the US was brightening, in Europe, the IASB's own constituency was giving it trouble.

News that Adair Turner would speak at one of accounting's most renowned institutes struck some in the profession as a little odd.

The Financial Services Authority, which Lord Turner heads, had remained largely quiet on accountancy standards and his decision to address the ICAEW [The Institute of Chartered Accountants in England and Wales] seemed to many a cue that he was about to enter the fray. He didn't disappoint. ...

His comments were squarely directed at new IASB plans to change the way banks account for bad loans – a key issue in the crisis. He later said he felt there was a risk the IASB might complicate its existing standards as it converges with US standards.

His was the most prominent of the voices so far expressing skepticism about the convergence process.

In July 2008, the Fédération des Experts Comptables Européens (FEE) said there were 'diminishing returns', from further convergence. Two months later Nigel Sleigh-Johnson, head of financial reporting at the ICAEW, said the process needed to be kept under 'close review'.

More recently, Stephen Haddrill, chief executive at the Financial Reporting Council, said the process should not be about 'translating American standards into an international shape'.

Significantly the Basel Committee on Banking Supervision last month also urged the IASB to stay the course and not reshape its standards to suit convergence objectives.

Tweedie, speaking from an IASB meeting in Brazil, told Reuters journalists that convergence cannot take place at 'all costs'.

'Ultimately, we have to speak for the international community. If we disagree with FASB, we have to do what we think is right,' Tweedie said. 'I don't think the United States wants to be isolated.'

Tweedie knows his success with international standards – now accepted by 131 nations across the world – each day places more pressure on the US to accept the standards.

Japan has now set a 2016 change date, at which point companies will no longer use US accounting rules.

However, within the IASB, it seems understood that the convergence ship has traveled too far to simply be turned around, however prominent the criticism.

Nations like India, Canada, Brazil and Japan have signed up to international standards, in part because they understood that the US would eventually get on board. The US is the last major piece of the jigsaw still to fall into place. If the US walks away, could the international regime take such a major blow?

Source: *Accountancy Age*, 11 February 2010

4.6 Limited US recognition of IFRSs

Although the IASB/FASB convergence project is not yet completed, at the beginning of 2008 the SEC adopted rules that permitted foreign private issuers (but not US domestic companies) to lodge, with the SEC, their financial statements prepared in accordance with IFRSs without the need to provide a reconciliation to their accounting results prepared in accordance with GAAP as used in the United States. Before this, such a reconciliation was required. Now, therefore, foreign companies that are listed across a number of stock exchanges internationally, including within the US, can lodge their reports in the US even though the reports have not been prepared in accordance with US accounting standards and do not provide a reconciliation to US GAAP. The ruling of the SEC requires that foreign private issuers that take advantage of this option must state explicitly and unreservedly in the notes to their financial statements that such financial statements are in compliance with IFRS as issued by the IASB (without modifications) and they must also provide an unqualified auditor's report that explicitly provides an opinion that the financial statements have been compiled in accordance with IFRSs as issued by the IASB. In explaining the basis for their decision to provide this concession to foreign companies the SEC stated (2007, p. 16):

> As discussed in the Proposing Release, continued progress towards convergence between U.S. GAAP and IFRS as issued by the IASB is another consideration in our acceptance of IFRS financial statements without a U.S. GAAP reconciliation. We believe that investors can understand and work with both IFRS and U.S. GAAP and that these two systems can co-exist in the U.S. public capital markets in the manner described in this rule making, even though convergence between IFRS and U.S. GAAP is not complete and there are differences between reported results under IFRS and U.S. GAAP.

Hence, effectively there are two types of financial statements being lodged within the US (as is the case in many other countries). Foreign companies can lodge their reports within the US in accordance with IFRSs whereas domestic US companies must lodge their reports in accordance with US GAAP. It is interesting that the SEC states that these two systems can co-exist. If different systems can co-exist then does that question the need for all countries to adopt IFRSs? What do you, the reader, think?

The following two press releases (Accounting Headlines 4.4 and 4.5) provide additional information about the decision taken in 2002 for the IASB and FASB to work towards converging their respective accounting standards, and the decision taken in late 2007 by the SEC to remove the requirement for foreign companies to provide a reconciliation to US GAAP.

Accounting Headline 4.4

Joint news release from the FASB and IASB

FASB and IASB agree to work together toward convergence of global accounting standards

LONDON, United Kingdom, October 29, 2002 – The Financial Accounting Standards Board (FASB) and International Accounting Standards Board (IASB) have issued a memorandum of understanding marking a significant step toward formalizing their commitment to the convergence of U.S. and international accounting standards. The FASB and IASB presented the agreement to the chairs of leading national standard setters at a two-day meeting being held in London. The agreement between the FASB and IASB represents their latest commitment, following their September joint meeting, to adopt compatible, high-quality solutions to existing and future accounting issues.

The agreement follows the decisions recently reached by both Boards to add a joint short-term convergence project to their active agendas. The joint short-term convergence project will require both Boards to use their best efforts to propose changes to U.S. and international accounting standards that reflect common solutions to certain specifically identified differences. Working within

▶

each Board's due process procedures, the FASB and IASB expect to issue an Exposure Draft to address some, and perhaps all, of those identified differences by the latter part of 2003. The elimination of those differences, together with the commitment by both Boards to eliminate or reduce remaining differences through continued progress on joint projects and coordination of future work programs, will improve comparability of financial statements across national jurisdictions.

Robert H. Herz, Chairman of the FASB, commented, 'The FASB is committed to working toward the goal of producing high-quality reporting standards worldwide to support healthy global capital markets. By working with the IASB on the short-term convergence project – as well as on longer-term issues – the chances of success are greatly improved. Our agreement provides a clear path forward for working together to achieve our common goal.'

Hailing the agreement, Sir David Tweedie, Chairman of the IASB, remarked, 'This underscores another significant step in our partnership with national standard setters to reach a truly global set of accounting standards. While we recognize that there are many challenges ahead, I am extremely confident now that we can eliminate major differences between national and international standards, and by drawing on the best of U.S. GAAP, IFRSs and other national standards, the world's capital markets will have a set of global accounting standards that investors can trust.'

Source: FASB and IASB, 29 October 2002

Accounting Headline 4.5

IASB press release
The IASB welcomes SEC vote to remove reconciliation requirement

The International Accounting Standards Board (IASB) welcomed the decision taken today by the US Securities and Exchange Commission (SEC) to remove the requirement for non-US companies reporting under International Financial Reporting Standards (IFRSs) as issued by the IASB to reconcile their financial statements to US generally accepted accounting principles (GAAP).

The development of a single, high quality language for financial reporting that is accepted throughout the world's capital markets has been the primary goal of the IASB since its inception in 2001 and today's decision is an important step towards achieving that objective.

The adoption of IFRSs by the European Union with effect from 2005, and similar decisions by Australia, Hong Kong and South Africa, led the way in a process that has resulted in over 100 countries now requiring or permitting the use of IFRSs. The SEC's decision follows those announced by other leading countries in 2007 to establish time lines for the acceptance of IFRSs in their domestic markets or accelerate convergence of national standards with IFRSs. Among those are Canada, India and Korea, all of which will adopt IFRSs by 2011. In Brazil listed companies will have to comply with IFRSs from 2010, and convergence between Japanese GAAP and IFRSs is expected by 2011. At the beginning of this year China introduced a completely new set of accounting standards that are intended to produce the same results as IFRSs.

Commenting on the SEC's decision Sir David Tweedie, Chairman of the IASB, said:

> We are delighted that the US Securities and Exchange Commission has decided to allow non-US issuers to file under IFRSs without the need

for reconciliation to US GAAP. The IASB remains strongly committed to its joint work with the US Financial Accounting Standards Board set out in the Memorandum of Understanding in February 2006 in order to achieve our goal of providing the world's integrating capital markets with a common language for financial reporting.

Source: IASB, 15 November 2007

4.7 Does the international standardization of accounting standards necessarily lead to the international standardization of accounting practice?

The standardization of accounting standards by a multitude of different countries, with different enforcement mechanisms, different forms of capital markets, different cultures and so forth might be considered by many people to lead to the standardization of accounting practice. Certainly this seems to be a central assumption of the IASB. But is this a realistic belief? Will international standardization of accounting standards lead to international standardization of accounting practice? Evidence provided by Kvaal and Nobes (2010) indicates that where there is still flexibility within options provided by individual IFRSs and IASs, companies in different countries tend to choose the options that reflect the requirements within their previous (pre-IFRS adoption) national accounting regulations. As such, Kvaal and Nobes (2010) indicate that despite the international standardization intended by the widespread adoption of IRFSs, national differences still persist and limit the international comparability of financial statements drawn up by companies in different countries:

> we document formally that there are different national versions of IFRS practice. Related to this, we show that companies not only have an opportunity to pursue pre-IFRS practices originating in their national GAAP, but also extensively use this opportunity.

> These findings are important for several reasons. For financial statement users, they imply that full international comparability has not yet arrived. Therefore, it has been suggested, investors might be misled by an apparent uniformity (Ball, 2006: 15). As long as accounting standards contain options and require use of judgment, some variation in accounting practice is inevitable. However, the existence of systematic differences in practice related to national borderlines

is clearly in conflict with the objective of international harmonisation and may mislead financial statement users who do not pay attention to them. Some differences within IFRS practice are observable and can be adjusted for by alert analysts (e.g. the location of dividends in a cash flow statement); other differences are easily observable but cannot be adjusted for without a large degree of estimation (e.g. the effects of the inventory flow method on profit, or the absence of a gross profit figure in a by-nature income statement); yet others are not observable (e.g. the application of criteria for making impairments or for capitalising development costs). Some users of financial statements might be misled by even the first type of differences, but many might be misled by the third type. The second and third types create difficulties for international comparative analysis. (Kvaal and Nobes, 2010, pp. 173–74)

In the discussion that follows we will see that there are a number of reasons why the standardization of accounting standards will not (and does not) necessarily lead to standardization in practice. Hence, consistent with Nobes (2006), we would argue that the study of international differences in accounting (and the reasons and motivations therefore) will remain an important area of research despite the ongoing standardization efforts of the IASB.[13] We will see that there are various reasons why international differences will survive (and have survived) beyond the introduction of IFRSs.

Differences in taxation systems

As one explanation of ongoing differences in accounting practices, Nobes (2006, p. 235) utilizes a comparison of differences in taxation systems between Germany and the UK to identify why financial accounting practices in the UK and Germany might be systematically different despite both countries adopting IFRS. He states:

> In Germany, companies are required to continue to prepare unconsolidated financial statements under the conventional rules of the Handelsgesetzbuch (HGB) for calculations of taxable income and distributable income. This is irrespective of any use of IFRS for consolidated or unconsolidated statements (Haller and Eierle, 2004). In some areas, the tax-driven accounting choices of the unconsolidated statements might flow through to consolidated IFRS statements. For example, asset impairments are tax deductible in Germany (but not in the UK), so there is a bias in favour of them. They might survive into IFRS consolidations in Germany, given the room for judgment in IFRS impairment procedures.
>
> In the UK, IFRS is allowed for individual company financial statements and therefore as a starting point for calculations of taxable income. The tax authorities generally expect the statements of a parent and other UK group members to use the same accounting policies as group statements. To take an example,

---

[13] As Nobes (2006) noted, there has historically been a number of accounting researchers who specialized in studying the reasons and rationale for differences in the accounting methods or practices being adopted in different countries. Many such researchers considered that their area of specialization might become defunct as a result of the global adoption of IFRSs. However, as this section will demonstrate, despite the widespread adoption of IFRSs there will continue to be many differences in the accounting methods adopted across different countries, and hence, many areas to consider for research into international accounting differences.

the recognition and measurement of intangible assets has tax implications. Consequently, given that IFRS requires considerable judgment in this area, individual companies using IFRS will have an incentive to make interpretations of IAS 38 (Intangible Assets) in order to minimise capitalisation and therefore tax, and then these will flow through to consolidated statements.

Differences in economic and political influences on financial reporting

There is also an expectation that differences in the economic and political forces operating within a country will have implications for various decisions and judgements made throughout the accounting process. As Ball (2006, p. 15) states:

> The fundamental reason for being sceptical about uniformity of implementation in practice is that the incentives of preparers (managers) and enforcers (auditors, courts, regulators, boards, block shareholders, politicians, analysts, rating agencies, the press) remain primarily local. All accounting accruals (versus simply counting cash) involve judgments about future cash flows. Consequently, there is much leeway in implementing accounting rules. Powerful local economic and political forces therefore determine how managers, auditors, courts regulators and other parties influence the implementation of rules. These forces have exerted a substantial influence on financial reporting practice historically, and are unlikely to suddenly cease doing so, IFRS or no IFRS. Achieving uniformity in accounting standards seems easy in comparison with achieving uniformity in actual reporting behaviour. The latter would require radical change in the underlying economic and political forces that determine actual behaviour.

Modifications made to IFRSs at a national level

As indicated earlier in this chapter, and an issue that is of concern to accounting regulators in the US, is that the IASB has no ability to enforce the application of its accounting standards in countries that have made the decision to adopt IFRSs. The effect of this is that regulatory bodies in particular countries may take the decision to modify a particular IFRS before it is released. This was the case in the EU in relation to their acceptance of IFRS 39. If modifications to IFRSs are made at a national level then this will result in international inconsistencies in accounting practice. As Ball (2006, p. 16) states:

> The most visible effect of local political and economic factors on IFRS lies at the level of the national standard adoption decision. This already has occurred to a minor degree, in the EU 'carve out' from IAS 39 in the application of fair value accounting to interest rate hedges. The European version of IAS 39 emerged in response to considerable political pressure from the government of France, which responded to pressure from domestic banks concerned about balance sheet volatility. Episodes like this are bound to occur in the future, whenever reports prepared under IFRS produce outcomes that adversely affect local interests.

In relation to local modifications to IFRSs, Veron also makes the following comment (2007, p. 41):

> If implementation is guided by nationally determined recommendations, then they may gradually diverge from one country to another ... The main promise of IFRS, of making the accounts of companies comparable for investors to make the right choices across countries and sectors, would be in jeopardy. The SEC's Chairman recently insisted that '*We have got to be able to demonstrate that IFRS is indeed a single set of international accounting standards, and not a multiplicity of standards going by the same name*'.

Differences in implementation, monitoring and enforcement

The argument here is that unless there is consistency in the implementation of accounting standards and subsequent enforcement mechanisms then we cannot expect accounting practices to be uniform despite the actions of the IASB. That is, inconsistencies internationally in how the adoption of accounting standards are implemented, monitored and enforced will lead to inconsistencies in how the standards are applied which in turn diminishes the international comparability of financial reports. In relation to the implementation of accounting standards, different countries will have varying levels of expertise in applying IFRSs. Using China as an example, Veron (2007, p. 20) states:

> In China as in other developing economies, any reference to financial statements prepared 'in accordance with IFRS' needs to be taken with a pinch of salt. The most daunting challenge there is not the standards' adoption, but their proper enforcement in a context of massive underdevelopment of the accounting profession, both quantitatively and qualitatively: China has no more than 70,000 practising accountants (many of them poorly trained), while the size of its economy would probably require between 300,000 and one million.

As Nobes (2006, pp. 242–43) explains when considering differences between accounting practice in Germany and the UK:

> Enforcement (including monitoring) of compliance with IFRS remains a national matter within the EU. It has been suggested (La Porta *et al.*, 1997) that enforcement of accounting rules is stronger in the UK than in Germany. Hope (2003) constructed an index of compliance and registered Germany substantially lower than the UK. Furthermore, a great deal of evidence has been amassed that compliance by German groups with international standards was lax despite an audited statement of compliance by directors (e.g. Street and Bryant, 2000, Street and Gray, 2001). By contrast, compliance with standards in the UK since the creation of the Financial Reporting Review Panel (FRRP) in 1990 is generally regarded as having been high (Brown and Tarca, 2005).

Questioning the logic behind any belief that the efforts of the IASB will realistically lead to international consistencies in accounting practice Ball (2006, pp. 16–17) states:

> Does anyone seriously believe that implementation will be of equal standard in all the nearly 100 countries that have announced adoption of IFRS in one way or another? The list of adopters ranges from countries with developed accounting and auditing professions and developed capital markets (such as Australia) to countries without a similarly developed institutional background (such as Armenia, Costa Rica, Ecuador, Egypt, Kenya, Kuwait, Nepal, Tobago and Ukraine).
>
> Even within the EU, will implementation of IFRS be at an equal standard in all countries? … It is well known that uniform EU economic rules in general are not implemented evenly, with some countries being notorious standouts. What makes financial reporting rules different?
>
> Accounting accruals generally require at least some element of subjective judgment and hence can be influenced by the incentives of managers and auditors. Consider the case of IAS 36 and IAS 38 which require periodic review of long term tangible and intangible assets for possible impairment to fair value. Do we seriously believe that managers and auditors will comb through firms' asset portfolios to discover economically impaired assets with the same degree of diligence and ruthlessness in all the countries that adopt IFRS? Will auditors, regulators, courts, boards, analysts, rating agencies, the press and other monitors of corporate financial reporting provide the same degree of oversight in all IFRS-adopting countries? In the event of a severe economic downturn creating widespread economic impairment of companies' assets, will the political and regulatory sectors of all countries be equally likely to turn a blind eye? Will they be equally sympathetic to companies failing to record economic impairment on their accounting balance sheets, in order to avoid loan default or bankruptcy (as did Japanese banks for an extended period)? Will local political and economic factors cease to exert the influence *on actual financial reporting practice* that they have in the past? Or will convergence among nations in adopted accounting standards lead to an offsetting divergence in the extent to which they are implemented?

Ball (2006) also discusses how the recent general trend inherent within IFRSs of adopting asset measurement bases tied to 'fair value' will in itself create inconsistencies because in many countries there is an absence of markets for many types of assets, including financial assets. In such countries with 'thinly trading markets' relatively more estimation of 'fair values' will be required. As Ball (2006, p. 17) states:

> To make matters worse, the countries in which there will be greater room to exercise judgment under fair value accounting, due to lower-liquidity markets and poorer information about asset impairment, are precisely the countries with weaker local enforcement institutions (audit profession, legal protection, regulation, and so on). Judgment is a generic property of accounting standard implementation, but worldwide reliance on judgment has been widely expanded under IFRS by the drift to fair value accounting and by the adoption of fair value standards in countries with illiquid markets.

The ultimate implication of the potential variation in accounting practice (for the reasons discussed in this section) is that investors might be misled into believing that IFRS adoption has created a consistency in international accounting practices. That is, the adoption of IFRSs might (incorrectly) be construed as a signal that a country has improved its quality of reporting. In a sense, the adoption of IFRSs brings a level of legitimacy to a country's financial reporting despite any limitations in the level of enforcement of the standards. As Ball (2006, pp. 22–23) states:

> Substantial international differences in financial reporting quality are inevitable, and my major concerns are that investors will be mislead into believing that there is more uniformity in practice than actually is the case and that, even to sophisticated investors, international differences in reporting quality now will be hidden under the rug of seemingly uniform standards … But the problem with IFRS adoption, as a signal to investors about the financial reporting quality of a preparer, is that it is almost costless for all countries to signal that they are of high quality: i.e., to adopt the highest available accounting standards on paper. Worse. IFRS adoption most likely costs less to the lower-quality countries, for two reasons. First, the lower-quality regimes will incur fewer economic and political costs of actually enforcing the adopted standards. It is the higher quality reporting regimes that are more likely to incur the cost of actually enforcing IFRS. Because they have the institutions (such as a higher-quality audit profession, more effective courts system, better shareholder litigation rules) that are more likely to require enforcement of whatever standards are adopted. Second, by wholesale adoption of IFRS, the lower-quality regimes can avoid the costs of running their own standard-setting body, which likely are proportionally higher than in larger economies.

Ball discussed the 'free rider' problem associated with IFRS.[14] If a 'symbol of legitimacy' – such as IFRSs – can be acquired at low cost then some countries with low accounting proficiency will make the choice to adopt IFRSs because of the reputational benefits such a choice may generate. However, such a choice will have costly implications for countries with higher levels of accounting proficiency and who put in place appropriate implementation, monitoring and enforcement mechanisms. As Ball (2006, p. 23) states:

> A classic 'free rider' problem emerges: it is essentially costless for low-quality countries to use the IFRS 'brand name,' so they all do. If IFRS adoption is a free good, what companies or countries will not take it? When it is costless to say otherwise, who is going to say: 'We will not adopt high standards'?

As a potential solution to the above problem, Ball (2006, p. 24) makes the following proposal:

> The only way to make the IFRS signal informative about quality is for the worldwide financial reporting system to incorporate a cost of signalling that the lower-quality agents are not prepared to pay. This would necessitate an effective worldwide enforcement mechanism under which countries that adopt but do not effectively implement IFRS are either penalised or prohibited from using the IFRS brand name. In the absence of an effective worldwide enforcement mechanism it is essentially costless for low-quality countries to use the IFRS 'brand name', and

---

[14] As explained in Chapter 3, a free-rider can be defined as a party that takes advantage of particular goods or services without incurring some of the associated production or establishment costs.

local political and economic factors inevitably will exert substantial influence on local financial reporting practice, IFRS adoption notwithstanding. If allowing all countries to use the IFRS label discards the information in accounting standards about reporting quality differences, then the available quality signal could become the quality of the enforcement of standards, not standards per se.

Accounting Headline 4.6 provides an example of where a European company appeared to depart from an IASB standard and the article emphasizes the inability of the IASB to force compliance with its standards. The article also makes reference to inconsistencies in how IFRSs are applied internationally.

Accounting Headline 4.6

Departure from IFRSs by EU company
Loophole lets bank rewrite the calendar

By *Floyd Norris*

It is not often that a major international bank admits it is violating well-established accounting rules, but that is what Société Générale has done in accounting for the fraud that caused the bank to lose 6.4 billion euros – now worth about $9.7 billion – in January.

In its financial statements for 2007, the French bank takes the loss in that year, offsetting it against 1.5 billion euros in profit that it says was earned by a trader, Jérôme Kerviel, who concealed from management the fact he was making huge bets in financial futures markets.

In moving the loss from 2008 – when it actually occurred – to 2007, Société Générale has created a furor in accounting circles and raised questions about whether international accounting standards can be consistently applied in the many countries around the world that are converting to the standards.

While the London-based International Accounting Standards Board writes the rules, there is no international organization with the power to enforce them and assure that companies are in compliance.

In its annual report released this week, Société Générale invoked what is known as the 'true and fair' provision of international accounting standards, which provides that

'in the extremely rare circumstances in which management concludes that compliance' with the rules 'would be so misleading that it would conflict with the objective of financial statements,' a company can depart from the rules.

In the past, that provision has been rarely used in Europe, and a similar provision in the United States is almost never invoked. One European auditor said he had never seen the exemption used in four decades, and another said the only use he could recall dealt with an extremely complicated pension arrangement that had not been contemplated when the rules were written.

Some of the people who wrote the rule took exception to its use by Société Générale.

'It is inappropriate,' said Anthony T. Cope, a retired member of both the I.A.S.B. and its American counterpart, the Financial Accounting Standards Board. 'They are manipulating earnings.'

John Smith, a member of the I.A.S.B., said: 'There is nothing true about reporting a loss in 2007 when it clearly occurred in 2008. This raises a question as to just how creative they are in interpreting accounting rules in other areas.' He said the board should consider repealing the 'true and

▶

fair' exemption 'if it can be interpreted in the way they have interpreted it.'

Société Générale said that its two audit firms, Ernst & Young and Deloitte & Touche, approved of the accounting, as did French regulators. Calls to the international headquarters of both firms were not returned, and Société Générale said no financial executives were available to be interviewed.

In the United States, the Securities and Exchange Commission has the final say on whether companies are following the nation's accounting rules. But there is no similar body for the international rules, although there are consultative groups organized by a group of European regulators and by the International Organization of Securities Commissions. It seems likely that both groups will discuss the Société Générale case, but they will not be able to act unless French regulators change their minds.

'Investors should be troubled by this in an I.A.S.B. world,' said Jack Ciesielski, the editor of *The Analyst's Accounting Observer*, an American publication. 'While it makes sense to have a "fair and true override" to allow for the fact that broad principles might not always make for the best reporting, you need to have good judgment exercised to make it fair for investors. SocGen and its auditors look like they were trying more to appease the class of investors or regulators who want to believe it's all over when they say it's over, whether it is or not.'

Not only had the losses not occurred at the end of 2007, they would never have occurred had the activities of Mr. Kerviel been discovered then. According to a report by a special committee of Société Générale's board, Mr. Kerviel had earned profits through the end of 2007, and entered 2008 with few if any outstanding positions.

But early in January he bet heavily that both the DAX index of German stocks and the Dow Jones Euro Stoxx index would go up. Instead they fell sharply. After the bank learned of the positions in mid-January, it sold them quickly on the days when the stock market was hitting its lowest levels so far this year.

In its annual report, Société Générale says that applying two accounting rules – IAS 10, 'Events After the Balance Sheet Date,' and IAS 39, 'Financial Instruments: Recognition and Measurement' – would have been inconsistent with a fair presentation of its results. But it does not go into detail as to why it believes that to be the case.

One rule mentioned, IAS 39, has been highly controversial in France because banks feel it unreasonably restricts their accounting. The European Commission adopted a 'carve out' that allows European companies to ignore part of the rule, and Société Générale uses that carve out. The commission ordered the accounting standards board to meet with banks to find a rule they could accept, but numerous meetings over the past several years have not produced an agreement.

Investors who read the 2007 annual report can learn the impact of the decision to invoke the 'true and fair' exemption, but cannot determine how the bank's profits would have been affected if it had applied the full IAS 39.

It appears that by pushing the entire affair into 2007, Société Générale hoped both to put the incident behind it and to perhaps de-emphasize how much was lost in 2008. The net loss of 4.9 billion euros it has emphasized was computed by offsetting the 2007 profit against the 2008 loss.

It may have accomplished those objectives, at the cost of igniting a debate over how well international accounting standards can be policed in a world with no international regulatory body.

Source: *New York Times*, 7 March 2008, p. C1

Hence, given the material provided in this section, we might question the belief that the global adoption of IFRSs will lead to consistency in international accounting practices. There will, we believe, continue to be international differences in accounting practice and such differences will continue to provide an interesting area of research for accounting academics. However, at a more fundamental level, is it really a good idea that there should be global consistency in accounting practice anyway? That is, is the central quest of the IASB that there be global standardization of accounting standards logically flawed? Is it appropriate to have a global 'one-size-fits-all' approach to financial reporting when there are international differences in the nature of capital, labour and product markets; differences in monitoring and enforcement mechanisms; differences in economic and political influence; and differences in cultures? The next section of this chapter explores various reasons why, in the absence of global harmonization and standardization efforts such as those being undertaken by the IASB, we would expect to find international differences in accounting practices.

4.8 Explanations of differences in accounting practices employed in different countries

Will financial accounting standards developed in London by the IASB necessarily meet the information needs of financial report users in all countries? Does it make sense that a given suite of accounting standards will be equally applicable for a service company operating in South America as it would for a mining company operating in Australia, or a manufacturing company in China? What do you, the reader think? In this regard, Chand and White (2007, p. 606) make the following comment:

> Once the IFRSs are adopted by a particular country, both the multinational and domestic enterprises may be required to follow the standards. A suite of standards developed with the needs of international users of financial reports in mind, specifically those seeking international comparability, will not necessarily meet the needs of users in a particular jurisdiction. The IASB cannot take cognisance of the individual national, cultural and political factors of all its member nations while preparing IFRSs. Transporting IASB standards to developing countries – which have their own disparate group of external information users that operate within internationally diverse cultural, social, and political environments – should not be expected to have optimum results (Hopwood, 2000, Ngangan *et al.*, 2005). Therefore, of critical importance is the fundamental question, who gains the most from harmonization/convergence?

The above point is interesting. Given that over 100 countries have now adopted IFRSs, is there any clear evidence that all countries have benefited from the adoption, or that the benefits are spread across different types or sizes of organizations within particular countries?

Authors such as Perera (1989) have argued that accounting practices within particular countries have traditionally evolved to suit the circumstances of a particular society, at a particular time. While there was a large variation in accounting systems adopted in different countries (prior to 2005 when many, but not all, countries adopted IFRSs), it has been commonly accepted that there were two main models of financial accounting which evolved within economically developed countries: these being the Anglo-American model and the continental European model (Mueller, 1967; Nobes, 1984).[15] The Anglo-American model is characterized by a system of accounting that is strongly influenced by professional accounting bodies rather than government, emphasizes the importance of capital markets (the entities within the countries that use this model of accounting are typically very reliant on public sources of equity and debt finance), and relies upon terms such as 'true and fair' or 'presents fairly', which in turn are based upon considerations of economic substance over and above legal form (legal form being bound by legislation).

The continental European model of accounting, on the other hand, typically is characterized by relatively small input from the accounting profession, little reliance upon qualitative requirements such as true and fair, and stronger reliance upon government. The accounting methods tend to be heavily associated with the tax rules in place, and the information tends to be of a nature to protect the interest of creditors, rather than investors *per se* (the entities within countries that use the continental European model have historically tended to obtain most of their long-term funds from family sources, governments or lenders, often banks).

Over time, numerous reasons have been given for differences in the accounting methods of different countries. Mueller (1968) suggests that such differences might have been caused by differences in the underlying laws of the country, the political systems in place (for example, a capitalistic/free-market system versus a centralized/communistic system), or their level of development from an economic perspective. As Mueller (1968, p. 95) explains:

> In society, accounting performs a service function. This function is put in jeopardy unless accounting remains, above all, practically useful. Thus, it must respond to the ever-changing needs of society and must reflect the social, political, legal and economic conditions within which it operates. Its meaningfulness depends on its ability to mirror these conditions.

Other reasons such as tax systems, level of education and level of economic development have also been suggested to explain historical differences in accounting practices (Doupnik and Salter, 1995). At present there is no single clear theory that explains why, in the absence of efforts to standardize accounting, we would expect to find international differences in accounting practices. Many different causes have been suggested. Nobes (1998) reviewed the literature and confirmed that numerous reasons have been proposed to explain the differences. These are summarized in Table 4.1.

According to Nobes, many of the factors in Table 4.1 are interrelated. A number are deemed to be 'institutional', and a number relate to the broader notion of culture. We will now consider individually some of the factors identified in Table 4.1. First, we will examine

---

[15] For example, France, Italy, Spain and Germany are often presented as examples of the Continental European group, while countries such as the US, UK, Ireland, the Netherlands, Canada, Australia and New Zealand are often presented as examples of the Anglo-American group.

TABLE 4.1 Reasons proposed for international accounting differences
1 Nature of business ownership and financing system
2 Colonial inheritance
3 Invasions
4 Taxation
5 Inflation
6 Level of education
7 Age and size of accountancy profession
8 Stage of economic development
9 Legal systems
10 Culture
11 History
12 Geography
13 Language
14 Influence of theory
15 Political systems, social climate
16 Religion
17 Accidents
Source: Nobes (1998, p. 163).

the impact that cultural factors (including religious influences) could have had on shaping accounting practices. We will then consider how institutional factors, such as different legal and financing systems, might also have caused accounting practices to vary between countries. Again, we emphasize that many (but not all – Kvaal and Nobes, 2010) differences in accounting practices may have been eliminated due to many countries adopting IFRSs. After reading the material that follows we perhaps might then question whether it was actually appropriate for such a diverse group of countries to seek to adopt one set of accounting standards (IFRSs).

Culture

Culture is a broad concept that would be expected to impact on legal systems, tax systems, the way businesses are formed and financed, and so on. For many years culture has been used in the psychology, anthropology and sociology literatures as the basis for explaining differences in social systems (Hofstede, 1980). In recent decades it has also been used to try to explain international differences in accounting systems. One of the earlier papers to consider the impacts of culture on accounting was written by Violet (1983) who argued that accounting is a 'socio-technical activity' that involves interaction between both human and non-human resources. Because the two interact, Violet claims that accounting cannot be considered culture free. Relating accounting to culture, Violet (1983, p. 8) claims:

> Accounting is a social institution established by most cultures to report and explain certain social phenomena occurring in economic transactions. As a social institution, accounting has integrated certain cultural customs and elements within the constraints of cultural postulates. Accounting cannot be

isolated and analyzed as an independent component of a culture. It is, like mankind and other social institutions, a product of culture and contributes to the evolution of the culture which employs it. Since accounting is culturally determined, other cultural customs, beliefs, and institutions influence it.

Takatera and Yamamoto (1987) have defined culture as 'an expression of norms, values and customs which reflect typical behavioural characteristics'. Hofstede (1980, p. 25) has defined culture as 'the collective programming of the mind which distinguishes the members of one human group from another'. It describes a system of societal or collectively held values (Gray, 1988) rather than values held at an individual level. 'Values' are deemed to determine behaviour. Gray (1988, p. 4) explains that the term 'culture' is typically reserved for societies as a whole, or nations, whereas 'subculture' is used for the level of an organization, profession (such as the accounting profession) or family.

Gray (1988, p. 5) argues that 'a methodological framework incorporating culture may be used to explain and predict international differences in accounting systems and patterns of accounting development internationally'. Any consideration of culture necessarily requires difficult choices as to the aspects of culture that are important to the issue under consideration, and, in turn, how one goes about measuring the relevant cultural attributes. As Perera (1989, p. 43) states, 'the study of culture is characterized by a unique problem arising from the inexhaustible nature of its components'.[16] Accounting researchers who have examined the possible impact of culture on the comparative shape of financial accounting practices in different countries have tended to draw on the work of Hofstede (1980, 1983) to understand differences in national cultures. Gray (1988, p. 5) explains:

> Hofstede's (1980, 1983) research was aimed at detecting the structural elements of culture and particularly those which most strongly affect known behaviour in work situations in organizations and institutions. In what is probably one of the most extensive cross-cultural studies ever conducted, psychologists collected data about 'values' from the employees of a multinational corporation located in more than fifty countries. Subsequent statistical analysis and reasoning revealed four underlying societal value dimensions along which countries could be positioned. These dimensions, with substantial support from prior work in the field, were labelled Individualism, Power Distance, Uncertainty Avoidance, and Masculinity. Such dimensions were perceived to represent a common structure in cultural systems. It was also shown how countries could be grouped into culture areas, on the basis of their scores on the four dimensions.[17]

Gray argues that the value systems of accountants in each country will be derived and related to the societal values of that country (which are reflected by Hofstede's initial cultural dimensions of Individualism, Power Distance, Uncertainty Avoidance and Masculinity, to

---

[16] Perera (1989, p. 43) further states that 'it is essential, therefore, that in analyzing the impact of culture upon the behaviour of the members of any particular subculture, a researcher must select the cultural components or dimensions most pertinent to the particular facet of cultural behaviour being studied'. This is clearly not a straightforward task.

[17] Hofstede's work is based on international surveys conducted within IBM. The attitude surveys were conducted between 1967 and 1973 and resulted in 117,000 responses from 88,000 employees in 66 countries (Baskerville, 2003). Hofstede was the senior researcher in charge of the survey.

which Hofstede later added a fifth dimension of Long-Term Orientation).[18] These social values held by accountants (which Gray terms the accounting subculture) will in turn, it is argued, impact on the development of the respective accounting systems at the national level. To the extent that Gray's arguments, and the propositions of Hofstede from which they are derived, are valid, at this point we can perhaps start to question whether accounting systems can be developed in a 'one-size-fits-all' perspective – an approach which the IASB has adopted. However, while it is argued that there should be some association between various value systems and accounting systems, over time, many events would typically have occurred that confound this possible relationship. For example, in relation to developing countries, Baydoun and Willett (1995, p. 72) state:

> It is quite possible that had accounting systems evolved independently in developing countries they would have a rather different form from any we now witness in present day Europe. However, most accounting systems used in developing countries have been directly imported from the West through a variety of channels: by colonialism in the past; and through Western multinational companies, the influence of local professional associations (usually founded originally by Western counterpart organizations) and aid and loan agencies from the industrialized countries.

Furthermore, as with any theoretical perspectives in social sciences, we need to bear in mind that Hofstede's propositions regarding the presence, nature and influence of 'cultural dimensions' are themselves open to challenge. For example, McSweeney, a high-profile and influential critic of Hofstede's theories (see, for instance, McSweeney, 2002a, 2002b, 2009a, 2009b), has argued that the 'national cultural model' proposed by Hofstede was developed using flawed research methods and questionable assumptions. In a recent paper, McSweeney (2009a, p. 934) posed the question:

> In the face of extensive empirical data of variations within countries across social and geographical contexts and also across time, how does the national culturalist literature continue to rely on spatial reductionism: on the 'fallacious assumption of cultural homogeneity within nations' (Tung, 2007: 41)?

McSweeney (2009a, p. 934) proceeded to provide, supported with a great depth of argumentation, the following reasons in response to the above question he had posed:

> It does so by making the following problematic moves. I: By denying agency. This is achieved by assuming that national culture is: (a) coherent; (b) stable; (c) pure; (d) by excluding any independent role of other cultural influences; and (e) excluding any independent role of non-cultural influences. II: By unwarranted depictions. This is done by: (a) conflating nation and state; (b) making unwarranted generalizations from singular instances and/or treating unrepresentative averages as nationally representative; and (c) confusing statistical averages with causal forces. And, III: By ignoring prior and pertinent intellectual developments elsewhere, it fails to engage with the peripheralization in

---

[18] Hofstede's theory, while being applied to accounting issues, is from the cross-cultural psychology literature and was of itself not directly concerned with accounting.

anthropology and cultural geography (and in other disciplines) of the assumptions of national and other spatial cultural uniformity. These moves are now addressed.

Specifically from the perspective of accounting research, Baskerville (2003) raises similar concerns over the validity and reliability of Hofstede's national cultural dimensions. In his study, Baskerville identifies and explores a number of theoretical and methodological issues in prior studies that, he concludes, have been problematic in developing reliable insights into the role of national cultures, including (p. 1):

> (i) the assumption of equating nation with culture (ii) the difficulties of, and limitations on, a quantification of culture represented by cultural dimensions and matrices; and (iii) the status of the observer outside the culture.

Despite these issues, McSweeney (2009a) notes that the 'national cultural model' is still in common use in many areas of organizational studies (and we might include accounting as one such discipline). He comments that the national cultural model (associated most commonly with Hofstede, but augmented by many other researchers) was in the past also used by researchers within several different social science disciplines. However, he highlights that in many of these disciplines, this model's explanations of the development, presence and influence of national cultural differences have now been largely found to lack credibility. McSweeney (2009a, p. 949) argues that the persistence of the national cultural model in organization studies research, despite it being discredited in other disciplines, seems to be due to many researchers in sub-disciplines within organization studies (such as accounting) being unwilling to engage with critiques of the model, and thus ignoring clear flaws in the model:

> Within organization studies, a knowledge community has been built around the model. It [the national cultural model] has achieved a scholarly identity, being employed in papers across a wide range of peer-reviewed journals. The consensus on fundamentals within the community and the embeddedness it has achieved within areas of organization studies have created defences against the impact of critiques. It is rare for users of the model to acknowledge critiques – far less to engage with them.
>
> Two characteristics of organization studies which enable the advocates of the model to avoid engagement with critique are described here. First, disregard is facilitated by the fragmentation of organization studies into many relatively autonomous communities with a high degree of internal consensus and self-referentiality (March, 2004, Whitley, 2000). The balkanization of organization studies is arguably greater than in many other disciplines (Pfeffer, 1993) and is certainly far in excess of the degree of separateness which existed in anthropology at the time of the model's demise in that discipline. Secondly, while it is, of course, not possible to examine a situation uninfluenced by categories, theories and hunches, a tendency to build one-sided stories has been a powerful factor. Such bias is a deleterious tendency to search for or interpret new information in a way that confirms one's preconceptions and avoid information and interpretations which contradict them (Nickerson, 1998). It is widely tolerated in organization studies (Miles and Michael, 1984). Within the national cultural

community this bias includes a tendency not to consider alternative explanations and a widespread readiness to cite, or to generally refer to, studies which support the model but neglect contradictory studies.

Consistent with these observations from McSweeney, researchers who have drawn on and applied Hofstede's propositions about national cultures to research into international differences in financial accounting have tended to do so largely uncritically. Specifically from an accounting perspective, Baskerville (2003, p. 11) raises similar concerns to some of those raised by McSweeney, and urges greater criticality by accounting researchers:

> Such problems have ramifications for the utilization of Hofstede's cultural indices, and implications for cross-cultural accounting research which should not be ignored.

> The use of Hofstede's indices of cultural dimensions appeared to give cross-cultural studies in accounting stature and scientific legitimacy, and respectability within accounting research. Those researchers who utilize these dimensions successfully should be prepared to include in their application of the cultural indices a consideration of how their research addressed the problems of the concept of nations versus cultures, and the problems inherent in the universalist approach as debated earlier last century during the formative years in anthropology.

Despite (or possibly because of) many accounting researchers failing to be adequately critical of the insights provided by national cultural models, Hofstede's propositions have been influential in developing this branch of comparative international accounting research. We will therefore now go on to explain key aspects of the theories in this area. But when reading about and considering these theories, you should bear in mind the criticisms we have just outlined about some of the assumptions underlying these theories.

Financial accounting theories in this area have principally used the initial four societal value dimensions identified by Hofstede. These can be summarized as follows (quoted from Hofstede, 1984):

Individualism versus *Collectivism*

Individualism stands for a preference for a loosely knit social framework in society wherein individuals are supposed to take care of themselves and their immediate families only. Its opposite, Collectivism, stands for a preference for a tightly knit social framework in which individuals can expect their relatives, clan, or other in-group to look after them in exchange for unquestioning loyalty (it will be clear that the word 'collectivism' is not used here to describe any particular social system). The fundamental issue addressed by this dimension is the degree of interdependence a society maintains among individuals. It relates to people's self concept: 'I' or 'we'.

With regard to the cultural dimension of *Individualism versus Collectivism* it is interesting to note that a great deal of economic theory is based on the notion of *self-interest* and the *rational economic person* (one who undertakes action to maximize personal wealth at the expense of others). This is very much based in the *Individualism dimension*. In a culture that exhibits *Collectivism* it is expected that members of the society would look after each other and issues of loyalty would exist.[19]

Large *versus* Small Power Distance

Power Distance is the extent to which the members of a society accept that power in institutions and organisations is distributed unequally. This affects the behaviour of the less powerful as well as of the more powerful members of society. People in Large Power Distance societies accept a hierarchical order in which everybody has a place, which needs no further justification. People in Small Power Distance societies strive for power equalisation and demand justification for power inequities. The fundamental issue addressed by this dimension is how a society handles inequalities among people when they occur. This has obvious consequences for the way people build their institutions and organisations.

Strong *versus* Weak Uncertainty Avoidance

Uncertainty Avoidance is the degree to which the members of a society feel uncomfortable with uncertainty and ambiguity. This feeling leads them to beliefs promising certainty and to sustaining institutions protecting conformity. Strong Uncertainty Avoidance societies maintain rigid codes of belief and behaviour and are intolerant towards deviant persons and ideas. Weak Uncertainty Avoidance societies maintain a more relaxed atmosphere in which practice counts more than principles and deviance is more easily tolerated. The fundamental issue addressed by this dimension is how a society reacts to the fact that time only runs one way and that the future is unknown: whether it tries to control the future or to let it happen. Like Power Distance, Uncertainty Avoidance has consequences for the way people build their institutions and organisations.

Masculinity *versus* Femininity

Masculinity stands for a preference in society for achievement, heroism, assertiveness, and material success. Its opposite, Femininity, stands for a preference for relationships, modesty, caring for the weak, and the quality of life. The fundamental issue addressed by this dimension is the way in which a society allocates social (as opposed to biological) roles to the sexes.

It is claimed that when countries are given scores on each of the four value dimensions, a number of countries can be clustered together, reflecting that they have similar cultural values.[20]

---

[19] Positive Accounting Theory, a theory developed by Watts and Zimmerman (and which we discuss in depth in Chapter 7), attempts to explain and predict managers' selection of accounting methods. In developing their theory, Watts and Zimmerman assume that individuals will *always* act in their own self-interest. Such an assumption would be invalid in a community which embraces a Collectivist perspective. In a similar vein, Hamid *et al.* (1993) suggest that finance theories developed in Western cultures will not apply in Islamic cultures. According to Hamid *et al.* (1993), the Islamic principles do not allow the payment of interest. They argue (p. 146) therefore that 'much of Western finance theory, in particular the capital asset pricing model, which draws upon interest-dependent explanations of risk, cannot be part of the (Islamic) accounting and finance package'.

[20] For example, of the many groups, one group with similar scores on each of the four societal values comprises Australia, Canada, Ireland, New Zealand, UK, and USA. Another group is Denmark, Finland, Netherlands, Norway and Sweden, while another group comprises Indonesia, Pakistan, Taiwan and Thailand. The claim is that people within these various groupings of countries share a similar culture and therefore share similar *norms* and *value systems*.

Returning to how Gray (1988, p. 5) developed Hofstede's value dimensions to provide insights in relation to comparative international financial accounting, Gray sought to relate these value dimensions to the values that he perceived to be in place within the accounting subculture. Gray developed four accounting values that were deemed to relate to the accounting subculture with the intention that the accounting values would then be directly linked to Hofstede's four societal values. Gray's four accounting values were defined as follows (1988, p. 8):

Professionalism versus Statutory Control

A preference for the existence of individual professional judgement and the maintenance of professional self-regulation, as opposed to compliance with prescriptive legal requirements and statutory control.

Uniformity versus Flexibility

A preference for the enforcement of uniform accounting practices between companies and the consistent use of such practices over time, as opposed to flexibility in accordance with the perceived circumstances of individual companies.

Conservatism versus Optimism

A preference for a cautious approach to measurement so as to cope with the uncertainty of future events, as opposed to a more optimistic, laissez-faire, risk-taking approach.

Secrecy versus Transparency

A preference for confidentiality and the restriction of disclosure of information about the business only to those who are closely involved with its management and financing, as opposed to a more transparent, open and publicly account-able approach.

Gray (1988) then developed a number of hypotheses relating Hofstede's four societal cultural dimensions to each one of his own four accounting values.[21] His first hypothesis was:

> **Hypothesis 1**: The higher a country ranks in terms of *Individualism* and the lower it ranks in terms of *Uncertainty Avoidance* and *Power Distance*, then the more likely it is to rank highly in terms of *Professionalism*.

The basis for the above hypothesis was that a preference for applying judgement (for example, determining whether something is *true and fair*) rather than strict rules is more likely where people tend to be individualistic; where people are relatively more comfortable with people using their own judgement, rather than conforming to rigid codes of rules; and

---

[21] Although Gray (1988) developed four hypotheses, he did not test them empirically. To test them, as others have subsequently done, one must determine whether an accounting system scores high or low in a particular country on the four dimensions developed by Gray.

where different people are allowed to make judgements rather than relying on strict rules 'from above' (lower Power Distance).

Gray's second hypothesis was:

> **Hypothesis 2**: The higher a country ranks in terms of *Uncertainty Avoidance* and *Power Distance* and the lower it ranks in terms of *Individualism*, then the more likely it is to rank highly in terms of *Uniformity*.

The basis for the second hypothesis is that communities that prefer to avoid uncertainty prefer more rigid codes of behaviour and greater conformity. A desire for uniformity is also deemed to be consistent with a preference for Collectivism (as opposed to Individualism) and an acceptance of a relatively more Power Distance society in which laws are more likely to be accepted.

Gray's third hypothesis was:

> **Hypothesis 3**: The higher a country ranks in terms of *Uncertainty Avoidance* and the lower it ranks in terms of *Individualism* and *Masculinity*, then the more likely it is to rank highly in terms of *Conservatism*.

As noted previously, Conservatism implies that accountants favour notions such as prudence (which traditionally means that profits and assets are calculated in a conservative manner with a tendency towards understatement rather than overstatement). The basis for the third hypothesis is that communities that have strong Uncertainty Avoidance characteristics tend to prefer a more cautious approach to cope with existing uncertainties. On the other hand, Conservatism is expected to be associated with communities that care less about individual achievement. Communities that tend to demonstrate masculine tendencies emphasize achievement – hence the expectation that lower levels of Masculinity will lead to higher preferences for conservative accounting principles. A more highly masculine community would be deemed to prefer to use methods of accounting that lead to higher levels of performance being reported.

Gray's fourth hypothesis was:

> **Hypothesis 4**: The higher a country ranks in terms of *Uncertainty Avoidance* and *Power Distance* and the lower it ranks in terms of *Individualism* and *Masculinity*, then the more likely it is to rank highly in terms of *Secrecy*.

The basis for the fourth hypothesis is that communities that have a higher preference for Uncertainty Avoidance prefer not to disclose too much information because this could lead to conflict, competition and security problems. Also, communities that accept higher Power Distance would accept restricted information, as this acts to preserve power inequalities. Also, a community that prefers a collective approach, as opposed to an individualistic approach, would prefer to keep information disclosures to a minimum to protect those close to the firm and to reflect limited concern for those external to the organization. A more *Masculine* community would be expected to provide more information about its financial position and performance to enable comparisons of the level of performance of different entities. (Masculine communities would be deemed to be more concerned with issues such as ranking the performance of one entity against another.) However, as a caveat to the general position that more Masculine communities disclose more accounting information, Gray (1988, p. 11) argues that 'a significant but less important link with masculinity also seems likely to the extent that more caring societies, where more emphasis is given to the quality of life, people and the environment, will tend to be more open, especially as regards socially related information'.[22] Table 4.2 summarizes the hypothesized relationships between Gray's accounting values and Hofstede's cultural values.

TABLE 4.2 Summary of the hypothesized relationships between Gray's accounting values and Hofstede's cultural values

| Cultural values | Accounting values (from Gray) | | | |
(from Hofstede)	Professionalism	Uniformity	Conservatism	Secrecy
Power Distance	–	+	?	+
Uncertainty Avoidance	–	+	+	+
Individualism	+	–	–	–
Masculinity	?	?	–	–

Note: '+' indicates a positive relationship; '–' indicates a negative relationship; and '?' indicates that the direction of the relationship is unclear.

Gray (1988) further hypothesized that relationships can be established between accounting values and the *authority* and *enforcement* of accounting systems (the extent to which they are determined and enforced by statutory control or professional means), and the *measurement* and *disclosure* characteristics of the accounting systems. According to Gray (1988, p. 12):

> Accounting value systems most relevant to the professional or statutory authority for accounting systems and their enforcement would seem to be the professionalism and uniformity dimensions, in that they are concerned with regulation and the extent of enforcement and conformity ... Accounting values most relevant to the measurement practices used and the extent of information disclosed are self-evidently the conservatism and the secrecy dimensions.

Gray's linkage between societal values, accounting values and accounting practice can be summarized, as in Figure 4.1 (as summarized in Fechner and Kilgore, 1994, p. 269).

One objective of Gray's research was to explain how differences between countries in respect of their culture may either impede any moves towards international harmonization of accounting standards, or may bring into question efforts to generate some form of harmonization or standardization.

---

[22] Socially related information would relate to such issues as health and safety issues, employee education and training, charitable donations, support of community projects and environmental performance. A more Feminine (less Masculine) society would tend to consider these issues more important. Hence, while Femininity might be associated with less financial disclosure, it is assumed to be associated with greater social disclosure.

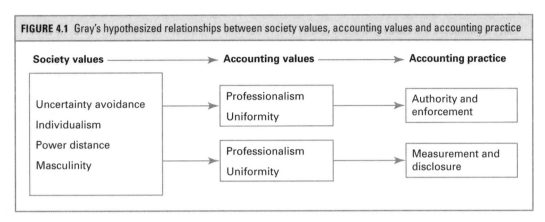

FIGURE 4.1 Gray's hypothesized relationships between society values, accounting values and accounting practice

Source: Fechner and Kilgore (1994, p. 269).

A number of other authors have also used Hofstede's cultural dimensions.[23] Zarzeski (1996) provides evidence that supports a view that entities located in countries classified as relatively more Individualistic and Masculine and relatively less in terms of Uncertainty Avoidance provide greater levels of disclosure. Zarzeski also considered issues associated with international profile and found that those entities with a relatively higher international profile tend to be less secretive than other entities. Further, entities from continental European countries, such as France and Germany, which have historically tended to rely more heavily on debt financing than, say, Anglo-American companies, have lower levels of disclosure than Anglo-American companies. In relation to the issue of secrecy, Zarzeski shows that local enterprises are more likely to disclose information commensurate with the secrecy of their culture than are international enterprises. In explaining this she states (p. 20):

> The global market is just a different 'culture' than the one the firm faces at home. When a firm does business in the global market, it is operating in a different 'culture' and therefore may need to have different 'practices'. Higher levels of financial disclosures may be necessary for international survival because disclosure of quality operations should result in lower resource costs. When enterprises from more secretive countries perceive economic gain from increasing their financial disclosures, cultural borrowing may occur. The culture being borrowed will be a 'global market culture', rather than a specific country culture.

Perera (1989) considered both Hofstede's cultural dimensions and Gray's accounting subcultural value dimensions and uses them to explain historical differences in the accounting practices adopted in continental European countries and Anglo-American countries. According to Perera (1989, p. 51), many countries in continental Europe are characterized by relatively high levels of uncertainty avoidance where rules or 'social codes' tend to shape behaviour, while the opposite applies in Anglo-American countries.

---

[23] Baydoun and Willett (1995, p. 72) identify a number of problems in testing the Hofstede–Gray theory. They emphasize that many accounting systems are imported from other countries with possibly different cultures. As they state: 'Due to the interference in what would otherwise have been the natural evolution of financial information requirements there are no uncontaminated examples of modern accounting practices in developing countries. Consequently great care has to be taken in using data from developing countries to draw inferences about relevance on the basis of the Hofstede–Gray framework.'

Baydoun and Willett (1995) used the Hofstede–Gray theory to investigate the use of the French United Accounting System (which was ranked lowly in terms of Professionalism and highly in terms of Uniformity as well as being considered as quite conservative) in Lebanon. According to Baydoun and Willett, following World War I the Allied Supreme Council granted France a mandatory authority over Lebanon. Lebanon was a French colony until 1943 and French troops remained there until 1946. Strong trading relations between France and Lebanon continued to exist and in 1983 the French government sponsored the transfer of the French Uniform Accounting System (UAS) to Lebanon. What was of interest is whether the French system was actually suited to the Lebanese cultural environment. Baydoun and Willett provided evidence to suggest that Lebanon and France ranked in a relatively similar manner in terms of Power Distance and Individualism. However, Lebanon was considered to rank lower in terms of Uncertainty Avoidance and higher in terms of Masculinity. On this basis (and we can refer back to Table 4.2), Baydoun and Willett (p. 81) conclude that 'it would appear that Lebanon's requirements are for less Uniformity, Conservatism and Secrecy in financial reporting practices'.[24]

Chand and White (2007) explored various cultural attributes within the Fijian society to determine whether the recent adoption of IFRSs within the Fijian context made sense. Their view was that rules-based standards would be more appropriate than the principles-based standards that have been developed by the IASB.

Religion

A great deal of the culture-based research, particularly that based on the work of Hofstede and Gray, tends to lead to countries being grouped together in terms of both community and accounting subculture – this is perceived as providing insights into the appropriateness of the harmonization/standardization process and, particularly, in identifying limits therein. That is, a feature of the work of Gray is that it relies on indigenous characteristics which are confined within the boundaries of the countries under review. In subsequent work, Hamid *et al.* (1993) considered the influence of one cultural input or factor, *religion*, on accounting practices. As they indicate, religion transcends national boundaries. They consider how Islamic cultures, which exist in numerous countries, had typically failed to embrace 'Western' accounting practices and they reflect upon how issues of religion had previously occupied minimal space in the accounting literature. They state (p. 134):

> The existing literature dealing with the interaction of business activity and Islam needs extending to capture the particular effects which compliance with Islamic beliefs have on the structure of business and finance within an Islamic framework. In particular, the incompatibility of many Western accounting practices with Islamic principles requires explanation. For jurisprudential Islamic law influences the conduct of businesses in a manner not accommodated

---

[24] In undertaking their work, Baydoun and Willett were, in a number of respects, critical of Gray's work. For example, they state (p. 82) that 'all of Gray's accounting values are defined in terms of preferences for particular courses of action, rather than in terms of apparent attributes of financial statements, such as the qualitative characteristics described in the FASB's conceptual framework project'. Also they state that Gray's theory does not clearly indicate what forms of financial statements might be preferred.

automatically by Anglo-American accounting practice. And many Western accounting practices draw upon assumptions which conflict with the tenets of Islam … There seems to be little understanding that, unlike the Western tradition, fundamental business ethics flow automatically from the practices of the religion, rather than from the codes (mainly of etiquette) devised and imposed upon members by professional associations.

Hamid *et al.*, (1993) point out that the Islamic tradition does have notions of stewardship – but to God rather than to suppliers of equity or debt capital. That is, Muslims believe that they hold assets not for themselves, but in trust for God. There are also other fundamental differences – for example, Islam precludes debt financing and prohibits the payment of interest, and this prohibition has significant implications for processes aimed at the international harmonization of accounting standards, particularly:

> in-so-far as harmonisation is perceived necessary to entail implementation of many standard Western accounting procedures in which interest calculations are integral. Many past and present Western standards entail discounting procedures involving a time value of money concept, which is not admitted by Islam.[25] (p. 144)

Hence, Hamid *et al.* (1993) appear to provide a logical argument that religion can have a major impact on the accounting system chosen. Religion can potentially affect how people do business and how they make decisions. As will be seen in Chapter 6, the conceptual framework projects developed in countries such as the United States, Australia, Canada, the United Kingdom and New Zealand (which, interestingly, have all been grouped together by Hofstede), and by the IASB's predecessor (the International Accounting Standards Committee, or IASC), are based on the underlying objective that financial report users require financial information as the basis for making *rational economic decisions* (and what is 'rational' may be culturally dependent). Such rational economic decisions also take into account the time value of money, which necessarily requires considerations of appropriate interest or discount rates. In some societies, such as Islamic states, this may not be a relevant objective. Further, any claims that particular frameworks of accounting are superior to others should only be made after considering the environments in which the frameworks are to be utilized.

Having examined several theories which seek to explain international accounting differences in terms of broad cultural (including religious) influences, we will now move on to explore five of the more concrete institutional factors which some theorists believe influence the shape of accounting practices in any nation at any point in time. As you may appreciate when reading the following sections, these institutional factors are both interrelated and can be linked to the broader cultural influences we have just examined. A useful exercise to help develop your understanding of both the cultural and institutional factors is for you to attempt, while reading the following sections, to associate (in a broad way) the institutional factors we discuss with cultural influences.

---

[25] For example, notions of discounting are found in 'Western' accounting standards dealing with employee benefits, lease capitalization, impairment of assets, and general insurers.

Legal systems

The first institutional factor we will examine is the legal systems operating in different countries. These can be divided into two broad categories: common law and Roman law systems.

In common law systems, there have historically been relatively few prescriptive statutory laws dealing with many areas of life. Instead, the body of law has been developed by judges applying both the limited amount of statutory law and the outcomes of previous judicial decisions to the facts of a specific case. Each judgement then becomes a legal precedent for future cases.

Conversely, in Roman law systems, parliamentary (statutory) law tends to be very detailed and covers most aspects of daily life. The implications of this for accounting is that in common law countries we would expect to find relatively few detailed accounting laws guiding accounting practices, and therefore historically the development of accounting practices would have been left much more to the professional judgement of accountants (and auditors). With Roman law systems, by contrast, we would expect to find a body of codified accounting laws prescribing in detail how each type of transaction or event should be treated in the accounts. In this type of system there was therefore much less need or scope for the use of professional judgement in preparing accounts or developing accounting practices.

As Nobes and Parker (2010) explain, the common law system was developed in England after the Norman Conquest of 1066, whereas the Roman law system was developed in continental European countries and spread to the former colonies of Belgium, France, Germany, Italy, Portugal and Spain. Countries where the development of legal systems and practices were heavily influenced by England tend to have common law systems. These countries include England and Wales, Ireland, India, the USA, Canada, Australia and New Zealand.[26]

Therefore, in the EU, we would expect England, Wales, Ireland and (partially) Scotland historically to have had relatively few codified accounting laws, with the development of accounting practices being left to the professional judgement of accountants. In the remainder of the EU we would expect accounting practice to have historically been developed through detailed codified accounting laws (or legally recognized regulations) with relatively little input from professional accountants. The adoption of IFRSs – which are often considered to be principles based – would have represented a significant change in practice for countries considered to have Roman law systems relative to countries that were classified as having common law systems.

Business ownership and financing system

A second key institutional factor which researchers have demonstrated has historically had an impact on the shape of a nation's accounting practices is the business ownership and financing system. Similarly to legal systems, this factor can be broadly divided into two distinct types – this time referred to as 'outsider' and 'insider' systems.

In 'outsider' systems, external shareholders (that is, those who are not involved in the management of the company) are a significant source of finance for much business

---

[26] Nobes and Parker (2004) point out that a very small number of countries (such as Scotland, South Africa and Israel) have developed legal systems which incorporate aspects of both common and Roman law.

activity. As these external shareholders will not be involved in the detailed management of the company, and will therefore not have access to the company's detailed management accounting information, they will need to be provided with separate financial accounting information to help them make their investment decisions. They may invest in the shares of a number of companies, and need a basis to evaluate the performance of any company – for example, by comparing it to the performance of other companies. To help ensure an effective and efficient allocation of finance to different companies in this type of outsider-financed system, it is important for external investors (and potential investors) to be provided with financial accounting information that reflects the underlying economic performance of a business in a fair, balanced and unbiased manner. Thus, given the significance of outsider finance, financial accounting will have historically developed with a primary aim of providing this fair, balanced and unbiased information to external shareholders – a process which requires rather extensive use of professional judgement (Nobes, 1998), for example, to handle regular developments or innovations in business practices which cannot easily be foreseen when writing accounting codes or legislation.

Conversely, in 'insider' systems of finance, provision of finance by external shareholders is much less significant. Instead, there has either been a dominance of family-owned businesses, and/or the dominant providers of long-term finance have historically been either banks or governments (Zysman, 1983). With family-owned businesses, the owners will tend to have access to the detailed internal management accounting information of the business, so there is no obvious need for financial accounts to provide information to aid investment decision-making by shareholders. In some countries (such as Germany) where banks have historically been the dominant source of long-term finance for large companies (rather than external shareholders), banks and companies have tended to develop long-term supportive relationships. These involve banks having a representative on the supervisory board of companies to whom they are major lenders, and these representatives are provided with the detailed management accounting information available to all members of the supervisory board. In the case of family-owned businesses, given that the predominant providers of finance are effectively 'insiders' to the business and have access to detailed management information, there will have been little pressure for financial accounting to have developed to provide information to aid external investment decisions in these countries (Nobes, 1998). Nobes and Parker (2010) explain that in systems where governments provide a significant amount of long-term business finance, government representatives will often become directors of the state-funded companies, and will thus have access to the inside management information. Thus, a characteristic shared by all countries in which insider systems of finance predominate is that the primary role of accounting has historically not been to provide fair, balanced and unbiased information to help outside investors make efficient and effective investment decisions. Thus, financial accounting in these countries has developed to fulfil a different role than in outsider-financed countries. One such role, which we will explore in the next section, is the provision of information to calculate taxation liabilities.

Countries which have historically been dominated by insider systems of finance have tended also to be countries with Roman law systems, while outsider-financed countries usually have common law systems (La Porta *et al.*, 1997). Thus, most continental European countries (with the exception of the Netherlands, which has a Roman law system but a large amount of outsider finance) have historically relied on insider forms of finance, with the result that financial accounting in these nations did not develop to serve the needs of investment decisions in capital markets. Conversely, the United Kingdom and Ireland (and the USA, Australia and New Zealand among other non-European states) have relied to a much greater extent on outsider forms of finance, with a primary role of accounting historically being to service the information needs of capital markets with fair, balanced and unbiased information.[27]

As an example of empirical research linking financing systems with differences in accounting practices, Pratt and Behr (1987) compared the standard-setting processes adopted in the United States and Switzerland. Differences in the standards and processes adopted were explained by differences in 'size, complexity, and diversity of capital transactions, the wide distribution of ownership, and the opportunistic nature of the capital market participants'.

Chand and White (2007) consider the ownership and financing systems that are common in Fiji and argue that the recent adoption of IFRSs in Fiji has created a level of inefficiency not previously experienced. That is, they argue that there is an inappropriate match between IFRSs and the financing systems inherent in Fiji.

Before leaving our discussion of the impact of different financing systems on the shape of accounting practices, we should emphasize that with the increasing scale of globalized businesses, multinational corporations based in any country are increasingly relying on financing from more than one nation. The funding needs of many of these companies in countries which have traditionally relied upon insider forms of finance have grown beyond the funding capacity of these insider sources of finance, with several companies now increasingly also relying upon outsider finance – from shareholders in both their home country and in other nations. Thus, the information requirements associated with outsider-financed systems are to a certain extent now becoming applicable to many large companies in continental European countries (Nobes and Parker, 2010).

Taxation systems

As we saw in the previous subsection, in countries with predominantly outsider systems of finance, financial accounting practices historically developed to provide a supposedly fair, balanced and unbiased representation of the underlying economic performance of a business to help improve the effectiveness of investment allocation decisions by external shareholders. Such a system requires that accounting reflects some sort of economic reality with, for example, each business selecting depreciation methods that most closely reflect the manner in which it uses its fixed assets.

Conversely, in countries with largely insider systems of finance this pressure for financial reports to have developed to reflect fairly some form of underlying economic reality is not present. Rather, financial reports have developed for different purposes, and one important purpose is the calculation of tax (Nobes and Parker, 2010). In most continental European countries that have traditionally relied heavily on insider forms of finance, for a company to claim an allowance for tax this allowance had to be included in its financial reports. For example, if a company wished to reduce its tax liability by taking

---

[27] As we will see in the final chapter of this book, many critical accounting theorists strongly disagree that accounting information is fair, balanced or unbiased.

advantage of the maximum permitted taxable depreciation allowances, it had to include these tax depreciation allowances in its financial reports. These tax depreciation allowances will be determined by taxation law, and will not necessarily bear any relationship to the amount or proportion of the fixed assets that have actually been used in any particular year. The financial accounting results will therefore be expected to be substantially affected and determined by the provisions of taxation law in many continental European countries that have historically relied upon insider systems of finance.

In outsider-financed countries, the tax accounts have historically been separate from the financial accounts. Thus, if a company wished to claim the maximum tax depreciation allowances permitted by taxation law in these countries, this would not affect the calculation of its reported profits in its financial reports. These financial accounts could therefore include a fair depreciation charge reflecting the utilization of assets without affecting the company's ability to claim the maximum tax depreciation allowances in its tax accounts, and the provisions of taxation law have not therefore exerted much influence on the financial accounts.

Given that (with the notable European exception of the Netherlands) there has tended to be a high correlation between insider-financed systems and Roman law countries (La Porta *et al.*, 1997), this has resulted in the detailed provisions of taxation law effectively becoming a large part of the detailed accounting regulations in many continental European countries which have codified Roman law systems. Again, the adoption of IFRSs in such countries represented a significant change to their traditional accounting practices for those companies required to adopt IFRSs (which in some countries does not include non-listed companies).

A further institutional factor that tended to differentiate between, and also reinforce the distinction between, Roman law insider-financed countries and common law outsider-financed systems is the strength of the accounting profession.

Strength of the accounting profession

Nobes and Parker (2010) explain that the strength of the accounting profession in any country has historically both been determined by, and helped to reinforce, the influence on financial accounting systems of the institutional factors we have discussed above. In a common law country, which has a predominantly outsider system of long-term finance and where tax law has historically had little influence on financial accounting, there will have been relatively few statutory laws determining the contents of financial reports. The primary purpose of these financial reports will have been to provide a fair, balanced and unbiased representation of the underlying economic performance of the business, and this will have required the exercise of professional judgement to cope with each different situation within and between businesses. Thus, in these countries there will have historically been demand for a large number of accountants who are able to apply professional judgement to determine the most suitable way of reflecting unique sets of transactions and events in financial accounting reports of many companies. This need for accountants who are able to, and have scope to, exercise professional judgement has led to the development of large and strong accounting professions in countries such as the United Kingdom, Ireland, the United States, Canada, Australia and New Zealand. As we saw in Chapter 2, strong accounting professions have then been effective in lobbying governments to ensure that accounting regulatory systems give scope for the exercise of professional judgement, thus possibly reinforcing the strength and influence of the accounting profession.

Conversely, in Roman law countries which have had largely insider systems of finance and where compliance with the details of tax laws exerts a substantial influence on the shape of financial accounts, there will have historically been little need or scope for the use of professional judgement when drawing up financial accounting statements. There has therefore been much less impetus for the development of accounting professions than in outsider-financed common law systems. The accounting professions in many continental European countries have therefore historically been smaller and weaker (in terms of influence) than their counterparts in the United Kingdom, Ireland, Australia or the United States. Nobes and Parker (2004) argue that these weaker accounting professions have had an impact in reinforcing accounting practices which require little exercise of professional judgement in these countries, because the effective implementation of flexible, judgemental accounting practices requires a reasonably large accounting profession which is comfortable with (and has sufficient experience of) applying professional judgements to complex accounting issues.

Accidents of history

As indicated earlier in this section, accounting systems tend to be regarded as following either an Anglo-American or a continental European model. The cultural and institutional differences we have discussed so far in this chapter support this view, with countries following the Anglo-American model tending historically to have common law systems, outsider financing, little influence of taxation law on financial accounting and a strong accounting profession accustomed to exercising a considerable amount of professional judgement – with the opposite applying in countries following the continental European model. If we accept that these influences have been significant in shaping a nation's accounting practices, we should expect accounting practices in countries with Anglo-American systems to have historically been broadly similar. However, this is not consistent with the evidence presented in the first section of this chapter when, for example, we saw that both the reported profits and the net assets of the multinational pharmaceutical company AstraZeneca were significantly different when calculated in accordance with UK accounting rules (and then with IFRS rules that have been largely derived from Anglo-American type accounting rules) than when calculated in accordance with US rules. If the cultural and institutional influences we have examined so far in this chapter, and which are broadly similar between the United Kingdom and the United States, are significant in shaping accounting practices, then there must be an important additional influencing factor that varies between the United Kingdom and the United States.

Nobes and Parker (2004) point to the importance of the additional factor of 'accidents of history', whose influence will be restricted to the accounting systems of the individual countries affected by the accidents. For example, following the Wall Street Crash of 1929, the United States established Securities Exchange legislation aimed at investor protection, while there was no such development at that time in the United Kingdom. This legislation included certain accounting requirements, which have been delegated to private sector accounting standard-setting bodies, and which have produced a detailed set of US accounting rules (as we would expect to see in a Roman law country). In contrast, following a series of high-profile accounting failures in the United Kingdom in the late 1980s, the United Kingdom established a more principles-based system of accounting regulation since the early 1990s. As Unerman and O'Dwyer (2004) highlight, in the aftermath of accounting failures at Enron in 2001, it was claimed by many in the United Kingdom that these different regulatory systems would have prevented Enron using in the United Kingdom the creative accounting techniques it followed in the United States. Going back to the case of AstraZeneca, studying the reconciliation provided in the financial reports between the results calculated using IFRS and US accounting rules, it is apparent that a substantial difference between the two sets of accounting regulations (in the case of this company) arises from differences between the US and the IFRS accounting treatment of mergers and acquisitions (including the calculation of goodwill). Different pressures in the countries that have adopted IFRSs (possibly including different lobbying efforts by interested parties in each country) resulted in IFRS and US accounting rules for mergers and acquisitions being somewhat different, although these differences are likely to reduce substantially in the future given the ongoing convergence efforts of the IASB and FASB.

In summarizing this chapter so far, we can see that a number of reasons, including culture, religion (which is a subset of culture) and institutional factors (which we could also imagine would be influenced by culture), have been advanced to explain the accounting systems in place in each country. This discussion has by no means been exhaustive in identifying the many factors proposed to explain why historically there were international differences in accounting systems, but nevertheless the referenced research indicates that one general approach to accounting, such as that used in the United Kingdom, Ireland, the Netherlands, the United States, Australia, New Zealand or Canada, may suit a particular environment, but not others. Therefore, it is probably somewhat naive to claim that there is any one 'best' system of accounting. With this view in mind we can reflect on the following claim: Former Chairman of the US Financial Accounting Standards Board, Dennis Beresford, was quoted as claiming that the US accounting and reporting system was regarded by many as 'the most comprehensive and sophisticated system in the world' (as quoted in Wyatt and Yospe, 1993). Perhaps in some countries (perhaps the majority), the US system might be considered as sophisticated – but in others it might be considered as quite irrelevant on cultural, religious or institutional grounds.

Despite various factors that seem to provide a logical rationale for international differences in accounting practices, there have been extensive efforts over several decades to reduce the differences between accounting systems in different countries. As we have seen, a great deal of this effort culminated in many diverse countries all adopting IFRSs. Having read the material already provided in this chapter we are now better placed to understand why accounting systems in different countries were dissimilar prior to recent efforts to globally standardize financial accounting. We are also now better placed to be able to consider whether we believe that the global standardization of accounting is appropriate. What do you the reader think? Is it really appropriate that diverse countries with different cultural attributes, different financing systems, religions, different taxation systems, different histories and so forth all adopt the same accounting standards? The next section of this chapter provides some concluding comments on the obstacles to ongoing standardization of accounting.

4.9 Concluding comments about obstacles to the ongoing standardization of financial accounting

As we have discussed, one key obstacle to the establishment and maintenance of international standardization of accounting is considered to be international cultural and institutional differences which we saw caused financial accounting to vary in the first place. As argued earlier, if these causal factors continue to vary between countries, then it is difficult to see how a single set of accounting rules – such as those published by the IASB – will be appropriate or suitable for all countries. That is, as accounting traditionally varied between different countries for reasons that could be theoretically explained (such as cultural, religious or institutional reasons), a key impediment to the continued standardization of accounting is the fact that these good reasons for accounting differences arguably continue to exist. While many countries (or, in the case of the EU, groups of countries) have either adopted IFRSs, or plan to adopt IFRSs in the near term, there is nothing that strictly stops them from abandoning IFRSs should it become apparent that they are not very relevant to their countries' financial accounting information needs. Of course it would be costly and difficult for a country to abandon IFRSs – but it is possible.

As an example of this obstacle to maintaining standardization efforts, Perera (1989, p. 52) considers the success of transferring accounting skills from Anglo-American countries to developing countries. He notes:

> The skill[s] so transferred from Anglo-American countries may not work because they are culturally irrelevant or dysfunctional in the receiving countries' context.

Perera (1989) also argues that international accounting standards themselves are strongly influenced by Anglo-American accounting models and, as such, these international standards tend to reflect the circumstances and patterns of thinking in a particular group of countries. He argues that these standards are likely to encounter problems of relevance in countries where different environments from those found in Anglo-American countries exist. Thus, for example, if the majority of German companies continue to rely on 'insider' forms of finance, and Germany continues to use a Roman law system, its previously used codified accounting regulations would probably be more appropriate for most German companies than the imposition of a form of the Anglo-American accounting system.[28] Nobes and Parker (2010) indicate that in such circumstances it may be considered more appropriate to have a dual system, where some companies in a country (perhaps the bulk of companies that are not listed and are not required to prepare consolidated accounts) are required to prepare financial reports in accordance with their historically developed domestic system, and listed companies are required to prepare an additional set of financial

---

[28] In a similar way, the imposition of a detailed codified accounting system would not be appropriate for Australia, the United Kingdom, the United States or Ireland, where the 'outsider' system of finance requires financial accounts to provide fair and balanced information reflecting some form of underlying economic reality.

reports (probably only the consolidated or group accounts) in accordance with Anglo-American-style international accounting rules.[29]

A further obstacle to harmonization has been explained by Nobes and Parker (2004) as the lack of a developed accounting profession in some countries. Thus, as discussed earlier, in countries where strong accounting professions have not developed there are likely to be initial problems implementing international accounting regulations based on the Anglo-American professional judgement model (such as IFRSs). Furthermore, some countries might have nationalistic difficulties in being seen to implement a system of international accounting standards which are regarded as being closely aligned to the Anglo-American systems.

A final potential and significant obstacle to the ongoing standardization of accounting is that, as we saw in Chapters 2 and 3, accounting regulations can and do have economic consequences (Nobes and Parker, 2010). Across time, governments of individual countries may regret giving control over a process that has real economic consequences – accounting standard-setting – to an international body (the IASB) over which they have little influence. We saw how this can impact on the process of international standardization in Chapter 3, when we examined the recent difficulties which have been experienced with the refusal of the EU to endorse fully at the outset the provisions of the revised IAS 39 and its replacement IRFS 9, partly because of the potential negative economic impact these provisions might have on banks in their countries.

Chapter summary

In this chapter we identified and considered historical differences in international accounting practices and we have seen that numerous reasons (generated from different theoretical perspectives) have been advanced to explain why such differences arose (including differences in culture, religions as a subset of culture, legal systems, financing systems, taxation systems, the strength of the accounting profession and accidents of history). Much of the existing research into comparative international accounting questions whether it is appropriate to have one system of accounting that is adopted uniformly throughout the world (which has been stated as a long-term objective of the IASB).

While many researchers question the relevance of 'Western-style' accounting standards across all countries, efforts by a number of international organizations are nevertheless continuing to encourage quite culturally disparate countries to adopt IASs/IFRSs. This implies that the members of some international organizations are either unaware of the literature or, alternatively, choose to reject it as irrelevant. As efforts by a number of countries continue in relation to the domestic implementation of international standards, it is to be expected that this debate will continue.

---

[29] In this regard, although companies in member states of the EU are required to follow accounting standards released by the IASB for the purposes of their consolidated financial reports, this requirement is restricted to companies listed on a stock exchange.

Questions

4.1 In the context of financial accounting, what is harmonization and/or standardization?

4.2 Global standardization of accounting requires the United States to adopt IFRSs. Do you think it is likely that the US will embrace IFRSs in the near term, and what do you think are some of the factors that might discourage the US from adopting IFRSs?

4.3 Just because different countries adopt IFRSs does this necessarily mean that the accounting procedures and practices they adopt will be consistent and comparable internationally?

4.4 Any efforts towards standardizing accounting practices on an international basis implies a belief that a 'one-size-fits-all' approach is appropriate. Is this naive?

4.5 While it is often argued that within particular countries there should be some association between various value systems and accounting systems, it is also argued (for example, by Baydoun and Willett, 1995) that over time many events would typically have occurred that confound this expected relationship. What type of events might confound the expected relationship?

4.6 Baydoun and Willett (1995, p. 72) identify a number of problems in testing the Hofstede–Gray theory. They emphasize that many accounting systems are imported from other countries with possibly different cultures. As they state: 'Due to the interference in what would otherwise have been the natural evolution of financial information requirements, there are no uncontaminated examples of modern accounting practices in developing countries. Consequently great care has to be taken in using data from developing countries to draw inferences about relevance on the basis of the Hofstede–Gray framework.' Explain the point of view being provided by Baydoun and Willett. Do you believe that they are correct?

4.7 In the early 1990s, US Financial Accounting Standards Board's chairperson Dennis Beresford claimed that the US accounting and reporting system was regarded by many as 'the most comprehensive and sophisticated system in the world'. Evaluate this statement. How do you think its validity might have changed in the aftermath of accounting failures at Lehman Brothers in 2008 and Enron, WorldCom and Andersen in 2001/2? Do you think that the US system would be regarded as sophisticated in all cultural contexts?

4.8 Prior to recent international actions to adopt IFRSs, would you expect that large international companies domiciled in a particular country would have adopted different accounting policies from companies that only operated within the confines of that country? Explain your answer.

4.9 Evaluate how reasonable it is to assume that the inflow of foreign investment into EU member states would have been restricted if the EU had not made compliance with IASs/IFRSs compulsory for all EU listed companies from 2005.

4.10 Explain barriers to ongoing standardization of financial accounting across all EU member states. Given these barriers, do you think that the EU has been naive in embracing the standardization process for all member states?

4.11 What are some perceived benefits that flow from the decision that a country will adopt IFRSs?

4.12 It is often argued that the accounting standards of the FASB are rule-based, whereas the accounting standards issued by the IASB are principles-based. Rules-based standards by their nature can be quite complex, particularly if they seek to cover as many situations as possible. Do you think it would be easier to circumvent the requirements of rules-based, or principles-based, accounting standards?

4.13 Is it appropriate for accounting standard-setting bodies to consider culture and religion when devising accounting regulations, particularly given that the output of financial reporting is expected to be objective and unbiased? Explain your view.

4.14 What are some possible reasons for historical differences in accounting rules operating within the Netherlands, the United States and the United Kingdom?

4.15 Does the standardization of accounting standards on a global basis necessarily equate with a standardization in accounting practice?

4.16 Critically evaluate the plausibility of using Hofstede's national cultural models to predict the nature of financial accounting practices in any particular country.

4.17 The IASC (1998, p. 50) stated that 'many developing and newly industrialised countries are using International Accounting Standards as their national requirements, or as the basis for their national requirements. These countries have a growing need for relevant and reliable financial information to meet the requirements both of domestic users and of international providers of the capital that they need.' Do you think that IASs/IFRSs will provide 'relevant and reliable information' that meets the needs of all financial statement users in all countries?

4.18 In considering the relevance of IFRSs to developing countries, Chand and White (2007, p. 606) state:

> While the forces of globalisation and convergence are moving accounting practices towards a unified, or at least harmonised regulatory framework for financial reporting, this is unlikely to best serve the diverse interests of the disparate user groups of financial reports.

Required:
Explain the reasons behind Chand and White's claim.

4.19 Ball (2006, p. 17) makes the following comment:

> In sum, even a cursory review of the political and economic diversity among IFRS-adopting nations, and of their past and present financial reporting practices, makes the notion that uniform standards alone will produce uniform financial reporting seem naive.

Required:
Explain the basis of Ball's comments.

4.20 Ball (2006, p. 22) provides the following statement:

> In the presence of local political and economic factors that exert substantial influence on local financial reporting practice, and in the absence of an effective

worldwide enforcement mechanism, the very meaning of IFRS adoption and the implications of adoption are far from clear. In the enthusiasm of the current moment, the IFRS 'brand name' currently is riding high, and IFRS adoption is being perceived as a signal of quality. I am not sure how long that perception will last.

Required:
Provide an argument as to whether you are inclined to agree or disagree with Ball's scepticism about the future 'value' associated with embracing IFRS.

4.21 The European Commission made the following statement in a press release issued in 2002:

> European Commission has welcomed the Council's adoption, in a single reading, of the Regulation requiring listed companies, including banks and insurance companies, to prepare their consolidated accounts in accordance with International Accounting Standards (IAS) from 2005 onwards (see IP/01/200 and MEMO/01/40). The Regulation will help eliminate barriers to cross-border trading in securities by ensuring that company accounts throughout the EU are more reliable and transparent and that they can be more easily compared. This will in turn increase market efficiency and reduce the cost of raising capital for companies, ultimately improving competitiveness and helping boost growth.

Required:
You are required to evaluate the above statement. In particular you should consider whether the adoption of IFRSs in various different countries, with different overview and enforcement mechanisms necessarily leads to the generation of financial information that is more 'reliable' and 'comparable'.

References

Ball, R. (2006) 'International Financial Reporting Standards (IFRS): Pros and cons for investors', *Accounting and Business Research* (International Accounting Policy Forum), 5–27.

Baskerville, R.F. (2003) 'Hofstede never studied culture', *Accounting, Organizations and Society*, **28** (1), 1–14.

Baydoun, N. & Willett, R. (1995) 'Cultural relevance of Western accounting systems to developing countries', *ABACUS*, **31** (1), 67–92.

Brown, P. & Tarca, A. (2005) 'A commentary on issues relating to the enforcement of International Financial Reporting Standards in the EU', *European Accounting Review*, **14** (1), 181–212.

Chand, P. & White, M. (2007) 'A critique of the influence of globalization and convergence of accounting standards in Fiji', *Critical Perspectives on Accounting*, **18** (5), 605–22.

Doupnik, T.S. & Salter, S.B. (1995) 'External environment, culture, and accounting practice: A preliminary test of a general model of international accounting development', *The International Journal of Accounting*, **30** (3), 189–207.

Fechner, H.H.E. & Kilgore, A. (1994) 'The influence of cultural factors on accounting practice', *The International Journal of Accounting*, **29**, 265–77.

G-20 (2010) *Annex II (Financial Sector Reporm) to the G-20 Toronto Summit Declaration*, Toronto: G-20.

Gray, S.J. (1988) 'Towards a theory of cultural influence on the development of accounting systems internationally', *ABACUS*, **24** (1), 1–15.

Haller, A. & Eierle, B. (2004) 'The adaptation of German accounting rules to IFRS: A legislative balancing act', *Accounting in Europe*, **1**, 27–50.

Hamid, S., Craig, R. & Clarke, F. (1993) 'Religion: A confounding cultural element in the international harmonization of accounting?', *ABACUS*, **29** (2), 131–48.

Hofstede, G. (1980) *Culture's Consequences: International Differences in Work-related Values*, Beverly Hills, CA: Sage.

Hofstede, G. (1983) 'Dimensions of national cultures in fifty countries and three regions', in: Derogowski, J.B., Dziuraweic, S. & Annis, R. (eds.), *Expiscations in Cross-Cultural Psychology*, Lisse: Swets and Zeitlinger.

Hofstede, G. (1984) 'Cultural dimensions in management and planning', *Asia Pacific Journal of Management* (January).

Hope, O.-K. (2003) 'Disclosure practices, enforcement of accounting standards, and analysts' forecast accuracy: An international study', *Journal of Accounting Research*, **41** (2), 235–72.

Hopwood, A.G. (2000) 'Understanding financial accounting practice', *Accounting, Organizations and Society*, **25** (8), 763–66.

IASC (1998) *Shaping IASC for the Future*, London: International Accounting Standards Committee.

IASCF (2010) *IASC Foundation Constitution*, London: IASC Foundation.

Irvine, H. (2008) 'The global institutionalization of financial reporting: The case of the United Arab Emirates', *Accounting Forum*, **32**, 125–42.

Kvaal, E. & Nobes, C. (2010) 'International differences in IFRS policy choice: A research note', *Accounting and Business Research*, **40** (2), 173–87.

La Porta, R., Lopez-de-Silanes, F., Shleifer, A. & Vishny, R.W. (1997) 'Legal determinants of external finance', *Journal of Finance*, **52** (3), 1131–50.

March, J.G. (2004) 'Parochialism in the evolution of a research community: The case of organization studies', *Management and Organization Review*, **1** (1), 5–22.

McSweeney, B. (2002a) 'The essentials of scholarship: A reply to Geert Hofstede', *Human Relations*, **55** (11), 1363–72.

McSweeney, B. (2002b) 'Hofstede's model of national cultural differences and their consequences: A triumph of faith – a failure of analysis', *Human Relations*, **55** (1), 89–118.

McSweeney, B. (2009a) 'Dynamic diversity: Variety and variation within countries', *Organization Studies*, **30** (9), 933–57.

McSweeney, B. (2009b) 'Incoherent culture', *European Journal of Cross-Cultural Competence and Management*, **1** (1), 22–27.

Miles, M.B. & Michael, H.A. (1984) *Qualitative Data Analysis*, Beverly Hills, CA: Sage.

Mueller, G.G. (1967) *International Accounting*, New York: Macmillan.

Mueller, G.G. (1968) 'Accounting principles generally accepted in the United States versus those generally accepted elsewhere', *The International Journal of Accounting Education and Research*, **3** (2), 91–103.

Ngangan, K., Saudagaran, S.M. & Clarke, F.L. (2005) 'Cultural influences on indigenous users' perceptions of the importance of disclosure items: Empirical evidence from Papua New Guinea', *Advances in International Accounting*, **18**, 27–51.

Nickerson, R.S. (1998) 'Confirmation bias: A ubiquitous phenomenon in many guises', *Review of General Psychology*, **2**, 175–220.

Nobes, C. (1984) *International Classification of Financial Reporting*, London: Croom Helm.

Nobes, C. (1998) 'Towards a general model of the reasons for international differences in financial reporting', *ABACUS*, **34** (2), 162–87.

Nobes, C. (2006) 'The survival of international differences under IFRS: Towards research agenda', *Accounting and Business Research*, **36** (3), 233–45.

Nobes, C. & Parker, R. (2004) *Comparative International Accounting*, Harlow: Pearson Education Limited.

Nobes, C. & Parker, R. (2010) *Comparative International Accounting*, Harlow: Pearson Education Limited.

Perera, H. (1989) 'Towards a framework to analyze the impact of culture on accounting', *The International Journal of Accounting*, **24** (1), 42–56.

Pfeffer, J. (1993) 'Barriers to the advance of organizational science: Paradigm development as a dependent variable', *Academy of Management Review*, **18** (4), 599–620.

Pratt, J. & Behr, G. (1987) 'Environmental factors, transaction costs, and external reporting: A cross national comparison', *The International Journal of Accounting Education and Research*, **22** (2), 1–24.

Purvis, S.E.C., Gernon, H. & Diamond, M.A. (1991) 'The IASC and its comparability project', *Accounting Horizons*, **5** (2), 25–44.

SEC (2007) *Acceptance from Foreign Private Issuers of Financial Statements Prepared in Accordance with International Financial Reporting Standards without Reconciliation to U.S. GAAP, RIN 3235-AJ90, SEC, Washington*, Washington: Securities and Exchange Commission.

Street, D.L. & Bryant, S.M. (2000) 'Disclosure level and compliance with IASs: A comparison of companies with and without U.S. listings and filings', *The International Journal of Accounting*, **35** (3), 305–29.

Street, D.L. & Gray, S.J. (2001) *Observance of International Accounting Statidards: Factors Explaining Non-compliance*, London: Association of Chartered Certified Accountants.

Takatera, S. & Yamamoto, M. (1987) 'The cultural significance of accounting in Japan', *Seminar on Accounting and Culture*, European Institute for Advanced Studies in Management, Brussels.

Tung, R.L. (2007) 'The cross-cultural research imperative: The need to balance cross-national and intra-national diversity', *Journal of International Business Studies*, **39** (1), 41–46.

Unerman, J. & O'Dwyer, B. (2004) 'Basking in Enron's reflexive goriness: Mixed messages from the UK profession's reaction', in Asia Pacific Interdisciplinary Research on Accounting Conference, Singapore.

Veron, N. (2007) *The Global Accounting Experiment*, Brussels: Bruegel Publishers.

Violet, W.J. (1983) 'The development of international accounting standards: An anthropological perspective',

The International Journal of Accounting Education and Research, **18** (2), 1–12.

Whitley, R. (2000) *The Intellectual and Social Organization of the Sciences*, 2nd edn, Oxford: Oxford University Press.

Wyatt, A.R. & Yospe, J.F. (1993) 'Wake-up call to American business: International accounting standards are on the way', *Journal of Accountancy* (July), 80–85.

Zarzeski, M.T. (1996) 'Spontaneous harmonization effects of culture and market forces on accounting disclosure practices', *Accounting Horizons*, **10** (1), 18–37.

Zysman, J. (1983) *Government, Markets and Growth: Financial Systems and the Politics of Change*, Ithaca, NY: Cornell University Press.

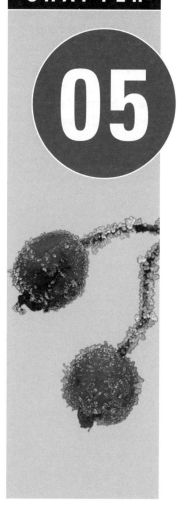

05

Normative Theories of Accounting 1: The Case of Accounting for Changing Prices and Asset Values

❖ LEARNING OBJECTIVES

Upon completing this chapter readers should:

❖ be aware of some particular limitations of historical cost accounting in terms of its ability to cope with various issues associated with changing prices and changing market conditions;

❖ be aware of a number of alternative methods of accounting that have been developed to address problems associated with changing prices

and market conditions in arriving at asset values, including fair value accounting;

❖ be able to identify some of the strengths and weaknesses of the various alternative accounting methods;

❖ understand that the calculation of income under a particular method of accounting will depend on the perspective of capital maintenance that has been adopted.

Opening issues

Various asset valuation approaches are often adopted in the financial statements of large corporations. Non-current assets acquired (or perhaps revalued) in different years will simply be added together to give a total euro value, even though the various costs or valuations might provide little reflection of the current values of the respective assets. For example, pursuant to IAS 16 'Property, Plant and Equipment' it is permissible for some classes of property, plant and equipment to be measured at cost, less a provision for depreciation, while other classes of property, plant and equipment may be measured at their current fair value (supposedly reflective of current market conditions). The different measurements are then simply added together to give a total value of property, plant and equipment – with the total neither representing cost nor fair value.

Issues to consider:

- What are some of the criticisms that can be made in relation to the practice of accounting wherein we add together, without adjustment, assets that have been acquired or valued in different years, when both the purchasing power of the euro and the market conditions that together give rise to valuations were conceivably quite different?

- What are some of the alternative methods of accounting (alternatives to historical cost accounting) that have been advanced to cope with the issue of changing prices and changing market conditions, and what acceptance have these alternatives received from the accounting profession?

- What are the strengths and weaknesses of the alternatives to historical cost?

5.1 Introduction

In Chapter 3 we considered various theoretical explanations about why regulation might be put in place. Perspectives derived from *public interest theory*, *capture theory* and the *economic interest theory of regulation* did not attempt to explain what form of regulation was most optimal or efficient. Rather, by adopting certain theoretical assumptions about individual behaviour and motivations, these theories attempted to explain which parties were most likely to try, and perhaps succeed in, affecting the regulatory process.

In this chapter we consider a number of *normative theories* of accounting. Based upon particular judgements about the types of information people *need* (which could be different from what they *want*), the various normative theories provide prescriptions about how the process of financial accounting *should* be undertaken.[1]

---

[1] Positive theories, by contrast, attempt to explain and predict accounting practice without seeking to prescribe particular actions. Positive accounting theories are the subject of analysis in Chapter 7.

Across time, numerous normative theories of accounting have been developed by a number of well-respected academics. However, these theories have typically failed to be embraced by the accounting profession, or to be mandated within financial accounting regulations. Relying in part on material introduced in Chapter 3, we consider why some proposed methods of accounting are ultimately accepted by the profession and/or accounting standard-setters, while many are dismissed or rejected. We question whether the rejection is related to the *merit* of their arguments (or lack thereof), or due to the *political nature* of the standard-setting process wherein various vested interests and economic implications are considered. In this chapter we specifically consider various prescriptive theories of accounting (normative theories) that were advanced by various people on the basis that historical cost accounting has too many shortcomings, particularly in times of rising prices and changing market conditions. Some of these shortcomings were summarized by the International Accounting Standards Committee (which was subsequently replaced by the International Accounting Standards Board) in IAS 29 'Financial Reporting in Hyperinflationary Economies':

> In a hyperinflationary economy, reporting of operating results and financial position in the local currency without restatement is not useful. Money loses purchasing power at such a rate that comparison of amounts from transactions and other events that have occurred at different times, even within the same accounting period, is misleading. (paragraph 2)

5.2 Limitations of historical cost accounting in times of rising prices

Over time, criticisms of historical cost accounting have been raised by a number of notable scholars, particularly in relation to its inability to provide useful information in times of rising prices and changing market conditions. For example, criticisms were raised by Sweeney, MacNeal, Canning and Paton in the 1920s and 1930s. From the 1950s the levels of criticism increased, with notable academics (such as Chambers, Sterling, Edwards and Bell) prescribing different models of accounting that they considered provided more useful information than was available under conventional historical cost accounting. Such work continued through to the early 1980s, but declined thereafter as levels of inflation throughout the world began to drop. Subsequently the debate changed to focus on the use of current market values – known as *fair values* – (supposedly reflecting current market conditions at the accounting date) for valuing assets, rather than amending historic costs simply to take account of inflation.[2]

Across time, these criticisms appear to have been accepted by accounting regulators – at least on a piecemeal basis. In recent years, for example, various accounting standards have been released that require or permit the application of fair values when measuring assets. These include: financial instruments (pursuant to IAS 39), property, plant and equipment (where the fair value model has been adopted pursuant to IAS 16 – this accounting standard

---

[2] For example, there is a great deal of debate about whether stock (inventory) measurement rules (which require inventory to be measured at the lower of cost and net realizable value pursuant to IAS 2) provide relevant information in situations where the market (fair) value of the inventory greatly exceeds its cost.

gives financial statement preparers a choice between the cost model and the fair value model in the measurement of property, plant and equipment), some intangible assets (where there is an 'active market' pursuant to IAS 38), investment properties (pursuant to IAS 14), and biological assets (pursuant to IAS 41) that are required to be valued at fair value as opposed to historical cost.

Historical cost accounting assumes that money holds a constant purchasing power. As Elliot (1986, p. 33) states:

> An implicit and troublesome assumption in the historical cost model is that the monetary unit is fixed and constant over time. However, there are three components of the modern economy that make this assumption less valid than it was at the time the model was developed.[3]

> One component is specific price-level changes, occasioned by such things as technological advances and shifts in consumer preferences; the second component is general price-level changes (inflation); and the third component is the fluctuation in exchange rates for currencies. Thus, the book value of a company, as reported in its financial statements, only coincidentally reflects the current value of assets.

Again it is emphasized that under our current accounting standards many assets can or must be measured at historical cost. For example, inventory (or stock) must be measured at cost – or net realizable value if it is lower – and property plant and equipment can be valued at cost where an entity has adopted the 'cost model' for a class of property, plant and equipment pursuant to IAS 16. While there was much criticism of historical cost accounting during the high inflation periods of the 1970s and 1980s, there were also many who supported historical cost accounting. The method of accounting predominantly used today is still based on historical cost accounting, although the conceptual frameworks we discuss in the next chapter, and some recent accounting standards (as noted above), have introduced elements of current value – or fair value – measurements. Hence, the accounting profession and reporting entities have tended to maintain at least partial support for this historical cost approach.[4] The very fact that historical cost accounting has continued to be applied by business entities has been used by a number of academics to support its continued use, which in a sense is a form of *accounting-Darwinism* perspective – the view that those things that are most efficient and effective will survive over time. For example, Mautz (1973) states:

> Accounting is what it is today not so much because of the desire of accountants as because of the influence of businessmen. If those who make management and investment decisions had not found financial reports based on

---

[3] As indicated in Chapter 2, the historical cost method of accounting was documented as early as 1494 by the Franciscan monk Pacioli in his famous work *Summa de Arithmetica, Geometrica, Proportioni et Proportionalita*.

[4] IAS 16 provides reporting entities with an option to adopt either the 'cost model' (measuring property, plant and equipment at historical cost) or the 'fair value model' for measuring classes of property, plant and equipment. The 'fair value model' requires the revaluation of the assets to their fair value (which in itself means that a modified version of historical cost accounting can be used), which is one way to take account of changing values. Basing revised depreciation on the revalued amounts is one limited way of accounting for the effects of changing prices.

historical cost useful over the years, changes in accounting would long since have been made.[5, 6]

It has been argued (for example, Chambers, 1966) that historical cost accounting information suffers from problems of irrelevance in times of rising prices. That is, it is questioned whether it is useful to be informed that something cost a particular amount many years ago when its current value (as perhaps reflected by its replacement cost, or current market value) might be considerably different. It has also been argued that there is a real problem of additivity. At issue is whether it is really logical to add together assets acquired in different periods when those assets were acquired with euros of different purchasing power.[7]

In a number of countries, organizations are permitted to revalue their non-current assets. What often happens, however, is that different assets are revalued in different periods (with the local currency – for example dollars or euros – having different purchasing power in each period), yet the revalued assets might all be added together, along with assets that have continued to be valued at cost, for the purposes of disclosure in the statement of financial position (formerly known as the balance sheet).[8]

There is also an argument that methods of accounting that do not take account of changing prices, such as historical cost accounting, can tend to overstate profits in times of rising prices, and that distribution to shareholders of historical cost profits can actually lead to an erosion of operating capacity. For example, assume that a company commenced operations at the beginning of the year 2012 with €100,000 in inventory comprising 20,000 units at €5.00 each. If at the end of the year all the inventory had been sold, there were assets (cash) of €140,000 and throughout the year there had been no contributions from owners, no borrowings and no distributions to owners, then profit under a historical cost system would be €40,000. If the entire profit of €40,000 was distributed to owners

---

[5] However, because something continues to be used does not mean that there is nothing else that might not be better. This is a common error made by proponents of decision usefulness studies. Such studies attempt to provide either support for, or rejection of, something on the basis that particular respondents or users indicated that it would, or would not, be useful for their particular purposes. Often there are things that might be more 'useful' – but they are unknown by the respondents. As Gray *et al.* (1996, p. 75) state: 'Decision usefulness purports to describe the central characteristics of accounting in general and financial statements in particular. To describe accounting as useful for decisions is no more illuminating than describing a screwdriver as being useful for digging a hole – it is better than nothing (and therefore "useful") but hardly what one might ideally like for such a task.'

[6] Reflective of the lack of agreement in the area, Elliot (1986) adopts a contrary view. Still relying upon metaphors associated with evolution, Elliot (1986, p. 35) states: 'There is growing evidence in the market place … that historical cost-basis information is of ever declining usefulness to the modern business world. The issue for the financial accounting profession is to move the accounting model toward greater relevance or face the fate of the dinosaur and the messenger pigeon.'

[7] Again, under existing accounting standards, assets such as property, plant and equipment can be measured at fair value or at cost. IAS 16 gives reporting entities the choice between applying the fair value model or the cost model to the different classes of property, plant and equipment. Hence, we are currently left with a situation where, even within a category of assets (for example, property, plant and equipment), some assets might be measured at cost while others might be measured at fair value.

[8] In relation to property, plant and equipment, IAS 16 requires that where revaluations to fair value are undertaken, the revaluations must be made with sufficient regularity to ensure that the carrying amount of each asset in the class does not differ materially from its fair value at the reporting date. Nevertheless, there will still be instances where some assets have not been revalued for three to five years but they will still be aggregated with assets that have been recently revalued.

in the form of dividends, then the financial capital would be the same as it was at the beginning of the year. Financial capital would remain intact.[9]

However, if prices had increased throughout the period, then the actual operating capacity of the entity may not have remained intact. Let us assume that the company referred to above wishes to acquire another 20,000 units of inventory after it has paid €40,000 in dividends, but finds that the financial year-end replacement cost has increased to €5.40 per unit. The company will only be able to acquire 18,518 units with the €100,000 it still has available. By distributing its total historical cost profit of €40,000, with no adjustments being made for rising prices, the company's ability to acquire goods and services has fallen from one period to the next. Some advocates of alternative approaches to accounting would prescribe that the profit of the period is more accurately recorded as €140,000, less 20,000 units at €5.40 per unit, which then equals €32,000. That is, if €32,000 is distributed to owners in dividends, the company can still buy the same amount of inventory (20,000 units) as it had at the beginning of the period – its purchasing power remains intact.[10] Despite the problems associated with measuring inventory at historical cost, as illustrated above, organizations are still required to measure their inventory at cost (or net realizable value if it is lower than cost) pursuant to IAS 2.

In relation to the treatment of changing prices we can usefully, and briefly, consider IAS 41 'Agriculture'. IAS 41 provides the measurement rules for biological assets (for example, for grapevines or cattle). The accounting standard requires that changes in the fair value of biological assets from period to period be treated as part of the period's profit or loss. In the development of the accounting standard there were arguments by some researchers (Roberts *et al.*, 1995) that the increases in fair value associated with changing prices should be differentiated from changes in fair value that are due to physical changes (for example, changes in the size or number of the biological assets). The argument was that only the physical changes should be treated as part of profit or loss. Although IAS 41 treats the total change in fair value as part of income it is interesting to note that IAS 41 'encourages' disclosures which differentiate between changes in the fair values of the biological assets which are based upon price changes and those based upon physical changes. As paragraph 51 of IAS 41 states:

> The fair value less costs to sell of a biological asset can change due to both physical changes and price changes in the market. Separate disclosure of physical and price changes is useful in appraising current period performance and future prospects, particularly when there is a production cycle of more than one year. In such cases, an entity is encouraged to disclose, by group or otherwise, the amount of the change in fair value less costs to sell included in profit or loss due

---

[9] While it might be considered that measuring inventory at fair value would provide relevant information, IAS 2 'Inventories' prohibits the revaluation of inventory. Specifically, IAS 2 requires inventory to be measured at the lower of cost and net realizable value.

[10] In some countries, such as the United States, an inventory cost flow assumption based on the last-in-first-out (LIFO) method can be adopted (this cost flow assumption is not allowed under IAS 2). The effect of employing LIFO is that cost of goods sold will be determined on the basis of the latest cost, which in times of rising prices will be higher, thereby leading to a reduction in reported profits. This does provide some level of protection (although certainly not complete) against the possibility of eroding the real operating capacity of the organization.

to physical changes and due to price changes. This information is generally less useful when the production cycle is less than one year (for example, when raising chickens or growing cereal crops).

In relation to the above disclosure guidance it is interesting to consider why the regulators considered that financial statement users would benefit from separate disclosure of price changes and physical changes in relation to agricultural assets when similar suggestions are not provided within other accounting standards relating to other categories of assets. This is somewhat inconsistent.

Returning to the use of historical cost in general, it has also been argued that historical cost accounting distorts the current year's operating results by including in the current year's income holding gains that actually accrued in previous periods.[11] For example, some assets may have been acquired at a very low cost in a previous period (and perhaps in anticipation of future price increases pertaining to the assets), yet under historical cost accounting the gains attributable to such actions will only be recognized in the subsequent periods when the assets are ultimately sold. As an illustration, let us assume that a reporting entity acquired some land in 2004 for €1,000,000. Its fair value increased to €1,300,000 in 2008 and then €1,700,000 in 2011. A decision is made to sell the land in 2012 for its new fair value of €1,900,000. If the land had been measured at cost then the entire profit of €900,000 would be shown in the 2012 financial year even though the increase in fair value accrued throughout the previous eight years. Arguably placing all the gain in the last year's profits distorts the results of that financial period as well as the results of preceding periods. Another potential problem of historical cost accounting is it can lead to a distortion of 'return-on-asset' measures. For example, consider an organization that acquired some machinery for €1 million and returned a profit of €100,000. Such an organization would have a return on assets of 10 per cent. If another organization later acquired the same type of asset for €2 million (due to rising prices) and generated a profit of €150,000, then on the basis of return on assets the second organization would appear less efficient, pursuant to historical cost accounting.

There is a generally accepted view that dividends should only be paid from profits (and this is enshrined within the corporations laws of many countries). However, one central issue relates to how we measure profits. There are various definitions of profits. One famous definition was provided by Hicks (1946), that is that profits (or 'income' as he referred to it) is the maximum amount that can be consumed during a period while still expecting to be as well off at the end of the period as at the beginning of the period. Any consideration of 'well-offness' relies upon a notion of capital maintenance – but which one? Different notions will provide different perspectives of profit.

There are a number of perspectives of capital maintenance. One version of capital maintenance is based on maintaining financial capital intact, and this is the position taken in historical cost accounting. Under historical cost accounting, dividends should normally only be paid to the extent that the payment will not erode financial capital, as illustrated in the earlier example of a company needing to replace 20,000 units of inventory where €40,000 is distributed to owners in the form of dividends and no adjustment is made to take account of changes in prices and the related impact on the purchasing power of the entity.

---

[11] Holding gains are those that arise while an asset is in the possession of the reporting entity.

Another perspective of capital maintenance is one that aims at maintaining purchasing power intact.[12] Under this perspective, historical cost accounts are adjusted for changes in the purchasing power of the euro (typically by use of the price index) which, in times of rising prices, will lead to a reduction in income relative to the income calculated under historical cost accounting. As an example, under general price level adjustment accounting (which we will consider more fully later in this chapter) the historical cost of an item is adjusted by multiplying it by the chosen price index at the end of the current period, divided by the price index at the time the asset was acquired. For example, if some land, which was sold for €1,200,000, was initially acquired for €1,000,000 when the price index was 100, and the price index at the end of the current period is 118 (reflecting an increase in prices of 18 per cent), then the adjusted cost would be €1,180,000. The adjusted profit would be €20,000 (compared to an historical cost profit of €200,000).[13] What should be realized is that under this approach to accounting where adjustments are made by way of a general price index, the value of €1,180,000 will not necessarily (except due to chance) reflect the current market value of the land. Various assets will be adjusted using the same general price index.

Use of actual current values (as opposed to adjustments to historical cost using price indices) is made under another approach to accounting that seeks to provide a measure of profits which, if distributed, maintains physical operating capital intact. This approach to accounting (which could be referred to as current cost accounting) relies upon the use of current values, which could be based on present values, entry prices (for example, replacement costs) or exit prices.

Reflective of the attention that the impact of inflation was having on financial statements, Accounting Headline 5.1 reproduces an article that appeared in *Accountancy* in January 1974 (a period of high inflation – and a time when debate in this area of accounting was widespread). The impact of high levels of inflation continued into the early 1980s in many western nations and its continued impact on accounting information is reflected in Accounting Headline 5.2, which reproduces a further *Accountancy* article, this time from 1980.

In the discussion that follows we consider a number of different approaches to undertaking financial accounting in times of rising prices. This discussion is by no means exhaustive but does give some insight into some of the various models that have been prescribed by various parties.[14]

---

[12] Gray *et al.* (1996, p. 74) also provide yet another concept of capital maintenance – one that includes environmental capital. They state 'it is quite a simple matter to demonstrate that company "income" contains a significant element of capital distribution – in this case "environmental capital". An essential tenet of accounting is that income must allow for the maintenance of capital. Current organizational behaviour clearly does not maintain environmental capital and so overstates earnings. If diminution of environmental capital is factored into the income figure it seems likely that no company in the western world has actually made any kind of a profit for many years.' We will consider this issue further in Chapter 9.

[13] Hence, if €20,000 is distributed as dividends, the entity would still be in a position to acquire the same land that it had at the beginning of the period (assuming that actual prices increased by the same amount as the particular price index used).

[14] For example, we will not be considering one approach to determining income based on present values which did not have wide support, but would be consistent with Hicks' income definition (and which might be considered as a *true income* approach). A present value approach would determine the discounted present value of the firm's assets and liabilities and use this as the basis for the financial statements. Under such an approach the calculated value of assets will depend upon various expectations, such as expectations about the cash flows the asset would return through its use in production (its value in use) or its current market value (value in exchange). Such an approach relies upon many assumptions and judgements, including the determination of the appropriate discount rate. Under a present value approach to accounting, profit would be determined as the amount that could be withdrawn, yet maintain the present value of the net assets intact from one period to the next.

Accounting Headline 5.1

An insight into some professional initiatives in the area of accounting for changing prices

CPP accounting – an end or a beginning?

There are two methods of inflation accounting, current purchasing power [CPP] accounting and replacement cost accounting [RCA], and the relative merits of the two were elaborated and discussed throughout [a] day-long conference, organised and jointly sponsored by the English Institute [of Chartered Accountants] and the *Financial Times*. After an introduction by the chairman, Sir Ronald Leach CBE FCA (also chairman of the Accounting Standards Steering Committee), in which he outlined the compromise reached between the Government and the Institute on the production of a provisional [accounting] standard for inflation accounting, Chris Westwick presented his case for the use of CPP accounting. Current purchasing power accounting involves substitution of the current pound in the accounts, whereas replacement cost accounting utilises revaluation of the company's assets on the basis of their replacement cost. Mr Westwick felt CPP accounting

would provide more information to the shareholder, being concerned with the maintenance of the shareholders' capital rather than the maintenance of physical assets (as in the RCA method), and therefore would be the more suitable technique to employ. He said that RCA placed too much importance on the business of the company, and not enough on making money for shareholders, also tending to ignore the gain on long-term money.

The second speaker was R. S. Allen, a director of J. A. Scrimgeour and a council member of the society of investment analysts; he likened CPP accounting to Esperanto – conceived in idealism but not practicable; he was, needless to say, putting the other point of view. Mr Allen favoured the RCA method as something within the shareholder's grasp, but also acceptable to management and appropriate, since inflation increases the value of assets.

Source: *Accountancy*, January 1974, p. 6.

Accounting Headline 5.2

The need for accounting for changing prices

SSSP 16 – a standard for all

... as the president of the Institute [of Chartered Accountants in England and Wales], David Richards FCA, made clear at the annual dinner of the Nottingham Society

of Charted Accountants on 14 March ... [that] useful as it may be, 'historic cost accounting has an unfortunate tranquillising side-effect in not a few boardrooms. The

> historic cost figures often look good – on paper – and they tend to induce a boardroom euphoria. It is only when these figures are adjusted for the effects of a diminishing pound that the more realistic picture of past performance of the company begins to emerge.'
>
> Arguably, current cost accounting, and a general awareness of the effects of inflation, are, if anything, more important to the small organisation than to the large. After the best part of a decade of high-level inflation, there is little excuse for the medium to large company being unaware of the problem, or lacking trained accounting staff to highlight it.
>
> Source: *Accountancy*, April 1980, p. 1.

5.3 Current purchasing power accounting

Current purchasing power (CPP) accounting (or as it is also called, general purchasing power accounting, general price level accounting, or constant dollar/euro accounting) can be traced to the early works of such authors as Sweeney (1964, but originally published in 1936) and has since been favoured by a number of other researchers. CPP accounting has also, at various times, been supported by professional accounting bodies throughout the world, but more in the form of supplementary disclosures to accompany financial statements prepared under historical cost accounting principles. CPP accounting was developed on the basis of a view that, in times of rising prices, if an entity were to distribute unadjusted profits based on historical costs the result could be a reduction in the real value of an entity – that is, in real terms the entity could risk distributing part of its capital (as we saw in an earlier example).

In considering the development of accounting for changing prices, the majority of research initially related to restating historical costs to account for changing prices by using historical cost accounts as the basis, but restating the accounts by use of particular price indices. This is the approach we consider in this section of the chapter. The literature then tended to move towards current cost accounting (which we consider later in this chapter), which changed the basis of measurement to current values as opposed to restated historical values. Consistent with this trend, the accounting profession initially tended to favour price-level-adjusted accounts (using indices), but then tended to switch to current cost accounting which required the entity to find the current values of the individual assets held by the reporting entity.[15, 16]

CPP accounting, with its reliance on the use of indices, is generally accepted as being easier and less costly to apply than methods that rely upon current valuations of particular

---

[15] Current values could be based on *entry* or *exit* prices. As we will see, there is much debate as to which 'current' value is most appropriate.

[16] Professional support for the use of replacement costs appeared to heighten around the time of the 1976 release of ASR 190 within the United States.

assets.[17] It was initially considered by some people that it would be too costly and perhaps unnecessary to attempt to find current values for all the individual assets. Rather than considering the price changes of specific goods and services, it was suggested on practical grounds that price indices be used.

Calculating indices

When applying general price level accounting, a price index must be applied. A price index is a weighted average of the current prices of goods and services relative to a weighted average of prices in a prior period, often referred to as a base period. Price indices may be broad or narrow – they may relate to changes in prices of particular assets within a particular industry (a specific price index), or they might be based on a broad cross-section of goods and services that are consumed (a general price index, such as a Consumer Price Index (CPI) or Retail Price Index (RPI)).

But which price indices should be used? Should we use changes in a general price index (for example, as reflected in the UK by the CPI or RPI) or should we use an index that is more closely tied to the acquisition of production-related resources? There is no clear answer. From the shareholders' perspective the CPI or RPI may more accurately reflect their buying pattern – but prices will not change by the same amount for shareholders in different locations. Further, not everybody will have the same consumption patterns as is assumed when constructing a particular index. The choice of an index can be very subjective. Where CPP accounting has been recommended by particular professional bodies, CPI/RPI-type indices have been suggested.

Because CPP relies upon the use of price indices, it is useful to consider how such indices are constructed. To explain one common way that indices may be constructed we can consider the following example which is consistent with how the UK Consumer Price Index is determined. Let us assume that there are three types of commodities (A, B and C) that are consumed in the following base year quantities and at the following prices:

| Year | Commodity A | | Commodity B | | Commodity C | |
	Price €	Quantity	Price €	Quantity	Price €	Quantity
Base year (2012)	10.00	100	15.00	200	20.00	250
2013	12.00		15.50		21.20	

From the above data we can see that prices have increased. The price index in the base year is frequently given a value of 100 and it is also frequently assumed that consumption

---

[17] However, many questions can be raised with regard to what the restated value actually represents after being multiplied by an index such as the general rate of inflation. This confusion is reflected in studies that question the relevance of information restated for changes in purchasing power.

quantities (or proportions between the different commodities) thereafter remain the same, such that the price index at the end of year 2011 would be calculated as:

$$100 \times \frac{(12.00 \times 100) + (15.50 \times 200) + (21.20 \times 250)}{(10.00 \times 100) + (15.00 \times 200) + (20.00 \times 250)} = 106.67100$$

From the above calculations we can see that the prices within this particular 'bundle' of goods have been calculated as rising on average by 6.67 per cent from the year 2012 to the year 2013. The reciprocal of the price index represents the change in general purchasing power across the period. For example, if the index increased from 100 to 106.67, as in the above example, the purchasing power of the euro would be 93.75 per cent (100/106.67) of what it was previously. That is, the purchasing power of the euro has decreased.

Performing current purchasing power adjustments

When applying CPP, all adjustments are done at the end of the period, with the adjustments being applied to accounts prepared under the historical cost convention. When considering changes in the value of assets as a result of changes in the purchasing power of money (due to inflation) it is necessary to consider monetary assets and non-monetary assets separately. Monetary assets are those assets that remain fixed in terms of their monetary value, for example cash and claims to a specified amount of cash (such as trade debtors and investments that are redeemable for a set amount of cash). These assets will not change their monetary value as a result of inflation. For example, if we are holding €10 in cash and there is rapid inflation, we will still be holding €10 in cash, but the asset's purchasing power will have decreased over time.

Non-monetary assets can be defined as those assets whose monetary equivalents will change over time as a result of inflation, and would include such things as plant and equipment and inventory. For example, inventory may cost €100 at the beginning of the year, but the same inventory could cost, say, €110 at the end of the year due to inflation. Relative to monetary assets, the purchasing power of non-monetary assets is assumed to remain constant even in the presence of inflation.

Most liabilities are fixed in monetary terms (there is an obligation to pay a pre-specified amount of cash at a particular time in the future independent of the change in the purchasing power of the particular currency) and hence liabilities would typically be considered as monetary items (monetary liabilities). Non-monetary liabilities, on the other hand, although less common, would include obligations to transfer goods and services in the future, items which could change in terms of their monetary equivalents.

Net monetary assets would be defined as monetary assets less monetary liabilities. In times of inflation, holders of monetary assets will lose in real terms as a result of holding the monetary assets, as the assets will have less purchasing power at the end of the period relative to what they had at the beginning of the period (and the greater the level of general price increases, the greater the losses). Conversely, holders of monetary liabilities will gain, given that the amount they have to repay at the end of the period will be worth less (in terms of purchasing power) than it was at the beginning of the period.

Let us consider an example to demonstrate how gains and losses might be calculated on monetary items (and under CPP, gains and losses will relate to net monetary assets rather than net non-monetary assets). Let us assume that an organization holds the following assets and liabilities at the beginning of the financial year:

	€
Current assets	
Cash	6,000
Inventory	9,000
	15,000
Non-current assets	
Land	10,000
Total assets	25,000
Liabilities	
Bank loan	5,000
Owners' equity	20,000

Let us also assume that the general level of prices has increased 5 per cent since the beginning of the year and let us make a further simplifying assumption (which will be relaxed later) that the company did not trade during the year and that the same assets and liabilities were in place at the end of the year as at the beginning. Assuming that general prices, perhaps as reflected by changes in the CPI, have increased by 5 per cent, then the CPI-adjusted values would be:

	Unadjusted	Price adjustment factor	Adjusted
	€		€
Current assets			
Cash	6,000		6,000
Inventory	9,000	0.05	9,450
	15,000		15,450
Non-current assets			
Land	10,000	0.05	10,500
Total assets	25,000		25,950
Liabilities			
Bank loan	5,000		5,000
Owners' equity	20,000		20,950

Again, monetary items are not adjusted by the change in the particular price index because they will retain the same monetary value regardless of inflation. Under CPP there is an assumption that the organization has not gained or lost in terms of the purchasing power attributed to the non-monetary assets, but, rather, it will gain or lose in terms of purchasing power changes attributable to its holdings of the net monetary assets. In the above example, to be as 'well off' at the end of the period the entity would need €21,000 in net assets (which equals €20,000 × 1.05) to have the same purchasing power as it had one year earlier (given the general increase in prices of 5 per cent). In terms of end-of-year euros, in the above illustration the entity is €50 worse off in adjusted terms (it only has net assets with an adjusted value of €20,950, which does not have the same purchasing power as €20,000 did at the beginning of the period). As indicated above, this €50 loss relates to the holdings of net monetary assets and not to the holding of non-monetary assets, and is calculated as the balance of cash, less the balance of the bank loan, multiplied by the general price level increase. That is, (€6,000 − €5,000) × 0.05. If the monetary liabilities had exceeded the monetary assets throughout the period, a purchasing power gain would have been recorded. If the amount of monetary assets held was the same as the amount of monetary liabilities held, then no gain or losses would result.

Again, it is stressed that under CPP no change in the purchasing power of the entity is assumed to arise as a result of holding non-monetary assets. Under general price level accounting, non-monetary assets are restated to current purchasing power and no gain or loss is recognized. Purchasing power losses (or gains) arise only as a result of holding net monetary assets. As noted at paragraph 7 of Provisional Statement of Standard Accounting Practice 7 (PSSAP 7), issued in the United Kingdom in 1974:

> Holders of non-monetary assets are assumed neither to gain nor to lose purchasing power by reason only of inflation as changes in the prices of these assets will tend to compensate for any changes in the purchasing power of the pound.

An important issue to consider is how the purchasing power gains and losses should be treated for income purposes. Should they be treated as part of the period's profit or loss, or should they be transferred directly to a reserve? Generally, where this method of accounting has been recommended it has been advised that the gain or loss should be included in income. Such recommendations are found in the US Accounting Research Bulletin No. 6 (issued in 1961); in the Accounting Principles Board (APB) Statement No. 3 (issued in 1969 by the American Institute of Certified Public Accountants (AICPA)); in the Financial Accounting Standards Board's (FASB) Exposure Draft entitled 'Financial Reporting in Units of General Purchasing Power'; and within Provisional Statement of Accounting Practice No. 7 issued by the Accounting Standards Steering Committee (UK) in 1974.

As a further example of calculating gains or losses in purchasing power pertaining to monetary items, let us assume four quarters with the following CPI index figures:

At the beginning of the year	120
At the end of the first quarter	125
At the end of the second quarter	130
At the end of the third quarter	132
At the end of the fourth quarter	135

Let us also assume the following movements in net monetary assets (total monetary assets less total monetary liabilities):

Opening net monetary assets		€100,000
Inflows:		
First quarter net inflow	20,000	
Second quarter net inflow	24,000	
Total inflows		44,000
Outflows:		
Third quarter net outflow	(17,000)	
Fourth quarter net outflow	(13,000)	
Total outflows		(30,000)
Closing net monetary assets		€114,000

In terms of year-end purchasing power euros, the purchasing power gain or loss can be calculated as:

	Unadjusted euros		Price index		Adjusted euros
Opening net monetary assets	€100,000	×	135/120	=	€112,500
Inflows:					
First quarter net inflow	€20,000	×	135/125	=	€21,600
Second quarter net inflow	€24,000	×	135/130	=	€24,923
Outflows:					
Third quarter net outflow	€(17,000)	×	135/132	=	€(17,386)
Fourth quarter net outflow	€(13,000)	×	135/135	=	€(13,000)
Net monetary assets adjusted for changes in purchasing power					€128,637

What the above calculation reflects is that to have the same purchasing power as when the particular transactions took place, then in terms of end-of-period euros, €128,637 in net monetary assets would need to be on hand at year end.[18] The actual balance on hand, however, is €114,000. Hence, there is a purchasing power loss of €14,637 which under CPP would be treated as an expense in the profit and loss account.

Let us now consider a more realistic example of CPP adjustments. We will restate the financial statements to reflect purchasing power as at the end of the current financial year.

---

[18] For example, we can consider the initial net monetary asset balance of €100,000 at the beginning of the period. For illustration, we can assume that this was represented by cash of €100,000. Given the inflation which has caused general prices to rise from a base of 120 to 135, to have the same general purchasing power at the end of the period an amount of cash equal to €112,500 would need to be on hand. The difference between the required amount of €112,500 and the actual balance of €100,000 is treated as a purchasing power loss relating to holding the cash. Conversely, if the net monetary balance had been (€100,000), meaning that monetary liabilities exceeded monetary assets, then we would have gained, as the purchasing power of what we must pay has decreased over time.

Let us assume that the entity commenced operation on 1 January 2012 and the unadjusted statement of financial position (or balance sheet) is as follows:

CPP plc statement of financial position as at 1 January 2012		
Current assets		
Cash	10,000	
Inventory	25,000	35,000
Non-current assets		
Plant and equipment	90,000	
Land	75,000	165,000
Total assets		200,000
Current liabilities		
Bank overdraft	10,000	
Non-current liabilities		
Bank loan	10,000	
Total liabilities		20,000
Net assets		180,000
Represented by:		
Shareholders' funds		
Paid up capital		180,000

As a result of its operations for the year, CPP plc had the historical cost income statement (profit and loss account) and balance sheet at year end as shown below:

CPP plc income statement for year ended 31 December 2012		
Sales revenue		200,000
Less:		
Cost of goods sold		
Opening inventory	25,000	
Purchases	110,000	
	135,000	
Closing inventory	35,000	100,000
Gross profit		100,000
Other expenses		
Administrative expenses	9,000	
Interest expense	1,000	
Depreciation	9,000	19,000
Operating profit before tax		81,000
Tax		26,000
Operating profit after tax		55,000
Opening retained earnings		0
Dividends proposed		15,000
Closing retained earnings		40,000

CPP plc statement of financial position as at 31 December 2012		
Current assets		
Cash	100,000	
Trade debtors	20,000	
Inventory	35,000	155,000
Non-current assets		
Plant and equipment	90,000	
Accumulated depreciation	(9,000)	
Land	75,000	156,000
Total assets		311,000
Current liabilities		
Bank overdraft	10,000	
Trade creditors	30,000	
Tax payable	26,000	
Provision for dividends	15,000	
	81,000	
Non-current liabilities		
Bank loan	10,000	
Total liabilities		91,000
Net assets		220,000
Represented by:		
Shareholders' funds		
Paid up capital		180,000
Retained earnings		40,000
		220,000

As we have already stated, under CPP gains or losses only occur as a result of holding net monetary assets. To determine the gain or loss, we must consider the movements in the net monetary assets. For example, if the organization sold inventory during the year, this will ultimately impact on cash. However, over time, the cash will be worth less in terms of its ability to acquire goods and services, hence there will be a purchasing power loss on the cash that was received during the year. Conversely, expenses will decrease cash during the year. In times of rising prices, more cash would be required to pay for the expense, hence in a sense we gain in relation to those expenses that were incurred earlier in the year (the logic being that if the expenses were incurred later in the year, more cash would have been required).

We must identify changes in net monetary assets from the beginning of the period until the end of the period.

Movement in net monetary assets from 1 January 2012 to 31 December 2012		
	1 January 2012	**31 December 2012**
Monetary assets		
Cash	10,000	100,000
Trade debtors		20,000
	10,000	120,000
Less:		
Monetary liabilities		
Bank overdraft	10,000	10,000
Trade creditors		30,000
Tax payable		26,000
Provision for dividends		15,000
Bank loan	10,000	10,000
Net monetary assets	(10,000)	29,000

To determine any adjustments in CPP plc we must identify the reasons for the change in net monetary assets.

Reconciliation of opening and closing net monetary assets	
Opening net monetary assets	(10,000)
Sales	200,000
Purchase of goods	(110,000)
Payment of interest	(1,000)
Payment of administrative expenses	(9,000)
Tax expense	(26,000)
Dividends	(15,000)
Closing net monetary assets	29,000

What we need to determine is whether, had all the transactions taken place at year end, the company would have had to transfer the same amount, measured in monetary terms, as it actually did. Any payments to outside parties throughout the period would have required a greater payment at the end of the period if the same items were to be transferred. Any receipts during the year will, however, be worth less in purchasing power.

To adjust for changes in purchasing power we need to have details about how prices have changed during the period, and we also need to know when the actual changes took place. We make the following assumptions:

- The interest expense and administrative expenses were incurred uniformly throughout the year.
- The tax liability did not arise until year end.

- The dividends were declared at the end of the year.
- The inventory on hand at year end was acquired in the last quarter of the year.
- Purchases of inventory occurred uniformly throughout the year.
- Sales occurred uniformly throughout the year.

We also assume that the price level index at the beginning of the year was 130. Subsequent indices were as follows:

31 December 2012	140
Average for the year	135
Average for first quarter	132
Average for second quarter	135
Average for third quarter	137
Average for fourth quarter	139

Rather than using price indices as at the particular dates of transactions (which would generally not be available) it is common to use averages for a particular period.

	Unadjusted	Index	Adjusted
Opening net monetary assets	(10,000)	140/130	(10,769)
Sales	200,000	140/135	207,407
Purchase of goods	(110,000)	140/135	(114,074)
Payment of interest	(1,000)	140/135	(1,037)
Payment of administrative expenses	(9,000)	140/135	(9,333)
Tax expense	(26,000)	140/140	(26,000)
Dividends	(15,000)	140/140	(15,000)
Closing net monetary assets	29,000		31,194

The difference between €29,000 and the amount of €31,194 represents a loss of €2,194. It is considered to be a loss, because to have the same purchasing power at year end as when the entity held the particular net monetary assets, the entity would need the adjusted amount of €31,194, rather than the actual amount of €29,000. This loss of €2,194 will appear as a 'loss on purchasing power' in the price-level-adjusted income statement (see below).

From the above balance sheet we can again emphasize that the non-monetary items are translated into euros of year-end purchasing power, whereas the monetary items are already stated in current purchasing power euros, and hence no changes are made to the reported balances of monetary assets.

One main strength of CPP is its ease of application. The method relies on data that would already be available under historical cost accounting and does not require the

Price-level-adjusted income statement for year ended 31 December 2012

Sales revenue	200,000	140/135	207,407
Less Cost of goods sold			
Opening inventory	25,000	140/130	26,923
Purchases	110,000	140/135	114,074
	135,000		140,997
Closing inventory	35,000	140/139	35,252
	100,000		105,745
Gross profit	100,000		101,662
Other expenses			
Administrative expenses	9,000	140/135	9,333
Interest expense	1,000	140/135	1,037
Depreciation	9,000	140/130	9,692
	19,000		20,062
Operating profit before tax	81,000		81,600
Tax	26,000	140/140	26,000
Operating profit after tax	55,000		55,600
Loss on purchasing power			2,194
			53,406
Opening retained earnings	0		0
Dividends proposed	15,000	140/140	15,000
Closing retained earnings	40,000		38,406

Price-level-adjusted statement of financial position as at 31 December 2012

Current assets			
Cash	100,000		100,000
Trade debtors	20,000		20,000
Stock	35,000	140/139	35,252
Total current assets	155,000		155,252
Non-current assets			
Plant and equipment	90,000	140/130	96,923
Accumulated depreciation	(9,000)	140/130	(9,692)
Land	75,000	140/130	80,769
Total non-current assets	156,000		168,000
Total assets	311,000		323,252
Current liabilities			
Bank overdraft	10,000		10,000
Trade creditors	30,000		30,000
Tax payable	26,000		26,000
Provision for dividends	15,000		15,000
Non-current liabilities			
Bank loan	10,000		10,000
Total liabilities	91,000		91,000
Net assets	220,000		232,252
Represented by:			
Shareholders' funds			
Paid up capital	180,000	140/130	193,846
Retained earnings	40,000		38,406
	220,000		232,252

reporting entity to incur the cost or effort involved in collecting data about the current values of the various non-monetary assets. CPI (or RPI) data would also be readily available. However, and as indicated previously, movements in the prices of goods and services included in a general price index might not be reflective of price movements involved in the goods and services involved in different industries. That is, different industries may be affected differently by inflation.

Another possible limitation is that the information generated under CPP might actually be confusing to users. They might consider that the adjusted amounts reflect the specific value of specific assets (and this is a criticism that can also be made of historical cost information). However, as the same index is used for all assets this will rarely be the case. Another potential limitation that we consider at the end of the chapter is that various studies (which have looked at such things as movements in share prices around the time of disclosure of CPP information) have failed to find much support for the view that the data generated under CPP are relevant for decision-making (the information when released caused little if any share price reaction).

Following the initial acceptance of CPP in some countries in the 1970s, there was a move towards methods of accounting that used actual current values. Support for CPP declined. We will now consider such approaches.

5.4 Current cost accounting

Current cost accounting (CCA) was one of the various alternatives to historical cost accounting that tended to gain the most acceptance. Notable advocates of this approach have included Paton (1922), and Edwards and Bell (1961). Such authors decided to reject historical cost accounting and CPP in favour of a method that considered actual valuations. As we will see, unlike historical cost accounting, CCA differentiates between profits from trading and those gains that result from holding an asset.

Holding gains can be considered as realized or unrealized. If a financial capital maintenance perspective is adopted with respect to the recognition of income, then holding gains or losses can be treated as income. Alternatively, they can be treated as capital adjustments if a physical capital maintenance approach is adopted.[19] Some versions of CCA, such as that proposed by Edwards and Bell, adopt a physical capital maintenance approach to income recognition. In this approach, which determines valuations on the basis of replacement costs,[20] operating income represents realized revenues, less the replacement cost of the assets in question. It is considered that this generates a measure of income which represents the maximum amount that can be distributed, while maintaining operating capacity intact. For example, assume that an entity acquired 150 items of

---

[19] In some countries non-current assets can be revalued upward by way of an increase in the asset account and an increase in a reserve, such as a revaluation reserve. This increment is typically not treated as income and therefore the treatment is consistent with a physical capital maintenance approach to income recognition (this approach is embodied within IAS 16 as it relates to property, plant and equipment, and within IAS 38 as it relates to intangible assets).

[20] We will also see later in this chapter that there are alternative approaches to current cost accounting that rely upon exit (sales) prices.

inventory at a cost of €10.00 each and sold 100 of the items for €15 each when the replacement cost to the entity was €12 each. We will also assume that the replacement cost of the 50 remaining items of inventory at year end was €14. Under the Edwards and Bell approach the operating profit that would be available for dividends would be €300, which is $100 \times (€15 - €12)$. There would be a realized holding gain on the goods that were sold, which would amount to $100 \times (€12 - €10)$, or €200, and there would be an unrealized holding gain in relation to closing inventory of $50 \times (€14 - €10)$, or €200. Neither the realized nor the unrealized holding gain would be considered to be available for dividend distribution.[21]

In undertaking CCA, adjustments are usually made at the year-end using the historical cost accounts as the basis of adjustments. If we adopt the Edwards and Bell approach to profit calculation, operating profit is derived after ensuring that the operating capacity of the organization is maintained intact. Edwards and Bell believe operating profit is best calculated by using replacement costs.[22, 23] As noted above, in calculating operating profit, gains that accrue from holding an asset (holding gains) are excluded and are not made available for dividends – although they are included when calculating what is referred to as business profit. For example, if an entity acquired goods for €20 and sold them for €30, then business profit would be €10, meaning that €10 could be distributed and still leave financial capital intact (this would be the approach taken in historical cost accounting). But if the replacement cost to the entity of the goods at the time they were sold was €23, then €3 would be considered a holding gain, and to maintain physical operating capacity only €7 could be distributed – current cost operating profit would be €7. No adjustment is made to sales revenue. This €7 distribution can be compared to what could be distributed under historical cost accounting. Because historical costs accounting adopts a financial capital maintenance approach, €10 could be distributed in dividends thereby maintaining financial capital (but nevertheless causing an erosion in the operating ability of the organization).

In relation to non-current assets, for the purposes of determining current cost operating profit, depreciation is based on the replacement cost of the asset. For example, if an item of machinery was acquired at the beginning of 2012 for €100,000 and had a projected life of 10 years and no salvage value, then assuming the straight-line method of depreciation is used, its depreciation expense under historical cost accounting would be €10,000 per year. If at the end of 2012 its replacement cost had increased to €120,000, then under current cost accounting a further €2,000 would be deducted to determine current cost operating profit. However, this €2,000 would be treated as a realized cost

---

[21] Comparing this approach to income calculations under historical cost accounting we see that if we add CCA operating profit of €300 and the realized holding gain of €200, then this will give the same total as we would have calculated for income under historical cost accounting.

[22] In a sense, the Edwards and Bell approach represents a 'true income' approach to profit calculation. They believe that profit can only be correctly measured (that is, 'be true') after considering the various asset replacement costs.

[23] Those who favour a method of income calculation that requires a maintenance of financial capital (advocates of historical cost accounting) treat holding gains as income, while those who favour a maintenance of physical capital approach to income determination (such as Edwards and Bell) tend to exclude holding gains from income. A physical capital perspective was adopted by most countries in their professional releases pertaining to CCA.

saving (because historical cost profits would have been lower if the entity had not already acquired the asset) and would be recognized in business profit (it would be added back below operating profit) and the other €18,000 would be treated as an unrealized cost saving and would also be included in business profit. As with CPP, no restatement of monetary assets is required as they are already recorded in current euros and hence in terms of end-of-period purchasing power euros.

As an example of one version of CCA (consistent with the Edwards and Bell proposals) let us consider the following example. CCA plc's balance sheet at the commencement of the year is provided below. This is assumed to be the first year of CCA plc's operations.

CCA plc statement of financial position as at 1 January 2012		
Current assets		
Cash	10,000	
Inventory	25,000	35,000
Non-current assets		
Plant and equipment	90,000	
Land	75,000	165,000
Total assets		200,000
Current liabilities		
Bank overdraft	10,000	
Non-current liabilities		
Bank loan	10,000	
Total liabilities		20,000
Net assets		180,000
Represented by:		
Shareholders' funds		
Paid up capital		180,000

The unadjusted income statement and balance sheet for CCA plc after one year's operations are provided below.

CCA plc income statement for year ended 31 December 2012		
Sales revenue		200,000
Less:		
Cost of goods sold		
Opening inventory	25,000	
Purchases	110,000	
	135,000	
Closing inventory	35,000	100,000
Gross profit		100,000

Other expenses		
Administrative expenses	9,000	
Interest expense	1,000	
Depreciation	9,000	19,000
Operating profit before tax		81,000
Tax		26,000
Operating profit after tax		55,000
Opening retained earnings		0
Dividends proposed		15,000
Closing retained earnings		40,000

CCA plc statement of financial position as at 31 December 2012		
Current assets		
Cash	100,000	
Trade debtors	20,000	
Inventory	35,000	155,000
Non-current assets		
Plant and equipment	90,000	
Accumulated depreciation	(9,000)	
Land	75,000	156,000
Total assets		311,000
Current liabilities		
Bank overdraft	10,000	
Trade creditors	30,000	
Tax payable	26,000	
Provision for dividends	15,000	
	81,000	
Non-current liabilities		
Bank loan	10,000	
Total liabilities		91,000
Net assets		220,000
Represented by:		
Shareholders' funds		
Paid up capital		180,000
Retained earnings		40,000
		220,000

We will assume that the inventory on hand at the year-end comprised 3,500 units that cost €10 per unit. The replacement cost at year end was €11.00 per unit. We will also assume that the replacement cost of the units actually sold during the year was €105,000 (as opposed to the historical cost of €100,000) and that the year-end replacement cost of the plant and equipment increased to €115,000. The plant and equipment has an expected life of 10 years with no residual value. The replacement cost of the land is believed to be €75,000 at year end.

CCA plc income statement for year ended 31 December 2012 Adjusted by application of current cost accounting		
Sales revenue		200,000
Less:		
Cost of goods sold		105,000
		95,000
Other expenses		
Administrative expenses	9,000	
Interest expense	1,000	
Tax	26,000	
Depreciation (€115,000 × 1/10)	11,500	47,500
Current cost operating profit		47,500
Realized savings		
Savings related to inventory actually sold		5,000
Savings related to depreciation actually incurred [(115,000 − 90,000) × 1/10]		2,500
Historical cost profit		55,000
Unrealized savings		
Gains on holding inventory – yet to be realized		3,500
Gains on holding plant and machinery – not yet realized through the process of depreciation [(115,000 − 90,000) × 9/10)]		22,500
Business profit		81,000
Opening retained earnings		0
Dividends proposed		15,000
Closing retained earnings		66,000

CCA plc statement of financial position as at 31 December 2012 Adjusted by application of current cost accounting		
Current assets		
Cash	100,000	
Trade debtors	20,000	
Inventory (3,500 × €11.00)	38,500	158,500
Non-current assets		
Plant and equipment	115,000	
Accumulated depreciation	(11,500)	
Land	75,000	178,500
Total assets		337,000

Current liabilities		
Bank overdraft	10,000	
Trade creditors	30,000	
Tax payable	26,000	
Provision for dividends	15,000	
	81,000	
Non-current liabilities		
Bank loan	10,000	
Total liabilities		91,000
Net assets		246,000
Represented by:		
Shareholders' funds		
Paid up capital		180,000
Retained earnings		66,000
		246,000

Consistent with the CCA model prescribed by Edwards and Bell, all non-monetary assets have to be adjusted to their respective replacement costs. Unlike historical cost accounting, there is no need for inventory cost flow assumptions (such as last-in-first-out; first-in-first-out; weighted average). Business profit shows how the entity has gained in financial terms from the increase in cost of its resources – something typically ignored by historical cost accounting. In the above illustration, and consistent with a number of versions of CCA, no adjustments have been made for changes in the purchasing power of net monetary assets (in contrast to CPP).[24]

The current cost operating profit before holding gains and losses, and the realized holding gains, are both tied to the notion of realization, and hence the sum of the two equates to historical cost profit.

Differentiating operating profit from holding gains and losses (both realized and unrealized) has been claimed to enhance the usefulness of the information being provided. Holding gains are deemed to be different from trading income as they are due to market-wide movements, most of which are beyond the control of management. Edwards and Bell (1961, p. 73) state:

> These two kinds of gains are often the result of quite different decisions. The business firm usually has considerable freedom in deciding what quantities of assets to hold over time at any or all stages of the production process and what quantity of assets to commit to the production process itself ... The difference

---

[24] Some variants of CCA do include some purchasing power changes as part of the profit calculations. For example, if an entity issued €1 million of debt when the market required a rate of return of 6 per cent, but that required rate subsequently rises to 8 per cent, then the unrealized savings would include the difference between what the entity received for the debt and what they would receive at the new rate. This unrealized saving would benefit the organization throughout the loan as a result of the lower interest charges.

between the forces motivating the business firm to make profit by one means rather than by another and the difference between the events on which the two methods of making profit depend require that the two kinds of gain be separated if the two types of decisions involved are to be meaningfully evaluated.

As with CPP, the CCA model described above has been identified as having a number of strengths and weaknesses. Some of the criticisms relate to its reliance on replacement values. The CCA model we have just described uses replacement values, but what is the rationale for replacement cost? Perhaps it is a reflection of the 'real' value of the particular asset. If people in the market are prepared to pay the replacement cost, and if we assume economic rationality, then the amount paid must be a reflection of the returns it is expected to generate. However, it might not be worth that amount (the replacement cost) to all firms – some firms might not elect to replace a given asset if they have an option. Further, past costs are sunk costs and if the entity were required to acquire new plant it might find it more efficient and less costly to acquire different types of assets. If it did buy it, then this might reflect that it is actually worth much more. Further, replacement cost does not reflect what it would be worth if the firm decided to sell it.

As was indicated previously, it has been argued that separating holding gains and losses from other results provides a better insight into management performance, as such gains and losses are due to impacts generated outside the organization; however, this can be criticized on the basis that acquiring assets in advance of price movements might also be part of efficient operations.

Another potential limitation of CCA is that it is often difficult to determine replacement costs. The approach also suffers from the criticism that allocating replacement cost via depreciation is still arbitrary, just as it is with historical cost accounting.

An advantage of CCA is better comparability of various entities' performance, as one entity's profits are not higher simply because it bought assets years earlier and therefore would have generated lower depreciation under historical cost accounting.

Chambers, an advocate of CCA based on exit values, was particularly critical of the Edwards and Bell model of accounting. He states (1995, p. 82) that:

> In the context of judgement of the past and decision making for the future, the products of current value accounting of the Edwards and Bell variety are irrelevant and misleading.

We now briefly consider some of the key principles underlying the alternative accounting model prescribed by Chambers and a number of others – a model that relies upon the use of *exit values*.

5.5 Exit price accounting: the case of Chambers' continuously contemporary accounting

Exit price accounting has been proposed by researchers such as MacNeal, Sterling and Chambers. It is a form of current cost accounting that is based on valuing assets at their net selling prices (exit prices) at the accounting date and on the basis of orderly sales. Chambers coined the term 'current cash equivalent' to refer to the cash that an entity would expect to receive through the orderly sale of an asset, and he held the view that information about current cash equivalents was fundamental to effective decision-making. He labelled his method of accounting continuously contemporary accounting, or CoCoA.

Although he generated some much cited research throughout the 1950s (such as Chambers, 1955) a great deal of his work culminated in 1966 in the publication of *Accounting, Evaluation and Economic Behavior*. This document argued that the key information for economic decision-making relates to capacity to adapt – which was argued to be a function of current cash equivalents (Chambers, 1966). The statement of financial position (balance sheet) is considered to be the prime financial statement under CoCoA, and should show the net selling prices of the entity's assets. Profit would directly relate to changes in adaptive capital, with adaptive capital reflected by the total exit values of the entity's assets. In other words, profit is directly tied to the increase (or decrease) in the current net selling prices of the entity's assets. No distinction is drawn between realized and unrealized gains. Unlike some other models of accounting, all gains are treated as part of profit. Profit is that amount that can be distributed, while maintaining the entity's adaptive ability (adaptive capital). CoCoA abandons notions of realization for recognizing revenue, and hence revenue recognition points change relative to historical cost accounting. Rather than relying on sales, revenues are recognized at such points as production or purchase.

As indicated previously in this chapter, how one calculates income is based, in part, on how one defines wealth. According to Sterling, an advocate of exit price accounting, (1970b, p. 189).

> The present [selling] price is the proper and correct valuation coefficient for the measurement of wealth at a point in time and income is the difference between dated wealths so calculated.

In developing the CoCoA model, Chambers made a judgement about what people need in terms of information. Like authors such as Edwards and Bell, and unlike some of the earlier work which documented existing accounting practices to identify particular principles and postulates (descriptive research),[25] Chambers set out to develop what he considered was a superior model of accounting – a model that represented quite a dramatic change from existing practice. We call this prescriptive or normative research. The research typically highlighted the limitations of historical cost accounting and then proposed an alternative on the basis of an argument that it would enable better decision-making. Chambers adopted a decision usefulness approach and within this approach he adopted a decision-models perspective.[26]

---

[25] As a specific example of the inductive (descriptive) approach to theory development we can consider the work of Grady (1965). This research was commissioned by the American Institute of Certified Public Accountants and documented the generally accepted conventions of accounting of the time.

[26] As indicated in Chapter 1, decision usefulness research can be considered to have two branches, these being the *decision-makers emphasis*, and the *decision-models emphasis*. The *decision-makers emphasis* relies upon undertaking research that seeks to ask decision-makers what information they want. Proponents of the *decision-models emphasis*, on the other hand, develop models based upon the researchers' perceptions about what is necessary for efficient decision-making. Information prescriptions follow (for example, that information should be provided about the market value of the reporting entity's assets). This branch of research typically assumes that different classes of stakeholders have identical information needs. Unlike the decision-makers emphasis, the decision-models emphasis does not ask the decision-makers what information they want, but, instead, it concentrates on what types of information are considered by the researcher to be useful for decision-making.

Chambers' approach is focused on new opportunities – the ability or capacity of the entity to adapt to changing circumstances and the most important item of information to evaluate future decisions is, according to Chambers, current cash equivalents. Chambers makes an assumption about the objective of accounting – to guide future actions. Capacity to adapt is the key and the capacity to adapt to changing circumstances is dependent upon the current cash equivalents (realizable values) of the assets on hand. The higher the current market value of the entity's assets the greater is the ability of the organization to adapt to changing circumstances.

However, Chamber's CoCoA model never gained widespread acceptance. Just as Chambers was critical of the Edwards and Bell model, Edwards and Bell were also critical of Chambers' approach. For example, Edwards (1975, p. 238) states:

> I am not convinced of the merit of adopting, as a normal basis for asset valua-tion in the going concern, exit prices in buyer markets. These are unusual val-ues suitable for unusual situations. I would not object in principle to keeping track of such exit prices at all times and, as Solomons (1966) has suggested, substituting them for entry values when they are the lesser of the two and the firm has taken a definite decision not to replace the asset, or even the function it performs.

Despite the lack of support at the time for Chambers' CoCoA model, some of its underlying principles are consistent with the arguments used today by those who support a move towards using *fair values* in the statement of financial position. An increasing requirement to use fair values as the basis of asset and liability valuations in some accounting standards is a controversial issue in both academic and practitioner debates. The next section of this chapter will focus on aspects of the current debate surrounding the use of *fair value accounting*.

5.6 Fair value accounting

Fair value is an asset (and liability) measurement concept that has been used in an increasing number of accounting standards in recent years. In the IASB's proposed accounting standard on fair value (due to be published in 2011, with a near identical accounting standard to be published by the FASB)[27] fair value is defined as:

> the price that would be received to sell an asset or paid to transfer a liability in an *orderly transaction* between *market participants* at the measurement date (IASB, 2010, p. 5, paragraph 1, emphasis in original)

If there is an active and liquid market in which assets are traded that are identical to the asset to be valued, then the fair value will be equivalent to the asset's market value. This

---

[27] At the time of writing this chapter, the IASB had published (in August 2010) a 'staff draft' of the proposed forthcoming IFRS on Fair Value Measurement. This was an interim stage between an exposure draft that had been published for comment in 2009 and the final publication of the IFRS expected in 2011. The 'staff draft' incorporates all the decisions made by the IASB (in conjunction with the FASB) up to March 2010.

technique of identifying a fair value is known as *mark to market*. However, the IASB (and FASB) recognize that there will be instances where assets for which fair values are required do not have markets where identical assets are actively traded, so a directly comparable market value is not available. In these circumstances the market price of a very similar asset or liability can be used or, where there is not an active market for the form of asset that is to be fair valued (so market values for an identical or similar asset cannot be observed), an alternative is to use an accepted valuation model to infer the fair value. This technique is known as *mark to model* and requires the identification of both an accepted valuation model and the inputs required by the model to arrive at a valuation. In practice, the best estimate of the exit price (realizable value), as preferred by Chambers, is taken as the fair value of the asset (IASB, 2010, p. 5, paragraph 2).

The IASB and FASB's proposed (similar) accounting standards on fair value measurement establish a *fair value hierarchy* in which the highest attainable level of inputs must be used to establish the fair value of an asset or liability. Levels 1 and 2 in the hierarchy are *mark to market* situations, with the highest level, level 1, being 'quoted prices (unadjusted) in active markets for identical assets or liabilities' (IASB, 2010, p. 14, paragraph 77) while level 2 are directly observable inputs other than level 1 market prices (level 2 inputs could include market prices for similar assets or liabilities, or market prices for identical assets but that are observed in less active markets). Level 3 inputs are *mark to model* situations where observable inputs are not available and risk-adjusted valuation models need to be used instead.

Permitting, and in some cases requiring, certain categories of assets and liabilities to be valued at fair value has been controversial. In this chapter we will focus on two of the key features of fair value that have attracted heated debate: first, the *volatility* and *procyclicality* that some argue can be (and has been) introduced into net asset and profit figures when the markets used to determine an asset's fair value are themselves volatile; and second, aspects of the *decision usefulness* normative position underlying the use of fair values. This decision usefulness position maintains that the role of financial accounting is to provide information that is useful to help investors make certain types of investment decisions (a normative position that is shared with Chambers, who advocated a similar exit value measurement basis). But before discussing these issues, it would be helpful to outline the situations when fair values are permitted and when they are required by accounting standards, and how any changes in fair values are recorded in the income statement.

Required and permitted uses of fair values

Under current IASB rules, within a range of International Accounting Standards (IASs) and International Financial Reporting Standards (IFRSs), many assets are required to be included in the statement of financial position at historical cost (less amortization or impairment where appropriate), some are required to be included at fair value, and there are some types of assets where organizations have the option of including the asset either at historical cost or fair value (Nobes and Parker, 2010, p. 204). Where an organization chooses to use fair value for a type of asset in this final category, it must then use fair values for all of the assets it has of the same type and cannot *usually* change back to using historical costs for this type of asset in the future.

FASB accounting rules in the United States have in the past been much more restrictive in the use of fair values than the IASB rules (Zeff, 2007), although there are moves towards much greater use of fair values. This is proving controversial – as shown in Accounting Headline 5.3.

Accounting Headline 5.3
Controversy of extension of fair value accounting in the United States
FASB in midst of 'religious war' on fair value

By Mario Christodoulou

A member of the US accounting standard setter has likened attempts to bring in fair value to a 'religious war' in a speech with regulators this week.

Lawrence Smith, board member with the Financial Accounting Standards Board (FASB), made the comment in a panel discussion with US audit regulator, the Public Company Accounting Oversight Board, in the midst of a far ranging consultation on the accounting principle.

FASB is pushing ahead with plans to bring in a full fair value measurement model which would force banks to value their financial assets at market prices. The proposals are being fought by banks who argue the rules would add volatility to balance sheets.

Smith said he is not a 'fair value zealot', but was swayed to the model when he saw the effect on deposits.

'That's what threw me over the edge,' he said.

'Some people have advised us that we shouldn't say this, but I'll say it – fair value, to some of us, is almost like a religious war out there and we are trying to deal with that as best we can.'

FASB is attempting to harmonise its accounting rules with international standards, despite clear differences in their approach to fair value. Whereas FASB's proposal measures assets measured at fair value, the international model allows some loans to be valued at amortised cost.

The contentious proposals was passed by a single vote, with the five-member FASB board split 3-2.

Smith's comment will likely widen the gap between FASB's proposal and its international counterpart, the International Accounting Standards Board (IASB). Failure to reach agreement on the standard will undermine US attempts to adopt international rules.

The US Securities and Exchange Commission is currently investigating the impact of international accounting rules on US markets. A key part of their final decision will depend on the level of convergence between US and international accounting rules, with fair value being among the most important projects on the table.

Source: *Accountancy Age,* 22 July 2010 (online)

Under both FASB and IASB rules certain types of liabilities also have to be included in the statement of financial position at fair value. This requirement covers liabilities held for trading and derivative liabilities.

Under IASB rules, gains or losses arising on fair valuing: derivatives (both assets and liabilities), investments held solely for trading (again, both assets and liabilities) and assets that an organization chooses to value at fair value (where it has the option to do so) are taken to profit or loss. These items are known as 'fair value through profit and loss', with the latter category (where the organization has taken the option to value at fair value instead of historical cost) termed 'designated at fair value through profit and loss'. In contrast any gains or losses arising from fair valuing investments that are, in principle, available for sale (in other words, investments that were not acquired solely for trading, such as shares owned in other companies, even where there is not an intention to sell these shares) are taken to the statement of comprehensive income and do not affect the reported profit or loss. This removes the effect of any volatility in the market values of these assets (which may be held for the long-term) from the profit or loss figure, but any volatility in the market values of other types of assets will lead to volatility in the profit or loss figure. Nobes and Parker (2010, p. 207) explain:

> The managers of companies do not generally like volatility, so they like to treat as few [financial/investment] assets as possible as 'trading'. Since some financial assets clearly cannot be held to maturity because they have no maturity date (e.g. shares), it is common for companies (except financial institutions) to treat most financial assets as available for sale. In contrast, the standard-setters believe that all financial assets should be treated as 'trading' … This is why the IASB added the option to IAS 39 for other financial assets to be treated in the same way as a trading asset.

In November 2009 the IASB published the first stage of a new IFRS for financial instruments – IFRS 9 – which is to eventually replace the existing accounting standard on this topic, IAS 39. Given the controversial nature of many aspects of accounting for financial instruments, the IASB unusually chose to develop IFRS 9, and withdraw the respective provisions of IAS 39, in three stages. The first of these stages includes rules on the use of fair values when accounting for financial assets (new rules on accounting for financial liabilities will be included in a later stage of IFRS 9). These requirements have to be implemented by companies, at the latest, for accounting periods beginning on or after 1 January 2013, although companies may implement them earlier. IFRS 9 will simplify the guidance on use of fair values so will change some of the fair value accounting rules outlined above. Specifically for financial assets (fair valuing rules for the other categories of assets and liabilities discussed above are not affected):

- The organization's 'business model' related to the financial asset, and the 'contractual cash flow characteristics' of the financial asset (IFRS 9, paragraph 4.1) will be used to determine the treatment of the asset.
- If an objective of the business model is solely to hold the asset to realize its contractual cash flows, and these only comprise payment of principal and interest, then at the accounting date the asset has to be valued at historical cost (or fair value at the date of acquisition if different), adjusted for amortization and impairment if relevant. (IFRS 9, paragraphs 4.2 and 5.2.2)
- All other financial assets must be included in the statement of financial position at fair value. (IFRS 9, paragraph 4.4)
- Any changes in the value of a financial asset (either one held at amortized or impaired historical cost, or one held at fair value) have to be recognized in the income statement

as part of the profit or loss for the period, unless the asset is an investment in the equity of another entity and is not held for trading (this still has to be recorded at fair value) and the organization has made an irrevocable election at the date of acquisition to treat gains or losses on this investment as part of comprehensive income. (IFRS 9, paragraphs 5.4.1, 5.4.2 and 5.4.4)

IFRS 9 reduces the ability of organizations to classify investments in a way that will enable volatility in the values of these investments to bypass the reported profit and loss figure by taking changes in values to the statement of comprehensive income. We will now move on to discuss the added volatility that use of fair values is claimed to have introduced into accounting results.

Fair values and added volatility and procyclicality in accounting measures

In using market prices, rather than inflation-adjusted historical costs, fair value measurements provide valuations for assets (and for any fair valued liabilities) that factor into the values current market conditions at the accounting date. This is a feature they share with realizable (exit) values – as championed years earlier by Chambers and others – and replacement cost values. One key outcome of this reliance on market values is that where the underlying asset markets that are used to derive the fair values for a type of asset suffer from volatility, this volatility will be reflected in the values of the fair valued assets (and liabilities) shown in the statement of financial position. In other words, using fair values can result in considerable volatility in the statement of financial position.

As we will see when we discuss conceptual frameworks in the next chapter, current accounting practice (in very broad terms) is to measure income (or profit) as the difference between the net asset figure in the statement of financial position at the start of the accounting period and the net asset figure at the end of the accounting period. Therefore, where use of fair value for a particular type of asset or liability introduces volatility into figures in the statement of financial position, this will also lead to volatility in figures in the income statement. Depending on the specific accounting treatment required in accounting standards for an individual type of asset or liability, this volatility can (and often is) within the profit or loss for the period.

During the sub-prime banking crisis it was claimed by many (especially banks themselves) that accounting requirements to value many of their assets at fair value exacerbated the crisis (Laux and Leuz, 2009; Power, 2010). This is a phenomenon termed procyclicality. It is argued that when markets for financial assets (such as shares, bonds and derivatives) are booming, the value of these assets held by banks, and shown at fair value in their statements of financial position, will similarly rise significantly above their historical cost – thus increasing the reported net assets and capital and reserves of the bank. As banking regulations usually set bank lending limits in terms of a proportion (or multiple) of capital and reserves, this increase in the reported fair value of the assets of a bank will enable a bank to lend more. Some of this additional lending may fuel further demand in the markets for financial assets – thus further increasing the market values of these assets held by banks and further increasing their reported capital and reserves. This, it is argued, will enable banks to lend even more and thus will help to create an upward spiral in financial assets prices and bank lending that becomes increasingly disconnected from the underlying real economic values of the assets in these markets (Laux and Leuz, 2009).

Conversely, it was argued by many at the time of the sub-prime banking crisis that when markets for financial assets are in free-fall (as they were at times during the crisis), fair value accounting exacerbates a downward spiral of assets prices and bank lending that is equally unreflective of (and significantly overstates) decreases in real underlying economic values (Laux and Leuz, 2009). The basis of this viewpoint is that requirements to mark to market financial assets held by banks may lead to a rapid erosion in the capital and reserves shown in the banks' statements of financial position. This will reduce their lending limits (where these are tied to their reported levels of capital and reserves) and will both reduce bank lending (thus reducing demand in financial markets, putting further downward pressure on asset prices in these markets) and will possibly require the banks to sell some of the financial assets they hold to release liquidity. This will put further downward pressure on the prices of financial assets, leading to a downward price spiral as these reduced prices further reduce the reported net assets of the banks.

Although these impacts of fair value accounting were widely articulated at the time of the sub-prime banking crisis, Laux and Leuz (2009) argue many of these claimed empirical effects were not caused by fair value accounting, so the *volatility and procyclicality* case against fair value accounting is not as clear cut as the above arguments indicate. Laux and Leuz (2009, p. 827) indicate that while there are some legitimate concerns about the impact of fair values:

> the concern about the downward spiral is most pronounced for FVA [fair value accounting] in its pure form but it does not apply in the same way to FVA as stipulated by US GAAP or IFRS. Both standards allow for deviations from market prices under certain circumstances (e.g., prices from fire sales). Thus, it is not clear that the standards themselves are the source of the problem.

The basis of this argument is that, as we saw earlier, both IFRSs and US GAAPs permit fair values to be determined using data other than direct market observations in many circumstances. These are referred to as level 2 and level 3 in the fair value measurement hierarchy. In situations where markets are demonstrably not providing values based on *orderly* transactions or for any other reason are not operating efficiently (for example, due to illiquidity in the markets), then rather than using level 1 fair value measurements (directly observed market prices for identical assets), then level 2 mark to market or level 3 mark to model valuations should be used. Laux and Leuz (2009) explain that during the sub-prime banking crisis, many banks moved to using level 2 and 3 valuations rather than level 1 valuations for many financial assets, and also took advantage of provisions to allow some assets to be reclassified from fair value to historical cost categories in special circumstances, thus acting as a 'damper' reducing the speed (or acceleration) of any procyclical effects. They also argue that any failure to provide fair values in financial statements during economic downturns *could* in itself cause markets to overreact and/or misprice company shares:

> it is also possible that market reactions are even more extreme if current market prices or fair-value estimates are not disclosed to the market. We are not aware of any empirical evidence that investors would be calmer under HCA. Investors are not naïve; they know about the problems, e.g., in the subprime-loan market, and hence will draw inferences even in the absence of fair-value disclosures (and in that case might assume the worst). Thus, lack of transparency could make matters worse. Furthermore, even if investors were to react more calmly

> under HCA, this may come at the price of delaying and increasing the underly-
> ing problems (e.g., excessive subprime lending). (Laux and Leuz, 2009, p. 828)

Apart from the mainly empirical question of whether fair values lead to unwarranted volatility in reported asset values, and give rise to undesirable procyclical outcomes, a key normative question is whether the move to the use of fair values improves the role and functioning of financial accounting. Much of this normative debate focuses on whether the purpose of financial accounting is to provide information to help a range of financial stakeholders make effective economic decisions (which would support the move to the use of fair values) or whether financial accounting should serve more of a traditional role of helping existing investors assess the effectiveness of the directors' stewardship of the assets owned by the firm (which would support greater use of historical cost accounting).

Fair value and the decision usefulness versus stewardship role of financial accounting

Whittington (2008) distinguished between what he refers to as two competing 'world views' underlying present-day normative positions on financial accounting. He terms these the *Fair Value View* and the *Alternative View*. He argues that under the Fair Value View, the sole purpose of financial accounting is seen as being to provide information useful for a range of financial stakeholders making economic decisions based on future cash flows. In contrast, proponents of the Alternative View believe that 'stewardship, defined as accountability to present shareholders is a distinct objective, ranking equally with decision usefulness' (p. 159). We will discuss some of the implications of these different world views in Chapter 6 when we look at Whittington's criticisms of aspects of current and proposed conceptual frameworks of accounting. For the purpose of our examination in this chapter of the use of fair values, a key aspect of Whittington's critique is that fair values provide information suited for a *decision usefulness* role for financial accounting whereas historical cost accounting provides information aligned to a *stewardship* role. For the former, in situations where there has to be a trade-off, relevant information (in terms of providing information that helps forecast future cash flows) is considered more important than reliability of accounting information, and it is assumed that:

> Market prices should give an informed, *non entity specific* estimate of cash
> flow potential, and *markets* are generally sufficiently complete and efficient
> to provide evidence for representationally faithful measurement on this basis.
> (Whittington, 2008, p. 158, emphasis in original)

As market values are considered to provide the most relevant decision-useful information, fair values in the statement of financial position are considered to be more important than information in the income statement. The former thus becomes the primary financial statement while income statements just record the difference in net asset (fair) value from one year to the next (Ronen, 2008).

In contrast, for a primarily stewardship role the reporting of the impact of transactions entered into by the firm is considered to be of key importance. This information is captured primarily in the income statement, with the statement of financial position recording the residual amounts of cash flows that have not yet been 'used up' (or have been used but not yet received or paid) in accordance with the realization and matching principles of accrual accounting (such as inventory purchased but not yet sold, the useful lives of tangible non-current assets that have not yet been used and can help generate income in future periods, and so on) (Ronen, 2008). For these purposes, reliability of measurement is important, and the application of prudence is regarded as important in enhancing the reliability of information (Whittington, 2008).

In considering issues of relevance versus reliability in fair value accounting, Ronen (2008, p. 186) argues that fair values do not measure the value of assets in their use to the specific firm. Therefore, despite the rationale of fair values being that they provide relevant decision-useful information, Ronen claims that fair values do not always provide the most relevant measures:

> Since the fair value measurements …are based on exit values, they do not reflect the value of the assets' employment within the specific operations of the firm. In other words, they do not reflect the use value of the asset, so they do not inform investors about the future cash flows to be generated by these assets within the firm, the present value of which is the fair value to shareholders. Thus, these exit values fall short of meeting the informativeness objective of financial statements. In a similar vein, they do not do well in serving the stewardship function, as they do not properly measure the managers' ability to create value for shareholders.
>
> Nonetheless, exit value measures have partial relevance. Specifically, they quantify the opportunity cost to the firm of continuing as a going concern, engaging in the specific operations of its business plan; the exit values reflect the benefits foregone by not selling the assets.

In assessing the reliability of fair value information, Ronen (2008, p. 186) explains that under fair value accounting, level 1 measurements can generally be considered reliable, but for level 2 and 3 measurements:

> Level 2 involves estimations of fair value based on predictable relationships among the observed input prices and the value of the asset or liability being measured. The degree of reliability one can attach to these derived measures would depend on the goodness of the fit between the observed input prices and the estimated value. Measurement errors and mis-specified models may compromise the precision of the derived estimates. Nonetheless, Level 2 is not as hazardous as Level 3. In the latter, unobservable inputs, subjectively determined by the firm's management, and subject to random errors and moral hazard, may cause significant distortions both in the balance sheet and in the income statement. Moreover, discounting cash flows to derive a fair value invites deception.

Looking at considerations of reliability in more depth, Power (2010) argues that reliability is understood differently by different people and is, in effect, socially constructed. He partially explains the rise of fair value accounting in terms of a specific perception of reliability grounded in the developing discipline of financial economics, which has been increasingly drawn upon by accounting regulators to give authority (from outside the discipline of accounting) to their pronouncements. He explains (p. 202) that despite the many unrealistic assumptions underlying financial economics, with these being widely articulated in the wake of the sub-prime banking crisis, financial economics has provided an attractive body of knowledge for accounting standard setters:

> Whitley (1986) suggests that the close links [of finance theory] with practice had more to do with financial economics as a reputational system and less to do with the direct applicability of its analytical core. This is consistent with Hopwood's (2009: 549) critique of the 'growing distance of the academic finance knowledge base from the complexities of practice and practical institutions.' Yet, as Abbott (1988) has argued, purely 'academic' knowledge has always played a significant role for professions, providing the rational theorisations needed by practice. Financial economics is almost the perfect example of this. (Power, 2010, p. 202)

> … proponents of fair values in accounting argue for their greater relevance to users of financial information, but the deeper point is that they also redefine the reliability of fair values supported by financial economics, both in terms of specific assumptions and in terms of its general cultural authority. Against sceptics, key accounting policy makers were able to acquire confidence in a knowledge base for accounting estimates rooted in a legitimised discipline. (Power, 2010, p. 205)

Power (2010, p. 201) argues that in this context, fair value – as a measurement basis grounded in financial economics' conceptions of the role of accounting as being to provide decision-useful information to a range of financial stakeholders – becomes the 'acceptable' measurement basis:

> once it is admitted that market prices may not reveal fundamental value, due to liquidity issues or other reasons, then it can be argued that the real foundation of fair value lies in economic valuation methodologies; level 3 methods are in fact the engine of markets themselves, capable of 'discovering' values for accounting objects which can only be sold in 'imaginary markets'. It follows that the [fair value] hierarchy is more of a liquidity hierarchy than one of method, but overall it expresses the imperative of market alignment which informs fair value enthusiasts.

> The sociology of reliability to emerge from these arguments suggests that subjectivity and uncertainty can be transformed into *acceptable fact* via strategies which appeal to broader values in the institutional environment which even opponents must accept. Accounting 'estimates' can acquire authority when they come to be embedded in taken-for granted routines. (Power, 2010, p. 201, emphasis in original)

As fair value accounting looks likely to grow in importance and influence, as an increasing number of accounting standards require its use, debates over issues such as the impact of fair values and normative questions about the desirability of different aspects of fair values are also likely to gain even greater prominence. Academic studies examining the reactions of users to fair value accounting disclosures should provide important evidence to inform this debate. Many such studies have in the past examined reactions to the earlier attempts at reflecting current values in financial statements, such as current cost and CPP accounting. We now move on to discuss insights provided by these studies.

5.7 The demand for price-adjusted and value-adjusted accounting information

One research method often used to assess the usefulness of particular disclosures is to look for a stock market reaction (share price reaction) around the time of the release of the information, the rationale being that if share prices react to the disclosures then such disclosures must have information content. That is, the information impacts on the decisions made by individuals participating in the capital market. A number of studies have looked at the stock market reaction to current cost and CPP information. Results are inconclusive, with studies such as Ro (1980, 1981), Beaver *et al.* (1980), Gheyara and Boatsman (1980), Beaver and Landsman (1987), Murdoch (1986), Schaefer (1984), Dyckman (1969), Morris (1975), and Peterson (1975) finding limited evidence of any price changes around the time of disclosure of current cost information. (However, Lobo and Song (1989) and Bublitz *et al.* (1985) provide limited evidence that there is information content in current cost disclosures.)

While the majority of share price studies show little or no reaction to price-adjusted accounting information, it is possible that the failure to find a significant share price reaction might have been due to limitations in the research methods used. For example, there could have been other information released around the time of the release of the CCA/CPP information. However, with the weight of research that indicates little or no reaction by the share market, we are probably on safe ground to believe that the market does not value such information when disclosed within the annual report. Of course there are a number of issues why the capital market might not react to such information. Perhaps individuals or organizations are able to obtain this information from sources other than corporate annual reports, and hence, as the market is already aware of the information, no reaction would then be expected when the annual reports are released.

Apart from analysing share price reactions, another way to investigate the apparent usefulness of particular information is to undertake surveys. Surveys of managers (for example Ferguson and Wines, 1986) have indicated limited corporate support for CCA, with managers citing such issues as the expense, the limited benefits from disclosure, and a lack of agreement as to the appropriate approach to explain the limited support for CCA.

In the United States, and in relation to the relevance of FASB Statement No. 33 (which required a mixture of CCA and CPP information), Elliot (1986, p. 33) states:

> FASB Statement No. 33 requires the disclosure of value information on one or two bases, either price level adjusted or current cost. Surveys taken since this rule became effective suggest that users do not find the information helpful, don't use it, and they say it doesn't tell them anything they didn't already know. Preparers of the information complain that it is a nuisance to assemble.

Given the above results, we can perhaps say that, in general, there is limited evidence to support the view that the methods used to account for changing prices have been deemed to be successful in providing information of relevance to financial statement users. This is an interesting outcome, particularly given that many organizations over time have elected to provide CCA/CPP information in their annual reports even when there was no requirement to do so, and also given that many organizations have actively lobbied for or against the particular methods of accounting. Adopting the method for disclosure purposes, or lobbying for it, implies that corporate management, at least, considered that the information was relevant and likely to impact on behaviour – a view at odds with some of the surveys and share price studies reported earlier.

In relation to research that has attempted to analyse the motivations underlying the corporate adoption of alternative accounting methods, an influential paper was Watts and Zimmerman (1978). That paper is generally considered to be one of the most important papers in the development of Positive Accounting Theory (which we consider in Chapter 7). The authors investigated the lobbying positions taken by corporate managers with respect to the FASB's 1974 Discussion Memorandum on general price level accounting (current purchasing power accounting). As we know from material presented in this chapter, if general price level accounting were introduced, then in times of rising prices, reported profits would be reduced relative to profits reported under historical cost conventions. The reduction in profits would be due to such effects as higher depreciation and purchasing power losses due to holding net monetary assets.

Watts and Zimmerman proposed that the political process was a major factor in explaining which corporate managers were more likely to favour or oppose the introduction of general price level accounting. The political process itself is seen as a competition for wealth transfers. For example, some groups may lobby government to transfer wealth away from particular companies or industries (for example, through increased taxes, decreased tariff support, decreased subsidies, increases in wages awarded, more stringent licensing arrangements) and towards other organizations or groups otherwise considered to be poorly treated. Apart from government, groups such as consumer groups (perhaps through product boycotts), employee groups (through wage demands or strikes) and community interest groups (through impeding operations or lobbying government) can act to transfer wealth away from organizations through political processes.

The perspective of Watts and Zimmerman was that entities deemed to be politically visible are more likely to favour methods of accounting that allow them to reduce their reported profits. High profitability itself was considered to be one attribute that could lead to the unwanted (and perhaps costly) attention and scrutiny of particular corporations.

The corporate lobbying positions in the submissions made to the FASB are explained by Watts and Zimmerman on the basis of self-interest considerations (rather than any consideration of such issues as the 'public interest').[28] The study suggests that large firms (and large firms are considered to be more politically sensitive) favour general price level accounting because it enables them to report lower profits.[29, 30]

Other research has also shown that companies might have supported CCA for the political benefits it provided. In times of rising prices, the adoption of CCA (as with

---

[28] As we discuss in Chapter 7, and as we already discussed in earlier chapters, one of the central assumptions of Positive Accounting Theory is that all individual action is motivated by self-interest considerations, with that interest being directly tied to the goal of maximizing an individual's own wealth.

[29] Ball and Foster (1982), however, indicate that size can be a proxy for many things other than political sensitivity (such as industry membership).

[30] Within the Watts and Zimmerman study many of the respondents were members of the oil industry and such industry members were also inclined to favour the introduction of general price level accounting. Consistent with the political cost hypothesis, 1974 (the time of the submissions) was a time of intense scrutiny of oil companies.

general price level accounting) can lead to reduced profits. In a New Zealand study, Wong (1988) investigated the accounting practices of New Zealand companies between 1977 and 1981 and found that corporations that adopted CCA had higher effective tax rates and larger market concentration ratios than entities that did not adopt CCA, both variables being suggestive of political visibility. In a UK study, Sutton (1988) found that politically sensitive companies were more likely to lobby in favour of CCA. Sutton investigated lobbying submissions made in the United Kingdom in relation to an exposure draft of a proposed accounting standard that recommended the disclosure of CCA information. Applying a Positive Accounting Theory perspective he found support for a view that organizations that considered they would benefit from the requirement tended to lobby in support of it. Those expected to benefit were:

- capital-intensive firms because it was expected that the adoption of CCA would lead to decreased profits (due to higher depreciation) and this would be particularly beneficial if the method was accepted for the purposes of taxation; and
- politically sensitive firms, as it would allow them to show reduced profits.

Examining possible perceived political 'benefits' of inflation-adjusted accounting information from a different perspective, Broadbent and Laughlin (2005) draw on debates in the United Kingdom in the 1970s to argue that the then British government considered CPP as likely to produce undesirable economic impacts compared to CCA. The main issue was that the government believed CPP accounts could foster disinvestment at a time when the UK economy needed investment. In support of their argument, Broadbent and Laughlin (2005) quote Bryer and Brignall (1985, p. 32) who state that in launching a governmental committee of inquiry to examine inflation accounting a government minister had commented that:

> inflation accounting ... involved issues much broader than pure account-ing matters. The committee would 'take into account a broad range of issues including the implications for investment and efficiency; allocation of resources through the capital market; the need to restrain inflation in the UK'. [31]

5.8 Professional support for various approaches to accounting for changing prices and asset values

Over time, varying levels of support have been given to different approaches to accounting in times of rising prices. CPP was generally favoured by accounting standard-setters from the 1960s to the mid-1970s, with a number of countries, including the United States, the United Kingdom, Canada, Australia, New Zealand, Ireland, Argentina, Chile and Mexico, issuing documents that supported the approach. For example, in the United States the American Institute of Certified Public Accountants (AICPA) supported general price level restatement in Accounting Research Study No. 6 released in 1961. The Accounting Principles Board also supported the practice in Statement No. 3.

---

[31] This quotation indicates the existence of broader perceived economic impacts of accounting regulation, as discussed in Chapter 3.

Early in its existence, the FASB also issued an exposure draft supporting the use of general purchasing power – 'Financial Reporting in Units of General Purchasing Power' – which required CPP to be disclosed as supplementary information.

From about 1975, preference tended to shift to CCA. In 1976 the SEC released ASR 190 which required certain large organizations to provide supplementary information about 'the estimated current replacement cost of inventories and productive capacity at the end of the fiscal year for which a balance sheet [now referred to as a Statement of Financial Position] is required and the approximate amount of cost of sales and depreciation based on replacement cost for the two most recent full fiscal years'. In Australia, a Statement of Accounting Practice (SAP 1) entitled 'Current Cost Accounting' was issued in 1983. Although not mandatory, SAP 1 recommended that reporting entities provide supplementary CCA information. In the United Kingdom, support for CCA was demonstrated by the Sandilands Committee (a government committee) in 1975. In 1980 the Accounting Standards Committee (UK) issued SSAP 16, which required supplementary disclosure of current cost data (SSAP 16 was withdrawn in 1985).

In the late 1970s and early 1980s many accounting standard-setters issued recommendations that favoured disclosure based upon a mixture of CPP and CCA. Such 'mixed' reporting recommendations were released in the United States, the United Kingdom, Canada, Australia, New Zealand, Ireland, West Germany and Mexico. For example, in 1979 the FASB released SFAS 33 which required a mixture of information, including:

- purchasing power gains and losses on net monetary assets;
- income determined on a current cost basis; and
- current costs of year-end inventory and property plant and equipment.

Around the mid-1980s, generally a time of falling inflation, accounting professions worldwide tended to move away from issues associated with accounting in times of changing prices (as demonstrated by the UK's withdrawal of SSAP 16 in 1985).

It is an interesting exercise to consider why particular methods of accounting did not gain and maintain professional support. Perhaps it was because (as indicated in Broadbent and Laughlin, 2005) the profession, like a number of researchers, questioned the relevance of the information, particularly in times of lower inflation. If they did question the relevance of the information to various parties (such as the capital market) it would be difficult for them to support regulation from a 'public interest' perspective, given the costs that would be involved in implementing a new system of accounting.[32]

Even in the absence of concerns about the relevance of the information, standard-setters might have been concerned that a drastic change in our accounting conventions could cause widespread disruption and confusion in the capital markets and therefore might not be in the public interest. Although there have been numerous accounting controversies and disputes over time (for example, how to account for goodwill or research and development, or how to account for investments in associates), such controversies typically impact on only a small subset of accounts. Adopting a new model of accounting would have much more widespread effects, which again might not have been in the public interest.

---

[32] Broadbent and Laughlin (2005) argue that the conception of 'public interest' will both vary from person to person (or interest group to interest group) and will also change over time.

It has also been speculated that the adoption of a new method of accounting could have had consequences for the amount of taxation that the government ultimately collected from businesses. As Zeff and Dharan (1996, p. 632) state:

> Some governments fear that an accounting regimen of generally lower reported profits under current cost accounting (with physical capital maintenance) would lead to intensified pressure for a concomitant reform of corporate income tax law.

Throughout the 1970s and 1980s, many organizations opposed the introduction of alternative methods of accounting (alternative to historical cost). Corporate opposition to various alternative methods of accounting could also be explained by the notion of self-interest as embraced within the economic interest theory of regulation. Under historical cost accounting, management has a mechanism available to manage its reported profitability. Holding gains might not be recognized for income purposes until such time as the assets are sold. For example, an organization might have acquired shares in another organization some years earlier. In periods in which reported profits are expected to be lower than management wants, management could elect to sell some of the shares to offset other losses. If alternative methods of accounting were introduced, this ability to manipulate reported results could be lost.[33] Hence such corporations might have lobbied government, the basis of the submissions being rooted in self-interest. Because there are typically corporate or business representatives on most standard-setting bodies, there is also the possibility that corporations/business interests were able to capture effectively the standard-setting process (Walker, 1987).

As we have already seen in this chapter, there is some evidence that accounting information adjusted to take account of changing prices might not be relevant to the decision-making processes of those parties involved in the capital market (as reflected by various share price studies) and hence the alternative models of accounting might not be favoured by analysts (accepting the private economic interest theory of regulation, analysts might have little to gain personally if the alternative methods of accounting were introduced).

Of course we will never know for sure why particular parties did not favour particular accounting models, but what we can see is that alternative explanations can be provided from public interest theory, capture theory or the economic interest theory of regulation – theories that were discussed at greater length in earlier chapters.

Throughout the CCA/CPP debates a number of key academics continued to promote their favoured methods of accounting (and some continued to do so throughout the 1990s). We can obviously speculate what drove them – was it the public interest or was it self-interest? What do you think?

We can see that the debate is far from settled as to which method of accounting is most appropriate in accounting for changing prices. While debate in this area has generally abated since the mid-1980s it is very possible that, if levels of inflation increase to their previously high levels, such debates will again be ignited. Various authors have

---

[33] In recent years the discretion of management in relation to the measurement of equity investments has been reduced. IAS 39 stipulates a general requirement that such investments shall be measured at fair value.

developed accounting models that differ in many respects. Some of these differences are due to fundamental differences of opinion about the role of accounting and the sort of information necessary for effective decision-making. Because information generated by systems of accounting based on the historical cost convention is used in many decisions, major change in accounting conventions would conceivably have widespread social and economic impacts. This in itself will restrict any major modifications/changes to our (somewhat outdated) accounting system. This perspective was reflected in the 1960s, and arguably the perspective is just as relevant now.

As an example of how the profession has typically been reluctant to implement major reforms, we can consider activities undertaken in 1961 and 1962, when the Accounting Research Division of AICPA commissioned studies by Moonitz (1961), and by Sprouse and Moonitz (1962) respectively. In these documents the authors proposed that accounting measurement systems be changed from historical cost to a system based on current values. However, prior to the release of the Sprouse and Moonitz study the Accounting Principles Board of AICPA stated in relation to the Moonitz and the Sprouse and Moonitz studies that 'while these studies are a valuable contribution to accounting principles, they are too radically different from generally accepted principles for acceptance at this time' (Statement by the Accounting Principles Board, AICPA, April 1962).

As we have seen in the earlier discussion of fair value accounting, there is widespread support among accounting standard-setters for an increasing use of fair values. However, many practitioners still question the growing use of fair value accounting.

While this chapter has emphasized various issues and debates associated with how best to measure the financial performance of an entity in times when prices are changing, we must remember that financial performance is only one facet of the total performance of an entity. As we see in Chapter 9, there is much debate about how to measure and report information on the social and environmental performance of reporting entities. As with the debate we have considered in this chapter, the debates about the appropriate methodology and relevance of social and environmental information are far from settled. As has been emphasized, the practice of accounting generates a multitude of interesting debates.

Chapter summary

This chapter has explored different models of accounting that have been developed to provide financial information in periods of rising prices and other changing market conditions that impact on asset values. These models have been developed because of the perceived limitations of historical cost accounting. Critics of historical cost accounting suggest that because historical cost adopts a capital maintenance perspective which is tied to maintaining financial capital intact, it tends to overstate profits in periods of rising prices. Historical cost accounting adopts an assumption that the purchasing power of currency remains constant over time. Debate about the best model of accounting to use in periods of rising prices was vigorous in the 1960s through to the mid-1980s. During this time, inflation levels tended to be relatively high. Since this time, inflation levels internationally have tended to be low and the debate about which model to adopt to adjust for rising prices has tended to wane. Nevertheless, there has been a general movement by regulators such as the IASB towards the use of fair values in various accounting standards – although the adoption of fair value tends to be on a piecemeal basis as particular accounting standards are developed. With this said, however, there are still various assets that are measured on the basis of historical costs.[34]

A number of alternative models have been suggested. For example, CPP was one of the earlier models to be developed. CPP was supported by a number of professional accounting bodies during the 1960s and 1970s, although support then tended to shift to CCA. CPP uses numbers generated by historical cost accounting as the basis of the financial statements and at the end of each period CPP applies a price index, typically a general price index, to adjust the historical cost numbers. For purposes of the statement of financial position, adjustments are made to non-monetary assets. Monetary items are not adjusted by the price index. However, although monetary items are not adjusted for disclosure purposes, holding monetary items will lead to gains or losses in purchasing power which are recognized in the period's profit or loss. No gains or losses are recorded in relation to holding non-monetary items. One of the advantages of using CPP is that it is easy to apply. It simply uses the historical cost accounting numbers that are already available and applies a price index to these numbers. A disadvantage is that the adjusted prices may provide a poor reflection of the actual value of the items in question.

Another model of accounting that we considered was current cost accounting (CCA). It uses actual valuations of assets, typically based on replacement costs, and operating income is calculated after consideration of the replacement costs of the assets used in the production and sale cycle. Non-monetary assets are adjusted to take account of changes in replacement costs, and depreciation expenses are also adjusted on the basis of changes in replacement costs. While not in use today, CCA attracted support from professional accounting bodies in the early 1980s. Opponents of CCA argued that replacement costs have little relevance if an entity is not considering replacing an asset and, further, that replacement costs might not accurately reflect the current market values of the assets in question.

A further issue we considered related to changing assets values was fair value accounting. This is currently a controversial practice both among professional accountants and researchers, and has generated heated debates over its advantages and disadvantages. However, its use looks set to continue growing.

Questions

5.1 What assumptions, if any, does historical cost accounting make about the purchasing power of the currency?

5.2 List some of the criticisms that can be made of historical cost accounting when it is applied in times of rising prices.

---

[34] For example, inventory and property, plant and equipment where the entity has elected to adopt the 'cost model'.

5.3   Why do you think that corporate management might prefer to be allowed to use historical costs rather than being required to value assets on the basis of current values?

5.4   As shown in this chapter, Mautz (1973) made the following statement:

> Accounting is what it is today not so much because of the desire of accountants as because of the influence of businessmen. If those who make management and investment decisions had not found financial reports based on historical cost useful over the years, changes in accounting would long since have been made.

Required:

Evaluate the above statement.

5.5   What is the 'additivity' problem inherent in historical cost accounting?

5.6   Explain the difference between income derived from the viewpoint of maintaining financial capital (as in historical cost accounting) and income derived from a system of ensuring that physical capital remains intact.

5.7   In current purchasing power accounting:

    a Why is it necessary to consider monetary assets separately from non-monetary assets?

    b Why will holding monetary assets lead to a purchasing power loss, but holding non-monetary assets does not lead to a purchasing power loss?

5.8   What are holding gains, and how are holding gains treated if current cost accounting is applied? Do we need to differentiate between realized and unrealized holding gains?

5.9   Should 'profits' that result from holding gains be allowed to be distributed to shareholders? Explain your view.

5.10 What are some of the major strengths and weaknesses of historical cost accounting?

5.11 What are some of the major strengths and weaknesses of current purchasing power accounting?

5.12 What are some of the major strengths and weaknesses of current cost accounting (applying replacement costs)?

5.13 Despite the efforts of authors such as Chambers, Edwards and Bell, and Sterling, historical cost accounting has maintained its position of dominance in how we do financial accounting. Why do you think that historical cost accounting has remained the principal method of accounting?

5.14 As indicated in this chapter, various studies have provided support for a view that CCA/CPP is of little relevance to users of financial statements. Nevertheless numerous organizations lobbied in support of the methods, as well as voluntarily providing such information in their annual reports. Why do you think this is so?

5.15 The IASB Framework for the Preparation and Presentation of Financial Statements does not prescribe a specific approach to measurement. However, in recent years accounting standards have been released which have shown a movement away from historical costs and a movement towards the use of fair values. Why do you think this is occurring? Further, why do you think that conceptual frameworks have not been amended to suggest an alternative to historical costs – such as the use of fair values?

5.16 According to Watts and Zimmerman (1978), what factors appeared to motivate corporate management to lobby in support of general price level accounting (current purchase power accounting)?

5.17 Critically evaluate the claimed procyclical role of fair value accounting. How persuasive are arguments that fair value accounting's procyclicality should reduce the use of fair value accounting?

5.18 Compare and contrast level 1, level 2 and level 3 fair value measurements. What implications do these different measurement techniques have for the reliability of fair value disclosures?

References

Abbott, A. (1988) *The System of Professions*, Chicago, IL: Chicago University Press.

Ball, R. & Foster, G. (1982) 'Corporate financial reporting: A methodological review of empirical research', *Studies on Current Research Methodologies in Accounting: A Critical Evaluation, the Journal of Accounting Research*, **20** (Supplement), 161–234.

Beaver, W., Christie, A. & Griffin, p. (1980) 'The information content of SEC ASR 190', *Journal of Accounting and Economics*, **2**, 127–57.

Beaver, W. & Landsman, W. (1987) *The Incremental Information Content of FAS 33 Disclosures*,. Stamford, CT: FASB.

Broadbent, J. & Laughlin, R. (2005) 'Government concerns and tensions in accounting standard setting: The case of accounting for the private finance initiative in the UK', *Accounting and Business Research*, **35** (3), 207–28.

Bryer, R. & Brignall, S. (1985) 'The GAAP in inflation accounting debate', *Accountancy*, **96**, 32–33.

Bublitz, B., Freka, T. & McKeown, J. (1985) 'Market association tests and FASB statement 33 disclosures: A re-examination', *Journal of Accounting Research*, (Supplement), 1–23.

Canning, J.B. (1929) *The Economics of Accountancy: A Critical Analysis of Accounting Theory*, New York: Ronald Press.

Chambers, R.J. (1955) 'Blueprint for a theory of accounting', *Accounting Research* (January), 17–55.

Chambers, R.J. (1966) *Accounting, Evaluation and Economic Behavior*, Englewood Cliffs, NJ: Prentice-Hall.

Chambers, R.J. (1995) 'An introduction to price variation and inflation accounting research', in: Jones, S., Romana, C. & Ratnatunga, J. (eds.) *Accounting Theory: A Contemporary Review*, Sydney: Harcourt Brace.

Dyckman, T.R. (1969) *Studies in Accounting Research No. 1: Investment Analysis and General Price Level Adjustments*, Evanston, IL: American Accounting Association.

Edwards, E. (1975) 'The state of current value accounting', *Accounting Review*, **50** (2), 235–45.

Edwards, E.O. & Bell, P.W. (1961) *The Theory and Measurement of Business*

Income, Berkeley, CA: University of California Press.

Elliot, R.K. (1986) 'Dinosaurs, passenger pigeons, and financial accountants', *World,* 32–35.

Ferguson, C. & Wines, G. (1986) 'Incidence of the use of current cost accounting in published annual financial statements', *Accounting Forum* (March).

Gheyara, K. & Boatsman, J. (1980) 'Market reaction to the 1976 replacement cost disclosures', *Journal of Accounting and Economics,* **2** (2), 107–25.

Grady, P. (1965) 'An inventory of generally accepted accounting principles for business enterprises', *Accounting Research Study No. 7,* New York: AICPA.

Gray, R., Owen, D. & Adams, C. (1996) *Accounting and Accountability: Changes and Challenges in Corporate Social and Environmental Reporting,* London: Prentice-Hall.

Hicks, J.R. (1946) *Value and Capital,* Oxford: Oxford: University Press.

Hopwood, A.G. (2009) 'Exploring the interface between accounting and finance', *Accounting, Organizations and Society,* **34** (5), 549–50.

IASB (2010) *Staff Draft of Proposed IFRS on Fair Value Measurement,* London: IFRS Foundation.

Laux, C. & Leuz, C. (2009) 'The crisis of fair-value accounting: Making sense of the recent debate', *Accounting, Organizations and Society,* **34** (6–7), 826–34.

Lobo, G. & Song, I. (1989) 'The incremental information in SFAS 33 income disclosures over historical cost income and its cash and accrual components', *Accounting Review,* **64** (2), 329–43.

MacNeal, K. (1970) *Truth in Accounting,* Lawrence, KS: Scholars Book Company.

Mautz, R.K. (1973) 'A few words for historical cost', *Financial Executive,* (January), 23–27 & 93–98.

Moonitz, M. (1961) 'The basic postulates of accounting', *Accounting Research Study No. 1,* New York: AICPA.

Morris, R.C. (1975) 'Evidence of the impact of inflation on share prices', *Accounting and Business Research* (Spring), 87–95.

Murdoch, B. (1986) 'The information content of FAS 33 returns on equity', *The Accounting Review,* **61** (2), 273–87.

Nobes, C. & Parker, R. (2010) *Comparative International Accounting,* Harlow: Pearson Education Limited.

Paton, W.A. (1922) *Accounting Theory,* Lawrence, KS: Scholars Book Co, reprinted 1973.

Peterson, R.J. (1975) 'A portfolio analysis of general price-level restatement', *The Accounting Review,* **50** (3), 525–32.

Power, M. (2010) 'Fair value accounting, financial economics and the transformation of reliability', *Accounting & Business Research,* **40** (3), 197–210.

Ro, B.T. (1980) 'The adjustment of security returns to the disclosure of replacement cost accounting information', *Journal of Accounting and Economics,* **2** (2), 159–89.

Ro, B.T. (1981) 'The disclosure of replacement cost accounting data and its effect on transaction volumes', *Accounting Review,* **56** (1), 70–84.

Roberts, D.L., Staunton, J. J. & Hagan, L. L. (1995) 'Accounting for self-generating and regenerating assets', *Discussion Paper No. 23.* Melbourne: Australian Accounting Research Foundation.

Ronen, J. (2008) 'To fair value or not to fair value: A broader perspective', *ABACUS,* **44** (2), 181–208.

Schaefer, T. (1984) 'The information content of current cost income relative to dividends and historical cost income', *Journal of Accounting Research,* **22** (2), 647–56.

Solomons, D. (1966) 'An overview of exit price accounting', *ABACUS,* **2** (2), 205–209.

Sprouse, R. & Moonitz, M. (1962) 'A tentative set of broad accounting principles for business enterprises', *Accounting Research Study No. 3,* New York: AICPA.

Sterling, R.R. (1970a) 'On theory construction and verification', *Accounting Review,* **45** (4), 444–57.

Sterling, R.R. (1970b) *Theory of the Measurement of Enterprise Income,* Lawrence, KS: University of Kansas Press.

Sutton, T.G. (1988) 'The proposed introduction of current cost accounting in the UK: Determinants of corporate preference', *Journal of Accounting and Economics,* **10** (2), 127–49.

Sweeney, H.W. (1964) *Stabilised Accounting,* originally published in 1936, New York: Holt Rinehart and Winston.

Walker, R.G. (1987) 'Australia's ASRB: A case study of political activity and regulatory capture', *Accounting and Business Research,* **17** (67), 269–86.

Watts, R.L. & Zimmerman, J. L. (1978) 'Towards a positive theory of the determination of accounting standards', *The Accounting Review,* **53** (1), 112–34.

Whitley, R. (1986) 'The transformation of business finance into financial economics: The roles of academic expansion and changes in U.S. capital markets', *Accounting, Organizations and Society,* **11** (2), 171–92.

Whittington, G. (2008) 'Fair value and the IASB/FASB conceptual framework project: An alternative view', *ABACUS,* **44** (2), 139–168.

Wong, J. (1988) 'Economic incentives for the voluntary disclosure of current cost financial statements', *Journal of Accounting and Economics,* **10** (2), 151–67.

Zeff, S.A. (2007) 'The SEC rules historical cost accounting: 1934 to the 1970s', *Accounting & Business Research,* **37** (Special issue), 49–62.

Zeff, S.A. & Dharan, B. G. (1996) *Readings and Notes on Financial Accounting,* New York: McGraw-Hill.

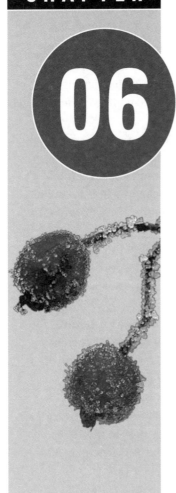

CHAPTER

06

Normative Theories of Accounting 2: The Case of Conceptual Framework Projects

❖ *LEARNING OBJECTIVES*

Upon completing this chapter readers should:

❖ understand the role that conceptual frameworks can play in the practice of financial reporting;

❖ be aware of the history of the development of the various existing conceptual framework projects;

❖ be able to identify, explain and critically evaluate the various building blocks that have been developed within various conceptual framework projects;

❖ be able to identify some of the perceived advantages and disadvantages that arise from the establishment and development of conceptual frameworks;

❖ be aware of some recent initiatives being jointly undertaken by the International Accounting Standards Board and the Financial Accounting Standards Board to develop an improved conceptual framework of financial reporting;

❖ be able to identify some factors, including political factors, that might help or hinder the development of conceptual framework projects;

❖ be able to explain which groups within society are likely to benefit from the establishment and development of conceptual framework projects.

Opening issues

For many years the practice of financial accounting lacked a generally accepted theory that clearly enunciated the objectives of financial reporting, the required qualitative characteristics of financial information, or provided clear guidance as to when and how to recognize and measure the various elements of accounting. In the absence of an accepted theory, accounting standards tended to be developed in a rather *ad hoc* manner with various inconsistencies between different standards. For example, various accounting standards relating to different classes of assets used different recognition and measurement criteria. It has been argued that the development of a conceptual framework would lead to improved financial reporting, and this improved reporting would provide benefits to the various financial statement readers as it would enable them to make more informed resource allocation decisions. Do you agree with this argument, and what is the basis of your view?

6.1 Introduction

In Chapter 5 we considered a number of normative theories developed by some notable accounting academics to address various accounting issues associated with how financial accounting *should* be undertaken in the presence of changing prices (typically increasing prices associated with inflation). These theories included current purchasing power accounting, current cost accounting and continuously contemporary accounting (or exit price accounting). As revealed in Chapter 5, the various normative theories, which represented quite significant departures from existing accounting practice, failed to be embraced by professional accounting bodies and regulators throughout the world, and with the decline in levels of inflation within most countries debate about the relative benefits of alternative approaches of accounting for changing prices has subsided in recent years. However, in recent times there has nevertheless been an increasing propensity for accounting standard-setters to adopt fair value as the basis for measuring many assets, and to thereby move away from using historical cost for many assets.

While the various normative theories discussed in Chapter 5, which were advanced to deal with changing prices, did not ultimately gain the support of accounting professions, professional accounting bodies within countries such as the United States, the United Kingdom, Canada, Australia and New Zealand, as well as the International Accounting Standards Committee (IASC, which subsequently became the International Accounting

Standards Board (IASB)), have undertaken work to develop conceptual frameworks for accounting, which in themselves can be considered to constitute *normative theories of accounting*. In this chapter we consider what is meant by the term 'conceptual framework' and we consider why particular professional bodies thought there was a need to develop them. We see that there are numerous perceived advantages and disadvantages associated with conceptual frameworks and we consider certain arguments that have been advanced to suggest that conceptual frameworks play a part in *legitimizing* the existence of the accounting profession. Countries that have adopted IFRSs (including all EU countries) in effect currently utilize the conceptual framework released by the IASB which is known as the *IASB Framework for the Preparation and Presentation of Financial Statements* (or simply known as the IASB Framework). Therefore, much of the discussion in this chapter will refer to the guidance provided in the IASB Framework. However, as this chapter will explain, there is currently a joint initiative being undertaken by the IASB and the US Financial Accounting Standards Board (FASB) in which both Boards are working together to develop a revised conceptual framework. This work is being undertaken in a number of stages and the expectation is that the framework will not be completed for a number of years. At various points in this chapter we will refer to some recent publications that have already emanated from the joint efforts of the IASB and FASB, as such publications provide an indication of what prescriptions might be embodied within our future conceptual framework.

6.2 What is a conceptual framework of accounting?

There is no definitive view of what constitutes a 'conceptual framework'. The FASB in the United States, which developed one of the first conceptual frameworks in accounting, defined its conceptual framework as 'a coherent system of interrelated objectives and fundamentals that is expected to lead to consistent standards' (Statement of Financial Accounting Concepts No. 1: *Objectives of Financial Reporting by Business Enterprises, 1978*).

In Chapter 1 we provided a definition of 'theory' (from the *Oxford English Dictionary*) as 'A scheme or system of ideas or statements held as an explanation or account of a group of facts or phenomena'. This definition was similar to that provided by the accounting researcher Hendriksen (1970, p. 1). He defined a theory as 'a coherent set of hypothetical, conceptual and pragmatic principles forming the general framework of reference for a field of inquiry'. Looking at these definitions of 'theory' and looking at the FASB's definition of its conceptual framework, it is reasonable to argue that the conceptual framework attempts to provide a theory of accounting, and one that appears quite structured. Because conceptual frameworks provide a great deal of *prescription* (that is, they prescribe certain actions, such as when to recognize an asset for financial statement purposes) they are considered to have *normative* characteristics. According to the FASB, the conceptual framework 'prescribes the nature, function and limits of financial accounting and reporting' (as stated in Statement of Financial Accounting Concepts No. 1: *Objectives of Financial Reporting by Business Enterprises, 1978*).

In recent years, the FASB and the IASB have been undertaking an initiative to develop, on a joint basis, an improved conceptual framework for financial reporting. In July 2006 the FASB and the IASB jointly published a discussion paper entitled *Preliminary Views on an Improved Conceptual Framework for Financial Reporting: The Objective of Financial*

Reporting and Qualitative Characteristics of Decision-useful Financial Reporting Information (IASB, 2006). That paper was the first in a series of publications jointly developed by the two Boards as part of a project to develop a common conceptual framework for financial reporting. The boards received nearly 200 responses to the discussion paper and in May 2008, after considering the various comments, they released an Exposure Draft for the proposed first two chapters of the new conceptual framework. The document was entitled: *Exposure Draft of an Improved Conceptual Framework for Financial Reporting* (IASB, 2008c) and this phase of the project specifically addressed the objective of financial reporting and the qualitative characteristics and constraints of decision-useful financial reporting information. According to the Exposure Draft (p. 12), the conceptual framework is:

> a coherent system of concepts that flow from an objective. The objective of financial reporting is the foundation of the framework. The other concepts provide guidance on identifying the boundaries of financial reporting; selecting the transactions, other events and circumstances to be represented; how they should be recognised and measured (or disclosed); and how they should be summarised and communicated in financial reports.

As the above definition indicates, the *objective of financial reporting* is the fundamental building block for the conceptual framework currently being jointly developed by the IASB and the FASB. Hence, if particular individuals or parties disagreed with the objective identified by the IASB and the FASB then they would most likely disagree with the various prescriptions provided within the revised conceptual framework. We will return later in the chapter to a discussion of the objective of financial reporting currently proposed by IABS/FASB.[1]

The view taken by people involved in developing conceptual frameworks tends to be that if the practice of financial reporting is to be developed logically and consistently (which might be important for creating public confidence in the practice of accounting) we first need to develop some consensus on important issues such as what we actually mean by *financial reporting* and what should be its scope; what organizational characteristics or attributes indicate that an entity should produce general purpose financial reports; what the *objective* of financial reporting is; what *qualitative characteristics* financial information should possess; what the elements of financial reporting are; what measurement rules should be employed in relation to the various elements of accounting; and so forth. It has been proposed that unless we have some agreement on fundamental issues, such as those mentioned above, accounting standards will be developed in a rather *ad hoc* or piecemeal manner with limited consistency between the various accounting standards developed over time.

It is perhaps somewhat illogical to consider how to account for a particular item of expenditure if we have not, as FASB and IASB propose, agreed in the first place on what the *objective* of financial accounting actually is, or indeed on issues such as what an *asset* is or what a *liability* is. Nevertheless, for many years accounting standards were developed

---

[1] As we will see later in the chapter, the objective of financial reporting as provided in the Draft Conceptual Framework document released by the IASB and FASB in 2008 is stated as follows (IASB, 2008c, p. 12): The objective of general purpose financial reporting is to provide financial information about the reporting entity that is useful to present and potential equity investors, lenders and other creditors in making decisions in their capacity as capital providers. Information that is decision-useful to capital providers may also be useful to other users of financial reporting who are not capital providers.

in many countries in the absence of conceptual frameworks. For example, the United Kingdom's Accounting Standards Board initiated a conceptual framework development project in 1991. However, recommendations related to the practice of accounting first started being released in the United Kingdom in the 1940s, followed some years later by accounting standards. By the time the United Kingdom's conceptual framework (entitled *The Statement of Principles*) was issued in 1999, there were already many accounting standards in place. In the absence of a conceptual framework, and reflective of the lack of agreement in many key areas of financial reporting, there was a degree of inconsistency between the various accounting standards that were being released within the United Kingdom. This absence of a conceptual framework led to a great deal of criticism. As Horngren (1981, p. 94) states:

> All regulatory bodies have been flayed because they have used piecemeal approaches, solving one accounting issue at a time. Observers have alleged that not enough tidy rationality has been used in the process of accounting policy-making. Again and again, critics have cited a need for a conceptual framework.

In developing a conceptual framework for accounting it is considered that there are a number of 'building blocks' that must be developed. The framework must be developed in a particular order, with some issues necessarily requiring agreement before work can move on to subsequent 'building blocks'. Figure 6.1 provides an overview of the framework developed in the late 1980s by the IASC, and which was later adopted by the IASC's successor – the IASB. While initially referred to as the IASC Framework, it is now referred to as the *IASB Framework for the Preparation and Presentation of Financial Statements* (or simply referred to as the IASB Framework). This is the framework that the IASB is to use until such time that the new conceptual framework being jointly developed by the IASB and the FASB is released.

The IASC/IASB view of a conceptual framework is also broadly consistent with the definitions in the conceptual frameworks developed by some individual countries, although the relative emphasis given to the different components tends to vary slightly from one framework to another.

As we can see, the first issue to be addressed is the definition of *financial reporting*. Unless there is some agreement on this it would be difficult to construct a framework for financial reporting. Having determined what financial reporting means, attention is then turned to the *subject* of financial reporting, specifically which entities are required to produce general purpose financial reports,[2] and the likely characteristics of the users of these reports. Attention is then turned to the *objective* of financial reporting. As we will see shortly, the objective of general purpose financial reporting provided in the IASB Framework is deemed to be:

> to provide information about the financial position, performance and changes in financial position of an entity that is useful to a wide range of users in making

---

[2] Conceptual frameworks of accounting relate to general purpose financial reporting (which meets the needs of a multitude of user groups, many of which have information needs in common) as opposed to special purpose financial reports (special purpose financial reports are specifically designed to meet the information needs of a specific user or group). We consider definitions of general purpose financial reporting in more depth later in this chapter.

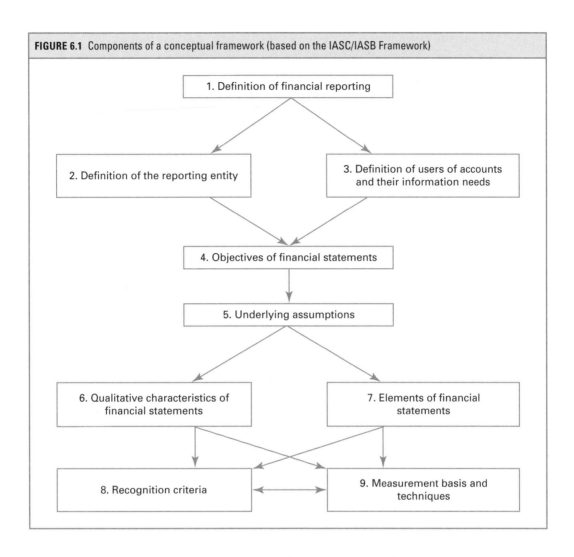

FIGURE 6.1 Components of a conceptual framework (based on the IASC/IASB Framework)

1. Definition of financial reporting

2. Definition of the reporting entity

3. Definition of users of accounts and their information needs

4. Objectives of financial statements

5. Underlying assumptions

6. Qualitative characteristics of financial statements

7. Elements of financial statements

8. Recognition criteria

9. Measurement basis and techniques

economic decisions (paragraph 12 of the IASC *Framework for the Preparation and Presentation of Financial Statements*).

If it is accepted that this is the objective of financial reporting, the next step is to determine the basic underlying assumptions and qualitative characteristics of financial information necessary to allow users to make economic decisions. We address these issues later in this chapter.

Over time, it is to be expected that perspectives of the role of financial reporting will change. Consistent with this view, there is an expectation by many, including accounting standard-setters, that the development of conceptual frameworks will continue. They will evolve over time. This view that conceptual frameworks will evolve over time is consistent with comments made by the IASB and FASB in relation to works being undertaken in developing the revised conceptual framework. They state (IASB, 2008c, p. 9):

> To provide the best foundation for developing principle-based common standards, the boards have undertaken a joint project to develop a common and improved conceptual framework. The goals for the project include updating

and refining the existing concepts to reflect changes in markets, business practices and the economic environment that occurred in the two or more decades since the concepts were developed.

In the discussion that follows we consider the history of the development of conceptual frameworks in different countries. We see that conceptual frameworks are largely prescriptive, or normative in approach, for example indicating how the elements of accounting (the elements being assets, liabilities, income, expenses and equity) are defined and when they *should* be recognized. However, we also see that in certain cases, because of apparent coercion by powerful interest groups, parts of certain conceptual frameworks became descriptive of current practice, with limited implications for changing existing accounting practices.

6.3 A brief overview of the history of the development of conceptual frameworks

A number of countries, such as the United States, the United Kingdom, Ireland, Canada, Australia and New Zealand have undertaken various activities directed to the development of a conceptual framework. The IASC also undertook work to develop a conceptual framework. There are many similarities (and some differences) between the various conceptual frameworks developed in the different jurisdictions.[3] It is arguable whether any standard-setter anywhere in the world has developed what could be construed as a complete conceptual framework.

One country particularly active in developing frameworks in relation to financial reporting was the United States. Initially, some of the work involved developing *prescriptive* theories of how accounting *should* be undertaken, while other research related to the development of *descriptive* theories of how accounting was generally performed. For example, in 1961 and 1962 the Accounting Research Division of the American Institute of Certified Public Accountants (AICPA) commissioned studies by Moonitz (1961) and Sprouse and Moonitz (1962). These theorists prescribed that accounting practice should move towards a system based on current values rather than historical cost. This work was considered 'too radically different from generally accepted principles' (AICPA, 1973) and was abandoned by the profession. The AICPA then commissioned Grady to develop a

---

[3] This raises issues associated with the possible duplication of effort and whether it might have been more cost efficient for the various countries to pool their resources and develop one unified conceptual framework. However, as Kenneth Most states in Staunton (1984, p. 87) when comparing the Australian and US conceptual frameworks, 'a conceptual framework differs from a straight-jacket; one size does not fit all. The kind of doctrinaire thinkers who have dominated the standard-setting process in this country [United States] are not subject to the same economic, sociological, and professional influences that would affect Australians faced with a similar task'. Consistent with this view, Chapter 4 considered how issues such as *culture* are used to explain differences between the rules released by standard-setters in different countries. However, with the increasing use of IFRSs internationally, and the related adoption of the IASB Framework, it appears that global uniformity (and therefore, a one-size-fits-all-approach), is deemed by accounting regulators to be more important than cultural differences which might influence the information requirements of particular nations or cultures. It would also appear that given the joint work being undertaken by the IASB and FASB then future years will see the introduction of a single conceptual framework for use internationally – again ignoring the view that different countries have different information demands and expectations.

theory of accounting. Grady (1965) was basically descriptive of existing practice (it was based on inductive reasoning – as described in Chapter 1 of this book), thereby being quite uncontroversial. His work led to the release of Accounting Principles Board (APB) Statement No. 4, *Basic Concepts and Accounting Principles Underlying the Financial Statements of Business Enterprises* in 1970. As it was not controversial and simply reflected generally accepted accounting principles of the time, APB Statement No. 4 had a high probability of being acceptable to the AICPA's constituency (Miller and Redding, 1986).

The Trueblood Report

Although APB Statement No. 4 did not cause great controversy, the accounting profession was under some criticism for the apparent lack of any real theoretical framework.[4] The generally accepted accounting principles of the time allowed for much diversity in accounting treatments, and this was seen by many to be a problem. There was an absence of agreement on key issues about the role and objectives of financial reporting, appropriate definition, recognition and measurement rules for the elements of accounting, and so on. Responding to the criticism, the AICPA formed the Trueblood Committee (named after the committee chairperson Robert Trueblood) in 1971. It produced a report, The Trueblood Report (released in 1973 by the AICPA), which listed 12 objectives of accounting and 7 qualitative characteristics that financial information should possess (relevance and materiality; form and substance; reliability; freedom from bias; comparability; consistency; understandability).

Objective 1 of the report was that financial statements are to provide information useful for making economic decisions. That is, there was a focus on the information needs of financial statement users. This objective, which was carried forward to subsequent documents, indicated that *decision usefulness* (as opposed to concepts such as *stewardship*) was a primary objective of financial statements.[5,6] This can be contrasted with previous perspectives of the role of accounting. For example, Accounting Terminology Bulletin No. 1 issued in 1953 by the AICPA made no reference to the information needs of users. It stated:

> Accounting is the art of recording, classifying and summarizing in a significant manner and in terms of money, transactions and events which are in part at least of a financial character, and interpreting the results thereof.

Objective 2 provided by the Trueblood Committee stated that financial statements are primarily to serve those users who have limited authority, ability or resources to obtain information and who rely on financial statements as the principal source of information

---

[4] In relation to APB Statement No. 4, Peasnell (1982, p. 245) notes that 'at best it was a defensive, descriptive document'.

[5] This focus on decision users' needs was also embraced in the earlier document, *A Statement of Basic Accounting Theory*, issued by the American Accounting Association in 1966. It was also embraced in APB Statement No. 4 released in 1970.

[6] 'Decision usefulness' and 'stewardship' are two terms that are often used in relation to the role of financial information. The 'decision usefulness' criterion is considered to be satisfied if particular information is useful (decision useful) for making particular decisions, such as decisions about the allocation of scarce resources. From an accounting perspective, stewardship refers to the process wherein a manager demonstrates how she or he has used the resources that have been entrusted to them. Traditionally, this was seen as one of the key roles of historical cost accounting.

about an organization's activities. This objective, which was also carried forward in subsequent work, was interesting in that it tended to be a departure from much research that was being carried on at the time. A great deal of research being undertaken in the late 1960s and thereafter had embraced the *efficient markets hypothesis* (discussed more fully in Chapter 10) that markets react quickly to impound the information content of publicly available information, whenever that information first becomes publicly available. Researchers working with the efficient markets hypothesis considered that as long as the information was publicly available to somebody, then, given an assumption of market efficiency, this information would quickly be dispersed among all interested users. The Trueblood Committee and subsequent committees responsible for development of conceptual frameworks within the United States and elsewhere did not appear to embrace this view of market efficiency.

The Trueblood Committee acknowledged that a variety of different valuation methods were used for different classes of assets and liabilities. This had been an issue that had concerned a number of researchers. However, the Trueblood Committee noted that they considered different valuation rules were relevant for different classes of assets, thereby ignoring the 'additivity problem' raised by such researchers. As we will see shortly, prescribing a particular valuation or measurement approach is an activity that those responsible for developing conceptual frameworks have been reluctant to undertake.

The FASB Conceptual Framework Project

In 1974 the Accounting Principles Board within the United States was replaced by the Financial Accounting Standards Board (FASB). The FASB embarked on its conceptual framework project early in its existence and the first release, Statement of Financial Accounting Concepts (SFAC) No. 1: *Objectives of Financial Reporting by Business Enterprises*, occurred in 1978. This was followed by the release of six more SFACs, with the latest one, SFAC No. 7: *Using Cash Flow Information and Present Values in Accounting Measurement*, being issued in 2000. The initial SFACs were quite normative (that is, they attempted to prescribe how accounting should be undertaken). However, when SFAC No. 5: *Recognition and Measurement in Financial Statements of Business Enterprises*, was released in 1984 the FASB appeared to opt for an approach largely descriptive of current practice. Rather than prescribe a particular valuation approach the FASB described some of the various valuation approaches commonly used: historical cost, current cost (replacement cost), current market value (exit value), net realizable value (amount gained from sale, less costs associated with the sale) and the present (discounted) value of future cash flows. The failure to take the lead and actually prescribe a particular valuation approach was referred to as a 'cop-out' by Solomons (1986). This view was also embraced by a number of others. For example, Nussbaumer (1992, p. 238) states:

> the issuance of SFAC 5 (December 1984) marked the greatest disappointment of the FASB's project for the conceptual framework. It did nothing more than describe present practice; it was not prescriptive at all. The recognition and measurement issues, which the FASB promised to deal with in SFAC 5, were not settled, and the measurement issue was sidestepped. … If the FASB cannot reach an agreement when there are only seven members, it is unlikely that the

profession as a whole will come to agreement on these issues either. The FASB should provide leadership to the profession on these issues and not compromise them for the sake of expediency.

In a similar vein, Miller (1990) argued that the FASB conceptual framework in accounting initially provided much needed reform to accounting. For example, SFAC No. 1 explicitly put financial report users' needs at the forefront of consideration. However, when SFAC No. 5 was released, 'momentum was lost when FASB did not have sufficient political will to face down the counter-reformation and endorse expanded use of current values in the recognition and measurement phase of the project' (Miller, 1990, p. 32). Interestingly, since SFAC 5 was released there has been very limited activity in the FASB conceptual framework project. SFAC 6 was released in 1985, but this was primarily a replacement of an early statement (SFAC 3). Only one further SFAC (SFAC 7) was released (in 2000). It would appear that measurement issues represented a real stumbling block for the project. Had the FASB supported one valuation method over and above others, this would have been a dramatic departure from current accounting practice and may not have been palatable to its constituents.[7] Although this is conjecture, perhaps the FASB went as far as it could politically. We consider this issue in more depth later in this Chapter.

The (UK) Corporate Report

If we turn our attention to other conceptual framework projects we see that their degree of progression has also been slow. In the United Kingdom an early move towards developing guidance in relation to the objectives and the identification of the users of financial statements, as well as the methods to be used in financial reporting, was provided by *The Corporate Report* – a discussion paper released in 1976 by the Accounting Standards Steering Committee of the Institute of Chartered Accountants in England and Wales. As we see in subsequent discussion in this chapter, *The Corporate Report* was particularly concerned with addressing the *rights* of the community in terms of their access to financial information about the entities operating in their community. The view taken was that if the community gives an organization permission to operate, then that organization has an *accountability* to the community and this accountability includes an obligation to provide information about its financial performance. This perspective of financial statement users was broader than that adopted in frameworks being developed in other countries and involved groups that did not have a direct financial interest in the organization, but were nevertheless affected by its ongoing operations.

The Corporate Report was also part of a UK Government Green Paper on Law Reform. The report ultimately did not become enshrined in law and its contents were generally not accepted by the accounting profession. In 1991 the UK Accounting Standards Board embarked on a project to develop a conceptual framework, largely consistent with the main principles underlying the FASB and IASC frameworks, and thereby abandoned the broader notions of *users' rights* raised in *The Corporate Report*.

---

[7] Current accounting practice requires that different measurement approaches be used for different classes of assets. For example, the lower of cost and net realizable value is used for inventory whereas marketable securities are to be valued at fair value. If a conceptual framework was released which required one basis of asset measurement for all assets then this would have significant implications for the revision of various accounting standards.

Development of conceptual frameworks in other nations

Other countries such as Australia, Canada and New Zealand have devoted resources to the development of a conceptual framework. In Australia, work on the conceptual framework started in the 1980s, with the first of four Statements of Accounting Concept being issued in 1990. The Australian conceptual framework had a number of similarities to the FASB project and, as with the FASB, prescribing a particular measurement principle was a major stumbling block. In Canada, initial efforts were incorporated in a document entitled *Corporate Reporting: Its Future Evolution*, which was released in 1980. This report was written by Edward Stamp and became known as *The Stamp Report*. This report appeared to rely heavily on *The Corporate Report* (possibly unsurprising as Stamp was also one of the authors of *The Corporate Report*), and like *The Corporate Report* was not embraced by the accounting profession. Subsequently, further work was undertaken towards developing a conceptual framework with a number of similarities to the FASB project. In 1990 the Accounting Research and Standards Board in New Zealand also commenced some work related to a conceptual framework. It has many similarities to other frameworks developed in other countries.

At the international level, the IASC published a conceptual framework in 1989, entitled *Framework for the Preparation and Presentation of Financial Statements*, which is also similar in many respects to the conceptual frameworks developed in the above countries. Given the centrality of International Accounting Standards/International Financial Reporting Standards in European and global financial reporting (particularly since January 2005), some argue that the IASB needs a more up-to-date conceptual framework to guide its accounting standard-setting process – something that the IASB responded to by jointly undertaking the initiative with the FASB to develop a new conceptual framework.

What the above information demonstrates is that a number of countries have devoted resources to the development of a conceptual framework. What also is apparent is that those responsible for the frameworks have either been reluctant to promote significant changes from accounting practice (which obviously limits their ability to generate significant changes in financial reporting), or, where frameworks have suggested significant changes, such changes have not been embraced by the accounting professions and many of their constituents. The reasons for this are provided in the discussion that follows.

Current efforts of the IASB and the FASB

From 2005 the IASB and the FASB have been jointly working towards the development of a revised conceptual framework that will be used by both parties. The need for this revised framework has arisen because of the 'convergence project' in which the IASB and the FASB are working together to converge their two sets of accounting standards. The ultimate aim is that the accounting standards of both the IASB and FASB will be of such comparable nature that the US will ultimately adopt IFRSs and there will be one set of accounting standards (IFRSs) that are used globally. As we indicated in Chapter 4, unlike many other countries, at this time the US has not adopted IFRSs and has retained the use of its own domestically developed accounting standards.

Prior to convergence many differences existed between the respective standards released by both boards (the IASB and the FASB). There were also many differences between the conceptual frameworks developed by the respective boards. Given that efforts are under way to converge accounting standards being released by the IASB with those being released by the FASB, there is a need for one uniform conceptual framework. In explaining the need for a revised conceptual framework, the FASB and IASB state (Bullen and Crook, 2005, pp. 2–3):

> The Boards will encounter difficulties converging their standards if they base their decisions on different frameworks … The FASB's current Concepts Statements and the IASB's Framework, developed mainly during the 1970s and 1980s, articulate concepts that go a long way toward being an adequate foundation for principles-based standards … Although the current concepts have been helpful, the IASB and FASB will not be able to realise fully their goal of issuing a common set of principles-based standards if those standards are based on the current FASB Concepts Statements and IASB Framework. That is because those documents are in need of refinement, updating, completion, and convergence. There is no real need to change many aspects of the existing frameworks, other than to converge different ways of expressing what are in essence the same concepts. Therefore, the project will not seek to comprehensively reconsider all aspects of the existing Concepts Statements and the Framework. Instead, it will focus on areas that need refinement, updating, or completing, particularly on the conceptual issues that are more likely to yield standard-setting benefits soon.

In considering the amount of time it will take to develop the converged conceptual framework, the FASB and IASB (Bullen and Crook, 2005, p. 16) state:

> This joint project is a major undertaking for both Boards and will take several years. In the intervening period, the Boards will look to their existing frameworks for guidance in setting standards.

The IASB and FASB are undertaking the work on the conceptual framework in eight phases, as listed below. At the time of writing this chapter (in 2010), phases A, B, C and D were active:

Phase	Topic
A	Objectives and qualitative characteristics.
B	Definitions of elements, recognition and derecognition
C	Measurement
D	Reporting entity concept
E	Boundaries of financial reporting, and presentation and disclosure
F	Purpose and status of the framework
G	Application of the framework to not-for-profit entities
H	Remaining issues, if any

Details of the progress on the revised conceptual framework can be found on the IASB's website (www.ifrs.org) and then following the links to the conceptual framework project (at the time of writing this chapter this was in the 'work plan for IFRS' link).

6.4 Building blocks of a conceptual framework

In this section we consider some of the guidance that has already been produced in existing conceptual framework projects. We consider issues such as definition of a reporting entity; perceived users of financial statements; the objectives of general purpose financial reporting; the qualitative characteristics that general purpose financial reports should possess; the elements of financial statements; and discussions of possible approaches to recognition and measurement of the elements of financial statements. We will primarily focus on the IASB Framework that is currently in place as this is the framework that is currently guiding accounting practice in those countries that made the decision to adopt IFRSs. Where appropriate, we will also make reference to current work being undertaken in the joint IASB/FASB conceptual framework project given that this work provides an indication of possible future guidance.

Definition of the reporting entity

One key issue in any discussion about financial reporting is what characteristics of an entity provide an indication of an apparent need for it to produce general purpose financial reports. The term *general purpose financial reports* refers to financial reports that comply with accounting standards and other generally accepted accounting principles and are released by reporting entities to satisfy the information demands of a varied cross-section of users. These reports can be contrasted with special purpose financial reports, which are provided to meet the information demands of a particular user or group of users. As stated earlier, the guidance that we consider in this chapter relates to general purpose financial reports.

Some researchers, such as Walker (2003), have been critical of the practicality of conceptual frameworks directed at general purpose financial statements, as a single set (or framework) of accounting concepts is unlikely to be able to address the diversity of information needs from a heterogeneous range of different stakeholders.

Clearly, not all entities should be expected to produce general purpose financial reports. For example, there would be limited benefits in requiring a small owner/manager to prepare general purpose financial reports (which comply with the numerous accounting standards) for, say, a small corner shop. There would be few external users with a significant stake or interest in the organization. Limited guidance is provided by some conceptual frameworks regarding the types of entities to whose financial reports the conceptual framework is relevant. For example, paragraph 8 of the IASC *Framework for the Preparation and Presentation of Financial Statements* – and remember that this framework has now been adopted as the IASB Framework – states that:

> The *Framework* applies to the financial statements of all commercial, indus-trial and business reporting entities, whether in the public or private sectors. A reporting entity is an entity for which there are users who rely on the financial statements as their major source of financial information about the entity.

Consistent with the discussion above, general purpose financial reports are considered in the IASB Framework (paragraph 6) to be statements which 'are directed towards the common information needs of a wide range of users'. However, these user needs are not well defined.

In May 2008 the IASB and FASB released a document entitled 'Preliminary Views – Conceptual Framework for Financial Reporting: The Reporting Entity' as part of the joint work being undertaken by the IASB and FASB. In providing background to the report, the IASB state (2008a, p. 1):

> The boards' existing conceptual frameworks do not include a reporting entity concept. The IASB's *Framework for the Preparation and Presentation of Financial Statements* defines the reporting entity in one sentence with no further explanation. The FASB's *Statements of Financial Accounting Concepts* do not contain a definition of a reporting entity or discussion of how to identify one. As a result, neither framework specifically addresses the reporting entity concept. The objective of this phase (Phase D) of the project is to develop a reporting entity concept for inclusion in the boards' common conceptual framework.

In March 2010, the IASB and FASB provided more details on the possible definition of the reporting entity when they published an exposure draft entitled: Conceptual Framework for Financial Reporting: The Reporting Entity (IASB, 2010). This explained (p. 9) that:

> A reporting entity is a circumscribed area of economic activities whose financial information has the potential to be useful to existing and potential equity investors, lenders and other creditors who cannot directly obtain the information they need in making decisions about providing resources to the entity and in assessing whether management and the governing board of that entity have made efficient and effective use of the resources provided.
>
> A reporting entity has three features:
>
> **a** economic activities of an entity are being conducted, have been conducted or will be conducted;
>
> **b** those economic activities can be objectively distinguished from those of other entities and from the economic environment in which the entity exists; and
>
> **c** financial information about the economic activities of that entity has the potential to be useful in making decisions about providing resources to the entity and in assessing whether the management and the governing board have made efficient and effective use of the resources provided.
>
> These features are necessary but not always sufficient to identify a reporting entity.

Hence, whether an entity is classified as a reporting entity is partly determined by the information needs of the users, and this relies upon professional judgement.

Users of financial reports

If conceptual frameworks are designed to meet the 'information needs of a wide range of users', to be effective it is necessary for the frameworks to identify the potential users and their main information needs. The definition of users provided at paragraph 9 of the IASB Framework encompasses investors, employees, lenders, suppliers, customers, government and their agencies, and the public, and is thereby broader than that used by the FASB in the United States. In the FASB's SFAC 1 the main focus of financial reports is present and potential investors and other users (with either a direct financial interest or somehow related to those with a financial interest, for example stockbrokers, analysts, lawyers or regulatory bodies). Within SFAC 1 there appears to be limited consideration of the public being a legitimate user of financial reports. However, in the IASB Framework, even though a range of users (along with the nature of their likely information needs) is identified, it is proposed that accounting information designed to meet the information needs of investors will usually also meet the needs of the other user groups identified. This claim is justified on the basis that 'investors are providers of risk capital to the entity' (paragraph 10), but the framework does not explain why information designed to be useful to providers of risk capital is also likely to be useful to the other types of stakeholders in most circumstances.

The issue as to which groups should be considered to be legitimate users of financial information about an organization is an argument that has attracted a great deal of debate. There are many, such as the authors of *The Corporate Report* (Accounting Standards Steering Committee, 1975), who hold that all groups affected by an organization's operations have *rights* to information about the reporting entity, including financial information, regardless of whether they are contemplating resource allocation decisions.

Indeed, many would question whether the need for information to enable financial resource allocation decisions is the only or dominant issue to consider in determining whether an organization has a public obligation to provide information about its performance (Unerman *et al.*, 2007).[8] Organizations, particularly large corporations, have many social and environmental impacts throughout society with such impacts not being restricted to those people who are investors, or who are considering investing within the organization. In large part the extent of an organization's impacts, and its ability to minimize harmful impacts, will be tied to the financial resources under its control and will also impact upon these resources (Hopwood *et al.*, 2010). As such, a reasonable argument can be made that various groups within society have a legitimate interest in information about an organization's financial position and performance, and to restrict the definition of users to investors might be a little bit too simplistic. The 2008 Exposure Draft released by the IASB and FASB as part of the conceptual framework project states (IASB, 2008b, p. 16):

> The primary user group includes both present and potential equity investors, lenders and other creditors, regardless of how they obtained, or will obtain, their interests. In the framework, the terms *capital providers* and *claimants* are used interchangeably to refer to the primary user group.
>
> Managers and the governing board of an entity (herein collectively referred to as management) are also interested in financial information about the entity. However, management's primary relationship with the entity is not that of a capital provider. Management is responsible for preparing financial reports; management is not their intended recipient. Other users who have specialised needs, such as suppliers, customers and employees (when not acting as capital providers), as well as governments and their agencies and members of the

---

[8] We consider this issue further in Chapter 9.

public, may also find useful the information that meets the needs of capital providers; however, financial reporting is not primarily directed to these other groups because capital providers have more direct and immediate needs.

As we can see from the above quote, the current work of the IASB and FASB appears to maintain a restricted view of the users of general purpose financial reports and tends to disregard information rights or needs of users who do not have a direct financial interest in the organization.

In considering the issue of the level of expertise expected of financial report readers, it has generally been accepted that readers are expected to have some proficiency in financial accounting. As a result, accounting standards are developed on the basis of this assumption. The FASB conceptual framework refers to the 'informed reader'. In the IASB Framework, paragraph 25 explains that:

> users are assumed to have a reasonable knowledge of business and economic activities and accounting and a willingness to study the information with reasonable diligence.

Consistent with this, in the recent conceptual framework project the IASB (2008c, p. 40) states:

> Users of financial reports are assumed to have a reasonable knowledge of business and economic activities and to be able to read a financial report. In making decisions, users also should review and analyse the information with reasonable diligence.

In considering the required qualitative characteristics that financial information should possess (for example, relevance, understandability), some assumptions about the ability of report users are required. It would appear that those responsible for developing conceptual frameworks have accepted that individuals without any expertise in accounting are not the intended audience of reporting entities' financial reports (even though such people may have a considerable amount of their own wealth invested). Having established the audience for general purpose financial statements, we now consider the objectives of such statements aimed at these users.

Objectives of general purpose financial reporting

Over time, a number of objectives have been attributed to information provided within financial statements.[9] A traditionally cited objective was to enable outsiders to assess the *stewardship* of management. That is, whether the resources entrusted to management have been used for their intended or appropriate purposes. It is generally accepted that historical cost accounting enables management to report effectively on the stewardship of the resources provided to the reporting entity.

---

[9] In a FASB Discussion Memorandum released in 1974, the FASB defines an objective as 'something toward which effort is directed, an aim, or end of action, a goal'. It is perhaps questionable whether information itself can have objectives. Certainly, users of information can have objectives which can be achieved (or not) as a result of using information. Nevertheless, it is common for accounting standard-setters to talk about the objectives of financial information and, as such, we maintain this convention.

Another objective of financial reporting, and one that has become a commonly accepted goal of financial reporting, is to assist in report users' economic decision-making. That is, in recent times, less emphasis has been placed on the stewardship function of financial reports. For example, the FASB notes in SFAC 1 that a major objective of financial reporting is that it:

> should provide information that is useful to present and potential investors and creditors and other users in making rational investment, credit and similar decisions.

This objective refers to 'rational' decisions. It is commonly accepted in the economics and accounting literature that a 'rational decision' is one that maximizes expected utility, with this utility typically considered to be related to the maximization of wealth. The FASB framework emphasizes the information needs of those who have a financial stake in the reporting entity. For example, the above objective refers to the needs of present and potential investors and creditors. It also refers to the needs of 'others', but the 'others' are also explained in terms of having financial interests in the reporting entity.

This focus on the information needs of financial report users has also been embraced in other conceptual frameworks. For example, in the IASB Framework the objective of financial reporting is 'to provide information about the financial position, performance, and changes in financial position of an enterprise that is useful to a wide range of users in making economic decisions' (paragraph 12).[10] The IASB Framework explains that economic decisions should be based on an assessment of an enterprise's future cash flows, indicating that the main objective of general purpose financial statements is to assist stakeholders in judging likely future cash flows. Moving towards a system of reporting a range of cash flow forecasts would clearly be a significant change to existing accounting practices which focus on reporting (some of) the effects of past transactions and events. However, the IASB Framework (paragraph 15) then explains that:

> Users are better able to evaluate this ability to generate cash and cash equivalents if they are provided with information that focuses on the financial position, performance and changes in financial position of an entity.

Therefore, while the objective of financial statements is to aid economic decisions which will be based on an evaluation of future cash flows, the IASB Framework argues that this objective of enabling stakeholders to evaluate cash flows will be effectively addressed through the information contained in balance sheets (now known as statements of financial position), profit and loss accounts (income statements) and cash flow/funds flow statements. Thus, there is no need for a radical change in the types of main financial statements that are needed if the objective of the financial statements as a whole (that is, the annual report and accounts) is to provide information that is useful for making economic decisions.

Once we move towards this notion of *decision usefulness*, an objective embraced within all conceptual framework projects, we might question whether historical cost information

---

[10] The more traditional stewardship role of financial statements is explicitly recognized as an additional objective in the IASB Framework, where paragraph 14 states that 'Financial statements also show the results of the stewardship of management, or the accountability of management for the resources entrusted to it'.

(which arguably is useful for assessing stewardship) is useful for financial report users' decisions, such as whether to invest in, or lend funds to, an organization. Arguably, such decisions could be more effectively made if information on current market values was made available. It is interesting to note that although the IASB Framework does not really address measurement issues, as we saw in Chapter 5 many recently released accounting standards require assets to be valued on the basis of fair values, and also various liabilities to be valued on the basis of present values. In effect, accounting regulators appear to be side-stepping the use of the conceptual framework as the foundation of developing the measurement principles of general purpose financial reporting and instead are using the ongoing release of new accounting standards as the means of bringing major change to accounting measurement principles. Such an approach seems to be inconsistent with the reasons why conceptual frameworks are established.

Apart from *stewardship* and *decision usefulness*, another commonly cited objective of financial reporting is to enable reporting entities to demonstrate *accountability* between the entity and those parties to which the entity is deemed to be accountable. Gray *et al.* (1996, p. 38) provide a definition of accountability, this being: 'the duty to provide an account or reckoning of those actions for which one is held responsible'. Issues that arise here are *to whom* is a reporting entity accountable, and *for what*? There are a multitude of opinions on this. Within the FASB project it would appear that those responsible for developing a framework considered that there is a duty to provide an account of the entity's financial performance to those parties who have a direct financial stake in the reporting entity. Emphasis seems to be placed on economic efficiencies. This can be contrasted with the guidance provided by *The Corporate Report* (UK), which argued that society effectively allows organizations to exist as long as they accept certain responsibilities, one being that they are accountable for their actions to society generally, rather than solely to those who have a financial stake in the entity. *The Corporate Report* makes the following statement at paragraph 25:

> The public's right to information arises not from a direct financial or human relationship with the reporting entity but from the general role played in our society by economic entities. Such organisations, which exist with the general consent of the community, are afforded special legal and operational privileges; they compete for resources of manpower, materials and energy and they make use of community owned assets such as roads and harbours.

Although *The Corporate Report* emphasized an accountability perspective of financial reporting, it was generally not accepted, and the UK position (through the ASB's subsequent conceptual framework project) was basically one of acceptance of the *decision-makers emphasis* with prime consideration being given to the needs of those with a financial interest or stake in the organization.

To understand the 'current thinking' of the IASB and the FASB in relation to the objective of financial reporting it is useful to consider the exposure draft released by the IASB as part of the ongoing efforts to develop a revised conceptual framework. In relation to the objective of financial reporting it states (IASB, 2008b, p. 14):

> The objective of general purpose financial reporting is to provide financial information about the reporting entity that is useful to present and poten-tial equity investors, lenders and other creditors in making decisions in their

capacity as capital providers. Information that is decision-useful to capital providers may also be useful to other users of financial reporting who are not capital providers.

As a normative theory of accounting, whether we are likely to accept the prescriptions provided by the new conceptual framework will be dependent upon whether we agree with the underlying key assumptions and objectives adopted as the basis of developing the theory. Hence, if we disagree with the objective of financial reporting as noted above then we would probably be inclined to dismiss much of the contents of the revised conceptual framework.

Before moving on to consider some of the suggested qualitative characteristics of financial information, for the sake of completeness we will briefly mention the underlying assumptions set out as a separate section in the IASB's framework, but not given such prominence in most other conceptual framework projects. These underlying assumptions are simply that for financial statements to meet the objectives of providing information for economic decision-making they should be prepared on the accrual and going concern basis. Specifically paragraphs 22 and 23 of the IASB Framework currently state:

> 22. In order to meet their objectives, financial reports are prepared on the accrual basis of accounting. Under this basis, the effects of transactions and other events are recognized when they occur (and not as cash or its equivalent is received or paid) and they are recorded in the accounting records and reported in the financial reports of the periods to which they relate. Financial reports prepared on the accrual basis inform users not only of past transactions involving the payment and receipt of cash but also of obligations to pay cash in the future and of resources that represent cash to be received in the future. Hence, they provide the type of information about past transactions and other events that is most useful to users in making economic decisions.
>
> 23. Financial reports are normally prepared on the assumption that an entity is a going concern and will continue in operation for the forseeable future. Hence, it is assumed that the entity has neither the intention nor the need to liquidate or curtail materially the scale of its operations; if such an intention or need exists, the financial report may have to be prepared on a different basis and, if so, the basis used is disclosed.

Qualitative characteristics of financial reports

If it is accepted that financial information should be useful for economic decision-making, as conceptual frameworks indicate, then a subsequent issue to consider (or in terms of the terminology used earlier, a subsequent 'building block' to consider) is the *qualitative characteristics* (attributes or qualities) that financial information should have if it is to be *useful* for such decisions (implying that an absence of such qualities would mean that the central objectives of general purpose financial reports would not be met).

Conceptual frameworks have dedicated a great deal of their material to discussing qualitative characteristics of financial information. The four primary qualitative characteristics that have been identified in the IASB Framework are *understandability, relevance, reliability* and *comparability*.

Understandability

In the IASB Framework, information is considered to be *understandable* if it is likely to be understood by users with some business and accounting knowledge (as discussed earlier in this chapter). However, this does not mean that complex information which is relevant to economic decision-making should be omitted from the financial statements just because it might not be understood by some users. Given that conceptual frameworks have been developed primarily to guide accounting standard-setters in the setting of accounting rules (rather than as a set of rules to which entities must refer when compiling their financial statements), this qualitative characteristic of *understandability* is perhaps best seen as a requirement (or challenge) for standard-setters to ensure that the accounting standards they develop for dealing with complex areas produce accounting disclosures which are understandable (irrespective of the complexity of the underlying transactions or events). Based on your knowledge of accounting practice, how successful do you think accounting standard-setters have been in this task?

Relevance

Under the IASB Framework, information is regarded as *relevant* if it:

> influences the economic decisions of users by helping them evaluate past, present or future events or confirming, or correcting, their past evaluations. (paragraph 26)

There are two main aspects to relevance – for information to be relevant it should have both *predictive value* and *feedback (or confirmatory) value*, the latter referring to the information's utility in confirming or correcting earlier expectations.

Materiality

Closely tied to the notion of *relevance* is the notion of *materiality*. This is embodied in various conceptual framework projects. For example, paragraph 30 of the IASB Framework states that an item is material if:

> its omission or misstatement could influence the economic decisions of users taken on the basis of the financial statements. … Materiality provides a cut-off point rather than being a primary qualitative characteristic which information must have if it is to be useful.

Considerations of materiality provide the basis for restricting the amount of information provided to levels that are comprehensible to financial statement users. It would arguably be poor practice to provide hundreds of pages of potentially relevant and reliable information to report readers – this would only result in an overload of information. Nevertheless, materiality is a heavily judgemental issue and at times we could expect that it might actually be used as a justification for failing to disclose some information that might be deemed to be potentially harmful to the reporting entity.

Reliability

Turning to another primary qualitative characteristic, something is deemed to be *reliable* if it 'is free from material bias and error and can be depended upon by users to represent faithfully' the underlying items it claims to represent (IASB Framework, paragraph 31).

Within the United States, SFAC 2 defines reliability as 'the quality of information that assures that information is reasonably free from error and bias and faithfully represents what it purports to represent'. SFAC 2 notes that reliability is a function of *representational faithfulness, verifiability* and *neutrality*. According to SFAC 2, representational faithfulness refers to the 'correspondence or agreement between a measure or description and the phenomenon that it purports to represent'. *Verifiability* is defined in SFAC 2 as 'the ability through consensus among measurers to ensure that information represents what it purports to represent, or that the chosen method of measurement has been used without error or bias'. *Neutrality* implies that the information was not constructed or compiled to generate a predetermined result.

In addition to freedom from bias and material error, the IASB Framework assesses reliability in terms of *faithful representation, substance over form, neutrality, prudence* and *completeness*. Where the economic substance of a transaction is inconsistent with its legal form, *substance over form* requires that the accounting represents the economic substance (or impact) of the transaction. *Prudence* in paragraph 37 of the IASB Framework requires 'a degree of caution in the exercise of judgement needed in making the estimates required under conditions of uncertainty', but this does not extend to 'excessive provisions, the deliberate understatement of assets or income, or the deliberate overstatement of liabilities or expenses' as this would conflict with the requirement of neutrality.

Introducing notions of *prudence* with the associated notions of *neutrality* and *representational faithfulness* has implications for how financial accounting has traditionally been practised. Traditionally, accountants adopted the doctrine of conservatism or prudence. In practice, this was usually taken to mean that asset values should never have been shown at amounts in excess of their realizable values (but they could be understated), and liabilities should never have been understated (although it was generally acceptable for liabilities to be overstated). That is, there was traditionally a bias towards undervaluing the *net assets* of an entity. It would appear that such a doctrine is not consistent with the qualitative characteristic of 'freedom from bias', as financial statements should, arguably, not be biased in one direction or another. In more recent conceptual framework projects (such as the UK ASB's *Statement of Principles*) and recently developed accounting standards in many jurisdictions, the requirement of prudence was 'softened' in favour of a greater focus on neutrality and representational faithfulness.

Comparability

The final primary qualitative characteristic in the IASB Framework is *comparability*. To facilitate the comparison of the financial statements of different entities (and for a single entity over a period of time), methods of measurement and disclosure must be consistent – but should be changed if no longer relevant to an entity's circumstances. Drawing on studies by Loftus (2003) and Booth (2003), Wells (2003) argues that a key role of a conceptual framework should be to produce consistent accounting standards which lead to comparable accounting information between different entities, as without such comparability it is difficult for users to evaluate accounting information.

Desirable characteristics such as consistency thus imply that there are advantages in restricting the number of accounting methods that can be used by reporting entities. However, other academics have argued that any actions which result in a reduction in the accounting methods that can be used by reporting entities lead potentially to reductions in the efficiency with which organizations operate (Watts and Zimmerman, 1986). For example, management might elect to use a particular accounting method because it believes that for their particular and perhaps unique circumstances the specific method of accounting best reflects their underlying performance. Restricting the use of the specific method can result in a reduction in how efficiently external parties can monitor the performance of the entity, and this in itself has been assumed to lead to increased costs for the reporting entity (this 'efficiency perspective', which has been applied in Positive Accounting Theory, is explored in Chapter 7).

If it is assumed, consistent with the *efficiency perspective* briefly mentioned above, that firms adopt particular accounting methods because the methods best reflect the underlying economic performance of the entity, then it is argued by some theorists that the regulation of financial accounting imposes unwarranted costs on reporting entities. For example, if a new accounting standard is released that bans an accounting method being used by particular organizations, this will lead to inefficiencies, as the resulting financial statements will no longer provide the best reflection of the performance of the organization. Many theorists would argue that management is best able to select appropriate accounting methods in given circumstances, and government and/or others should not intervene.

Balancing relevance and reliability

Returning to the specific requirements of the IASB Framework, it is considered important for information to possess each of the four primary qualitative characteristics if it is to be useful in aiding economic decision-making. However, it appears that the IASB Framework gives greater prominence to *reliability* and *relevance* than to *understandability* or *comparability*. In balancing *relevance* and *reliability*, paragraph 32 notes that 'Information might be relevant but so unreliable in nature or representation that its recognition may be potentially misleading.'

Another consideration that needs to be addressed when deciding whether to disclose particular information is thus the potential constraints on producing relevant and reliable information. The IASB Framework discusses two such constraints: *timeliness* and *balancing costs and benefits*. In relation to the former, paragraph 43 recognizes that for much accounting information there will be a trade-off between being able to produce information quickly (and thereby enhancing the *relevance* of the information) and measuring this information accurately (and therefore *reliably*), as the production of accurate information often requires corroboration that occurs sometime later. In these circumstances, it is a judgemental matter regarding how to balance *relevance* and *reliability* – that is, how long to wait against the extent of reliability required). In other words, the longer we take to ensure information is reliable (perhaps through various forms of auditing) the less relevant the information may become in terms of helping users to make decisions (as they will be basing these decisions on information that is not current).

The other major constraint, consideration of costs and benefits of disclosure, is a highly subjective activity and requires decisions about many issues. Paragraph 44 of the IASB Framework requires that 'the benefits derived from information should exceed the cost of providing it'. But from whose perspective are we to consider costs and benefits? Are costs and benefits attributable to some user groups more or less important than others, and so on? Any analysis of costs and benefits is highly judgemental and open to critical comment.

As we have done elsewhere in this chapter, it is interesting to consider the 'latest thinking' of the IASB and FASB in relation to the desired qualitative characteristics of financial reporting. In the Exposure Draft released in 2008 as part of the joint initiative of the IASB and FASB (IASB, 2008b, p. 13) it is stated:

> For financial information to be useful, it must possess two fundamental qualitative characteristics – *relevance* and *faithful representation.*

Therefore, although the existing IASB Framework for the Preparation and Presentation of Financial Statements has four primary qualitative characteristics of financial reporting (these being relevance, reliability, understandability and comparability) the draft conceptual framework being developed by the IASB and FASB has reduced the four 'primary qualitative characteristics' to two 'fundamental qualitative characteristics' – these being relevance and faithful representation.

Within the 2008 Exposure Draft the qualitative characteristic of reliability was replaced by 'faithful representation' – in previous documents 'faithful representation' had been seen as a component of reliability. In relation to faithful representation, the Exposure Draft states (IASB, 2008b, p. 36):

> Faithful representation is attained when the depiction of an economic phenomenon is complete, neutral, and free from material error. Financial information that faithfully represents an economic phenomenon depicts the economic substance of the underlying transaction, event or circumstances, which is not always the same as its legal form.

In explaining why it has been proposed that 'relevance' be replaced as a primary qualitative of financial reporting, it is stated (IASB, 2008b, p. 47):

> Given the nature and extent of the longstanding problems with the qualitative characteristic of *reliability*, as well as previous efforts to address them, the boards concluded that the term itself needed reconsideration. Because further efforts to explain what *reliability* means were not likely to be productive, the boards sought a term that would more clearly convey the intended meaning.
>
> *Faithful representation* – the faithful depiction in financial reports of economic phenomena – is essential if information is to be decision-useful. To represent economic phenomena faithfully, accounting representations must be complete, neutral and free from material error. Accordingly, the boards proposed that faithful representation encompasses all the key qualities that the previous frameworks included as aspects of reliability.

The other two primary qualitative characteristics identified in the IASB Framework, these being understandability and comparability, have been renamed as 'enhancing qualitative characteristics' in the draft document released by the IASB. Two additional 'enhancing qualitative characteristics' have also been included (thereby giving a total of four 'enhancing qualitative characteristics), these being verifiability and timeliness. IASB (2008b, p. 38) explains:

> Enhancing qualitative characteristics are complementary to the fundamental qualitative characteristics. Enhancing qualitative characteristics distinguish

more useful information from less useful information. The enhancing qualitative characteristics are *comparability, verifiability, timeliness* and *understandability*. These characteristics enhance the decision-usefulness of financial reporting information that is relevant and faithfully represented.

Can financial statements provide neutral and unbiased accounts of an entity's performance and position?

A review of existing conceptual frameworks such as the IASB Framework or the framework proposed in joint work currently being undertaken by the IASB and the FASB, as reflected by some of the material provided above, indicates that conceptual frameworks provide a perspective that accounting can, if performed properly, provide an objective (neutral and representationally faithful) view of the performance and position of a reporting entity. Reflecting on this apparent perspective, Hines (1991, p. 314) states:

> it appears that the ontological assumption underpinning the Conceptual Framework is that the relationship between financial accounting and economic reality is a unidirectional, reflecting or faithfully reproducing relationship: economic reality exists objectively, intersubjectively, concretely and independently of financial accounting practices; financial accounting reflects, mirrors, represents or measures the pre-existent reality.

In fact, the role of a well-functioning system of accounting has been compared with that of cartography (map making). That is, just as an area can be objectively 'mapped', some have argued that so can the financial position and performance of an organization (Solomons, 1978). But as we would appreciate, the practice of accounting is heavily based on professional judgement. As we will see in the subsection dealing with recognition, the elements of financial accounting are, in some jurisdictions and in the IASB Framework, explicitly tied to assessments of probabilities. Clearly, there is a degree of subjectivity associated with such assessments. Cartography is not based on subjective assessments of probabilities.[11]

Although conceptual frameworks argue for attributes such as *neutrality* and *representational faithfulness*, we should perhaps take time to question whether it is valid or realistic to believe that financial accounting provides an objective perspective of an entity's performance. In Chapter 3 we considered research that investigated the economic consequences of accounting regulations. It was argued that before an accounting standard-setting body releases new or amended reporting requirements it attempts to consider the economic consequences that would follow from the decision to release an accounting standard. Even if a proposed accounting rule was considered the *best* way to account (however this is determined – which of course would be an issue provoking much debate), if this proposed accounting rule would lead to significant costs being imposed on particular parties (for example, preparers) then plans to require the approach could be abandoned

---

[11] If it was, we could imagine the carnage that might occur if a map of the ocean simply told a ship's captain that it was probable that a reef was safe for crossing.

by the standard-setters. Once a profession starts considering the *economic consequences* of particular accounting standards it is difficult to perceive that the accounting standards, and therefore accounting, can really be considered objective or neutral.

Tied to issues associated with economic implications, there is a body of literature (Positive Accounting Theory, which we have already briefly discussed and which we consider in Chapter 7) that suggests that those responsible for preparing financial statements will be driven by self-interest to select accounting methods that lead to outcomes that provide favourable outcomes for their own personal wealth. That is, this literature predicts that managers and others involved in the accounting function will always put their self-interest ahead of the interests of others.[12] *If* we accept this body of literature, we would perhaps dismiss notions of objectivity or neutrality as being unrealistic. Self-interest perspectives are often used to explain the phenomenon of 'creative accounting' – a situation where those responsible for the preparation of financial reports select accounting methods that provide the most desired outcomes from their own perspective (such as apparently may have occurred at Enron and Lehman Brothers).

Accounting standards and conceptual frameworks form the foundation of general purpose financial reporting. As we have noted in earlier chapters, accounting standards and conceptual frameworks are developed through public consultation, which involves the release of exposure drafts and, subsequently, a review of the written submissions made by various interested parties, including both the preparers and users of the financial information. Consequently, the process leading to finalized accounting standards and conceptual frameworks can be considered to be political. The political solutions and compromises impact on the financial information being presented and that information is, therefore, an outcome of a political process – a process where parties with particular attributes (power) may be able to have a relatively greater impact on final reporting requirements than other parties. This can be considered to have implications for the objectivity or neutrality of the financial information being disclosed. Hines (1989, p. 80) argues that many individuals not involved in the standard-setting process would be very surprised to find out just how political the development of accounting standards actually is. She states 'an accounting outsider might find it remarkable that accounting knowledge should be articulated not only by professional accountants, but also by accounting information users – much like doctors and patients collaborating on the development of medical knowledge'.

Hines is one author who has written quite a lot of material on what she sees as the apparent 'myth' of accounting neutrality. Hines (1988) argues that parties involved in the practice and regulation of accounting impose their own judgements about what attributes of an entity's performance should be emphasized (for example, *profits* or *return on assets*) and, also, what attributes of an entity's operations (for example, expenditure on employee health and safety initiatives) are not important enough to emphasize or highlight separately. The accountant can determine, under the 'guise' of objectivity, which attributes of an entity's operations are important and which can be used as a means of comparing the performance

---

[12] One example that is often provided by proponents of Positive Accounting Theory is managers being provided with a bonus tied to the output of the accounting system, for example, to profits. It would be argued in such a case that managers will have incentives to increase reported profits, rather than be objective.

of different organizations. For example, we are informed in the United States' SFAC No. 1 that reported earnings measures an *enterprise's performance* during a period (paragraph 45) – but clearly there are other perspectives of organizational performance (clearly some that would take a more social, as opposed to financial, form).[13] Hines emphasizes that in *communicating reality*, accountants simultaneously *construct reality*.

> If people take a definition or description of reality, for example, an organisational chart, or a budget, or a set of financial statements, to be reality, then they will act on the basis of it, and thereby perpetuate, and in so doing validate, that account of reality. Having acted on the basis of that definition of reality, and having thereby caused consequences to flow from that conception of reality, those same consequences will appear to social actors, in retrospect, to be proof that the definition of reality on which they based their actions was real … Decisions and actions based on that account predicate consequences, which, in retrospect, generally confirm the validity of the subsequent account. For example, say an investigator, or a newspaper report, suggested that a 'healthy' set of financial statements is not faithfully representational, and that a firm 'really' is in trouble. If this new definition of reality is accepted by, say, creditors, they may panic and precipitate the failure of the firm, or through the court, they may petition for a liquidation. A new definition of reality, if accepted, will be 'real in its consequences', because people will act on the basis of it. (Hines, 1991, p. 322)

Until accountants determine something is worthy of being the subject of the accounting system, then, in a sense, the issue or item does not exist. There is no transparency, and as such there is no perceived accountability in relation to the item. This perspective is adopted by Handel (1982, p. 36), who states:

> Things may exist independently of our accounts, but they have no human existence until they become accountable. Things may not exist, but they may take on human significance by becoming accountable … Accounts define reality and at the same time they are that reality … The processes by which accounts are offered and accepted are the fundamental social process … Accounts do not more or less accurately describe things. Instead they establish what is accountable in the setting in which they occur. Whether they are accurate or inaccurate by some other standards, accounts define reality for a situation in the sense that people act on the basis of what is accountable in the situation of their action. The account provides a basis for action, a definition of what is real, and it is acted on so long as it remains accountable.[14]

Hence, in concluding this subsection of the chapter we can see that there are a number of arguments that suggest that characteristics such as neutrality, while playing a part in the

---

[13] And of course financial 'performance' is very much tied to the judgements about which particular accounting methods should be employed, over how many years an asset should be amortized, and so forth. Further, because accounting rules can change over time, this in itself can lead to a change in reported profits and hence a change in apparent 'performance'.

[14] As quoted in Hines (1991).

development of conceptual frameworks, do not, and perhaps may never be expected to, reflect the underlying characteristics of financial reports. As with much of the material presented in this book, whether we accept these arguments is a matter of personal opinion. As a concluding comment to challenge the belief in the objectivity or neutrality of accounting practice, we can reflect on the following statement of Baker and Bettner (1997, p. 293):

> Accounting's capacity to create and control social reality translates into empowerment for those who use it. Such power resides in organizations and institutions, where it is used to instill values, sustain legitimizing myths, mask conflict and promote self-perpetuating social orders. Throughout society, the influence of accounting permeates fundamental issues concerning wealth distribution, social justice, political ideology and environmental degradation. Contrary to public opinion, accounting is not a static reflection of economic reality, but rather is a highly partisan activity.[15]

Definition of the elements of financial reporting

Having considered perspectives on the required qualitative characteristics of financial information, the next building block we can consider is how the elements of financial reporting are defined. The definitions provided within conceptual frameworks indicate the characteristics or attributes that are required before an item can be considered as belonging to a particular class of element (for example, before it can be considered to be an *asset*). Recognition criteria (which we consider in the next subsection of this chapter), on the other hand, are employed to determine whether the item can actually be included within the financial reports (that is, whether a particular transaction or event should be recognized as affecting the accounts).

Alternative approaches have been adopted in defining the elements of financial reporting. In the United States, ten elements of financial reporting are identified in SFAC 3, and subsequently in SFAC 6.[16] These elements are assets, liabilities, equity, investments, distributions, comprehensive income, revenues, expenses, gains and losses. The IASC's 1989 Framework (which subsequently became the IASB Framework) identifies five elements, split into two broad groups. The first group are elements relating to *financial position*, comprising the elements of *assets, liabilities* and *equity*. The second group includes elements relating to *performance* and comprises *income* and *expenses*. In the United Kingdom, the elements defined in the ASB's 1999 framework were somewhere between the US and the IASB frameworks, being *assets, liabilities, ownership interest, gains, losses, contributions from owners* and *distributions to owners*.

In the FASB conceptual framework, rather than simply having a single element entitled *income* (or *gains* as in the ASB's framework), two elements are provided, *revenues* and *gains*, where revenues relate to the 'ongoing major or central operations' of the entity, while

---

[15] The view that the practice of accounting provides the means of maintaining existing positions of power and wealth by a favoured 'elite' is further investigated in Chapter 12 which considers the works of a body of theorists who are labelled *critical theorists*.

[16] SFAC 3 was superseded by SFAC 6. SFAC 3 related to business enterprises. SFAC 6 includes non-business entities.

gains relate to 'peripheral or incidental transactions'. Clearly, the FASB classification system requires some judgement to be made about whether an item does or does not relate to the central operations of the entity. Such differentiation admits the possibility that managers might opportunistically manipulate whether items are treated as part of the ongoing operations of the entity or whether they are treated as peripheral or incidental.

Conceptual framework approaches to determining profit

There are different approaches that can be applied to determining profits (revenues less expenses). Two such approaches are commonly referred to as the *asset/liability approach*, and the *revenue/expense approach*. The asset/liability approach links profit to changes that have occurred in the assets and liabilities of the reporting entity, whereas the revenue/expense approach tends to rely on concepts such as the matching principle, which is very much focused on actual transactions and which gives limited consideration to changes in the values of assets and liabilities.

In the asset/liability approach, the principal consideration in determining how to account for any transaction (or other event) is to determine what impact this transaction or event has had on increasing or decreasing the values of assets or liabilities. The amount of the impact of any transaction or event that has not affected the value of assets or liabilities is effectively treated as a gain or loss (income or expense). This approach therefore treats the statement of financial position (formerly known as the balance sheet) as the primary financial statement, and anything that does not belong in the statement of financial position is put through the statement of comprehensive income (formerly the profit and loss account). For example, where an entity incurs expenditure, the decision process regarding how to treat this expenditure in the financial statements is first to ask: has this expenditure given rise to a new asset (or an increase in the value of an existing asset)? Where all of the expenditure is deemed to have created an asset, all of the expenditure will be reflected in the statement of financial position as an increase in the book value of an asset, and there will be no immediate impact on the net income. In situations where it is deemed that the value of an asset created (in accordance with the definition of asset discussed below) is lower than the expenditure incurred, an increase in book value of the assets within the statement of financial position will be the value of the asset created, and the difference between this value of the asset created and the amount of the expenditure incurred will be reflected in the statement of comprehensive income as an expense. Thus, if an entity incurs €1,000 expenditure on purchasing goods for resale, but by the date these goods are received by the entity their realizable value has fallen to €800, then €800 of this expenditure will be reflected in the statement of financial position as an asset and the balance of the transaction (€200) will be reflected as a loss (or expense) in the income statement.

Conversely, the revenue/expense approach treats the income statement as the principal financial statement, with the first consideration for any transaction or event being: how much of this transaction or event can (and should) be treated as income or expenses in accordance with the accruals and prudence concepts. Any amount not treated as income or expenditure is then placed in the statement of financial position as an asset or liability – with assets broadly representing the amount of expenditure that has not yet been consumed at the accounting date (and the amount of income that has not yet been received in cash), while liabilities represent expenditure that has been consumed in advance of payment (and income received in advance). Thus, in the example at the end of the last paragraph, the decision process would be: How much of the €1,000 expenditure should be treated as an expense immediately – the €200 that is unlikely to be recovered in future sales. The balance of €800 would then be placed in the statement of financial position as an asset representing the amount of expenditure that has yet to be matched against income (or consumed by selling the goods) at the accounting date.

As is the case in the above simplified example, for many transactions and events the asset/liability approach will produce the same accounting results as the revenue/expense approach, but the decision processes in arriving at this result are fundamentally different. However, for many more complex transactions and events, the two approaches will result in different accounting treatments – and we should remember that the main role of conceptual frameworks is to help standard-setters determine the most appropriate accounting treatments to be set out in accounting standards.

Most conceptual framework projects, including the IASB Framework and the FASB Framework, adopt the asset/liability approach. Within these frameworks the definitions of elements of financial statements must thus start with definitions of assets and liabilities, as the definitions of all other elements flow from these definitions of assets and liabilities. This should become apparent as we consider each of the elements of accounting – something that we now are about to do. In relation to the 'asset and liability view' of profit determination, the FASB and IASB (Bullen and Crook, 2005, pp. 7–8) state:

> In both [FASB and IASB] frameworks, the definitions of the elements are consistent with an 'asset and liability view,' in which income is a measure of the increase in the net resources of the enterprise during a period, defined primarily in terms of increases in assets and decreases in liabilities.

> That definition of income is grounded in a theory prevalent in economics: that an entity's income can be objectively determined from the change in its wealth plus what is consumed during a period (Hicks, 1946, pp. 178–179). That view is carried out in definitions of liabilities, equity, and income that are based on the definition of assets, that is, that give 'conceptual primacy' to assets. That view is contrasted with a 'revenue and expense view,' in which income is the difference between outputs from and inputs to the enterprise's earning activities during a period, defined primarily in terms of revenues (appropriately recognized) and expenses (either appropriately matched to them or systematically and rationally allocated to reporting periods in a way that avoids distortion of income.) ... Some recent critics advocate a shift back to the revenue and expense view. However, in a recent study about principle-based standards, mandated by the 2002 Sarbanes-Oxley legislation, the U.S. Securities and Exchange Commission said the following:

>> ... the revenue/expense view is inappropriate for use in standard-setting – particularly in an objectives-oriented regime ... Historical experience suggests that the asset/liability approach most appropriately anchors the standard-setting process by providing the strongest conceptual mapping to the underlying economic reality. (page 30).

>> ... the FASB should maintain the asset/liability view in continuing its move to an objectives-oriented standard-setting regime (page 42).

Definition of assets

In the IASB Framework, paragraph 49(a) defines an asset as:

> a resource controlled by the entity as a result of past events and from which future economic benefits are expected to flow to the entity.

This definition, which is similar to that adopted by the FASB, identifies three key characteristics:

1 There must be an expected future economic benefit.
2 The reporting entity must control the resource that gives rise to these future economic benefits.
3 The transaction or other event giving rise to the reporting entity's control over the future economic benefits must have occurred.

The IASB Framework makes clear that the future economic benefits can be distinguished from the source of the benefit – a particular object or right. The definition refers to the benefit and not the source. Thus, whether an object or right is disclosed as an asset will be dependent upon the likely economic benefits flowing from it. In the absence of the benefits, the object should not be disclosed as an asset. As paragraph 59 of the IASB Framework states:

> There is a close association between incurring expenditure and generating assets but the two do not necessarily coincide. Hence, when an entity incurs expenditure, this may provide evidence that future economic benefits were sought but is not conclusive proof that an item satisfying the definition of an asset has been obtained.

Conceptual frameworks do not require that an item must have a value in exchange before it can be recognized as an asset. The economic benefits may result from its ongoing use (often referred to as value-in-use) within the organization.

The characteristic of *control* relates to the capacity of a reporting entity to benefit from the asset and to deny or regulate the access of others to the benefit. The capacity to control would normally stem from legal rights. However, legal enforceability is not a prerequisite for establishing the existence of control. Hence, it is important to realize that control, and not legal ownership, is required before an asset can be shown within the body of an entity's balance sheet. Frequently, controlled assets are owned but this is not always the case. As paragraph 57 of the IASB Framework states:

> In determining the existence of an asset, the right of ownership is not essential; thus, for example, property held on a lease is an asset if the entity controls the benefits which are expected to flow from the property. Although the capacity of an entity to control benefits is usually the result of legal rights, an item may nonetheless satisfy the definition of an asset even where there is no legal control.

While the above definition of an asset is the definition that currently should be used by the IASB when developing new (or amending existing) accounting standards, this definition might change in future years. Given the central importance of the asset definition to financial reporting, any change therein will conceivably have broad implications for financial reporting. In relation to joint work being undertaken by the FASB and IASB, the FASB and IASB state in their 'Project Update: Conceptual Framework – Phase B: Elements and Recognition' that the existing definition of assets, which relies upon the terms 'control', 'expected', and 'flow' of benefits, has a number of shortcomings. The Boards noted the following (FASB, 2010b):

> The Boards agreed that the current frameworks' existing asset definitions have the following shortcomings:
>
> - Some users misinterpret the terms 'expected' (IASB definition) and 'probable' (FASB definition) to mean that there must be a high likelihood of future economic benefits for the definition to be met; this excludes asset items with a low likelihood of future economic benefits.
> - The definitions place too much emphasis on identifying the future flow of economic benefits, instead of focusing on the item that presently exists, an economic resource.
> - Some users misinterpret the term 'control' and use it in the same sense as that used for purposes of consolidation accounting. The term should focus on whether the entity has some rights or privileged access to the economic resource.
> - The definitions place undue emphasis on identifying the past transactions or events that gave rise to the asset, instead of focusing on whether the entity had access to the economic resource at the balance sheet date.
>
> The Boards have tentatively adopted the following working definition of an asset:
>
> - An *asset* of an entity is a present economic resource to which the entity has a right or other access that others do not have.
>
> Accompanying text will amplify the asset definition by describing *present, economic resource,* and *right or other access that others do not have*:
>
> - *Present* means that on the date of the financial statements both the economic resource exists and the entity has the right or other access that others do not have.
> - An *economic resource* is something that is scarce and capable of producing cash inflows or reducing cash outflows, directly or indirectly, alone or together with other economic resources. Economic resources that arise from contracts and other binding arrangements are unconditional promises and other abilities to require provision of economic resources, including through risk protection.
> - A *right or other access that others do not have* enables the entity to use the economic resource and its use by others can be precluded or limited. A right or other access that others do not have is enforceable by legal or equivalent means.

Whether the above definition replaces the existing definition is something that future years will reveal. You should consider the extent to which the above definition may have some limitations of its own.

Definition of liabilities

Paragraph 49(b) of the IASB Framework defines a liability as:

> a present obligation of the entity arising from past events, the settlement of which is expected to result in an outflow from the entity of resources embodying economic benefits.

This definition is also very similar to the definition provided in other conceptual frameworks and, as with the definition of assets, there are three key characteristics:

1 There must be an expected future disposition or transfer of economic benefits to other entities.

2 It must be a present obligation.

3 A past transaction or other event must have created the obligation.

As indicated, the definition of a liability provided above does not restrict 'liabilities' to situations where there is a legal obligation. Liabilities should also be recognized in certain situations where equity or usual business practice dictates that obligations to external parties currently exist. As paragraph 60 of the IASB Framework states:

> An essential characteristic of a liability is that the entity has a present obligation. An obligation is a duty or responsibility to act or perform in a certain way. Obligations may be legally enforceable as a consequence of a binding contract or statutory requirement. This is normally the case, for example, with amounts payable for goods and services received. Obligations also arise, however, from normal business practice, custom and a desire to maintain good business relations or act in an equitable manner. If, for example, an entity decides as a matter of policy to rectify faults in its products even when these become apparent after the warranty period has expired, the amounts that are expected to be expended in respect of goods already sold are liabilities.

Hence the liabilities that appear within an entity's statement of financial position (formerly called the balance sheet) might include obligations that are legally enforceable as well as obligations that are deemed to be equitable or constructive. When determining whether a liability exists, the intentions or actions of management need to be taken into account. That is, the actions or representations of the entity's management or governing body, or changes in the economic environment, directly influence the reasonable expectations or actions of those outside the entity and, although they have no legal entitlement, they might have other sanctions that leave the entity with no realistic alternative but to make certain future sacrifices of economic benefits. Such present obligations are sometimes called 'equitable obligations' or 'constructive obligations'. An equitable obligation is governed by social or moral sanctions or custom rather than legal sanctions. A constructive obligation is created, inferred or construed from the facts in a particular situation rather than contracted by agreement with another entity or imposed by government.

Determining whether an equitable or a constructive obligation exists is often more difficult than identifying a legal obligation, and in most situations judgement is required to determine if an equitable or a constructive obligation exists. One consideration is that the entity has no realistic alternative to making the future sacrifice of economic benefits and this implies that there is no discretion. In cases where the entity retains discretion to avoid making any future sacrifice of economic benefits, a liability does not exist and is not recognized. It follows that a decision of the entity's management or governing body, of itself, is not sufficient for the recognition of a liability. Such a decision does not mark the inception of a present obligation since, in the absence of something more, the entity retains the ability to reverse the decision and thereby avoid the future sacrifice of economic benefits. For example, an entity's management or governing body may resolve that the entity will offer to repair a defect it has recently discovered in one of its products, even though the nature of the defect is such that the purchasers of the product would not expect the entity to do so. Until the entity makes public that offer, or commits itself in some other way to making the repairs, there is no present obligation, constructive or otherwise, beyond that of satisfying the existing statutory and contractual rights of customers.

Requiring liability recognition to be dependent upon there being a present obligation to other entities has implications for the disclosure of various provision accounts, such as a provision for maintenance. Generally accepted accounting practice in some countries has required such amounts to be disclosed as a liability, even though it does not involve an obligation to an external party. This issue is partially addressed in paragraph 64 of the IASB Framework. It states:

> when a provision involves a present obligation and satisfies the rest of the definition, it is a liability even if the amount has to be estimated. Examples include provisions for payments to be made under existing warranties and provisions to cover pension obligations.

Thus, the IASB Framework requires estimated (and therefore uncertain) present obligations, which have resulted from past events and are likely to result in an outflow of economic resources, to be treated as liabilities. In more recent conceptual frameworks (such as the ASB's UK and Irish framework, which has now effectively been superseded by the older IASB Framework given the adoption of IASs/IFRSs in the EU from 2005) there tends to be an explicit requirement that uncommitted provisions not be classified as liabilities.

As with the asset definition, the IASB and FASB have recently suggested a revised definition of a liability. As FASB (2010b) states:

> The Boards agreed that the current frameworks' existing liability definitions have the following shortcomings:
>
> ■ Some users misinterpret the terms 'expected' (IASB definition) and 'probable' (FASB definition) to mean that there must be a high likelihood of future outflow of economic benefits for the definition to be met; this excludes liability items with a low likelihood of a future outflow of economic benefits.
>
> ■ The definitions place too much emphasis on identifying the future outflow of economic benefits, instead of focusing on the item that presently exists, an economic obligation.
>
> ■ The definitions place undue emphasis on identifying the past transactions or events that gave rise to the liability, instead of focusing on whether the entity has an economic obligation at the balance sheet date.
>
> ■ It is unclear how the definition applies to contractual obligations.

The Boards have tentatively adopted the following working definition of a liability:

- A *liability* of an entity is a present economic obligation for which the entity is the obligor.

Accompanying text will amplify the liability definition by describing *present, economic obligation,* and *obligor*:

- *Present* means that on the date of the financial statements both the economic obligation exists and the entity is the obligor.

- An *economic obligation* is an unconditional promise or other requirement to provide or forgo economic resources, including through risk protection.

- An entity is the *obligor* if the entity is required to bear the economic obligation and its requirement to bear the economic obligation is enforceable by legal or equivalent means.

Again, as with the proposed definition of assets, the suggested change in the liability definition could potentially have significant implications for financial reporting. For example, the above definition could act to exclude constructive or equitable obligations that are not enforceable against the entity. This would be a major departure from existing practice. Again, whether the above proposed definition ultimately becomes part of the revised conceptual framework is a matter of debate.

Definition of equity

Paragraph 49(c) of the IASB Framework defines equity as 'the residual interest in the assets of the entity after deducting all its liabilities'. That is, equity equals assets minus liabilities (and in a company, equity would be represented by 'shareholders' funds'). This definition is essentially the same as that provided by the FASB. The residual interest is a claim or right to the net assets of the reporting entity. As a residual interest, it ranks after liabilities in terms of a claim against the assets of a reporting entity. Consistent with the *asset/liability approach* to determining profits (discussed earlier in this section), the definition of equity is directly a function of the definitions of assets and liabilities. Profit or loss, income and expenses are then calculated in terms of changes in equity (that is, changes in net assets).

Definition of income

Consistent with the *asset/liability approach*, the definition of income (and expenses) provided in the IASB Framework is dependent upon the definitions given to assets and liabilities. Paragraph 70(a) defines income as:

> increases in economic benefits during the accounting period in the form of inflows or enhancements of assets or decreases of liabilities that result in increases in equity, other than those relating to contributions from equity participants.

This definition is broadly consistent with that provided by the FASB, except that the FASB definition in SFAC 3 and 6 restricts revenues to the transaction or events that relate to the 'ongoing major or central operations' of the entity.

Income can therefore be considered as relating to transactions or events that cause an increase in the net assets of the reporting entity, other than owner contributions. Strictly speaking, in applying the definition of income, increases in the market values of all assets could be treated as income. However, this is not always the case.

Within the IASB Framework, income can be recognized from normal trading relations, as well as from non-reciprocal transfers such as grants, donations, bequests or where liabilities are forgiven.

The IASB Framework further subdivides income into revenues and gains. Pursuant to the IASB Framework, 'revenue' arises in the course of the ordinary activities of an entity and is referred to by a variety of different names including sales, fees, interest, dividends, royalties and rent. 'Gains' represent other items that meet the definition of income and may, or may not, arise in the course of the ordinary activities of an enterprise. Gains include, for example, those arising on the disposal of non-current assets. There will be a degree of professional judgement involved in determining whether a component of income should be classified as revenue or as a gain. Conceptually, it is not clear why the IASB Framework subdivides income into revenues and gains and there is minimal justification provided for this subdivision within the framework.

Definition of expenses

As with income, the definition of expenses is dependent upon the definitions of assets and liabilities. Paragraph 70(b) of the IASB Framework defines expenses as:

> decreases in economic benefits during the accounting period in the form of out-
> flows or depletions of assets or incurrences of liabilities that result in decreases
> in equity, other than those relating to distributions to equity participants.

There is no reference within the IASB Framework to traditional notions of 'matching' expenses with related revenues. The definition provided by the FASB in SFAC 3 and 6 is also similar, but restricts expenses to transactions or events relating to 'ongoing major or central operations'.[17]

Expenses may therefore be considered as transactions or events that cause reductions in the net assets or equity of the reporting entity, other than those caused by distributions to the owners. They include losses (reductions in net assets) caused by events that are not under the control of an entity – such as the uninsured element of losses caused by fires or floods, or losses caused by unhedged changes in foreign exchange rates.

Reviewing the above definition of expenses (which we know is a direct function of the definitions given to assets and liabilities) we can see that if a resource is used up or damaged by an entity, but that entity does not *control* the resource – that is, it is not an *asset* of the entity – then to the extent that no liabilities or fines are imposed, no expenses will be recorded by the entity. For example, if an entity pollutes the environment but incurs no related fines, then no expense will be acknowledged, and reported profits will not be affected, no matter how much pollution was emitted or how much damage was done to resources that are shared with others (and hence, not controlled by the reporting entity).

---

[17] The definition of expenses provided in SFAC 3 and 6 is 'outflows or other using up of the assets of the entity or incurrences of liabilities of an entity (or a combination of both) during a period that result from delivering or producing goods, rendering services, or carrying out other activities that constitute the entity's ongoing major or central operations'.

This has been seen as a limitation of financial accounting and a number of experimental approaches have been adopted by a number of entities to recognize the externalities their operations can generate, but which would normally be ignored by traditional systems of accounting, including those proposed by the various conceptual framework projects. (Approaches used to incorporate externalities into financial accounting, often referred to as *full-cost accounting*, are explored in Chapter 9.)

The IASB Framework does not have a separate definition of profits, but, rather, only defines income and expenses as elements of performance. Profit is a presentational issue and is represented as the difference between the two elements, income and expenses.

Recognition of the elements of financial reporting

Having considered definitions of the elements of financial reporting (these being assets, liabilities, equity, income and expenses), the next building block we can consider is the recognition criteria for these elements. Recognition criteria are employed to determine whether an item can actually be included within any of the elements of the financial reports. For example, should an item of expenditure be recognized as an asset? Issues of recognition are tied to issues of measurement, which we consider in the next subsection of this chapter. Under conceptual frameworks such as the IASB Framework, an item cannot be recognized if it cannot be reliably measured.

Paragraph 83 of the IASB Framework specifies in relation to all elements of accounting that:

> An item that meets the definition of an element should be recognized if:
>
> **a** it is probable that any future economic benefit associated with the item will flow to or from the entity; and
>
> **b** the item has a cost or value that can be measured with reliability.

Thus, recognition is dependent upon the degree of probability that a future flow of economic benefits will arise which can be reliably measured. Obviously, considerations of *probability* can be very subjective, such that different people in different organizations might make different probability assessments for similar items. This will have implications for issues such as comparability – a qualitative characteristic of financial reporting. The IASB Framework provides relatively little guidance in judging probability, other than stating (in paragraph 85) that:

> Assessments of the degree of uncertainty attaching to the flow of future economic benefits are made on the basis of the evidence available when the financial statements are prepared.

Other paragraphs in the IASB Framework also mention that recognition depends upon materiality, and that given the interconnectedness of the definitions of the various elements, recognition of a transaction or event in respect of one element requires recognition in all elements related to that transaction or event. For example, if an event occurs which leads to the recognition that the value of a fixed asset has decreased (for example, depreciation) then the impact of this event on both assets and expenses must be recognized.

As noted above, issues of recognition are often regarded as standing side-by-side with issues of measurements. For example, Sterling (1985) argues that it is illogical to discuss how or when to recognize an element of accounting if we are not sure what measurement characteristics are to be recognized in relation to assets. What do you think of Sterling's argument that considering recognition issues in advance of measurement issues is akin to 'putting the cart before the horse'?

Measurement principles

While the recognition of the elements of financial reporting require that the elements must be measurable with reasonable accuracy, conceptual frameworks have tended to provide very limited prescription in relation to measurement issues. Assets and liabilities are often (and certainly in practice under IASs/IFRSs) measured in a variety of ways depending upon the particular class of assets or liabilities being considered. Given the way assets and liabilities are defined and used to derive measurements of income or profit, this has direct implications for reported profits. For example, liabilities are frequently recorded at present value, face value or on some other basis. In relation to assets, there are various ways these are measured – for example, inventory is to be measured at the lower of cost and net realizable value, some non-current assets such as property, plant and equipment can be measured at historical cost less a provision for depreciation, while other assets such as financial assets are to be measured at fair value.

Issues associated with measurement appeared to represent a stumbling block in the development of the FASB conceptual framework. While the FASB framework was initially promoted as being prescriptive, when SFAC 5 was issued in 1984 the FASB appeared to side-step the difficult measurement issues, and, rather, the statement provided a description of various approaches to measuring the elements of accounting. SFAC 5 simply notes that there are generally accepted to be five alternative measurement bases applied in practice: historical cost, current replacement cost, current market value, net realizable value, and present value. As noted previously in this chapter, such a descriptive approach was generally considered to represent a 'cop-out' on behalf of the FASB (Solomons, 1986). The IASB Framework explicitly recognizes the same variety of acceptable measurement bases as the FASB framework, with the exception of current market value (which could be regarded as comprising elements of current replacement cost and net realizable (sale) value).

As previously indicated in this chapter, the IASB and the FASB are currently involved in joint efforts to develop a new refined conceptual framework. In relation to measurement FASB and IASB (Bullen and Crook, 2005, p. 12) state:

> Measurement is one of the most underdeveloped areas of the two frameworks … Both frameworks (the IASB and FASB Frameworks) contain lists of measurement attributes used in practice. The lists are broadly consistent, comprising historical cost, current cost, gross or net realizable (settlement) value, current market value, and present value of expected future cash flows. Both frameworks indicate that use of different measurement attributes is expected to continue. However, neither provides guidance on how to choose between the listed measurement attributes or consider other theoretical possibilities. In other words, the frameworks lack fully developed measurement concepts … The long-standing unresolved controversy about which measurement attribute to adopt – particularly between historical-price and current-price measures – and the unresolved puzzle of unit of account are likely to make measurement one of the most challenging parts of this project.

Phase C of the joint IASB and FASB Conceptual Framework Project is to address measurement issues. In this work the IASB and FASB initially identified (in April 2007) nine potential measurement bases, these being: *past entry price, past exit price, modified past amount, current entry price, current exit price, current equilibrium price, value in use, future entry price*, and *future exit price* (FASB, 2010a). However, possibly as an indication of how controversial measurement issues can be, at the time of writing this chapter in 2010, over three years after the IASB and the FASB identified the nine potential measurement bases, few definitive decisions seem to have been taken regarding which measurement basis (or bases) should be recommended for the new conceptual framework. The FASB project website page that outlines key discussions and decisions on this part of the new conceptual framework (FASB, 2010a) indicates that there has been considerable discussion, with only tentative decisions. The most recent (at the time of writing this chapter) tentative decisions on measurement bases were reached in July 2010 and further indicate the compromises that are likely to be needed in reaching decisions on appropriate measurement bases. As the following summary of these July 2010 decisions indicates, these appear to begin to question, for example, the primacy of the statement of financial position as discussed above:

> The Boards reached the following tentative decisions relating to the development of preliminary views for the measurement chapter of the Conceptual Framework:
>
> 1 **Implications of the objective of financial reporting for measurement** – The financial statements are complements, and all of them provide information that is useful to users of financial reports. Therefore, the best way to satisfy the objective of financial reporting through measurement is to consider the effect of a particular measurement selection on all of the financial statements, instead of emphasizing the statement of financial position over the statement of comprehensive income or vice versa.
>
> 2 **General implications of the fundamental qualitative characteristics for measurement** – An explanation of how the fundamental qualitative characteristics of useful financial information (relevance and faithful representation) must be considered in selecting measurements should be developed within the measurement chapter. The Board discussed specific points supporting this tentative decision that will be developed further.
>
> 3 **Specific implications of the fundamental qualitative characteristics for historical cost and fair value** – The objective of selecting a measurement for a particular item is to maximize the information about the reporting entity's prospects for future cash flows subject to the ability to faithfully represent it at a cost that is justified by the benefits. Because neither historical cost nor fair value clearly and accurately describes the set of possible measurement methods that are to be considered, those terms should not be used in the measurement chapter.
>
> 4 **What should the measurement chapter accomplish** – The measurement chapter should list and describe possible measurements, arrange or classify the measurements in a manner that facilitates standard-setting decisions, describe the advantages and disadvantages of each measurement in terms of the qualitative characteristics of useful financial information, and discuss at a conceptual level how the qualitative

characteristics and cost constraint should be considered together in identifying an appropriate measurement. Without prescribing specific measurements for particular assets and liabilities, the measurement chapter should include cases or examples that demonstrate how the measurement chapter's concepts might be applied. (FASB, 2010a)

It is important to bear in mind that the above factors are only 'tentative decisions' and may well have changed by the time any conclusion is reached about the most appropriate measurement bases for assets, liabilities, income and expenditure (such a decision might take several years to reach). However, it is interesting to note that the IASB/FASB 4th point above, that indicates a possible mixed or eclectic approach recognizing that different measurement bases might be appropriate for use in different circumstances, resonates with some normative accounting theory that was proposed over 50 years ago and that was very influential until the movement towards empirical research in accounting (such as positive accounting theories explored in the next chapter) began to displace normative approaches. Professor Geoffrey Whittington (2008b), a highly respected accounting professor from the University of Cambridge, and a former board member of the IASB, points out that as far back as the early 1960s Edwards and Bell (1961) had recommended an eclectic approach to measurement of income – an approach the IASB and FASB lately may be moving towards with their July 2010 tentative decision noted above, made some 2 years after Whittington's paper was published:

> The implications for measurement of the Edwards and Bell approach are also at variance with the current IASB/FASB approach in the conceptual framework revision project because, unlike the IASB and FASB [at the time Whittington was writing this article], they do not aspire to identify a *single* ideal method of measurement. Rather, they see merit in a variety of valuation methods and income measures … This eclectic approach arises from their basic model, which recognises the fundamental uncertainty of the environment in which financial reporting takes place, and the role of financial reports in reducing, but not eliminating, that uncertainty by providing an objective account of the entity's progress to date. Their approach can be classified as an information approach rather than a measurement approach (Beaver and Demski, 1979, Hitz, 2007): they view accounting as providing useful information to be fed into models of valuation or decision making, rather than providing direct measurements of discounted cash flows or other economic phenomena. (Whittington, 2008b, pp. 79–80)

In this argument, Whittington also demonstrates the importance of studying a range of accounting theories – as even old theoretical perspectives can help us understand and develop current practices.

Having considered the definition, recognition and measurement of the elements of financial statements we will now consider some potential benefits that arise as a result of the development of conceptual frameworks.

6.5 Benefits associated with having a conceptual framework

Conceptual frameworks are costly to develop and open to many forms of political interference. In some respects their degree of progress, while initially promising, has for many years been rather slow and disappointing. It will be interesting to see how successful the joint initiative of the IASB and the FASB is relative to previous initiatives. Is it worth continuing with these frameworks? In this section we consider some perceived advantages that have been advanced by standard-setting bodies as being likely to follow from the development of a conceptual framework (we will also consider some criticisms). The perceived advantages include:

1 Accounting standards should be more consistent and logical because they are developed from an orderly set of concepts. That is, the accounting standards will be developed on the basis of agreed principles. The view is that in the absence of a coherent theory the development of accounting standards could be somewhat *ad hoc*. As the FASB and IASB (Bullen and Crook, 2005, p. 1) state:

> To be principles-based, standards cannot be a collection of conventions but rather must be rooted in fundamental concepts. For standards on various issues to result in coherent financial accounting and reporting, the fundamental concepts need to constitute a framework that is sound, comprehensive, and internally consistent.

2 The standard-setters should be more accountable for their decisions because the thinking behind specific requirements should be more explicit, as should any departures from the concepts that may be included in particular accounting standards.

3 The process of communication between the standard-setters and their constituents should be enhanced because the conceptual underpinnings of proposed accounting standards should be more apparent when the standard-setters seek public comment on them. Preparers and auditors will have a better understanding of why they are reporting/auditing. There is also a perspective that having a conceptual framework should alleviate some of the political pressure that might otherwise be exerted when accounting standards are developed – the conceptual framework could, in a sense, provide a defence against political attack.

4 The development of accounting standards should be more economical because the concepts developed will guide the standard-setters in their decision-making.

5 Where accounting concepts cover a particular issue, there might be a reduced need for developing additional accounting standards.

6 Conceptual frameworks have had the effect of emphasizing the 'decision usefulness' role of financial reports, rather than just restricting concern to issues associated with stewardship.

In terms of some possible disadvantages of conceptual frameworks, as with all activities based, at least in part, on lobbying processes and political actions, there will always be some parties potentially disadvantaged relative to others. Perhaps some smaller organizations feel that they are overburdened by reporting requirements because analysts have been able to convince regulators that particular information was necessary for an efficiently functioning economy.

Another criticism raised regarding the conceptual framework projects relates to their focus. Being principally economic in focus, general purpose financial reports typically ignore transactions or events that have not involved market transactions or an exchange of property rights. That is, transactions or events that cannot be linked to a 'market price' are not recognized. For example, a great deal of recent literature has been critical of traditional financial accounting for its failure to recognize the environmental externalities caused by business entities (see Deegan and Rankin, 1997; Gray and Bebbington, 2001; Gray *et al.*, 1996; Hopwood *et al.*, 2010; Rubenstein, 1992; Unerman *et al.*, 2007).

Following on from the above point, it has been argued that by focusing on economic performance, this, in itself, further reinforces the importance of economic performance relative to various levels of social or environmental performance – and this is perhaps becoming more of a problem as it becomes increasingly apparent that organizations should be embracing the concept of sustainable development. Several writers such as Hines (1988) and Gray and Bebbington (2001) have argued that the accounting profession can play a large part in influencing the forms of social conduct acceptable to the broader community. As has been indicated previously, accounting can both reflect and construct social expectations. For example, if profits and associated financial data are promoted as the best measure of organizational success, it could be argued that dominant consideration – by both the organization and the community – will only be given to activities that impact on this measure. If accountants were encouraged to embrace other types of performance indicators, including those that relate to environmental and other social performance, this may conceivably filter through to broadening people's expectations about organizational performance (Hopwood *et al.*, 2010). Nevertheless, at the present time, profitability, as indicated by the output of the accounting system, is typically used as a guide to the success of the organization.

Another criticism of conceptual frameworks is that they simply represent a codification of existing practice (Dean and Clarke, 2003; Hines, 1989), putting in place a series of documents that describe existing practice, rather than prescribing an 'ideal' or logically derived approach to accounting. Hines (1989) also argues that accounting regulations, as generated by the accounting regulators, are no more than the residual of a political process and as such do not represent any form of *ideal* model.

It has also been argued that conceptual frameworks have a more important objective from the perspective of the accounting standard-setters and one that does not provide benefits to financial statement users. Hines (1989) provides evidence that conceptual framework projects were actually initiated at times when professions were under threat – that they are 'a strategic manoeuvre for providing legitimacy to standard-setting boards during periods of competition or threatened government intervention' (1989, p. 89).

In supporting her case, Hines referred to the work undertaken in Canada. The Canadian Institute of Chartered Accountants (CICA) had done very little throughout the 1980s in relation to its conceptual framework project. It had commenced the development of a framework in about 1980, a period Hines claimed was 'a time of pressures for reform and criticisms of accounting standard-setting in Canada' (Hines, 1989, p. 88). However, interest 'waned' until another Canadian professional accounting body, the Certified General Accountants Association, through its Accounting Standards Authority of Canada, commenced developing a conceptual framework in 1986. This was deemed to represent a threat to CICA 'who were motivated into action'. Solomons (1983) also provides an argument that conceptual frameworks are a defence against political interference by other interest groups.

Whittington (2008a) provides a critique of the current IASB/FASB approach to developing their new conceptual framework, focusing on the potential role of fair value as a measurement basis – which he argues is in many ways inappropriate. As a key part of this critique, Whittington argues that in its objectives of providing information to help make investment decisions, the proposed conceptual framework (in common with the existing IASB Framework) does not adequately prioritize the information needs of existing (rather than potential future) investors. This is in contrast to some of the criticisms outlined above, that indicate a range of stakeholders other than investors will also be interested in information from general purpose financial statements. However, in common with some of these other perspectives, Whittington's arguments call for a greater emphasis on the stewardship role of financial statements rather than focusing on information to aid economic decision-making (of which stewardship may be considered a subset) – although Whittington is calling for general purpose financial statements that help evaluate the stewardship duties that managers have to existing owners rather than those they have to a broader range of current stakeholders in a business. As Whittington (2008a, pp. 144–45) explains, in the IASB/FASB consultation process it became apparent that:

> this sidelining of the stewardship objective was clearly unacceptable to many from countries that were recent adopters of IFRS and inherited a loftier view of stewardship's role … The objection to the subsuming of stewardship into the decision usefulness objective is, as expressed in the alternative view put forward by IASB members, that accountability entails more than the prediction of future cash flows. Its stewardship dimension is concerned with monitoring the past as well as predicting the future and is sometimes as much concerned with the integrity of management as with its economic performance (e.g., with respect to management remuneration and related party transactions). It is therefore concerned more with the past than is decision-usefulness, although the needs of the two typically overlap: information about the past conduct of management may be relevant to predicting future cash flows and the proper assessment of stewardship will entail estimating future prospects in order to evaluate the consequences of management's past policies. The difference between the two objectives is therefore typically one of emphasis rather than mutual exclusiveness, but both objectives need to be recognized if a proper balance is to be attained.

Whittington goes on to explain how fair values, which he states appear to underlie the new conceptual framework (in common with aspects of its predecessor frameworks), serve an economic decision-usefulness role much more than they serve a stewardship role. He contrasts what he refers to as the IASB/FASB preferred *Fair Value View* with an *Alternative View*:

> The Fair Value View emphasizes the role of financial reporting in serving investors in capital markets. It seeks accounting information that has a forward-looking content, impounding future cash flows from a non entity specific market perspective. It is most likely to achieve this when the reference markets are complete and competitive; ideally, perfect markets would be accessible.

> The Alternative View also seeks to serve investors, broadly defined, but it gives priority to existing shareholders and regards stewardship as an important and distinct function of financial reporting. It too seeks accounting information that is relevant to forecasting future cash flows, but it assumes that this will often be achieved by providing information that is useful input to investors'

valuation models, rather than direct valuation of future cash flows. Such information may be entity specific. This approach assumes that information asymmetry and imperfect and incomplete markets are common.

6.6 Conceptual frameworks as a means of legitimizing standard-setting bodies

While accounting standard-setters have promoted the benefits of conceptual frameworks, some of which have been discussed above, a number of writers (including Hines and Solomons, as identified above) have suggested that conceptual frameworks are created primarily to provide benefits to the parties that actually develop or commission the frameworks. It has been argued that conceptual frameworks have been used as devices to help ensure the ongoing existence of the accounting profession by 'boosting' their public standing (Dopuch and Sunder, 1980, p. 17). As Hines (1989, p. 74) suggests:

> One of the main obstacles against which accountants have continually had to struggle in the professionalism quest has been the threat of an apparent absence of a formal body of accounting knowledge, and that creating the perception of possessing such knowledge has been an important part of creating and reproducing their social identity as a profession … Viewing these attempts (at establishing conceptual frameworks) as claims to accounting knowledge, which are used as a political resource in reducing the threat of government intervention and competing with other groups, in order to maintain and increase professionalism and social mobility seems to explain these projects better than viewing them from a technical/functional perspective.

It is argued that conceptual frameworks provide a means of increasing the ability of a profession to self-regulate, thereby counteracting the possibility that government intervention will occur. Hines (1991, p. 328) states:

> Conceptual Frameworks presume, legitimise and reproduce the assumption of an objective world and as such they play a part in constituting the social world … Conceptual Frameworks provide social legitimacy to the accounting profession.
>
> Since the objectivity assumption is the central premise of our society … a fundamental form of social power accrues to those who are able to trade on the objectivity assumption. Legitimacy is achieved by tapping into this central proposition because accounts generated around this proposition are perceived as 'normal'. It is perhaps not surprising or anomalous then that Conceptual Framework projects continue to be undertaken which rely on information qualities such as 'representational faithfulness', 'neutrality', 'reliability', etc., which presume a concrete, objective world, even though past Conceptual Frameworks have not succeeded in generating Accounting Standards which achieve these qualities. The very talk, predicated on the assumption of an objective world to which accountants have privileged access via their 'measurement expertise', serves to construct a perceived legitimacy for the profession's power and autonomy.

If we accept the argument of Hines, we would perhaps reject notions that the accounting profession was attempting to uncover any *truths* or *ideals*, and, rather, we would consider that the development of conceptual frameworks was a political action to ensure the survival of the profession. Reflecting on the role of conceptual frameworks in assisting a professional accounting body to survive, Horngren (1981, p. 87) notes:

> The useful life of the FASB is not going to rest on issues of technical competence. The pivotal issue will be the ability of the board to resolve conflicts among the various constituencies in a manner perceived to be acceptable to the ultimate constituent, the 800-pound gorilla in the form of the federal government, particularly the SEC (of course, the federal gorilla is also subject to pressure from its constituents). The ability will be manifested in the FASB's decisions, appointments and conceptual framework. So the conceptual framework is desirable if the survival of the FASB is considered to be desirable. That is, the framework is likely to help provide power to the board. After all, the board has no coercive power. Instead, the board must really rely on power by persuasion.

Chapter summary

In this chapter we have considered the development of conceptual frameworks. We have seen that conceptual frameworks are made up of a number of building blocks that cover issues of central importance to the financial reporting process. From a technical or functional perspective it has been argued by accounting standard-setters that the development of a conceptual framework will lead to improvements in financial reporting practices, which will in turn lead to reports that are deemed more useful for the economic decisions made by the report users. With a well-formulated conceptual framework there is an expectation that information will be generated that is of more relevance to report users, as well as being more reliable. The use of a logically derived conceptual framework will also lead to the development of accounting standards that are consistent with each other. Further, there is a view that conceptual frameworks will allow constituents to understand more fully how and why particular accounting standards require specific approaches to be adopted, and will provide preparers with guidance when no specific accounting standards exist.

In considering the success of conceptual frameworks there are numerous authors who suggest that the frameworks have been a failure and have questioned whether such work should continue (Dopuch and Sunder, 1980). It has appeared that issues such as those relating to measurement have been very real stumbling blocks for the ongoing development of conceptual frameworks. The progress, or in some cases the lack of it, emphasizes the political nature of the accounting standard-setting process and shows that where constituents do not support particular approaches the standard-setters will quite often abandon particular endeavours.

While we can question the technical accomplishments of conceptual frameworks, some authors have suggested that technical advances were not the goal of the standard-setters. Rather, they have suggested that conceptual frameworks are actually established to bolster the ongoing existence and position of accountants in society. As Hines (1989, p. 79) states:

> Since professional powers, professional prestige and financial rewards are legitimised in society by being assumed to be founded on a formal body

of knowledge unique to the profession, the possibility of the loss of this mystique poses a threat to the successful advancement or social reproduction of the profession. The phenomenon of the proliferation of conceptual framework projects in the UK, USA, Canada and Australia is better understood as a response to such a threat than in the functional/technical terms in which the Conceptual Frameworks have been articulated and discussed.

Whether we accept that conceptual frameworks are developed to improve the practice of accounting, or that such frameworks are primarily created to assist those within the accounting profession, is obviously a matter of personal opinion. Having read this chapter you should be better informed to make a judgement.

Questions

6.1 What is a conceptual framework of accounting?

6.2 Do you think we need conceptual frameworks? Explain your answer.

6.3 What advantages or benefits have been advanced by standard-setters to support the development of conceptual framework projects? Do you agree that in practice such benefits will be achieved?

6.4 Conceptual framework projects identify a number of qualitative criteria that financial information should possess if it is to be useful for economic decision making. Two such attributes include neutrality and representational faithfulness. Do you believe that financial information can, in reality, be neutral and representationally faithful? Explain your answer.

6.5 Is the notion of 'prudence' as described in the IASB Framework consistent with the notion of 'neutrality' as also described within the IASB Framework?

6.6 The two main qualitative characteristics that financial information should possess have been identified as relevance and reliability. Is one more important than the other, or are they equally important? Explain why.

6.7 What are some possible objectives of general purpose financial reporting? Which objective appears to have been embraced within existing conceptual framework projects?

6.8 Which groups within society are likely to benefit from the development of a conceptual framework of accounting?

6.9 Would you consider that conceptual frameworks have been successful in achieving their stated objectives? Why, or why not?

6.10 Conceptual frameworks have yet to provide prescription in relation to measurement issues. Why do you think this is the case?

6.11 The Corporate Report (UK) referred to the 'public's right to information'. How does this differ from the perspectives adopted in other conceptual framework projects?

6.12 According to the IASB Framework, what level of proficiency in accounting are financial statement readers expected to possess? Do you agree with this position?

6.13 Hines (1991) states that 'in communicating reality, accountants simultaneously create reality'. What does she mean?

6.14 In this chapter we discussed how accounting standard-setters typically find it difficult to get support for newly developed requirements if those requirements represent major changes from existing practice. Why do you think this is the case and do you think the potential lack of support would influence the strategies adopted by accounting standard-setters?

6.15 If ultimately adopted do you think that the newly proposed definitions of assets and liabilities, as proposed in the joint work being undertaken by the IASB and FASB (and reproduced in this chapter), will have major implications for general purpose financial reporting? Why?

6.16 The definition of financial statement users provided at paragraph 9 of the IASB Framework encompasses investors, employees, lenders, suppliers, customers, government and their agencies, and the public. How much consideration, in your opinion, is really given within the IASB Framework to the information needs and expectations of 'the public'? Does the conceptual framework really prescribe the disclosure of information that members of the community would find useful in assessing the contribution that a corporation makes to the community?

6.17 Within the joint conceptual framework project being undertaken by the IASB and FASB, the following objective of general purpose financial reporting has been proposed (IASB, 2008b, p. 14):

> The objective of general purpose financial reporting is to provide financial information about the reporting entity that is useful to present and potential equity investors, lenders and other creditors in making decisions in their capacity as capital providers. Information that is decision-useful to capital providers may also be useful to other users of financial reporting who are not capital providers.

Given the above definition, how would general purpose financial reports be of relevance to people who are trying to assess the social and environmental performance of an organization?

6.18 Do you agree with a one-size-fits-all approach to international financial accounting – that is, that all countries should adopt the same accounting standards and conceptual framework? Explain your answer.

6.19 The FASB and IASB (Bullen and Crook, 2005, p. 12) state:

> The long-standing unresolved controversy about which measurement attribute to adopt – particularly between historical-price and current-price measures – and the unresolved puzzle of unit of account are likely to make measurement one of the most challenging parts of this project.

Required:

Provide an explanation of why measurement will be one of the most 'challenging' components of the conceptual framework being jointly developed by the FASB and IASB.

6.20 Hines (1991, p. 328) made the following statement:

> Conceptual Frameworks presume, legitimise and reproduce the assumptions of an objective world and as such they play a part in constituting the social world … Conceptual Frameworks provide social legitimacy to the accounting profession. Since the objectivity assumption is the central premise of our society … a fundamental form of social power accrues to those who are able to trade on the objectivity assumption. Legitimacy is achieved by tapping into this central proposition because accounts generated around this proposition are perceived as 'normal'. It is perhaps not surprising or anomalous then that Conceptual Framework projects continue to be undertaken which rely on information qualities such as 'representational faithfulness', 'neutrality', 'reliability', etc., which presume a concrete, objective world, even though past Conceptual Frameworks have not succeeded in generating Accounting Standards which achieve these qualities. The very talk, predicated on the assumption of an objective world to which accountants have privileged access via their 'measurement expertise', serves to construct a perceived legitimacy for the profession's power and autonomy.

Required:

You are to explain and evaluate Hines' statement.

References

Accounting Standards Steering Committee (1975) *The Corporate Report*, London: Institute of Chartered Accountants in England & Wales.

AICPA (1973) 'Report of study group on objectives of financial statements', *The Trueblood Report*, New York: American Institute of Certified Public Accountants.

Baker, C. & Bettner, M. (1997) 'Interpretive and critical research in accounting: A commentary on its absence from mainstream accounting research', *Critical Perspectives on Accounting*, **8** (1), 293–310.

Beaver, W.H. & Demski, J.S. (1979) 'The nature of income measurement', *The Accounting Review*, **54** (1), 38–46.

Booth, B. (2003) 'The conceptual framework as a coherent system for the development of accounting standards', *ABACUS*, **39** (3), 310–24.

Bullen, H.G. & Crook, K. (2005) 'Revisiting the concepts: A new conceptual framework project', joint FASB/IASB project report. Available at: www.fasb.org

Dean, G.W. & Clarke, F.L. (2003) 'An evolving conceptual framework?', *ABACUS*, **39** (3), 279–97.

Deegan, C.M. & Rankin, M. (1997) 'The materiality of environmental information to users of accounting reports', *Accounting, Auditing and Accountability Journal*, **10** (4), 562–83.

Dopuch, N. & Sunder, S. (1980) 'FASB's statement on objectives and elements of financial accounting: A review', *The Accounting Review*, **55** (1), 1–21.

Edwards, E.O. & Bell, P.W. (1961) *The Theory and Measurement of Business Income*, Berkeley, CA: University of California Press.

FASB (2010a) *Project Update: Conceptual Framework – Measurement* [Online], updated 28 July 2010' Financial Accounting Standards Board. Available at: http://www.fasb.org/project/cf_phase-c.shtml#background [accessed 9 August 2010].

FASB (2010b) *Project Update: Conceptual Framework – Elements and Recognition* [Online], updated 15 March 2010, Financial Accounting Standards Board. Available at: http://www.fasb.org/project/cf_phase-b.shtml#objective [accessed 9 August 2010].

Grady, P. (1965) 'An inventory of generally accepted accounting principles for business enterprises', *Accounting Research Study No. 7*, New York: AICPA.

Gray, R. & Bebbington, J. (2001) *Accounting for the Environment*, London: Sage.

Gray, R., Owen, D. & Adams, C. (1996) *Accounting and Accountability: Changes and Challenges in Corporate Social and Environmental Reporting*, London: Prentice-Hall.

Handel, W. (1982) *Ethnomethodology: How People Make Sense*, Hemel Hempstead: Prentice-Hall.

Hendriksen, E. (1970) *Accounting Theory*, Homewood, IL: Richard D. Irwin.

Hicks, J.R. (1946) *Value and Capital*, Oxford: Oxford University Press.

Hines, R. (1988) 'Financial accounting: In communicating reality, we construct reality', *Accounting Organizations and Society*, 13 (3), 251–62.

Hines, R. (1989) 'Financial accounting knowledge, conceptual framework projects and the social construction of the accounting profession', *Accounting, Auditing and Accountability Journal*, 2 (2), 72–92.

Hines, R. (1991) 'The FASBs conceptual framework, financial accounting and the maintenance of the social world', *Accounting Organizations and Society*, 16 (4), 313–51.

Hitz, J.-M. (2007) 'The decision usefulness of fair value accounting: A theoretical perspective', *European Accounting Review*, 16 (2), 323–62.

Hopwood, A.G., Unerman, J. & Fries, J. (eds.) (2010) *Accounting for Sustainability: Practical Insights*, London: Earthscan.

Horngren, C.T. (1981) 'Uses and limitations of a conceptual framework', *Journal of Accountancy*, 151 (4), 86–95.

IASB (2006) *Preliminary Views on an Improved Conceptual Framework for Financial Reporting: The Objective of Financial Reporting and Qualitative Characteristics of Decision-useful Financial Reporting Information*, London: International Accounting Standards Committee Foundation.

IASB (2008a) 'Discussion Paper – Preliminary Views on an Improved Conceptual Framework for Financial Reporting: The Reporting Entity', London: International Accounting Standards Board.

IASB (2008b) *Exposure Draft of an Improved Conceptual Framework for Financial Reporting: Chapter 1: The Objective of Financial Reporting, Chapter 2: Qualitative Characteristics and Constraints of Decision-useful Financial Reporting Information*, London: International Accounting Standards Committee Foundation.

IASB (2008c) *Exposure Draft of an Improved Conceptual Framework for Financial Reporting: Chapter 2 Qualitative Characteristics and Constraints of Decision-useful Financial Reporting Information*, London: International Accounting Standards Board.

IASB (2010) *Exposure Draft of Conceptual Framework for Financial Reporting: The Reporting Entity*, London: International Accounting Standards Committee Foundation.

Loftus, J.A. (2003) 'The CF and accounting standards: The persistence of discrepancies', *ABACUS*, **39** (3), 298–309.

Miller, P.B.W. (1990) 'The conceptual framework as reformation and counterreformation', *Accounting Horizons*, (June), 23–32.

Miller, P.B.W. & Redding, R. (1986) *The FASB: The People, the Process, and the Politics*, Homewood IL: Irwin.

Moonitz, M. (1961) 'The basic postulates of accounting', *Accounting Research Study No. 1*, New York: AICPA.

Nussbaumer, N. (1992) 'Does the FASBs conceptual framework help solve real accounting issues?', *Journal of Accounting Education*, **10** (1), 235–42.

Peasnell, K.V. (1982) 'The function of a conceptual framework for corporate financial reporting', *Accounting and Business Research*, **12** (4), 243–56.

Rubenstein, D.B. (1992) 'Bridging the gap between green accounting and black ink', *Accounting Organizations and Society*, **17** (5), 501–508.

Solomons, D. (1978) 'The politicization of accounting', *Journal of Accountancy*, **146** (5), 65–72.

Solomons, D. (1983) 'The political implications of accounting and accounting standard setting',

Accounting and Business Research, **13** (56), 107–18.

Solomons, D. (1986) 'The FASBs conceptual framework: An evaluation', *Journal of Accountancy*, **161** (6), 114–24.

Sprouse, R. & Moonitz, M. (1962) 'A tentative set of broad accounting principles for business enterprises', *Accounting Research Study No. 3*, New York: AICPA.

Staunton, J. (1984) 'Why a conceptual framework of accounting?', *Accounting Forum*, **7** (2), 85–90.

Sterling, R.R. (1985) 'An essay on recognition', *The University of Sydney Accounting Research Centre.*

Unerman, J., Bebbington, J. & O'Dwyer, B. (eds.) (2007) *Sustainability Accounting and Accountability*, London: Routledge.

Walker, R.G. (2003) 'Objectives of financial reporting', *ABACUS*, **39** (3), 340–55.

Watts, R.L. & Zimmerman, J.L. (1986) *Positive Accounting Theory*, Englewood Cliffs, NJ: Prentice-Hall.

Wells, M. (2003) 'Forum: The accounting conceptual framework', *ABACUS*, **39** (3), 273–78.

Whittington, G. (2008a) 'Fair value and the IASB/FASB conceptual framework project: An alternative view', *ABACUS*, **44** (2), 139–68.

Whittington, G. (2008b) 'What the "Old Guys" can tell us: Edwards and Bell's *The Theory and Measurement of Business Income*', *The Irish Accounting Review*, **15** (1), 73–84.

07

Positive Accounting Theory

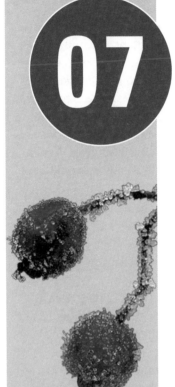

Upon completing this chapter readers should understand:

❖ how a positive theory differs from a normative theory;

❖ the origins of Positive Accounting Theory (PAT);

❖ the perceived role of accounting in minimizing the transaction costs of an organization;

❖ how accounting can be used to reduce the costs associated with various political processes;

❖ how particular accounting-based agreements with parties such as debtholders and managers can provide incentives for managers to manipulate accounting numbers;

❖ some of the criticisms of PAT.

> ## Opening issues
>
> Corporate management often expends considerable time and effort making submissions to accounting regulators on proposed introductions of, or amendments to, mandated accounting requirements (such as accounting standards). For example, as we discussed in Chapter 3, elements of the revised IAS 39 (which required market valuations for financial instruments) were opposed by many banks in Europe. The banks argued that these elements of IAS 39 failed to take account of the underlying economic realities of the manner in which these banks operated, and would result in financial statements that would not reflect the underlying economic reality. Executives of many banks lobbied against the introduction of these elements of IAS 39. What would have motivated such opposition?

7.1 Introduction

In previous chapters of this book we have considered numerous issues as they relate to financial accounting, including theories to explain the needs and demand for financial accounting regulations as well as explanations for international differences in financial accounting. We have also considered normative theories of accounting – specifically theories that prescribe how to undertake financial accounting in times of changing prices (or asset values), and conceptual framework projects which provide prescription about how elements of accounting should be defined and measured, and when they should be recognized.

In this chapter we change the focus and consider a theory that seeks to explain why managers within organizations will elect to adopt particular accounting methods in preference to others. That is, we will not be considering theories (normative theories) that tell us how we should be undertaking financial accounting. Rather, we will be considering a theory (a positive theory) that explains why managers elect to embrace particular accounting methods.

Quite often in financial accounting we will have a choice between alternative accounting methods to account for a particular transaction or event – that is, even with our many accounting standards there is still a degree of flexibility in how to account for specific items or events. The theory discussed in this chapter – Positive Accounting Theory – provides a particular perspective about why managers, when confronted with a choice between competing accounting methods, would elect to adopt or support particular accounting methods in preference to others. As we will see in this chapter, Positive Accounting Theory relies in large part on assumptions from economic theory. For example, the theory assumes that 'markets' are efficient and that all individual action is driven by self-interest. As with most theories of accounting, there will be supporters and there will also be opponents of the theory. The chapter will conclude with a review of some criticisms of Positive Accounting Theory.

7.2 Positive Accounting Theory defined

As indicated in Chapter 1, a *positive theory* is a theory that seeks to explain and predict particular phenomena. According to Watts (1995, p. 334), the use of the term *positive research* was popularized in economics by Friedman (1953) and was used to distinguish research which sought to *explain* and *predict* (which is positive research), from research which aimed to provide *prescription* (as we have explained in previous chapters, prescriptive research is often labelled *normative* research). Positive Accounting Theory, the topic discussed in this chapter and the theory popularized by Watts and Zimmerman, is one of several positive theories of accounting.[1] As indicated in Chapter 1, we will refer to the general class of theories that attempt to explain and predict accounting practice in lowercase (that is, as positive theories of accounting), and will refer to Watts and Zimmerman's particular positive theory of accounting as Positive Accounting Theory (that is, in uppercase). Hence, while it might be confusing, we must remember that Watts and Zimmerman's Positive Accounting Theory is an example of *one* particular positive theory of accounting. This confusion might not have arisen had Watts and Zimmerman elected to adopt an alternative name (or 'trademark') for their particular theory. According to Watts and Zimmerman (1990, p. 148):

> We adopted the label 'positive' from economics where it was used to distinguish research aimed at explanation and prediction from research whose objective was prescription. Given the connotation already attached to the term in economics we thought it would be useful in distinguishing accounting research aimed at understanding accounting from research directed at generating prescriptions … The phrase 'positive' created a trademark and like all trademarks it conveys information. 'Coke', 'Kodak', 'Levi's' convey information.

As Watts and Zimmerman (1986, p. 7) state, Positive Accounting Theory (hereafter referred to as PAT):

> is concerned with explaining accounting practice. It is designed to explain and predict which firms will and which firms will not use a particular method … but it says nothing as to which method a firm should use.[2]

Positive theories can be contrasted with normative theories. In Chapters 5 and 6 we considered different normative theories of accounting. Normative theories prescribe how a particular practice *should* be undertaken and this prescription might be a significant departure from existing practice. A normative theory is generated as a result of the

---

[1] Legitimacy theory, institutional theory and stakeholder theory, all covered in Chapter 8, are other examples of positive theories. For example, legitimacy theory predicts that in certain circumstances organizations will use positive or favourable disclosures in an effort to gain, maintain or restore the *legitimacy* of an organization. These other positive theories are not grounded in classical economic theory, whereas Positive Accounting Theory is.

[2] Similarly, in Chapter 8 we see that three other positive theories, stakeholder theory (the managerial version), institutional theory, and legitimacy theory, provide alternative explanations (alternative to PAT) about what drives an organization to make particular disclosures. These theoretical perspectives also do not prescribe particular actions, or methods of disclosure.

particular theorist applying some norm, standard or objective against which actual practice should strive to achieve.

We see in this chapter that PAT focuses on the relationships between the various individuals involved in providing resources to an organization and how accounting is used to assist in the functioning of these relationships. Examples are the relationships between the owners (as suppliers of equity capital) and the managers (as suppliers of managerial labour), or between the managers and the firm's debt providers (that is, the creditors). Many relationships involve the delegation of decision-making from one party (the principal) to another party (the agent) – this is referred to as an agency relationship.

When decision-making authority is delegated, this can lead to some loss of efficiency and consequent costs. For example, if the owner (principal) delegates decision-making authority to a manager (agent) it is possible that the manager may not work as hard as would the owner, given that the manager might not share directly in the results of the organization. Any potential loss of profits brought about by the manager under-performing is considered to be a cost that results from the decision-making delegation within this agency relationship – an agency cost. The agency costs that arise as a result of delegating decision-making authority from the owner to the manager are referred to in PAT as *agency costs of equity*.

PAT, as developed by Watts and Zimmerman and others, is based on the central economics-based assumption that the actions of all individuals are driven by *self-interest*, and that individuals will always act in an opportunistic manner to the extent that their actions will increase their wealth. Notions of loyalty, morality and the like are not incorporated in the theory (as they typically are not incorporated in other accounting or economic theories). Given an assumption that self-interest drives all individual actions (which in many people's mind is an overly simplistic and inaccurate assumption), PAT predicts that organizations will seek to put in place mechanisms that align the interests of the managers of the firm (the agents) with the interests of the owners of the firm (the principals). As we see later in this chapter, some of these methods of aligning interests will be based on the output of the accounting system (such as providing the manager with a share of the organization's *profits*). Where such accounting-based 'alignment mechanisms' are in place, there will be a need for financial statements to be produced. Managers are predicted to 'bond' themselves to prepare these financial statements.[3] This is costly in itself, and in PAT would be referred to as a 'bonding cost'. If we assume that managers (agents) will be responsible for preparing the financial statements, then PAT also would predict that there would be a demand for those statements to be audited or monitored, otherwise agents would, assuming self-interest (a maintained assumption of PAT), try to overstate profits, thereby increasing their absolute share of profits. In PAT, the cost of undertaking an audit is referred to as a 'monitoring cost'.

To address the agency problems that arise within an organization, there may be various bonding and monitoring costs incurred. If it was assumed, contrary to the assumptions of PAT, that individuals always worked for the benefit of their employers, then there would not be such a demand for such activities – other than perhaps to review the efficiency with

---

[3] From the PAT perspective, *bonding* occurs when the agent gives a guarantee to undertake, or not to undertake, certain activities.

which the manager was operating the business. As PAT assumes that not all opportunistic actions of agents can be controlled by contractual arrangements or otherwise, there will always be some residual costs associated with appointing an agent.

Having provided this introductory overview of PAT we now turn to the origins and development of PAT. We return to the issue of how accounting can be used to reduce conflicts within the firm later in this chapter. The following discussion shows that PAT developed out of the economics literature and was heavily reliant on assumptions about the efficiency of markets (from the efficient markets hypothesis); on research that considered the reactions of capital markets to accounting information (which was developed from models such as the capital assets pricing model); and on the role of contractual arrangements in minimizing conflicts within an organization (from agency theory).

7.3 The origins and development of Positive Accounting Theory

Positive research in accounting started coming to prominence around the mid-1960s and appeared to become the dominant research paradigm within financial accounting in the 1970s and 1980s. Prior to this time the dominant type of accounting research was normative accounting research – research that sought to provide prescription based on the theorists' perspective of the underlying objective of accounting. High-profile normative researchers of this time included Sterling, Edwards, Bell and Chambers and the focus of much of the research was how to undertake accounting in times of rising prices.[4] Such normative research did not rely on examining existing practice – that is, it did not tend to be empirical.

Watts (1995, p. 299) provides an insight into the trends in accounting research that occurred from the 1950s to 1970s. As evidence of the trends, and relying on the works of Dyckman and Zeff (1984), he documents the number of publications accepted by two dominant academic accounting journals – *The Accounting Review* and the *Journal of Accounting Research*.[5] He states:

> The introduction of positive research into accounting in the mid-1960s represented a paradigm shift. Prior to that time, the most common type of paper published in the leading English language academic journal of the time (The Accounting Review) was normative (like the works of Edwards and Bell, Chambers and Sterling). In the period 1956–1963, 365 of Accounting Review articles were of this type. These papers use assumptions about phenomena and objectives to deduce their prescriptions. They do not use systematic evidence

[4] We considered the work of these theorists in Chapter 5. As indicated in Chapter 5 as well as in Chapter 1, researchers such as Sterling, Chambers and many others were particularly critical of positive research, and particularly of Positive Accounting Theory. Among their many criticisms was the criticism that PAT, while attempting to explain and predict accountants' behaviour, provided no prescription about what methods accountants should adopt to provide useful information to the readers of accounting reports.

[5] By relying on only two journals it could easily be argued, given that there are many other accounting journals, that the data may not be representative of all accounting research being undertaken. Further, evidence would indicate that the editors of these journals developed an extremely favourable disposition towards positive research, a disposition not necessarily shared by editors of other journals. Nevertheless, there was certainly a significant movement towards positive research in the 1960s and 1970s.

and/or advance hypotheses for formal testing. Only 3% of the articles published in Accounting Review in 1956–1963 were empirical and most were not designed to test hypotheses. Virtually none of the papers in this time period were attempts to explain current accounting using mathematical modelling or less formal techniques. Today, almost all papers in Accounting Review are in the positive tradition and the same is true of most other leading academic journals (all of which started in 1963 or later).[6]

In reflecting on what caused the shift in paradigm from normative to positive research, Watts (1995, p. 299) argues that:

> The paradigm shift is associated with changes in US business schools in the late 1950s and early 1960s. Reports on business education commissioned by the Ford Foundation and the Carnegie Corporation of New York were catalysts for those changes ... Hypothesis forming and testing were viewed as essential for good research.[7]

The above quote refers to the 'essential' nature of 'hypothesis forming and testing'. This in itself represents a biased view about what constitutes 'good research'. A hypothesis would be formed to test a prediction, for example that under specific conditions accountants would select a particular method of accounting – this type of issue is something that fascinates researchers working within a PAT framework. The reason that normative researchers, on the other hand, would not form and test hypotheses is that such researchers would not be as concerned with what is (which could be tested empirically) – rather they would be concerned with what should be. Hence, normative researchers do not necessarily develop any predictive hypotheses – but this in itself should not be used to dismiss their work as not being 'good research'.

Nevertheless, there was a view from opponents of normative research that, in failing to provide 'falsifiable' predictions (or hypotheses), normative researchers failed to meet the requirements necessary to advance knowledge. As we indicated in Chapter 1, there is a subset of the research community known as the falsificationists (the leader of which was considered to be Karl Popper). They consider that knowledge develops through trial and error and that 'sound research' should generate propositions or hypotheses that are of a form that allows them to be rejected if evidence supporting the propositions or hypotheses is not available (that is, the hypothesis should be falsifiable). If falsifiable hypotheses are not generated from the theory then falsificationists would believe that the theory is deficient.

It was also argued that around the mid-1960s and throughout the 1970s, computing facilities improved markedly such that it became increasingly practical to undertake large-scale statistical analysis – an approach used within the positive research paradigm. As Watts and Zimmerman (1986, p. 339) state:

> Computers and large machine-readable data bases (CRSP and Compustat) became available in the 1960s. And, partially in response to the lowered cost

---

[6] As we might imagine, there are many researchers who do not favour the positive research paradigm, and hence would challenge Watts' view that journals that publish positive research are 'leading' academic journals.

[7] As indicated in Chapter 1, a paradigm can be described as an approach to knowledge advancement that adopts particular theoretical assumptions, research goals and research methods (Kuhn, 1962).

of empirical work, finance and economic positive theories became available for accounting researchers' use. This led to the development of positive accounting research and to researchers trained in the methodology of positive theory.[8]

Watts considers that one paper which was crucial to the acceptance of the positive research paradigm was Ball and Brown (1968). According to Watts (1995, p. 303), the publication of this paper in the *Journal of Accounting Research* caused widespread interest in accounting-related capital market research (research which seeks to explain and predict share price reaction to the public release of accounting information), and led to ever-increasing numbers of papers being published in the area (we will consider this paper shortly). Reflecting on the subsequent shift in publications towards positive research, Watts (1995, p. 303) states:

> Empirical papers as a proportion of papers published in Journal of Accounting Research rose from 13 per cent in 1967 to 31 per cent in 1968 and to 60 per cent by 1972. Normative papers in Journal of Accounting Research fell from 24 per cent in 1967 to seven per cent in 1968 and by 1972 to zero. The Accounting Review (which is another leading journal) followed suit and stopped publishing normative papers. The empirical papers in the capital markets area were in the positivist tradition. The normativists challenged the evidence and its interpretation, but did not supply their own counter-evidence. They did not have the training nor likely the desire to compete in this dimension.

Role of the efficient markets hypothesis

One development from the 1960s that was crucial to the development of PAT was the work of theorists such as Fama, particularly work that related to the development of the efficient markets hypothesis (EMH). The EMH is based on the assumption that capital markets react in an efficient and unbiased manner to publicly available information.[9] The perspective taken is that security prices reflect the information content of publicly available information and this information is not restricted to accounting disclosures. The capital market is considered to be highly competitive, and as a result newly released

---

[8] Chapter 12 (which considers the views of the *critical theorists*) provides alternative views about why positive accounting flourished in the 1970s and 1980s. These theorists (for example Mouck, 1992; Tinker *et al.*, 1991) believe that many accounting researchers provide research results and perspectives that aim to legitimize and maintain particular political ideologies. As an example, in the late 1970s and in the 1980s, there were moves by particular governments around the world towards deregulation. This was particularly the case in the United States and the United Kingdom. Around this time researchers working within the Positive Accounting Theory framework, and researchers who embraced the efficient markets hypothesis, came to prominence. The researchers typically took an anti-regulation stance, a stance that matched the views of the government of the time. Coincidentally, perhaps, the critical theorists show that such research, which supported calls for deregulation, tended to attract considerable government-sourced research funding, thereby providing further resources for the theory's development.

[9] Research that subsequently tested the EMH predominantly adopted the assumption of *semi-strong form market efficiency*. Under the assumption of semi-strong form efficiency the market price of a firm's securities reflects all publicly available information. According to Watts and Zimmerman (1986, p. 19) the available evidence is generally consistent with the semi-strong form of EMH. Two other forms of market efficiency (with less empirical support) have also been advanced. A *weak form* of market efficiency assumes that existing security prices simply reflect information about past prices and trading volumes. The *strong form* of market efficiency assumes that security prices reflect all information known to anyone at that point in time (including information which is not publicly available). We consider capital markets research (and the EMH) more fully in Chapter 9.

public information is expected to be quickly impounded into share prices. As Watts and Zimmerman (1986, p. 6) state:

> Underlying the EMH is competition for information. Competition drives investors and financial analysts to obtain information on the firm from many sources outside the firm's accounting reports and even outside the firm itself. For example, analysts obtain weekly production data on automobile firms and interview management. Analysts also interview competitors about a corporation's sales and creditors about the corporation's credit standing.

If accounting results are released by an organization, and these results were already anticipated by the market (perhaps as a result of interim announcements), then the expectation is that the price of the security will not react to the release of the accounting results. Consistent with traditional finance theory, PAT assumes that the price of a security is determined on the basis of beliefs about the present value of future cash flows pertaining to that security, and when these beliefs change (as a result of particular 'new' information becoming available) the expectation is that the security's price will also change.[10]

Because share prices are expected to reflect information from various sources (as the information relates to predicting future cash flows), there was a view that management cannot manipulate share prices by changing accounting methods in an opportunistic manner. If the change in accounting method does not signal a change in cash flows, then early proponents of the EMH would argue that the capital market will not react. Further, because there are many sources of data used by the capital market, if managers make less than truthful disclosures, which are not corroborated or contradict other available information, then, assuming that the market is efficient, the market will question the integrity of the managers. Consequently, the market will tend to pay less attention to subsequent accounting disclosures made by such managers. Watts and Zimmerman (1986) rely upon this perspective to argue against the need for extensive accounting regulation. Because accounting information is only one source of information, because markets are assumed to be efficient in evaluating information, and because of the existence of other potentially non-corroboratory evidence, there is believed to be limited benefit in imposing accounting regulation.[11]

Share price reactions to unexpected earnings announcements

Researchers such as Ball and Brown (1968) and Beaver (1968) sought to investigate empirically stock market reactions to accounting earnings announcements. Utilizing monthly information about earnings announcements in the *Wall Street Journal* and information about share returns, Ball and Brown investigated whether unexpected changes in accounting earnings lead to abnormal returns on an organization's securities. Relying

---

[10] In studies that investigate the reaction of the capital market to earnings announcements, it is generally assumed that accounting earnings are highly correlated with cash flows, hence new information about accounting earnings is deemed to indicate new information about cash flows.

[11] As we indicated in Chapter 3, advocates of a 'free-market' approach to regulation (that is, people who adopt an anti-regulation stance) typically use arguments that various markets (such as capital markets and managerial labour markets) are efficient and will penalize managers who fail to provide information which efficiently reflects the performance of their organization. Hence, markets will 'encourage' full disclosure and there is therefore perceived to be no need for regulatory requirements or intervention.

upon the EMH, Ball and Brown proposed that if the earnings announcements were useful to the capital market (that is, if there was *new* or *unexpected* information in the announcement), then share prices would adjust to reflect the new information. As they stated (1968, p. 159):

> If security prices do in fact adjust rapidly to new information as it becomes available, then changes in security prices will reflect the flow of information to the market. An observed revision of stock prices associated with the release of the income report would thus provide evidence that the information reflected in income numbers is useful.

Hence Ball and Brown needed to determine whether the earnings announcement contained any information that was unexpected and therefore potentially 'useful'. Using statistical modelling they calculated an estimate of what was the *expected earnings* of the entity in the absence of the earnings announcement. They also needed a model to estimate what the market return from holding the entity's securities would have been in the absence of the information. That is, they needed to be able to determine what *normal* returns would have been on the securities so that they could then determine whether any *abnormal* returns arose (which would have been assumed to relate to the information disclosure).

In determining what the normal returns would have been, had there been no unexpected information in the earnings announcement, reliance is placed on the market model which is derived from the capital assets pricing model (CAPM).[12] These models are more fully discussed in Chapter 10. Briefly, on the basis of past information, the CAPM provides an indication of the expected rate of return on securities by applying a linear model.[13] The expected return on a particular stock is calculated by considering the risk-free rate of return (for example, the return from holding government bonds), plus a risk/return component which is based on how the returns on the particular security have fluctuated historically relative to the movements in the overall (diversified) stock market. The difference between the expected return and the actual return constitutes the abnormal return. The results of the Ball and Brown study were generally supportive of the view that if earnings (or profit) announcements provided unexpected information, the capital market reacted to the information, the reaction taking the form of abnormal returns on the entity's securities.

By indicating that earnings (or profit) announcements (mainly based on historical cost accounting) were impacting on share prices, Ball and Brown provided evidence that they considered was consistent with a view that historical cost information was useful to the market.[14] This was in direct conflict with various normative theorists (such as Chambers)

---

[12] Share returns would generally be calculated by taking into account the change in price of the security during the period, as well as any dividends received during the period.

[13] The development of the CAPM is generally credited to the works of Sharpe (1964) and Lintner (1965).

[14] Much research has followed Ball and Brown (1968). For example, subsequent research has shown that the relationship between the information content in earnings announcements and changes in share prices tends to be more significant for small firms. That is, in general, larger firms' earnings announcements have relatively less information content (for example). This is consistent with the EMH and is explained by the fact that larger firms tend to have more information being circulated about them, as well as attracting more attention from such parties as security analysts. Hence, on average, earnings announcements for larger firms tend to be more anticipated, and hence already impounded in the share price prior to the earnings announcement.

who had argued that historical cost information is rather useless and misleading.[15] The capital market apparently thought otherwise (if we accept that the change in share price reflected the *usefulness* of the accounting information).[16] In this respect, Watts and Zimmerman (1986, p. 161) state:

> Some critics charge that, because earnings are calculated using several different methods of valuation (e.g. historical cost, current cost, and market value), the earnings numbers are meaningless and stock prices based on those numbers do not discriminate between efficient and less efficient firms. Given the EMH, evidence is inconsistent with this criticism. Positive stock price changes are associated with positive unexpected earnings and negative stock prices with negative unexpected earnings. Therefore, since the stock price is an unbiased estimate of value, earnings changes are measures of value changes.

Throughout the 1970s and subsequent years, many other studies were published that documented the relationship between accounting earnings and security returns (and a number of these are considered in Chapter 10). However, while supportive of the EMH, the literature was unable to explain *why* particular accounting methods might have been selected in the first place. That is, the research provided no hypotheses to *predict* and *explain* accounting choices – rather the existing research simply considered the market's reaction to the ultimate disclosures.

Use of agency theory to help explain and predict managerial choice of accounting policies

Much of the research based on the EMH assumed that there were zero contracting and information costs, as well as assuming that the capital market could efficiently 'undo' the implications of management selecting different accounting methods.[17] For example, if an entity elected to switch its inventory cost flow assumptions and this led to an increase in reported income, then the market was assumed to be able to 'see through' this change and, to the extent that there were no apparent cash flow implications (for example, through changing taxes), there would be no share price reaction. Hence, if the particular accounting

---

[15] Ball and Brown's results were also considered to be important because they emphasize that accounting numbers were not the sole (or predominant) source of information about an organization. This was in contrast to the views held by many normative theorists who considered that accounting data were the sole, or at least the most important, source of information about an organization, hence their concerns about getting the accounting numbers 'right'.

[16] What should also be appreciated is that research such as that undertaken by Ball and Brown and subsequent researchers actually represents a joint test of the EMH, as well as the procedures used to estimate *expected returns* and *normal returns*. That is, failure to generate significant results (or indeed, success in generating significant results) may be due to misspecification problems in the calculation of expected earnings and normal returns, rather than problems with the hypothesis itself.

[17] As shown later in this chapter, however, subsequent arguments were developed to support a contrary view that a change in accounting method may have cash flow consequences (and therefore, consequences for share prices). For example, the new accounting method may be considered to provide information more efficiently about the performance of the firm, and hence may enable the firm to attract more funds at lower cost (perhaps because investors consider the available information to be more reliable). Further, and as shown shortly, many contractual arrangements with associated cash flows (for example, there might be an agreement that the manager gets paid a percentage of profits) are tied to accounting numbers and hence changing those numbers can ultimately change cash flows (and hence, change firm value if we believe that the value of a firm's securities represent expectations about the net present value of the future expected cash flows of the firm).

method had no direct taxation implications, and assuming that markets were efficient and able to understand the effects of using alternative accounting methods, there was an inability to explain why one method of accounting was selected by management in preference to another. As Watts and Zimmerman (1990, p. 132) state:

> An important reason that the information perspective (e.g. Ball and Brown, 1968) failed to generate hypotheses explaining and predicting accounting choice is that in the finance theory underlying the empirical studies, accounting choice *per se* could not affect firm value. Information is costless and there are no trans-action costs in the CAPM frameworks. Hence if accounting methods do not affect taxes they do not affect firm value. In that situation there is no basis for predicting and explaining accounting choice. Accounting is irrelevant.

Yet, evidence indicated that corporate managers expended considerable resources lobbying regulators in regard to particular accounting methods that could potentially be included in accounting standards. To such individuals, the choice of accounting method *did* matter. Further, there was evidence (for example, Kaplan and Roll, 1972) that firms within an entire industry often elected to switch accounting methods at a particular time.

A key to explaining managers' choice of particular accounting methods came from agency theory. Agency theory provided a necessary explanation of why the selection of particular accounting methods might matter, and hence was an important facet in the development of PAT. Agency theory focused on the relationships between principals and agents (for example, the relationship between shareholders and corporate managers), a relationship which, due to various information asymmetries, created much uncertainty. Agency theory accepted that transaction costs and information costs exist.

Jensen and Meckling (1976) was a key paper in the development of agency theory and was a paper that Watts and Zimmerman greatly relied upon when developing PAT. Jensen and Meckling defined the agency relationship (1976, p. 308) as:

> A contract under which one or more (principals) engage another person (the agent) to perform some service on their behalf which involves delegating some decision-making authority to the agent.[18]

Relying upon traditional economics literature (including accepting assumptions such as that all individuals are driven by desires to maximize their own wealth) Jensen and Meckling considered the relationships and conflicts between agents and principals and how efficient markets and various contractual mechanisms can assist in minimizing the cost to the firm of these potential conflicts.

Within agency theory, a well-functioning firm was considered to be one that minimizes its agency costs (those costs inherent in the principal–agent relationship). As indicated earlier in this chapter, if there is no mechanism to make an agent pay for actions that are undertaken and which adversely impact upon the owners (principals), then that agent (or manager) will, it is assumed, have an incentive to consume many perquisites, as well as to use confidential information for personal gain at the expense of the principals (the owners).

---

[18] This *contract* does not have to be a written contract. That is, it may simply constitute implicit terms about how the principal expects the manager to the behave.

It is the incentive problems that are at the heart of agency theory. As Lambert (2001, pp. 5–6) states:

> agency theory models are constructed based on the philosophy that it is important to examine incentive problems and their 'resolution' in an economic setting in which the potential incentive problem actually exists. Typical reasons for conflicts of interest include (i) effort aversion by the agent, (ii) the agent can divert resources for his private consumption or use, (iii) differential time horizons, e.g., the agent is less concerned about the future period effects of his current period actions because he does not expect to be with the firm or the agent is concerned about how his actions will affect others' assessments of his skill, which will affect compensation in the future, or (iv) differential risk aversion on the part of the agent.

It is assumed within agency theory that principals will assume that the agent (like the principal and, indeed, all individuals) will be driven by self-interest, and therefore the principals will anticipate that the manager, unless restricted from doing otherwise, will undertake self-serving activities that could be detrimental to the economic welfare of the principals. In the absence of any contractual mechanisms to restrict the agents' potentially opportunistic behaviour, the principal will pay the agent a lower salary in anticipation of the opportunistic actions.[19] This lower salary will compensate the owners for the adverse actions that the managers are considered likely to undertake (this is referred to as price protection). Hence, the perspective is that it is the agents who, on average, pay for the principals' expectations of their opportunistic behaviour. The agents are therefore assumed to have an incentive to enter into contractual arrangements that appear to be able to reduce their ability to undertake actions detrimental to the interests of the principals. Consistent with this, Watts and Zimmerman (1986, p. 184) state:

> This [perspective] provides the prime insight in the Jensen and Meckling analysis: the agent, not the principal, has the incentive to contract for monitoring. The outside shareholders do not care if monitoring (often involving accounting and auditing) is conducted. Competition in the capital markets leads to price protection and ensures that outside investors earn a normal return. Owner-managers (the agents) have the incentive to offer guarantees to limit their consumption of perks, for owner-managers receive all the gains … With competition and rational expectations, owner-managers who have incentives to take value reducing actions (opportunistic actions) such as over-consuming perks, shirking, or stealing when they sell outside shares, bear the costs of those dysfunctional actions. Hence they have incentives to contract to limit those actions and to have their actions monitored. The incentive is reduced (but not eliminated) by price protection in managerial labour markets.[20]

---

[19] Or if shares are being sold in a company, the shareholders will, in the absence of contractual constraints on the manager, pay a lower price for shares in the organization.

[20] In this context, reference is made to the owner–manager to imply that the manager might have some ownership in the organization but does not own the entire organization. This quote also reflects the beliefs that Positive Accounting Theorists have about the efficiency of markets – such as capital markets or labour markets. It is assumed that such markets can efficiently adjust required rates of return to anticipated levels of risk – such as the risks associated with managers being opportunistic.

That is, if it is assumed that managers would prefer higher salaries, then there will be an incentive for them to agree to enter into contractual arrangements that minimize their ability to undertake activities that might be detrimental to the interests of the owners (many of these contractual arrangements will be tied to accounting numbers). The managers (agents) will have incentives to provide information to demonstrate that they are not acting in a manner detrimental to the owners (principals).[21]

In reflecting upon why many accounting researchers embraced agency theory as part of their research, Lambert (2001, p. 4) states:

> The primary feature of agency theory that has made it attractive to accounting researchers is that it allows us to explicitly incorporate conflicts of interest, incentive problems, and mechanisms for controlling incentive problems into our models. This is important because much of the motivation for accounting and auditing has to do with the control of incentive problems. For example, the reason we insist on having an 'independent' auditor is that we do not believe we can trust managers to issue truthful reports on their own. Similarly, much of the motivation for focusing on objective and verifiable information and for conservatism in financial reporting lies with incentive problems. At the most fundamental level, agency theory is used in accounting research to address two questions: (i) how do features of information, accounting, and compensation systems affect (reduce or make worse) incentive problems and (ii) how does the existence of incentive problems affect the design and structure of information, accounting, and compensation systems?

The perspective of the firm as a 'nexus of contracts'

In the agency theory literature, the firm itself is considered to be a *nexus of contracts* and these contracts are put in place with the intention of ensuring that all parties, acting in their own self-interest, are at the same time motivated towards maximizing the value of the organization. The view of the firm as a nexus of contracts is consistent with Smith and Watts' (1983, p. 3) definition of a corporation. They define the corporation as:

> a set of contracts among various parties who have a claim to a common output. These parties include stockholders, bondholders, managers, employees, suppliers and customers. The bounds of the corporation are defined by the set of rights under the contracts. The corporation has an indefinite life and the set of contracts which comprise the corporation evolves over time.

Agency theory does not assume that individuals will ever act other than in self-interest, and the key to a well-functioning organization is to put in place mechanisms (contracts) that ensure that actions that benefit the individual also benefit the organization.[22] The firm will have many contracts negotiated with various individuals and parties and these

---

[21] These arguments about managers' opportunistic behaviour are 'on average' arguments. Principals would not know with certainty whether specific agents will adopt particular opportunistic strategies which are detrimental to the principals' economic welfare. Rather, the principals who believe that everybody is motivated by their own self-interest will assume, on average, that the agent will adopt such strategies, and the principal will price protect accordingly. Hence, the agent who does not commit to restrict the available set of actions will be penalized (in the form of lower salary) even though they individually may not ultimately elect to undertake actions detrimental to the principal.

[22] As shown later in this chapter, one way to align the interests of the manager with those of the owners of the firm might be for the manager to be given a share of profits in the organization. Hence, the manager would be motivated to increase profits (to increase his or her own wealth) and such self-interested activity will also provide benefits to the owners, who, all things being equal, will benefit from higher accounting earnings.

contracts will aim to reduce the many conflicts of interests and related uncertainties that might otherwise arise (that is, the firm will be a nexus of contracts). Apart from internal mechanisms (for example, compensation contracts with managers that pay managers a bonus tied to accounting profits), there will be other market-wide mechanisms that are also assumed to constrain the opportunistic actions of the managers. That is, apart from the effects of various contractual arrangements within 'the firm', the literature of the 1970s also proposed that various markets, such as the market for corporate control and the market for managers, provided incentives for managers to work in the interests of the owners (Fama, 1980).[23] As Bushman and Smith (2001, p. 238) state:

> Corporate control mechanisms are the means by which managers are disciplined to act in the investors' interest. Control mechanisms include both internal mechanisms, such as managerial incentive plans, director monitoring, and the internal labor market, and external mechanisms, such as outside shareholder or debtholder monitoring, the market for corporate control, competition in the product market, the external managerial labor market, and securities laws that protect outside investors against expropriation by corporate insiders.

As indicated above, agency theory provides an explanation for the existence of the firm. The establishment of the firm is seen as an alternative and efficient way to produce or supply goods and services relative to individuals dealing with 'the market' by way of a series of separate transactions.[24] As Emanuel *et al.* (2003, p. 151) state:

> The firm is an alternative to the market when the costs of using the market become excessive. When a firm replaces the market, authority substitutes for the price mechanism in determining how decisions are made … Accounting, together with employment contracts, compensation arrangements, debt contracts and the board of directors including its audit and compensation committees comprise a package of structures that have evolved to govern the firm. These institutional devices become the firm's efficient contracting technology. As accounting is part of that contracting technology, the accounting controls and systems and board structures that evolve and get implemented are efficient and the accounting methods that are used in calculating the numbers in the contractual arrangements are, likewise, efficient.

In explaining the existence of firms from an agency theory perspective, reliance is often placed on the early work of Ronald Coase. As Emanuel *et al.* (2003, p. 152) state:

> Coase (1937) suggests that the firm is an alternative form of organisation for managing the very same transactions [that otherwise could be made with market participants]. For example, a firm could make its raw materials as opposed

---

[23] See Chapter 3 for an overview of the implications for managers that flow from an efficiently functioning 'market for managers' and 'market for corporate takeovers'. In Chapter 3 we show that an assumption about efficiency in these markets provides a justification for some people to argue against regulating accounting disclosures.

[24] For example, if we wanted a new car we can either buy it from a firm that specializes in making cars (and which has developed efficient contracting mechanisms between the various providers of the factors of production), or we can individually negotiate via 'the market' with suppliers of tyres, seats, engines, windscreens, radios, frames, mechanics, and so forth. It is accepted that it is more efficient, because of contracting efficiencies inherent within a firm, to acquire the car from a firm specializing in car production rather than to coordinate the production of the car ourselves.

to acquiring them through the market. Coase indicates that firms exist because there are costs of using the pricing mechanism. Examples of these costs are the costs of discovering what the relevant prices are, the costs of determining quality, and the costs of negotiating and concluding a separate contract for each exchange transaction. Further, there are costs associated with drawing up a long-term contract because, due to uncertainty (i.e., where knowledge of future possible states of the world and all involved relationships are incomplete) and bounded rationality (i.e., the limitations of humans to make economic decisions because of their limited ability to receive, store, retrieve, and process information), complete contracting is not feasible (Williamson, 1975, 1985, 1988, 1996). Coase suggests that economies of scale in long-term contracting are what cause activity to be organised in firms ... The Coasian and Williamson analysis suggests that firms exist because they are contracting-cost-efficient. Economic Darwinism ensures that competition will weed out inefficient structures and ill-designed organisations. Over the long-term, the institutional structure that survives is the firm's efficient contracting technology. As accounting is part of that contracting technology, the accounting controls and systems that the firm uses and the accounting methods that are used to reduce conflicts of interests between parties to the firm and that align with the firm's value-increasing activities are, likewise, efficient. In respect of the accounting methods, Watts and Zimmerman (1990, p. 134) describe these procedures as efficient accounting choices because they 'are the result of a similar economic equilibrium'.

From this theoretical perspective, firms therefore exist because they are an efficient way to coordinate the activities of various agents. As we have explained, each of the agents employed within a firm is assumed to act in their own self-interest. Principals will be aware of this 'self-interest'. Unless agents can show that they are working in the interests of the principals, the principals will pay the agents lower rewards for their work in anticipation of the agent taking actions that are costly to the principal. Knowing this, agents are predicted to have incentives to provide information to show they are working to the benefit of the owners (principals) so as to receive higher payments. This prediction (from agency theory), combined with the view that markets were efficient, was traditionally used by researchers as a basis for arguments against the regulation of accounting. Managers (agents) are deemed, even in the absence of regulation, to have incentives to provide information that best reflects the underlying performance of the entity. Failure to do so will have negative implications for their reputation and hence will negatively impact on the total amount of income they can receive from within the organization, or elsewhere. Referring to the work of Fama, Watts and Zimmerman (1986, p. 192) argue:

> Fama (1980) suggests that information on managers' opportunistic value-reducing behavior eventually becomes known and affects their reputation. As a consequence, if managers consume a large quantity of perks (e.g., shirks), it eventually becomes known and they acquire a reputation. Such managers are expected to over-consume perks in the future, and their future compensation is reduced. Hence, even if managers' compensation is not adjusted in the period in which they over-consume, they still bear a cost for that over-consumption – the

present value of the reductions in their future compensation. This effect is mitigated if the manager is close to retirement and does not have any deferred compensation (i.e., compensation paid after retirement).

The emergence of Positive Accounting Theory

By the mid- to late-1970s, theory had therefore been developed that proposed that markets were efficient and that contractual arrangements were used as a basis for controlling the efforts of self-interested agents. The existence of firms was also explained on the basis of the firms' efficiency in terms of reducing total transaction costs. This research provided the necessary basis for the development of PAT. PAT emphasized the role of accounting in reducing the agency costs of an organization (including the conflicts that exist between owners and managers). It is also emphasized that efficiently written contracts, with many being tied to the output of the accounting system, were a crucial component of an efficient corporate governance structure.

One of the first papers to document how considerations of contracting costs,[25] as well as how considerations of the political process, impacted on the choice of accounting methods was Watts (1977), which did not attract great attention. However, in the subsequent year, Watts and Zimmerman (1978) was published and this paper has become accepted as the key paper in the development and acceptance of PAT. It attempted to explain the lobbying positions taken by US corporate managers in relation to the FASB's 1974 Discussion Memorandum on general price level adjustments (GPLAs). According to Watts and Zimmerman (1978, p. 113):

> In this paper, we assume that individuals act to maximise their own utility. In doing so they are resourceful and innovative. The obvious implication of this assumption is that management lobbies on accounting standards based on its own self-interest.[26]

As indicated in Chapter 5, general price level accounting, through the use of a general price index, makes adjustments to historical cost profits to take into account the effects of changing prices. In times of inflation this typically has the effect of decreasing income, as well as increasing assets.

Watts and Zimmerman considered how particular organizational attributes might affect whether the managers of an organization supported, or opposed, a particular accounting requirement. Among the factors considered, two were the possibility that managers were paid bonuses tied to reported profits (which they referred to as the management compensation hypothesis), and the possibility that the organization was subject to high

---

[25] Contracting costs are costs that arise as a result of 'contracting' or formulating an agreement with another party (for example, a manager) wherein one party provides a particular service for a particular payment. The contracting costs include: the costs of finding the other party to the contract; negotiating the agreement; costs associated with monitoring that the agreement has been carried out in the manner expected; possible renegotiation costs; and so on.

[26] Watts and Zimmerman, like many other economists, ignored non-financial aspects of individual's utility functions and simply assumed that an individual's utility, or well-being, is maximized when their wealth is maximized. Perhaps non-financial aspects of an individual's utility function were ignored because such aspects were considered too difficult to model.

levels of political scrutiny (which they referred to as the political cost hypothesis). In relation to the issue of political scrutiny and the associated costs, Watts and Zimmerman (1978, p. 115) state:

> To counter potential government intrusions, corporations employ a number of devices, such as social responsibility campaigns in the media, government lobbying and selection of accounting procedures to minimise reported earnings. By avoiding the attention that 'high' profits draw because of the public's association of high reported profits and monopoly rents, management can reduce the likelihood of adverse political actions and, thereby, reduce its expected costs (including the legal costs the firm would incur opposing the political actions). Included in political costs are the costs labour unions impose through increased demands generated by large reported profits. The magnitude of the political costs is highly dependent on firm size.

The results of Watts and Zimmerman (1978) did not provide support for the management compensation hypothesis.[27] This was probably due to the fact that the Discussion Memorandum required GPLA disclosures to be provided as a supplement to the financial statements and did not require the financial statements themselves to be altered (and the bonus plans were expected to be tied to the numbers presented in the financial statements). However, significant findings were presented in relation to the political cost hypothesis.[28] More specifically, larger firms (who were deemed to be subject to higher political scrutiny) tended to support the Discussion Memorandum – an approach which would indicate (in times of rising prices) that the profits of the firm, adjusted for the effects of inflation, were lower than were otherwise reported.[29] The view of Watts and Zimmerman was that, by presenting lower adjusted profits, these firms would attract less political attention and hence there would be less likelihood that parties would attempt to transfer wealth away from the firm (perhaps in the form of calls for increased taxes, for less tariff protection, for higher wages and so on). In concluding their paper, Watts and Zimmerman (1978, p. 131) state:

> The single most important factor explaining managerial voting behavior on General Price Level Accounting is firm size (after controlling for the direction of change in earnings). The larger firms, ceteris paribus, are more likely

---

[27] Specifically, the prediction provided within Watts and Zimmerman (1978, p. 116) in relation to management compensation plans was that 'a change in accounting standards which increase the firm's reported earnings would, *ceteris paribus*, lead to greater incentive income. But this would reduce the firm's cashflows and share prices would fall. As long as per manager present value of the after tax incentive income is greater than the decline in each manager's portfolio, we expect management to favour such an accounting change.'

[28] Political costs are costs that particular groups external to the organization may be able to impose on the organization as a result of particular political actions. The costs could include increased taxes, increased wage claims or product boycotts.

[29] The prediction provided by Watts and Zimmerman (1978, p. 118) in relation to political costs was 'that managers have greater incentives to choose accounting standards which report lower earnings (thereby increasing cash flows, firm value and their welfare) due to tax, political, and regulatory considerations than to choose accounting standards which report higher earnings and, thereby, increase their incentive compensation. However, this prediction is conditional upon the firm being regulated or subject to political pressure. In small (i.e., lower political costs) unregulated firms, we would expect that managers do have incentives to select accounting standards which report higher earnings, if the expected gain in incentive compensation is greater than the foregone expected tax consequences. Finally, we expect managers to also consider the accounting standard's impact on the firm's bookkeeping costs (and hence their own welfare).'

to favour GPLA if earnings decline. This finding is consistent with our government intervention argument since the larger firms are more likely to be subjected to government interference and, hence, have more to lose than smaller organisations.

Following the work of Watts and Zimmerman (1978), research in the area of PAT flourished. Much of this research sought to address some of the limitations inherent in Watts and Zimmerman's work. For example, subsequent research acknowledged that reported profits are affected by many different accounting choices (rather than just the one choice, such as the choice to use GPLA), some of which may be income increasing, while others are income decreasing (thereby potentially offsetting each other). Zmijewski and Hagerman (1981) was an early paper that considered this issue and they undertook research in an endeavour to predict management's choice in relation to four accounting methods choices, those relating to how to account for depreciation, stock (or inventory), investment tax credits and past pension costs.

In 1990 Watts and Zimmerman published an article in *The Accounting Review* that considered ten years of development of Positive Accounting Theory ('Positive Accounting Theory: A Ten Year Perspective'). They identified three key hypotheses that had become frequently used in the PAT literature to explain and predict whether an organization would support or oppose a particular accounting method. These hypotheses can be called the management compensation hypothesis (or bonus plan hypothesis), the debt hypothesis (or debt/equity hypothesis) and the political cost hypothesis. Watts and Zimmerman (1990, p. 138) explain these hypotheses as follows:

> The bonus plan hypothesis is that managers of firms with bonus plans [tied to reported income] are more likely to use accounting methods that increase current period reported income. Such selection will presumably increase the present value of bonuses if the compensation committee of the board of directors does not adjust for the method chosen. The choice studies to date find results generally consistent with the bonus plan hypothesis.

Hence, all things being equal, this hypothesis predicts that if a manager is rewarded in terms of a measure of performance such as accounting profits, that manager will prefer accounting methods that have a greater impact on increasing profits to the extent that this leads to an increase in his or her bonus. Turning our attention to the 'debt hypothesis', they state (p. 139):

> The debt/equity hypothesis predicts [that] the higher the firm's debt/equity ratio, the more likely managers use accounting methods that increase income. The higher the debt/equity ratio, the closer (i.e. tighter) the firm is to the constraints in the debt covenants.[30] The tighter the covenant constraint, the greater [is] the probability of a covenant violation and of incurring costs

---

[30] In this chapter there will be a number of instances where we refer to debt covenants. Covenants can be considered as undertakings provided by a borrower as part of a contract associated with a loan, and these undertakings (covenants) either specifically restrict the borrower from taking particular actions, or specifically require the borrower to take particular actions.

from technical default. Managers exercising discretion by choosing income increasing accounting methods relax debt constraints and reduce the costs of technical default.[31]

Hence, all things being equal, if a firm has entered into agreements with lenders, and these agreements involve accounting-based debt covenants (such as stipulating a maximum allowable debt/equity or debt/asset constraint) then managers have an incentive to adopt accounting methods that relax the potential impacts of the constraints (such as adopting accounting methods that increase reported income and assets). Turning our attention to the third hypothesis of their study – the 'political costs hypothesis' – Watts and Zimmerman state (1990, p. 139):

> The political cost hypothesis predicts [that] large firms rather than small firms are more likely to use accounting choices that reduce reported profits. Size is a proxy variable for political attention. Underlying this hypothesis is the assumption that it is costly for individuals to become informed about whether accounting profits really represent monopoly profits and to 'contract' with others in the political process to enact laws and regulations that enhance their welfare. Thus rational individuals are less than fully informed. The political process is no different from the market process in that respect. Given the cost of information and monitoring, managers have incentive to exercise discretion over accounting profits and the parties in the political process settle for a rational amount of ex post opportunism.

Hence, all things being equal, if managers consider that they are under considerable political scrutiny, this could motivate them to adopt accounting methods that reduce reported income. Reducing reported profits could decrease the possibility that people will argue that the organization is exploiting other parties by applying business practices that generate excessive profits for the benefits of owners while at the same time providing limited returns to other parties involved in the transactions, such as employees. As an indication of how reported profits can be used as a means to criticize companies for exploiting others, and how the profits can also be used to justify a call for government action, we can consider Accounting Headline 7.1 which is critical of the role of Goldman Sachs and other investment banks in making profits from allegedly exploiting commodities in a way that impacts negatively on the poor. Read the article and then consider whether the position taken by the World Development Movement would have been as strong if Goldman Sachs had not recorded such high profits.

Researchers using the above three hypotheses (the management bonus hypothesis, the debt/equity hypothesis, and the political cost hypothesis), and there have been many such researchers, often adopted the perspective that managers (or agents) will act opportunistically when selecting particular accounting methods (for example, managers

---

[31] As indicated here, Watts and Zimmerman made the assumption that 'the higher the debt/equity ratio, the closer (i.e. tighter) the firm is to the constraints in the debt covenants'. This assumes that all organizations have entered into debt agreements that have covenants restricting the amount of total debt relative to the amount of total assets or total equity. While this assumption might have been reasonable back in the 1970s/80s when most large companies had entered into such arrangements, Mather and Peirson (2006) provide evidence that while the majority of large companies do still agree to debt covenants, less than half of the recently negotiated covenants restrict total liabilities to a proportion of either total assets or equity. Hence the predictive power of the hypotheses may not be as great as it once was. Nevertheless, it provides a useful prediction for companies known to have leverage constraints.

Accounting Headline 7.1

An instance of profits being used to justify a claim that a company is exploiting others

Hedge funds accused of gambling with lives of the poorest as food prices soar

By Katie Allen

Financial speculators have come under renewed fire from anti-poverty campaigners for their bets on food prices, blamed for raising the costs of goods such as coffee and chocolate and threatening the livelihoods of farmers in developing countries ...

The World Development Movement's (WDM) Great Hunger Lottery report says 'risky and secretive' financial bets on food prices have exacerbated the effect of poor harvests in recent years. It argues that volatility in food prices has made it harder for producers to plan what to grow, pushed up prices for British consumers and in poorer countries risks sparking civil unrest, like the food riots seen in Mexico and Haiti in 2008.

Deborah Doane, WDM director, said: 'Investment banks, like Goldman Sachs, are making huge profits by gambling on the price of everyday foods. But this is leaving people in the UK out of pocket, and risks the poorest people in the world starving.'

'Nobody benefits from this kind of reckless gambling except a few City wheeler-dealers. British consumers suffer because it pushes up inflation, because of unpredictable oil and raw material prices, and the world's poorest people suffer because basic foods become unaffordable.'

The group used figures in Goldman Sachs' annual report to estimate that the bank made a profit of $1bn (£650m) through speculating on food last year. The bank, however, says the 'overwhelming majority' of its activities in commodity markets are on behalf of clients and that the WDM's profit estimates are 'ludicrously overstated'.

The charity is urging the UK government to take the lead within the European Union in demanding more transparency and tighter controls in commodities markets. It says 800 people have pledged to call the Financial Services Authority watchdog this week to complain about speculators' growing influence on food prices and demand changes similar to those in the US.

Source: *The Guardian*, 19 July 2010, p. 21
©Guardian News and Media Limited 2010

---

will select particular accounting methods because the choice will lead to an increase in profit and therefore to an increase in *their* bonus). Watts and Zimmerman (1978) was mainly grounded in the *opportunistic perspective*. However, a lot of the subsequent PAT research also adopted an *efficiency perspective*. This perspective proposes that managers will elect to use a particular accounting method because the method most efficiently provides a record of how the organization performed. For example, the manager might have selected a particular depreciation method, not because it will lead to an increase in his or her bonus (the opportunistic perspective), but because the method most correctly reflects the use of the underlying asset. The following discussion considers the *opportunistic* and *efficiency* perspectives of PAT. In practice it is often difficult to determine whether opportunistic or efficiency considerations drove the managers' choice of a particular method – and this has been one limitation of much of this research.

7.4 Opportunistic and efficiency perspectives

As noted above, research that applies PAT typically adopts either an *efficiency perspective* or an *opportunistic perspective*. Within the *efficiency perspective*, researchers explain how various contracting mechanisms can be put in place to minimize the agency costs of the firm, that is, the costs associated with assigning decision-making authority from the principal (for example, the owner) to the agent (for example, the manager). The efficiency perspective is often referred to as an *ex ante* perspective – *ex ante* meaning before the fact – as it considers what mechanisms are put in place up-front, with the objective of minimizing future agency and contracting costs. For example, many organizations throughout the world voluntarily prepared publicly available financial statements before there was any regulatory requirement to do so. These financial statements were also frequently subjected to an audit, even when there also was no regulatory requirement to do so (Morris, 1984).[32] Researchers such as Jensen and Meckling (1976) argue that the practice of providing audited financial statements leads to real cost savings as it enables organizations to attract funds at lower cost. As a result of the audit, external parties have more reliable information about the resources and obligations of the organization, which therefore enables the organization to attract funds at a lower cost than would otherwise be possible, thereby increasing the value of the organization.

Within this efficiency (*ex ante*) perspective of PAT it is also argued that the accounting practices adopted by firms are often explained on the basis that such methods best reflect the underlying financial performance of the entity. Different organizational characteristics are used to explain why different firms adopt different accounting methods. For example, the selection of a particular asset depreciation rule from among alternative approaches is explained on the basis that it best reflects the underlying use of the asset. Firms that have different patterns of use in relation to an asset will be predicted to adopt different depreciation or amortization policies. That is, organizations will differ in the nature of their business, and these differences will in turn lead to differences in the accounting methods (as well as other policies) being adopted. By providing measures of performance that best reflect the underlying performance of the firm, it is argued that investors and other parties will not need to gather as much additional information from other sources. This will consequently lead to cost savings.

As an illustration of research that adopts an efficiency perspective, Whittred (1987) sought to explain why firms voluntarily prepared publicly available consolidated financial statements in a period when there was no regulation that required them to do so. He found that when companies borrowed funds, security for debt often took the form of guarantees

---

[32] Benston (1969) provides evidence that all the firms listed on the New York Stock Exchange in 1926 published balance sheets when there was no direct requirement to do so. Further, 82 per cent were audited by a CPA when there was also no direct statutory requirement to do so.

provided by other entities within the group of organizations. Consolidated financial statements were described as being a more efficient means of providing information about the group's ability to borrow and repay debts than providing lenders with separate financial statements for each entity in the group.[33]

If it is assumed, consistent with the efficiency perspective, that firms adopt particular accounting methods because the methods best reflect the underlying economic performance of the entity (thereby reducing the risks of investors and therefore decreasing the firm's cost of capital), then it is argued by PAT theorists that the regulation of financial accounting imposes unwarranted costs on reporting entities. For example, if a new accounting standard is released that bans an accounting method being used by particular organizations, proponents of PAT would see this as leading to inefficiencies as the resulting financial statements will no longer provide the best reflection of the performance of the organization. Many PAT theorists would argue that management is best able to select appropriate accounting methods in given circumstances, and government should not intervene in the process.[34]

The *opportunistic perspective* of PAT, on the other hand, takes as given the negotiated contractual arrangements of the firm (some of which are discussed later in this chapter) and seeks to explain and predict certain opportunistic behaviours that will subsequently occur. Initially, the particular contractual arrangements might have been negotiated because they were considered to be most efficient in aligning the interests of the various individuals within the firm thereby providing cost savings for the firm. However, it is not possible or efficient to write complete contracts that provide guidance on all accounting methods to be used in all circumstances – hence there will always be some scope for managers to be opportunistic.

The opportunistic perspective is often referred to as an *ex post* perspective – *ex post* meaning after the fact – because it considers opportunistic actions that could be undertaken once various contractual arrangements have been put in place. For example, in an endeavour to minimize agency costs (an efficiency perspective), a contractual arrangement might be negotiated that provides the managers with a bonus based on the profits generated by the entity. Once it is in place, the manager could elect to adopt particular accounting methods that increase accounting profits, and therefore the size of

---

[33] These results were also supported by Mian and Smith (1990). Using US data they found that the inclusion of financial subsidiaries in consolidated financial statements prior to Financial Accounting Standard 94 (which required the subsidiaries to be included within consolidated statements) was directly related to whether guarantees of debt were in existence between members of the group of companies. As Watts (1995, p. 332) indicates, the fact that two independent studies (Mian and Smith, 1990; Whittred, 1987) in different time periods and in different countries found the same results provides a stronger case that the efficiency perspective appears to explain this type of accounting choice.

[34] In this regard we can consider IAS 38 'Intangibles'. This accounting standard requires all research expenditure to be expensed as incurred regardless of whether the expenditure is considered likely to lead to future economic benefits (IAS 38 does, however, allow development expenditure to be carried forward subject to certain stringent requirements). The requirement that all research be expensed as incurred is highly conservative and does not allow financial report readers to differentiate between entities that have undertaken valuable research (in terms of generating future economic benefits) and those entities that have pursued failed research projects. For financial accounting purposes all research (good and bad) is to be treated the same. Arguably, this does not enhance the 'efficiency' of general purpose financial reports in terms of assessing the past and future economic performance of respective reporting entities.

the bonus (an opportunistic perspective). Managers might elect to adopt a particular asset depreciation method that increases income (for example, electing to depreciate an asset over a longer useful life), even though it might not reflect the actual use of the asset. It is assumed within PAT that managers will opportunistically select particular accounting methods whenever they believe that this will lead to an increase in their personal wealth. PAT also assumes that principals would predict a manager to be opportunistic. With this in mind, principals often stipulate the accounting methods to be used for particular purposes. For example, a bonus plan agreement may stipulate that a particular depreciation or amortization method such as straight-line amortization has to be adopted to calculate income for the determination of the bonus. However, as noted previously, it is assumed to be too costly to stipulate in advance all accounting rules to be used in all circumstances. Hence PAT proposes that there will always be scope for agents opportunistically to select particular accounting methods in preference to others. Across time there have been many reported cases of organizations that have been found to have overstated their reported earnings and assets. For example, consider Accounting Headline 7.2, which relates to overstatement of profits at a large Dutch supermarket group. The opportunistic perspective provided by PAT provides some possible reasons for the overstatement of reported assets and profits. Perhaps the entity inflated its profits and assets in an attempt to circumvent restrictions that had been put in place by lenders – for example, lenders might have stipulated debt-to-asset constraints or minimum earnings requirements (perhaps in the form of negotiated interest-coverage clauses in a debt agreement). As the level of debt increases, the tendency towards opportunistic overstatement of assets and income would be expected to increase (if we accept the arguments provided by PAT). The extent of the opportunistic accounting activities often only becomes evident following corporate failure, at which time the extent of asset overstatement will be highlighted.

Accounting Headline 7.2

Overstatement of profits
Dutch supermarket admits £317m error

Ahold, the Dutch-based supermarket giant, has admitted that it overstated its profits by at least $500m (£317m).

As a consequence, the company said its chief executive and chief financial officer would be leaving, while an investigation into its US food distribution division has begun.

It has also postponed its annual results, which were meant to have been announced on 5 March.

The news sent shock waves through the market as Ahold's share price tumbled 40%.

The trouble is believed to be centred around US Foodservice, Ahold's distribution service, over the way it accounted for income.

The company is already saddled with massive debt problems fuelled by an aggressive acquisition strategy, which has made merging different accounting practices together difficult.

Source: *Accountancy Age*, 24 February 2003

The following discussion addresses the various contractual arrangements that may exist between owners and managers, and between debtholders and managers, particularly those contractual arrangements based on the output of the accounting system. Again, these contractual arrangements are initially assumed to be put in place to reduce the agency costs of the firm (the efficiency perspective). However, it is assumed by Positive Accounting Theorists that once the arrangements are in place, parties will, if they can, adopt manipulative strategies to generate the greatest economic benefits to themselves (the opportunistic perspective). The following material also considers the political process and how firms might use accounting to minimize the costs of potential political scrutiny.

While some researchers tend to utilize either the *efficiency* or *opportunistic* perspectives of PAT to explain particular accounting choices, it should be noted that in reality it is often difficult to conclude firmly that an accounting choice was driven solely by an efficiency or an opportunistic motivation. As Fields *et al.* (2001) state:

> Unconstrained accounting choice is likely to impose costs on financial state-ment users because preparers are likely to have incentives to convey self-serving information. For example, managers may choose accounting methods in self-interested attempts to increase the stock [share] price prior to the expiration of stock options they hold. On the other hand, the same accounting choices may be motivated by managers' objective assessment that the current stock price is undervalued (relative to their private information). In practice, it is difficult to distinguish between the two situations, but it is the presence of such mixed motives that makes the study of accounting choice interesting.

7.5 Owner–manager contracting

If the manager owned the firm, then that manager would bear the costs associated with their own perquisite consumption. Perquisite consumption could include consumption of the firm's resources for private purposes (for example, the manager may acquire an overly expensive company car, acquire overly luxurious offices, stay in overly expensive hotel accommodation) or the excessive generation and use of idle time. As the percentage ownership held by the manager decreases, that manager begins to bear proportionately less of the cost of his or her own perquisite consumption. The costs begin to be absorbed by the other (non-manager) owners of the firm.

As noted previously, PAT adopts as a central assumption that all action by individuals is driven by self-interest, and that the major interest of individuals is to maximize their own wealth. Such an assumption is often referred to as the 'rational economic person' assumption. If all individuals are assumed to act in their own self-interest, then owners would expect the managers (their agents) to undertake activities that may not always be in the interest of the owners (the principals). Further, because of their position within the firm, the managers will have access to information not available to the principals (this problem is frequently referred to as 'information asymmetry') and this may further increase the manager's ability to undertake actions beneficial to themselves at the expense of the owners. The costs of the divergent behaviour that arises as a result of the agency relationship (that is, the relationship between the principal and the agent appointed to perform duties on behalf of the principal) are, as indicated previously, referred to as agency costs (Jensen and Meckling, 1976).

It is assumed in PAT that the principals hold expectations that their agents will undertake activities that may be disadvantageous to the value of the firm, and the principals will price this into the amounts they are prepared to pay the manager. That is, in the absence of controls to reduce the ability of the manager to act opportunistically, the principals expect such actions and, as a result, will pay the manager a lower salary. That is, the principals will price protect. This lower salary compensates the principals for the expected opportunistic behaviour of the agents. The manager will therefore bear some of the costs of the potential opportunistic behaviours (the agency costs) that they may, or may not, undertake. If it is expected that managers would derive greater satisfaction from additional salary than from the perquisites that they will be predicted to consume, then managers may be better off if they are able to commit themselves contractually not to consume perquisites. That is, they commit or bond themselves contractually to reducing their set of available actions (some of which would not be beneficial to owners). Of course, the owners of the firm would need to ensure that any contractual commitments can be monitored for compliance before agreeing to increase the amounts paid to the managers. In a market where individuals are perfectly informed it could be assumed that managers would ultimately bear the costs associated with the bonding and monitoring mechanisms (Jensen and Meckling, 1976). However, markets are typically not perfectly informed.

Managers may be rewarded on a fixed basis (that is, a set salary independent of performance), on the basis of the results achieved, or on a combination of the two. If the manager was rewarded purely on a fixed basis, then assuming self-interest, that manager would not want to take great risks as he or she would not share in any potential gains. There would also be limited incentives for the manager to adopt strategies that increase the value of the firm (unlike equity owners whose share of the firm may increase in value). Like debtholders, managers with a fixed claim would want to protect their fixed income stream. Apart from rejecting risky projects, which may be beneficial to those with equity in the firm, the manager with a fixed income stream may also be reluctant to take on optimal levels of debt, as the claims of the debtholders would compete with the manager's own fixed income claim.

Assuming that self-interest drives the actions of the managers, it may be necessary to put in place remuneration schemes that reward the managers in a way that is, at least in part, tied to the performance of the firm. This will be in the interest of the manager as that manager will potentially receive greater rewards and will not have to bear the costs of the perceived opportunistic behaviours (which may not have been undertaken anyway). If the performance of the firm improves, the rewards paid to the manager correspondingly increase. Bonus schemes tied to the performance of the firm will be put in place to align the interests of the owners and the managers. If the firm performs well, both parties will benefit.

Bonus schemes generally

It is common practice for managers to be rewarded in a way that is tied to the profits of the firm, sales of the firm, or return on assets, that is, for their remuneration to be based on the output of the accounting system. Table 7.1 describes some of the accounting-based remuneration plans found to have been used in Australia. It is also common for managers to be rewarded in line with the market price of the firm's shares. This may be through holding an equity interest in the firm, or perhaps by receiving a cash bonus explicitly tied to movements in the market value of the firm's securities.

TABLE 7.1 Accounting performance measures used within Australia as a basis for rewarding managers

- Percentage of after-tax profits of the last year
- Percentage of after-tax profits after adjustment for dividends paid
- Percentage of pre-tax profits of the last year
- Percentage of division's profit for the last year
- Percentage of division's sales for the last year
- Percentage of the last year's accounting rate of return on assets
- Percentage of previous year's division's sales, plus percentage of firm's after-tax profits
- Percentage of previous year's division's sales plus percentage of division's pre-tax profits
- Percentage of previous two years' division's sales, plus percentage of last two years' division's pre-tax profit
- Percentage of previous year's firm's sales, plus a percentage of firm's after-tax profit
- Average of pre-tax profit for the last two years
- Average of pre-tax profit for the last three years
- Percentage of the last six months' profit after tax

Source: Deegan (1997).

Accounting-based bonus plans

As indicated above, the use of accounting-based bonus schemes is quite common. In considering their use within the United States, Bushman and Smith (2001, p. 250) state:

> The extensive and explicit use of accounting numbers in top executive compensation plans at publicly traded firms in the U.S. is well documented. Murphy (1998) reports data from a survey conducted by Towers Perrin in 1996–1997. The survey contains detailed information on the annual bonus plans for 177 publicly traded U.S. companies. Murphy reports that 161 of the 177 sample firms explicitly use at least one measure of accounting profits in their annual bonus plans. Of the 68 companies in the survey that use a single performance measure in their annual bonus plan, 65 use a measure of accounting profits. While the accounting measure used is often the dollar value of profits, Murphy also reports common use of profits on a per-share basis, as a margin, return, or expressed as a growth rate. Ittner *et al.* (1997), using proxy statements and proprietary survey data, collect detailed performance measure information for the annual bonus plans of 317 U.S. firms for the 1993–1994 time period. The firms are drawn from 48 different two-digit SIC codes. Ittner et al. document that 312 of the 317 firms report using at least one financial measure in their annual plans. Earnings per share, net income and operating income are the most common financial measure, each being used by more than a quarter of the sample.

Given that the amounts paid to the manager may be directly tied to accounting numbers (such as profits/sales/assets), any changes in the accounting methods being used by the organization will affect the bonuses paid (unless the bonuses have been explicitly tied to the accounting numbers that would be derived from the use of the accounting methods in place when the bonus schemes were originally negotiated – this is sometimes referred to as using 'frozen GAAP').[35] Such a change may occur as a result of a new accounting standard being issued. For example, IAS 38 permits some development (but not research) expenditure to be capitalized as an intangible asset in certain circumstances. Consider the consequences if a new rule was issued that required all research *and* development expenditure to be written off. With such a change, profits for some firms which previously capitalized development expenditure could decline, and the bonuses paid to managers may also change. If it is accepted, consistent with classical finance theory, that the value of the firm is a function of the future cash flows of the firm, then the value of the organization may change (perhaps because less expenditure will be incurred in relation to development). Hence, once we consider the contractual arrangements within a firm, Positive Accounting Theorists would argue that we can start to appreciate that a change in accounting method can lead to a change in cash flows, and hence a change in the value of the organization (because as we have already emphasized, the value of an organization is considered to relate directly to expectations about the present value of the organization's future cash flows). This perspective is contrary to the views of early proponents of the EMH who argued that changes in accounting methods would not impact on share prices unless they had direct implications for expenses such as taxation.

As a recent case in point we can speculate on how the adoption of IAS 38 'Intangibles' in some countries (and, as indicated above, among other things this standard requires that all research expenditure must be expensed as incurred) will impact upon the research and development activities of various organizations. For example, subject to certain requirements, Australian, New Zealand, French and Scandinavian listed companies could, prior to 2005, capitalize research expenditure. With the adoption of International Financial Reporting Standards (IFRSs) from 2005 this is no longer permitted and all research expenditure must be expensed as incurred (subject to certain requirements, development expenditure can be capitalized). As a result there might be some expectation that the accounting standard will impact on the amount of research being conducted by some firms in those countries. With specific reference to the 'bonus hypothesis', there could be an expectation that if a manager is being paid a bonus tied to accounting profits, and given the 'harsh' treatment required in relation to research expenditure ('harsh' because it has to be written off as incurred), the existence of a management bonus may motivate managers to reduce the level of research expenditure thereby increasing the size of their bonus. Such a strategy of reducing research expenditure might be even greater the closer the manager is to retirement – the reason for this being that the time-lag between the research expenditure and the subsequent economic benefits might be longer than the period until the manager retires (we will return to this 'horizon problem' shortly). Through the related impacts upon

---

[35] Where an accounting-based contractual arrangement is to be calculated according to the accounting rules in place at the reporting date (and these rules may change as new accounting standards are issued), then such agreements are considered to be relying on 'rolling GAAP' (also called 'floating GAAP').

cash flows, such a change in research activity in turn can be expected to impact on the value of the reporting entities' equity (share price). This example demonstrates how a change in an accounting standard can have real implications for an organization's share price.

Of course it is possible that the bonus might be based on the 'old' accounting rules in place at the time the remuneration contract was negotiated (perhaps through a clause in the management compensation contract) such that a change in generally accepted accounting principles will not impact on the bonus, but this will not always be the case. Contracts that rely on accounting numbers may rely on 'floating' generally accepted accounting principles. This would suggest that should an accounting rule change, and should it affect an item used within a contract negotiated by the firm, the value of the firm (through changes in related cash flows) might consequently change. PAT would suggest that if a change in accounting policy had no impact on the cash flows of the firm, then a firm would be indifferent to the change.

In explaining the use of accounting-based bonus schemes, Emanuel *et al.* (2003, p. 155) state:

> Accounting earnings are often used to calculate the manager's payoff (Healy, 1985, Sloan, 1993, Smith and Watts, 1982) because it is a more efficient measure of the manager's performance than other measures such as stock prices and realised cash flows. There are two reasons for this. First, stock prices are influenced more by market factors that are outside the control of management and, hence, are less effective in isolating that part of performance that results from the manager's actions (Sloan, 1993). Secondly, realised cash flows do not take into account the manager's actions at the time those actions are put in place to increase the value of the firm. Hence, realised cash flows do not provide a timely measure of the effect of the manager's actions on firm performance, especially when performance is measured over short intervals (Dechow, 1994). Further, accounting earnings possess a variety of desirable characteristics that other performance measures do not have, including objectivity, reliability, verifiability and conservatism (Watts and Zimmerman, 1986, pp. 205–207). Since accounting earnings are efficient in measuring firm performance, they play an important role in determining the reward and punishment of performance. We observe the existence of earnings-based bonus plans that provide an efficient means of aligning the manager's and shareholders' interests so that the manager does not participate in activities that are opportunistic, because such actions detract from firm value maximisation. To the extent that earnings are a good measure of future cash flows and all things else are constant, higher earnings lead to higher firm value and more compensation to the manager. Besides compensation, accounting performance measures affect other rewards and punishments of the firm's employees, such as continued employment and promotion (Blackwell et al., 1994).

Incentives to manipulate accounting numbers

In considering the costs of implementing incentive schemes based on accounting output, there is a possibility that rewarding managers on the basis of accounting profits may induce them to manipulate the related accounting numbers to improve their apparent performance and, importantly, their related rewards (the opportunistic perspective). That is, accounting profits may not always provide an unbiased measure of firm performance or value. Healy (1985) provides an illustration of when managers may choose to manipulate accounting numbers opportunistically due to the presence of accounting-based bonus schemes. He found that when schemes existed that rewarded managers after a pre-specified level of earnings had been reached, the managers would adopt accounting methods consistent with maximizing that bonus. In situations where the profits were not expected to reach the minimum level required by the bonus plan, the managers appeared to adopt strategies that further reduced income in that period (frequently referred to as 'taking a bath'), but would lead to higher income in subsequent periods – periods when the profits may be above the required threshold for the bonus to be paid. As an example, the manager might write off an asset in one period, when a bonus was not going to be earned anyway, such that there would be nothing further to depreciate in future periods when profit-related bonuses might be paid.[36]

Investment strategies that maximize the present value of the firm's resources will not necessarily produce uniform periodic cash flows or accounting profits. It is possible that some strategies may generate minimal accounting returns in early years, yet still represent the best alternatives available to the firm. Rewarding management on the basis of accounting profits may discourage them from adopting such strategies. That is, it may encourage management to adopt a short-term, as opposed to long-term, focus.

In Lewellen *et al.* (1987) it was shown that US managers approaching retirement were less likely to undertake research and development expenditure if their rewards were based on accounting-based performance measures, such as profits. This was explained on the basis that all research and development had to be written off as incurred pursuant to US accounting standards, and hence undertaking research and development would lead directly to a reduction in profits. Although the research and development expenditure would be expected to lead to benefits in subsequent years, the retiring managers might not have been there to share in the gains. That is, the employment horizon of the manager is short relative to the 'horizon' relating to the continuation of the organization (which might be assumed to be indefinite). This difference in 'horizons' is often referred to as a 'horizon problem'. Hence, the *self-interested manager* who was rewarded on the basis of accounting profits was predicted not to undertake research and development in the periods close to the point of retirement because the manager would not share in any associated gains. This may, of course, have been detrimental to the ongoing operations (and value) of the business. In such a case it would have been advisable from an *efficiency perspective* for an organization that incurred research and development expenditure to take retiring managers off a profit-share bonus scheme, or alternatively to calculate 'profits' for the purpose of the plan after adjusting for research and development expenditures. Alternatively, managers approaching retirement could have been rewarded in terms of

---

[36] Holthausen *et al.* (1995) utilized private data on firms' compensation plans also to investigate managers' behaviour in the presence of management compensation plans. Their results confirmed those of Healy (1985), except that they did not find any evidence to support the view that management will 'take a bath' when earnings are below the lower pre-set bound.

market-based schemes that are tied to the long-term performance of the organization. For example, perhaps the manager of a company involved in research and development, and who is expected to retire in the near future, should be allocated options to buy shares in the company (share options) that cannot be exercised for say three or four years after he or she retires. That way, the manager would be encouraged to put in place projects that will be successful after he or she leaves the organization. Market-based schemes are addressed below.

Market-based bonus schemes

Firms involved in activities such as mining, or high-technology research and development, may have accounting earnings that fluctuate greatly. Successful long-term strategies may be put in place that will not provide accounting earnings for a number of periods. In such industries, Positive Accounting Theorists may argue that it is more appropriate to reward the manager in terms of the market value of the firm's securities, which are assumed to be influenced by expectations about the net present value of expected future cash flows. This may be done either by basing a cash bonus on any increases in share prices, or by providing the manager with shares or options to shares in the firm. If the value of the firm's shares increases, both the manager and the owners will benefit (their interests will be aligned). Importantly, the manager will be given an incentive to increase the value of the firm. In a survey of Australian managers, Deegan (1997) provides evidence that 21 per cent of the managers surveyed held shares in their employer.

As already indicated in this chapter, offering managers incentives that are tied to accounting profits might have the adverse effect of inducing them to undertake actions that are not in the interests of shareholders. This might particularly be the case in relation to expenditure on research and development. As already explained, within the United States, all research and development is required to be expensed as incurred, and hence there is an immediate downward impact on profits when a firm undertakes research and development.[37] Apart from the initial impacts on profits, there is also evidence that capital markets frequently do not put a great amount of value on research and development expenditure because of the many uncertainties inherent in such expenditure (Lev and Sougiannis, 1996; Kothari et al., 2002) – that is, the market is considered to undervalue the benefits attributable to research and development. In relation to the personal motivations of chief executive officers (CEOs) in the United States, Cheng (2004, p. 307) states:

> CEOs consider the benefits and costs of R&D spending, and [consistent with the maintained assumption of self-interest] they invest in R&D only when the expected personal benefits dominate the personal costs. Their expected costs of R&D spending include the negative impact of R&D spending on short-term accounting and stock performance, since these measures affect CEO compensation and job security (Dechow and Skinner, 2000, Murphy, 1999). The negative impact of R&D spending on current accounting earnings is due to the fact that

---

[37] By contrast, IAS 38 'Intangible Assets' requires expenditure on research expenditure to be expensed as incurred, but does allow development expenditure to be capitalized to the extent that future economic benefits are deemed 'probable' and the cost can be measured reliably.

R&D spending is typically immediately expensed under US GAAP. Therefore, CEOs who want to boost current accounting earnings have incentives to reduce R&D spending (e.g., Baber et al., 1991, Dechow and Skinner, 2000). In addition, CEOs may consider R&D investments as less desirable than other investments in terms of the impact of the investments on short-term stock prices [because of the tendency of capital markets to undervalue R&D expenditures]. Relative to other investments, R&D projects are associated with higher information asymmetry between managers and shareholders (e.g., Clinch, 1991) and greater uncertainty of the future benefits (e.g., Chan et al., 2001, Kothari et al., 2002). As a result, current stock prices likely do not fully reflect the future benefits of R&D spending (Lev and Sougiannis, 1996). Therefore, CEOs concerned with short-term stock prices may reduce R&D spending to increase other investments with benefits more fully (or better) reflected in current stock prices.

The above impacts are heightened as the manager approaches retirement. As Cheng (2004, p. 308) states:

> CEOs are concerned with short-term accounting and stock performance, and these concerns generate incentives for CEOs to reduce R&D spending. Such incentives become stronger when CEOs approach retirements or face earnings shortfalls (Baber et al., 1991, Dechow and Sloan, 1991). As the CEO approaches retirement, it is less likely for the CEO to benefit from current R&D investments. Meanwhile, the CEOs career concern diminishes, and the CEO becomes more short-term oriented (Gibbons and Murphy, 1992) due to weakened concern about the discipline from the managerial labor markets. Likewise, when facing deteriorating economic performance, the CEO is more concerned with the expected personal costs of R&D spending, since poor performance may trigger such results as job termination and corporate takeover, which may disentitle the CEO to the future of current R&D spending. Thus CEOs have incentives to reduce R&D spending in order to reverse a poor performance, especially if an expected shortfall is small and thus more easily reversed.

Given that there would conceivably be incentives for senior management to reduce spending on research and development (particularly if they are offered bonuses tied to accounting profit) it is perhaps predictable that additional contractual agreements might be put in place to reduce this motivation to reduce research and development. One approach would be to have those people who are responsible for determining senior management salaries (often done by way of a compensation committee that is established within the organization and on which non-managerial directors often serve) specifically to adjust management salaries in such a way that the salary is directly tied to research and development activity. As Cheng (2004, p. 308) states:

> When CEO incentives to reduce R&D spending become stronger, compensation committees may adjust CEO compensation arrangements to mitigate such incentives. This adjustment should affect CEO's consideration of the expected personal benefits and expected personal costs of R&D spending in favour of R&D expenditures. One possible adjustment is to establish a greater positive association between changes in R&D spending and changes in CEO

compensation. Such a greater association makes increasing R&D spending more beneficial to the CEO, and reducing R&D spending more costly to the CEO.

The results of Cheng (2004) indicate that compensation committees do often establish a link between changes in research and development spending and changes in CEOs' total compensation. Further, the compensation being offered to the retiring managers is often by way of the provision of share options. Granting share options to the managers also increases the longer-term focus of managers thereby further motivating the CEOs to embrace optimal levels of research and development activity.[38]

In considering the use of share options, and as with accounting-based bonus schemes, there are also problems associated with the manager being rewarded in ways that are influenced by share price movements. First, the share price will be affected not only by factors controlled by the manager, but also by outside, market-wide factors. That is, share prices may provide a 'noisy' measure of management performance – 'noisy' in the sense that they are affected not only by the actions of management but also largely by general market movements over which the manager has no control. Further, only the senior managers would be likely to have a significant effect on the cash flows of the firm, and hence the value of the firm's securities. Therefore, market-related incentives may only be appropriate for senior management. Offering shares to lower-level management may be demotivational as their own individual actions would have little likelihood (relative to senior management) to impact on share prices, and therefore their personal wealth. Consistent with this, it is often more common for senior managers, relative to other employees, to hold shares in their employer. Within the Deegan (1997) sample, 35 per cent of senior management, 16 per cent of middle management and 6 per cent of lower management held shares in their employer.

Reflecting the way executives often share in the performance of an organization, Accounting Headline 7.3 shows how the advertising agency WPP rewards its chief executives by way of a scheme tied to the market value of the organization's securities. It would be expected that rewarding the executives in the manner outlined should align the interests of the executives (agents) with those of the shareholders (principals) – a view consistent with agency theory and PAT. It would be expected that such schemes would be restricted to senior management as they have the greatest ability to have an impact on share prices. However, as Accounting Headline 7.3 also shows, there has been considerable criticism from shareholders in recent years of the size of executive share option schemes. From the perspective of PAT this might indicate that shareholders believe the size of some such schemes now potentially dilute the value of shareholders' existing shares (through the issue of new shares at a substantial discount to future market values) by so much that the agency benefits of these share options are outweighed by their cost to existing shareholders.

---

[38] As a particular example of the use of share options, Cheng (2004, p. 321) refers to the options provided to the CEO of a large US corporation. According to Cheng, 'the CEO of the company was scheduled to retire on 1 April 2000 at age 64. The compensation committee approved to grant 1,500,000 stock options to the CEO in 1997 in order to provide a stock option-based incentive to continue his contributions to the improvement of the share price through and beyond retirement, and half the options would not become exercisable until the CEO became 66.'

Accounting Headline 7.3

The use and criticism of market based incentives

WPP's Sir Martin Sorrell sees off revolt over bonus scheme

By *Richard Wray*

The WPP chief executive, Sir Martin Sorrell, has seen off an investor revolt against a controversial bonus scheme that could see him pocket £60m over the next five years.

Just under a quarter of shareholders who voted before today's annual meeting in Dublin refused to back the scheme, which replaces and exceeds a similarly controversial scheme that garnered a protest back in 2004.

Sorrell, who has topped the Guardian's survey of Britain's highest paid FTSE 100 directors in previous years, was asked after the meeting whether he thought he was worth such enormous sums.

'That is not for me to say,' he said. 'Shareowners are asked to vote on it, unlike other companies in our sector that don't get shareholder approval at all for option allocations with no performance restrictions and take advantage of low points in the market [to allot executive share options]. This is all transparent and open.'

WPP has spent months meeting with senior investors to build support for its new leadership equity acquisition plan (Leap III).

But the plan was criticised by corporate governance experts. Before today's meeting, the Association of British Insurers, whose members control about a fifth of the stockmarket, issued a 'red top' health warning about the scheme, while the corporate governance advisers PIRC urged investors to vote against it due to concerns the payout could be 'excessive'.

WPP's annual meeting, however, was far from a rough ride for Sorrell. It was the first meeting since WPP moved its headquarters to the Republic of Ireland for tax purposes, and the company swapped its traditional venue of Claridge's in London for the Four Seasons hotel in Dublin.

As a result, the 15 people on the podium were outnumbered less than three to one by the audience and a significant number of the attendees were WPP employees.

Despite a video link back to the UK, there were no questions asked of the board.

Sorrell, however, hit back after the meeting at the suggestion that the company has received an easy ride because of its move to Ireland.

'There is no less scrutiny, there is more transparency now than there has ever been,' he said. 'Dublin is not the antipodes.'

… City investors have become far more vocal in their opposition to what they see as unwarranted or excessive executive remuneration packages. Shell's annual meeting in the Netherlands last month saw 59% of shareholders oppose its remuneration report after bonuses were paid to directors despite performance targets being missed. That followed the outrage at RBS over Sir Fred Goodwin's pension payout.

But WPP insiders at the annual meeting believe the company has become unfairly caught up in the furore over pay. They pointed out that Sorrell must invest $19m (£12.5m) of his own cash in WPP shares and the company must outperform 90% of its peer group – compared with 75% in the previous scheme – for it to pay out in full.

Source: *Guardian*, 3 June 2009, p. 22
©Guardian News and Media Limited 2010

In general it is argued that the likelihood of accounting-based or market-based performance measures or reward schemes being put in place will, in part, be driven by considerations of the relative 'noise' of market-based versus accounting-based performance measures. The relative reliance upon accounting-based or market-based measures may potentially be determined on the basis of the relative sensitivity of either measure to general market (largely uncontrollable) factors. Sloan (1993) indicates that CEO salary and bonus compensation appears to be relatively more aligned with accounting earnings in those firms where:

- share returns are relatively more sensitive to general market movements (relatively noisy);

- accounting earnings have a high association with the firm-specific movement in the firm's share values;

- accounting earnings have a less positive (more negative) association with market-wide movements in equity values.

While the above arguments have discussed how or why managers might work in the interests of owners if they are offered rewards that are tied to the value of the shares of the organization, there is also an argument that if managers are provided with an equity interest in the organization then this will have other positive impacts in terms of encouraging the managers to increase the level of disclosure. Without an equity interest in the organization, managers might be motivated to withhold information from shareholders and other interested stakeholders. As Nagar *et al.* (2003, p. 284) state:

> Managers avoid disclosing private information because such disclosure reduces their private control benefits. For instance, a lack of information disclosure limits the ability of capital and labour markets to effectively monitor and discipline managers (Shleifer and Vishny, 1989). The disclosure agency problem can thus be regarded as a fundamental agency problem underlying other agency problems. Practitioners also echo the view that managers exhibit an inherent tendency to withhold information from investors, even in the 'high disclosure' environment of US capital markets. A panellist at the recent STERN Stewart Executive Roundtable states, 'all things equal, the managers of most companies would rather not disclose things if they don't have to. They don't want you to see exactly what they're doing; to see the little bets they are taking' (Stern Stewart, 2001, p. 37).

In relation to the concern that managers might be motivated to restrict disclosure, Nagar *et al.* (2003) suggest that providing managers with equity interests (for example, shares or share options) in the organization will act to reduce the 'non-disclosure tendency'. Specifically, they state (p. 284):

> Stock [share] price-based incentives elicit both good news and bad news disclosures from managers. Managers have incentives to release good news and bad news because it boosts stock price. On the other hand, the potential negative investor interpretation of silence (Milgrom, 1981, Verrecchia, 1983), and litigation costs (which reduce the value of the managers' ownership interest) are incentives to release bad news. Therefore, we argue that managerial stock

> price-based incentives, both as periodic compensation and aggregate share-
> holdings, help align long-run managerial and investor disclosure preferences
> and mitigate disclosure agency problems ... Our basic premise is that stock
> price-based incentives are contractual mechanisms that align managerial dis-
> closure preferences with those of shareholders.

The results of Nagar *et al*'s study are consistent with their expectations. Their results
show that offering managers equity-based incentives increases the managers' propensity
to disclose information. Specifically, they found that firm disclosures, measured both by
the frequency of earnings forecasts and analysts' ratings of the firms' disclosures, increase
as the proportion of CEO compensation tied to the share prices, and the value of CEO
shareholdings, increase.

In considering the use of share-based versus accounting-based bonus schemes,
accounting-based rewards have the advantage that the accounting results may be based on
sub-unit or divisional performance, but one would need to ensure that individuals do not
focus on their division at the expense of the organization as a whole.

PAT assumes that if a manager is rewarded on the basis of accounting numbers (for
example, on the basis of a share of profits) then the manager will have an incentive to
manipulate the accounting numbers. Given such an assumption, the value of audited
financial statements becomes apparent. Rewarding managers in terms of accounting
numbers (a strategy aimed at aligning the interests of owners and managers) may not
be appropriate if management was solely responsible for compiling those numbers. The
auditor will act to arbitrate on the reasonableness of the accounting methods adopted.
However, it must be remembered that there will always be scope for opportunism.

The above arguments concentrate on how management's rewards will be directly
affected as particular accounting methods are chosen. Management might also be rewarded
in other indirect ways as a result of electing to use particular accounting methods. For
example, DeAngelo (1988) provided evidence that when individuals face a contest for their
positions as managers of an organization they will, prior to the contest, adopt accounting
methods that lead to an increase in reported profits (and the increased reported earnings
could not be associated with any apparent increase in cash flows) thereby bolstering
their case for re-election. DeAngelo also showed that where the existing managers were
nevertheless unsuccessful in retaining their positions within the organization, the newly
appointed managers were inclined to recognize many expenses as soon as they took office
(that is, using terminology we introduced earlier in this chapter: 'take a bath') in a bid to
highlight the poor 'state of affairs' they had inherited. Such strategies as those described
above would be consistent with the opportunistic perspective applied within PAT. The
view that incoming CEOs may 'take a bath' was also confirmed by Wells (2002) who states
(p. 191):

> There is support for the view that incoming CEOs take an 'earnings bath' in
> the year of the CEO change ... Tests of earnings management yield evidence of
> income decreasing earnings management in the year of the CEO change, with
> the strongest results for CEO changes categorised as 'non-routine'. In this set-
> ting, the incoming CEO is typically not associated with past decisions, implicit
> criticism of which may be embodied in downwards earnings management.

Moreover, the outgoing CEO is unable to constrain such behaviour. This highlights an important corporate governance issue, namely the effect of the CEO succession process in constraining the opportunities for incoming management to undertake earnings management in the period subsequent to the CEO change.[39]

Apart from using particular incentive schemes to motivate employees to work in the interests of owners in the current period, particular remuneration plans can also be used to retain key employees. For example, offering managers share options that cannot be exercised for a number of years, and which would be forfeited on departure from the organization, can not only act to motivate them to increase the organization's value, but can also act as an incentive for managers to remain within the firm (Deegan, 1997). As Balsam and Miharjo (2007, p. 96) state:

> Equity compensation, or more precisely, forfeitable equity compensation, can reduce voluntary executive turnover by imposing a cost on the executive, which a prospective employer may not be willing to reimburse … The vast majority of publicly traded corporations provide equity compensation, usually stock options, to their executives in an effort to retain them and motivate them to act in the shareholders' interests. Equity compensation provides a direct link between executive compensation and shareholder wealth and consequently aligns the interests of a firms' executives with those of its shareholders.

Balsam and Miharjo (2007) provide evidence that offering executives share options that cannot be exercised for a number of periods does have the effect of retaining strongly performing executives. By contrast, they provide little incentive for retaining poorly performing managers as poor performance will translate to lower share prices and hence may make the options worthless – therefore eliminating any retention effects.

Having considered the contractual relationship between managers and principals, and how accounting can be used as a means of reducing the costs associated with potential conflict, we can now consider the relationship between debtholders and managers. We will see that accounting can be used to restrict the implications of this conflict and thereby enable an organization to attract funds at a lower cost than might otherwise be possible.

7.6 Debt contracting

When a party lends funds to another organization the recipient of the funds may undertake activities that reduce or even eliminate the probability that the funds will be repaid. These costs that relate to the divergent behaviour of the borrower are referred to in PAT as the *agency costs of debt* and, under PAT, lenders will anticipate divergent behaviour. For example, the recipient of the funds may pay excessive dividends, leaving few assets in the organization to service the debt. Alternatively, the organization may take on

---

[39] Information reported on Crikey.com (entitled 'ANZ boss joins the "clear the decks" club', 26 October 2007) also provides evidence of how newly appointed chief executive officers of 13 large Australian listed companies – including ANZ Bank – made significant asset write-downs in the initial stages of their appointment.

additional and perhaps excessive levels of debt. The new debtholders would then compete with the original debtholder for repayment.

Further, the firm that has borrowed the funds may also invest in very high-risk projects. This strategy would also not be beneficial to the debtholders (who can also be referred to as creditors). The debtholders have a fixed claim (that is, they are receiving a set rate of interest) and hence if the project generates high profits they will receive no greater return, unlike the owners, who will share in the increased value of the firm. If the project fails, which is more likely with a risky project, the debtholders may receive nothing. The debtholders therefore do not share in any 'upside' (the profits), but suffer the consequences of any significant losses (the 'downside').

In the absence of safeguards that protect the interests of debtholders, the holders of debt will assume that management will take actions – such as those described above – that might not always be in the debtholders' interest, and, as a result, it is assumed that they will require the firm to pay higher costs of interest to compensate the debtholders for the high-risk exposure (Smith and Warner, 1979).

If the firm agrees not to pay excessive dividends, not to take on high levels of debt and not to invest in projects of an excessively risky nature, then it is assumed that this will reduce the risks of lenders and as a result the firm will be able to attract debt capital at a lower cost than would otherwise be possible. To the extent that the benefits of lower interest costs exceed the costs that may be associated with restricting how management can use the available funds, management will elect to sign agreements that restrict their subsequent actions. Again, signing such an agreement that includes restrictive debt covenants would be an efficient strategy from the firm's perspective as it will likely lead to a reduction in the firm's cost of attracting funds.

Apart from explicitly agreeing not to undertake certain actions (such as taking on excessive levels of debts or agreeing not to invest in particularly risky ventures), management might also agree to adopt particular accounting methods if such adoption leads to a reduction in the cost of attracting debt capital. For example, Zhang (2008) argues that managers might agree to adopt conservative accounting methods because they believe that this might reduce the perceived risks faced by the lender. Conservative accounting methods bias the organization towards more readily recognizing losses than gains, consistent with the traditional 'doctrine of conservatism'. Conservative accounting practices would also restrict the organization from undertaking numerous (or perhaps, any) asset revaluations. The effect of conservative accounting methods is that both profits, and net assets (and therefore equity), would tend to be understated (that is, they provide 'conservative measures' of financial position and financial performance) relative to organizations that do not adopt conservative accounting methods. It also means that debt covenants restricting the amount of debt relative to assets (or debt to equity), or the amount of times profits must cover interest (known as an interest coverage clause) will tend to be more restrictive or binding for those organizations that adopt conservative accounting methods. As Zhang (2008) argues, the more binding covenants will provide an earlier warning of default risk, and thereby will reduce the risk exposure of the lending party (for example, a bank). The reason for this is that because management will have less ability to circumvent restrictive covenants (for example, by undertaking asset revaluations), such covenants will create a technical default of a loan agreement earlier than if management has the scope to loosen the restrictions, perhaps through undertaking an asset revaluation. The earlier the lender can take actions to safeguard its funds, the lower the risk of the lender.

Zhang (2008) reports that borrowers who adopt conservative accounting methods attract funds at lower rates of interest (a benefit to the borrower). This is consistent with Ahmed *et al.* (2002) who also finds that adopting conservative accounting methods leads to a reduction in the cost of attracting capital. Zhang (2008) also found that borrowers who adopt more conservative accounting methods are also more likely to violate debt contracts, and to violate them sooner (and the early default signal creates lower risk for lenders – which explains why they are prepared to loan the money at lower cost).

Historical evidence on Australian public debt contracts is provided by Whittred and Zimmer (1986) who find that for public debt contracts written between 1962 and 1985:[40]

> with few exceptions, trust deeds for public debt place restrictions on the amount of both total and secured liabilities that may exist. The constraints were most commonly defined relative to total tangible assets; less often relative to share-holders' funds. The most frequently observed constraints were those limiting total and secured liabilities to some fraction of total tangible assets (p. 22).[41]

While Whittred and Zimmer provided information about public debt issues, Cotter (1998b) provided evidence of private debt contracts negotiated between Australian listed companies and banks between 1993 and 1995. She finds that (p. 187):

> Leverage covenants are frequently used in bank loan contracts, with leverage most frequently measured as the ratio of total liabilities to total tangible assets. In addition, prior charges covenants that restrict the amount of secured debt owed to other lenders are typically included in the term loan agreements of larger firms, and are defined as a percentage of total tangible assets.[42]

Hence, it is clear that for a number of years that both private and public debt contracts within Australia have included restrictive covenants that are directly linked to accounting numbers. Where covenants restrict the total level of debt that may be issued – as was found by both Whittred and Zimmer (1986) and Cotter (1998b) – this is assumed to lead to a reduction in the risk to existing debtholders. This is further assumed to translate to lower interest rates being charged by the 'protected' debtholders. Where the covenants (or debt contract clauses) in a debt contract are breached then this is referred to as a 'technical default' of the borrowing agreement. Where such a breach occurs, and depending on the

---

[40] When we note that something is a 'public issue' it means that the particular security (such as a debenture, unsecured note, or convertible note) was made available for the public to invest in (with the terms of the issue typically provided within a publicly available prospectus document). Investors in a public debt issue would have a trustee who is to act in the interests of all the public investors. By contrast, a private debt issue involves an agreement between a limited number of parties (perhaps just one party, such as a bank) to provide debt capital to an organization.

[41] It is common in debt contracts that the measure of assets to be used excludes intangible assets. In part this is due to the concern that if an organization becomes financially distressed then many of its intangible assets (such as brand-names, patents, goodwill) may have little market value.

[42] Cotter (1998a) notes that in the 1990s banks became the major source of corporate debt. This can be contrasted with the earlier period reviewed by Whittred and Zimmer (1986). In the early 1980s Australian corporations placed relatively greater reliance on raising debt through public funding, rather than privately dealing with institutions such as banks.

terms within the debt contract, the debtholder could have the right to demand immediate repayment, or the right to seize particular assets over which it has security. Alternatively, the debtholder could agree to renegotiate the terms of the contract and not enforce the conditions of the breach but, as we indicate below, renegotiation would typically only be available in the case of private debt agreements given that the negotiation for privately raised debt would involve a limited number of parties.

In relation to debt restrictions incurred within debt contracts, Cotter (1998a) found that the definition of assets commonly used within debt agreements allowed for assets to be revalued. However, for the purposes of the debt restriction, some banks restricted the frequency of revaluations to once every two or three years, while others tended to exclude revaluations undertaken by directors of the firm. These restrictions lessened the ability of firms to loosen debt constraints by revaluing assets. Cotter (1998a) also found that apart from debt-to-assets constraints, interest coverage and current ratio clauses were frequently used in debt agreements. These clauses typically required that the ratio of net profit, with interest and tax added back, to interest expense be at least a minimum number of times. In the Cotter study, the number of times which interest had to be covered ranged from one and a half to four times. The current ratio clauses reviewed by Cotter required that current assets had to be between one and two times the size of current liabilities, depending upon the size and industry of the borrowing firm.

In more recent research, Mather and Peirson (2006) undertook an analysis of public and private debt issues made between 1991 and 2001. They showed that relative to the earlier samples used by Whittred and Zimmer, more recent public debt issues in Australia show a 'significant reduction in the use of debt to asset constraints such as covenants restricting the total liabilities/total tangible assets, or total secured liabilities to total tangible assets, with only 28 per cent of the sample of recent contracts including these covenants' (p. 292). However, Mather and Peirson provide evidence that while there is a reduction in the use of covenants that restrict the amount of total liabilities relative to assets, there appears to be a greater variety of covenants being used relative to earlier years. Among the other covenants they find in debt contracts are requirements stipulating required minimum interest coverage, minimum dividend coverage, minimum current ratio, and required minimum net worth. Again, as we know, if these minimum accounting-based requirements are not met, then the borrower is considered to be in technical default of the debt agreement and the lenders may take action to retrieve their funds. As we should appreciate, the purpose of the various debt covenants is to provide lenders with regular and timely indicators of the possibility of a borrower defaulting on repaying its debts. A violation of a debt covenant signals an increase in the likelihood of default. However, it needs to be appreciated that the covenant measures are simply indicators of the chances that an organization will not repay borrowed funds, and just because an organization is in technical default of a covenant is not a perfect indicator that the entity would not have repaid the borrowed funds.

When debt contracts are written, and where they utilize accounting numbers, the contract can rely upon either the accounting rules in place when the contracts were signed (often called 'frozen GAAP'), or the contract might rely upon the accounting rules in place at each year's reporting date (referred to as 'rolling GAAP' or 'floating GAAP'). Mather and Peirson (2006) find that in all the public debt contracts they studied, other than one, rolling (or floating) GAAP was to be used to calculate the specific ratios used within the contracts. The use of rolling GAAP increases the risk to borrowers in the sense that if a new accounting standard is released by the IASB that changes the treatment of particular assets, liabilities, expenses or income then this has the potential to cause an organization to be in technical default of a loan agreement. For example, a new accounting standard might be released that requires a previously recognized asset to be fully expensed to the income statement. This could have obvious implications for debt to asset constraints, or interest coverage requirements. This in itself could motivate an organization to actively lobby accounting standard-setters against a particular draft accounting standard. As Mather and Peirson (2006, p. 294) state:

> The use of rolling GAAP … means that new (or revisions to) accounting standards might cause breaches of covenants not anticipated at the time of contract negotiation.

When comparing the use of covenants in public and private debt issues, Mather and Peirson found that the mean number of accounting-based covenants used in the sample of public debt contracts is smaller (mean of 1.5) than the mean number of covenants (mean of 3.5) found in the sample of private debt contracts. That is, there were more restrictions based on privately negotiated debt agreements. Similarly, where debt covenants restricted total liabilities to total tangible assets, Mather and Peirson find that 'the limits imposed in public debt contracts (a mean total liabilities/total tangible assets of 82.2 per cent) appear to be less restrictive that those in private debt contracts (mean limit of 75.2 per cent)'. The fact that private debt contracts are more restrictive than public debt contracts can be explained from an efficiency perspective. Where a covenant is violated then an organization is in technical default of the debt contract. If an organization is in technical default it often has the option to try to negotiate with the debtholders to come up with a compromise that does not involve immediate repayment of the debt. However, it is very difficult to come up with a negotiated outcome in a public debt issue as there are so many diverse parties involved – some of which might not even be able to be contacted – and therefore it is relatively difficult or nearly impossible to have a successful renegotiation – hence we would expect to find the covenant restrictions to be less restrictive in public debt contracts relative to private debt contracts.[43] As Mather and Peirson (2006, p. 305) state:

> In comparison to our sample of recent public debt contracts, private debt contracts contain a greater number, variety and, collectively, more restrictive set of financial covenants. We also document differences in accounting rules associated with financial covenants used in these contracts. Tailoring of the definition of liabilities and earnings in private debt contracts make them more restrictive compared with the definitions in public debt contracts. Our findings support theory that suggests that covenant restrictive and renegotiation–flexible contracts are more suited to borrowers contracting with financial intermediaries

---

[43] As Mather and Peirson (2006) point out, a trustee would typically be appointed to look after the interests of individual investors in a public debt issue. However, individual investors would still be required to approve any course of action ensuing from a technical breach of a debt covenant.

in private debt markets than to public debt-markets that are characterized by diverse and numerous investors.

As with management compensation contracts, PAT assumes that the existence of debt contracts (which are initially put in place as a mechanism to reduce the agency costs of debt and can be explained from an *efficiency perspective*) provides management with a subsequent (*ex post*) incentive to manipulate accounting numbers, with the incentive to manipulate the numbers increasing as the accounting-based constraint approaches violation. As Watts (1995, p. 323) states:

> Early studies of debt contract-motivated choice test whether firms with higher leverage (gearing) are more likely to use earnings-increasing accounting methods to avoid default (leverage hypothesis). The underlying assumptions are that the higher the firm's leverage the less [is the] slack in debt covenants and the more likely the firm is to have changed accounting methods to have avoided default. This change is usually interpreted as opportunistic since technical default generates wealth transfers to creditors but it could also be efficient to the extent that it avoids real default and the deadweight loss associated with bankruptcy.

For example, if the firm contractually agreed that the debt to total tangible assets ratio should be kept below a certain figure, then if that figure was likely to be exceeded (causing a technical default of the loan agreement), management may have an incentive either to inflate assets or deflate liabilities. This is consistent with the results reported in Christie (1990) and Watts and Zimmerman (1990). To the extent that such an action was not objective, management would obviously be acting opportunistically and not to the benefit of individuals holding debt claims against the firm. Debt agreements typically require financial statements to be audited.

Other research to consider how management might manipulate accounting numbers in the presence of debt agreements includes that undertaken by DeFond and Jiambalvo (1994) and Sweeney (1994). Both of these studies investigated the behaviour of managers of firms known to have defaulted on accounting-related debt covenants. DeFond and Jiambalvo (1994) provided evidence that the managers manipulated accounting accruals in the years before and the year after violation of the agreement. Similarly, Sweeney (1994) found that as a firm approaches violation of a debt agreement, managers have a greater propensity to adopt income-increasing strategies relative to firms that are not approaching technical default of accounting-based debt covenants. The income-increasing accounting strategies included changing key assumptions when calculating pension liabilities and adopting last-in-first-out cost flow assumptions for inventory.

Sweeney (1994) also showed that managers with an incentive to manipulate accounting earnings might also strategically determine when they will first adopt a new accounting requirement. When new accounting standards are issued there is typically a transition period (which could be a number of years) in which organizations can voluntarily opt to implement a new accounting requirement. After the transitional period the use of the new requirement becomes mandatory. Sweeney showed that organizations that defaulted on their debt agreements tended to adopt income-increasing requirements early, and deferred the adoption of accounting methods that would lead to a reduction in reported earnings.

Research by Dhaliwal (1982) and Holthausen (1990) has also shown that firms with high leverage ratios (debt to equity), and who are thereby assumed to be approaching the violation of debt agreements, tend to oppose the introduction of accounting methods that have the potential to introduce high variability in reported earnings. This is because the high variability might increase the possibility of defaulting on accounting-based debt agreements in particular years.

Debt contracts occasionally restrict the accounting techniques that may be used by the firm, hence requiring adjustments to published accounting numbers. For example, and as stated above, Cotter (1998a) showed that bank loan contracts sometimes did not allow the component related to asset revaluations to be included in the definition of 'assets' for the purpose of calculating ratios, such as 'debt to assets' restrictions. These revaluations were, however, permitted for external reporting purposes. Therefore, loan agreements sometimes require the revaluation component (or other accounting adjustments that are allowed by accounting standards) to be removed from the published accounting numbers prior to the calculation of any restrictive covenants included within the debt contract.

Within financial reporting, management usually has available a number of alternative ways to account for particular items. Hence management has at its disposal numerous ways to minimize the effects of existing accounting-based restrictions. Therefore, it may appear optimal for debtholders to stipulate in advance *all* accounting methods that management must use. However, and as noted previously, it would be too costly, and for practical purposes impossible, to write 'complete' contracts up front. As a consequence, management will always have some discretionary ability, which may enable it to loosen the effects of debtholder-negotiated restrictions. The role of external auditors (if appointed) would be to arbitrate on the reasonableness of the accounting methods chosen.

Apart from using debt covenants (such as debt-to-asset constraints or minimum interest coverage requirements), which may or may not be breached, another contractual mechanism which is becoming increasingly used is something known as 'performance pricing'. Referring to US data, Beatty and Weber (2003, p. 120) state:

> Performance pricing is a relatively new feature in bank debt contracts that explicitly makes the interest rate charged on a bank loan a function of the borrower's current creditworthiness. Asquith *et al.* (2002) document that performance-pricing features typically measure the borrower's creditworthiness using financial ratios such as debt to earnings before interest, taxes, depreciation and amortisation (EBITDA), leverage and interest coverage. That is, the interest rate charged in the contract does not remain fixed over the length of the loan, but varies inversely with changes in measures of financial performance. Compared to covenants under which accounting information affects loan rates only when the borrower violates a single threshold, performance pricing creates a more continuous and direct link between accounting information and interest rates. Thus, performance pricing likely gives managers additional incentives to make income-increasing accounting method changes.

Beatty and Weber (2003) explore whether the existence of accounting-based performance pricing increases borrowers' tendencies to adopt income-increasing accounting method changes.

Beatty and Weber (2003) also note that debt contracts often prohibit borrowers from using voluntary accounting method changes to affect contract calculations. Hence they expect that borrowers who change their accounting methods are more likely to make income-increasing changes if their debt contracts allow the changes to affect contract calculations.

While we have previously argued in this chapter that borrowers would typically agree to various contractual restrictions (including restrictions on the accounting methods they are permitted to use) in an effort to reduce the interest costs and other borrowing costs that they are required to pay, Beatty and Weber (2003) also suggest that some borrowers might actually agree to pay higher costs of interest in return for being allowed greater flexibility in choosing accounting methods. That is, if we accept that restrictions placed on borrowers (which have the effect of reducing the ability of the borrower to transfer wealth away from the lenders and thereby potentially reduce the agency costs of debt) lead to a reduction in cost, then conversely we could speculate that in some circumstances some managers might be prepared to pay for increased flexibility – that is, there could be a value in having the ability to select alternative accounting measures – and managers might be prepared to pay for this flexibility.

In discussing their results, Beattie and Weber find that 75 borrowers from their sample of 125 US borrowing corporations had at least one contract that allowed voluntary accounting method changes to affect contract calculations. Predictably, they find that such firms, with contracts that allowed voluntary changes in the accounting methods used, were more likely to adopt income-increasing accounting methods than other firms that have debt contracts that do not allow debt covenants to be calculated by use of new accounting methods. Further, they find that the likelihood that such firms will adopt income-increasing methods increases as the cost of technical violation of debt contracts increases. In relation to the existence of accounting-based performance pricing, their results show that borrowers who change their accounting methods are more likely to make income-increasing accounting changes if their debt contracts include accounting-based performance pricing.

Having discussed how managers might have incentives to adopt income-increasing accounting methods, we can now briefly consider the role of independent auditors. In relation to auditors, and following discussion so far provided in this chapter, there would arguably be a particular demand for financial statement auditing (that is, monitoring by external parties) when:

- management is rewarded on the basis of numbers generated by the accounting system (therefore giving managers an incentive to adopt increasing accounting numbers to increase personal financial rewards); and
- when the firm has borrowed funds, and accounting-based covenants are in place to protect the investments of the debtholders.

Consistent with the above, it could also be argued that as the managers' share of equity in the business decreases, and as the proportion of debt to total assets increases, there will be a corresponding increase in the demand for auditing. In this respect, Ettredge *et al.* (1994) show that organizations that voluntarily elect to have interim financial statements audited tend to have greater leverage, and lower management shareholding in the firm.

In the discussion that follows we will consider how expectations about the *political process* can also impact on managers' choice of accounting methods.

7.7 Political costs

As indicated previously in this chapter, firms (particularly larger ones) are sometimes under scrutiny by various groups, for example, by government, employee groups, consumer groups, environmental lobby groups and so on. For example, the size of a firm is often used as an indication of market power and this in itself can attract the attention of regulatory bodies such as the Belgian Competition Council, the Danish Competition Authority, the European Commission, the Finish Competition Authority, the German Bundeskartellamt, the Irish Competition Authority, the Netherlands Competition Authority, the Norwegian Competition Authority, the Swedish Competition Authority, the UK Competition Commission or the US Federal Trade Commission – among many other such authorities throughout the world.

Government and interest groups may publicly promote the view that a particular organization (typically large) is generating excessive profits and not paying its 'fair share' to other segments of the community (for example, the wages it is paying are too low, its product prices are too high, its financial commitment to environmental and community initiatives is too low, its tax payments are too low, and so on). Watts and Zimmerman (1978, 1986) highlight the highly publicized claims about US oil companies made by consumers, unions and government within the United States in the period of the late 1970s. The claims were that oil companies were making excessive reported profits and were in effect exploiting the nation. It is considered that such claims may have led to the imposition of additional taxes in the form of 'excess profits' taxes.

Consistent with the early work of Watts and Zimmerman (1978), it has been argued that to reduce the possibility of adverse political attention and the associated costs of this attention (for example, the costs associated with increased taxes, increased wage claims, or product boycotts), politically sensitive firms (typically large firms) should adopt accounting methods that lead to a reduction in reported profits.[44] However, the view that lower reported profits will lead to lower political scrutiny (and ultimately to lower wealth transfers away from the firm) assumes that parties involved in the political process are unable or not prepared to 'unravel' the implications of the managers' various accounting choices. That is, managers can somehow *fool* those involved in the political process by simply adopting one method of accounting (income decreasing) in preference to another. In this regard, Fields *et al.* (2001, p. 260) state:

> In order for earnings management to be successful the perceived frictions must exist and at least some users of accounting information must be unable or unwilling to unravel completely the effects of the earnings management. … Political cost-based motivations implicitly assume that users of accounting information (e.g, trade unions or government agencies) may be unable to undo completely the effects of earnings management.

---

[44] Difficulties with using firm size to proxy for political costs, including the likelihood that it can proxy for many other effects, such as industry membership, are discussed in Ball and Foster (1982).

But, why would it be the case that external parties can potentially be 'fooled' by management as a result of management's choices of alternative accounting methods when elsewhere it has been assumed (consistent with the EMH) that individuals within other markets, such as the capital market, can efficiently unravel management's choices of accounting methods?

In relation to political costs, and from an economic perspective, there is a view that in political markets there is limited expected 'pay-off' that can result from the actions of individuals (Downs, 1957). For example, if an individual seeks to know the real reasons why government elected to adopt a particular action from among many possible actions, then gathering such information would be costly. Yet that individual's vote would have very little likelihood of affecting the existence of the government. Hence, individuals will elect to remain *rationally uninformed*. However, should particular interest groups form, then such information costs can be shared and the ability to investigate government actions can increase. A similar perspective is taken with groups other than government, for example representatives of labour unions, consumer bodies and so on. Officials of these bodies represent a diverse group of people, with the individual constituents again having limited incentive to be fully informed about the activities of the office-bearers.

Because PAT assumes that *all* actions by *all* individuals (including officials of interest groups, politicians and so on) are driven by self-interest, representatives of interest groups are predicted to adopt strategies that maximize their own welfare in the knowledge that their constituents will have limited motivation to be fully informed about their activities.

With the above arguments in mind, we can consider the actions of politicians. Because politicians know that highly profitable companies could be unpopular with a large number of their constituency, the politicians could 'win' votes by taking actions against such companies. However, Watts and Zimmerman (1979) argue that politicians will claim that the actions they have taken were in the 'public interest' as obviously they need to disguise the fact that such actions best served the politicians' own interests. As Watts and Zimmerman (1979, p. 283) argue:

> In recent years economists have questioned whether the public interest assumption is consistent with observed phenomena. They have proposed an alternative assumption – that individuals involved in the political process act in their own self-interest (the self-interest assumption). This assumption yields implications which are more consistent with observed phenomena than those based on the public interest assumption.[45]

To justify their own actions, politicians may simply rely on the reported profits of companies to provide an *excuse* for their actions, knowing that individual constituents are unlikely to face the cost of investigating the politicians' motives, or the cost of investigating how the corporation's profits were determined (that is, whether the profit resulted because a particular accounting method was used in a less than objective manner). To reduce the *excuses* of politicians, potentially politically sensitive firms are predicted to anticipate

---

[45] In Chapter 3 of this book we considered different theories of regulation. One theory, public interest theory, suggests that regulators are not driven by self-interest but, rather, elect to put in place regulations that are in the best interest of society. By contrast, economic interest group theories of regulation assume that everybody, including regulators, are motivated by their own self-interest and hence regulators put in place regulations that best serve themselves rather than society generally. This latter theory ties in best with the assumptions embodied within PAT.

politicians' actions and therefore the management of politically vulnerable firms have an incentive to reduce their reported profits. As Watts and Zimmerman (1979, p. 281) state:

> Government commissions often use the contents of financial statements in the regulatory process (rate setting, anti-trust, etc.). Further, Congress often bases legislative actions on these statements. This, in turn, provides management with incentives to select accounting procedures which either reduce the costs they bear or increase the benefits they receive as a result of the actions of government regulators and legislators.

Interestingly, when the media report a company's profitability they seldom give any attention to the accounting methods used to calculate the profit. In a sense, profit is held out as some form of objective measure of organizational performance (much like governments might rely on profits to support a particular action). Media reports of high corporate profitability can potentially trigger political costs for a firm. In the discussion above we discussed how representatives of interest groups might use profits as a justification for particular actions. In this respect we can consider Accounting Headline 7.4. The article refers to the high profits of banks in the UK and highlights how, despite making significant profits, banks are defying calls to increase lending to small business, to pay higher tax on their profits and bonuses, and to be broken up into smaller banks because of a perception that very large banks pose a threat to the economy if they fail. In a sense, the reported accounting profits could be used as an excuse to push for greater regulation of bank lending practices, 'windfall' taxes and greater controls on the size of banks. Perhaps if reported profits were not so high there would be less chance that demands for increased regulation and government action would be made. As Watts and Zimmerman (1978, p. 115) state:

> By avoiding the attention that high profits draw because of monopoly rents, management can reduce the likelihood of adverse political actions and, thereby, reduce its expected costs (including the legal costs the firm would incur opposing the political actions). Included in political costs are the costs labour unions impose through increased demands generated by large reported profits.

Accounting Headline 7.4
Profits as a consideration in the political process
HSBC rejects bid to force lending as profits soar

By Jill Treanor

Britain's biggest bank, HSBC, intends to defy any government-imposed targets for lending to businesses and households despite ministers' fears that the drought in credit is threatening the economic recovery.

As HSBC kicked off the bank reporting season with a more than doubling in first half profits to $11.1bn (£7.2bn), it also revealed that its total lending fell. Customers in the UK repaid some £33bn more than it had paid out in new loans during the first six months of the year, it said.

But the bank shrugged off the clamour for more credit by saying lending targets would not work. And with the government also considering breaking up banks 'too big to fail', HSBC risked further conflict when chief executive Michael Geoghegan said the financial system needed banks like HSBC that were 'big enough to cope'.

HSBC's better than expected results helped bolster the stock market, helping the FTSE 100 gain 139 points to close at 5,397. HSBC's shares rose 5.3%.

While the government considers ways to bolster lending, including the threat of taxing profits or setting lending targets to banks such as HSBC which did not need to be bailed out, HSBC declared lending targets would not work.

Douglas Flint, finance director of HSBC, said: 'It is very difficult to see how you construct a target and have it be effective.'

Both George Osborne, the chancellor, and Vince Cable, the business secretary, have spelt out concerns that if banks do not lend then any economic recovery could stall. Small businesses continue to complain that loans are hard to get while banks insist demand is drying up.

Stephen Alambritis from the Federation of Small Businesses (FSB) said banks were now lending at the rate of £500m a month, down from the £900m a month in 2008 before the banking crisis struck. Banks were putting up hurdles to loans 'the size of Becher's Brook', he said.

HSBC insisted demand in the UK was down. Overdraft usage was down 45%, and UK loan applications were down by 20%. But it said it approves nearly 70% of all business applications, the same rate as over the past three years, and stressed new lending to small business was up 38% to £1.3bn. New mortgage lending was £7bn in the first half of the year, which it says reflected its willingness to lend as its market share is now 8%, against its traditional 3% share. The bank also received support from the British Chambers of Commerce which said: 'The current lending situation is much more complicated than simply forcing banks to lend when demand among business is muted.'

The bank tried to deflect criticism about bonuses by insisting that while it was setting aside 24% of the revenues in its investment bank to pay out bonuses and salaries – which amounts to some $2.5bn (£1.5bn) – in the first six months, this was less than the 35% it would have used before the banking crisis.

The investment banking arm had its second best half year on record, making $5.6bn of profits, down from the previous record of $6.2bn which was recorded the same time last year. Despite the fall in profits, the amount set aside to pay staff was higher than a year ago, although the bank insisted this was because of the cost of the bonus tax in the UK and France.

Even so, the bank is likely to pay out big bonuses to its top bankers. Last year Stuart Gulliver, the head of the investment bank, was the highest paid member of staff with a £10m pay deal.

Source: *Guardian,* 3 August 2010, p. 1
©Guardian News and Media Limited 2010

Numerous studies have considered how particular accounting methods can be used in an endeavour to decrease political costs. We have already considered the work of Watts and Zimmerman. Other research has been undertaken by Jones (1991) who, in a US study, considered the behaviour of 23 domestic firms from five industries that were the subject of government import-related investigations over the period from 1980 to 1985. These government investigations by the International Trade Commission sought to determine whether the domestic firms were under threat from foreign competition. Where this threat is deemed to be unfair, the government can grant relief by devices such as tariff protection. In making its decision the government relies upon a number of factors, including economic measures such as profits and sales. The results of the study show that in the year of the investigations the sample companies selected accounting strategies that led to a decrease in reported profits. Such behaviour was not evidenced in the year before or the year after the government investigation (perhaps indicating that the politicians are fairly 'short sighted' when undertaking investigations).

In a UK study, Sutton (1988) found that politically sensitive companies were also more likely to lobby in favour of current cost accounting.[46] In a New Zealand study, Wong (1988) investigated the practice of New Zealand companies between 1977 and 1981 and found that those that adopted current cost accounting (which had the effect of reducing reported profits) had higher effective tax rates and larger market concentration ratios than other firms. Effective tax rates and market concentration rates were both used as a measure of political sensitivity.

Apart from adopting income-reducing accounting techniques, authors such as Ness and Mirza (1991) have argued that particular voluntary social disclosures in an organization's annual report can be explained as an effort to reduce the political costs of the disclosing entities. Ness and Mirza (1991) studied the environmental disclosure practices of a number of UK companies. They considered that companies in the oil industry had developed particularly poor reputations for their environmental practices and that such a reputation could be used by various interest groups to transfer wealth away from the firm (and presumably away from the managers). Such wealth transfers might be generated if certain groups lobbied government to impose particular taxes (perhaps related to their environmental performance), or perhaps if particular employee groups took actions to insist that the companies put in place strategies to improve their environmental performance and reputation. Ness and Mirza argued that if firms voluntarily provide environmental disclosures (typically of a positive or self-laudatory nature) then this may lead to a reduction in future wealth transfers away from the firm. They found, consistent with their expectations, that oil companies provided greater environmental disclosures within their annual reports than did companies operating in other industries. They argued that this was the case as oil companies had more potentially adverse wealth transfers at stake.

---

[46] While a number of studies considered in this chapter investigate the choice between alternative accounting methods, it should be noted that in recent years there has been an increased focus on studying the manipulation of accounting accruals. Relative to investigating the selection of particular accounting methods (for example, the use of straight line depreciation versus reducing balance depreciation), the study of the accruals is more difficult and requires the use of modelling techniques to identify discretionary (those controlled by management) and non-discretionary accruals (Jones, 1991). The use of accruals can also be explained from either an *efficiency* or *opportunistic* perspective (Guay *et al.*, 1996).

Before concluding our discussion on political costs it is useful to consider Accounting Headline 7.5 that highlights anger of many consumer groups as energy companies reported record profits while many of their consumers were left struggling in the face of steep price rises. These high prices meant that many people had difficulty affording fuel for such basic requirements as heating. Arguably, a time when high fuel costs were adversely affecting so many people was not the most politically favourable time for energy companies such as Centrica and Shell to report record profits.

Accounting Headline 7.5

High profits as consumers face price rises

Energy prices: Consumer anger over Centrica's £992m profit

By Mark Milner and Terry Macalister

The parent company of British Gas provoked further consumer anger yesterday when it revealed a profit of nearly £1bn made in the first six months of the year less than 24 hours after it raised household gas bills by a record 35%.

News that Centrica's 800,000 shareholders are being awarded a 16% increase in their dividend payout added to the backlash.

'British Gas customers, still reeling from 35% price hikes, might have expected Centrica to be losing money,' said Adam Scorer, campaigns director at consumer watchdog, energywatch. 'They will be staggered at the rude health of Centrica's half-year profit.'

'Customers will be outraged to learn that while they ponder how to make ends meet Centrica's shareholders are enjoying an increase in their dividends.'

Shell also stoked the furore over high fuel prices by posting a profit of nearly $8bn (£4bn) in the second quarter of the year, the equivalent of £2m an hour.

Rising fuel and food bills are increasing pressure on the government, with calls for windfall taxes on energy companies. ...

Charities said yesterday that the latest increases in domestic energy prices would push hundreds of thousands more people into fuel poverty. National Energy Action [NEA] said British Gas's increase in gas prices, accompanied by a 9% rise in electricity bills, would push average household bills up to £1,320 a year, more than double the figure in January 2003.

'Across the UK fuel poverty could affect 6 million households by the end of the year,' Zoe Mcleod of NEA said. 'Ministers may well be on holiday now, but they need to stop their sunbathing and plan ahead to protect vulnerable households from the cold this winter.'

Centrica has blamed the need to increase household bills on the more than doubling of wholesale energy prices. Yesterday it said its £992m operating profit was down almost 20% compared with the same period last year, while the profit from British Gas's residential business fell from £533m to £166m.

Tony Woodley, joint leader of the Unite union attacked the utility sector in the wake of Centrica's figures. 'This combination of massive profits and eye-watering price rises proves that the privatised pro-vision of basic utilities has failed the public,' he said. 'They should be taken back into some form of ownership by the community.'

Woodley also criticised Shell. 'These latest vast profits now put the case for a windfall tax on big oil companies beyond argument,' he said. 'The government should grasp the nettle and do what it did in 1997 by taxing grotesque profits and put the proceeds into helping the millions of people struggling with their fuel bills'. ...

Shell says it is investing more heavily in new oil and gas production than ever before to meet rising demand and says a windfall tax would damage its ability to provide sup-plies into the future. The company also says the government should not tax profit made in other parts of the world.

The company later produced figures showing it was paying up to 75% tax on some North Sea oil fields and had handed over £500m in overall UK taxation during 2007. Centrica said it was paying a similar level of tax on its North Sea production and its overall tax rate was now 58%.

Shell declined to say how much it had earned from motorists at its network of pet-rol stations. It said it was "one of the cheap-est" suppliers and its overall refining and marketing business had been having a rough period with big profits coming from explora-tion and production.

Source: *Guardian*, 1 August 2008, p. 2
©Guardian News and Media Limited 2010

The extracts in Accounting Headline 7.5 emphasize how accounting profits can be used to justify actions being taken against an organization. If Centrica's and Shell's profits had not been so high, then perhaps such calls for action would not have been made. This is consistent with Watts and Zimmerman's political cost hypothesis.

To this point, we have shown that PAT indicates that the selection of particular and alternative accounting methods may impact on the cash flows associated with debt contracts, the cash flows associated with management compensation plans, and the political costs of the firm. PAT indicates that these impacts can be used to explain why firms elect to use particular accounting methods in preference to others. PAT also indicates that the use of particular accounting methods may have opposing effects. For example, if a firm was to adopt a policy that increased income (for example, it may capitalize an item, rather than expensing it as incurred), then this may reduce the probability of violating a debt constraint. However, it may increase the political visibility of the firm due to the higher profits. Managers are assumed to select the accounting methods that best balance the conflicting effects (and also that maximize their own wealth).

We have demonstrated in this chapter that PAT became the dominant theory used by accounting researchers in the 1970s.[47] It represented a challenge to many normative theorists and conflicted with the views of many established researchers. Many individuals openly criticized PAT. In the concluding section of this chapter we now consider some of these criticisms of PAT.

---

[47] While its popularity is still high, many accounting schools are now actively promoting alternative theories.

7.8 Some criticisms of Positive Accounting Theory

One widespread criticism of PAT is that it does not provide *prescription* and therefore does not provide a means of improving accounting practice. It is argued that simply explaining and predicting accounting practice – which is the aim of PAT – is not enough. Using a medical analogy, Sterling (1990, p. 130) states:

> PAT cannot rise above giving the same answers because it restricts itself to the descriptive questions. If it ever asked how to solve a problem or correct an error (both of which require going beyond a description to an evaluation of the situation), then it might go on to different questions and obtain different answers after the previous problem was solved. If we had restricted the medical question to the description of the smallpox virus, for example, precluding prescriptions to be vaccinated, we would need more and more descriptive studies as the virus population increased and mutations appeared. Luckily Edward Jenner was naughtily normative, which allowed him to discover how cowpox could be used as a vaccine so smallpox was eventually eliminated, which made room for different questions on the medical agenda.

Howieson (1996, p. 31) provides a view that by failing to provide prescription, Positive Accounting Theorists may alienate themselves from practising accountants. As he states:

> an unwillingness to tackle policy issues is arguably an abrogation of academics' duty to serve the community which supports them. Among other activities, practitioners are concerned on a day-to-day basis with the question of which accounting policies they should choose. Traditionally, academics have acted as commentators and reformers on such normative issues. By concentrating on positive questions, they risk neglecting one of their important roles in the community.

A second criticism of PAT is that it is not *value free*, as it asserts. If we are to look at various research that has adopted PAT, we will see a general absence of prescription (that is, there is no guidance as to what people *should* do – rather it explains or predicts what they *will* do). This is normally justified by Positive Accounting Theorists by saying that they do not want to impose their views on others, but rather would prefer to objectively provide information about the expected implications of particular actions and let people decide for themselves what they should do (for example, they may provide evidence to support a prediction that organizations close to breaching accounting-based debt covenants will adopt accounting methods that increase the firm's reported profits and assets). However, as a number of accounting academics have pointed out, selecting a theory to adopt for research (such as PAT) is based on a value judgement; what to research is based on a value judgement; believing that all individual action is driven by self-interest is a value judgement and, so on.[48] Equally, whether one accepts that 'stealing by the owner-manager is analogous to the owner-manager's over consumption of perks', as Watts and Zimmerman (1986, p. 185)

---

[48] In Chapter 12 we also see that some researchers argue that Positive Accounting Theorists adopt a conservative right-wing ideology in promoting the virtues of markets, the rights of shareholders (the capitalist class) and so on.

note, is a matter of personal opinion. Also, Watts and Zimmerman appear to have taken a normative position when they identify the objective of accounting research. According to them, 'the objective of accounting theory is to explain and predict accounting practice' (1986, p. 2). Clearly, there are many other views about the role of accounting theory. Hence, no research, whether conducted under PAT or otherwise, is value free. While Watts and Zimmerman did continue to argue for a number of years that PAT was value free, they did eventually concede (1990, p. 146) that:

> Positive theories are value laden. Tinker et al (1982, p. 167) argue that all research is value laden and not socially neutral. Specifically, 'Realism operating in the clothes of positive theory, claims theoretical supremacy because it is born of fact, not values' (p. 172). We concede the importance of values in determining research: both the researcher's and user's preferences affect the process.

Following from the above points, a third criticism of PAT relates to the fundamental assumption that *all action* is driven by a desire to maximize one's wealth. To many researchers such an assumption represents a far too negative and simplistic perspective of humankind. In this respect, Gray *et al.* (1996, p. 75) state that PAT promotes 'a morally bankrupt view of the world'. Given that everybody is deemed to act in their own self-interest, the perspective of self-interest has also been applied to the research efforts of academics. For example, Watts and Zimmerman (1990, p. 146) argue that:

> Researchers choose the topics to investigate, the methods to use, and the assumptions to make. Researchers' preferences and expected payoffs (publications and citations) affect their choice of topic, methods, and assumptions.

Many academics would challenge this view and would argue that they undertake their research because of real personal interest in an issue. Another implication of the self-interest issue is that incorporation of this self-interest assumption into the teaching of undergraduate students (as has been done in many universities throughout the world) has the possible implication that students think that when they subsequently have to make decisions in the workplace it is both acceptable and predictable for them to place their own interests above those of others. It is perhaps questionable whether such a philosophy is in the interests of the broader community.[49] Nevertheless, while assuming that all action is driven by a desire to maximize one's own wealth is not an overly kind assumption about human nature, such an assumption has been the cornerstone of many past and existing theories used within the discipline of economics (and this is not a justification).

A further criticism of the economic assumptions underlying PAT comes from its reliance on the assumption of the efficiency of markets – again this assumption is a long-standing cornerstone of much economic theory, which does not in itself justify it as a valid assumption. The credibility of economic theories (and therefore arguably also of PAT)

---

[49] It certainly is not consistent with any quests towards ecologically and socially sustainable development – an issue which we address in Chapter 9. To embrace sustainable development – which is defined as development that meets the needs of the present world without compromising the ability of future generations to meet their own needs (World Commission on Environment and Development, 1987) – we need to consider the interests of future generations. If we accept and promote a view that self-interest drives all current actions – as PAT researchers and many other economics researchers do – then such an assumption holds very little hope for any real quests towards sustainable development.

relying upon this assumption was widely called into question following the sub-prime banking crisis and ensuing global financial crisis. For example, Adair Turner, the Chair of the UK banking regulator, the Financial Services Authority (FSA) stated that:

> we have had a very fundamental shock to the 'efficient market hypothesis' which has been the DNA of the FSA and securities and banking regulators throughout the world. The idea that more complete and more liquid markets are definitionally good and the more of them we have the more stable the system will be, that was asserted with great confidence up to three years ago. (Prospect, 2009, p. 39)

McSweeney (2009) points out a number of areas in which positivistic accounting models have been called into question in light of the sub-prime banking crisis and the failure of markets to behave in a manner that is a fundamental assumption underlying much economic (and positive accounting) theory. *If* Positive Accounting Theorists are unwilling to adequately reflect on the ongoing plausibility of the key assumptions underlying their models, and adapt their models accordingly, then they risk these models becoming discredited as those outside the academic accounting world realize the models are implausible.

Another criticism of PAT is that since its general inception in the 1970s the issues being addressed have not shown great development. Since the early days of Watts and Zimmerman (1978) there have been three key hypotheses: the debt hypothesis (which proposes that organizations close to breaching accounting-based debt covenants will select accounting methods that lead to an increase in profits and assets); the bonus hypothesis (which proposes that managers on accounting-based bonus schemes will select accounting methods that lead to an increase in profits); and the political cost hypothesis (which proposes that firms subject to political scrutiny will adopt accounting methods that reduce reported income). A review of the recent PAT literature indicates that these hypotheses continue to be tested in different environments and in relation to different accounting policy issues – even after the passing of over 30 years since Watts and Zimmerman (1978). In this respect, Sterling (1990, p. 130) posed the following question:

> What are the potential accomplishments [of PAT]? I forecast more of the same: twenty years from now we will have been inundated with research reports that managers and others tend to manipulate accounting numerals when it is to their advantage to do so.

In commenting on the perceived lack of development of PAT, Fields *et al.* (2001, p. 301) state:

> Fundamentally, we believe it is necessary to step back from the current research agenda, and to develop the 'infrastructure' surrounding the field. In a sense, the accounting choice field has been a victim of its own perceived success, and has outrun the development of theories, statistical techniques and research design that are necessary to support it. We therefore are calling for a return to work in these basic areas, before the field is able to advance further.

Also, much of the research within PAT considers individual accounting choices (for example, whether an entity will revalue a particular class of non-current assets) when in practice the organization will have a vast number of accounting choices, many of which might have opposing effects on financial performance and position. That is, while researchers might be studying whether an entity elects to adopt an accounting method that increases income, at the same time the entity might also be adopting another (unresearched) accounting method that reduces income. Considering one accounting method choice from the portfolio of all the accounting choices being made within the firm provides a very incomplete picture. In this regard Fields *et al.* (2001, p. 288) state:

> Most of the work [in PAT] examines the choice of a particular accounting method within the context of the goals driving the accounting choice, whereas managers may make multiple accounting method choices to accomplish a specific goal. As a result, examining only one choice at a time may obscure the overall effect obtained through a portfolio of choices.

Fields *et al.* (2001, p. 290) further state:

> In addition to the problem of addressing multiple accounting choices, generally as reflected in accruals, there is also the issue of multiple, and potentially conflicting, motivations for the accounting choices. Most of the work discussed focuses on a single motive for accounting choice decisions. For example, the compensation literature focuses on the question of whether managers use accounting discretion to maximize their compensation. Implicitly, the results suggest that managers' actions come at the expense of shareholders. But if this is so, why do compensation contracts allow discretion? One plausible answer is that managers' actions are not only anticipated, but also desirable from shareholders' perspective. For example, the same accounting choices that maximize managers' compensation may also decrease bond covenant violations or increase asset valuations. However, such motives are typically not included in the analysis. By focusing on one goal at a time, much of the literature misses the more interesting question of the interactions between and tradeoffs among goals. Moreover, it is not clear whether the conclusions are attributable to the specific motivation being analyzed; generally results consistent with one hypothesis are consistent with many. For example, what may appear to be an opportunistic choice of an earnings increasing accounting method choice (to benefit managers at the expense of other stakeholders in the firm), may be in fact a response to avoid a bond covenant violation (and thus benefits all other stakeholders at the expense of the creditors). Finally, with only few exceptions, research in the 1990s generally focuses on motives identified in the 1970s and 1980s. Typically the usual suspects are rounded up. However, we suspect that new insights may be gained by investigating additional motives. The problem of multiple conflicts can be viewed, in turn, as a special case of the familiar 'correlated omitted variable' problem in econometrics.

Another criticism is that the measurements or proxies being used within the literature are often far too simplistic. As Fields *et al.* (2001, p. 272) state:

> Most work investigating the debt hypothesis in the 1980s used crude proxies such as the leverage ratio for the proximity of the firm to violation of its debt covenants. However, Lys (1984) documents that because leverage is determined

endogenously, it is a poor proxy for default risk, unless there is a control for the risk of the underlying assets. On the other hand, Duke and Hunt (1990) determine that the debt to equity ratio is a good proxy for the closeness to some covenant violations, including retained earnings, net tangible assets and working capital, but not for other covenants. In the 1990s researchers began studying firms that actually violated covenants in order to avoid the use of proxies.

A further criticism is that PAT is scientifically flawed. It has been argued that as the hypotheses generated pursuant to PAT (for example, the debt hypothesis, the bonus hypothesis and the political cost hypothesis) are frequently not supported (they are falsified), then scientifically PAT should be rejected. Christenson (1983, p. 18) states:

> We are told, for example, that 'we can only expect a positive theory to hold on average' [Watts and Zimmerman, 1978, p. 127, n. 37]. We are also advised 'to remember that as in all empirical theories we are concerned with general trends' [Watts and Zimmerman, 1978, pp. 288–9], where 'general' is used in the weak sense of 'true or applicable in most instances but not all' rather than in the strong sense of 'relating to, concerned with, or applicable to every member of a class' [American Heritage Dictionary, 1969, p. 548] … A law that admits exceptions has no significance, and knowledge of it is not of the slightest use. By arguing that their theories admit exceptions, Watts and Zimmerman condemn them as insignificant and useless.

As a study of people, however (accounting is a process undertaken by people and the accounting process itself cannot exist in the absence of accountants), it is hard to consider that any model or theory could ever fully explain human action. In fact, ability to do so would constitute a dehumanizing action. Are there any theories of human activity or choice processes that always hold? In defence of the fact that PAT predictions do not always hold, Watts and Zimmerman (1990, p. 148) state:

> But accounting research using this methodology has produced useful predictions of how the world works. A methodology that yields useful results should not be abandoned purely because it may not predict all human behaviour. Do we discard something that works in some situations because it may not work in every circumstance?

Another criticism of PAT is that the positive researchers believe that they can generate laws and principles expected to operate in different situations, and that there is one underlying 'truth' that can be determined by an independent, impartial observer who is not influenced by individual perceptions, idiosyncrasies or biases (Tinker *et al.*, 1982, p. 167). That is, the apparent perspective is that reality exists objectively, and one observer's view of that reality will be the same as all other people's views. This is referred to as the 'realist philosophy'. A number of researchers have challenged this philosophy (for example, Hines, 1988). They have argued that in undertaking large-scale empirical research, positive researchers ignore many organization-specific relationships and the information collected is only the information that the researchers consider relevant. A different person would possibly consider that other information is more relevant. Many researchers critical of the 'realist perspective' argue that more insights might be gained by undertaking in-depth case studies. Positive researchers would provide a counter-argument, however, that case study research is very specific to a particular time and place and therefore cannot be generalized to a broader population. Such arguments about research methodology abound in the literature with potentially very limited likelihood that researchers operating across different paradigms will ever agree on what constitutes valid research. As Watts and Zimmerman (1990, p. 149) concede when defending their research against numerous criticisms:

> To most researchers, debating methodology is a 'no win' situation because each side argues from a different paradigm with different rules and no common ground. Our reason for replying here is that some have mistaken our lack of response as tacit acceptance of the criticisms.

While the above criticisms do, arguably, have some merit, PAT does continue to be used by many accounting researchers. Respected accounting research journals continue to publish PAT research (although the numbers appear to be declining). A number of the leading accounting research schools throughout the world continue to teach it. What must be remembered is that all theories of accounting will have limitations. They are, of necessity, abstractions of the 'real world'. Whether individually we prefer one theory of accounting in preference to another will be dependent upon our assumptions about many of the issues raised within this chapter.

However, as pointed out earlier in this section, several of the fundamental assumptions underlying PAT were called into question in light of market failures surrounding the sub-prime banking crisis and ensuing global financial crisis. Therefore, even though our preference for one theoretical perspective over another will depend upon our own assumptions about many issues, we need to ensure that we maintain a 'reality check' on these assumptions otherwise accounting research risks stagnating and losing credibility (Unerman and O'Dwyer, 2010). As Hopwood (2007, p. 1367) explained in his *Presidential Scholar* plenary address to the 2006 American Accounting Association annual meeting, accounting theory needs to be continually developed in order to remain useful in a changing world:

> There were … there have been … and there are now people who think that they know what accounting – and auditing for that matter – is. How wrong these people are. They are the ones who list the attributes of the status quo, seemingly wanting to confine the new to being within the boundaries of the old. They have no conception that accounting and accounting research have repeatedly changed across time, and when things change they become what they were not, at least in part. Accounting has been a craft that has had no essence. It has changed significantly across time, adopting new forms, methods, and roles. Likewise for accounting research. Historically, it too has developed in relation to a diverse series of circumstances and pressures, taking on different forms in different places and at different moments of time, repeatedly adopting approaches that were novel and contentious. Moreover, both accounting and accounting research will continue to do just that, regardless of the pleas and efforts of those who act in the name of the status quo. Indeed the very role of accounting research is in part to make both accounting and our knowledge of it different – to move forward our understandings of accounting and, at times, the practice of accounting itself.

Chapter summary

Apositive theory seeks to explain and predict particular phenomena. In this chapter we considered Positive Accounting Theory (PAT), a theory that seeks to explain and predict managers' choices of accounting methods. PAT focuses on relationships between various individuals within and outside an organization and explains how financial accounting can be used to minimize the costly implications associated with each contracting party operating in his or her own self-interest. The economic perspective that all individual behaviour is motivated by self-interest is central to PAT, and PAT predicts that contractual arrangements will be put in place to align the interests of the various self-interested parties. Many of these contractual arrangements will use the output of the accounting system.

PAT became a dominant research paradigm in the 1970s and 1980s and its development owed much to previous research work that had been undertaken, including work on the efficient markets hypothesis (EMH) and agency theory. The EMH provided evidence that capital markets react to new information but it provided little explanation for why managers might elect to use particular accounting methods in preference to others. PAT was developed to fill this void.

Applying agency theory, PAT focused on relationships between principals and agents. PAT proposed that agents have incentives to enter various contracts. Firms themselves were considered as a nexus of contracts between many self-interested individuals. The contractual arrangements are initially put in place for efficiency reasons with well-developed contracts reducing the overall agency costs that could arise within the firm. Further, agents are predicted to adopt those accounting methods that most efficiently reflect their own performance. Regulation is considered to introduce unnecessary costs and inefficiencies into the contractual arrangements, particularly as it often acts to reduce the methods of accounting that would otherwise be adopted.

Early work within PAT relied upon three central hypotheses: the bonus hypothesis, the debt hypothesis and the political cost hypothesis. The bonus hypothesis predicts that from an efficiency perspective many organizations will elect to provide their managers with bonuses tied to the performance of the firm, with these bonuses often being directly related to accounting numbers (for example, management might be rewarded with a share of profits). Offering performance-based rewards will motivate the self-interested manager to work also in the best interests of the owners. However, under the opportunistic perspective, PAT predicts that once bonus schemes are in place, managers will, to the extent that they can get away with it, manipulate performance indicators such as profits to generate higher individual rewards.

The debt hypothesis predicts that to reduce the cost of attracting debt capital firms will enter into contractual arrangements with lenders which reduce the likelihood that the managers can expropriate the wealth of the debtholders. Arranging such agreements prior to obtaining debt finance is deemed to be an efficient way to attract lower cost funds. However, once a debt contract is in place, the opportunistic perspective of PAT predicts that firms, particularly those close to breaching debt covenants, will adopt accounting methods that act to minimize or loosen the effects of the debt constraint.

The political cost hypothesis explores the relationships between a firm and various outside parties who, although perhaps not having any direct contractual relationships, can nevertheless impose various types of wealth transfers away from the firm. It is argued that high profits can attract adverse and costly attention to the firm, and hence managers of politically vulnerable firms look for ways to reduce the level of political scrutiny. One way is to adopt accounting methods that lead to a reduction in reported profits. Most tests of the political cost hypothesis use size of the firm as a proxy for the existence of political scrutiny.

The chapter also provided a number of criticisms of PAT. Included among the various criticisms was a challenge to the central PAT assumption that *all* individual action is driven by self-interest. Furthermore, the validity of several of the fundamental economics-based assumptions underlying PAT were called into question in light of the market failures at the time of the sub-prime banking crisis and ensuing global financial crisis.

Questions

7.1 Early positive research investigated evidence of share price changes as a result of the disclosure of accounting information. However, such research did not explain why particular accounting methods were selected in the first place. How did Positive Accounting Theory fill this void?

7.2 Explain the *management bonus hypothesis* and the *debt hypothesis* of Positive Accounting Theory.

7.3 If a manager is paid a percentage of profits, does this generate a motive to manipulate profits? Would this be anticipated by principals and, if so, how would principals react to this expectation?

7.4 What is an *agency relationship* and what is an *agency cost*? How can agency costs be reduced?

7.5 Explain the *political cost hypothesis* of Positive Accounting Theory.

7.6 Explain the *efficiency perspective* and the *opportunistic perspective* of Positive Accounting Theory. Why is one considered to be *ex post* and the other *ex ante*?

7.7 Would managers who have negotiated debt contracts with accounting-based covenants based around 'rolling GAAP' be relatively more likely to lobby an accounting standard-setter about a proposed accounting standard than would a manager from a firm who has negotiated accounting-based debt covenants that use 'frozen GAAP'? Why?

7.8 Organizations typically have a number of contractual arrangements with debtholders, with many covenants written to incorporate accounting numbers.

   a Why would an organization agree to enter into such agreements with debtholders?

   b On average, do debtholders gain from the existence of such agreements?

7.9 Positive Accounting Theorists typically argue that managers can reduce political costs by simply adopting an accounting method that leads to a reduction in reported income. Does this imply anything about the perceived efficiency of those parties involved in the political process and, if so, what perception is held?

7.10 If a reporting entity has a choice of either *expensing* or *capitalizing* an item of expenditure, and if the entity is subject to a high degree of political scrutiny, then what choice would be predicted by the *political cost hypothesis* of Positive Accounting Theory? Explain your answer.

7.11 Assume that Kahuna Company SA decides to undertake an upward revaluation of its non-current assets just prior to the end of the financial year, the effect being that the total assets of the company increases, as does the total shareholders' equity. You are required to:

    a explain the decision of management to undertake an asset revaluation in terms of the *debt hypothesis* of Positive Accounting Theory

    b explain the decision of management to undertake an asset revaluation in terms of the *management compensation hypothesis* of Positive Accounting Theory

7.12 Mather and Peirson (2006) report that public debt contracts tends to have both a lower average number of accounting-based debt covenants as well as less binding debt covenants (for example, in relation to debt-to-assets constraints in both public and private debt agreement, the covenants in the public debt agreements were found to be 'looser', meaning that the ratio percentage is typically higher in the public debt contract). Why would this be the case?

7.13 Positive Accounting Theory assumes that all individual action is driven by self-interest, with the self-interest being tied to wealth maximization.

    a Is this a useful and/or realistic assumption?

    b Adopting this assumption, why would politicians introduce particular regulations?

    c Why would researchers study particular issues?

7.14 What are some of the criticisms of PAT? Do you agree with them? Why or why not?

7.15 Zhang (2008) argues that if a borrower adopts conservative accounting methods then this will reduce the risk exposure of the lender and will lead to a reduced interest cost for the borrower. What is the basis of this argument?

7.16 Read Accounting Headline 7.6. As you will see, National Express had negotiated an agreement with lenders that its borrowing would not be higher than '3.5 times its earnings before interest, tax, depreciation and amortisation (EBITDA)'. However as profits dropped this covenant came close to being breached, meaning that the lenders ultimately could demand repayment of the funds if they choose to invoke their right to do so. From a PAT theory perspective, why would National Express have agreed to this interest cover requirement rather than other types of covenants, such as a restriction on the organization's total liabilities to total tangible assets? Further, why would the banks have negotiated to have this interest cover agreement included within the debt agreement?

7.17 Adopting a Positive Accounting perspective, consider the following issues:

    a If a new accounting standard impacts on profits, should this impact on the value of the firm, and if so, why?

    b Will the imposition of a particular accounting method have implications for the *efficiency* of the organization?

Accounting Headline 7.6

An example of a debt covenant
Richard Bowker resigns as chief executive of National Express

By Dan Milmo

Richard Bowker has resigned as chief executive of National Express as the public transport group struggles to hold on to its £1.4bn east coast rail franchise.

Bowker will step down in August to take up a chief executive post at an unnamed company overseas. His position became increasingly precarious in recent weeks as the government rebuffed attempts to renegotiate Britain's most expensive rail contract.

... National Express requires a rights issue of around £400m to pay down its £1.2bn debt burden, according to market watchers, and investors are understood to be against the move unless the east coast situation is resolved.

Bowker oversaw the record £1.4bn bid for the London-to-Edinburgh route, which committed the group to annual payments that rise from £85m in 2008 to £395m by 2015, leading to industry speculation that his departure would also be a pre-condition to a rights issue. The contract has become a financial millstone that is expected to lose the company £90m over the next two years. In order to meet its targets the franchise requires passenger revenue growth of around 10% per year, but the latest figures showed a 0.3% increase in turnover as the recession hits demand and forces business passengers – a key earner for the route – to trade down to standard class tickets.

... National Express is up against the boundaries of a debt covenant that limits its borrowings to no more than 3.5 times its earnings before interest, tax, depreciation and amortisation (EBITDA). Faced with rising east coast payments and the burden of an underperforming Spanish coach business, National Express is widely expected to approach shareholders in a cash call before December, when its debt guidelines are tested again.

The group is also a takeover target, having announced the rejection of a nil-premium approach from rival FirstGroup earlier this week. National Express said it did not consider it appropriate to enter into talks with FirstGroup while it deals with its borrowings and the east coast contract. However, analysts believe that a deal could be attractive to both sets of shareholders if the east coast contract is scrapped or negotiated before a takeover is agreed.

Source: *Guardian*, 1 July 2009, p. 20
©Guardian News and Media Limited 2010

7.18 Applying Positive Accounting Theory, and after reading Accounting Headline 7.7, answer the following questions:

    a From an efficiency perspective, why could the introduction of new rules on share option accounting be costly for an organization?

    b Why could the introduction of the new rules on share option accounting be costly for a manager?

    c What would motivate the regulators to develop the new rules?

Accounting Headline 7.7

Introduction of accounting regulation for accounting for share options

Are you getting your fair shares?

By Joanna Osborne, senior IFRS technical partner at KPMG

Last month, the IASB issued IFRS2 on share-based payment, which will affect UK-listed companies preparing their first group financial statements under IFRS and applies to share-based payments active at 1 January 2005.

In the UK, share-based payments are already required to be expensed under UITF17. But whereas this expense is the difference between the underlying share price at grant date and the employee contribution (intrinsic value), IFRS2 requires share-based payments to be expensed at fair value.

This, alongside other differences to current UK practice, will mean a significant increase in the frequency and amount of expenses recorded for share-based payments in company accounts from 2005.

IFRS2 seeks to measure the fair value of services received from employees by reference to the fair value of a share option, multiplied by the number of options that ultimately vest. This measure will mean a greater hit on the accounts, as the fair value of an option will be recorded as higher than the intrinsic value of the share.

To understand this, compare two different employee packages, one comprising cash plus an option to acquire a share at today's price in three years' time, and one comprising ownership of the share itself.

In the first package you can earn interest on the cash for three years, although you don't receive the generally small amount from dividends that you would in the second package. The major bonus of this package is the one-way nature of the share option.

In effect it is a free bet on whether the share price will be higher than today's price in three years' time. If you hold an actual share you suffer a loss if the price goes down. If you have an option, you don't have to exercise it and suffer that loss still have the cash and subsequent interest. If the share price rises you gain with either package.

It is, however, complicated to determine the fair value of a share option at grant date because it involves predicting, among other things, future share price movements. But there are well-established and accessible mathematical techniques, for example the Black-Scholes and the binomial models, that are used by option traders to predict the future movements in share price and therefore to derive the fair value of an option.

... The long-awaited arrival of IFRS2 is going to make the means of payment of bonuses largely neutral in profit and loss account terms between cash and shares or share options. But a significant increase in the amount of expense recorded for share-based payments is inevitable.

Source: *Accountancy Age (UK)*, 8 March 2004

7. 19 Read Accounting Headline 7.4 (earlier in the chapter) and explain why publicity such as this might be costly to an organization. How would Positive Accounting theorists expect the banks to react to such publicity?

References

Ahmed, A.S., Billings, B.K., Morton, R.M. & Stanford-Harris, M. (2002) 'The role of accounting conservatism in mitigating bondholder-shareholder conflicts over dividend policy and in reducing debt costs', *Accounting Review*, **77** (4), 867–90.

Asquith, P., Beatty, A. & Weber, J. (2002) 'Performance pricing in private debt contracts', Working Paper, Massachusetts Institute of Technology, Cambridge, MA.

Baber, W.R., Fairfield, P.M. & Haggard, J. (1991) 'The effect of concern about reported income on discretionary spending decisions: The case of research and development', *Accounting Review*, **66** (4), 818–29.

Ball, R. & Brown, P. (1968) 'An empirical evaluation of accounting income numbers', *Journal of Accounting Research*, **6** (2), 159–78.

Ball, R. & Foster, G. (1982) 'Corporate financial reporting: A methodological review of empirical research', *Studies on Current Research Methodologies in Accounting: A Critical Evaluation, Journal of Accounting Research*, **20** (Supplement), 161–234.

Balsam, S. & Miharjo, S. (2007) 'The effect of equity compensation on voluntary executive turnover', *Journal of Accounting and Economics*, **43** (1), 95–119.

Beatty, A. & Weber, J. (2003) 'The effects of debt contracting on voluntary accounting method changes', *Accounting Review*, **78** (1), 119.

Beaver, W. (1968) 'The information content of annual earnings announcements', *Journal of Accounting Research*, **6** (Supplement), 67–92.

Benston, G.J. (1969) 'The value of the SECs accounting disclosure requirements', *The Accounting Review*, (July), 515–32.

Blackwell, D.W., Brickley, J.A. & Weisback, M.S. (1994) 'Accounting information and internal performance evaluation: Evidence from Texas banks', *Journal of Accounting and Economics*, **17** (3), 331–58.

Bushman, R.M. & Smith, A.J. (2001) 'Financial accounting information and corporate governance', *Journal of Accounting and Economics*, **32** (1–3), 237–333.

Chan, L.K.C., Lakonishok, J. & Sougiannis, T. (2001) 'The stock market valuation of research and development expenditures', *Journal of Finance*, **56** (6), 2431–56.

Cheng, S. (2004) 'R&D expenditures and CEO compensation', *Accounting Review*, **79** (2), 305–28.

Christenson, C. (1983) 'The methodology of positive accounting', *The Accounting Review*, **58** (January), 1–22.

Christie, A. (1990) 'Aggregation of test statistics: An evaluation of the evidence on contracting and size hypotheses', *Journal of Accounting and Economics*, **12**, 15–36.

Clinch, G. (1991) 'Employee compensation and firms' research and development activity', *Journal of Accounting Research*, **29** (1), 59–78.

Coase, R.H. (1937) 'The nature of the firm', *Economica*, **4** (16), 386–405.

Cotter, J. (1998a) *Asset Revaluations and Debt Contracting*, University of Queensland.

Cotter, J. (1998b) 'Utilisation and restrictiveness of covenants in Australian private debt contracts', *Accounting and Finance*, **38** (2), 181–96.

DeAngelo, L. (1988) 'Managerial competition, information costs, and corporate governance: The use of accounting performance measures in proxy contests', *Journal of Accounting and Economics*, **10** (January), 3–36.

Dechow, P. (1994) 'Accounting earnings and cash flows as measures of firm performance: The role of accounting accruals', *Journal of Accounting and Economics*, **18**, 3–24.

Dechow, P.M. & Skinner, D.J. (2000) 'Earnings management: Reconciling the views of accounting academics, practitioners, and regulators', *Accounting Horizons*, **14** (2), 235–50.

Dechow, P.M. & Sloan, R.G. (1991) 'Executive incentives and the horizon problem', *Journal of Accounting & Economics*, **14** (1), 51–89.

Deegan, C. (1997) 'The design of efficient management remuneration contracts: A consideration of specific human capital investments', *Accounting and Finance*, **37** (1), 1–40.

DeFond, M. & Jiambalvo, J. (1994) 'Debt covenant violation and manipulation of accruals', *Journal of Accounting and Economics*, **17**, 145–76.

Dhaliwal, D.S. (1982) 'Some economic determinants of management lobbying for alternative methods of accounting: Evidence from the accounting for interest costs issue', *Journal of Business Finance & Accounting*, **9** (2), 255–65.

Downs, A. (1957) *An Economic Theory of Democracy*, New York: Harper and Row.

Duke, J.C. & Hunt III, H.G. (1990) 'An empirical examination of debt covenant restrictions and accounting-related debt proxies', *Journal of Accounting and Economics*, **12** (1–3), 45–63.

Dyckman, A. & Zeff, S. (1984) 'Two decades of the Journal of Accounting Research', *Journal of Accounting Research*, **22**, 225–97.

Emanuel, D., Wong, J. & Wong, N. (2003) 'Efficient contracting and accounting', *Accounting & Finance*, **43** (2), 149–66.

Ettredge, M., Simon, D., Smith, D. & Stone, M. (1994) 'Why do companies purchase timely quarterly reviews?', *Journal of Accounting and Economics*, **18** (2), 131–56.

Fama, E. (1980) 'Agency problems and the theory of the firm', *Journal of Political Economy*, **88**, 288–307.

Fields, T.D., Lys, T.Z. & Vincent, L. (2001) 'Empirical research on accounting choice', *Journal of Accounting and Economics*, **31** (1–3), 255–307.

Friedman, M. (1953) *The Methodology of Positive Economics: Essays in Positive Economics*, Chicago: University of Chicago Press.

Gibbons, R. & Murphy, K.J. (1992) 'Optimal incentive contracts in the presence of career concerns: Theory and evidence', *Journal of Political Economy*, **100** (3), 468.

Gray, R., Owen, D. & Adams, C. (1996) *Accounting and Accountability: Changes and Challenges in Corporate Social and Environmental Reporting*, London: Prentice-Hall.

Guay, W.R., Kothari, S.P. & Watts, R.L. (1996) 'A market-based evaluation of discretionary accrual models', *Journal of Accounting Research*, **34** (Supplement), 83–105.

Healy, P.M. (1985) 'The effect of bonus schemes on accounting decisions', *Journal of Accounting and Economics*, **7**, 85–107.

Hines, R. (1988) 'Financial accounting: In communicating reality, we construct reality', *Accounting Organizations and Society*, **13** (3), 251–62.

Holthausen, R.W. (1990) 'Accounting method choice: Opportunistic behavior, efficient contracting, and information perspectives', *Journal of Accounting and Economics*, **12** (1–3), 207–18.

Holthausen, R.W., Larcker, D.F. & Sloan, R.G. (1995) 'Annual bonus schemes and the manipulation of earnings', *Journal of Accounting and Economics*, **19**, 29–74.

Hopwood, A.G. (2007) 'Whither accounting research?', *Accounting Review*, **82** (5), 1365–74.

Howieson, B. (1996) 'Whither financial accounting research: A modern-day Bo-Peep?', *Australian Accounting Review*, **6** (1), 29–36.

Ittner, C.D., Larcker, D.F. & Rajan, M.V. (1997) 'The choice of performance measures in annual bonus contracts', *Accounting Review*, **72** (2), 231.

Jensen, M.C. & Meckling, W.H. (1976) 'Theory of the firm: Managerial behavior, agency costs and ownership structure', *Journal of Financial Economics*, **3** (October), 305–60.

Jones, J. (1991) 'Earnings management during import relief investigations', *Journal of Accounting Research*, **29**, 193–228.

Kaplan, R.S. & Roll, R. (1972) 'Investor evaluation of accounting information: Some empirical evidence'. *Journal of Business*, **45**, 225–57.

Kothari, S.P., Laguerre, T. & Leone, A. (2002) 'Capitalizing versus expensing: Evidence on the uncertainty of future earnings from capital expenditure versus R&D outlay', *Review of Accounting Studies*, **7** (4), 355–82.

Kuhn, T.S. (1962) *The Structure of Scientific Revolutions*, Chicago: University of Chicago Press.

Lambert, R.A. (2001) 'Contracting theory and accounting', *Journal of Accounting and Economics*, **32** (1–3), 3–87.

Lev, B. & Sougiannis, T. (1996) 'The capitalization, amortization, and value-relevance of R&D', *Journal of Accounting and Economics*, **21** (1), 107–38.

Lewellen, W., Loderer, C. & Martin, K. (1987) 'Executive compensation and executive incentive problems : An empirical analysis', *Journal of Accounting and Economics*, **9** (3), 287–310.

Lintner, J. (1965) 'The valuation of risk assets and the selection of risky investments in stock portfolios and capital budgets', *Review of Economics and Statistics*, **47**, 13–37.

Lys, T. (1984) 'Mandated accounting changes and debt covenants: The case of oil and gas accounting', *Journal of Accounting and Economics*, **6** (1), 39–65.

Mather, P. & Peirson, G. (2006) 'Financial covenants in the markets for public and private debt', *Accounting & Finance*, **46** (2), 285–307.

McSweeney, B. (2009) 'The roles of financial asset market failure denial and the economic crisis: Reflections on accounting and financial theories and practices', *Accounting, Organizations and Society*, **34** (6–7), 835–48.

Mian, S.L. & Smith, C.W. (1990) 'Incentives for consolidated financial reporting', *Journal of Accounting and Economics*, **12**, 141–71.

Milgrom, P.R. (1981) 'Good news and bad news: Representation theorems and applications', *The Bell Journal of Economics*, **12** (2), 380–91.

Morris, R. (1984) 'Corporate disclosure in a substantially unregulated environment', *ABACUS* (June), 52–86.

Mouck, T. (1992) 'The rhetoric of science and the rhetoric of revolt in the story of positive accounting theory', *Accounting, Auditing and Accountability Journal*, 35–56.

Murphy, K.J. (1999) 'Executive compensation', *Handbook of Labor Economics (3B)*. Amsterdam: North-Holland.

Nagar, V., Nanda, D. & Wysocki, P. (2003) 'Discretionary disclosure and stock-based incentives', *Journal of Accounting and Economics*, **34** (1–3), 283–309.

Ness, K. & Mirza, A. (1991) 'Corporate social disclosure: A note on a test of agency theory', *British Accounting Review*, **23**, 211–17.

Prospect (2009) 'Adair Turner roundtable', *Prospect*.

Sharpe, W.F. (1964) 'Capital asset prices: A review of market equilibrium under conditions of risk', *Journal of Finance*, **19**, 425–42.

Shleifer, A. & Vishny, R.W. (1989) 'Management entrenchment: The case of manager-specific investments', *Journal of Financial Economics*, **25** (1), 123–39.

Sloan, R.G. (1993) 'Accounting earnings and top executive compensation', *Journal of Accounting and Economics*, **16**, 55–100.

Smith, C.W. & Warner, J.B. (1979) 'On financial contracting: An analysis of bond covenants', *Journal of Financial Economics* (June), 117–61.

Smith, C.W. & Watts, R. (1982) 'Incentive and tax effects of executive compensation plans', *Australian Journal of Management* (December), 139–57.

Smith, C.W. & Watts, R.L. (1983) 'The structure of executive contracts and the control of management', Unpublished manuscript, University of Rochester.

Sterling, R.R. (1990) 'Positive accounting: An assessment', *ABACUS*, **26** (2), 97–135.

Stern Stewart (2001) 'Stern Stewart roundtable on capital structure and stock repurchase', *Journal of Applied Corporate Finance*, **14** (1), 8–41.

Sutton (1988) 'T.G., the proposed introduction of current cost accounting in the UK', *Journal of Accounting and Economics*, **10**, 127–49.

Sweeney, A.P. (1994) 'Debt-covenant violations and managers accounting responses', *Journal of Accounting and Economics*, **17**, 281–308.

Tinker, A., Lehman, C. & Neimark, M. (1991) 'Falling down the hole in the middle of the road: Political quietism in corporate social reporting', *Accounting, Auditing and Accountability Journal*, **4** (1), 28–54.

Tinker, A.M., Merino, B.D. & Neimark, M.D. (1982) 'The normative origins of positive theories: Ideology and accounting thought', *Accounting Organizations and Society*, **7** (2), 167–200.

Unerman, J. & O'Dwyer, B. (2010) *The Relevance and Utility of Leading Accounting Research*, ACCA Research Report No. 120, London: Certified Accountants Educational Trust.

Verrecchia, R.E. (1983) 'Discretionary disclosure', *Journal of Accounting and Economics*, **5**, 179–94.

Watts, R.L. (1977) 'Corporate financial statements: A product of the market and political processes', *Australian Journal of Management* (April), 53–75.

Watts, R.L. (1995) 'Nature and origins of positive research in accounting', in: Jones, S., Romano, C. & Ratnatunga, J. (eds.) *Accounting Theory: A Contemporary Review*, Sydney: Harcourt Brace, 295–353.

Watts, R.L. & Zimmerman, J.L. (1978) 'Towards a positive theory of the determination of accounting standards', *The Accounting Review*, **53** (1), 112–34.

Watts, R.L. & Zimmerman, J.L. (1979) 'The demand for and supply of accounting theories: The market for excuses', *The Accounting Review*, **54** (2), 273–305.

Watts, R.L. & Zimmerman, J.L. (1986) *Positive Accounting Theory*, Englewood Cliffs, NJ: Prentice-Hall.

Watts, R.L. & Zimmerman, J.L. (1990) 'Positive accounting theory: A ten year perspective', *The Accounting Review*, **65** (1), 131–56.

Wells, P. (2002) 'Earnings management surrounding CEO changes', *Accounting & Finance*, **42** (2), 169–93.

Whittred, G. (1987) 'The derived demand for consolidated financial reporting', *Journal of Accounting and Economics*, **9** (December), 259–85.

Whittred, G. & Zimmer, I. (1986) 'Accounting information in the market for debt', *Accounting and Finance*, **28** (1), 1–12.

Williamson, O.E. (1975) *Markets and Hierarchies: Analysis and Antitrust Implications*, New York: Free Press.

Williamson, O.E. (1985) *The Economic Institutions of Capitalism*, New York: Free Press.

Williamson, O.E. (1988) 'Corporate finance and corporate governance', *Journal of Finance,* **43** (3), 567–91.

Williamson, O.E. (1996) *The Mechanisms of Governance*, New York: Oxford University Press.

Wong, J. (1988) 'Economic incentives for the voluntary disclosure of current cost financial statements', *Journal of Accounting and Economics*, **10** (2), 151–67.

World Commission on Environment and Development (1987) *Our Common Future (The Brundtland Report)*, Oxford: Oxford University Press.

Zhang, J. (2008) 'The contracting benefits of accounting conservatism to lenders and borrowers', *Journal of Accounting and Economics*, **45** (1), 27–54.

Zmijewski, M. & Hagerman, R. (1981) 'An income strategy approach to the positive theory of accounting standard setting/choice', *Journal of Accounting and Economics*, **3**, 129–49.

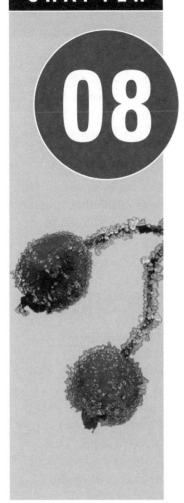

08

Unregulated Corporate Reporting Decisions: Considerations of Systems-Oriented Theories

Opening issues

In *The Independent* newspaper on 26 July 2010 a headline read: 'Cable tells banks to increase lending'. The article explained that the UK Secretary for State for Business, Innovation and Skills, Dr Vince Cable, was particularly critical of UK banks for failing to provide adequate lending to UK businesses and he argued that this failure had resulted in damage for many businesses as they tried to recover from the impact of the global recession. The newspaper article stated that Dr Cable warned the banks that they were 'not acting in the national interest'.

Would you expect the banks to react to such negative media publicity and, if so, why? Further, would you expect the banks to make any disclosures within their annual reports or on their corporate websites in relation to these 'high profile' accusations of damaging behaviour? What form would you expect these disclosures to take?

8.1 Introduction

In Chapter 7 we considered a number of theoretical arguments as to why corporate management might elect voluntarily to provide particular information to parties outside the organization. These arguments were grounded within *Positive Accounting Theory*. In this chapter we consider some alternative theoretical perspectives that address this issue. Specifically, we consider *legitimacy theory*, *stakeholder theory* and *institutional theory*.

As has been stressed throughout this book, and particularly in Chapter 1, theories are abstractions of reality and hence particular theories cannot be expected to provide a full account or description of particular behaviour. Hence, it is sometimes useful to consider the perspectives provided by alternative theories. Different researchers might study the same phenomenon but elect to adopt alternative theoretical perspectives.[1] The choice of one theoretical perspective in preference to others will, at least in part, be due to particular value judgements of the authors involved. As O'Leary (1985, p. 88) states:

> Theorists' own values or ideological predispositions may be among the factors that determine which side of the argument they will adopt in respect of disputable connections of a theory with evidence.

Legitimacy theory, stakeholder theory and institutional theory are three theoretical perspectives that have been adopted by a number of researchers in recent years. These theories are sometimes referred to as 'systems-oriented theories'. In accordance with Gray *et al.* (1996, p. 45):

> a systems-oriented view of the organisation and society ... permits us to focus on the role of information and disclosure in the relationship(s) between organisations, the State, individuals and groups.

---

[1] For example, some researchers operating within the Positive Accounting Theory paradigm (for example, Ness and Mirza, 1991) argue that the voluntary disclosure of social responsibility information can be explained as a strategy to reduce political costs. Social responsibility reporting has also been explained from a legitimacy theory perspective (for example, Deegan *et al.*, 2002), and from a stakeholder theory perspective (for example, Swift, 2001).

Systems-oriented theories have also been referred to as 'open-systems theories'. Commenting on the use of open-systems theorizing, Suchman (1995, p. 571) states:

> Open-system theories have reconceptualised organisational boundaries as porous and problematic … Many dynamics in the organizational environment stem not from technological or material imperatives, but rather, from cultural norms, symbols, beliefs and rituals. Corporate disclosure policies are considered to represent one important means by which management can influence external perceptions about their organisation.

Within a *systems-based perspective*, the entity is assumed to be influenced by, and in turn to have influence upon, the society in which it operates. This is simplistically represented in Figure 8.1.

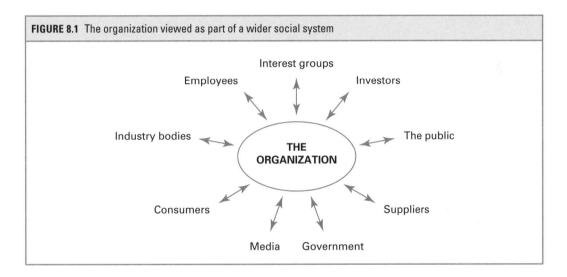

FIGURE 8.1 The organization viewed as part of a wider social system

Within legitimacy theory, stakeholder theory and institutional theory, accounting disclosure policies are considered to constitute a strategy to influence the organization's relationships with the other parties with which it interacts. In recent times, stakeholder theory and legitimacy theory have frequently been applied to explain why organizations make certain social responsibility disclosures within their annual reports, or within other corporate reports.[2] These theories could, however, also be applied to explain why companies adopt particular financial accounting techniques. We will mainly focus on these two theories in this chapter, but towards the end of the chapter we will also explore some insights from the more recent application of institutional theory to the analysis of voluntary corporate reporting. To the extent that these theories provide explanations and predictions of particular managerial decisions, such as decisions to disclose information, they can also be considered to be positive theories (as opposed to normative theories which are theories used to provide prescription about how certain activities – such as accounting – *should* be undertaken).

---

[2] Social responsibility disclosures are considered more fully in Chapter 9. However, at this stage they can be defined as disclosures that provide information about the interaction of an organization with its physical and social environment, inclusive of community involvement, the natural environment, human resources, energy and product safety (Gray and Bebbington, 2001; Gray *et al.*, 1996).

8.2 Political economy theory

According to Gray *et al.* (1996), legitimacy theory and stakeholder theory are both derived from a broader theory which has been called *political economy theory*. The other theory we consider in this chapter – institutional theory – can also be linked to political economy theory. The 'political economy' itself has been defined by Gray *et al.* (1996, p. 47) as 'the social, political and economic framework within which human life takes place'. The perspective embraced is that *society*, *politics* and *economics* are inseparable, and economic issues cannot meaningfully be investigated in the absence of considerations about the political, social and institutional framework in which the economic activity takes place. It is argued that by considering the *political economy* a researcher is able to consider broader (societal) issues that impact on how an organization operates, and what information it elects to disclose. According to Guthrie and Parker (1990, p. 166):

> The political economy perspective perceives accounting reports as social, political, and economic documents. They serve as a tool for constructing, sustaining, and legitimising economic and political arrangements, institutions, and ideological themes which contribute to the corporation's private interests. Disclosures have the capacity to transmit social, political, and economic meanings for a pluralistic set of report recipients.

Guthrie and Parker (1990, p. 166) further state that corporate reports cannot be considered as neutral, unbiased (or representationally faithful) documents, as many professional accounting bodies might suggest, but rather, corporate reports are 'a product of the interchange between the corporation and its environment and attempt to mediate and accommodate a variety of sectional interests'.[3] This view is consistent with Burchell *et al.* (1980, p. 6) who suggest that accounting can 'not be seen as a mere assembly of calculative routines, it functions as a cohesive and influential mechanism for economic and social management'.

Political Economy Theory has been divided (perhaps somewhat simplistically, but nevertheless usefully) into two broad streams which Gray *et al.* (1996, p. 47) have labelled 'classical' and 'bourgeois' political economy. Classical political economy theory is related to the works of philosophers such as Karl Marx, and explicitly places 'sectional (class) interests, structural conflict, inequity, and the role of the state at the heart of the analysis' (Gray *et al.*, 1996, p. 47). This can be contrasted with 'bourgeois' political economy theory which, according to Gray *et al.* (1995, p. 53), largely ignores these elements and, as a result, is content to perceive the world as essentially pluralistic.[4]

---

[3] As we would appreciate, various professional accounting bodies throughout the world have released documents (normally as part of a conceptual framework project) indicating that financial reporting should embrace the attributes of *neutrality* and *representational faithfulness*. Proponents of political economy theories would argue that there are a multitude of political and social issues that make such a perspective unrealistic.

[4] A pluralistic perspective assumes (typically implicitly) that many classes of stakeholders have the power to influence various decisions by corporations, government and other entities. Within this perspective, accounting is not considered to be put in place to favour specific interests (sometimes referred to as 'elites'). By using 'society' as the topic of focus rather than subgroups within society, theories such as legitimacy theory, which is derived from the bourgeois branch of political economy theory, ignore 'struggles and inequities within society' (Puxty, 1991).

Classical political economy theory tends to perceive accounting reports and disclosures as a means of maintaining the favoured position (for example, the wealth and power) of those who control scarce resources (capital), and as a means of undermining the position of those without scarce capital. It focuses on the structural conflicts within society.[5]

According to Cooper and Sherer (1984), the study of accounting should recognize *power* and *conflict* in society, and consequently should focus on the effects of accounting reports on the distribution of income, wealth and power in society. This is consistent with Lowe and Tinker (1977) who argue that the majority of accounting research is based on a *pluralist* conception of society. According to Lowe and Tinker, this pluralistic view assumes (incorrectly, they argue) that power is widely diffused and that society is composed of many individuals whose preferences are to predominate in social choices, such that no individual is able consistently to influence that society (or the accounting function therein) and no one group dominates all others. Researchers such as Lowe and Tinker (1977) and Cooper and Sherer (1984) oppose such a view and provide a counter-perspective that the *pluralist* view ignores a great deal of evidence which suggests that the majority of people in society are controlled by a small but 'well-defined elite' – an elite that uses accounting (as well as other mechanisms) as a means of maintaining their position of dominance. We further consider the works of authors who take this view when we consider *critical accounting perspectives* in Chapter 12. We show that such researchers tend to be extremely critical of current accounting and reporting techniques.

According to Gray *et al.* (1996), and as briefly noted above, *bourgeois political economy*, on the other hand, does not explicitly consider structural conflicts and *class struggles* but rather 'tends to be concerned with interactions between groups in an essentially pluralistic world (for example, the negotiation between a company and an environmental pressure group, or between a local authority and the state)'. It is this branch of political economy theory from which legitimacy theory and stakeholder theory derive. Neither theory questions or studies the various class structures (and possible struggles) within society.[6] However, institutional theory can be applied within either a classical or a bourgeois conception of political economy. We now turn our attention to legitimacy theory.

8.3 Legitimacy theory

Legitimacy theory asserts that organizations continually seek to ensure that they are perceived as operating within the bounds and norms of their respective societies, that is, they attempt to ensure that their activities are perceived by outside parties as being 'legitimate'. These bounds and norms are not considered to be fixed, but change over time, thereby requiring organizations to be responsive to the ethical (or moral) environment in

---

[5] For example, in considering the practice of social responsibility reporting, classical political economists would typically argue that the growth of environmental disclosure by companies since the late 1980s can be seen as an attempt to act *as if* in response to environmental groups while, *actually*, attempting to wrest the initiative and control of the environment agenda from these groups in order to permit capital to carry on doing what it does best – making money from capital (Gray *et al.*, 1996, p. 47).

[6] Positive Accounting Theory, the focus of Chapter 7, also does not consider issues associated with inequities within society or the role of accounting in sustaining these inequities.

which they operate. Lindblom (1993) distinguishes between *legitimacy*, which is considered to be a status or condition, and *legitimation*, which she considers to be the process that leads to an organization being adjudged *legitimate*. According to Lindblom (p. 2), legitimacy is:

> a condition or status which exists when an entity's value system is congruent with the value system of the larger social system of which the entity is a part. When a disparity, actual or potential, exists between the two value systems, there is a threat to the entity's legitimacy.

Legitimacy is a relative concept – it is relative to the social system in which the entity operates and is *time* and *place* specific. As Suchman (1995, p. 574) states:

> Legitimacy is a generalised perception or assumption that the actions of an entity are desirable, proper, or appropriate *within* some socially constructed system of norms, values, beliefs, and definitions.

Within legitimacy theory, 'legitimacy' is considered to be a resource on which an organization is dependent for survival (Dowling and Pfeffer, 1975; O'Donovan, 2002). It is something that is conferred upon the organization by society, and it is something that is desired or sought by the organization. However, unlike many other 'resources', it is a 'resource' that the organization is considered to be able to impact or manipulate through various disclosure-related strategies (Woodward *et al.*, 1996).

Consistent with resource dependence theory (see Pfeffer and Salancik, 1978), legitimacy theory would suggest that whenever managers consider that the supply of the particular resource – legitimacy – is vital to organizational survival, then they will pursue strategies to ensure the continued supply of that resource. As we will see shortly, strategies aimed at gaining, maintaining or repairing legitimacy (often referred to as legitimation strategies) may include targeted disclosures, or perhaps controlling or collaborating with other parties who in themselves are perceived by society to be legitimate and therefore able to provide 'legitimacy by association' (Deegan and Blomquist, 2006; Oliver, 1991).

For an organization seeking to be perceived as legitimate it is not the actual conduct of the organization that is important, it is what society collectively knows or perceives about the organization's conduct that shapes legitimacy. Information disclosure is vital to establishing corporate legitimacy. As Suchman (1995, p. 574) states:

> An organisation may diverge dramatically from societal norms yet retain legitimacy because the divergence goes unnoticed. Legitimacy is socially constructed in that it reflects a congruence between the behaviours of the legitimated entity and the shared (or assumed shared) beliefs of some social group; thus legitimacy is dependent on a collective audience, yet independent of particular observers.

Consistent with the view that 'legitimacy' is based on *perceptions*, Nasi *et al.* (1997, p. 300) state:

> A corporation is legitimate when it is judged to be 'just and worthy of support' (Dowling and Pfeffer, 1975). Legitimacy therefore is not an abstract measure of the 'rightness' of the corporation but rather a measure of societal perceptions of the adequacy of corporate behaviour (Suchman, 1995). It is a measure of the

attitude of society toward a corporation and its activities, and it is a matter of degree ranging from highly legitimate to highly illegitimate. It is also important to point out that legitimacy is a social construct based on cultural norms for corporate behaviour. Therefore, the demands placed on corporations change over time, and different communities often have different ideas about what constitutes legitimate corporate behaviour.

Legitimacy, public expectations and the social contract

Legitimacy theory relies upon the notion that there is a 'social contract' between the organization in question and the society in which it operates. The 'social contract' is not easy to define, but the concept is used to represent the multitude of implicit and explicit expectations that society has about how the organization should conduct its operations.[7] It can be argued that traditionally profit maximization *was* perceived to be the optimal measure of corporate performance (Abbott and Monsen, 1979; Heard and Bolce, 1981; Patten, 1991, 1992; Ramanathan, 1976). Under this notion, a firm's profits were viewed as an all-inclusive measure of *organizational legitimacy* (Ramanathan, 1976). However, public expectations have undergone significant change in recent decades. Heard and Bolce (1981) note the expansion of the advocacy movement in the United States during the 1960s and 1970s, and the significant increase in legislation related to social issues, including the environment and employees' health and safety, which was enacted in the United States within the same period. With heightened social expectations it is anticipated that successful business corporations will react and attend to the human, environmental and other social consequences of their activities (Heard and Bolce, 1981).

It has been argued that society increasingly expects business to 'make outlays to repair or prevent damage to the physical environment, to ensure the health and safety of consumers, employees, and those who reside in the communities where products are manufactured and wastes are dumped ...' (Tinker and Neimark, 1987, p. 84). Consequently, companies with a poor social and environmental performance record may increasingly find it difficult to obtain the necessary resources and support to continue operations within a community that values a clean environment. Perhaps this was not the case a number of decades ago.

It is assumed within legitimacy theory that society allows the organization to continue operations to the extent that it generally meets their expectations – that is, to the extent it complies with the social contract. Legitimacy theory emphasizes that the organization must appear to consider the rights of the public at large, not merely those of its investors. Failure to comply with societal expectations (that is, comply with the terms of the 'social contract') may lead to sanctions being imposed by society, for example in the form of legal restrictions imposed on an organization's operations, limited resources (for example, financial capital and labour) being provided and/or reduced demand for its products (sometimes through organized consumer boycotts).

Consistent with legitimacy theory, organizations are not considered to have any inherent right to resources. Rather, the right to access resources must be earned. *Legitimacy* (from

---

[7] It can be argued that requirements imposed by the law reflect the explicit terms of the social contract, while uncodified community expectations (and these will be perceived to be different by different people) constitute the implicit terms of the social contract.

society's perspective) and the right to operate go hand in hand. As Mathews (1993, p. 26) states:

> The social contract would exist between corporations (usually limited companies) and individual members of society. Society (as a collection of individuals) provides corporations with their legal standing and attributes and the authority to own and use natural resources and to hire employees. Organisations draw on community resources and output both goods and services and waste products to the general environment. The organisation has no inherent rights to these benefits, and in order to allow their existence, society would expect the benefits to exceed the costs to society.

Accounting Headline 8.1 provides a copy of a newspaper article in which an executive of one of the large pharmaceutical companies concedes that his organization needs to change its practices to more fully meet the 'social contract'. It is interesting to note that the notion of a social contract is something that is increasingly being referred to by managers (and we will see further evidence of this later in this chapter).

Accounting Headline 8.1

The social contract between a pharmaceutical company and the community

Profits before the poor? Drugs giant offers an answer to the toxic question facing a 'heartless' industry

By *Sarah Boseley*

For Andrew Witty, it's a question of redefining the unwritten contract that major drug companies have with society. For critics of big pharma, it's about addressing widely felt concerns about an industry that has often seemed heartless. Either way, the changes proposed by the chief executive of GlaxoSmithKline [GSK] goes to the core of one of the most toxic debates of our time.

The most serious charge against such firms is that they put profits ahead of poor people's lives. It's an allegation GSK has not escaped, even though it has cut the prices of its Aids drugs in developing countries and has promised efforts to develop a malaria vaccine.

The low point came in 2001, when GSK was among 39 multinational companies that took legal action against the South African government to try to prevent it importing cheap drugs. Amid an international outcry, the drug companies backed down. 'I don't think anybody can claim that was handled well,' said chief executive Andrew Witty.

… Witty says drug companies have an obligation to respond to society's needs and demands. 'It's been obvious for a while, I think, that efforts have to be made to really reassert and strengthen that contract with society.'

That goes to the very core of the business. Drug companies are criticised for failing to deliver for the rich world as well as the poor – for the UK and US as well as Tanzania or Ethiopia. They stand accused of focusing their efforts on making 'me-too' blockbusters – barely altered copies of other companies' billion dollar sellers for indigestion or heart disease – rather than working on diseases where there are few treatments, such as Alzheimer's.

Transparency is a major issue. Witty has pledged to publish all clinical trial data, whether positive or negative – and be open about GSK's payments to doctors.

He has also signalled his willingness to negotiate on price, in a climate where value for money is increasingly discussed and other countries are contemplating setting up a version of Nice, the National Institute for Healthcare and Clinical Excellence, which decides whether drugs are cost-effective for the NHS.

Another part of the social contract is ending practices that cause public anxiety, he said. About eight weeks ago, GSK announced without fanfare that it would commit never again to experiment on great apes.

... Critics of the drug companies acknowledged yesterday that GSK was making strides, but said it could go further, for instance, on the point of giving away 20% of profits in the 60 least developed countries – GSK currently has operations in only 18 of them and earns around £30 million a year from them.

'I recognize the fact that GSK is seeking to meet concerns,' said Michelle Childs, director of policy and advocacy at Médecins sans Frontières, who welcomed the move to open to pool patents on chemical compounds that could help the development of treatments for neglected diseases. But, she said, she would challenge GSK to go further. 'He is saying there is no need for a patent pool for HIV. Our position is that there is an urgent need for a patent pool for HIV because of the rising prices of new first and second line drugs for patients who develop resistance.' Buying cut-price drugs from GSK would not necessarily be the best move for the poorest countries, she added.

Generic companies were capable of producing drugs at lower prices than big pharma could manage, because of the lower costs of manufacture. GSK's combination HIV drug Combivir had been reduced from $730 (£506) in 2001 per patient per year and now sells at $197 in the least developed countries.

Source: *Guardian*, 14 February 2009, p. 13
©Guardian News and Media Limited 2010

The idea of a 'social contract' is not new, having been discussed by philosophers such as Thomas Hobbes (1588–1679), John Locke (1632–1704), and Jean-Jacques Rousseau (1712–1778). Shocker and Sethi (1974, p. 67) provide a good overview of the concept of a social contract:

> Any social institution – and business is no exception – operates in society via a social contract, expressed or implied, whereby its survival and growth are based on:
>
> 1 the delivery of some socially desirable ends to society in general, and
>
> 2 the distribution of economic, social, or political benefits to groups from which it derives its power.

In a dynamic society, neither the sources of institutional power nor the needs for its services are permanent. Therefore, an institution must constantly meet the twin tests of legitimacy and relevance by demonstrating that society requires its services and that the groups benefiting from its rewards have society's approval.

It is emphasized that the social contract is a theoretical construct, and hence an individual cannot simply go and find a copy of the social contract 'negotiated' between an organization and the society in which it operates. Different managers will have different perceptions about how society expects the organization to behave across the various attributes of its activities (that is, they will have different perspectives of the contract) – and this in itself can explain, at least in part, why some managers will elect to do things differently from other managers. If a manager undertakes certain actions that are subsequently found to be unacceptable to the community (for example, sourcing clothing from 'sweatshops' in developing countries – an issue that recently outraged many people within the community) then legitimacy theory would explain this in terms of the manager misinterpreting the terms of the social contract and this misinterpretation may subsequently have adverse impacts on the organization's survival. Consider the implications for Nike, GAP and other clothing and footwear manufacturers when the media ran campaigns about their association with various abusive 'sweatshops'.

The social contract is considered to be made up of numerous terms (or clauses) – some explicit and some implicit. Gray *et al.* (1996) suggest that legal requirements provide the explicit terms of the contract, while other non-legislated societal expectations embody the implicit terms of the contract. That is, there is an imperfect correlation between the law and societal norms (as reflected by the social contract) and according to Dowling and Pfeffer (1975) there are three broad reasons for the difference. First, even though laws are reflective of societal norms and values, legal systems are slow to adapt to changes in the norms and values in society. Secondly, legal systems often strive for consistency whereas societal norms and expectations can be contradictory. Thirdly, it is suggested that while society may not be accepting of certain behaviours, it may not be willing or structured enough to have those behavioural restrictions codified within law. It is in relation to the composition of the implicit terms of the 'contract' that we can expect managers' perceptions to vary greatly.

As indicated in Deegan and Rankin (1996, p. 54), Deegan (2002, p. 293) and Deegan (2007, pp. 133–35), in accordance with legitimacy theory if an organization cannot justify its continued operation then in a sense the community may revoke its 'contract' to continue its operations. Again, as indicated earlier, this may occur through consumers reducing or eliminating the demand for the products of the business, factor suppliers eliminating the supply of labour and financial capital to the business, and/or constituents lobbying government for increased taxes, fines or laws to prohibit actions that do not conform with the expectations of the community.

Given the potential costs associated with conducting operations deemed to be outside the terms of the 'social contract', Dowling and Pfeffer (1975) state that organizations will take various actions to ensure that their operations are perceived to be legitimate. That is, they will attempt to establish congruence between 'the social values associated with or implied by their activities and the norms of acceptable behaviour in the larger social system of which they are a part' (Dowling and Pfeffer, 1975, p. 122).

Legitimacy and changing social expectations

As community expectations change, organizations must also adapt and change. That is, if society's expectations about performance change, then arguably an organization will need to show that what it is doing is also changing (or perhaps it will need explicitly to communicate and justify why its operations have not changed). This need to identify community expectations, and then meeting these changing expectations of society, is reflected in the following extracts from Nokia's 2009 Sustainability Report:

> The feedback from stakeholder engagement activities and our success in various external recognition arenas (see our Recognition and Awards section) indicates that our stakeholders believe we have made progress in many areas of sustainability. In the future, our stakeholders are looking to us to provide more data and metrics to support our sustainability activities, such as in reporting emissions, and increasing the number of recycled devices. We are also expected to anticipate trends and continue to play a leading role in addressing emerging sustainability issues such as biodiversity and environmental impact of the whole supply chain. (p. 19)

> We constantly strive to activate new channels concerning the ways in which we meet our existing expectations, while at the same time we continue to identify new trends down the road. This window into the future is an important part of our ongoing success as it allows us to understand where systematic improvements can be made (p. 21)

In relation to the dynamics associated with changing community expectations, Lindblom (1993, p. 3) states:

> Legitimacy is dynamic in that the relevant publics continuously evaluate corporate output, methods, and goals against an ever evolving expectation. The legitimacy gap will fluctuate without any changes in action on the part of the corporation. Indeed, as expectations of the relevant publics change the corporation must make changes or the legitimacy gap will grow as the level of conflict increases and the levels of positive and passive support decreases.

The term 'legitimacy gap' – as used in the above quote – is a term that has been utilized by many researchers to describe the situation where there appears to be a lack of correspondence between how society believes an organization should act and how it is perceived that the organization has acted. In relation to how legitimacy gaps arise, Sethi (1978) describes two major sources of the gaps. First, societal expectations might change, and this will lead to a gap arising even though the organization is operating in the same manner as it always had. As an example of this source of a legitimacy gap, Nasi *et al.* (1997, p. 301) state:

> For American tobacco companies in the 1970s, for example, the increasing awareness of the health consequences of smoking resulted in a significant and widening legitimacy gap (Miles and Cameron, 1982). The tobacco companies had not changed their activities, and their image was much the same as it had been, yet they suddenly faced a significantly different evaluation of their role in society; they faced a significant and widening legitimacy gap.

As we have already emphasized, community expectations are not considered static, but rather, change across time thereby necessitating the organization to be responsive to current and future changes to the environment in which they operate. While organizations might change towards community expectation, if the momentum of their change is slower than the changing expectations of society, then legitimacy gaps will arise.

Legitimacy itself can be threatened even when an organization's performance is not deviating from society's expectations of appropriate performance. This might be because the organization has failed to make disclosures that show it is complying with society's expectations, which in themselves might be changing across time. That is, legitimacy is assumed to be influenced by disclosures of information, and not simply by (undisclosed) changes in corporate actions. As noted above, if society's expectations about performance change, then arguably an organization will need to show that what it is doing is also changing (or perhaps it will need explicitly to communicate and justify why its operations have not changed).

The second major source of a legitimacy gap, according to Sethi (1977), occurs when previously unknown information becomes known about the organization – perhaps through disclosure being made within the news media. In relation to this possibility, Nasi *et al.* (1997, p. 301) make an interesting reference to 'organizational shadows'. They state:

> The potential body of information about the corporation that is unavailable to the public – the corporate shadow … – stands as a constant potential threat to a corporation's legitimacy. When part of the organisational shadow is revealed, either accidentally or through the activities of an activist group or a journalist, a legitimacy gap may be created.

In relation to the above source of a legitimacy gap, we can consider how society reacted to media revelations made about certain sportswear companies' use of sweatshops in Asia (for example, Nike); revelations about the pollution being caused by mining companies' tailings dams in remote environments (for example, BHP Billiton's operations in Papua New Guinea); or revelations about how the products of particular companies affect consumer health (for example, the reaction to the McDonald's investigation as told within the movie *Supersize Me*). All these revelations arguably had significant cost implications for the respective companies involved – and to solve the legitimacy problems the organizations typically relied upon various disclosure strategies.

The notion of a legitimacy gap has been depicted diagrammatically by O'Donovan (2002). His depiction is reproduced in Figure 8.2. In explaining the diagram, O'Donovan states:

> The area marked X [in Figure 8.2] represents congruence between corporate activity and society's expectations of the corporation and its activities, based on social values and norms. Areas Y and Z represent incongruence between a corporation's actions and society's perceptions of what these actions should be. These areas represent 'illegitimacy' or legitimacy gaps (Sethi, 1978). The aim of the corporation is to be legitimate, to ensure area X is as large as possible, thereby reducing the legitimacy gap. A number of legitimation tactics and disclosure approaches may be adopted to reduce the legitimacy gap.

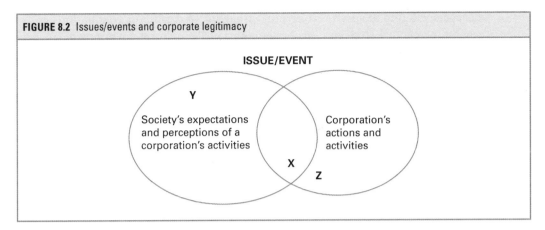

FIGURE 8.2 Issues/events and corporate legitimacy

ISSUE/EVENT

Y

Society's expectations and perceptions of a corporation's activities

Corporation's actions and activities

X

Z

Source: O'Donovan (2002, p. 347).

Much of the work that has been undertaken within the social and environmental accounting area, and which has embraced legitimacy theory, has typically addressed actions undertaken by organizations to *regain* their legitimacy after some form of legitimacy threatening event occurs. But as authors such as Suchman (1995) and O'Donovan (2002) indicate, legitimation strategies might be used to either *gain, maintain,* or *repair* legitimacy. According to O'Donovan (2002, p. 349):

> Legitimation techniques/tactics chosen will differ depending upon whether the organisation is trying to gain or extend legitimacy, to maintain its current level of legitimacy, or to repair or to defend its lost or threatened legitimacy.

While researchers have proposed that legitimation tactics might differ depending upon whether the entity is trying to *gain, maintain,* or *repair* legitimacy, the theoretical development in this area remains weak. Although the literature provides some general commentary, there is a lack of guidance about the relative effectiveness of legitimation strategies with regard to either gaining, maintaining, or regaining legitimacy. In terms of the general commentary provided within the literature, gaining legitimacy occurs when an organization moves into a new area of operations in which it has no past reputation. In such a situation the organization suffers from the 'liability of newness' (Ashforth and Gibbs, 1990) and it needs to proactively engage in activities to win acceptance.

The task of *maintaining* legitimacy is typically considered easier than *gaining* or *repairing* legitimacy (Ashforth and Gibbs, 1990; O'Donovan, 2002). One of the 'tricks' in maintaining legitimacy is to be able to anticipate changing community perceptions. According to Suchman (1995, p. 594), strategies for maintaining legitimacy fall into two groups – forecasting future changes, and protecting past accomplishments. In relation to monitoring or forecasting changing community perceptions, Suchman (1995, p. 595) states:

> Managers must guard against becoming so enamoured with their own legitimating myths that they lose sight of external developments that might bring those myths into question. With advanced warning, managers can engage in pre-emptive conformity, selection, or manipulation, keeping the organization and its environment in close alignment; without such warning,

managers will find themselves constantly struggling to regain lost ground. In general, perceptual strategies involve monitoring the cultural environment and assimilating elements of that environment into organizational decision processes, usually by employing boundary-spanning personnel as bridges across which the organization can learn audience values, beliefs, and reaction.

In relation to protecting past (legitimacy enhancing) accomplishments, Suchman (1995, p. 595) states:

> In addition to guarding against unforeseen challenges, organizations may seek to buttress the legitimacy they have already acquired. In particular, organizations can enhance their security by converting legitimacy from episodic to continual forms. To a large extent this boils down to (a) policing internal operations to prevent miscues, (b) curtailing highly visible legitimation efforts in favour of more subtle techniques, and (c) developing a defensive stockpile of supportive beliefs, attitudes and accounts.

In relation to *maintaining* legitimacy, the greater the extent to which the organization trades on its level of legitimacy the more crucial it will be for that organization to ensure that it does not deviate from the high standards that it has established. For example, compare an armaments manufacturer with, say, The Body Shop (a shop that has developed a reputation for sound social and environmental practices). The products of armaments manufacturers are designed to kill – such an organization arguably has less to worry about in terms of its legitimacy than The Body Shop. The Body Shop trades on its reputation for caring about the environment, society and the welfare of animals. If, perhaps, an organization within the supply chain of The Body Shop – and without the knowledge of The Body Shop – undertook activities that were somehow related to animal testing or with particular environmental damage and such facts were found out by the media, for example, then this could be extremely costly to the organization. It has a lot of *investment in legitimacy* to lose.

In considering *repairing* legitimacy, Suchman (1995, p. 597) suggests that related legitimation techniques tend to be reactive responses to often unforeseen crises. In many respects, *repairing* and *gaining* legitimacy are similar. As O'Donovan (2002, p. 350) states:

> Repairing legitimacy has been related to different levels of crisis management … The task of repairing legitimacy is, in some ways, similar to gaining legitimacy. If a crisis is evolving proactive strategies may need to be adopted, as has been the case for the tobacco industry during the past two decades … Generally, however, the main difference is that strategies for repairing legitimacy are reactive, usually to an unforseen and immediate crisis, whereas techniques to gain legitimacy are usually ex ante, proactive and not normally related to crisis.

In the discussion that follows we will consider the strategies that can be used by corporate management in an effort to *gain, maintain* or *regain* legitimacy. As we have already indicated, our theoretical development has not developed sufficiently to link specific legitimation techniques with efforts to either gain, maintain, or regain legitimacy. Most of the proposed legitimation techniques appear to relate to regaining legitimacy in the light of particular crises – something that has tended to be the focus of many researchers working within the social and environmental accounting area (and who embrace legitimacy theory). Nevertheless, all legitimation strategies rely upon disclosure.

Dowling and Pfeffer outline the means by which an organization may, perhaps when confronted with legitimacy-threatening events, legitimate its activities (1975, p. 127):

■ The organization can adapt its output, goals and methods of operation to conform to prevailing definitions of legitimacy.

■ The organization can attempt, through communication, to alter the definition of social legitimacy so that it conforms to the organization's present practices, output and values.

■ The organization can attempt, through communication, to become identified with symbols, values or institutions that have a strong base of legitimacy.

Consistent with Dowling and Pfeffer's strategy of 'communication', Lindblom (1993) proposes that an organization can adopt a number of strategies where it perceives that its legitimacy is in question because its actions (or operations) are at variance with society's expectations and values. Lindblom (1993) identifies four courses of action (there is some overlap with Dowling and Pfeffer) that an organization can take to obtain, maintain, or repair legitimacy in these circumstances.

The organization can:

■ seek to educate and inform its 'relevant publics' about (actual) changes in the organization's performance and activities which bring the activities and performance more into line with society's values and expectations;

■ seek to change the perceptions that 'relevant publics' have of the organization's performance and activities – but not change the organization's actual behaviour (while using disclosures in corporate reports to indicate falsely that the performance and activities have changed);

■ seek to manipulate perception by deflecting attention from the issue of concern onto other related issues through an appeal to, for example, emotive symbols, thus seeking to demonstrate how the organization has fulfilled social expectations in other areas of its activities; or

■ seek to change external expectations of its performance, possibly by demonstrating that specific societal expectations are unreasonable.

Use of accounting reports in legitimation strategies

According to Lindblom (1993), and Dowling and Pfeffer (1975), the public disclosure of information in such places as annual reports can be used by an organization to implement each of the above strategies. Certainly, this is a perspective that many researchers of social responsibility reporting have adopted, as we show shortly. For example, a firm may provide information to counter or offset negative news which may be publicly available, or it may simply provide information to inform the interested parties about attributes of the organization that were previously unknown. In addition, organizations may draw attention to strengths, for instance environmental or community awards won or safety initiatives that have been implemented, while sometimes neglecting or down-playing information concerning negative implications of their activities, such as pollution or workplace accidents.

In considering the various proposed legitimizing techniques identified above we can see that the techniques might be symbolic (and not actually reflect any real change in activities), or they might be substantive (and reflect actual change in corporate activities). As Ashforth and Gibbs (1990) indicate, the use of substantive management techniques might 'involve real, material change in organizational goals, structures, and processes or socially institutionalized practices' (p. 178). By contrast, symbolic management techniques of legitimation involve the portrayal of corporate behaviour in a manner to 'appear consistent with social values and expectations', but the actual operating policies of the organization may not change (Ashforth and Gibbs, 1990, p. 180). For example, companies may publish policies on various issues including the environment, but may not enforce or set in place mechanisms for the full adoption of such policies. Other techniques relating to symbolic management techniques may include offering excuses for behaviour or apologies (Ashforth and Gibbs, 1990).

According to Ashforth and Gibbs, it is not necessary for corporations to use either substantive or symbolic management techniques exclusively and they may adopt a mix of substantive and/or symbolic legitimating techniques which they apply with varying levels of intensity. As an example of the potential use of 'legitimizing symbols' we can consider research reported by Deegan and Blomquist (2006).

Deegan and Blomquist investigated the development of the Australian Minerals Industry Code for Environmental Management by the Mineral Council of Australia. Many Australian mining companies signed up to this Code of Conduct. This Code had among its many requirements a reporting requirement that required signatories to the Code to prepare and release a publicly available environmental report within two years of signing the Code. Concerned about the quality of reporting being undertaken within the minerals industry, WWF-Australia (formerly known as the World Wide Fund for Nature) undertook an exercise in which they assessed the quality of the reports being released by the signatories of the Code. WWF assessed the reports using particular reporting criteria that WWF had developed. WWF's results were reported in a document they released which was entitled 'Mining Environmental Reports: Ore or Overburden?' In explaining how the establishment of the Code and the subsequent involvement of WWF might have contributed to the legitimacy of the minerals industry, Deegan and Blomquist referred to the work of Richardson and Dowling (1986). Richardson and Dowling refer to 'legitimating symbols' and 'procedural legitimation' – with both being linked to one another. According to Richardson and Dowling (1986, p. 102):

> Procedural legitimation represents a process of negotiation through which the values of a community and their connotative link to particular social relations and artifacts is created and institutionalized, as legitimating symbols. In the process, both value standards and social structures are subject to change.

In discussing their results, Deegan and Blomquist (2006) state:

> The legitimating symbol in this case was the Australian Minerals Industry Code for Environmental Management. As Richardson and Dowling emphasise,

legitimating symbols are open to 'challenge and change' and they can only sustain their existence through the support and affirmation of those parties that are perceived by the community as having high 'value standards' (a process of procedural legitimation involving a third party). WWF would arguably be perceived as having high 'value standards' and hence, their participation in the process would add to the legitimacy of the Code and increase the community perception that the Code had some form of 'higher order reality' that was independent of the creating body (the Mineral Council of Australia). Indeed, the comments made by the interviewees [from the Australian Minerals Council who were involved with the development of the Code] was consistent with the view that the WWF's involvement assisted the social standing of the Code. By reviewing the reporting policies of Code signatories, the WWF was effectively treating the Code as a 'value standard' which it was 'sanctioning' (Giddens, 1979) – something that would appear to be beneficial to the industry. While data was not collected from non-signatories at the time, it is conceivable that WWF's 'sanctioning' of the Code might have encouraged other organisations to subsequently become signatories. Certainly, the membership numbers increased subsequent to WWF's involvement (though obviously many factors could have contributed to this increase).

Consistent with the positions taken both by Dowling and Pfeffer and by Lindblom, Hurst (1970) suggests that one of the major functions of accounting, and subsequently accounting reports, is to legitimate the existence of the corporation. Such views highlight the strategic nature of financial statements and other related disclosures.

Corporate views on the importance of the social contract

The view within legitimacy theory that organizations will be penalized if they do not operate in a manner consistent with community expectations (that is, in accordance with the social contract) is a view being embraced publicly by corporate managers in many European and other nations. This is reflected, for example, in some statements made by Total S.A. (the large French-based multinational oil company) in its stand-alone *Environment and Society Report* of 2009. In the report the Chief Executive Officer of Total, Christophe de Margerie, states (p. 1):

> Our activities, our size and our financial strength understandably raise high expectations, in areas as various as employment, the environment, local development, safety, access to energy, financial transparency, ethics and more.

> We must acknowledge and take heed of these expectations. Doing so is a moral and civic duty and, more prosaically, an industrial and business one.

This view is also reflected in the supermarket chain Tesco's 2010 *Corporate Responsibility Report* (p. 52):

> Our business exists to serve our stakeholders, who have a wide range of expectations. Sometimes these expectations can conflict. We listen to the views of all our stakeholders and take them into account when trying to balance different considerations.

> Feedback from our stakeholders is used to review the issues on our CR [corporate responsibility] agenda which we adjust when new issues of significance emerge. Our Community Plans are developed to respond to local stakeholder priorities.

Similarly, the need to engage in dialogue with stakeholders to indentify their expectations (or the terms of the social contract) is reflected in the 2010 *Sustainability Report* of the European, African and Asian telecommunications company Vodafone Group Plc (p. 7):

> Listening and responding to our stakeholders – the people who affect our business or who are affected by it – is a core part of our sustainability management. Their feedback helps us understand their expectations, enables us to prioritise issues effectively and informs our sustainability strategy.

In common with many companies' social and environmental reports, this theme was reflected in many places throughout Vodafone's *Sustainability Report*. For example (p. 9):

> What we learn from stakeholder engagement feeds into our process to identify the issues that are most significant – or 'material' – to Vodafone. We use a 'materiality matrix' … to map the issues that our stakeholders are most concerned about against those which have the biggest financial or reputational impact on our business.

The above statements illustrate that the notions embodied within legitimacy theory are reflective of the public positions being taken by European corporate executives. Management appears to consider that meeting the expectations of the community in which it operates can protect or enhance profitability while failure to do so can be detrimental to ongoing operations and survival. The last quote given above (from Vodafone's report) specifically links these notions of legitimacy to the corporation's reputation.

Reputation risk management

In recent years, the role of social and environmental responsibility and reporting within corporate legitimation strategies has become more focused, at least in part, on the significance of these practices for managing risks to the reputation of an organization. In other words, the gaining and maintaining of legitimacy is often now expressed in terms of its role in building or maintaining an organization's reputation. This explicit use of the term *reputation* makes much clearer the financial importance of legitimacy. When it is put in terms of *reputation risk management* it often indicates that managers regard their company's reputation to be a resource of considerable (if normally unquantified) value in generating future profits, and any damage to this reputation will therefore affect future profitability. Accounting Headline 8.2 provides an example of how a damaged reputation for social and environmental impacts can have potentially significant financial costs. This example shows how damage to the oil multinational BP's social and environmental reputation arising from the world's largest accidental oil spill, when the BP Deepwater Horizon oil rig exploded in the Gulf of Mexico in April 2010, appears to have led to a loss of lucrative oil exploration contracts. A *reputation risk management* perspective on voluntary social and environmental

---

Accounting Headline 8.2

Financial costs of damage to social and environmental reputation

BP frozen out of Arctic oil drilling race

By Terry Macalister

BP has been forced to abandon hopes of drilling in the Arctic, currently the centre of a new oil rush, due to its tarnished reputation following the Gulf of Mexico spill.

The company confirmed tonight that it was no longer trying to win an exploration licence in Greenland, despite earlier reports of its interest. 'We are not participating in the bid round,' said a spokesman at BP's London headquarters who declined to discuss its reasons for the reverse.

The setback, which follows the announcement this week of a major find in the region by British rival Cairn Energy, is the first sign that the Gulf of Mexico disaster may have permanently damaged BP's ability to operate – not just in US waters, but in other environmentally-sensitive parts of the world.

... 'With the Greenpeace ship already harassing Cairn off Greenland – a company which has an exemplary safety record – everyone realised it would be political madness to give the green light to BP,' one source said.

BP has traditionally been at the forefront of breaking into new frontiers such as Russia and Angola, as well as drilling the deepest wells in the Gulf of Mexico, but the blowout and enormous environmental damage in the southern states has completely changed its external image and its own ambitions.

There has long been speculation since the Deepwater Horizon accident in April that BP could find itself persona non grata, particularly in sensitive environmental regions such as the Arctic.

... There will be another round of bidding for drilling off Greenland next year and the year after, but BP's reverse this week shows that it will be difficult for the firm to secure future exploration licences in the area.

Source: *Guardian*, 26 August 2010, p. 1
©Guardian News and Media Limited 2010

---

disclosures in annual reports assumes that threats to corporate legitimacy can result in damage to the value of a company's reputation, and such risks to reputation need to be minimized through active management.

The following examples of how the term *reputation* is used in Vodafone's 2010 *Sustainability Report* provide a further illustration of some of the many areas where issues of social and environmental responsibility can impact upon the value of a corporation's reputation:

> We want Vodafone to be recognised as a green brand by everyone, not just experts in sustainability. Our 'perception' target requires us to deliver a wide range of sustainability initiatives to engage effectively with consumers. In 2009/10, we held 18 workshops for over 180 consumers and employees – in the Czech Republic, Germany, Greece, Ireland, Italy, Spain and the UK – to help us

> understand how to establish Vodafone's reputation as a 'green' communications company. (p. 29)
>
> In 2009/10, we investigated 171 significant security issues – both internal and external – involving senior management or posing a serious risk to our reputation. These represented a loss to the business of at least £50,000. Incidents mainly related to organised subscription fraud, handset theft and phishing attacks. (p. 52)
>
> Vodafone's Tax Risk Policy, developed in 2008/09, is designed to ensure tax risks – financial and reputational – are assessed, tracked, recorded and managed consistently across the Group. It was rolled out to our local tax teams in 2009/10. (p. 53)
>
> There is a clear moral imperative for us to ensure Vodafone suppliers adopt fair and environmentally acceptable practices. This is complemented by very practical commercial considerations. For example, we rely on our suppliers to treat their staff well. Any failure to do so poses a reputational risk for us, but may also mean that a supplier delivers poor quality goods or is even closed for breaching legislation. Similarly, a supplier's failure to minimise its environmental impacts may impact our reputation and can add to expenditure through fuel costs, emission levies, or clean-up costs. (p. 54)

Academic studies have explored how companies have used reputation risk management as a justification, or motive, for their social and environmental responsibility and reporting. These reputation risk management theory perspectives are relatively new, so we will cover them fairly briefly. An important starting point to our explanation of reputation risk management theory is to stress the distinction, within reputation theories, between legitimacy and reputation. Deephouse and Carter (2005) explain that legitimacy is a condition that an organization (or any other body) will either have or will not have (so it is a binary concept), whereas reputation is a relative concept that reflects how much more or less legitimate one organization is regarded in comparison to other organizations:

> it appears that a central element of legitimacy, as currently understood, is meeting and adhering to the expectations of a social system's norms, values, rules, and meanings ... Regardless of the source of these expectations (Ruef and Scott, 1998), social actors generally accept and take for granted legitimate organizations (Suchman, 1995).
>
> In contrast to legitimacy, reputation has been assessed in past definitions in terms of relative standing or desirability ... quality ... esteem ... and favourableness ... [For example] Lawrence (1998) proposed that the reputation of a forensic accountant indicates expertise vis-à-vis other accountants. Thus, central to a reputation is a comparison of organizations to determine their relative standing. For any two organizations, they will either have the same reputation or, more likely, one will have a better reputation than the other.

One perspective on this theoretical distinction between legitimacy and reputation is that reputation can be regarded as a more nuanced understanding of some of the attributes that researchers have long regarded as part of an organization's legitimacy (Unerman, 2008).

Therefore, some of the social and environmental reporting studies that in the past have examined reporting practices from the perspective of legitimacy theory (and we discuss several of these empirical studies in the next subsection) might, if they had been conducted more recently, have been regarded as studies of reputation as well as legitimacy.

A study that focused specifically on reputation risk management theory was undertaken by Bebbington *et al.* (2008). In explaining the role and scope of their study, Bebbington *et al.* (2008, p. 338) state:

> One emerging explanation for CSR reporting, suggested by reporting proponents … practitioners … and researchers … of CSR reporting, is that it could be conceived as both an outcome of and part of reputation risk management (hereafter RRM) processes. While such an explanation has intuitive appeal, the proposition has yet to have considerable impact on the social accounting literature. This paper focuses on exploring this proposition by way of a three-stage investigation. First, the RRM thesis is examined on its own terms, drawing from literature that specifically focuses on reputation. Second, an exploratory study is undertaken, using a single report, to provide a glimpse into the plausibility of the RRM thesis as it pertains to CSR reporting. Third, drawing from the previous two investigations, the paper seeks to develop an understanding of the linkages between existing theoretical explanations for reporting (focusing on legitimacy and stakeholder theory) and the RRM thesis. As such the paper is exploratory in nature.

Bebbington *et al.* (2008) draw on a wide range of academic literature to help develop their perspective on reputation risk management theory. In particular they explore theoretically how reputation risk management strategies can be used as part of a strategy aimed at restoring an organization's image. They then use this theory to help analyse Shell's 2002 social and environmental report, showing how reputation-related disclosures in the report appear to be grouped together by Shell into what Bebbington *et al.* (2008, p. 351) term 'constellations of reputation'. They also show how their insights are complementary to those provided by other theories – such as legitimacy theory. We will now return to legitimacy theory to discuss a range of studies that have tested this theory.

Empirical tests of legitimacy theory

In recent years, numerous accounting researchers who have elected to study social and environmental reporting practices have used legitimacy theory.[8] A number of papers have identified specific types of social responsibility disclosures that have appeared within annual reports. The respective researchers have attempted to explain these disclosures on the basis that they form part of the portfolio of strategies undertaken by accountants and their managers to bring legitimacy to, or maintain the legitimacy of, their respective organizations. We now consider a number of such papers.

---

[8] However, it needs to be appreciated that legitimacy theory could be utilized as a basis for explaining various types of disclosures other than those relating to social and environmental performance issues. For whatever reason, social and environmental accounting researchers have tended to embrace legitimacy theory more so than other accounting researchers.

An early study that sought to link legitimacy theory to corporate social disclosure policies was conducted by Hogner (1982). This longitudinal study examined corporate social reporting in the annual reports of the US Steel Corporation over a period of 80 years, commencing in 1901, the data being analysed for year to year variation. Hogner showed that the extent of social disclosures varied from year to year and he speculated that the variation could represent a response to society's changing expectations of corporate behaviour.

Patten (1992) focused on the change in the extent of environmental disclosures made by North American oil companies, other than just Exxon Oil Company, both before and after the *Exxon Valdez* incident in Alaska in 1989 – which before the 2010 BP Deepwater Horizon explosion and oil spill had been one of the largest oil spills in history and had a significant effect on many creatures and the environments they inhabited. Patten (1992) argued that if the Alaskan oil spill resulted in a threat to the legitimacy of the petroleum industry, and not just to Exxon, then legitimacy theory would suggest that companies operating within that industry would respond by increasing the amount of environmental disclosures in their annual reports. Patten's results indicate that there were increased environmental disclosures by the petroleum companies for the post-1989 period, consistent with a legitimation perspective. This disclosure reaction took place across the industry, even though the incident itself was directly related to one oil company. He argued (p. 475):

> it appears that at least for environmental disclosures, threats to a firm's legitimacy do entice the firm to include more social responsibility information in its annual report.

Deegan and Rankin (1996) utilized legitimacy theory to try to explain systematic changes in corporate annual report environmental disclosure policies around the time of proven environmental prosecutions. The authors examined the environmental disclosure practices of a sample of Australian firms that were successfully prosecuted by environmental protection authorities (EPAs) for breaches of various environmental protection laws during the period 1990 to 1993 (any prosecutions by these agencies were reported in the EPAs' annual reports which were publicly available). The annual reports of a final sample of 20 firms, prosecuted a total of 78 times, were reviewed to ascertain the extent of the environmental disclosures. These annual reports were matched by industry and size to the annual reports of a control group of 20 firms that had not been prosecuted.

Of the 20 prosecuted firms, 18 provided environmental information in their annual report, but the disclosures were predominantly of a positive nature providing 'good news' about the organizations' performance, and the disclosures were of a qualitative nature. Only two organizations made any mention of the prosecutions. Deegan and Rankin found that prosecuted firms disclosed significantly more environmental information (of a favourable nature) in the year of prosecution than any other year in the sample period. Consistent with the view that companies increase disclosure to offset any effects of EPA prosecutions, the EPA-prosecuted firms also disclosed more environmental information, relative to non-prosecuted firms. The authors concluded that the public disclosure of proven environmental prosecutions has an impact on the disclosure policies of firms involved.

Accounting Headline 8.3

Negative media coverage of the pharmaceutical industry's product safety record

Drugs early-warning system 'not working'

By Stephen Foley

The UK's biggest pharmaceutical companies have called on the Government to do more to ensure that doctors report side effects from new drugs, in an attempt to head off growing public concern about the side effects of blockbuster drugs. ...

Drug safety has become one of the central concerns of an inquiry into the influence of the pharmaceutical industry by the House of Commons Health Select Committee. The issue has been given added impetus since the inquiry began last summer by the withdrawal of Vioxx, the arthritis painkiller linked to heart attacks, and shrill criticism in the US of other drugs on the market. ...

John Patterson – who was appointed to the board of AstraZeneca last month, charged with reviewing the company's approach to drug safety – rejected MPs' suggestions that the drug industry is more concerned with finding new uses for existing drugs than with monitoring their safety. He said: 'We

have a legal, moral and ethical duty to follow the safety of our products.'

The Select Committee, chaired by David Hinchcliffe, is hoping to publish recommendations from its inquiry by the end of March. Previous sessions have heard criticism of the drug industry for 'disease-mongering' to promote drugs such as antidepressants or pills for erectile dysfunction, and of other marketing practices.

However, the executives before the committee yesterday insisted that the 'checks and balances' on the industry were about right. They said patients were missing out because new medicines are slow to be adopted in the UK, where doctors are perceived as more conservative and where the National Health Service reviews new products for cost effectiveness before allowing them to be prescribed.

Source: *The Independent*, Friday 14 January 2005, p. 50
©The Independent Newspaper

With the results of Patten (1992) and Deegan and Rankin (1996) in mind we can consider Accounting Headline 8.3, which documents concerns about the attitudes of pharmaceutical companies towards product safety. Read the accounting headline and then consider how legitimacy theory could be used to predict how companies in the industry might react to such publicity. Do you think that companies in the pharmaceutical industry would be deemed to have breached their 'social contract', and, if so, do you think that they might use their annual reports in an attempt to reinstate their legitimacy?

In another study that embraced legitimacy theory, Deegan and Gordon (1996) reviewed annual report environmental disclosures made by a sample of companies from 1980 to 1991. They investigated the objectivity of corporate environmental disclosure practices and trends in environmental disclosures over time. They also sought to determine if environmental disclosures were related to concerns held by environmental groups about particular industries' environmental performance. The results derived by the Deegan and Gordon (1996) study indicated, among other findings, that during the period covered by the study: (1) increases in corporate environmental disclosures over time were positively associated with increases in the levels of environmental group membership; (2) corporate environmental disclosures were overwhelmingly self-laudatory; and (3) there was a positive correlation between the environmental sensitivity of the industry to which the corporation belonged and the level of corporate environmental disclosure.[9] These results were deemed to be consistent with legitimacy theory.

Gray, *et al.* (1995) performed a longitudinal review of UK corporate social and environmental disclosures for the period 1979 to 1991. In discussing the trends in corporate environmental disclosure policies, they made use of legitimacy theory with specific reference to the strategies suggested by Lindblom (1993), which we considered earlier in this chapter. After considering the extent and types of corporate disclosures, they stated (p. 65):

> The tone, orientation and focus of the environmental disclosures accord closely with Lindblom's first, second and third legitimation strategies [which we provided earlier in this chapter]. A significant minority of companies found it necessary to 'change their actual performance' with respect to environmental interactions (Lindblom's first strategy) and use corporate social reporting to inform their 'relevant publics' about this. Similarly, companies' environmental disclosure has also been an attempt, first, to change perceptions of environmental performance – to alter perceptions of whether certain industries were 'dirty' and 'irresponsible' (Lindblom's second strategy) and, second, as Lindblom notes, to distract attention from the central environmental issues (the third legitimation strategy). Increasingly, companies are being required to demonstrate a satisfactory performance within the environmental domain. Corporate social reporting would appear to be one of the mechanisms by which the organisations satisfy (and manipulate) that requirement.

In relation to trends found in regard to health and safety disclosures Gray *et al.* (p. 65) stated:

> We are persuaded that companies were increasingly under pressure from various 'relevant publics' to improve their performance in the area of health and safety and employed corporate social reporting to manage this 'legitimacy gap'. That is, while the disclosure did not, as such, demonstrate improved health and safety records (lack of previous information makes such assessment impossible), it did paint a picture of increasing concern being given by companies to the matter of protecting and training their workforce. This disclosure then helped add to the image of a competent and concerned organization which took its responsibilities in this field seriously. As such, health and safety disclosure appears to be a strong illustration of Lindblom's second legitimation strategy – 'changing perceptions'.

---

[9] Environmental sensitivity was determined by use of a questionnaire sent to environmental lobby groups in which office-bearers were required to rate industries (on a 0 to 5 scale) on the basis of whether the industry had been made the focus of action as a result of its environmental performance/implications.

Deegan *et al.* (2000) also utilized legitimacy theory to explain how the social disclosures included within the annual reports of companies in selected industries changed around the time of major social incidents or disasters that could be directly related to their particular industry. The results of this study were consistent with legitimacy theory and showed that companies did appear to change their disclosure policies around the time of major company- and industry-related social incidents. The authors argued that 'the results highlight the strategic nature of voluntary social disclosures and are consistent with a view that management considers that annual report social disclosures are a useful device to reduce the effects upon a corporation of events that are perceived to be unfavourable to a corporation's image' (p. 127).

Deegan *et al.* (2002) undertook a further longitudinal study examining disclosures on social and environmental issues in the annual reports of BHP (now BHP Billiton), a large Australian company, over the period 1983 to 1997. This study demonstrated positive correlations between media attention for certain social and environmental issues (which was taken as a proxy for social concerns with these issues) and the volume of disclosures on these issues. However, in a UK-based study of the annual report disclosures of five companies over a 20-year period from 1975, Campbell *et al.* (2003) found that 'Those companies that would be (according to legitimacy theory) expected to disclose more (because of society's negative perceptions) do not always do so and those companies with a lesser apparent legitimacy gap sometimes disclose more' (p. 573).

Applying legitimacy theory to financial (as opposed to social and environmental) disclosure practices, in a US study the choice of an accounting framework was deemed to be related to a desire to increase the legitimacy of an organization. Carpenter and Feroz (1992) argued that the State of New York's (government) decision to adopt generally accepted accounting procedures (GAAP) (as opposed to a method of accounting based on cash flows rather than accruals) was 'an attempt to regain legitimacy for the State's financial management practices' (p. 613). According to Carpenter and Feroz, New York State was in a financial crisis in 1975, with the result that many parties began to question the adequacy of the financial reporting practices of all the associated government units. To regain legitimacy the State elected to implement GAAP (which incorporates accruals-based accounting). As Carpenter and Feroz (1992, pp. 635, 637) state:

> The state of New York needed a symbol of legitimacy to demonstrate to the public and the credit markets that the state's finances were well managed. GAAP, as an institutionalized legitimated practice, serves this purpose ... We argue that New York's decision to adopt GAAP was an attempt to regain legitimacy for the state's financial management practices. Challenges to the state's financial management practices, led by the state comptroller, contributed to confusion and concern in the municipal securities market. The confusion resulted in a lowered credit rating. To restore the credit rating, a symbol of legitimacy in financial management practices was needed.

> It is debatable whether GAAP was the solution for the state's financial management problem. Indeed, there is strong evidence that GAAP did not solve the state's financial management problems.

New York needed a symbol of legitimacy that could be easily recognised by the public. In the realm of financial reporting, 'GAAP' is the recognised symbol of legitimacy.

According to Carpenter and Feroz, few people would be likely to oppose a system that was 'generally accepted' – general acceptance provides an impression of legitimacy. As they state (p. 632):

> In discussing whether to use the term 'GAAP' instead of 'accrual' in promoting the accounting conversion efforts, panel members argued that no one could oppose a system that is generally accepted. The name implies that any other accounting principles are not accepted in the accounting profession. GAAP is also seemingly apolitical.

As has been emphasized in this chapter, legitimacy theory proposes a relationship between corporate disclosures (and other corporate strategies) and community expectations, the view being that management reacts to community concerns and changes therein. But we are left with a question – how does management determine community expectations? There is evidence that management might rely on sources such as the media to determine community expectations. For example, Brown and Deegan (1998) investigated the relationship between the print media coverage given to various industries' environmental effects and the levels of annual report environmental disclosures made by a sample of firms within those industries. The basis of the argument was that the media can be particularly effective in driving the community's concern about the environmental performance of particular organizations and, where such concern is raised, organizations will respond by increasing the extent of disclosure of environmental information within the annual report.

Brown and Deegan used the extent of media coverage given to a particular issue as a measure (or proxy) of community concern. They made explicit reference to *media agenda setting theory*. Media agenda setting theory proposes a relationship between the relative emphasis given by the media to various topics and the degree of salience these topics have for the general public (Ader, 1995, p. 300).[10] In terms of causality, increased media attention is believed to lead to increased community concern for a particular issue. The media are not seen as mirroring public priorities; rather, they are seen as shaping them.[11] That is, media agenda setting theory posits that the media shapes public awareness, with the media agenda preceding public concern for particular issues (McCombs and Shaw, 1972). The view taken is that the public needs the media to tell them how important an issue within the 'real world' is as, for many issues, individuals do not learn this from available real world cues. Neuman (1990) identifies a distinction between 'obtrusive' and 'unobtrusive' issues. He notes, for example, that inflation is seen as a 'classic example' of an obtrusive issue because the public would become aware of it every time they went to the store and they do not need

---

[10] For an explanation of media agenda setting theory see Ader (1995), Blood (1981), Eyal *et al.* (1981), Mayer (1980), McCombs (1981), McCombs and Shaw (1972), Zucker (1978).

[11] An extreme but somewhat interesting view of the media's power of influence is provided by White (1973, p. 23). In relation to the United States he states that 'the power of the press in America is a primordial one. It sets the agenda of public discussion; and this sweeping political power is unrestrained by any law. It determines what people will talk and think about – an authority that in other nations is reserved for tyrants, priests, parties and mandarins.'

the media to report the official statistics to realize that this issue affects their lives. Unobtrusive issues, on the other hand, would include foreign events (such as polluting activities undertaken at off-shore locations, or workplace practices in remote factories) which cannot be experienced or known by the public without the media functioning as a conduit (Neuman, 1990; Zucker, 1978). It is argued that the media's agenda setting effect is most apparent in relation to unobtrusive events. Utilizing a joint consideration of media agenda setting theory and legitimacy theory, the arguments provided in Brown and Deegan (1998) can be summarized as:

- management uses the annual report as a tool to legitimize the ongoing operations of the organization (from legitimacy theory);
- community concerns with the environmental performance of a specific firm (or indeed, any aspect of corporate performance) in an industry will also impact on the disclosure strategies of firms across that industry (consistent with Patten, 1992, who adopted legitimacy theory); and
- the media are able to influence community perceptions about issues such as the environment (from media agenda setting theory); and
- if management respond to community concerns, and if it is accepted that community concerns are influenced by media attention given to particular social and environmental issues, then we should find a relationship between the extent of disclosure of social and environmental issues within the annual report and the media attention given to those issues.

The results in Brown and Deegan (1998) indicate that for the majority of the industries studied, higher levels of media attention (as determined by a review of a number of print media newspapers and journals) are significantly associated with higher levels of annual report environmental disclosures.

O'Donovan (1999) also considered the role of the media in shaping community expectations, and how corporate management responds to potentially damaging media attention. O'Donovan (1999) provides the results of interviews with senior executives from three large Australian companies. The executives confirmed that, from their perspective, the media does shape community expectations, and that corporate disclosure is one way to correct 'misperceptions held or presented by the media'.

Within the context of companies that source their products from developing countries, Islam and Deegan (2010) undertook a review of the social and environmental disclosure practices of two leading multinational sportswear and clothing companies, these being Nike and Hennes & Mauritz. Islam and Deegan found a direct relationship between the extent of global news media coverage of a critical nature being given to particular social issues relating to the industry, and the extent of social disclosure. In particular, they found that once the news media started running a campaign that exposed poor working conditions and the use of child labour in developing countries, it appeared that the multinational companies then responded by making various disclosures identifying initiatives that were being undertaken to ensure that the companies did not source their products from factories that had abusive or unsafe working conditions, or used child labour. Islam and Deegan argued that the evidence was consistent with the view that the news media influenced the expectations of Western consumers (consistent with media agenda setting theory), thereby causing a legitimacy problem for the companies. The companies then responded to the legitimacy crisis by providing disclosures within their annual report that particularly focused on working conditions and the use of child labour in developing countries. Islam and Deegan showed that prior to the time at which the news media started running stories about the labour conditions in developing countries (and the media attention to these issues appeared to commence in the early 1990s), there was a general absence of disclosures being made by the companies. This was despite the fact that evidence suggests that poor working conditions and the use of child labour existed in developing countries for many years prior to the newspapers commencing coverage on the issues. Islam and Deegan speculate that had the Western news media not run stories exposing the working conditions in developing countries – which created a legitimacy gap for the multinational companies – then the multinational companies would not have embraced initiatives to improve working conditions, nor provided disclosures about the initiatives being undertaken in relation to working conditions in developing countries.

A range of other studies have investigated managerial attitudes towards the role of corporate reporting in legitimation strategies. While legitimacy theory has been supported in many studies, there are some studies in which legitimacy theory has not been supported.[12] For example, Wilmshurst and Frost (2000) conducted a questionnaire survey among a sample of chief financial officers (CFOs) which asked these executives to rank the importance of various factors in environmental disclosure decisions. Wilmshurst and Frost then analysed environmental disclosures within the annual reports of the companies for whom their sample of CFOs worked, and found (p. 22) 'the influences of the competitor response to environmental issues and customer concerns to have predictive power'. This provided 'limited support for the applicability of legitimacy theory'.

O'Dwyer (2002) interviewed 29 senior executives from 27 large Irish companies and found that managerial motives for engaging in corporate social and environmental reporting were only sometimes consistent with a legitimacy theory explanation. This was despite many managers perceiving clear threats to their organizations' legitimacy in the eyes of a range of powerful stakeholders. O'Dwyer states (2002, p. 416) that detailed and close questioning revealed:

> an overwhelming perception of CSD [corporate social disclosure] as an unsuccessful legitimation mechanism. Therefore, while CSD is sometimes perceived as being employed as part of a legitimacy process, its employment in this manner is ultimately viewed as failing to aid in securing a state of legitimacy for organisations. Furthermore, despite the predominant view [among senior managers] that CSD is incapable of facilitating the achievement of a state of legitimacy, research into the CSD practices [of the companies interviewed] subsequent to the interviews … reveals that many of the interviewees' companies continue to engage in some form of CSD. In conjunction with the

---

[12] As we emphasized in Chapter 1, empirical testing of particular theories cannot always be expected to support those theories. There can be various reasons for this, including errors in measurement caused by the researchers, inappropriate definition and measurement of variables, biased representations being received from those being interviewed and so forth. Further, even if the researchers have undertaken their research in an appropriate and rigorous manner, theories about human behaviour cannot always be expected to provide perfect predictions of that behaviour – hence previously 'successful' theories might not be supported in some studies.

interviewees' perspectives, this questions the pervasive explanatory power of legitimacy theory with respect to the motives for CSD when considered in the Irish context.

Conversely, in a different interview-based study which discussed a range of hypothetical situations with a sample of six managers, O'Donovan (2002) found support for legitimacy theory.

While a great deal of legitimizing activity might be at a corporate level, some will also be taken at an industry level thereby attempting to bring legitimacy to the industry in general. For example, Deegan and Blomquist (2006) – referred to earlier in this chapter – provided evidence that the Australian minerals industry developed their industry-wide environmental management code so as to bring legitimacy to the industry generally.

Before concluding our discussion of legitimacy theory it needs to be appreciated that if a company makes disclosures because of concerns about its legitimacy, then the disclosures are effectively being motivated by survival or profitability considerations rather than being motivated by a desire to demonstrate greater accountability for its own sake. In recent years many companies have made it much clearer than they did in the past that a key motivation for them adopting corporate social and environmental responsibility strategies, and for engaging in the accounting and reporting that goes with these, is that this will help them either make more profit, reduce costs, and/or more effectively manage risks (Hopwood *et al.*, 2010). Some researchers have been critical of this motivation because it will only result in partial accountability, with many issues that are important to a range of stakeholders potentially remaining unreported. However, these motivations seem to have resulted in recent years in many more companies providing some social and environmental disclosures in their corporate reports, and this could be regarded as increasing accountability – even though the motivation might not be a desire simply to provide greater accountability (Hopwood *et al.*, 2010). Having read this section, do you regard the use of disclosures to aid greater accountability and the use of disclosures to win, maintain or repair legitimacy as mutually exclusive? Or do you think there could be a combination of these motives underlying any disclosure decisions?

Distinguishing legitimacy theory from Positive Accounting Theory

Some writers have suggested that the propositions generated by legitimacy theory (that annual report disclosure practices can be used in a strategic manner to manage an organization's relations with the community in which it operates) are very similar to the propositions generated by the political cost hypothesis which is developed through Positive Accounting Theory (which we discussed in Chapter 7).[13] While there are some similarities, legitimacy theory relies upon the central notion of an organization's 'social contract' with society and predicts that management will adopt particular strategies (including reporting strategies) in a bid to assure the society that the organization is complying with the society's

---

[13] As Chapter 7 indicates, Positive Accounting Theory proposes that managers are motivated to undertake actions that will maximize their own wealth. To the extent that mechanisms have been put in place to align the interests of the managers with the goals of maximizing the value of the organization, the manager will adopt those accounting and disclosure methods that minimize the wealth transfers away from the organization – wealth transfers that might be due to various political processes.

values and norms (which are predicted to change over time). Unlike Positive Accounting Theory, legitimacy theory does not rely upon the economics-based assumption that *all* action is driven by individual self-interest (tied to wealth maximization) and it emphasizes how the organization is part of the social system in which it operates. Also, unlike Positive Accounting Theory, legitimacy theory makes no assumptions about the efficiency of markets, such as the capital market and the market for managers.

8.4 Stakeholder theory

We now turn to stakeholder theory. It has both an ethical (moral) or normative branch (which is also considered as prescriptive), and a positive (managerial) branch.[14] We first consider the ethical branch. We then consider the positive (managerial) branch, which explicitly considers various groups (of stakeholders) that exist in society, and how the expectations of particular stakeholder groups may have more (or less) impact on corporate strategies. This in turn has implications for how the stakeholders' expectations are considered or managed.

In the discussion that follows we see that there are many similarities between legitimacy theory and stakeholder theory, and as such, to treat them as two totally distinct theories would be incorrect. As Gray *et al.* (1995, p. 52) state:

> It seems to us that the essential problem in the literature arises from treating each as competing theories of reporting behaviour, when 'stakeholder theory' and 'legitimacy theory' are better seen as two (overlapping) perspectives of the issue which are set within a framework of assumptions about 'political economy'.

As Deegan (2002, p. 295) indicates, both theories conceptualize the organization as part of a broader social system wherein the organization impacts upon, and is impacted by, other groups within society. While legitimacy theory discusses the expectations of society in general (as encapsulated within the 'social contract'), stakeholder theory provides a more refined resolution by referring to particular groups within society (stakeholder groups). Essentially, stakeholder theory accepts that because different stakeholder groups will have different views about how an organization should conduct its operations, there will be various social contracts 'negotiated' with different stakeholder groups, rather than one contract with society in general. While implied within legitimacy theory, the managerial branch of Stakeholder theory explicitly refers to issues of stakeholder power, and how a stakeholder's relative power affects their ability to 'coerce' the organization into complying with the stakeholder's expectations.

---

[14] Stakeholder theory itself is a confusing term as many different researchers have stated that they have used stakeholder theory in their research. Yet when we look at the research we see that different theories with different aims and assumptions have been employed – yet they have all been labelled as *stakeholder theory*. As Hasnas (1998, p. 26) states, 'stakeholder theory is somewhat of a troublesome label because it is used to refer to both an empirical theory of management and a normative theory of business ethics, often without clearly distinguishing between the two'. More correctly, perhaps, we can think of the term stakeholder theory as an *umbrella term* that actually represents a number of alternative theories that address various issues associated with relationships with stakeholders, including considerations of the rights of stakeholders, the power of stakeholders, or the effective management of stakeholders.

Hence, as we have already stated above, this chapter treats legitimacy theory and stakeholder theory as largely overlapping theories that provide consistent but slightly different insights into the factors that motivate managerial behaviour (Gray *et al.*, 1995; O'Donovan, 2002). Differences between the theories largely relate to issues of resolution, with stakeholder theory focusing on how an organization interacts with particular stakeholders, while legitimacy theory considers interactions with 'society' as a whole. A consideration of both theories is deemed to provide a fuller explanation of management's actions. As Gray *et al.* (1995, p. 67) state in relation to social disclosure-related research:

> The different theoretical perspectives need not be seen as competitors for explanation but as sources of interpretation of different factors at different levels of resolution. In this sense, legitimacy theory and stakeholder theory enrich, rather than compete for, our understandings of corporate social disclosure practices.

It should be noted, however, that some researchers (for example, Nasi *et al.*, 1997; Suchman, 1995) maintain that the theories are more discrete in nature than this chapter, and some others, assume. For example, Nasi *et al.* (1997, p. 296) argue that although the perspectives 'are not precisely competing, each leads to a different general prediction regarding the likelihood and evolution of a corporate response in the face of a social issue'. They further state (p. 303) that:

> although the perspectives agree on the need and reality of issues management activities, they disagree on the nature of the issues management and on managerial motivation for the issues management.

The ethical branch of stakeholder theory

The moral or ethical (also referred to as the 'normative') perspective of stakeholder theory argues that all stakeholders have the right to be treated fairly by an organization, and that issues of *stakeholder power* are not directly relevant. That is, the impact of the organization on the life experiences of a stakeholder should be what determines the organization's responsibilities to that stakeholder, rather than the extent of that stakeholder's (economic) power over the organization. As Hasnas (1998, p. 32) states:

> When viewed as a normative (ethical) theory, the stakeholder theory asserts that, regardless of whether stakeholder management leads to improved financial performance, managers should manage the business for the benefit of all stakeholders. It views the firm not as a mechanism for increasing the stockholders' financial returns, but as a vehicle for coordinating stakeholder interests, and sees management as having a fiduciary relationship not only to the stockholders, but to all stakeholders. According to the normative stakeholder theory, management must give equal consideration to the interests of all stakeholders and, when these interests conflict, manage the business so as to attain the optimal balance among them. This of course implies that there will be times when management is obliged to at least partially sacrifice the interests of the stockholders to those of the other stakeholders. Hence, in its

normative form, the stakeholder theory does imply that business has true social responsibilities.

Within the ethical branch of stakeholder theory there is a view that stakeholders have intrinsic rights (for example, to safe working conditions, fair pay), and these rights should not be violated.[15] That is, each group of stakeholders merits consideration for its own sake and not merely because of its ability to further the interests of some other group, such as the shareholders (Donaldson and Preston, 1995, p. 66). As Stoney and Winstanley (2001, p. 608) explain, fundamental to the ethical branch of stakeholder theory is a:

> concern for the ethical treatment of stakeholders which may require that the economic motive of organizations – to be profitable – be tempered to take account of the moral role of organizations and their enormous social effects on people's lives.

Obviously, a normative discussion of *stakeholder rights* requires some definition of *stakeholders*. One definition of stakeholders that we can use is that provided by Freeman and Reed (1983, p. 91):

> Any identifiable group or individual who can affect the achievement of an organisation's objectives, or is affected by the achievement of an organisation's objectives.

Clearly, many people (or other organizations) can be classified as stakeholders if we apply the above definitions (for example, shareholders, creditors, government, media, employees, employees' families, local communities, local charities, future generations and so on). With this in mind, Clarkson (1995) sought to divide stakeholders into *primary* and *secondary* stakeholders. A primary stakeholder was defined as 'one without whose continuing participation the corporation cannot survive as a going concern' (p. 106). Secondary stakeholders were defined as 'those who influence or affect, or are influenced or affected by, the corporation, but they are not engaged in transactions with the corporation and are not essential for its survival' (p. 107). According to Clarkson, primary stakeholders are the ones that must primarily be considered by management, because for the organization to succeed in the long run it must be run for the benefit of all primary stakeholders. Clarkson's definition of primary stakeholders would be similar to the definition of stakeholders applied by many researchers working within a managerial perspective of stakeholder theory, but this focus on primary stakeholders would be challenged by proponents of the ethical branch of stakeholder theory – who would argue that all stakeholders have a right to be considered by management.

The broader ethical (and normative) perspective that all stakeholders (both *primary* and *secondary*) have certain minimum rights that must not be violated can be extended to a notion that all stakeholders also have a right to be provided with information about how the organization is affecting them (perhaps through pollution, community

---

[15] We can contrast this perspective with that provided in Friedman (1962). He states: 'few trends could so thoroughly undermine the very foundation of our free society as the acceptance by corporate officials of a social responsibility other than to make as much money for their stockholders as possible. This is a fundamentally subversive doctrine' (p. 133).

sponsorship, provision of employment safety initiatives, etc.), even if they choose not to use the information, and even if they cannot directly have an impact on the survival of the organization (see, for example, O'Dwyer, 2005).

In considering the notion of *rights to information* we can briefly consider Gray *et al.*'s (1996) perspective of accountability as used within their 'accountability model'. They define accountability (p. 38) as:

> The duty to provide an account (by no means necessarily a financial account) or reckoning of those actions for which one is held responsible.

According to Gray *et al.* accountability involves two responsibilities or duties:

1 the responsibility to undertake certain actions (or to refrain from taking actions); and

2 the responsibility to provide an account of those actions.

Under their accountability model, reporting is assumed to be *responsibility* driven rather than *demand* driven. The view being projected is that people in society have a right to be informed about certain facets of the organization's operations.[16] By considering *rights*, it is argued that the model avoids the problem of considering users' *needs* and how such needs are established (Gray *et al.*, 1991). Applying the accountability model to corporate social reporting, Gray *et al.* (1991, p. 15) argue that:

> the role of corporate social reporting is to provide society-at-large (the principal) with information (accountability?) about the extent to which the organisation (the agent) has met the responsibilities imposed upon it (has it played by the rules of the game?).

That is, the role of a corporate report is to inform society about the extent to which actions for which an organization is deemed to be responsible have been fulfilled. Under the accountability model, the argument is that the principal (society) can elect to be entirely passive with regard to their demand for information. Nevertheless the agent (the organization) is still required to provide an account – the passive, non-demanding principal is merely electing not to use the information directly. Gray *et al.* state (p. 6) that 'if the principal chooses to ignore the account, this is his prerogative and matters not to the agent who, nevertheless, must account'.

Hurst (1970) also emphasizes the importance of accountability. He states (p. 58) that 'an institution which wields practical power – which compels men's wills or behaviour – must be accountable for its purposes and its performance by criteria not in the control of the institution itself'. The need to demonstrate accountability has also been stressed by the Research and Policy Committee of the Committee for Economic Development (a US-based organization). The committee states (1974, p. 21) that 'the great growth of corporations in

---

[16] Within the model they refer to society as the 'principal' and the organization (that owes the accountability) as the 'agent'. However, according to Gray *et al.* (1991, p. 17), their 'principal–agent model must be distinguished from "agency theory" or "economic principal–agent theory" as employed in, for example, Jensen and Meckling (1976), Ronen (1979), Fellingham and Newman (1979), Jensen (1983, 1993), Watts and Zimmerman (1986). Economic agency theory is grounded in neo-classical economics and takes its assumptions from it. Most significant among these are the assumptions about the single-minded greed of the principal and agent who are actively seeking to gain at the other's expense. The principal–agent model we are using makes no such assumptions and adopts no assumptions from economics, but rather owes its genesis to jurisprudence (Macpherson, 1973)'.

size, market power, and impact on society has naturally brought with it a commensurate growth in responsibility; in a democratic society, power sooner or later begets equivalent accountability'.

Gray *et al.* (1996) make use of the concept of the social contract to theorize about the responsibilities of business (against which there is a perceived accountability). Under their perspective they also perceive the law as providing the explicit terms of the social contract, while other non-legislated societal expectations embody the implicit terms of the contract.

In considering the above normative perspectives of how organizations *should* behave with respect to their stakeholders (relating to intrinsic rights including rights to information) it should be noted that these perspectives pertain to how the respective researchers believe organizations *should* act, which is not necessarily going to be the same as how they actually *do* act.[17] Hence, the various perspectives cannot be validated or confirmed by empirical observation – as might be the case if the researchers were providing descriptive or predictive (positive) theories about organizational behaviour. As Donaldson and Preston (1995, p. 67) state:

> In normative uses, the correspondence between the theory and the observed facts of corporate life is not a significant issue, nor is the association between stakeholder management and conventional performance measures a critical test. Instead a normative theory attempts to interpret the function of, and offer guidance about, the investor-owned corporation on the basis of some underlying moral or philosophical principles.

While we can now understand that there are researchers who promote a perspective that all stakeholders should be considered as important in their own right, irrespective of the resources they individually control, this ethical or moral view is not necessarily embraced by all. An alternative view is provided by the *managerial branch* of stakeholder theory.

The managerial branch of stakeholder theory

We now turn to perspectives of stakeholder theory that attempt to explain when corporate management will be likely to attend to the expectations of particular (typically powerful) stakeholders. According to Gray *et al.* (1996), this alternative perspective tends to be more 'organization-centred'. Gray *et al.* (1996, p. 45) state:

> Here (under this perspective), the stakeholders are identified by the organisation of concern, by reference to the extent to which the organisation believes the interplay with each group needs to be managed in order to further the interests of the organisation. (The interests of the organisation need not be restricted to conventional profit-seeking assumptions.) The more important the stakeholder to the organisation, the more effort will be exerted in managing the relationship. Information is a major element that can be employed by the organisation to

---

[17] Nevertheless, Donaldson and Preston (1995) argue that observation suggests that corporate decisions are frequently made on the basis of ethical considerations, even when doing so could not enhance corporate profit or shareholder gain. According to Donaldson and Preston, such behaviour is deemed to be not only appropriate, but desirable. They argue that corporate officials are not less morally obliged than any other citizens to take ethical considerations into account, and it would be unwise social policy to preclude them from doing so.

manage (or manipulate) the stakeholder in order to gain their support and approval, or to distract their opposition and disapproval.

Unlike the ethical branch of stakeholder theory, such (organization-centred) theories can and are often tested by way of empirical observation.

As we learned earlier, within legitimacy theory the audience of interest is typically defined as *the society*. Within a descriptive managerial branch of stakeholder theory the organization is also considered to be part of the wider social system, but this perspective of stakeholder theory specifically considers the different stakeholder groups within society and how they should best be managed if the organization is to survive (hence we call it a 'managerial' perspective of stakeholder theory).[18] Like legitimacy theory, it is considered that the expectations of the various stakeholder groups will impact on the operating and disclosure policies of the organization. The organization will not respond to all stakeholders equally (from a practical perspective, they probably cannot), but rather will respond to those stakeholders that are deemed to be 'powerful' (Bailey *et al.*, 2000; Buhr, 2002). Nasi *et al.* (1997) build on this perspective to suggest that the most powerful stakeholders will be attended to first. This is consistent with Wallace (1995, p. 87) who argues that 'the higher the group in the stakeholder hierarchy, the more clout they have and the more complex their requirements will be'.

A stakeholder's (for example, owner's, creditor's or regulator's) power to influence corporate management is viewed as a function of the stakeholder's degree of control over resources required by the organization (Ullman, 1985). The more critical the stakeholder's resources are to the continued viability and success of the organization, the greater the expectation that the stakeholder's demands will be addressed. A successful organization is considered to be one that satisfies the demands (sometimes conflicting) of the various powerful stakeholder groups.[19] In this respect Ullman (1985, p. 2) states:

> our position is that organisations survive to the extent that they are effective. Their effectiveness derives from the management of demands, particularly the demands of interest groups upon which the organisation depends.

Power in itself will be stakeholder-organization specific, but may be tied to such things as command of limited resources (finance, labour), access to influential media, ability to legislate against the company or ability to influence the consumption of the organization's goods and services. The behaviour of various stakeholder groups is considered a constraint on the strategy that is developed by management to match corporate resources as best it can with its environment.

Some researchers have considered stakeholder power in conjunction with other stakeholder attributes. For example, Mitchell *et al.* (1997) provide a framework to identify

---

[18] By comparison, Donaldson and Preston (1995) refer to the *instrumental perspective* of stakeholder theory in which the principal focus of interest is the proposition that corporations practising stakeholder management will be relatively successful in conventional performance terms. This is obviously similar to our 'managerial' perspective of stakeholder theory.

[19] In considering the managerial perspective of stakeholder theory, Hasnas (1998, p. 32) states: 'when viewed as an empirical theory of management designed to prescribe a method for improving a business's performance, the stakeholder theory does not imply that business has any social responsibilities.'

stakeholders according to the relative importance of each type of stakeholder in terms of an organization meeting its objectives. They argue that there are three features of a stakeholder that need to be considered, these being power, legitimacy and urgency. Power refers to the extent that a stakeholder can exert its influence on the organization. A stakeholder has legitimacy when its demands conform to the norms, values and beliefs of the wider community. Urgency is the extent to which stakeholder demands require immediate attention from a firm. The greater the extent to which organizations believe stakeholders possess these three attributes, the greater their importance to an organization. Building on this perspective, Parthiban *et al.* (2007) also found that organizations are more likely to respond to the expectations of stakeholders with power, legitimacy and urgency.

Freeman (1984) discusses the dynamics of stakeholder influence on corporate decisions. A major role of corporate management is to assess the importance of meeting stakeholder demands in order to achieve the strategic objectives of the firm. Further, as Friedman and Miles (2002) also point out, the expectations and power relativities of the various stakeholder groups can change over time. Organizations must therefore continually adapt their operating and disclosure strategies. Roberts (1992, p. 598) states:

> A major role of corporate management is to assess the importance of meeting stakeholder demands in order to achieve the strategic objectives of the firm. As the level of stakeholder power increases, the importance of meeting stakeholder demands increases also.

If we accept the view that a 'good' management is one that can successfully attend to various and sometimes conflicting demands of various (important) stakeholder groups, then we might, consistent with Evan and Freeman (1988), actually redefine the purpose of the firm. According to Evan and Freeman (1988), 'the very purpose of the firm is, in our view, to serve as a vehicle for coordinating stakeholders. It is through the firm that each stakeholder group makes itself better off through voluntary exchanges' (p. 82).

As indicated above, as the level of *stakeholder power* increases, the importance of meeting stakeholder demands increases. Some of this demand may relate to the provision of information about the activities of the organization. According to a number of writers, for example Ullman (1985) and Friedman and Miles (2002), the greater the importance to the organization of the respective stakeholder's resources/support, the greater the probability that the particular stakeholder's expectations will be incorporated into the organization's operations. From this perspective, various activities undertaken by organizations, including public reporting, will be directly related to the expectations of particular stakeholder groups. Furthermore, organizations will have an incentive to disclose information about their various programmes and initiatives to the respective stakeholder groups to indicate clearly that they are conforming with those stakeholders' expectations. Organizations must necessarily balance the expectations of the various stakeholder groups. Unerman and Bennett (2004) are among others who argue that as these expectations and power relativities can change over time, organizations must continually adapt their operating and reporting behaviours accordingly.

Within the managerial perspective of stakeholder theory, information (including financial accounting information and information about the organization's social performance) 'is a major element that can be employed by the organization to manage (or manipulate) the stakeholder in order to gain their support and approval, or to distract their opposition and disapproval' (Gray *et al.*, 1996, p. 46). This is consistent with the legitimation strategies suggested by Lindblom (1993) as discussed earlier in this chapter. In relation to corporate social disclosures, Roberts (1992, p. 599) states:

> social responsibility activities are useful in developing and maintaining satisfactory relationships with stockholders, creditors, and political bodies. Developing a corporate reputation as being socially responsible through performing and disclosing social responsibility activities is part of a strategy for managing stakeholder relationships.[20]

Empirical tests of stakeholder theory

Utilizing stakeholder theory to test the ability of stakeholders to impact on corporate social responsibility disclosures, Roberts (1992) found that measures of stakeholder power and their related information needs could provide some explanation about levels and types of corporate social disclosures.

Neu *et al.* (1998) also found support for the view that particular stakeholder groups can be more effective than others in demanding social responsibility disclosures. They reviewed the annual reports of a number of publicly traded Canadian companies operating in environmentally sensitive industries for the period from 1982 to 1991. A measure of correlation was sought between increases and decreases in environmental disclosure and the concerns held by particular stakeholder groups. The results indicated that the companies were more responsive to the demands or concerns of financial stakeholders and government regulators than to the concerns of environmentalists. They considered that these results supported a perspective that where corporations face situations where stakeholders have conflicting interests or expectations, the corporations will elect to provide information of a legitimizing nature to those stakeholders deemed to be more important to the survival of the organization, while down-playing the needs or expectations of less 'important' stakeholders.

In another study that investigated how stakeholder power influences corporate disclosure decisions, Islam and Deegan (2008) investigated the social and environmental disclosure practices of a major trade organization operating within a developing country. Specifically, they investigated the social and reporting practices of the Bangladesh Garments and Manufacturing Enterprise Association (BGMEA). This organization is authorized by the government in Bangladesh to provide export licences to garment manufacturers thereby enabling local garment manufacturers to sell their products to foreign buyers, many of which are large multinational companies. Islam and Deegan interviewed senior executives from BGMEA. The executives indicated that the operating and disclosure policies of BGMEA and its member organizations were particularly influenced by the demands and expectations of multinational buying companies (such as

---

[20] Again, we find that a large number of the accounting-related studies that use stakeholder theory (as with legitimacy theory) have researched issues associated with social and environmental disclosures. While these theories could be applied to financial disclosures, most researchers of financial accounting practices have, at least to date, tended to use other theories, such as Positive Accounting Theory. Issues associated with firms' capital structures have been studied from a stakeholder theory perspective by Barton *et al.* (1989) and Cornell and Shapiro (1987).

Nike, Gap, Reebok, Hennes & Mauritz) – the group they considered to be their most powerful stakeholders. The senior executives also stated that they believed that the demands and expectations of the multinational buying companies directly responded to the expectations of Western consumers, and that the expectations of Western consumers were influenced by the Western news media (consistent with media agenda setting theory, as discussed earlier in this chapter). In this regard, the executives of BGMEA noted that prior to the mid-1990s, multinational companies placed no requirements or restrictions on the Bangladesh manufacturing companies in relation to factory working conditions, or the use of child labour. However, once the Western news media began running stories on poor working conditions in 'sweatshop' factories, and running stories on the use of child labour, this caused concern for Western consumers who thereafter started to boycott the products of the large multinational sportswear and clothing companies. The Western consumers were key stakeholders of the multinational companies. At this point the multinational companies started imposing operating and reporting requirements on suppliers in terms of their employee conditions and use of child labour. Reflective of the changes in perceived pressures, and the resultant reactions of BMGEA and their members, one of the senior executives of BGMEA stated (Islam and Deegan, 2008, p. 860):

> The 1990 multinational buyers only wanted product, no social compliances were required and no restriction was placed on the employment of child labour. Now multinational buying companies have changed their attitudes towards us, perhaps because of the pressures from western consumers. We had to change ourselves following buyers' requirements and to fit with global requirements and restrictions. Western consumers and human right organisations pressured foreign buyers, and then foreign buyers pressured us.

Stakeholder theory of the 'managerial' variety does not directly provide prescriptions about what information *should* be disclosed other than indicating that the provision of information, including information within an annual report, can, if thoughtfully considered, be useful to the continued operations of a business entity. Of course, if we accept this view of the world, we would still be left with the difficult problem of determining who are our most important (powerful) stakeholders, and what their respective information demands are.[21]

As we have noted, organizations typically have a multitude of stakeholders with differing expectations about how the organization should operate. Read Accounting Headlines 8.4 and 8.5. Accounting Headline 8.4 is critical of UK banks in terms of the high levels of bank

---

[21] Again it is emphasized that this will not always be an easy exercise. For example, and for the purpose of illustration (perhaps at an extreme), we may find that a company has elected to provide an elderly woman who lives in a modest house nearby with a report that details when coal dust can be expected to be released from the company's furnaces so that she can ensure that no washing is left out at this time. At face value such a person may not appear to be a powerful stakeholder and we as outsiders might question why the company provides such disclosures. However, we may find that the woman has a daughter who is a popular high-profile radio personality who will readily complain on air, at some cost to the company in terms of community support, each time her mother's washing is put out and is subsequently covered with coal ash. Through her connections the elderly woman is a powerful stakeholder and, to alleviate her problems, coal-dust release information is provided so that she can schedule her washing. In relation to this illustration it should be noted that an ethical/moral view of stakeholder information rights would perhaps be that this person has a right to information, regardless of the fact that her daughter works in the media.

Accounting Headline 8.4

Stakeholders' concern about an attribute of an organization's performance

Vince Cable hits out at 'rip-off' banks

By Rosamond Hutt, Press Association

Business Secretary Vince Cable today accused high street banks of 'ripping off' their customers as it was disclosed some are charging up to 167% interest on unauthorised overdrafts.

Mr Cable also said customers were losing out because of a lack of competition in a marketplace dominated by a small number of big banks.

He was speaking after a survey for the BBC's Panorama programme revealed that the average interest charged on unauthorised overdrafts was as much as 167%.

The research also found banks were demanding an average 32% interest on authorised overdrafts, despite advertised rates of around 19%.

Mr Cable said: 'When we talk about restructuring the banks what's going to come out of this is a more competitive system where the customers are not ripped off.'

'One of the negative side effects of this crisis is that our banking system that was already very concentrated is now even more concentrated so there's less competition, less choice and bigger temptation for banks to earn margins at the expense of their customers.'

Christine Ross, head of financial planning at SG Hambros which carried out the research on overdrafts, said consumers should read the fine print for hidden charges.

'What we found is that unless individuals really scrutinise the small print the overdraft rates charged are far higher than they could even imagine,' she said.

Bank customers complained to Panorama about the Halifax, claiming it was charging an effective annual rate of interest of 3,650% on an overdraft of just £10.

It was reported that instead of charging advertised interest on overdrafts, the bank was charging a flat fee of £1 a day.

This means that customers with small overdrafts end up paying a disproportionately high rate of interest over the course of a year.

In a statement, the Halifax said customers said they 'want a clear overdraft charging structure' and the £1 a day represents 'a simple set of daily fees'.

The bank said it offers a 'buffer zone' for overdrafts of less than £10 that is free and that the vast majority of its customers do not go into overdraft.

Source: *The Independent*, 19 July 2010
©The Independent Newspaper

fees being charged on various accounts. In your view would bank customers with small overdrafts be considered to be powerful stakeholders such that, without the intervention of the UK Secretary of State for Business and/or the widely viewed television programme *Panorama*, their concerns would be met by the banks voluntarily reducing the level of their fees (adopting the managerial branch of stakeholder theory)? How would this view be different if we were adopting a moral/ethical perspective of stakeholder theory?

Accounting Headline 8.5

A further example of stakeholders' concern about attributes of an organization's performance

How Goldman gambled on starvation

By Johann Hari

Speculators set up a casino where the chips were the stomachs of millions. What does it say about our system that we can so casually inflict so much pain?

By now, you probably think your opinion of Goldman Sachs and its swarm of Wall Street allies has rock-bottomed at raw loathing. You're wrong. There's more. It turns out that the most destructive of all their recent acts has barely been discussed at all. Here's the rest. This is the story of how some of the richest people in the world – Goldman, Deutsche Bank, the traders at Merrill Lynch, and more – have caused the starvation of some of the poorest people in the world.

It starts with an apparent mystery. At the end of 2006, food prices across the world started to rise, suddenly and stratospherically. Within a year, the price of wheat had shot up by 80 per cent, maize by 90 per cent, rice by 320 per cent. In a global jolt of hunger, 200 million people – mostly children – couldn't afford to get food any more, and sank into malnutrition or starvation. There were riots in more than 30 countries, and at least one government was violently overthrown. Then, in spring 2008, prices just as mysteriously fell back to their previous level. Jean Ziegler, the UN Special Rapporteur on the Right to Food, calls it 'a silent mass murder', entirely due to 'man-made actions.'

Earlier this year I was in Ethiopia, one of the worst-hit countries, and people there remember the food crisis as if they had been struck by a tsunami. 'My children stopped growing,' a woman my age called Abiba Getaneh, told me. 'I felt like battery acid had been poured into my stomach as I starved. I took my two daughters out of school and got into debt. If it had gone on much longer, I think my baby would have died.'

Most of the explanations we were given at the time have turned out to be false. It didn't happen because supply fell: the International Grain Council says global production of wheat actually increased during that period, for example. It isn't because demand grew either: as Professor Jayati Ghosh of the Centre for Economic Studies in New Delhi has shown, demand actually fell by 3 per cent. Other factors – like the rise of biofuels, and the spike in the oil price – made a contribution, but they aren't enough on their own to explain such a violent shift.

To understand the biggest cause, you have to plough through some concepts that will make your head ache – but not half as much as they made the poor world's stomachs ache.

For over a century, farmers in wealthy countries have been able to engage in a process where they protect themselves against risk. Farmer Giles can agree in January to sell his crop to a trader in August at a fixed price. If he has a great summer, he'll lose some cash, but if there's a lousy summer or the global price collapses, he'll do well from the deal. When this process was tightly regulated and only companies with a direct interest in the field could get involved, it worked.

Then, through the 1990s, Goldman Sachs and others lobbied hard and the regulations were abolished. Suddenly, these contracts were turned into 'derivatives' that could be bought and sold among traders who had nothing to do with agriculture. A market in 'food speculation' was born.

... Until deregulation, the price for food was set by the forces of supply and demand for food itself. (This was already deeply imperfect: it left a billion people hungry.) But after deregulation, it was no longer just a market in food. It became, at the same time, a market in food contracts based on theoretical future crops – and the speculators drove the price through the roof.

Here's how it happened. In 2006, financial speculators like Goldmans pulled out of the collapsing US real estate market. They reckoned food prices would stay steady or rise while the rest of the economy tanked, so they switched their funds there. Suddenly, the world's frightened investors stampeded on to this ground.

So while the supply and demand of food stayed pretty much the same, the supply and demand for derivatives based on food massively rose – which meant the all-rolled-into-one price shot up, and the starvation began. The bubble only burst in March 2008 when the situation got so bad in the US that the speculators had to slash their spending to cover their losses back home.

When I asked Merrill Lynch's spokesman to comment on the charge of causing mass hunger, he said: 'Huh. I didn't know about that.' He later emailed to say: 'I am going to decline comment.' Deutsche Bank also refused to comment. Goldman Sachs were more detailed, saying they sold their index in early 2007 and pointing out that 'serious analyses ... have concluded index funds did not cause a bubble in commodity futures prices', offering as evidence a statement by the OECD.

How do we know this is wrong? As Professor Ghosh points out, some vital crops are not traded on the futures markets, including millet, cassava, and potatoes. Their price rose a little during this period – but only a fraction as much as the ones affected by speculation. Her research shows that speculation was 'the main cause' of the rise.

... If we don't re-regulate, it is only a matter of time before this all happens again. How many people would it kill next time? The moves to restore the pre-1990s rules on commodities trading have been stunningly sluggish. In the US, the House has passed some regulation, but there are fears that the Senate – drenched in speculator-donations – may dilute it into meaninglessness. The EU is lagging far behind even this, while in Britain, where most of this 'trade' takes place, advocacy groups are worried that David Cameron's government will block reform entirely to please his own friends and donors in the City.

Only one force can stop another speculation-starvation-bubble. The decent people in developed countries need to shout louder than the lobbyists from Goldman Sachs.

Source: *The Independent*, 2 July 2010
©The Independent Newspaper

Accounting Headline 8.5 provides a view that the derivatives trading activities of some investment banks were a key reason for food prices to rise substantially such that many impoverished people in developing countries could not afford to buy enough food and faced possible starvation. As with Accounting Headline 8.4, would you consider these impoverished people in developing countries to be powerful stakeholders, such that their concerns would be met voluntarily by the investment banks (adopting the managerial perspective of stakeholder theory)? Again, how would this view be different if we were adopting a moral/ethical perspective of stakeholder theory?

As a concluding issue it should be realized that in the above discussion we have separately considered the normative moral/ethical perspective of stakeholder theory and the managerial (power-based) perspective of stakeholder theory. By discussing them separately it could be construed that management might either be ethically/morally aware or solely focused on the survival of the organization, whereas in practice there is likely to be a continuum of possible positions between these two absolute points. By considering the two perspectives separately we are likely to get a partial view only, as it is unlikely that the managers of any company will be at one or other of the absolute extremes of the continuum. Instead, the managers of many companies will arguably be driven by both ethical considerations and performance-based decisions – not just one or the other. As Wicks (1996) argues, many people have embraced a conceptual framework in which ethical considerations and market considerations are seen as constituting a categorically and independent realism. Wicks argues that this view is unrealistic since it implies that people cannot introduce 'moral imaginations when they act in the market world'. In terms of future research in stakeholder theory, Rowley (1998) provides some interesting advice. He states:

> The blurring of normative and descriptive analysis is problematic for the field, however, dividing them into separate camps is equally hazardous. I believe that if our most challenging issues 10 years from now are to be different from today, we will need to collectively understand the complementary roles that normative and descriptive research play in our research questions. Like market and society we cannot think of one without the other (p. 2).

Again, we are left with a view that particular theories (of accounting) can provide us with only a partial view, and hence it is sometimes useful to consider the insights provided by different theoretical perspectives. One additional systems-oriented theoretical perspective, which has only recently begun to be applied to an analysis of voluntary corporate reporting decisions, is *institutional theory*. Institutional theory explains that organizations are faced with institutional pressures and as a result of these pressures organizations within a field tend to become similar in their forms and practices.

8.5 Institutional theory

Broadly speaking, institutional theory considers the forms that organizations take, and provides explanations for why organizations within a particular 'organizational field' tend to take on similar characteristics and form (Larrinaga-Gonzalez, 2007).[22] While a

---

[22] DiMaggio and Powell (1983, p. 147) define an 'organization field' as 'those organizations that, in the aggregate, constitute a recognized area of institutional life: key suppliers, resource and product consumers, regulatory agencies, and other organizations that produce similar services or products'.

theory such as legitimacy theory discusses how particular disclosure strategies might be undertaken to gain, maintain or regain legitimacy, institutional theory explores how – at a broader level – particular organizational forms might be adopted in order to bring legitimacy to an organization. According to Carpenter and Feroz (2001, p. 565):

> Institutional theory provides another lens through which to view economic resource dependency incentives for accounting rule choice. Institutional theory views organizations as operating within a social framework of norms, values, and taken-for-granted assumptions about what constitutes appropriate or acceptable economic behaviour (Oliver, 1997). According to Scott (1987), 'organizations conform [to institutional pressures for change] because they are rewarded for doing so through increased legitimacy, resources, and survival capabilities' (p. 498).

Institutional theory has been developed within the management academic literature (more specifically, in organizational theory) since the late 1970s, by researchers such as DiMaggio and Powell (1983), Meyer and Rowan (1977), Powell and DiMaggio (1991) and Zucker (1977, 1987).

A major paper in the development of institutional theory was DiMaggio and Powell (1983). These authors investigated why there was such a high degree of similarity between organizations. Specifically, in undertaking their research they state (p. 148):

> We ask why there is such startling homogeneity of organizational forms and practices; and we seek to explain homogeneity, not variation. In the initial stages of their life cycle, organizational fields display considerable diversity in approach and form. Once a field becomes well established, however, there is an inexorable push towards homogenization.

According to DiMaggio and Powell, there are various forces operating within society that cause organizational forms to become similar. As they state (1983, p. 148):

> Once disparate organizations in the same line of businesses are structured into an actual field (as we shall argue, by competition, the state, or the professions), powerful forces emerge that lead them to become more similar to one another.

While institutional theory has become a major and powerful theoretical perspective within organizational analysis, it has also been adopted by some accounting researchers. Several management accounting researchers, such as Covaleski and Dirsmith (1988), Broadbent *et al.* (2001), and Brignall and Modell (2000), have used institutional theory. It has also been used by some researchers who investigate aspects of audit, such as Rollins and Bremser (1997), and others who research aspects of the development and role of the accounting profession, such as Fogarty (1996). More directly related to financial accounting theory, Fogarty (1992) applied institutional theory to an analysis of the accounting standard-setting process. Dillard *et al.* (2004, p. 506) state that:

> Institutional theory is becoming one of the dominant theoretical perspectives in organization theory and is increasingly being applied in accounting research to study the practice of accounting in organizations.

A key reason why institutional theory is relevant to researchers who investigate voluntary corporate reporting practices is that it provides a complementary perspective, to both stakeholder theory and legitimacy theory, in understanding how organizations understand and respond to changing social and institutional pressures and expectations. Among other factors, it links organizational practices (such as accounting and corporate reporting) to the values of the society in which an organization operates, and to a need to maintain organizational legitimacy. There is a view that organizational form and practices might tend towards some form of homogeneity – that is, the structure of the organization (including the structure of its reporting systems) and the practices adopted by different organizations tend to become similar to conform to what society, or particular powerful groups, consider to be 'normal' (Larrinaga-Gonzalez, 2007). Organizations that deviate from being of a form that has become 'normal' or expected will potentially have problems in gaining or retaining legitimacy. As Dillard *et al.* (2004, p. 509) state:

> By designing a formal structure that adheres to the norms and behaviour expectations in the extant environment, an organization demonstrates that it is acting on collectively valued purposes in a proper and adequate manner.

Dillard *et al.* (2004, p. 507) explain that institutional theory:

> concerns the development of the taken for granted assumptions, beliefs and values underlying organizational characteristics ... [with accounting-based studies] suggesting the importance of social culture and environment on the practice of accounting; the use of accounting practices as rationalizations in order to maintain appearances of legitimacy; and the possibilities of decoupling these rationalizing accounting practices from the actual technical and administrative processes.

Institutional theory therefore provides an explanation of how mechanisms through which organizations may seek to align perceptions of their practices and characteristics with social and cultural values (in order to gain or retain legitimacy) become institutionalized in particular organizations. Such mechanisms could include those proposed by both stakeholder theory and/or legitimacy theory, but could conceivably also encompass a broader range of legitimating mechanisms. This is why these three theoretical perspectives should be seen as complementary rather than competing.

There are two main dimensions to institutional theory. The first of these is termed *isomorphism* while the second is termed *decoupling*. Both of these can be of central relevance to explaining voluntary corporate reporting practices. We will consider isomorphism first.

Isomorphism

The term 'isomorphism' is used extensively within institutional theory and DiMaggio and Powell (1983, p. 149) have defined it as 'a constraining process that forces one unit in a population to resemble other units that face the same set of environmental conditions'. That is, organizations which adopt structures or processes (such as reporting processes) that are at variance with other organizations might find that the differences attract criticism. Carpenter and Feroz (2001, p. 566) further state:

> DiMaggio and Powell (1983) label the process by which organizations tend to adopt the same structures and practices as isomorphism, which they describe

as a homogenization of organizations. Isomorphism is a process that causes one unit in a population to resemble other units in the population that face the same set of environmental conditions. Because of isomorphic processes, organizations will become increasingly homogeneous within given domains and conform to expectations of the wider institutional environment.

Dillard *et al.* (2004, p. 509) explain that 'Isomorphism refers to the adaptation of an institutional practice by an organization'. As voluntary corporate reporting by an organization is an institutional practice of that reporting organization, the processes by which voluntary corporate reporting adapts and changes in that organization are isomorphic processes.

DiMaggio and Powell (1983) set out three different isomorphic processes (processes whereby institutional practices such as voluntary corporate reporting adapt and change). These three isomorphic processes are referred to as coercive isomorphism, mimetic isomorphism and normative isomorphism. We will discuss each of these in turn.

Coercive isomorphism

Coercive isomorphism arises where organizations change their institutional practices because of pressure from those stakeholders upon whom the organization is dependent (that is, this form of isomorphism is related to 'power'). According to DiMaggio and Powell (1983, p. 150):

> Coercive isomorphism results from both formal and informal pressures exerted on organizations by other organizations upon which they are dependent and by cultural expectations in the society within which organizations function. Such pressures may be felt as force, as persuasive, or as invitations to join in collusion.

DiMaggio and Powell provide two general hypotheses that relate to coercive isomorphism. These are:

- **Hypothesis 1**: The greater the dependence of an organization on another organization, the more similar it will become to that organization in structure, climate, and behavioural focus.

- **Hypothesis 2**: The greater the centralization of organization A's resource supply, the greater the extent to which organization A will change isomorphically to resemble the organizations on which it depends for resources.

This above form of isomorphism (coercive isomorphism) is related to the managerial branch of stakeholder theory (discussed earlier), whereby a company will, for example, use 'voluntary' corporate reporting disclosures to address the economic, social, environmental and ethical values and concerns of those stakeholders who have the most power over the company. The company is therefore coerced (in this case usually informally) by its influential (or powerful) stakeholders into adopting particular voluntary reporting practices.

The idea of coercive isomorphism has been applied to various practices adopted by organizations. For example, applying coercive isomorphism to government's selection of accounting procedures, Carpenter and Feroz (2001, p. 571) state:

> Other organizations that can provide resources, such as the credit markets, can exercise power over government entities. This power can be used to dictate the use of certain institutional rules – such as GAAP.

A company could be coerced into adapting its existing voluntary corporate reporting practices (including the issues upon which they report) to bring them into line with the expectations and demands of its powerful stakeholders (while possibly ignoring the expectations of less powerful stakeholders). Because these powerful stakeholders might have similar expectations of other organizations as well, there will tend to be conformity in the practices being adopted by different organizations – institutional practices will tend towards some form of uniformity. In relation to the ability to create change, Tuttle and Dillard (2007, p. 393) state:

> Change is imposed by an external source such as a powerful constituent (e.g., customer, supplier, competitor), government regulation, certification body, politically powerful referent groups, or a powerful stakeholder. The primary motivator is conformance to the demands of powerful constituents and stems from a desire for legitimacy as reflected in the political influences exerted by other members of the organisational field. These influences may be formal or informal and may include persuasion as well as invitations to collude. If the influencing group has sufficient power, change may be mandated.

In the mid-1990s there was a great deal of concern by Western consumers that multinational clothing companies were often sourcing their products from developing countries where local supply factories were using child labour (Islam and Deegan, 2008). As a result of pressure (coercive pressure) from the consumers, the Western news media, and from various lobby groups, most organizations thereafter put in place processes to help in assuring that supply factories did not use child labour.

It has also been argued that funding bodies such as the World Bank, which often loans funds for projects being undertaken in developing bodies, has the power to coerce borrowers to adopt accounting and reporting rules that comply with its requirements. In this way, those entities that receive funding from the World Bank tend to adopt the same reporting practices – a case of coercive isomorphism. As Neu and Ocampo (2007, p. 367) state:

> These organizations [such as the World Bank] operate in a variety of different institutional fields thereby 'spanning' fields. They also possess the economic capital necessary both to enter distant fields and to facilitate the diffusion of specific practices. The economic capital of the World Bank and International Monetary Fund, as evidenced by their lending activities, provides them with the ability to encourage coercive isomorphism (DiMaggio and Powell, 1983) thereby changing the day-to-day practices of previously autonomous fields. ... Contained within the loan agreements are requirements that borrower countries adopt and utilize specific accounting practices such as budgeting, auditing and financial reporting practices. In this way, the lending agreements facilitate the diffusion of accounting/financial practices across heterogeneous fields.

Mimetic isomorphism

The second isomorphic process specified by DiMaggio and Powell (1983) is mimetic isomorphism. This involves organizations seeking to emulate (or copy) or improve upon the institutional practices of other organizations, often for reasons of competitive advantage in terms of legitimacy. In explaining mimetic isomorphism, DiMaggio and Powell (1983, p. 151) state:

> Uncertainty is a powerful force that encourages imitation. When organizational technologies are poorly understood, when goals are ambiguous, or when the environment creates symbolic uncertainty, organizations may model themselves on other organizations.

According to DiMaggio and Powell, when an organization encounters uncertainty then it might elect to model itself on other organizations. In providing an example of modelling (mimetic isomorphism) they state (1983, p. 151):

> One of the most dramatic instances of modelling was the effort of Japan's modernizers in the late nineteenth century to model new governmental initiatives on apparently successful western prototypes. Thus, the imperial government sent its officers to study the courts, Army, and police in France, the Navy and postal system in Great Britain, and banking and art education in the United States. American corporations are now returning the compliment by implementing (their perceptions of) Japanese models to cope with thorny productivity and personnel problems in their own firms. The rapid proliferation of quality circles and quality-of-work-life issues in American firms is, at least in part, an attempt to model Japanese and European successes. These developments also have a ritual aspect; companies adopt these 'innovations' to enhance their legitimacy, to demonstrate that they are at least trying to improve working conditions.

DiMaggio and Powell (1983) provide two general hypotheses that relate to mimetic isomorphism. These are:

- **Hypothesis 3**: The more uncertain the relationship between means and ends the greater the extent to which an organization will model itself after organizations it perceives to be successful.

- **Hypothesis 4**: The more ambiguous the goals of an organization, the greater the extent to which the organization will model itself after organizations that it perceives to be successful.

Applying the idea of mimetic isomorphism to corporate social reporting Unerman and Bennett (2004) explain:

> Some institutional theory studies … have demonstrated a tendency for a number of organisations within a particular sector to adopt similar new policies and procedures as those adopted by other leading organisations in their sector. This process, referred to as 'mimetic isomorphism', is explained as being the result of attempts by managers of each organisation to maintain or enhance external stakeholders' perceptions of the legitimacy of their organisation, because any

organisation which failed (at a minimum) to follow innovative practices and procedures adopted by other organisations in the same sector would risk losing legitimacy in relation to the rest of the sector (Broadbent et al., 2001, Scott, 1995). Drawing upon these observations, in the absence of any legislative intervention prescribing detailed mechanisms of debate, a key motivating force for many managers to introduce mechanisms allowing for greater equity in the determination of corporate responsibilities would therefore be their desire to maintain, or enhance, their own competitive advantage. They would strive to achieve this by implementing stakeholder dialogue mechanisms which their economically powerful stakeholders were likely to perceive as more effective than those used by their competitors. It is unlikely that these managers would readily embrace mechanisms designed to facilitate widespread participation in the determination of corporate responsibilities unless their economically powerful stakeholders expected the interests of economically marginalized stakeholders to be taken into account in this manner, and these managers are only likely to implement the minimum procedures which they feel their economically powerful stakeholders would consider acceptable.

The above argument links pressures for mimetic isomorphism with pressures underlying coercive isomorphism. Unerman and Bennett (2004) maintain that in this case, without coercive pressure from stakeholders, it is unlikely there would be pressure to mimic or surpass the social reporting practices (institutional practices) of other companies.

Normative isomorphism

The final isomorphic process explained by DiMaggio and Powell (1983) is normative isomorphism. This relates to the pressures arising from group norms to adopt particular institutional practices. In the case of corporate reporting, the professional expectation that accountants will comply with accounting standards acts as a form of normative isomorphism for the organizations for whom accountants work to produce accounting reports (an institutional practice) which are shaped by accounting standards. In terms of voluntary reporting practices, normative isomorphic pressures could arise through less formal group influences from a range of both formal and informal groups to which managers belong – such as the culture and working practices developed within their workplace. These could produce collective managerial views in favour of or against certain types of reporting practices, such as collective managerial views on the desirability or necessity of providing a range of stakeholders with social and environmental information through the medium of corporate reports. DiMaggio and Powell provide two general hypotheses that relate to normative isomorphism. They are:

- **Hypothesis 5**: The greater the reliance on academic credentials in choosing managerial and staff personnel, the greater the extent to which an organization will become like other organizations in its field.

- **Hypothesis 6**: The greater the participation of organizational managers in trade and professional associations, the more likely the organization will be, or will become, like other organizations in its field.

The above two hypotheses stress that particular groups with particular training will tend to adopt similar practices (including reporting practices), or else appear to be out of line with their 'group' – which in itself might lead to formal or informal sanctions being imposed by 'the group' on those parties that deviate from the accepted or expected behaviour. As another example of normative isomorphism, Palmer *et al.* (1993) found that chief executive officers (CEOs) who attended elite business schools were likely to adopt an approach to organizing a business known as the multi-divisional form (MDF) of organization (the organization being separately organized into different product divisions). The multi-divisional form of organization was taught as a part of conventional wisdom in elite business schools. This emphasis was passed on to students who subsequently became CEOs. The actions of these similarly trained executives resulted in organizational similarity within specific types of organizational fields.

Having described the three forms of isomorphic processes (coercive, mimetic and normative isomorphism), it is interesting to note that such processes are not necessarily expected to make the organizations more efficient. As DiMaggio and Powell (1983, p. 153) state:

> It is important to note that each of the institutional isomorphic processes can be expected to proceed in the absence of evidence that they increase internal organizational efficiency. To the extent that organizational effectiveness is enhanced, the reason will often be that organizations are rewarded for being similar to other organizations in their fields. This similarity can make it easier for organizations to transact with other organizations, to attract career-minded staff, to be acknowledged as legitimate and reputable, and to fit into administrative categories that define eligibility for public and private grants and contracts. None of this, however, insures that conformist organizations do what they do more efficiently that do their more deviant peers.

Related to the above point, Carpenter and Feroz (2001, p. 569) state:

> Institutional theory assumes that organizations adopt structures and management practices that are considered legitimate by other organizations in their fields, regardless of their actual usefulness. Legitimated structures or practices can be transmitted to organizations in a field, through tradition (organization imprinting at founding), through imitation, by coercion, and through normative pressures ... Institutional theory is based on the premise that organizations respond to pressure from their institutional environments and adopt structures and/or procedures that are socially accepted as being the appropriate organizational choice ... Institutional techniques are not based on efficiency but are used to establish an organization as appropriate, rational, and modern ... By designing a formal structure that adheres to the prescription of myths in the institutional environment, an organization demonstrates that it is acting in a proper and adequate manner. Meyer and Rowan (1977) maintain that myths of generally accepted procedures – such as generally accepted accounting procedures (GAAP) – provide a defence against the perception of irrationality and enhanced continued moral and/or financial support from external resource providers.

While three types of isomorphism have been described above, in practice it will not necessarily be easy to differentiate between the three. As Carpenter and Feroz (2001, p. 573) state:

> DiMaggio and Powell (1983) point out that it may not always be possible to distinguish between the three forms of isomorphic pressure, and in fact, two or more isomorphic pressures may be operating simultaneously making it nearly impossible to determine which form of institutional pressure was more potent in all cases.

In applying the various notions of isomorphism embraced within institutional theory to accounting, the decision to disclose particular items of information may be more about 'show' (or 'form') than about 'substance'. As Carpenter and Feroz (2001, p. 570) state in relation to accounting practices adopted by government:

> One manifestation of organizations in need of institutional legitimacy is the collecting and displaying of huge amounts of information that have no immediate relevance for actual decisions. Hence those state governments that have adopted GAAP, yet do not use GAAP information in making financial management decisions (e.g. budgetary decisions), may have adopted GAAP for purposes of institutional legitimacy.

Carpenter and Feroz (2001) utilized institutional theory to explain four US state governments' decisions to switch from a method of accounting based on recording cash flows to methods of accounting based on GAAP. In describing the results of their analysis, they state (p. 588):

> Our evidence shows that an early decision to adopt GAAP can be understood in terms of coercive isomorphic pressures from credit markets, while late adopters seem to be associated with the combined influences of normative and mimetic institutional pressures … The evidence presented in the case studies suggests that severe, prolonged financial stress may be an important condition affecting the potency of isomorphic pressures leading to an early decision to adopt GAAP for external financial reporting.

They further state (p. 592):

> All states were subject to normative isomorphic pressures from the accounting profession, coercive isomorphic pressures from the credit markets, and from the federal government to adopt GAAP from 1975 through 1984. Coercive isomorphic institutional pressures were significantly increased in 1984 with the passage of the Single Audit Act (SAA) and the formation of the Government Accounting Standards Board (GASB). Since it is likely that both normative and coercive isomorphic pressures act in concert to move state governments to GAAP adoption, it may be impossible to empirically distinguish the two forms of isomorphic pressure … We note that all state governments were subject to potent institutional pressure to adopt GAAP after 1973. These institutional pressures were created by the federal government, professional accounting associations, and representatives of the credit markets. Thus state governments

were subjected to at least two forms of isomorphic pressures: normative and coercive … We predict that all state governments in the USA will eventually bow to institutional pressures for change and adopt GAAP for external financial reporting. Our prediction is based on insights from institutional theory, coupled with insight on the potency of the institutional pressures for change identified in our four case studies.

Decoupling

We will now turn our attention to the other dimension of institutional theory (other than isomorphism), this being 'decoupling'. *Decoupling* implies that while managers might perceive a need for their organization to be seen to be adopting certain institutional practices, and might even institute formal processes aimed at implementing these practices, actual organizational practices can be very different from these formally sanctioned and publicly pronounced processes and practices. Thus, the actual practices can be decoupled from the institutionalized (apparent) practices.

In terms of voluntary corporate reporting practices, this decoupling can be linked to some of the insights from legitimacy theory whereby social and environmental disclosures can be used to construct an organizational image that might be very different from the actual organizational social and environmental performance. Thus, the organizational image constructed through corporate reports might be one of social and environmental responsibility when the actual managerial imperative is maximization of profitability or shareholder value. As Dillard *et al.* (2004, p. 510) put it:

> Decoupling (Meyer and Rowan, 1977) refers to the situation in which the formal organizational structure or practice is separate and distinct from actual organizational practice. In other words, the practice is not integrated into the organization's managerial and operational processes. Formal structure has much more to do with the presentation of an organizational-self than with the actual operations of the organization (Carruthers, 1995). Ideally, organizations pursue economic efficiency and attempt to develop alignment between organizational hierarchies and activities. However, an organization in a highly institutionalized environment may face conflicts and inconsistencies between the demands for efficiency and the need to conform to 'ceremonial rules and myths' of the institutional context (Meyer and Rowan, 1977). In essence, institutionalized, rationalized elements are incorporated into the organization's formal management systems because they maintain appearances and thus confer legitimacy whether or not they directly facilitate economic efficiency.

In concluding this overview of institutional theory we can summarize some of the above points by stating that there will be various forces that cause organizations to take on particular forms or adopt particular reporting practices. While theories such as legitimacy theory and stakeholder theory explain why managers might embrace specific strategies (such as making particular disclosures to offset the legitimacy-threatening impacts of particular events), institutional theory tends to take a broader macro view to explain why organizations take on particular forms, or particular reporting practices. Institutional theory also provides an argument that, while organizations might put in place particular processes, such processes might be more for 'show' rather than for influencing corporate conduct. In our discussion of legitimacy theory we discussed how managers might undertake particular activities – such as disclosure activities – to alter perceptions of legitimacy. By contrast, researchers who adopt institutional theory typically embrace a view that managers are expected to conform with norms that are largely imposed upon them. Nevertheless, it needs to be appreciated that there is much overlap between institutional theory, legitimacy theory and stakeholder theory.

Chapter summary

This chapter provides a number of perspectives about why management voluntarily elects to make particular disclosures. Specifically, it reviews legitimacy theory (and within this it briefly looks at the newly emergent reputation risk management theory), stakeholder theory and institutional theory – three theories that can be classified as systems-oriented theories. Systems-oriented theories see the organization as being part of a broader social system.

Legitimacy theory, stakeholder theory and institutional theory are all linked to political economy theory, wherein the political economy constitutes the social, political and economic framework within which human life takes place and social, political and economic issues are considered as inseparable. Political economy theory can be classified as either classical or bourgeois. Bourgeois political economy theory ignores various tensions within society and accepts the world as essentially pluralistic with no particular class dominating another. Legitimacy theory and stakeholder theory adopt the bourgeois perspective. Institutional theory can adopt either the bourgeois or classical perspective.

Legitimacy theory relies upon the notion of a social contract, which is an implied contract representing the norms and expectations of the community in which an organization operates. An organization is deemed to be legitimate to the extent that it complies with the terms of the social contract. Legitimacy and the right to operate are considered to go hand in hand. Accounting disclosures are considered to represent one way in which an organization can legitimize its ongoing operations. Where legitimacy is threatened, disclosures are one strategy to restore legitimacy. In practice, policies to maintain or restore corporate legitimacy are sometimes articulated in terms of reputation risk management.

Two different categories of stakeholder theory have been reviewed, these being the ethical (or normative) branch and the managerial branch. The ethical branch of stakeholder theory discusses issues associated with rights to information, rights that should be met regardless of the power of the stakeholders involved. Within the ethical branch, disclosures are considered to be responsibility driven. The managerial branch of stakeholder theory, on the other hand, predicts that organizations will tend to satisfy the information demands of those stakeholders who are important to the organization's ongoing survival. Whether a particular stakeholder receives information will be dependent upon how powerful they are perceived to be, with power often considered in terms of the scarcity of the resources controlled by the respective stakeholders. The disclosure of information is considered to represent an important strategy in managing stakeholders.

Institutional theory provides a complementary, and partially overlapping, perspective to both legitimacy theory and stakeholder theory. It explains that managers will be subject to pressures to change, or adopt, certain voluntary corporate reporting practices. These pressures can be a combination of coercive, mimetic and/or normative, and the resulting institutional image can sometimes be more apparent than real.

Questions

8.1 Explain the notion of a *social contract* and what relevance the social contract has with respect to the *legitimacy* of an organization.

8.2 What is organizational legitimacy and why might it be considered to be a 'resource'?

8.3 Explain why organizational legitimacy is place and time specific.

8.4 What does the notion of legitimacy and social contract have to do with corporate disclosure policies?

8.5 How would corporate management determine the terms of the *social contract* (if this is indeed possible) and what would be the implications for a firm if it breached the terms of the contract?

8.6 If an organization's management considered that the organization might not have operated in accordance with community expectations (it broke the terms of its *social contract*), consistent with legitimacy theory, what actions would you expect management to undertake in the subsequent period?

8.7 If an organization was involved in a major accident or incident, would you expect it to use vehicles such as an annual report to try to explain the incident? If so, explain *how* and *why* it would use the annual report in this way.

8.8 What is a 'legitimacy gap' and why could such a gap suddenly occur?

8.9 What is the difference between legitimizing strategies that are 'symbolic' and those that are 'substantive'? Is one type more effective than the other?

8.10 Consistent with the material provided in this chapter, would you expect management to make disclosures in relation to real-world events or, alternatively, in relation to how it believed the community perceived the real-world events? Why?

8.11 Explain the difference between *legitimacy* and *reputation*.

8.12 Legitimacy theory, stakeholder theory and institutional theory are considered to be systems-oriented theories. What does this mean?

8.13 This chapter divided stakeholder theory into the *ethical branch* and the *managerial branch*. Explain the differences between the managerial and ethical branches of stakeholder theory in terms of the alternative perspectives about when information will, or should, be produced by an organization.

8.14 Under the *managerial perspective* of stakeholder theory, when would we expect an organization to meet the information demands of a particular stakeholder group?

8.15 Read Accounting Headline 8.5 on p. 358, an article that relates to claimed impacts of derivatives trading by wealthy investment banks on the lives of impoverished people in developing countries. After reading the accounting headline:

    a Apply the managerial perspective of stakeholder theory to explain whether management would care about the concerns of the *UN Special Rapporteur on the Right to Food*.

    b If we applied an ethical perspective of stakeholder theory, *should* they care?

    c If society considered that the investment banks' policies were unreasonable, would you expect the banks to use their annual reports to defend their position (legitimacy)?

8.16 Explain the concepts coercive isomorphism, mimetic isomorphism and normative isomorphism. How can these concepts be used to explain voluntary corporate reporting practices?

8.17 Larringa-Gonzalez (2007, p. 151) states the following:

> The results of KPMG surveys of corporate social reporting reveal that while, in 1993, 13 per cent of the top 100 companies in 10 countries published a separate report about their environmental and social impacts, this figure almost tripled to 33 per cent (for 16 countries) in the 2005 survey. At the same time casual observation leads to the conclusion that in the 1990s 'environmental' and/or 'health and safety' reports dominated the reporting scene. More recently, however, most companies publish an 'environmental and social' or 'sustainability' report. In particular, from the 2002 survey to the 2005 survey, the percentage of separate reports (for the global top 250 companies) that correspond to the label 'sustainability' and 'social and environmental' have increased from 24 per cent to 85 per cent, with a corresponding decline (from 73 per cent to 13 per cent) for environmental, health and safety reports.

Required:
You are to use institutional theory to explain these large-scale shifts in both report production, and the names being given to the reports.

8.18 To what extent do stakeholder, legitimacy and institutional theories provide competing, mutually exclusive, explanations of voluntary corporate reporting practices?

8.19 An article entitled 'The killing fields' appeared in the *Sunday Morning Post* (Hong Kong) on 7 August 2005. The article refers to practices used to produce furs from racoon dogs, foxes, spotted mountain cats and rabbits. Within the four-page article, the following comments are made:

> Wu Zhenyu, 55, describes the trade that draws him 2,000 km from his home in Liaoning to a town where he spends two months at a time selling furs. 'We wait

until the coldest part of winter, when their fur is at its thickest, to kill the foxes,' he says. you kill them, the important thing is to make sure you don't damage the fur. Some farmers kill them by electrocution, but many others beat the fox to death with a bamboo stick.' Asked if he thinks beating the animals is cruel, he laughs and shrugs. 'People murder each other all the time. Isn't that cruel?' ... For fur lovers it is a cut-price paradise. For animal welfare groups alarmed at China's rapidly expanding fur trade, it is a nightmare ... Buoyed by the revival of fur in the fashion industry in recent years, the Chinese mainland is, according to estimates by business experts, manufacturing up to 80 per cent of the fur coats sold around the world ... China is the fastest growing fur exporter in the world, but it is not just the scale of the fur trade on the mainland that concerns animal welfare groups such as Peta (People for Ethical Treatment of Animals) and Animals Asia, they are also alarmed at the lack of regulations and the cruelty the trade involves ... Female foxes are confined in small, stinking coops with litters of cubs and fed twice a day on bowls of grey slop. Nearby, racoon dogs and silver foxes show signs of severe distress, ramming their heads and trunks repeatedly against the crude wire than encloses them from birth until about four months old, when they are killed for their fur. In one cage a young fox stands protectively over the body of a month-old cub lying lifeless, its paws covered in flies dangling through the bottom of the cage ... Buy a jacket labelled 'Made in Italy' and its rabbit fur lining may have started as an 18 yuan pelt in Chongfu ... 'Our fur goes everywhere in the world', says Tan, tucking into a bowl of steamed rabbit meat, a bountiful dish in Guanhu thanks to him. 'We can't keep up with this demand. We are very happy about this' ... Peta and other animal welfare groups hope the approach of the 2008 Beijing Olympics will turn the eyes of the world on every aspect of Chinese life and encourage the government to introduce effective legislation to ensure animals are humanely treated. In the first campaign of its kind in China, Peta this year launched a Pamela Anderson poster offensive in Shanghai's underground train stations to try to dissuade wealthy women from wearing fur. The campaign showed the Baywatch star, one of the best-known western female faces on the mainland, baring a naked back to the camera with the slogan: 'Give fur the cold shoulder.' ... 'A lot of cruelty is effectively being outsourced to China. We shouldn't go down the path to encourage it or to make it less cruel. We should try to end it', Smillie (education director for Hong Kong-based Animals Asia) says. 'Why should we regulate it and give them a slightly bigger cage or better access to water?'. 'The animals don't have a semblance of a normal life. Even if you bring in regulations, who is going to check on them?'.

Required:

a After reading the above extract, and adopting a legitimacy theory perspective, explain:

   i Why it might be possible that 'cruel' animal practices would be tolerated in some countries, but not others.

   ii How (or if) European garment retailers might respond if it becomes widely known that their fur garments are produced from a supply chain that includes farms with high levels of animal cruelty. In doing so, consider the past experiences of companies like Nike, and the legitimizing mechanisms they utilized when negative issues associated with their supply chain came to light.

b From a stakeholder theory perspective explain whether the animal welfare groups in China are likely to affect the practices of the fur traders.

c Consider media agenda setting theory to explain whether you think that the prominent four-page article appearing in the major Hong Kong newspaper could impact on the views of Hong Kong residents?

References

Abbott, W. & Monsen, R. (1979) 'On the measurement of corporate social responsibility: Self-reported disclosures as a method of measuring corporate social involvement', *Academy of Management Journal*, **22** (3), 501–15.

Ader, C. (1995) 'A longitudinal study of agenda setting for the issue of environmental pollution', *Journalism & Mass Communication Quarterly*, **72** (3), 300–11.

Ashforth, B.E. & Gibbs, B.W. (1990) 'The double-edge of organizational legitimation', *Organization Science*, **1** (2), 177–94.

Bailey, D., Harte, G. & Sugden, R. (2000) 'Corporate disclosure and the deregulation of international investment', *Accounting, Auditing & Accountability Journal*, **13** (2), 197–218.

Barton, S., Hill, N. & Sundaram, S. (1989) 'An empirical test of stakeholder theory predictions of capital structure', *Financial Management* (Spring), 36–44.

Bebbington, J., Larrinaga-Gonzalez, C. & Moneva-Abadía, J.M. (2008) 'Corporate social reporting and reputation risk management', *Accounting, Auditing & Accountability Journal*, **21** (3), 337–61.

Blood, R.W. (1981) *Unobtrusive Issues and the Agenda-setting Role of the Press*, doctoral dissertation, Syracuse University, Syracuse, NY.

Brignall, S. & Modell, S. (2000) 'An institutional perspective on performance measurement and management in the "New Public Sector"', *Management Accounting Research*, **11** (3), 281–306.

Broadbent, J., Jacobs, K. & Laughlin, R. (2001) 'Organizational resistance strategies to unwanted accounting and finance changes: The case of general medical practice in the UK', *Accounting, Auditing & Accountability Journal*, **14** (5), 565–86.

Brown, N. & Deegan, C. (1998) 'The public disclosure of environmental performance information-a dual test of media agenda setting theory and legitimacy theory', *Accounting and Business Research*, **29** (1), 21–41.

Buhr, N. (2002) 'A structuration view on the initiation of environmental reports', *Critical Perspectives on Accounting*, **13** (1), 17–38.

Burchell, S., Clubb, C., Hopwood, A., Hughes, J. & Naphapiet, J. (1980) 'The roles of accounting in organizations and society', *Accounting, Organization & Society*, **5** (1), 5–28.

Campbell, D., Craven, B. & Shrives, P. (2003) 'Voluntary social reporting in three FTSE sectors: A comment on perception and legitimacy', *Accounting, Auditing & Accountability Journal*, **16** (4), 558–81.

Carpenter, V. & Feroz, E. (1992) 'GAAP as a symbol of legitimacy: New York State's decision to adopt generally accepted accounting principles', *Accounting, Organizations and Society*, **17** (7), 613–43.

Carpenter, V.L. & Feroz, E.H. (2001) 'Institutional theory and accounting rule choice: An analysis of four US state governments' decisions to adopt generally accepted accounting principles', *Accounting, Organizations and Society*, **26** (7–8), 565–96.

Carruthers, B.G. (1995) 'Accounting, ambiguity, and the new institutionalism', *Accounting, Organizations and Society*, **20** (4), 313–28.

Clarkson, M. (1995) 'A stakeholder framework for analyzing and evaluating corporate social performance', *Academy of Management Review*, **20** (1), 92–118.

Committee for Economic Development (1974) *Measuring Business Social Performance: The Corporate Social Audit*, New York: Committee for Economic Development.

Cooper, D.J. & Sherer, M.J. (1984) 'The value of corporate accounting reports-arguments for a political economy of accounting', *Accounting, Organizations and Society*, **9** (3/4), 207–32.

Cornell, B. & Shapiro, A. (1987) 'Corporate stakeholders and corporate finance', *Financial Management* (Spring), 5–14.

Covaleski, M.A. & Dirsmith, M.W. (1988) 'An institutional perspective on the rise, social transformation, and fall of a university budget category', *Administrative Science Quarterly*, **33**, 562–87.

Deegan, C. (2002) 'The legitimising effect of social and environmental disclosures – a theoretical foundation', *Accounting, Auditing & Accountability Journal*, **15** (3), 282–311.

Deegan, C. (2007) 'Organizational legitimacy as a motive for sustainability reporting', in: Unerman, J., Bebbington, J. & O'Dwyer, B. (eds.) *Sustainability Accounting and Accountability*, Abingdon: Routledge, 127–49.

Deegan, C. & Blomquist, C. (2006) 'Stakeholder influence on corporate reporting: An exploration of the interaction between WWF-Australia and the Australian minerals industry', *Accounting, Organizations and Society*, **31** (4–5), 343–72.

Deegan, C. & Gordon, B. (1996) 'A study of the environmental disclosure practices of Australian corporations', *Accounting and Business Research*, **26** (3), 187–99.

Deegan, C. & Rankin, M. (1996) 'Do Australian companies report environmental news objectively? An analysis of environmental disclosures by firms prosecuted successfully by the environmental protection authority', *Accounting, Auditing and Accountability Journal*, **9** (2), 52–69.

Deegan, C., Rankin, M. & Tobin, J. (2002) 'An examination of the corporate social and environmental disclosures of BHP from 1983–1997', *Accounting, Auditing & Accountability Journal*, **15** (3), 312–43.

Deegan, C., Rankin, M. & Voght, P. (2000) 'Firms disclosure reactions to major social incidents: Australian evidence', *Accounting Forum*, **24** (1), 101–30.

Deephouse, D.L. & Carter, S.M. (2005) 'An examination of differences between organizational legitimacy and organizational reputation', *Journal of Management Studies*, **42** (2), 329–60.

Dillard, J.F., Rigsby, J.T. & Goodman, C. (2004) 'The making and remaking of organization context: Duality and the institutionalization process', *Accounting, Auditing & Accountability Journal*, **17** (4), 506–42.

DiMaggio, P.J. & Powell, W.W. (1983) 'The iron cage revisited: Institutional isomorphism and collective rationality in organizational fields', *American Sociological Review*, **48**, 146–60.

Donaldson, T. & Preston, L. (1995) 'The stakeholder theory of the corporation-concepts, evidence, and implications', *Academy of Management Review*, **20** (1), 65–92.

Dowling, J. & Pfeffer, J. (1975) 'Organizational legitimacy: Social values and organizational behavior', *Pacific Sociological Review*, **18** (1), 122–36.

Evan, W. & Freeman, R. (1988) 'A stakeholder theory of the modern corporation: Kantian capitalism', in: Beauchamp, T. & Bowie, N. (eds.) *Ethical Theory and Business*, Englewood Cliffs, NJ: Prentice-Hall, 75–93.

Eyal, C.H., Winter, J.P. & DeGeorge, W.F. (1981) 'The concept of time frame in agenda setting', in: Wilhoit, G.C. (ed.) *Mass Communication Yearbook*. Beverly Hills, CA: Sage Publications.

Fellingham, J. & Newman, D. (1979) 'Monitoring decisions in an agency setting', *Journal of Business Finance and Accounting*, **6** (2), 203–22.

Fogarty, T.J. (1992) 'Financial accounting standard setting as an institutionalized action field: Constraints, opportunities and dilemmas', *Journal of Accounting and Public Policy*, **11** (4), 331–55.

Fogarty, T.J. (1996) 'The imagery and reality of peer review in the US: Insights from institutional theory', *Accounting, Organizations & Society*, **18**, 243–67.

Freeman, R. (1984) *Strategic Management: A Stakeholder Approach*, Marshall, MA: Pitman.

Freeman, R. & Reed, D. (1983) 'Stockholders and stakeholders: A new perspective on corporate governance', *Californian Management Review*, **25** (2), 88–106.

Friedman, A. & Miles, S. (2002) 'Developing stakeholder theory', *Journal of Management Studies*, **39** (1), 1–21.

Friedman, M. (1962) *Capitalism and Freedom*, Chicago: University of Chicago Press.

Giddens, A. (1979) *Central Problems on Social Theory: Action, Structure and Contradiction in Social Analysis*, London: McMillan Press.

Gray, R. & Bebbington, J. (2001) *Accounting for the Environment*, London: Sage Publications.

Gray, R., Kouhy, R. & Lavers, S. (1995) 'Corporate social and environmental reporting: A review of the literature and a longitudinal study of UK disclosure', *Accounting, Auditing and Accountability Journal*, **8** (2), 47–77.

Gray, R., Owen, D. & Adams, C. (1996) *Accounting and Accountability: Changes and Challenges in Corporate Social and Environmental Reporting*, London: Prentice-Hall.

Gray, R., Owen, D. & Maunders, K.T. (1991) 'Accountability, corporate social reporting and the external social audits', *Advances in Public Interest Accounting*, **4**, 1–21.

Guthrie, J. & Parker, L. (1990) 'Corporate social disclosure practice: A comparative international analysis', *Advances in Public Interest Accounting*, **3**, 159–75.

Hasnas, J. (1998) 'The normative theories of business ethics: A guide for the perplexed', *Business Ethics Quarterly*, **8** (1), 19–42.

Heard, J. & Bolce, W. (1981) 'The political significance of corporate social reporting in the United States of America', *Accounting Organizations and Society*, **6** (3), 247–54.

Hogner, R.H. (1982) 'Corporate social reporting: Eight decades of development at US Steel', *Research in Corporate Performance and Policy*, **4**, 243–50.

Hopwood, A.G., Unerman, J. & Fries, J. (eds.) (2010) *Accounting for Sustainability: Practical Insights*, London: Earthscan.

Hurst, J.W. (1970) *The Legitimacy of the Business Corporation in the Law of the United States 1780–1970*, Charlottesville: University Press of Virginia.

Islam, M.A. & Deegan, C. (2008) 'Motivations for an organization within a developing country to report social responsibility information: Evidence from Bangladesh', *Accounting, Auditing & Accountability Journal*, **21** (6), 850–74.

Islam, M.A. & Deegan, C. (2010) 'Media pressures and corporate disclosure of social responsibility performance information: A study of two global clothing and sports retail companies', *Accounting & Business Research*, **40** (2), 131–48.

Jensen, M.C. (1983) 'Organisation theory and methodology', *The Accounting Review*, **58** (April), 319–39.

Jensen, M.C. (1993) 'The modern industrial revolution, exit and failure of internal control systems', *Journal of Finance*, 831–80.

Jensen, M.C. & Meckling, W.H. (1976) 'Theory of the firm: Managerial behavior, agency costs and ownership structure', *Journal of Financial Economics*, **3** (October), 305–60.

Larrinaga-Gonzalez, C. (2007) 'Sustainability reporting: Insights from neoinstitutional theory', in: Unerman, J., Bebbington, J. & O'Dwyer, B. (eds.) *Sustainability, Accounting and Accountability*, Abingdon: Routledge.

Lawrence, T.B. (1998) 'Examining resources in an occupational community: Reputation in Canadian forensic accounting', *Human Relations*, **51** (9), 1103–31.

Lindblom, C.K. (1993) 'The implications of organisational legitimacy for corporate social performance and disclosure', *Critical Perspectives on Accounting Conference*, New York.

Lowe, E.A. & Tinker, A. (1977) 'Sighting the accounting problematic: Towards an intellectual emancipation of accounting', *Journal of Business Finance and Accounting*, **4** (3), 263–76.

Macpherson, C.B. (1973) *Democratic Theory: Essays in Retrieval*, Oxford: Oxford University Press.

Mathews, M.R. (1993) *Socially Responsible Accounting*, London: Chapman and Hall.

Mayer, H. (1980) 'Power and the press', *Murdoch University News*, **7** (8).

McCombs, M. (1981) 'The agenda-setting approach', in: Nimmo, D. & Sanders, K. (eds.) *Handbook of Political Communication*. Beverly Hills, CA: Sage.

McCombs, M. & Shaw, D. (1972) 'The agenda setting function of mass media', *Public Opinion Quarterly*, **36**, 176–87.

Meyer, J.W. & Rowan, B. (1977) 'Institutionalized organizations: Formal structure as myth and ceremony', *American Journal of Sociology*, **83**, 340–63.

Miles, R.H. & Cameron, K.S. (1982) *Coffin Nails and Corporate Strategies*, Englewood Cliffs, NJ: Prentice-Hall.

Mitchell, R.K., Agle, B.R. & Wood, D.J. (1997) 'Toward a theory of stakeholder identification and salience: Defining the principle of who and what really counts',

Academy of Management Review, **22** (4), 853–86.

Nasi, J., Nasi, S., Phillips, N. & Zyglidopoulos, S. (1997) 'The evolution of corporate social responsiveness- an exploratory study of Finnish and Canadian forestry companies', *Business & Society*, **38** (3), 296–321.

Ness, K. & Mirza, A. (1991) 'Corporate social disclosure: A note on a test of agency theory', *British Accounting Review*, **23**, 211–17.

Neu, D. & Ocampo, E. (2007) 'Doing missionary work: The World Bank and the diffusion of financial practices', *Critical Perspectives on Accounting*, **18** (3), 363–89.

Neu, D., Warsame, H. & Pedwell, K. (1998) 'Managing public impressions: Environmental disclosures in annual reports', *Accounting Organizations and Society*, **25** (3), 265–82.

Neuman, W.R. (1990) 'The threshold of public attention', *Public Opinion Quarterly*, **54** (2), 159–76.

O'Donovan, G. (1999) 'Managing legitimacy through increased corporate environmental reporting: an exploratory study', *Interdisciplinary Environmental Review*, **1** (1), 63–99.

O'Donovan, G. (2002) 'Environmental disclosures in the annual report: Extending the applicability and predictive power of legitimacy theory', *Accounting, Auditing & Accountability Journal*, **15** (3), 344–71.

O'Dwyer, B. (2002) 'Managerial perceptions of corporate social disclosure: An Irish story', *Accounting, Auditing & Accountability Journal*, **15** (3), 406–36.

O'Dwyer, B. (2005) 'Stakeholder democracy: Challenges and contributions from social accounting', *Business Ethics: A European Review*, **14** (1), 28–41.

O'Leary, T. (1985) 'Observations on corporate financial reporting in the name of politics', *Accounting, Organizations and Society*, **10** (1), 87–102.

Oliver, C. (1991) 'Strategic responses to institutional processes', *Academy of Management Review*, **16** (1), 145–79.

Oliver, C. (1997) 'Sustainable competitive advantage: Combining institutional and resource-based views', *Strategic Management Journal*, **18** (9), 697–713.

Palmer, D.A., Jennings, P.D. & Zhou, X. (1993) 'Late adoption of the multidivisional form by large U.S. corporations: Institutional, political, and economic accounts', *Administrative Science Quarterly*, **38** (1), 100–31.

Parthiban, D., Bloom, M. & Hillman, A.J. (2007) 'Investor activism, managerial responsiveness, and corporate social performance', *Strategic Management Journal*, **28** (1), 91–100.

Patten, D.M. (1991) 'Exposure, legitimacy and social disclosure', *Journal of Accounting and Public Policy*, **10**, 297–308.

Patten, D.M. (1992) 'Intra-industry environmental disclosures in response to the Alaskan oil spill: A note on legitimacy theory', *Accounting, Organizations and Society*, **15** (5), 471–75.

Pfeffer, J. & Salancik, G. (1978) *The External Control of Organizations: A Resource Dependence Perspective*, New York: Harper and Row.

Powell, W.W. & DiMaggio, P.J. (eds.) (1991) *The New Institutionalism in Organizational Analysis*, Chicago: University of Chicago Press.

Puxty, A. (1991) 'Social accountability and universal pragmatics', *Advances in Public Interest Accounting*, **4**, 35–46.

Ramanathan, K.V. (1976) 'Toward a theory of corporate social accounting', *The Accounting Review*, **21** (3), 516–28.

Richardson, A.J. & Dowling, J.B. (1986) 'An integrative theory of organizational legitimation', *Scandinavian Journal of Management Studies*, **3** (2), 91–109.

Roberts, R. (1992) 'Determinants of corporate social responsibility disclosure: An application of stakeholder theory', *Accounting, Organizations and Society*, **17** (6), 595–612.

Rollins, T.P. & Bremser, W.G. (1997) 'The SEC's enforcement actions against auditors: An auditor reputation and institutional theory perspective', *Critical Perspectives on Accounting*, **8** (3), 191–206.

Ronen, J. (1979) 'The dual role of accounting: A financial economic perspective', in: Bicksler, J. L. (ed.) *Handbook of Financial Economics*, Amsterdam: North Holland.

Rowley, T. '(1998) A normative justification for stakeholder theory', *Business and Society*, **37** (1), 105–107.

Ruef, M. & Scott, W.R. (1998) 'A multi-dimensional model of organizational legitimacy: Hospital survival in changing institutional environments', *Administrative Science Quarterly*, **43** (4), 877–904.

Scott, W.R. (1987) 'The adolescence of institutional theory', *Administrative Science Quarterly*, **32** (4), 493–511.

Scott, W.R. (1995) *Institutions and Organisations*, Thousand Oaks, CA: Sage.

Sethi, S.P. (1977) 'Dimensions of corporate social performance: An analytical framework', in: Carroll, A. B. (ed.) *Managing Corporate Social Responsibility*, Boston, MA: Little, Brown.

Sethi, S.P. (1978) 'Advocacy advertising: The American experience',

California Management Review, **21** (1), 55–67.

Shocker, A.D. & Sethi, S.P. (1974) 'An approach to incorporating social preferences in developing corporate action strategies', in: Sethi, S. P. (ed.) *The Unstable Ground: Corporate Social Policy in a Dynamic Society*, Los Angeles, CA: Melville, 67–80.

Stoney, C. & Winstanley, D. (2001) 'Stakeholding: Confusion or utopia: Mapping the conceptual terrain', *Journal of Management Studies*, **38** (5), 603–26.

Suchman, M.C. (1995) 'Managing legitimacy: Strategic and institutional approaches', *Academy of Management Review*, **20** (3), 571–610.

Swift, T. (2001) 'Trust, reputation and corporate accountability to stakeholders', *Business Ethics: A European Review*, **10** (1), 16–26.

Tinker, A. & Neimark, M. (1987) 'The role of annual reports in gender and class contradictions at General Motors: 1917–1976', *Accounting, Organisations and Society*, **12** (1), 71–88.

Tuttle, B. & Dillard, J. (2007) 'Beyond competition: Institutional isomorphism in U.S. accounting research', *Accounting Horizons*, **21** (4), 387–409.

Ullman, A. (1985) 'Data in search of a theory: A critical examination of the relationships among social performance, social disclosure, and economic performance of US firms', *Academy of Management Review*, **10** (3), 540–57.

Unerman, J. (2008) 'Strategic reputation risk management and corporate social responsibility reporting', *Accounting, Auditing & Accountability Journal*, **21** (3), 362–64.

Unerman, J. & Bennett, M. (2004) 'Increased stakeholder dialogue and the internet: Towards greater corporate accountability

380 **Chapter 08** Unregulated Corporate Reporting Decisions

or reinforcing capitalist hegemony?', *Accounting, Organizations and Society*, **29** (7), 685–707.

Wallace, G. (1995) 'Balancing conflicting stakeholder requirements', *Journal for* *Quality and Participation*, **18** (2), 84–98.

Watts, R.L. & Zimmerman, J.L. (1986) *Positive Accounting Theory*, Englewood Cliffs, NJ: Prentice-Hall.

White, T. (1973) *The Making of the President* *1972*, New York: Bantam Press.

Wicks, A. (1996) 'Overcoming the separation thesis: The need for a reconsideration of business and business research', *Business and Society*, **35** (1), 89–118.

Wilmshurst, T. & Frost, G. (2000) 'Corporate environmental reporting: A test of legitimacy theory', *Accounting,* *Auditing & Accountability Journal*, **13** (1), 10–26.

Woodward, D.G., Edwards, P. & **Birkin, F.** (1996) 'Organizational legitimacy and stakeholder information provision', *British Journal of Management*, **7** (4), 329–47.

Zucker, H.G. (1978) 'The variable nature of news media influence', in: Rubin, B. D. (ed.) *Communication* *Yearbook No. 2*, New Brunswick, NJ: Transaction Books, 225–45.

Zucker, L.G. (1977) 'The role of institutionalization in cultural persistence', *American Sociological* *Review*, **42**, 726–43.

Zucker, L.G. (1987) 'Institutional theories of organizations', *Annual Review of* *Sociology*, **13**, 443–64.

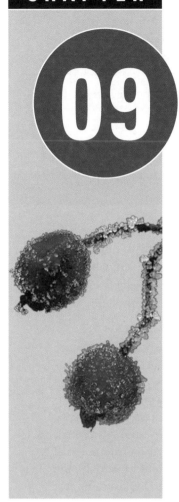

09

Extended Systems of Accounting: The Incorporation of Social and Environmental Factors within External Reporting

❖ **LEARNING OBJECTIVES**

Upon completing this chapter readers should:

❖ be aware of various perspectives about the responsibilities of business;

❖ be able to provide an explanation of the relationship between organizational responsibility and organizational accountability;

❖ be aware of the relationship between accounting and accountability;

❖ be aware of various theoretical perspectives that can explain why organizations might voluntarily elect to provide publicly available information about their social and environmental performance;

❖ be aware of the theoretical underpinnings of some recent initiatives in social and environmental accounting;

❖ be able to explain the concept of *sustainable development* and be able to explain how organizations are reporting their progress towards the goal of sustainable development;

❖ be able to identify some of the limitations of traditional financial accounting in enabling users of reports to assess a reporting entity's social and environmental performance.

Opening issues

1 Many companies throughout the world publish reports that discuss their economic, environmental and social performance. There are also numerous instances of companies publicly stating their commitment to sustainable development. For example, on the first page of Royal Dutch Shell plc's 2009 *Sustainability Report* the Anglo-Dutch multinational oil company states, under the heading *How we report on sustainable development*:

> We began reporting voluntarily on our environmental and social performance with the first Shell Report that covered 1997. Our reporting focuses on the environmental and social challenges that most affect business performance and matter most to our key stakeholders. These include local communities, non-governmental organisations, shareholders, investors, customers, governments, employees, media, academics, contractors and suppliers. We use a thorough process to select content for our reporting based on information from internal and external sources. Throughout the year we also provide information to the Dow Jones Sustainability Indexes, FTSE4Good, the Carbon Disclosure Project and other organisations that help investors understand the economic, environmental and social performance of companies.

> Internal controls such as audit trails and statistical checks help assure the accuracy of the Shell Sustainability Report. An External Review Committee of independent experts helps make sure our reporting is balanced, relevant and responsive to stakeholders' interests … This report is supported on the Shell website by additional environmental and social performance data and more detailed information on our approach to sustainable development and related issues.

Moves towards sustainable development require organizations explicitly to consider various facets of their economic, social and environmental performance. But why would companies, such as Shell, embrace sustainability as a corporate goal rather than simply aiming for increased and continued profitability? Furthermore, if an entity embraces 'sustainability reporting' (perhaps through releasing a stand-alone *Sustainability Report* and/or reporting on key sustainability issues throughout their annual report), what does this imply about the perceived accountability of business?

2 For many years, the global professional accountancy body, the Association of Chartered Certified Accountants (ACCA), has commissioned research seeking to advance social and environmental (or sustainability) accounting practices, and has sponsored annual social and environmental reporting awards in several countries. In recent years, many other professional accountancy bodies throughout the world have followed ACCA's lead by sponsoring research and actively fostering awareness among their members about these practices. Are social and environmental reporting issues really within the domain of professional accounting bodies? If not, who should be responsible for formulating social and environmental (or sustainability) reporting guidelines?

3 Consider your own opinions: what sort of social and environmental information do you think organizations should disclose (a normative question), and to whom should they make the disclosures (who are the relevant stakeholders)? Do you think your views about organizations' accountabilities would be the same as those of your fellow readers of this book? Just how subjective do you consider such assessments to be?

9.1 Introduction

The first seven chapters of this book predominantly focused on issues related to the role of externally published financial accounting information in providing information about the economic/financial performance of an entity. Given the title of this book – Financial Accounting Theory – such a focus on financial accounting would be anticipated. As we can appreciate from studying financial accounting, in most countries financial accounting is heavily regulated according to applicable corporations laws, stock exchange requirements and accounting standards. By contrast, there is a relative lack of regulatory requirements relating to the public disclosure of information about the social and environmental performance of an entity – the topic of attention in this chapter. This is despite growing concerns about issues such as climate change and the very real contribution large corporations make to this problem (and the capacity they have to help devise solutions). Nevertheless, for a number of years many organizations within Europe and throughout the world have been voluntarily providing public disclosures – in addition to the limited number of mandatory disclosures required by a few countries – about the social and environmental impact of their operations. Some of these organizations provide reasonably comprehensive accounts of their sustainability performance.[1]

In Chapter 8 we examined some issues related to accountability for the broader (non-financial) aspects of an organization's activities, by exploring theories that explain

---

[1] To gain an insight into the many and varied organizations that are producing social and environmental reports we can refer to various websites. At an international level CorporateRegister.com provides a link to corporations throughout the world that are producing social and environmental reports. Its website is located at www.CorporateRegister.com.

voluntary (unregulated) reporting practices. In this chapter we will develop our theoretical understanding of these issues, by examining aspects of the rapidly growing body of research that investigates the *social and environmental reporting* practices which are being adopted by an increasingly large number of organizations.

These social and environmental reporting practices are now often referred to as *sustainability reporting*, with the latter covering aspects of (the more traditional) financial/economic sustainability (or performance) of the reporting organization in addition to its social and environmental sustainability (or performance). Although there are some prominent academics who argue that it is misleading to use the term 'sustainability reporting' because the business practices which are being reported upon are far from being ecologically or socially sustainable (Gray, 2010) (this is a point we will return to in Chapter 12), as the term is currently commonly used in practice we will use the terms *sustainability reporting* and *social and environmental reporting* interchangeably in this chapter. We will use these terms to refer to the provision, to a range of stakeholders, of information about the performance of an entity with regard to its interaction with its physical and social environment, inclusive of information about an entity's support of employees, local and overseas communities, safety record and use of natural resources.

Social and environmental reporting is also commonly referred to as *corporate social responsibility reporting*. Corporate social responsibility itself has been defined in a variety of ways. A fairly accepted definition would be consistent with the definition provided by the Commission of European Communities (2001, p. 6). It defines corporate social responsibility as:

> a concept whereby companies integrate social and environmental concerns in their business operations and in their interaction with their stakeholders on a voluntary basis. Being socially responsible means not only fulfilling legal expectations, but also going beyond compliance and investing 'more' into human capital, the environment and the relations with stakeholders.

Because the area of social and environmental reporting is relatively new and continually evolving (and also generally unregulated), it is a very exciting area for accountants to be involved in. We are starting to see new 'breeds' of accountants – *environmental accountants* and *social accountants* – who work alongside 'traditional' financial accountants.

9.2 Brief overview of the historical development of social and environmental reporting practices

The public disclosure of information about the social and environmental impact of operations has become widespread among companies in many countries since the early 1990s, when a number of large companies made considerable advances in reporting aspects of their environmental impact. Subsequently, from about the mid-1990s, reporting about aspects of the social impact of organizations' operations became an increasingly popular practice (Buhr, 2007). Development of these practices in the early and mid-1990s tended to take the form of disclosures within the annual report (accompanying the annual financial accounts) about the environmental (and subsequently social) policies, practices and/or impacts of the reporting organization.

As these reporting practices became more widespread, and social and environmental disclosures made by some organizations became more extensive, some of the 'leading edge' reporting organizations began separating their detailed social and environmental disclosures from their annual report and financial statements – by publishing a separate stand-alone social and environmental report (while still providing a summary of these disclosures in their annual reports). These separate, stand-alone, reports were produced by a few corporations from the early 1990s and became more common from the late 1990s. They have now become standard practice among many large multinational companies in several industrial sectors and countries. Since the late 1990s, many corporations also made increasing use of the Internet to disseminate information about aspects of their social and environmental policies and performance (Adams and Frost, 2004). The Internet has also been used by a number of organizations to engage in dialogue with a variety of stakeholders about various social and environmental issues (Rinaldi and Unerman, 2009).

Although, as we have outlined in the previous paragraphs, social and environmental reporting practices have only become widespread in many countries since the early to mid-1990s, this does not tell the whole story of the development of these practices (Buhr, 2007). Some studies have found and analysed voluntary non-financial disclosures in a variety of different forms of corporate reports for periods commencing long before the 1990s' development of social and environmental reporting practices, and have demonstrated that forms of social and environmental reporting have existed for many decades.

For example, Guthrie and Parker (1989) examined social disclosures in the Australian company Broken Hill Proprietary (BHP – now part of one of the largest mining and minerals multinationals in the world, BHP Billiton) for a 100-year period from 1885; Unerman (2000b, 2000a) found evidence of social disclosures in a variety of reports produced annually by the Anglo-Dutch oil company Shell dating back to 1897 – with these disclosures becoming more prevalent from the 1950s; Hogner found evidence of social reporting practices at US Steel dating back to 1905; Tinker and Neimark (1987, 1988) and Niemark (1992) analysed social-type disclosures in the annual reports of the US company General Motors from 1916; and Adams and Harte (1998) analysed forms of social reporting in UK banks and retailers from 1935. There have also been several studies examining social and environmental disclosures in company reports from the 1960s and 1970s – such as Buhr (1998) and Campbell (2000). There was also a reasonable amount of practitioner attention paid in the 1970s to the information needs of a broad range of stakeholders, as evidenced by reports such as the UK's Corporate Report (Accounting Standards Steering Committee, 1975), although this interest largely faded in the 1980s. Thus the development of social and environmental reporting from the early 1990s might, more accurately, be considered a renaissance of non-financial reporting practices rather than a completely new phenomenon.

While we have been using the terminology 'social and environmental reporting' and 'sustainability reporting', another related term that gained prominence for a period from the late-1990s to the mid-2000s was *triple bottom line reporting*. Triple bottom line reporting has been defined by Elkington (1997) as reporting which provides information about the economic, environmental and social performance of an entity. The large multinational company Shell was responsible for popularizing the term 'triple bottom line reporting' as it was the first organization in the 1990s to release what it referred to as a triple bottom line report.

More recently the notion of 'triple bottom line reporting' has been displaced by recognition that social and environmental reports need to provide a more integrated picture of an organization's social, environmental and economic impacts and sustainability. It is now more widely accepted that the outcomes of most managerial decisions do not affect only the economic performance *or* the social performance *or* the environmental performance of the organization. Rather, there is a complex interplay between the direct and indirect social, environmental and economic impacts from any organizational action, and social and environmental reporting practices have developed to provide indications regarding this more complex integrated understanding of the interrelated sustainability impacts flowing from organizational strategies and actions (Hopwood *et al.*, 2010).

Because corporations are increasingly referring to 'sustainability' and 'sustainable development' as part of their business agendas we will now consider this term in more depth.

9.3 Developing notions of sustainability and sustainable development

Since the 1970s there has been much discussion in various forums about the implications of continued economic development for the environment and, relatedly, for humankind. Sustainable development is not something that will be easily achieved and many consider that, at least at this stage, it is nothing more than an ideal.

A significant step in placing *sustainability* on the agenda of governments and businesses worldwide was a report initiated by the General Assembly of the United Nations. The report entitled *Our Common Future* was presented in 1987 by the World Commission of Environment and Development chaired by Gro Harlem Brundtland, the then Norwegian Prime Minister. This important document subsequently became known as *The Brundtland Report*. The brief of the report was to produce a global agenda for change in order to combat or alleviate the ongoing pressures on the global environment – pressures considered as being clearly unsustainable. It was generally accepted that business organizations must change the way they do business and they must learn to question traditionally held business goals and principles (perhaps with encouragement from governments). The Brundtland Report defined sustainable development as:

> development that meets the needs of the present world without compromising the ability of future generations to meet their own needs. (World Commission on Environment and Development, 1987)

The Brundtland Report clearly identified that equity issues, and particularly issues associated with intergenerational equity, are central to the sustainability agenda. That is, it is argued that globally we must ensure that our generation's consumption patterns do not negatively impact on future generations' quality of life. Specifically, we should be in a position to say that the planet that we leave to our children is in as good a shape as the planet we inherited (and preferably in better shape). The move towards sustainability implies that something other than short-term self-interest should drive decision-making (this is a normative position). It implies that wealth creation for current generations should not be held as *the* all-consuming pursuit, and that consumption and personal wealth creation by us (now), while perhaps being considered as economically 'rational' (using the definition often applied in the economics literature), is not necessarily rational from a global and intergenerational perspective.[2]

There is evidence from a number of sources that, for many years, the ecological impacts of human (including business) activities has exceeded the earth's capacity to absorb these impacts (see, for example, Meadows *et al.*, 2004; Venetoulis *et al.*, 2004; Stern, 2007, 2009). This evidence demonstrates that our current levels of consumption (and other activities) are achieved at the expense of a degraded biosphere in which our children, grandchildren and great grandchildren will have to live. If we continue to 'consume' the world's environmental resources at this level, a time is likely to come where the biosphere will have been degraded to the extent that it can no longer support human life in anywhere near the numbers currently living. This is clearly an unsustainable position for nature, society and business profitability, and the scientific evidence shows that if we do not take any action to reduce our levels of greenhouse gas emissions, a catastrophic climate change 'tipping point' is likely to occur within the next 50 years. As with any complex situation, where numerous different natural systems interact, small parts of the body of evidence on climate change will not be consistent with the whole picture. However, taking individual small indicators out of context does not credibly challenge the overwhelming scientific consensus which, as Accounting Headline 9.1 argues, is that climate change from human activities is real, and urgent action needs to be taken to avoid reaching the catastrophic 'tipping point'.

Implicit in the above definition of sustainability is another requirement that intra-generational equity issues also need to be addressed – that is, the needs of all 'of the present world' inhabitants need to be met, which requires strategies to alleviate the poverty and starvation that currently besets the peoples of various countries. While from a moral perspective efforts should clearly be undertaken with a view to eradicating poverty and starvation (again, this is a normative assertion), from a broader perspective communities cannot be expected to focus on local or global environmental issues (necessary for sustainability) if they are in desperate need of money (for example, if they are starving, can they really be expected to keep their forests intact when such forests provide a means of 'free' heating and income?). Decisions by particular impoverished nations, such as to remove significant tracts of rainforest, can have significant global implications. Any vision of sustainability clearly needs to address poverty on a global scale.[3]

A further significant event that followed *The Brundtland Report* was the 1992 *Earth Summit* in Rio de Janeiro which was attended by government representatives from around the world as well as numerous social and environmental experts and non-government organizations. The *Earth Summit* again placed the issue of sustainable development at the

---

[2] Hence, the quest towards sustainable development ultimately relies upon people not being driven solely by their own short-term self-interest, and not putting wealth creation above all else. If we believed the assumptions embraced by Positive Accounting Theorists, as described in Chapter 7, that all action is driven by self-interest, then there would be little hope that people will ever consider the needs of future generations. Let's hope the assumptions of PAT theorists are not always right – or else this planet is in very big trouble!

[3] As another example of this, the severe landslide in the Philippines in February 2006 which claimed hundreds of victims was in part due to the removal of trees from illegal logging.

Accounting Headline 9.1

Scientific consensus on severity and urgency of climate change from human activities

Obama must take a lead on climate change – and soon

Scepticism is a healthy attitude to adopt to many, if not all, untested propositions. Sceptics throughout history, by applying their reasoned judgment and hard-headed critical faculties, have exposed lies, delusions and superstition.

Which is why scepticism is entirely the wrong word to apply to those who deny that emissions of carbon dioxide from human activity are leading to rises in average global temperatures, with potentially disastrous consequences. True sceptics respond to evidence.

Last week more evidence was published to support the established case for man-made global warming. Research, led by the US National Oceanic and Atmospheric Administration, drew on data from 11 possible indicators of climate and found that each one suggested warming consistent with expected effects of rising concentrations of greenhouse gases. Snow cover in the northern hemisphere is shrinking, glaciers are retreating, sea levels are rising, oceans and the atmosphere are warming. As it was put by Peter Stott, head of climate monitoring at the Met Office, which participated in the study: 'The fingerprints are clear'.

The data in this study were not included in the 2007 UN Intergovernmental Panel on Climate Change report that has been the main target of attack by climate change deniers. The IPCC's authority was badly damaged by 'climategate' – the leak of emails between scientists at the University of East Anglia, purporting to show a conspiracy to suppress inconvenient data.

In fact, as subsequent inquiries have shown, the emails proved at worst a cavalier and somewhat arrogant attitude on the part of scientists to critics of their work and a secretive, siege mentality in response to climate deniers. The actual scientific case for global warming was unscathed.

And yet, somehow the whole affair had a disproportionate effect in stifling public urgency over climate change. It did not help that the Copenhagen summit, shortly afterwards, billed in advance as the vital last chance opportunity for global action, resulted in an opaque compromise cobbled together at the eleventh hour mainly so heavyweight politicians in attendance could claim to have done some kind of deal.

That did little to advance the cause of public confidence or understanding. Since then, economic crisis and budget austerity have cleared pretty much all other considerations off political agendas in the developed world.

Democrats in the US Senate have now abandoned President Obama's climate bill, a modest affair to introduce some cap-and-trade mechanism to reduce emissions. Federal climate regulation now looks dead for the foreseeable future.

It is both baffling and sadly predictable that it should be so hard to turn a matter of near certain scientific urgency into political action. It is also profoundly depressing that the chances of concerted global action to protect the environment seem to be receding.

Source: *The Observer, Editorial,* 1 August 2010, p. 26
©Guardian News and Media Limited 2010

forefront of international politics and business. Globally, the Summit attracted considerable media attention. An important outcome of the *Earth Summit* was Agenda 21, which was deemed to be an action plan for the twenty-first century and which placed sustainability as the core consideration for ongoing national and global development.

In the same year as the *Earth Summit* (1992) the European Union (EU) released a document entitled *Towards Sustainability* as part of its *Fifth Action Programme*. One of the suggestions of the programme was for the accounting profession to take a role in implementing costing systems that internalize many environmental costs. As we discuss later in this chapter, traditional financial accounting typically ignores social and environmental costs and benefits. Specifically, the EU called for a 'redefinition of accounting concepts, rules, conventions and methodology so as to ensure that the consumption and use of environmental resources are accounted for as part of the full cost of production and reflected in market prices' (European Commission, 1992, Vol. II, Section 7.4, p. 67). The rationale for the EU's proposal was that if the prices reflected the 'full costs' of production, including environmental costs, then such costs would flow through the various production and consumption cycles, and as a result of the higher costs there would be an inclination towards more sustainable consumption patterns.[4] Although, as noted earlier in this chapter, ACCA has taken a lead on these types of sustainability issues for many years, it is only comparatively recently that other professional accountancy bodies have followed ACCA's lead by promoting among their members the importance of a range of accounting for sustainability practices.

In 2002 a follow-up to the Rio de Janeiro *Earth Summit* was held in Johannesburg. One of the outcomes of this *2002 Earth Summit* was the launch of a revised set of guidelines for the process of reporting the social and environmental impact of an organization's operations. These guidelines are known as the *Sustainability Reporting Guidelines* and were developed by a broad range of organizations under the auspices of the *Global Reporting Initiative* (GRI). We will discuss these guidelines and the GRI in more depth later in this chapter.

Since the important early developments of notions of sustainability in the late 1980s/early 1990s, many governments, industry and professional associations and non-government organizations have released various documents addressing the need for shifts towards sustainable development. Indeed, sustainability appears to have become a central part of the language of government and business worldwide, and the definition provided within *The Brundtland Report* has attracted widespread acceptance. As an example, consider the following statement in the introduction to Nokia's sustainability reporting principles within its 2009 *Sustainability Report* (p. 31):

> Nokia has published corporate responsibility reports since 2002 and we have reported our environmental activities continually since 1999. Sustainability means balancing economic, environmental and social priorities so that the needs of the present do not compromise the needs of the future. For Nokia this means taking environmental and social considerations into account in managing our operations, and developing mobile solutions that make a positive impact.

---

[4] There is an ethical issue here in that the higher priced goods will thereafter only be available to the wealthier. That is, the supply of those goods with a high 'environmental price' will be restricted to the wealthier people.

A more detailed explanation about a particular organization's commitment to sustainability is given in the following extract from the UK Co-operative Group's *Sustainability Report 2009* (p. 10):

> The Co-operative seeks to deliver value to its stakeholders in an ecologically sustainable and socially responsible manner.
>
> The Co-operative recognises the need to manage and develop its businesses in a sustainable manner – ie, business development that meets the needs of the present without compromising the ability of future generations to meet their own needs.
>
> We will seek to be transparent and accountable in our pursuit of sustainable development: reporting on progress (or the lack of it), securing independent verification and setting clear priorities and targets for all material activities.
>
> We recognise that there are physical limits to the resources of the Earth (both in terms of generating materials and absorbing wastes), and that any business activity that exceeds these limits is, by definition, unsustainable in the long term and will need to be reconstituted. Nature cannot withstand a progressive build-up of waste derived from the Earth's crust, nor can it withstand a progressive build-up of society's waste, particularly substances that cannot degrade into harmless materials. In addition, the productive area of Nature should not be diminished in terms of quality (diversity) or quantity (volume) and must be enabled to grow. These we recognise as the minimum conditions for ecological sustainability.
>
> There are ethical components of sustainable development for which business should be accountable. These extend far beyond legislative compliance. Unlike for ecological sustainability, there exists much less consensus as to what constitutes socially responsible business practice. Therefore, when considering such matters, The Co-operative will undertake stakeholder dialogue and be guided by the views arising, particularly those of members and customers, given their vital roles in governance and economic viability, respectively. More broadly, The Co-operative will be guided by the long-established co-operative values of self-help, self-responsibility, democracy, equality, equity and solidarity, along with the pursuit of legislative compliance.

From the perspective of a global bank, the Group Chairman's introduction to HSBC's *Sustainability Report 2009* (p. 2) explained that:

> At HSBC, sustainability is not just about how we do business, it is part of our very raison d'être. As a leading international and emerging markets bank, we are especially aware of our responsibility to manage our business across the world for the long term by making a real contribution to social and economic development, and by protecting the environment in which we operate.
>
> … While it is vital that we support social and economic development, we also recognise that this inevitably leads to competing demands on the world's resources. This brings challenges for those who finance that development. We are, therefore, working with the energy sector, for example, to recognise

and balance the increasing demands for power with emerging environmental concerns, and we continue to screen all our Project Financing in line with the Equator Principles.

... Each one of our 300,000 employees is an important contributor to our sustainable future. We seek to reward them appropriately in order to meet the long-term goals of our business, and also to create a working environment where financial reward is not the only motivating factor.

... This report touches on each of these themes and covers in more detail the ways in which HSBC affects the social, economic and environmental issues our customers and communities face. It describes the different ways in which we are building sustainability issues into the fabric of our culture, from how we manage our carbon footprint, to the way we treat and support our employees globally, and to how we build social and environmental criteria into business decisions.

... As HSBC faces the opportunities and challenges of this new decade, I would only reinforce the Board's commitment to running our business for the long term – and to playing our part in creating a sustainable future for our customers, employees and the communities we serve.

The above quotes show that sustainability is something that is in the minds of business on a global scale and as such it is something of which students of business and accounting should be aware. Adopting perspectives provided by several of the theories we explored in Chapter 8, we can further argue that if sustainability becomes part of the expectations held by society (that is, if it becomes part of the 'social contract'), then it must become a business goal. As the concept of sustainable development continues to become part of various communities' expectations, communities will expect to be provided with information about how organizations, governments and other entities have performed against the central requirements of sustainability.

9.4 Reporting on integrated understandings of sustainability and sustainable development

Integrated sustainability reporting, if properly implemented, is often perceived as providing information that enables report readers to assess how sustainable an organization's or a community's operations are. The perspective taken is that for an organization (or a community) to be sustainable (a long-run perspective) it must achieve an optimum balance between financial security (as evidenced through such measures as profitability); minimizing (or ideally eliminating) its negative environmental impacts; and acting in conformity with societal expectations or else risk losing its 'community licence to operate' (a concept that was discussed in Chapter 8).

These three aspects of sustainability tend to converge over longer time horizons. In the short term, it is possible to generate financial profits while negatively impacting upon society and the environment. In the medium term, given that businesses operate within society, negative impacts on society caused by some business activities might lead to a breakdown in social functions which are necessary to continued business profitability.

The argument here is that most businesses rely on the effective functioning of many social systems – such as physical infrastructure (transport systems, utilities and so on), well-ordered markets and a respect for property rights (law and order). If any of these systems breaks down then future profitability will be threatened.

Although some businesses might evolve to address, and thereby earn profits from, breakdowns in some social systems, these are unlikely to address all the problems arising for many businesses from large-scale social breakdown and will add financial costs to many businesses which will have to buy additional services from the market. For example, *if* a narrow focus on profit maximization by many businesses contributed to increased unemployment and poverty in many sections of society, and then *if* this led to a breakdown in law and order, then while some businesses could profit from supplying additional private security services to those with wealth who were threatened by the breakdown in law and order, many other businesses could suffer a negative economic outcome as their activities/markets might be negatively affected through the breakdown in law and order, and they might have to pay for additional private security services.

We stress that this scenario is just one of many possible outcomes from a business focus on profit maximization, and many people would argue that other scenarios are more likely to occur. Nevertheless, it is a possible scenario, and highlights one (of many) possible ways in which a narrow focus on short-term profit maximization could contribute to a breakdown in social systems.[5] As this scenario demonstrates, in the medium term if a narrow focus on profit maximization leads to a breakdown in social systems, then this might be neither socially nor financially/economically sustainable.

In the longer term, the convergence of economic, social and environmental sustainability is reasonably clear. This argument is that the economy (including business activities) and all social systems operate within the natural environment. As outlined earlier in this chapter, if business (and other human) activities contribute to the destruction of the biosphere, then there will be no humans left to run businesses, buy the products of businesses or operate social systems. In an extreme scenario, destruction of the environment leads to destruction of the human race, following which there would clearly be no profits or social systems. Thus, in the longer term, environmental sustainability is necessary for both social and economic sustainability, so attention to minimizing negative impacts in respect of the environment is necessary to ensure a sustainable social and economic future.

In a less extreme but still very worrying scenario, an influential report by the UK economist Lord Stern (2007) has estimated that the economic costs arising from levels of climate change that are likely to be seen if we do not change our current business and social activities could amount to a reduction of somewhere between 5 per cent and 20 per cent of per-capita consumption:

> analyses that take into account the full ranges of both impacts and possible outcomes – that is, that employ the basic economics of risk – suggest that BAU

---

[5] Some people would argue that an actual example of largely unrestrained profit maximization leading to a breakdown in many social systems occurred in Russia during the 1990s – in the period of 'cowboy capitalism' following the collapse of the Soviet Union, when a small proportion of the population became very wealthy while vast numbers had little to eat.

[business as usual] climate change will reduce welfare by an amount equivalent to a reduction in consumption per head of between 5 and 20%. Taking account of the increasing scientific evidence of greater risks, of aversion to the possibilities of catastrophe, and of a broader approach to the consequences than implied by narrow output measures, the appropriate estimate is likely to be in the upper part of this range. (p. x)

One implication of these arguments is that it is necessary to sacrifice some short-term economic profitability to ensure long-term sustainable economic profits within a sustainable social and ecological system. Lord Stern's review (2007, p. xiii) estimated that the costs of taking the urgent environmental action needed now to avert the likelihood of catastrophic climate change in the coming decades would amount to perhaps 1 per cent of global GDP per annum. This is a much lower figure than the above estimates of the costs that future generations will have to bear if we do not take the necessary action, and that will drive down long-term business profitability.

However, Dillard *et al.* (2005, p. 81) explain that, in practice, an obstacle to an integrated approach to sustainability is that 'social systems (i.e., humans and their intentionality) have come to dominate and exploit natural systems' – in particular economics (profit) based social systems are dominant. They argue that moves towards sustainability will therefore require an explicit reversal of this socially constructed dominance of the economic over the ecological. We can only ponder whether such a reversal can occur. Based on your own assumptions about what drives human behaviour, what do you think?

An example of the apparent dominance of economic over ecological and social elements of sustainability in business strategic and operational decision-making, and one that also demonstrates the potential for a shorter-term impact of social and ecological unsustainability on economic sustainability, is provided by the major explosion on BP's Deepwater Horizon oil platform in the Gulf of Mexico on 20 April 2010. The immediate social impact of the explosion was that it killed 11 workers who were on board the oil platform. In the following weeks and months, despite many expensive attempts by BP and the US government to stop the massive on-going leak of oil into the Gulf of Mexico, a major ecological and social disaster unfolded. As Accounting Headline 9.2 shows, the accident caused the largest accidental oil spill in history and the pollution devastated many eco-systems in the Gulf, including killing many birds, fish, plants and other elements of the food chain – both in the sea and along large stretches of coastline. This, in turn, had a major impact on the livelihoods of many Gulf communities that relied on the coastline and the sea for their living (such as fishermen and hoteliers). The cost of stemming the leak, cleaning up part of the pollution, and paying fines and compensation to those whose earnings were affected cost BP many billions of dollars – on top of a negative impact on BP's reputation, especially among US citizens and politicians. Accounting Headline 9.3 reports on investigations by the US Congress that indicated a culture at BP dominated by a drive for short-term cost saving, and it is interesting to contrast any short-term cost savings BP might have made by taking less care over the safety aspects of their drilling operations on the Deepwater Horizon against the massive costs (both direct and in term of loss of reputation) from the outcome of the accident.

Accounting Headline 9.2

Economic feedback of social and environmental impacts

A deadly addiction: figures confirm BP well blowout is history's biggest accidental marine spill

By Damian Carrington

We thought it was big, but now we know it is huge – the greatest accidental marine oil spill in all history. The latest calculations of the vast quantity of oil polluting the Gulf of Mexico after the blowout of BP's Macondo well conclude that 4.9m barrels poured into the ocean. The scientists making the estimate believe it is accurate to within 10%, so even the smallest leak would be a third bigger than the 3.3m barrels released into Mexico's Bay of Campeche when the Ixtoc I oil rig blew out in 1979. The largest ever was the 11m barrels deliberately spilled by retreating Iraqi troops in 1991.

... For the families of the 11 men who died on the Deepwater rig nothing has changed. For BP, it can start to make some calculations of the fines it may face: $5bn, or over $20bn if it is found to have been grossly negligent. Harder to estimate is the compensation the company will have to pay to those who lost their livelihoods because of the spill, from fishermen to strippers. BP's efforts to cap their payments by offering one-off deals in return for signing away the right to sue seems in bad taste, but the hard-up may be tempted and in any case the relationship between the residents of the Gulf states and big oil is complex. Many have lived well off the industry and when a federal ban on some drilling was imposed the court case to overturn it had a good deal of popular support.

But the biggest unknown is what will happen to the Gulf itself and the coastal wetlands that fringe it and that is because BP buried much of the oil below the surface. By injecting at least 1.8m gallons of dispersant chemicals into the plumes of oil, BP kept the oil out of sight and may have prevented some oiling of the shores. But the consequences for the food chain in the gulf are completely unknown, and the dispersant is just as toxic as the oil.

Also unknown is how the oil will interact with the huge 'dead zones' that afflict the gulf. These result from the wasted farm fertiliser washed down the Mississippi and other rivers into the gulf, where it spawns algal blooms which consume all the oxygen in the water. This year's dead zone is likely to be the biggest ever, greater than the state of Massachusetts, and early research shows the oil will make it worse.

More difficult to call is the consequence of a hurricane ripping through the gulf, as is likely before the end of the season in November. Such a storm could drive oil on to land, causing further damage, but it could also break up and disperse the oil, speeding its decomposition. Another positive factor is the gulf's latitude: the warm ocean there speeds the evaporation and digestion of the oil by bacteria.

Source: *Guardian*, 4 August 2010
©Guardian News and Media Limited 2010

Accounting Headline 9.3

Short-term economic cost savings leading to large social and ecological costs

Gulf oil spill: 'I don't recall', says BP chief to Congress

By Suzanne Goldenberg

It was, for Tony Hayward and members of a powerful congressional committee investigating the oil spill catastrophe in the Gulf, a mutually frustrating experience.

The much-awaited inquisition of the BP chief executive saw him resort yesterday to the favourite defence of corporate America when hauled up before committees of Congress: 'I don't recall.'

The strategy may have been legally prudent for Hayward, who was testifying under oath, but it did little to salvage the reputation of a man in the running for title of most reviled executive in America.

It also wiped out any goodwill which he may have generated by having started off his testimony with an apology.

Seven hours after the executive first walked into the wood-panelled room, the most significant admission the committee could wring out was that, maybe, someone at BP should have realised the drilling of the well was going horribly wrong.

... Members scoffed at Hayward's claim that he had in his three years as chief executive been devoted to improving safety, pulling out press clippings from 2007 in which he complained of 'excessive caution', and having too many people in decision-making. He also got short shrift for saying he was 'distraught' about what had happened, following a request by Waxman for a 'yes or no' on whether Hayward had kept to an expressed commitment at his appointment to focus 'like a laser' on safety. 'I don't want to know whether you're distraught; I want to know whether you've kept your commitment.'

The anger was fuelled by what Waxman called an astonishing culture of 'corporate complacency'. The committee reviewed 30,000 pages of documents from BP, but while it was widely known it had a 'nightmare well' in the Deepwater Horizon, none of those concerns percolated up to Hayward. 'We could find no evidence you paid any attention to the tremendous risks,' Waxman said.

Through the day, that was the theme. Members would read out emails from BP engineers pointing to a disaster waiting to unfold. There were emails acknowledging a problem on the well, and others suggesting BP gleefully over-rode those concerns. 'Who cares, it's done, end of story, will probably be fine,' said one email, which authorised a short-cut in positioning the well. 'It appears to me BP knowingly risked well failure to save a few million dollars,' said Waxman. 'Don't you feel any responsibility for those decisions?'

Hayward replied: 'I feel a great deal of responsibility for the accident.' But if the committee wanted further information on decisions to ignore warning signs, he would be of little help. 'I can't pass judgment on those decisions. I am not prepared to draw conclusions about this accident, until such time as this investigation is complete,' he said. 'I simply was not involved in the decision-making process. I haven't drawn a conclusion.'

Source: *Guardian*, 18 June 2010, p. 6
©Guardian News and Media Limited 2010

9.5 Stages of sustainability reporting

Having established that social and environmental reporting (or sustainability reporting) is not a new phenomenon, and having discussed the concept of sustainable development, we will now turn our attention to various assessments or decisions that need to be made in the process of reporting aspects of an organization's social and environmental performance. Such decisions relate to the following issues:

- *Why* does the entity wish to disclose publicly information about its social and environmental performance (its motivation for disclosure)?
- Who are the stakeholders *to whom* the social and environmental disclosures will be directed?
- *What* information and issues should the social and environmental disclosures address (what are the information needs of the stakeholders)?
- *How* should the reports be compiled, in terms of the format of the information to be disclosed?

The first issue above – *why* would an entity decide to report? – relates to managers' motivations to report. For example, an organization would need to consider whether it is reporting because it believes it has an accountability to various stakeholders, or whether, perhaps, it is reporting because it wants to win the support of powerful stakeholders. That is, the broad objectives driving any particular organization to undertake sustainability reporting can range from an ethically motivated desire to ensure that the organization benefits, or does not negatively impact upon, society and the natural environment, through to an economically focused motive to use social and environmental reporting to protect or enhance shareholder economic value. We discussed aspects of this range of motives in Chapter 8, when we explored the ethical/moral (or normative) and the managerial branches of stakeholder theory. In this chapter we will add to these perspectives by introducing additional research studies that address the broad objectives (or motives) which seek to explain why organizations engage in social and environmental reporting. Once it is determined why an entity decides to report, this decision will in turn inform the decision as *to whom* the information will be directed (the second bullet point above).

Referring back to our discussion in Chapter 8 of the ethical/moral and the managerial branches of stakeholder theory, it should be clear that if a corporation's social and environmental reporting is motivated exclusively by managerial reasoning and strategizing, then the stakeholders to whom that corporation's social and environmental reporting is directed might be narrowly defined as those stakeholders who hold and exercise the greatest economic power over the corporation. Conversely, social and environmental reporting motivated by ethical/moral reasoning (the ethical branch of stakeholder theory as described in Chapter 8) will seek to address the information needs of a broader range of stakeholders. Specifically, a broader 'ethical' approach to reporting would direct the reports towards those stakeholders most affected by the operations of the organization.

Once the organization has determined which stakeholders are the target recipients of the reports they can then consider the information demands of these particular stakeholders. This will then inform *what* types of information will be disclosed (the third bullet point above) and *what* issues the social and environmental reporting should address. Identifying what issues an entity is held responsible and accountable for by its stakeholders involves dialogue between the organization and its identified target stakeholders. Several research studies have addressed aspects of this process of communication with stakeholders.

The final stage in the social and environmental reporting process is then the production of a report (or more than one form of report) in a format that addresses these issues (or stakeholders' information needs). This is a very broad stage that involves many more detailed stages regarding *how* the report(s) should be compiled. In this stage several elements of the social and environmental reporting process diverge considerably from the financial reporting processes embodied in financial accounting conceptual frameworks, although some issues (such as reliability of information) are important in both.

In the following pages of this chapter we will structure our examination of sustainability reporting in accordance with the *why – to whom – for what – how* stages of social and environmental reporting explained above. We will begin with a detailed exploration of motives (or objectives, or the *why* question) for organizations in general, and business corporations specifically, to engage in corporate social responsibility and sustainability reporting.

9.6 Objectives of the social and environmental reporting process – the *why* stage

Social and environmental reporting – the topic of this chapter – is predominantly a voluntary process given the general lack of regulation in the area. Even with the lack of regulation in most countries, many organizations publicly release information about their social and environmental performance. This leads to the obvious question of why do they choose to do it? What motivates them to release this information voluntarily? Answers to such questions are directly tied to our beliefs about what drives individual behaviour.

As we have seen from previous chapters, different researchers will have differing views about why companies adopt particular operating and reporting strategies. For example:

1 In Chapter 8 we considered legitimacy theory and the associated notion of a 'social contract'. Adopting this perspective we could argue that an entity would undertake certain social activities (and provide an account thereof) if management perceived that the particular activities were expected by the communities in which it operates. That is, it is part of the social contract, or as companies often state, part of their licence to operate.

2 In Chapter 8 we also considered stakeholder theory. We learned that one version of stakeholder theory (the *managerial/positive* version and *not* the *ethical/normative* version) predicts that management is more likely to focus on meeting the expectations of powerful stakeholders. Powerful stakeholders are those who control resources that are both scarce and essential to the achievement of the organization's (or its managers') objectives. For most businesses, powerful stakeholders will be those who have the greatest potential to influence the firm's ability to generate maximum financial returns (or profits) – in other words, those stakeholders with the most economic power and influence over the firm. Under this *managerial* stakeholder perspective, management would be expected to embrace those economic, social and environmental activities

expected by the powerful stakeholders, and to provide an account of those activities to these stakeholders. Chapter 8 also showed that there was an ethical branch of stakeholder theory. This branch adopts a normative position and prescribes that an organization should consider the rights of all parties affected by the operation of the entity regardless of the power they can exercise. Under this perspective, the definition of stakeholders would be broader and would be consistent with the definition provided by Freeman (1984). Freeman defines a stakeholder as 'any group or individual who can affect *or is affected by* the achievement of the firm's objectives' (emphasis added). Hence, the answer to the 'why report' question is directly a function of whether management embraces ethical or managerial reasoning.

3 In Chapter 8 we further considered the accountability model developed by Gray *et al.* (1996). Under this normative model, which has much in common with the ethical branch of stakeholder theory, organizations have many responsibilities (at a minimum, as required by law but expanded by society's expectations that have not also been codified within the law), and with every organizational responsibility comes a set of rights for stakeholders. These include rights to information (accountability) from the organization to demonstrate how it has performed in relation to the responsibilities it has to its stakeholders. Obviously, determining responsibilities is not a straightforward exercise – different people will have different perspectives of the responsibilities of business, and hence the accountability of business. The accountability model is related to the ethical branch of stakeholder theory.

4 We also considered institutional theory in Chapter 8. This perspective assumes that the managers of an organization will develop or adopt new practices (such as corporate social responsibility and/or social and environmental reporting) because of a variety of institutional pressures. For example: other organizations developing new practices in these areas and managers being concerned that, if they do not emulate these other organizations, they will risk disapproval from some of their economically powerful stakeholders.

5 Another perspective we considered briefly in Chapter 8 was reputation risk management. This perspective refines some of the above perspectives that assume the main managerial motivation for voluntary reporting is maximization of profits. With reputation risk management it is assumed that the reputation of any organization has an economic value, and managers will use voluntary reporting practices (such as sustainability reporting) to seek to protect and enhance the value and income generating potential of the organization's reputation among its economically powerful stakeholders.

6 In Chapter 7 we considered Positive Accounting Theory. This theory predicts that all people are driven by self-interest.[6] As such, this theory predicts that particular social

---

[6] As such, and as already indicated, it is probably not a theory that provides a great deal of hope in terms of moves towards sustainable development – moves which, if we accept *The Brundtland Report* definition of sustainability discussed earlier in this chapter, would require current generations to consider forgoing consumption and wealth generation to ensure that future generations' needs are met. Sacrificing current consumption and wealth creation for the benefit of future generations and Positive Accounting Theory's central assumption of self-interest could be deemed to be mutually inconsistent.

and environmental activities, and their related disclosure, would only occur if they had positive wealth implications for the managers involved.

Hence, from the discussion above there could be various motivations for managers to decide to voluntarily disclose information – inclusive of information about social and environmental performance. These various theoretical perspectives on the broad reasons why organizations might engage in voluntary social and environmental reporting practices are not mutually exclusive. Furthermore, as emphasized throughout this book, the acceptance of particular theories to explain particular actions is, at least in part, tied to one's own value system.

While the above discussion of possible motivations to report is tied to particular theories it is interesting to consider some factors that industry believes motivates corporations to be socially responsible, and to provide an account of their social and environmental performance. Drawing on the insights provided by a number of surveys and reports by business-related organizations, Hopwood *et al.* (2010, pp. 10–15) explain the following components that contribute to 'the business case for embedding sustainability into decision-making':

■ The role of improved sustainability management in winning and retaining customers who have personal commitments and concerns about the social and environmental sustainability impacts of businesses.

■ The competitive advantage that a focus on improved sustainability management can bring, for example through identifying opportunities for innovation and new products.

■ Attracting, motivating and retaining skilled staff who have personal concerns about sustainability issues – with these valued staff often preferring to work for organizations that demonstrate a commitment to sustainability.

■ Managing risks arising from sustainability issues as demonstrated, for example, with the BP Deepwater Horizon example discussed earlier in this chapter.

■ Driving operational efficiencies through direct cost savings linked to social and environmental factors – such as reduced energy usage through improved efficiency in energy use and reduced waste.

■ Maintaining an organization's licence to operate – linked to the social contract discussed in Chapter 8.

■ Accessing capital, where an increasing number of investors and lenders are adopting social and environmental sustainability screening factors in their investment and lending decisions.

■ The impact on the valuable reputation and brand image of a business from positive or negative sustainability incidents – such as the BP Deepwater Horizon incident discussed earlier and the supply chain ethics issues discussed in Chapter 8 where some clothing companies in the past suffered reputational damage as a result of poor labour practices at their suppliers.

Any consideration of what motivates managers to report particular information cannot be considered in the absence of a consideration of the accountabilities of business. As indicated within the accountability model proposed by Gray *et al.* (1996) – as described in Chapter 8 and as briefly referred to above – whether the management of an organization elects to disclose particular information (that is, whether they will provide an account), will at least in part, be linked to their own perceptions about whether they believe they are accountable for particular types of performance. That is, the act of providing particular accounts (that is, accounting) is directly tied to perceptions about the responsibilities and associated accountabilities of business.

A narrow view of business responsibilities

Moves by many companies throughout the world to implement reporting mechanisms that provide information about the social and environmental performance of their entities imply that the management of these organizations consider that they have an accountability not only for their economic performance, but also for their social and environmental performance. While this is a view held by many individuals, it is not necessarily a view that is accepted universally. For example, if we were to adopt a fairly extreme view that corporations do not have social or moral responsibilities beyond simply generating profits for the benefits of owners, then we might not see the need to produce social and environmental accounts except to the extent that such accounts might enhance corporate profitability. For example, consider the views of the famous economist Milton Friedman. In his widely cited book, *Capitalism and Freedom*, Friedman (1962) rejected the view that corporate managers have any moral obligations beyond maximizing their profits. In relation to the view that organizations have social responsibilities he noted (p. 133) that such a view:

> shows a fundamental misconception of the character and nature of a free economy. In such an economy, there is one and only one social responsibility of business, to use its resources and engage in activities designed to increase its profits as long as it stays within the rules of the game, which is to say, engages in open and free competition, without deception or fraud.[7]

Arguably, Milton Friedman would not have been a strong advocate for social and environmental reporting – unless of course it could be linked to enhancing business profitability.

If we were to accept that an entity has a responsibility and accountability for its social and environmental performance, then as accountants we would accept a duty to provide an account of an organization's social and environmental performance. However, if we accept the Friedman view then we will not be motivated to provide such an account. For example, if we adopt a perspective that the dominant accountability of a corporation is to its shareholders in terms of its financial performance then we might believe that corporations only need to provide an account of their financial performance. There will be no motivation to provide social and environmental performance information to a

---

[7] According to Clarkson (1995, p. 103), 'Friedman chose to interpret social issues and social responsibilities to mean non-business issues and non-business responsibilities. He, like so many neo-classical economists, separated business from society, which enabled him to maintain that "the business of business is business". By placing the two abstractions of business and society into separate compartments, Friedman was able to deny the necessity, or even the validity, of the concept of corporate social responsibility, decrying it as a fundamentally subversive doctrine'.

broader group of stakeholders. Indeed, this is a view which arguably has been embraced by many regulators in the past who have fixated on putting in place extensive regulations in relation to financial accounting, but who have tended to ignore the regulation of social and environmental accounting. Such regulators would seem to question the relevance of social and environmental accountability.

Such a narrow approach to accountability, in which prime attention appears to be given to the needs and expectations of shareholders and other individuals with a financial stake in the organization (rather than stakeholders generally), is commonly referred to as a 'shareholder primacy' view of corporate reporting. This approach to regulating external reporting is found in many countries. Likewise, if students who study 'accounting' at university are simply taught about how to account for organizations from a financial perspective, without consideration of social or environmental performance, then those in charge of the programmes must in themselves be embracing a perspective that the major responsibility and accountability of a business organization is restricted to its financial performance. Is this a reasonable assumption to make?

Somewhat surprisingly, many students of accounting complete their accounting qualifications without ever considering issues associated with the accountability of business. But the practice of accounting which, at a fairly simplistic level, can be defined as the provision of information about the performance of an entity to a particular stakeholder group, cannot be divorced from a consideration of the extent of an entity's responsibility and accountability. That is, an organization will provide an account of those things for which it is deemed to be accountable. One cannot be considered without the other (so we should be left wondering how a study of accounting can be undertaken without a detailed consideration of the concept of corporate accountabilities).

Some argue that managers and organizations which embrace the stakeholder primacy perspective will actually benefit everybody within society because if the actions of all individuals (and businesses) are motivated solely by a self-interested desire to maximize personal wealth, then the resulting economic growth and the wealth generated by the successful individuals will 'trickle down' to the less successful. With this view, they argue, the conditions of all in society will be improved if all people in society actively pursue their own self-interest, with this being a morally desirable outcome. Indeed, this 'trickle down' theory is commonly repeated as a key moral justification for the capitalist system. The main problem with this moral justification for a narrow and exclusive focus on maximizing shareholder wealth (or shareholder value) is that there is little, if any, evidence to show that it occurs. As Gray (2005, pp. 6–7) states:

> It is disturbing … to discover that there is no direct evidence to support this precarious construction. The view relies, for its empirical support, on the generalised argument that, for example, we are all better off than we have ever been; that we are all getting better off all the time; and that this increase in well-being has coincided with the triumph of international capitalism. Such arguments are, at best, contestable. Whilst for many in the West this statement has a superficial veracity, it ignores the growing gap between rich and poor…

A considerable amount of economic evidence shows that not only is there lack of support for the existence of a generalized 'trickle down' effect, but the reverse may have occurred.

Hence many people question whether the social and environmental responsibilities of corporations should be left largely unregulated. For example, Hutton (1996, p. 172) provides evidence that in the largely free-market economic conditions of the United Kingdom in the 1980s, the real (inflation-adjusted) incomes of the wealthiest tenth of the population rose by more than 50 per cent, while the poorest 15 per cent of the population experienced a real-terms fall in their incomes.

Despite an apparent lack of empirical support for this 'moral' position underlying a narrow focus on shareholder value, we could be excused for thinking that many individuals working within the contemporary financial press hold the same view as Friedman. The financial press continues to praise companies for increased profitability and to criticize companies who are subject to falling profitability. They often do this with little or no regard to any social costs or social benefits being generated by the operations of the particular entities – costs and benefits not directly incorporated within reported profit. Indeed, it is not uncommon to see a report in the financial press that a particular company generated a sound profit *despite* increased wage costs. In such a context there is an implication that returns to one stakeholder (employees) are somehow bad, but gains to other stakeholders (the owners of capital) are good. As Collison (2003, p. 7) states:

> Financial description of the factors of production in the business media, and even in textbooks, makes clear that profit is an output to be maximised while recompense to labour is a cost to be minimised. Furthermore, a high cost of capital may be described as an exogenous constraint on business, rather than as an indication of the size of resource flows to providers of capital. *Financial Times* contributors are fond of words like 'ominous' to describe real wage rises: such words are not used to describe profit increases.

However, actions motivated purely by short-term economic considerations may, sometimes, result in a social and/or environmental outcome that is welcomed by many in society. Georgakopoulos and Thomson (2005) provide an example of this in the decision of some Scottish fish farms to institute organic farming practices. They state (p. 50) that:

> The shift to organic production was unproblematic and relatively inexpensive. It was not a reaction to protest movements nor was organic salmon regarded as a safer, healthy, product. The decision was not subjected to systematic account-ing evaluations. The shift to organic production was driven by the prospect of higher market prices and securing sales in a climate of declining market prices and volumes for 'unorganic' salmon.

A broader view of business responsibilities

Returning to the narrow view (Friedman, 1962) that the maximization of profits (or shareholder value) should be management's top priority, it should be noted that there is (as you might expect) a contrary view embraced by many researchers working in the area of corporate social and environmental reporting. This is that organizations, public or private, *earn* their right to operate within the community. This right, which we considered in Chapter 8, is provided by the society in which they exist, and not solely by those parties with a direct financial interest (such as the shareholders who directly benefit from increasing profits) or by government. That is, business organizations themselves are artificial entities that society chooses to create. Donaldson (1982) notes that if society chooses to create organizations, they can also choose either not to create them or to create different entities. The view held is that organizations do not have an inherent right to resources. As Mathews (1993, p. 26) states:

> Society (as a collection of individuals) provides corporations with their legal standing and attributes and the authority to own and use natural resources and to hire employees. Organisations draw on community resources and output both goods and services and waste products in the general environment. The organisation has no inherent rights to these benefits and, in order to allow their existence, society would expect the benefits to exceed the costs to society.

Consequently, the corporation receives its permission to operate from society, and is ultimately accountable to society for how it operates and what it does (Benston, 1982).

If society (and not just shareholders) considers that increasing profits is the overriding duty of organizations, then this factor alone may be sufficient (as Friedman argues) to ensure the business's survival. However, if society has greater expectations (such as that the organization must provide goods or services that are safe; that it must not exploit its employees; that it must not exploit its physical environment; and so on) then it is arguable whether an organization that is preoccupied with profitability alone could flourish.

Supporting this reasoning, a report based on a survey of chief executives from the Global Fortune 500 (the world's largest companies by revenue), which was published by the Judge Institute of Management at the University of Cambridge (Brady, 2003, p. 5), showed that:

> Despite recent financial scandals (Enron, WorldCom etc), [chief executives] predict that in the near future social credibility will be as important as financial credibility, and environmental credibility will only be marginally less important.

In the years since the Judge Institute report was published, an increasing number of businesses in many countries throughout the world have come to recognize the importance of social and environmental sustainability, and the interlinkages between these factors and the financial sustainability of their business. This has been reflected in a movement by an ever-growing number of major companies to voluntarily engage in a range of practices to improve their social and environmental performance, and to employ a range of accounting for sustainability practices to help them identify and report upon this performance (Hopwood *et al.*, 2010).

In this section we have addressed the *why* stage of social and environmental reporting – which is the initial stage where companies consider arguments in favour of engaging in corporate social responsibility and sustainability reporting. Consistent with some of the insights we developed in Chapter 8, we have seen that these motivations can range from a desire to maximize financial returns for shareholders and/or managers by using social and environmental reporting strategically as a tool to maintain and enhance the support of economically powerful stakeholders, through to a desire to discharge duties of accountability for the social and environmental impact that the organization (potentially) has on a wide range of stakeholders. Different managers will be driven by different motivations to report. We explored notions of sustainability to explain that shareholder interests of profit maximization tend to converge with interests of social and environmental sustainability over longer time horizons. Thus, in the long term, companies aiming for sustainable financial profits need to ensure they (and other businesses) are also socially and environmentally sustainable. This can make it difficult in practice to discern the true motives for *why* a company's executives develop and implement corporate social and environmental responsibility programmes and policies, and engage in social and environmental reporting, where the reasons for sustainability are explained in terms both of a need to avoid negative impacts on society and the environment and as being necessary to ensure future profitability.

Having considered several perspectives regarding *why* organizations might be motivated to report on their social and environmental impacts, we will now turn to the second broad stage of the sustainability reporting process – identifying the stakeholders whose information needs are to be addressed.[8]

9.7 Identifying stakeholders – the *who* stage

The range of stakeholders whose needs and expectations are considered by an organization when it is determining its corporate social responsibility policies, and when compiling its social and environmental reports, will be directly related to its motives for adopting these policies and practices. For an organization whose managers are motivated exclusively by the maximization of shareholder economic value, and who therefore might only use social and environmental reporting to win or maintain the approval of economically powerful stakeholders, the stakeholders to be addressed by social and environmental reporting might be restricted to the economically powerful stakeholders.

Economically powerful stakeholders can vary over time for a single organization. For example, for a company that requires a large number of semi-skilled employees and sells its products in reasonably competitive markets, consumers may have considerable economic power in times of economic recession but may lose some of this power in times of economic boom (when consumer demand grows faster than supply). Conversely, the semi-skilled workforce may become more economically powerful during an economic boom, if unemployment falls and a general shortage of semi-skilled workers arises. In this case, the economically powerful stakeholders whose views the company will seek to address in accordance with the managerial branch of stakeholder theory may shift from the company's consumers to its employees.

---

[8] Stakeholders have been defined in various ways. For our purposes we broadly define stakeholders as parties impacted by, or having an impact upon, the organization in question. This is also consistent with definitions provided by Freeman (1984) and Gray *et al.* (1996).

In contrast to the narrow focus on economically powerful stakeholders provided by the managerial branch of stakeholder theory, a much wider range of stakeholders will be considered if we follow the ethical branch of stakeholder theory. Organizations whose corporate social responsibility and whose sustainability reporting are motivated by broader ethical considerations of reducing the negative impact (or maximizing the positive impact) which the organization has on every person and entity affected by the organization's operations might consider the following as stakeholders to whom the organization is accountable: all humans from current and future generations upon whom their operations could have an impact (no matter how remote these people are from the organization), all animals living today and in the future upon whom the organization's operations could impact, and any other elements of nature potentially affected by the organization's operations. What is being emphasized is that the question about 'who' the social and environmental reports will be targeted at will ultimately be dependent upon management's views about their responsibilities and accountabilities. These views may vary from manager to manager.

The theoretical position that ethically motivated organizations should take account of the views and needs of all stakeholders (present and future) upon whom their operations might potentially impact represents a philosophical ideal rather than a practical and attainable aim. In practice, the operations of many organizations are likely to have some form of impact on many people, animals and other elements of nature, and to try to take account of all of these potential effects, and to seek to communicate to all those potentially affected, would be an impossible task (Unerman, 2007).

This impossibility arises partially because in our highly complex and interrelated world many activities have the potential to lead to numerous unintended and unforeseeable consequences (Beck, 1992, 1999). Where these future consequences of current actions are unforeseeable, it is difficult to conceive of how an organization could take them into account when determining the stakeholders affected (now and in the future) by its current operations, and thereby the stakeholders to whom the organization is accountable today. This impossibility also partially arises because, when it comes to the communication element of accountability (which, after all, is what this chapter is about), it is not possible to communicate effectively today with many non-human elements of nature or with future generations.

Thus, even when an organization's corporate social responsibility and social and environmental reporting is motivated by ethical rather than managerial reasoning, the organization will always need to identify a subset from all of the stakeholders who might be affected by their operations. The social and environmental needs and expectations of this subset of stakeholders will then determine the social and environmental responsibilities and accountability of the organization, and the social and environmental reporting which addresses these accountability duties (Unerman, 2007).

Some theorists, such as Gray *et al.* (1997) and Unerman and Bennett (2004), argue that an ethical approach to identifying, from a large number of stakeholders, those stakeholders to whom an organization is responsible and accountable requires consideration and prioritization of the views and interests of those stakeholders upon whose lives the organization's operations were likely to have the largest impact. These will not always be the stakeholders who are closest to the organization's operations in economic (or even in physical/geographical) terms.

The practical implications of this theoretical approach to stakeholder prioritization (in accordance with the ethical branch of stakeholder theory) is that organizations whose corporate social responsibility and social and environmental reporting are motivated by a desire to minimize the negative social and environmental impact of its operations will prioritize stakeholders' needs according to the extent of the impacts that the organization's operations are likely to have on any stakeholder's life. In determining its policies and practices, the organization will then seek to minimize its negative impacts on as many of these stakeholders as possible – addressing the needs and expectations of those stakeholders upon whom its operations have a potentially larger impact before the needs and expectations of stakeholders upon whom it is likely to have a lesser impact. However, O'Dwyer (2005) demonstrates how problematic this process of stakeholder prioritization can be in practice, as stakeholders who some would regard as highly dependent on the organization may, for reasons of expediency, be omitted from the prioritized subset of stakeholders defined and determined by the organization's managers.

Stakeholder identification in practice

As an example of how some organizations are defining their stakeholders in practice, in the *Sustainability Report 2009* of the Co-operative Group in the UK (which includes the Co-operative Bank), the organization defines its main stakeholders as comprising the following six groups (p. 10):

1 **Members** Anyone who is aged 16 or over, who lives in the UK, shares The Co-operative's Values and Principles and agrees to invest at least £1 can become a member. At the end of 2009, The Co-operative had 3.3 million economically active members who received a dividend payment, and 470,000 democratically active members (pages 90–91).

2 **Customers** Approximately 21 million customers visit The Co-operative Food each week and CFS has approximately nine million.

3 **Employees** At the end of 2009, The Co-operative had 113,391 staff, of whom 101,699 were employed by the Trading Group, and the remaining 11,692 were employed by CFS (page 100). Of these, 89,000 were co-operative members.

4 **Co-operative Movement** There are over 800 million co-operators across the world, and The Co-operative, as one of the largest co-operatives worldwide, seeks to deliver value to the rest of the Co-operative Movement in line with the sixth co-operative principle, 'co-operation between co-operatives' (inside front cover).

5 **Suppliers** Relationships with The Co-operative's suppliers range from infrequent purchases to ongoing strategic partnerships across the different business areas. In 2009, the number of suppliers of goods and services to The Co-operative, with whom yearly spend exceeded £50,000, totalled 1,800.

6 **Wider society** Amongst other groups, 'Wider society' encompasses the communities within which The Co-operative trades, local and national governments, NGOs, industry organisations, multi-stakeholder groups, charities and external expert organisations.

In an earlier *Sustainability Report* in 2003, the Co-operative Group explicitly explained why the identified stakeholders do not include the environment, stating that (p. 13):

> Unlike some organisations, [The Co-operative] does not define 'The Environment' as a separate Partner. The relationship between business and the 'Natural World' is essentially non-negotiable (in contrast to the relationship with suppliers, staff, etc.). The activities of [The Co-operative] and its Partners are ultimately governed by nature's limited capacity to generate resources and assimilate waste. For this reason, [The Co-operative] assesses the degree to which value is delivered to each Partner in an ecologically sustainable (and socially responsible) manner.

Broader evidence regarding how organizations are defining, and prioritizing, their stakeholders is provided by Owen *et al.* (2005). As part of a UK survey investigating managerial attitudes towards the provision of social and environmental information, they asked managers to rate the importance of a variety of different stakeholder groups as recipients of stand-alone sustainability reports on a scale from 0 (not important) to 5 (very important). According to the managers who were surveyed, shareholders were considered to be the most important audience for this information (mean importance of 3.95 out of 5) followed by: employees (3.83), environmental pressure groups (3.68), governmental regulators (3.58), local communities (3.48), customers (3.20), non-equity investors (2.80) and suppliers (2.65). This managerial ranking of important stakeholders can vary between different countries. For example, Adams (2002) shows that views regarding which stakeholders are the most important varied between a sample of UK and German managers.

In practice, whichever approach to stakeholder prioritization is taken by an organization – whether prioritizing stakeholders on the basis of those stakeholders most able to exert an influence on the organization's profits (or shareholder value), prioritizing stakeholders on the basis of those whose lives are most affected by the organization's activities, or adoption of a position somewhere on the continuum between these extreme positions – once the organization has identified the stakeholders whose social and environmental needs and expectations it will address, it then has to identify *what* are the information needs and expectations of these stakeholders. This takes us to the third stage of the *'why – to whom – for what – how'* process of social and environmental reporting.

9.8 Identifying stakeholder information needs and expectations – the *'what* do we report?' stage

A useful starting point to begin addressing the question *'For what social and environmental issues do stakeholders wish to hold organizations responsible and accountable?'* is to identify whether there is actually any demand among stakeholders for social and environmental information.[9]

---

[9] However, it needs to be appreciated that unless particular stakeholders know that particular information exists, or know how they might use the information, then they might not show any demand for it. To explain this point by analogy, somebody required to dig a hole in soil might demand a screwdriver if they have never been exposed to a shovel. According to Gray *et al.* (1991, p. 15) even if particular stakeholders do not read particular accounts, the entity nevertheless has a responsibility to provide an account.

Stakeholder demands for, and reactions to, social and environmental information

Obviously, for any form of public reporting to be useful in shaping community perceptions (one of the goals of corporate disclosure according to legitimacy theory) there needs to be an external demand for, or a reaction to, the particular information being disclosed. As Deegan and Rankin (1997) point out, the ability to shape perceptions through annual report or social and environmental report disclosures (as would be suggested by legitimacy theory, which was discussed in Chapter 8) is possible only if members of society actually use the reported information. Deegan and Rankin (1997) examined the issue of whether people actually use or rely upon the environmental performance information provided within annual reports. They solicited, by way of a questionnaire survey, the views of shareholders, stockbrokers and research analysts, accounting academics, representatives of financial institutions and a number of organizations performing a general review or oversight function regarding:

■ the materiality of environmental issues to certain groups in society who use annual reports to gain information;

■ whether environmental information is sought from annual reports; and

■ how important environmental information is to the decision-making process compared to other social responsibility information and information about the organization's financial performance and position.

Deegan and Rankin (1997) found, at statistically significant levels, that shareholders and individuals within organizations with a review or oversight function – these included consumer associations, employee groups, industry associations and environmental groups – considered that environmental information was material to the particular decisions they undertook. In addition, shareholders, accounting academics and individuals from organizations with a review or oversight function were found to seek environmental information from the annual report to assist in making their various decisions. The annual report was perceived by the total group of respondents to be significantly more important (in the mid-1990s) than any other source of information concerning an organization's interaction with the environment.[10] This study shows that various stakeholder groups within society *do* demand information about the social and environmental performance of organizations and thus, at a very broad level, there are issues for which stakeholders hold organizations responsible and accountable.

Another approach to determining whether people demand or react to certain disclosures is to review share price reactions to particular disclosures. The underlying theory used in many of these studies is derived from capital markets research and the use of the efficient markets hypothesis, which proposes that the information content of news announcements, if relevant to the marketplace, will be immediately and unbiasedly

---

[10] Since the mid-1990s many companies have started releasing very detailed stand-alone sustainability reports, often hundreds of pages in length. As such, if the Deegan and Rankin study was undertaken now then it is likely that the annual report would not be considered as the most important source of information about an entity's social and environmental performance for many corporations. However, as we will see later in this chapter, in the past few years there has been a move back towards integrating some aspects (the key aspects?) of social and environmental reporting in the annual report (Hopwood *et al.*, 2010).

impounded within share prices (capital markets research is explained in Chapter 10). That is, if an item of information about an organization can be associated with a change in the share price of that organization, then it is assumed that the information is of importance to investors and they have reacted to the disclosure of the information (with the reaction being reflected by the change in share price). We will consider share price reaction studies in more depth in the next chapter.

As an example of a share price study, Ingram (1978) and Anderson and Frankle (1980) found that the share market does react to social disclosure, with Ingram concluding the reaction to be a function of, among other things, the industry to which the organization belongs and the types of social disclosures being made.

Belkaoui (1976) and Jaggi and Freedman (1982) studied investors' reactions to pollution disclosures. Belkaoui observed a positive share market reaction to firms that provided evidence of responsible pollution control procedures compared to firms that could not demonstrate responsibility. He concluded that the results verified the existence of an 'ethical investor', that is, an investor who responds to demonstrations of social concern and invests in corporations that are socially responsible.

Jaggi and Freedman (1982) studied the market impact of pollution disclosures made by firms operating within highly polluting industries. Consistent with Belkaoui's results, Jaggi and Freedman observed a positive share market reaction to those firms that could demonstrate greater pollution controls.

What needs to be appreciated is that the above discussion illustrates that there are alternative ways to determine whether people use particular information. One way is to ask people, perhaps through a questionnaire as in the Deegan and Rankin study, while another possibility is to infer that people used the information by simply looking at a share price reaction around the time particular information is released by an organization.

The above studies examined the market's reaction to disclosures made by the organizations themselves. In contrast, Shane and Spicer (1983) undertook a study which investigated the market's response to environmental performance information emanating from a source outside the firm, specifically that produced by the New York-based organization, the Council on Economic Priorities – an organization that provides independent ranking on organizations' social and environmental performance. Shane and Spicer found that organizations identified by the Council on Economic Priorities as having poor pollution-control performance rankings were more likely to have significant negative security returns on the day the rankings were publicly released compared to organizations with higher pollution-control performance rankings. Shane and Spicer considered that the results were consistent with an assumption that the information released by the Council on Economic Priorities permitted investors to discriminate between organizations with different pollution-control performance records.

Similarly, Lorraine *et al.* (2004) examined share price reaction in the United Kingdom to 'publicity about fines for environmental pollution as well as commendations about good environmental achievements' (p. 7) over a five-and-a-half-year period. They found that while there was little market reaction on the day fines or commendations were announced publicly, there was a significant impact on share prices within a week of these announcements.

Examining market reactions to negative environmental performance information from sources both inside and outside the firm, Freedman and Patten (2004) found that where corporations (in the USA) published information in their annual reports about high levels of pollution emissions from their factories, the share price reaction was lower than for companies which were known to emit high levels of pollution but did not report this in their annual reports.

In further research, Blacconiere and Patten (1994) examined the market reaction to Union Carbide's devastating and widely reported chemical leak in India in 1984. Using a sample of 47 US firms, they observed a significant intra-industry market reaction to the event. However, firms with more extensive environmental disclosures in their annual reports before the disaster experienced a smaller negative reaction than those with less extensive disclosures.

From the limited evidence provided above, it would appear that investors *do* react to an organization's social responsibility disclosures, and therefore the broad answer to the *accountable for what* question is *accountable for some level of social responsibility practices and/or impacts.*

A further source of significant stakeholder demand for social and environmental information has, in recent years, come from banking and insurance institutions. These financial stakeholders have become a key user of such information, particularly about organizations' environmental performance. In some countries, banks will not provide funds to organizations unless information about their environmental policies and performance is provided (Bhimani and Soonawalla, 2010; Coulson 2007). The reason for this, in part, would be that an organization that has demonstrated poor environmental performance is considered to be a higher risk in terms of compliance with environmental laws and in terms of potential costs associated with rectifying environmental damage caused. Further, in some industries it is possible that collateral provided for loans (such as land) might be contaminated because of poor environmental management systems. An increasing number of investment analysts also evaluate the social and environmental performance of corporations as part of their investment analysis (Brigham *et al.*, 2010).

Another increasing source of demand for corporate social and environmental information is the growing socially responsible investment (SRI) market, and fund managers are also using their power to demand that corporations provide social and environmental performance information (Brigham *et al.*, 2010). As the financial benefits of good social and environmental governance (for example through improved risk management) have begun to be recognized by mainstream (non-SRI) investment managers, they have also started to demand higher levels of information about the social and environmental sustainability risks, polices and practices of the companies in which they invest (or in which they are considering investing). For example, in a study of investment decision-making practices at the global financial services company Aviva plc, Brigham *et al.* (2010, pp. 204 and 207) observed:

> A core part of Aviva's business involves the investment of funds received from policy-holders. This part of the business, Aviva Investors, manages global assets of around UK£236 billion in 15 countries. Aviva is therefore able to exert influence on sustainability outcomes through the way in which it invests

the monies entrusted to it. Sustainable investment practices are thus a prime example of how sustainability criteria are embedded in core business areas at Aviva. Aviva Investors seeks to integrate material environmental, social and governance (ESG) issues within all assets under management. ... AGM voting is seen as an important way of encouraging improvements in corporate disclosure and narrative reporting on ESG issues. Aviva Investors votes against the reports and accounts at the AGM if the company has not met the required standards of reporting. In 2008, Aviva voted on corporate responsibility disclosure at 558 AGMs for FTSE350 and FTSE EuroFirst 300 Index companies, indicating how the company is actively involved in shaping ESG policies in other companies.

... Aviva Investors' deployment of SRI criteria indicates how the company has chosen to mobilize its considerable position in the investment business to encourage sustainability in the companies in which it chooses to invest. ... Aviva mobilizes the specific power available to an institutional investor, although always within the constraints of the capital markets. No doubt, many of its customers would be unwilling to see such strategies implemented if they were to yield significantly poorer returns on investment. However, this is a further example of how Aviva has chosen to embed positive sustainability policies within its mainstream corporate strategy. Given that recent history has indicated such investment choices have had good profitability, a win–win situation has developed. Indeed, it might be seen that the reaction against excessive short-termism can be helpfully progressed by taking a long-term position both financially and in terms of sustainability.

Due to supply chain pressures, many organizations are also now demanding that suppliers provide them with details of their social and environmental performance prior to entering supply arrangements (Unerman and O'Dwyer, 2010). Supply chain considerations have in the past negatively impacted on a number of organizations with corporations such as Nike being prime examples.

Hence, while we have referred to only a very small proportion of the studies of demand for environmental performance information, it is very clear that there is a demand. For reasons discussed at the beginning of this section, this demand indicates that many stakeholders do hold organizations responsible and accountable for some social and/or environmental issues. But identifying that stakeholders do use, and therefore that there is a demand for, social and environmental information, does not tell us precisely *for what* issues the stakeholders of a particular organization will hold that organization responsible and accountable. To identify these issues at the level of an individual organization requires the organization to enter into some form of dialogue with its stakeholders.

Identifying information needs through dialogue with stakeholders

As we saw in the *for whom* section earlier in this chapter, managers motivated to engage in corporate social responsibility (and sustainability reporting) for strategic managerial economic reasons (following the managerial branch of stakeholder theory) will tend to identify relevant stakeholders as being those who are able to exert the most influence over their company's ability to generate profits (or maximize shareholder value). Such managers will seek to convince these economically powerful stakeholders that their organization's policies and actions accord with the social, environmental, economic and ethical views and expectations of these stakeholders, with social and environmental reporting being one of the mechanisms that may be used to convince these stakeholders. For social and environmental reporting to be effectively used to convince these stakeholders that the organization has operated in accordance with their expectations, the organization will need to know and understand these expectations – which will define what information is provided in the organization's social and environmental reports.

Conversely, following the ethical branch of stakeholder theory, managers who seek to minimize their organization's negative impact on a wide range of stakeholders will need to know and understand how their organization is likely to impact upon the lives of a range of stakeholders. The attitudes and experiences of these stakeholders regarding actual and potential organizational impacts are an important element of developing this knowledge and understanding. With an awareness of these views and expectations, managers can then focus their social responsibility policies and actions accordingly, and direct their social and environmental reporting towards providing an account to these stakeholders regarding how the organization has acted in relation to these responsibilities.

Furthermore, ethical reasoning indicates that people should be allowed to participate in making decisions on issues and matters that are likely to affect their lives. Therefore, where managers are motivated by broader ethical considerations, they will actively encourage all those stakeholders who are (or might be) affected by the organization's activities to participate in decision-making regarding these activities. To be able to participate in this manner, a wide range of stakeholders will need information about the effects the organization has (or is likely to have) on them, and managers will need to provide this information. In this situation, the answer to the *accountable for what* question is clearly *accountable to all stakeholders for the impact that the organization's actions have (or may have) upon these stakeholders.*

In these cases, and for any position on the continuum between these cases, managers need to understand their relevant stakeholders' views, needs and expectations to determine *for what* economic, social and environmental issues they will provide an account. Ascertaining these views, needs and expectations is likely to be more straightforward where corporate social responsibility has been motivated by a strategic economic desire to maintain or increase the support of economically powerful (or influential) stakeholders, as many of these stakeholders will often be close to, and therefore relatively easily identifiable by, the organization. For many commercial organizations, these powerful stakeholders will often be located in developed nations (or will be part of wealthy elites in developing nations) and will be accessible through commercial mass media such as television/radio, newspaper articles and the Internet.

However, for organizations whose social responsibility and social and environmental reporting are motivated by ethical reasoning to minimize the organization's impact on those most affected by its operations (and to allow these stakeholders to participate in decisions on issues which significantly affect their lives), ascertaining these stakeholders' views, needs and expectations is likely to be more problematic. First, there is likely to be a broader range of stakeholders whose views need to be ascertained. Second, while many of the stakeholders who are significantly affected by an organization's activities (such as employees) might be close to the organization, many others (such as those affected indirectly but substantially by environmental damage caused by the organization's operations, or workers of subcontractors in remote parts of the world) are likely to be remote from the organization itself. Third, as demonstrated by O'Dwyer (2005), some of the stakeholders who are considerably affected by an organization's operations might feel constrained by concerns about the consequences of 'upsetting' the organization if they express their 'true' feelings, in which case the organization can be regarded as being in a position of power which prevents open and honest dialogue with some stakeholders. Fourth, Adams (2004, p. 736) reports that there is often a 'lack of stakeholder awareness of, and even concern for, corporate impacts', and this can reduce the capacity of some stakeholders to engage in dialogue with the organization. Finally, if, following the reasoning discussed earlier in this chapter, we include future generations, non-humans and nature within our definition of stakeholders who are potentially significantly negatively affected by an organization's current operations, it is difficult to conceive of how any organization today could engage in dialogue effectively with these stakeholders to ascertain directly their views, needs and expectations regarding current organizational policies and practices.[11]

To overcome some (but not all) of these difficulties, organizations need to use a variety of channels of communication to engage in active (and not just reactive) dialogue with their stakeholders (Unerman, 2007). For example, some companies have made use of the interactive communication facilities of the Internet to solicit the views of anyone worldwide regarding the social, environmental, ethical and economic responsibilities that should be applied to their organization (Rinaldi and Unerman, 2009). However, as Unerman and Bennett (2004) have contended, because access to the Internet is not available to all those potentially affected by an organization's activities (particularly in many developing nations), Internet-based communication with stakeholders needs to be supplemented with other channels of communication that, between them, are accessible (and likely to be accessed by) a large proportion of the stakeholders upon whom an organization's operations might have an impact.

Such communications can include, for example, face-to-face meetings with a variety of stakeholders, questionnaire surveys, opinion polls, focus groups and invitations to write to the company about specific issues. O'Dwyer (2005, p. 286) indicates that whatever channels of communication are used to engage stakeholders in dialogue, to be effective these communication channels need to be adapted to the 'cultural differences encountered' between different groups of stakeholders. Another approach to discovering stakeholder expectations – and which relates to the above discussion – is to undertake a 'social audit'. We will refer to social audits later in this chapter.

Identifying stakeholder information needs and expectations in practice

In addressing processes of stakeholder dialogue, in late 1999 the Institute of Social and Ethical Accountability (ISEA) launched a social and environmental accountability

---

[11] These views are, however, often 'represented' by a variety of campaign groups.

'framework' AA1000, which places communication between the organization and its stakeholders at the core of social and environmental accountability practices. A central part of this framework, which has evolved since its launch, is guidance on the process of understanding stakeholders' information needs and expectations (in other words, understanding *for what* issues stakeholders consider the organization to be responsible and accountable). The ISEA website states:

> Launched in 1999, the AA1000 framework is designed to improve accountability and performance by **learning through stakeholder engagement.**
>
> It was developed to address the need for organisations to integrate their stakeholder engagement processes into daily activities. It has been used worldwide by leading businesses, non-profit organisations and public bodies.
>
> The Framework helps users to establish a systematic stakeholder engagement process that generates the **indicators, targets, and reporting systems** needed to ensure its effectiveness in overall organisational performance. (ISEA, 2005, emphasis in original)

In reflecting on the benefits to companies from complying with AA1000, Simon Zadek, a representative of ISEA, stated (as quoted in Environmental Accounting and Auditing Reporter, 2000, p. 2):

> There is an increasing body of evidence that organisations which listen to their stakeholders are more likely to be successful in the long term. AA1000's continuous cycle of consultation with stakeholders is designed to encourage transparency, clear goal-setting and the building of trust in relationships with people. Organisations which adhere to its principles and processes will be able to draw strength from association with this quality standard and, ultimately, can expect to achieve competitive advantage. Companies like Railtrack and Monsanto must wish, in retrospect, they had invested in these kinds of processes to help avoid billions being wiped off their market values.

The following extract from the 2010 *Vodafone Group Plc Sustainability Report* (p. 7) provides an example of the importance accorded to understanding stakeholder needs and expectations by some companies, and gives examples of several channels of communication used to understand stakeholders' views, needs and expectations:

Engaging with stakeholders

> Listening and responding to our stakeholders – the people who affect our business or who are affected by it – is a core part of our sustainability management. Their feedback helps us understand their expectations, enables us to prioritise issues effectively and informs our sustainability strategy.
>
> Details on how we engage with key stakeholder groups can be found on our website. Examples of specific engagement this year are also included elsewhere in this Report:
>
> **Investors and industry analysts** – through one-to-one meetings (including an annual investor roadshow) with our Group Corporate Responsibility Director, and by briefings with analysts …

Governments and regulators – by being transparent in stating our views and developing public policy positions on issues relevant to our business, for example communicating the findings of our Carbon Connections report to key EU officials …

Non-governmental organisations – through, for example, our Social Investment Fund programmes …, face-to-face meetings and The Vodafone Foundation …

Industry – through initiatives such as the ICT for Energy Efficiency (ICT4EE) industry forum in Europe, the GSMA's1 'Green Manifesto' and the Corporate Leaders' Group on Climate Change …, and as a member of the World Business Council for Sustainable Development, the Global eSustainability Initiative and CSR Europe.

Consumers – through public perception surveys on sustainability and specific issues such as mobiles, masts and health …, and focus groups on green issues for our industry …

Suppliers – through our assessments and collaborations to improve performance (see page 54)

Employees – through our Global People Survey and annual Performance Dialogues …

Local communities – through consultation on our network deployment activities …

We also engage with stakeholders in each of our local markets on the issues that are most relevant to them

Negotiating a consensus among competing stakeholder needs and expectations

In practice, as discussed earlier, many organizations are faced with a variety of values and expectations held by different stakeholders (Lewis and Unerman, 1999), and often these values and expectations will be incompatible with each other – so the organization will not be able to meet all of the expectations. As indicated by the managerial branch of stakeholder theory, where an organization is motivated to engage in these practices for strategic economic reasons (for example, to maximize shareholder value) then managers will usually choose to address the social, environmental and economic values and expectations of their most economically powerful stakeholders. As Gray *et al.* (1996, p. 45) state:

> Here (under this perspective), the stakeholders are identified by the organisation of concern, by reference to the extent to which the organization believes the interplay with each group needs to be managed in order to further the interests of the organisation. (The interests of the organisation need not be restricted to conventional profit-seeking assumptions.) The more important the stakeholder to the organisation, the more effort will be exerted in managing the relationship. Information is a major element that can be employed by the organisation to manage (or manipulate) the stakeholder in order to gain their support and approval, or to distract their opposition and disapproval.

Conversely, where, following the ethical branch of stakeholder theory, an organization's social responsibility and sustainability reporting is motivated by a desire to address the interests of those stakeholders upon whom the organization has the largest impact, it will need to identify and select the interests of those stakeholders upon whom the organization's activities have the largest negative impact. Given that there may be incompatible views among different stakeholders regarding the nature and extent of an organization's impacts, and regarding the priority among different stakeholders' interests, in practice the process of arriving at a consensus set of social, environmental and economic responsibilities is highly problematic (Unerman, 2007).

Unerman and Bennett (2004) addressed this issue. They suggested that while democratically ideal procedures for arriving at a consensus view among all of the stakeholders of any organization regarding that organization's social, environmental and economic responsibilities are probably impossible to fully implement in practice,[12] processes of stakeholder dialogue and debate could move part of the way towards a democratic ideal. The theoretically ideal procedures suggested by Unerman and Bennett draw on some of the theories of the German philosopher Jürgen Habermas (1992), and would require all those potentially affected by an organization's actions to engage in open and honest dialogue with each other (and not just with the organization) about these impacts and the moral acceptability of these impacts. They also require that a person only argues for outcomes which they would consider to be morally acceptable if they were placed in the position of someone negatively affected by that outcome (a requirement that moral positions should only be taken seriously if the person arguing for them believes they should apply universally). A final important requirement is that all stakeholders are prepared to listen to the arguments of others, and are prepared to modify their views in light of stronger arguments.

Gray *et al.* (1997) provide an alternative view on the role of stakeholders in determining corporate responsibilities. They argue that the model where an organization identifies, and then solicits the views of, a range of its stakeholders places the organization in a position of control over this process. The alternative position, termed the *polyvocal citizenship perspective*, outlined by Gray *et al.* (1997), views the organization as the product of a variety of relationships with different stakeholders, with these stakeholders' views determining the 'reality' (or the nature of the existence) of the organization. As the nature of the organization's existence, under this perspective, is determined by the stakeholders (very broadly defined), these stakeholders' social values and expectations will automatically be at the core of the organization. However, in practice, the 'entity' tends to be placed at the core of the management of accountability relationships, with managers determining the range of stakeholders to whom they are responsible and accountable.

While 'in theory' it makes sense for organizations to provide information to meet the specific needs of the respective stakeholders – meaning a one-size-fits-all approach might not be appropriate – many organizations do nevertheless use reporting guidelines generated by particular organizations such as the Global Reporting Initiative (GRI) to guide them on

---

[12] For example, in the case analysed by O'Dwyer (2005, p. 286) 'several stakeholders complained they had little opportunity to engage in dialogue with each other. It was widely claimed that stakeholders needed to learn from each other across the organization as opposed to merely enabling the board to learn from them and then isolate them'.

what to disclose. The rationale for adopting such guidelines as the basis for determining what to disclose would be based on a belief that organizations such as the GRI have done extensive research to determine the information needs of a cross-section of stakeholders. But in providing the basis for a general purpose sustainability report, such reporting guidelines will not necessarily meet the specific needs of particular stakeholders. This is similar to the position in financial reporting wherein conceptual frameworks and accounting standards are used to produce general purpose financial reports which are regarded as meeting most of the information needs of readers. For specific information needs, the stakeholders might request the organization to produce special purpose financial reports.

In summarizing this section on 'what do we report', such decisions will directly be affected by whether managers decide to provide information to a broad group of stakeholders or, alternatively, whether they restrict their consideration to a narrow (and perhaps powerful) group of stakeholders. What appears to be clear is that there is a demand for social and environmental information. To determine the types of information required, organizations can undertake various strategies to find out what information different categories of stakeholders require. In practice not all demands for information can be met.

In the next section, we move on from our discussion of theoretical perspectives regarding mechanisms that organizations can use to determine 'for what' issues their stakeholders hold them responsible and accountable to consider some theoretical perspectives regarding *how* social and environmental reports can be constructed to meet this 'set' of prioritized (or consensus) stakeholder expectations.

9.9 Theoretical perspectives on some social and environmental reporting procedures – the *how* stage

Because there is a general lack of regulation in the area of social and environmental reporting, as well as an absence of an accepted conceptual framework for social and environmental reporting, there is much variation in how this reporting is being done in practice. Some reporting approaches represent quite radical changes from how financial accounting has traditionally been practised. In this section we start by analysing whether the rules and procedures of financial accounting alone could provide suitable mechanisms for capturing and reporting the social and environmental impacts of organizations. If financial accounting practices are unable to capture and report on these social and environmental impacts effectively, then it is necessary to develop other (or additional) social and environmental reporting mechanisms. We will discuss one of the more influential (and more detailed) sustainability reporting guidelines, the *Global Reporting Initiative*, which can be regarded as a form of conceptual framework for social and environmental reporting. We complete this section by briefly discussing some perspectives on how to account for the social and environmental externalities caused by business entities.

Some possible limitations of traditional financial accounting in capturing and reporting social and environmental performance

In commencing our discussion of 'how' to report social and environmental information we will consider the potential role of financial accounting systems in providing such information. Financial accounting is often criticized on the basis that it ignores many of the social and environmental *externalities* caused by the reporting entity. Hence, its suitability for assisting in the disclosure of social and environmental information is questioned. Gray (2005, p. 3) has more profound criticisms of the relationship between financial accounting and sustainability when he argues that:

> Few ideas could be more destructive to the notion of a sustainable planet than a system of economic organisation designed to maximise those things which financial reporting measures [for example, increasing sales, profits, growth, and so on]. Few notions could be more fundamentally antagonistic to financial reporting and all its cosmetic adjustments than a planet wishing to seek sustainability.

Some of the reasons why traditional financial accounting may not be able to reflect the social and environmental impact of organizations effectively could include:

1 As conceptual frameworks, such as the IASB *Framework for the Preparation and Presentation of Financial Statements* emphasize, financial accounting focuses on the information needs of those parties involved in making resource allocation decisions. That is, the focus tends to be restricted to stakeholders with a financial interest in the entity, and the information that is provided consequently tends to be primarily of a financial or economic nature. This has the effect of denying or restricting access to information by people who are affected in a way that is not financial. But as we have seen, companies can elect to voluntarily provide social and environmental information. Owen *et al.* (2005) show that guidance developed in the UK during the first few years of the twenty-first century for a new Operating and Financial Review, to be published alongside the main financial statements, indicated that additional information about social and environmental factors *could* be included in any company's Operating and Financial Review to address the information needs of a wider group than simply those with a financial interest.

2 Following on from the above discussion, one of the cornerstones of financial accounting is the notion of 'financial materiality' which has tended to preclude the reporting of social and environmental information given the difficulty associated with quantifying social and environmental costs. 'Materiality' is an issue involving a great deal of professional judgement and is often judged in terms of the magnitude of the financial value of an item in relation to the size of other accounting metrics (such as turnover, net profit and/or net assets). If something is not judged to be material, it does not need to be disclosed in the financial reports. Unfortunately, this has often meant that if something cannot be quantified (as is the case for many social and environmental externalities) it is generally not considered to be material and therefore does not warrant separate disclosure. This obviously implies that materiality may not be a relevant criterion for the disclosure of social and environmental performance data. Yet many accountants have been conditioned through their education and training to adopt the *materiality* criterion to decide whether any information should be disclosed. In a review of British companies, Gray *et al.* (1998) indicate that companies frequently provide little or no information about environmental expenses because individually the expenditure is not

considered to be *material*. However, in recent years a number of companies have used materiality criteria to justify disclosure of some social and environmental impacts in annual financial reports, given growing recognition of the potential financial materiality flowing from social and environmental risks (Hopwood *et al.*, 2010; Unerman and O'Dwyer, 2010). The financial materiality of such risks was demonstrated very clearly with the multi-billion dollar costs to BP arising from the explosion on its Deepwater Horizon oil rig in April 2010, as discussed earlier in this chapter.

3 As highlighted in Gray *et al.* (1996), another issue that arises in financial accounting is that reporting entities frequently discount liabilities, particularly those that will not be settled for many years, to their present value. This tends to make future expenditure less significant in the present period. For example, if our current activities are creating a need for future environmental expenditure of a remedial nature, but that work will not be undertaken for many years, then as a result of discounting we will recognize little or no cost now (which does appear to be at odds with the sustainability agenda). For example, if we were anticipating that our activities would necessitate a clean-up bill of €100 million in 30 years' time to remove some contamination, and if we accept that our normal earnings rate is, say, 10 per cent, then the current expenses to be recognized in our financial statements under generally accepted accounting principles would be €5.73 million. While discounting makes good *economic* sense, Gray *et al.* (1996) argue that it does tend to make the clean-up somewhat trivial (and therefore, not that important) at the current time, perhaps thereby providing little current discouragement for an entity contemplating undertaking activities that will damage the environment but which will not be remediated for many years.

4 Financial accounting adopts the 'entity assumption', which requires the organization to be treated as an entity distinct from its owners, other organizations and other stakeholders. If a transaction or event does not directly impact on the entity, the transaction or event is to be ignored for accounting purposes. This means that the externalities caused by reporting entities will typically be ignored, thereby meaning that performance measures (such as profitability) are incomplete from a broader societal (as opposed to a 'discrete entity') perspective and accounting reports based on these performance measures fail to reflect all three strands of sustainability discussed earlier in this chapter. Arguably any moves towards accounting for sustainability would require a modification to, or a move away from, the entity assumption such that the costs borne by other parties outside the organization, as a result of consuming the outputs of the entity, would be factored into profit calculations, rather than being ignored as is currently the case.[13]

5 A related area in which our traditional financial accounting system potentially generates a rather strange outcome is the treatment of tradable pollution permits. In both the EU and an increasing number of countries outside the EU, a key tool to reduce greenhouse gas emissions from large users of energy is to provide these organizations with permits, sometimes free of charge, which allow the holder to release

---

[13] As an example, many companies make significant contributions to climate change and therefore to problems confronting current and future generations. Traditionally, such 'costs' have been ignored entirely when calculating corporate profits. However, moves to introduce 'carbon taxes' will act to internalize at least some of these costs.

a pre-specified amount of a particular pollutant. If the original recipient of the permit is not going to emit as much as the licence allows, then that party is allowed to sell the permit to another party (this is intended to act as an incentive for large-scale energy users to reduce their carbon emissions).[14] Lovell *et al.* (2010) state that the total value of such permits traded within the EU scheme in 2008 was €63 billion, indicating a sizeable activity for many large European corporations. As such, what we are finding in some jurisdictions is that particular organizations have the potential to treat tradable pollution permits as assets. This may make sense from an 'economic' perspective – but it is questionable whether something that will allow an organization to pollute is an asset from a broader 'societal' perspective. The IASB and FASB are currently undertaking a joint 'Emissions Trading Scheme Project' with the intention of publishing an exposure draft for a new accounting standard on this issue by late 2011. Since the introduction of emissions trading schemes in a number of jurisdictions, academic research has investigated some of the accounting implications of these types of schemes (see, for example, Bebbington and Larrinaga-Gonzalez, 2008; Engels, 2009; Freedman and Stagliano, 2008; Lohmann, 2009; Lovell *et al.*, 2010).

6 In financial accounting and reporting, expenses are defined in such a way as to exclude the recognition of any impacts on resources that are not controlled by the entity (such as the environment) unless fines or other cash flows result. For example, under the IASB's *conceptual framework* (the IASB Framework, as discussed in Chapter 6), *expenses* for financial reporting purposes are defined as:

> decreases in economic benefits during the accounting period in the form of out-flows or depletions of assets or incurrences of liabilities that result in decreases in equity, other than those relating to distributions to equity participants [paragraph 70b].

An understanding of *expenses* therefore requires an understanding of *assets*. Assets are defined as resources '*controlled* by the entity as a result of past events and from which future economic benefits are expected to flow to the entity' (paragraph 49a, emphasis added). The recognition of assets therefore relies upon *control*, and hence environmental resources such as air and water, which are shared and therefore not controlled by the organization, cannot be considered as 'assets' of that organization. Thus their use, or abuse, is not considered as an expense. This is an important limitation of financial accounting and one that must be emphasized. As indicated in Deegan (1996), and using a rather extreme example, under traditional financial accounting if an entity were to destroy the quality of water in its local environs, thereby killing all local sea creatures and coastal vegetation, then to the extent that no fines or other related cash flows were incurred, reported profits would not be directly affected.[15] No externalities would be recognized, and the reported assets/profits of

---

[14] As an example, details of the EU 'Greenhouse Gas Emission Trading Scheme' (ETS), which became operational in January 2005, can be found at http://ec.europa.eu/environment/climat/emission/index_en.htm.

[15] To prove this to yourself, ask yourself what accounts you would debit and credit if your company inadvertently released toxic water into the local river system thereby killing thousands of endangered species of plants and animals while at the same time no fines or penalties were imposed for the reckless action.

the organization would not be affected. Adopting conventional financial reporting practices, the performance of such an organisation could, depending upon the financial transactions undertaken, be portrayed as being very successful. In this respect Gray and Bebbington (1992, p. 6) provide the following opinion of traditional financial accounting:

> there is something profoundly wrong about a system of measurement, a system that makes things visible and which guides corporate and national decisions, that can signal success in the midst of desecration and destruction.[16]

Another point, considered more fully in Chapter 12, is that 'profits' as calculated by applying accounting standards provide a measure of possible future returns (dividends) to one stakeholder group – shareholders. In commending organizations for high profits we are, perhaps, putting the interests of the investors (the owners) above the interests of other stakeholders. From this perspective, financial accounting acts to support the interests of those with power (often proxied by financial wealth), and to undermine others (such as employees). Promoting performance indicators such as 'profits' will, it is argued, maintain the 'favoured' position of those in command of financial resources.

Consider Accounting Headline 9.4, which provides information about the reaction to an organization cutting jobs in an endeavour to cut 'costs'. Our traditional

---

Accounting Headline 9.4
_____

An illustration of activities that concurrently increase profits and 'social costs'

France braced for huge street protests over economic crisis

By Angelique Chrisafis

France is bracing for a wave of street protests in the second general strike over Nicolas Sarkozy's handling of the economic crisis.

Traditional public sector strikers such as teachers, transport workers and hospital staff will join an unprecedented new protest movement by private sector workers from banks and supermarkets to multinationals. Together they are protesting against both Sarkozy's cuts to France's public sector and welfare state, and accusing him of failing to protect workers from the economic crisis. Most of those involved fear the dreaded French scourge: unemployment, which is now rising at the fastest rate in more than a decade.

… Many across the left and right accuse Sarkozy of comforting the rich while workers suffer. When the French oil giant Total announced job cuts just after reporting record profits, more than 80% of the public voiced their disgust in a recent poll.

Source: *Guardian*, 19 March 2009
©Guardian News and Media Limited 2010

---

[16] Motivated by their concern about the limitations of traditional financial accounting, Gray and Bebbington have sought to develop alternative methods of accounting – methods that embrace the sustainability agenda. See, for example, Gray and Bebbington (2001).

systems of financial accounting ignores social costs that arise as a result of 'axing' employees and thereby making them unemployed. Putting people out of work might increase the profits of the entity but the hardship this causes and the social security payments thereafter paid by government will not be reflected within the financial statements of the reporting entity.

7 There is also the issue of 'measurability'. For an item to be recorded for financial accounting purposes it must be measurable with reasonable accuracy. As paragraph 83 of the IASB *Framework for the Preparation and Presentation of Financial Statements states*:

> An item that meets the definition of an element should be recognised if:
>
> **a** it is probable that any future economic benefit associated with the item will flow to or from the entity; and
>
> **b** the item has a cost or value that can be measured with reliability.

Trying to place a value on the externalities caused by an entity often relies on various estimates and 'guesstimates', thereby typically precluding their recognition from the financial accounts on the basis of the potential inaccuracy of the measurement.

Despite the above difficulties, there have been various experimental approaches throughout the world aiming to develop a 'full-cost' approach to profit calculation by placing an economic 'value' on the social and environmental impact of individual organizations. A number of companies have, in the past, experimented with full-cost accounting, including Dow Europe, BSO/Origin (Netherlands), Volvo, Ontario Hydro, and IBM. Some academic studies have also developed theoretical approaches in this area (see, for example, Bebbington and Gray, 2001; Gray, 1992). These approaches represent a dramatic departure from conventional accounting.

Nevertheless, the drawbacks with the current state of reporting (which we discussed above) indicate that financial accounting and reporting does not seem to possess suitable mechanisms for capturing and reporting upon the social and environmental impacts of organizations. Hence, in discussing 'how' to report social and environmental information we could justifiably have concerns about doing it through existing financial reporting systems. Financial accounting and reporting alone is therefore unsuitable as a mechanism to provide an account of these social and environmental impacts and to meet stakeholders' information needs and expectations. Consequently, non-financial accounting and reporting needs to be used, possibly in conjunction with aspects of financial accounting and reporting, to provide a suitable social and environmental account to these stakeholders.

Various attempts have been made in recent years to provide a systematic framework and guidance for organizations seeking to report upon their non-financial social and environmental impacts and performance, sometimes in conjunction with their economic performance. Among these, the most widely adopted have been the *Global Reporting Initiative* guidelines.

The Global Reporting Initiative

Despite (or perhaps because of) the deficiencies in the ability of traditional financial reporting to capture and reflect the social and environmental impacts of organizational activities, many organizations have developed a variety of practices which seek to report on these broader impacts. The inclusion of particular items for disclosure tends to be based on particular managers' perceptions of the information needs of particular stakeholder groups (Solomon and Lewis, 2002), while much reliance also tends to be placed on what is acknowledged as best reporting practice (as perhaps evidenced by an entity winning a reporting award for its disclosures).

As an attempt to codify best reporting practice, several bodies have been active in developing social and environmental reporting guidelines. At an international level, one source of reporting guidance that has taken a dominant position in the social and environmental (and sustainability) reporting domain is the Global Reporting Initiative's Sustainability Reporting Guidelines (commonly referred to as the GRI Guidelines).[17]

According to a report published by the long-established sustainability and business network Ceres entitled: *The 21st Century Corporation: The Ceres Roadmap for Sustainability* (2010, p. 35):

> The GRI Guidelines have become the de facto standard for sustainability reporting. In 2009, over 1,100 reports officially registered their sustainability reports with the GRI. Using these guidelines enables consistent, comparable disclosure on sustainability performance, risks and opportunities.
>
> Companies should use the GRI framework's principles and indicators to disclose their performance. The GRI has 15 sector supplements including oil and gas, financial services, and public agencies, as well as specific issue guides on areas such as human rights. These additional guidance documents are designed to help organizations navigate more deeply into sustainability reporting. Companies find additional sector-relevant disclosure guidance developed by regulatory agencies, and other national bodies in the countries where they operate.

These guidelines are therefore generally accepted as representing current 'best practice'. The first version of the GRI Guidelines was released in 2000 (following the release of draft guidelines in 1999). A second version of the guidelines (referred to as G2) was released in 2002. The third generation of the guidelines (referred to as G3) was released in 2006 and was developed as a result of multi-stakeholder collaboration that occurred in 2004 and 2005. It provides 49 'core indicators' and 30 'additional indicators' that can be used by reporting organizations. According to GRI (2006, p. 24):

> Core Indicators have been developed through GRI's multi-stakeholder processes, which are intended to identify generally applicable Indicators and are assumed to be material for most organizations. An organization should report on Core Indicators unless they are deemed not material on the basis of the GRI Reporting Principles. Additional Indicators represent emerging practice or address topics that may be material for some organizations, but are not material for others.[18]

---

[17] See www.globalreporting.org for details of the GRI and the sustainability reporting guidelines.

[18] The guidelines provide a number of external factors (such as issues raised by stakeholders, and local, national and international regulations) and internal factors (such as major risks to the organization, organizational values, goals and targets) that need to be considered in determining the 'materiality' of an item.

[19] Indicators provide a measure to enable evaluation and subsequent decision-making with regard to the particular aspect being measured. Within the G3 Guidelines an 'indicator aspect' is defined as 'The general types of information that are related to a specific indicator category (e.g., energy use, child labor, customers)'.

[20] Interested readers should go to the GRI Guidelines (www.globalreporting.org) to review the details of the specific indicators pertaining to each aspect.

The sustainability performance indicators (both 'core' and 'additional') are organized under the categories of economic performance, environmental performance and social performance (with the social indicators being further subdivided into labour practices and decent work performance indicators, investment and procurement practices, social performance indicators, and product responsibility performance indicators). Under each category there is required to be a 'Disclosure on Management Approach' (which covers such things as policies, responsibilities, goals). This disclosure is then followed by the indicators (which, as we have indicated, are divided into the 'core' and 'additional' indicators).

While the GRI guidelines are argued by many to have brought about improvements to sustainability reporting, it must be acknowledged that, not being mandatory, organizations can be selective about what indicators they choose to use in their reporting. However, the GRI includes an indicator called 'Application Levels' which organizations can use to reflect (in an icon on their report) how comprehensive their sustainability reports are in comparison with the whole range of issues and sustainability indicators covered in the GRI guidelines.

The key categories and subcategories of the draft G3 Guidelines, together with details of the 'indicator aspects' covered within the respective categories, are provided in Exhibit 9.1.[19]

EXHIBIT 9.1 An overview of the categories of indicators used within the GRI Sustainability Reporting Guidelines

A. Economic performance

The economic dimension of sustainability concerns the organisation's impacts on the economic conditions of its stakeholders and on economic systems at the local, national and global levels.

Economic performance indicators[20]

- Aspect: Economic Performance (four core indicators)
- Aspect: Market Presence (two core and one additional indicator)
- Aspect: Indirect Economic Impacts (one core and one additional indicator)

B. Environmental performance

The environmental dimension of sustainability concerns the organisation's impacts on living and non-living natural systems, including ecosystems, land, air and water. The structure of environmental indicators covers input (material, energy, water) and output (emissions, effluents, waste) related performance. In addition the indicators cover performance related to biodiversity, environmental compliance and other relevant information such as environmental expenditure and the impacts of products and services.

Environmental performance indicators

- Aspect: Materials (two core indicators)
- Aspect: Energy (two core and three additional indicators)
- Aspect: Water (one core and two additional indicators)

- Aspect: Biodiversity (two core and three additional indicators)
- Aspect: Emissions, Effluents and Waste (seven core and three additional indicators)
- Aspect: Products and services (two core indicators)
- Aspect: Compliance (one core indicator)
- Aspect: Transport (one additional indicator)
- Aspect: Overall (one additional indicator)

C. Social performance

The social dimension of sustainability concerns an organisation's impacts on the social systems within which it operates. The GRI social performance indicators identify key performance aspects surrounding labour practices, human rights and broader issues affecting consumers, community and other stakeholders in society. (Unlike economic and environmental performance, the G3 Guidelines divide social performance into four subgroups of performance indicators.)

Social performance indicators

C.1 Social performance: labor practices and decent work performance indicators

- Aspect: Employment (two core and one additional indicator)
- Aspect: Labor/Management Relations (two core indicators)
- Aspect: Occupational Health and Safety (two core and two additional indicators)
- Aspect: Training and Education (one core and two additional indicators)
- Aspect: Diversity and Opportunity (two core additional indicators)

C.2 Social performance: human rights performance indicators

- Aspect: Investment and Procurement Practices (two core and one additional indicator)
- Aspect: Non-discrimination (one core indicator)
- Aspect: Freedom of Association and Collective Bargaining (one core indicator)
- Aspect: Child Labor (one core indicator)
- Aspect: Forced and compulsory labour (one core indicator)
- Aspect: Security Practices (one additional indicator)
- Aspect: Indigenous rights (one additional indicator)

C.3 Social performance: society performance indicators

- Aspect: Community (one core indicator)
- Aspect: Corruption (three core indicators)
- Aspect: Public Policy (one core and one additional indicator)
- Aspect: Anti-Competitive Behaviour (one additional indicator)
- Aspect: Compliance (one core indicator)

> C.4 Social performance: product responsibility performance indicators
> - Aspect: Customer Health and Safety (one core and one additional indicators)
> - Aspect: Products and Service Labeling (one core and two additional indicators)
> - Aspect: Marketing Communications (one core and one additional indicator)
> - Aspect: Customer Privacy (one additional indicator)
> - Aspect: Compliance (one core indicator)

Source: Adapted from *Global Reporting Initiative* (2006).

The GRI guidelines consist of principles for defining report content and ensuring the quality of reported information as well as standard disclosures comprising performance indicators and other disclosure items. The guidelines also include guidance on specific technical issues in reporting. The 2006 (G3) guidelines comprise two main parts, these being:

- Part 1 – Defining report content, quality, and boundary
- Part 2 – Standard disclosures

The guidelines also include an introduction that provides an overview of sustainability reporting and addresses such issues as the purpose of preparing a sustainability report. The guidelines also provide an overview of issues associated with having the report reviewed by an independent third party. In relation to defining report content (which is included within Part 1), reference is made to a number of reporting principles, these being:

a **Materiality** 'The information in a report should cover topics and indicators that reflect the organization's significant economic, environmental, and social impacts, or that would substantively influence the assessments and decisions of stakeholders.' (GRI, 2006, p. 8)

b **Stakeholder inclusiveness** 'The reporting organization should identify its stakeholders and explain in the report how it has responded to their reasonable expectations and interests.' (GRI, 2006, p. 10)

c **Sustainability context** 'The reporting organization should present the organization's performance in the wider context of sustainability.' (GRI, 2006, p. 11)

d **Completeness** 'Coverage of the material topics and indicators, and definition of the report boundary should be sufficient to reflect significant economic, environmental, and social impacts and enable stakeholders to assess the reporting organization's performance in the reporting period.' (GRI, 2006, p. 12)

In relation to the 'quality of reported material', reference is made to a number of 'reporting principles for defining quality':

a **Balance** 'The report should reflect positive and negative aspects of the organization's performance to enable a reasoned assessment of overall performance.' (GRI, 2006, p. 13)

b **Comparability** 'Issues and information should be selected, compiled and reported consistently. Reported information should be presented in a manner that enables stakeholders to analyze changes in the organization's performance over time, and could support analysis relative to other organizations.' (GRI, 2006, p. 14)

c **Accuracy** 'The reported information should be sufficiently accurate and detailed for stakeholders to assess the reporting organization's performance.' (GRI, 2006, p. 15)

d **Timeliness** 'Reporting occurs on a regular schedule and information is available for stakeholders to make informed decisions.' (GRI, 2006, p. 16)

e **Clarity** 'Information should be made available in a manner that is understandable and accessible to stakeholders using the report.' (GRI, 2006, p. 16)

f **Reliability** 'Information and processes used in the preparation of a report should be gathered, recorded, compiled, analyzed and disclosed in a way that could be subject to examination and that establishes the quality and materiality of the information.' (GRI, 2006, p. 17)

As we can see, the above principles and qualitative characteristics are very similar to the qualitative characteristics that are typically promoted in relation to financial reporting. It is interesting to consider whether sustainability reporting should have similar attributes to financial reporting – what do you think?

In relation to Part 2 of the guidelines – to do with 'standard disclosures' – there are three different types of disclosures contained in this section, these being (GRI, 2006, p. 19):

1 **Strategy and Profile**: Disclosures that set the overall context for understanding organizational performance such as its strategy, profile, and governance.

2 **Management Approach**: Disclosures that cover how an organization addresses a given set of topics in order to provide context for understanding performance in a specific area.

3 **Performance Indicators**: Indicators that elicit comparable information on the economic, environmental, and social performance of the organization. [we have already detailed above summaries of the various indicators]

Readers are encouraged to go to the GRI's website to review the entire guidelines for themselves. The guidelines are expected to evolve continually over time. Clearly the GRI guidelines have evolved to provide extensive guidance on the issue of 'how' to report.

Apart from the GRI a number of other organizations have also released reporting guidelines, for example:

- Public Environmental Reporting Initiative (USA) (1992), The PERI Guidelines.
- Global Environmental Management Initiative (USA) (1994), Environment Reporting in a Total Quality Management Framework.
- Institute of Chartered Accountants in England and Wales (1996), Environmental Issues in Financial Reporting.
- United Nations Environment Programme (and SustainAbility) (1996), Engaging Stakeholders – Second International Progress Report on Company Environmental Reporting.
- UK Government's Advisory Committee on Business and the Environment (UK) (1997), Environmental Reporting and the Financial Sector – An Approach to Good Practice.

- European Chemical Industry Council (1998), Responsible Care: Health Safety and Environmental Reporting Guidelines.

- Environmental Task Force of the European Federation of Accountants (1999), FEE Discussion Paper: Towards a Generally Accepted Framework for Environmental Reporting.

- Business in the Community (UK) (2001), Winning with Integrity: A Guide to Social Responsibility.

- Association of British Insurers (2002), Disclosure Guidelines on Socially Responsible Investment.

- Group of 100 (2003), Sustainability: A Guide to Triple Bottom Line Reporting.

- The Prince of Wales's Accounting for Sustainability Project (from 2006 onwards) an evolving set of guidance on Accounting for Sustainability and Connected (sustainability) Reporting.

Since the mid-2000s, some 'leading edge' sustainability reporters have used the ideas underlying some of the above frameworks to re-integrate into their annual reports disclosures about their most material social and environmental impacts. You will recall that we discussed earlier in this chapter that it became increasingly common from the 1990s for large companies to produce separate stand-alone sustainability reports, moving into these reports much of the social and environmental information that had previously been published alongside the financial information in the annual report (sometimes these sustainability reports were referred to as *triple bottom line reports*). As a growing number of companies, and their investors, have recently come to recognize the importance of social and environmental sustainability for long-term financial sustainability, they have also recognized that it is important for the report focusing on the information needs of investors – the annual report – to provide a connected picture of the organization's most material economic, social and environmental sustainability policies, practices, risks and outcomes (Hopwood *et al.*, 2010). Some organizations, such as the large Danish pharmaceutical company Novo Nordisk, have gone even further in their re-integration of their social and environmental disclosures with their financial reports, by publishing a single sustainability and financial report that is both GRI and IFRS compliant (Dey and Burns, 2010).

In summarizing this section about 'how' to report we have seen that there are a number of limitations with financial accounting practices that tend to preclude financial accounting as a means of producing information about social and environmental performance of reporting entities. Given these limitations, alternative processes have been suggested such as the Global Reporting Initiative's Sustainability Reporting Guidelines. Before we conclude our discussion about 'how' to report we will consider another proposed approach to accounting for social and environmental performance. This approach – which has not been widely embraced – requires an entity to calculate a cost for the social and environmental externalities it creates.

Accounting for externalities

Reporting guidance such as that provided by the GRI provides numerous sustainability-related key performance indicators (KPIs) but does not consider the issue of trying to 'cost' the externalities caused by business. For example, the GRI does not provide guidance about placing a cost on such things as the pollution being generated by an organization, or any adverse health effects caused by the products or processes of a reporting entity. As explained earlier, generally accepted financial accounting practices also ignore the social and environmental externalities generated by a reporting entity. However, a very limited number of organizations have attempted to put a cost on the environmental externalities and benefits caused by their operations.[21] These costs and benefits are then usually taken from (or added to) traditionally calculated profits to come up with some measure of 'real profit'. This is an interesting approach that represents a departure from generally accepted accounting principles, and is based on many estimates and 'guesstimates'. For example, the Dutch computer consultancy organization BSO/Origin provided some environmental accounts in which a notional value was placed on the environmental costs imposed by the organization upon society. (The last set of accounts prepared by BSO/Origin addressing 'environmental costs' was released in 1995.) This value was then deducted from profits determined using conventional financial accounting to provide a measure of 'net value added'. Obviously, quantifying environmental effects/impacts in financial terms requires many assumptions. As BSO/Origin stated in its 1994 environmental report:

> This is the fifth year that BSO/Origin has presented an environmental account as well as a financial report. This is done on the basis of the 'extracted value' concept, the burden a product places on the ecosystem from the moment of its manufacture until the moment of its decomposition. This burden is expressed in terms of the costs which would have been incurred either to undo the detrimental effect to the point where the natural ecosystem could neutralise it, or to develop a responsible alternative. The entries are based on absolute data as supplied by the cells, educated guesstimates and extrapolations. The purpose is not to provide precise calculations accurate to the last decimal point, but to fulfil the principle of complete accounting, in which extracted as well as value added is included.

By including environmental costs and benefits in their profit calculations, organizations may be contributing to ongoing debates questioning the validity of profitability calculations which omit important social costs such as damage done to the environment. A number of companies have experimented with methods designed to determine the notional costs of the externalities being generated by their activities. These include Baxter International Inc. (USA), IBM (UK), Interface Europe, Anglian Water (UK), Wessex Water (UK) and Landcare Ltd (NZ).

The approaches adopted by some of these organizations include determining a notional 'sustainable cost'. This is explained by Gray and Bebbington (1992, p. 15) as:

> the amount an organisation must spend to put the biosphere at the end of the accounting period back into the state (or its equivalent) it was in at the beginning of the accounting period. Such a figure would be a notional one, and disclosed as a charge to a company's profit and loss account. Thus we would be presented with a broad estimate of the extent to which the accounting profits had been generated from a sustainable source … our estimates suggest that the

---

[21] An externality can be defined as 'an impact that an entity has on parties external to the organisation' (Deegan, 2005, p. 1186). From an accounting perspective, an 'externality' is not recognized in the financial statements. In part, this is because of the 'entity principle' embraced within financial accounting.

sustainable cost calculations would produce the sort of answer which would demonstrate that no Western company had made a profit of any kind in the last 50 years or so.

According to Bebbington and Gray (2001, p. 567) the sustainable cost calculation involves two elements, these being:

1 a consideration of the costs required to ensure that inputs to the organization have no adverse environmental impacts in their production. These are costs which arise in addition to those costs already internalized in the most environmentally sound products and services which are currently available; and

2 the costs required to remedy any environmental impacts which arise even if the organization's inputs had a zero environmental impact.

After considering the brief overview provided above, we can conclude that there is great diversity in how organizations account for their social and environmental impacts. This diversity is expected given the lack of regulation in this area of reporting. We will conclude this chapter by considering social audits. Social audits provide data which are then typically used in an entity's social and environmental reports. A social audit typically relies upon engaging a multitude of stakeholder groups.

9.10 Social audit

In this chapter, and in Chapter 8, we discussed the importance of organizations complying with community expectations. As we argued, if an organization does not comply with community expectations (often referred to as breaching the 'social contract'), or the expectations of particularly powerful stakeholders, then this can have negative implications for the survival of an organization. One way of seeing whether the organizations' performance is conforming with the expectations of various stakeholder groups is to undertake and then report what is referred to as a 'social audit'.

According to Elkington (1997, p. 88) the purpose of social auditing is for an organization to assess its performance in relation to society's requirements and expectations. This is often done by directly soliciting the views of various stakeholder groups. Obviously, different management teams will be interested in the views of different stakeholder groups. Managers that take a broader ethical perspective to identifying their stakeholders will typically seek the opinions and views of a broader cross-section of stakeholders. Social audits allow a company to examine its social impacts and to establish whether it is meeting its own social objectives. The results of a social audit often form the basis of an entity's publicly released social accounts (thereby increasing the apparent transparency of the organization), and the outcomes of social audits can be considered as an important part of the ongoing dialogue with various stakeholder groups. The Body Shop provides an insight into its social audit. According to The Body Shop Social Performance Report 2007 (p. 2, 3):

> Our social audit program is one way we can listen to all our stakeholders and evaluate how well they feel we are fulfilling and demonstrating our values every day. Importantly, through this process we also gather feedback and ideas that contribute to positive organizational change and our plans for the future

> ... Our social performance data is collected through a bi-annual stakeholder survey process. We ask our stakeholders to share their thoughts on how well they believe we fulfill and demonstrate our company goals and values based on their experience. We evaluate the numbers and written comments to identify opportunities for organizational improvement. Feedback and comments are an important part of the survey process because they help us understand the sources of stakeholder satisfaction and dissatisfaction with our values ... Our social audit process is externally verified and includes an independent assurance statement.

In discussing who they involved in the social audit, The Body Shop Social Performance Report 2007 stated (p. 4):

> In 2006, over a period of four months from March to June, more than 17,000 stakeholders participated in our social audit program. The key stakeholder groups were our staff (all businesses), The Body Shop customers, The Body Shop At Home consultants, Children's Centre families, suppliers and community organisations. The largest group of participants were our customers, followed by our staff. There was lower participation within the supplier and community organization stakeholder groups.

In relation to employees, The Body Shop's social audit asked the employees a number of questions on each of the following issues, upon which they reported the findings:

- Company values and ethos;
- Care, honesty and respect;
- Equal employment opportunity;
- Pride and Trust;
- Communication;
- Pay, benefits and recognition;
- Career development;
- Commitment to environmental issues.

Many of us might question whether the social audit data presented in The Body Shop Social Performance Report 2007 represents 'accounting' results. As we have explained in this chapter, and in Chapter 8, it really gets back to the issue of 'accountability'. The concept of 'accounting' cannot really be considered independently to the concept of 'accountability'. If the management of organizations, such as some of those discussed in this chapter, accept that they have a responsibility (accountability) in relation to the financial, social and environmental aspects of their company's performance then they will choose to provide a financial account (that is, financial reports), a social account, and an environmental account (all of which might be provided within a sustainability report, or provided separately). That is, their 'accounting systems' will embrace a broader perspective of 'accountability' rather than restricting the analysis to financial accounting.

Reflective of the interest in social accounting and social auditing, a social accounting standard was released in 1998 by the organization known as Social Accountability International, which until recently was known as the Council on Economic Priorities Accreditation Agency (Social Accountability International is a non-profit affiliate of the

Council on Economic Priorities).[22] The standard entitled SA8000 (SA stands for Social Accountability) focuses on issues associated with human rights, health and safety, and equal opportunities. It requires the audit of performance at each site against the principles of the UN Declaration of Human Rights, the International Labour Organization conventions and the UN Convention on the Rights of the Child.

Once activities such as social audits are undertaken they can then act as a catalyst for organizations, and, importantly, for senior management to embrace new values. A 'sustainable organization' needs to ensure that it complies with community expectations. As such, activities such as social audits make good business sense. Undertaking a social audit, particularly if the audit is undertaken by a credible, independent party, should act to increase the perceived transparency of the organization. A newspaper article, reproduced as Accounting Headline 9.5, supports this view in relation to the activities of Camelot – the organization responsible for running lotteries within the United Kingdom. Camelot was seeking another term to run the lotteries, but had been the subject of much public criticism about how they were using the substantial funds that they were attracting. They elected to undertake a social audit to highlight the positive aspects of its operations and to help it achieve its aim of having the government renew its licence to run lotteries.

Accounting Headline 9.5

Implementing social audits as a possible means of establishing corporate legitimacy – the case of Camelot

Camelot puts itself on trial

By Roger Crowe

Camelot, the National Lottery Operator, has decided to conduct a social audit in an effort to rescue its reputation before bidding for a new licence in 2001.

The exercise will aim to give an independent seal of approval to the way the lottery has been run, countering accusations that Camelot has made too much money, failed customers and charities and abused its monopoly position.

It follows Camelot's appointment in July of the campaigner Sue Slipman to the new post of director of social responsibility. Ms Slipman will be responsible for the audit until next month. She has described it as 'a challenging project'.

The £250,000 audit will report the views of six groups including staff, retailers and the general public, on how the lottery company is carrying out its responsibilities.

The decision to follow companies such as Body Shop and Shell in seeking external scrutiny of its social role was taken by the board in June.

---

[22] The website of Social Accountability International states: 'Our mission is to promote human rights for workers around the world as a standards organization, ethical supply chain resource, and programs developer. SAI promotes workers' rights primarily through our voluntary SA8000 system. Based on the International Labor Organization (ILO) standards and U.N. Human Rights Conventions, SA8000 is widely accepted as the most viable and comprehensive international ethical workplace management system available. SAI works with an array of stakeholders who are instrumental in the ever-continuing effort to improve and implement the SA8000 system.'

Companies such as BP and BT, as well as some of the international accountancy firms, have focused on social auditing as a means of justifying controversial actions and protecting reputations.

PricewaterhouseCoopers (PWC), the international audit and consultancy firm, is preparing to launch a Reputation Assurance Service which aims to help multinationals assess their social and environmental impact. Glen Peters, the firm's director of futures, said that managing a company's reputation will be one of the greatest challenges of the next decade. He expects 1,000 companies in the US and Europe to embrace the notion of wider accountability over the next five years.

Six large companies have been testing the PWC system, which will be launched in January. They are using the approach to examine their responsibilities to five groups – shareholders, employees, customers, society in general, and 'partners', including suppliers.

Mr Peters said big businesses were interested in such an exercise because of the need to back up promises such as 'the customer is number one' and 'employees are our most valuable asset'.

'Reputation is going to be a business's most important asset', he said. 'Businesses will need to adopt a systematic approach to protecting their reputations.'

Camelot has adopted a social audit after facing a furore over bonuses for directors and accusations of misconduct against its technical supplier, GTech.

The lottery operator has commissioned the New Economics Foundation (NEF) to manage the audit. The NEF pioneered the concept in Britain, initially with Traidcraft, the Third World crafts importer, then the cosmetics chain, Body Shop.

Adrian Henriques, head of social audit at NEF, said: 'Social auditing is becoming part of the mainstream. It is about determining what impact a company has on society and how society affects the company.'

Richard Brown, director of government relations at Camelot, said it was crucial that an external agency such as the NEF was involved to counter accusations that this was merely a public relations exercise. 'NEF will ensure that all stakeholder groups are involved in ongoing dialogue which is externally verified.'

Mr Brown said the decision to undertake the audit was not driven solely by the campaign to win a second licence term for the lottery. 'It is responding to changing values of the 1990s', he said. 'But it is also an important way of telling people there are plenty of things we can be proud of.'

He suggested the row over directors' bonuses might have been avoided if Camelot had been carrying out a social audit from the start, because the board would have understood how controversial the pay packages were.

Mr. Brown dismissed worries about the link with GTech, which was originally a partner in the lottery consortium but is now merely a supplier.

'If people have concerns about GTech, we would like to know about it.'

One unusual feature of the Camelot audit will be the establishment of a permanent 'stakeholder council' which will oversee the process and continue to monitor action or issues arising from it.

The audit will take about 18 months to complete and is not expected to be published until 2000, when applications for the new lottery licence will be submitted.

Source: *Guardian,* 21 September 1998
©Guardian News and Media Limited 2010

In this section we have examined a variety of perspectives related to *how* organizations can and do provide information to meet the identified needs and expectations of their stakeholders.

Chapter summary

This chapter has reviewed various issues associated with corporate social and environmental reporting. Since around the early 1990s many organizations throughout the world have been providing an increasing amount of information about their social and environmental performance in a variety of reports. Concerns associated with sustainability (which relates to economic, social and environmental performance issues) have increased since the early 1990s and the evolution of corporate social and environmental performance reporting appears to be related to these concerns, as developments in reporting are probably a reflection of changing community expectations about the performance and responsibilities of business. In examining various theoretical issues associated with social and environmental reporting, we structured our discussion to follow the *why – to whom – for what – how* stages of the sustainability reporting process.

In the *why* stage we explored various aspects of the motivations for organizations to engage in corporate social responsibility and social and environmental reporting. When a firm voluntarily discloses information publicly about its social and environmental performance this may imply that the managers are acknowledging that they are accountable to a broad group of stakeholders in relation to not only their financial performance, but also their social and environmental performance. However, as this chapter indicates, not all people consider that managers have social responsibilities to a broad group of stakeholders. Some researchers believe that the prime responsibility of managers is to shareholders alone and, within these confines, to maximizing shareholder (financial) value. However, this narrow perspective of corporate responsibility seems to be becoming less widely accepted, as an interrelated understanding of social, environmental and economic sustainability becomes more widely accepted.

For the *who* (or *to whom*) stage, we examined the range of stakeholders that different organizations are likely to wish to address in their social and environmental (or sustainability) reporting strategies. This range of stakeholders is likely to be directly related to an organization's motives for engaging in social and environmental reporting. It will be very broad for organizations which operate in a manner consistent with the ethical branch of stakeholder theory. Conversely, organizations following the managerial branch of stakeholder theory will tend to focus on the demands and expectations of a narrower range of stakeholders – those with the most power over the organization.

Having addressed issues relating to the identification of stakeholders to whom an organization's social and environmental reporting will be directed, we then explored some theoretical perspectives regarding the mechanisms which organizations may use to identify *what* information these stakeholders need, or *for what* issues these stakeholders believe the organization is socially and environmentally responsible and accountable. We first drew on several studies which demonstrated that stakeholders do appear to make use of information about the social and environmental performance of organizations, and we were thus able to conclude that stakeholders do want some social and environmental performance information. We then analysed theoretical perspectives on processes of stakeholder dialogue, which can be used by organizations to develop an understanding of what social and environmental information is likely to be demanded by their stakeholders. We demonstrated the difficulties involved in seeking to reach an acceptable consensus view among a wide range of stakeholders regarding the social, environmental and economic responsibilities of an organization – and the consequent accountability duties related to these responsibilities.

Finally, in the *how* stage, we reviewed perspectives on some of the processes involved in the production of social and environmental reports, including the limitations of conventional financial reporting for capturing and reflecting the social and environmental impact of an organization's policies and practices, key aspects of the *Global Reporting Initiative*, and some issues related to social auditing. Evidence shows that the practice of sustainability reporting is seen as a major issue in corporate accountability and reporting in the twenty-first century.

Questions

9.1 What has the environment to do with accounting?

9.2 What is accountability and what is its relationship to:

    a accounting?

    b an organization's responsibilities?

9.3 What is sustainable development?

9.4 Do conventional financial accounting practices and definitions encourage or assist corporations to adopt socially and environmentally sustainable business practices? Explain your answer.

9.5 Would advocates of Positive Accounting Theory (as explained in Chapter 7) believe that organizations will embrace sustainable development in the way described by *The Brundtland Report*? Explain your view.

9.6 What is an externality, and why do financial accounting practices typically ignore externalities?

9.7 What is a social audit and why would a profit-seeking entity bother with one?

9.8 Of what relevance to the accounting profession is sustainable development?

9.9 Why do you think that the accounting profession has generally not released any accounting standards pertaining to the disclosure of environmental information?

9.10 Evidence shows that business entities and business associations typically make submissions to government which argue in favour of maintaining the voluntary status of social and environmental performance reporting. That is, they typically oppose the introduction of legislation to require them to report information about their social and environmental performance. Why do you think this is the case?

9.11 Collison (2003, p. 861) states that: 'Attention to the interests of shareholders above all other groups is implicit in much of what is taught to accounting and finance students. The very construction of a profit and loss account … is a continual, and usually unstated, reminder that the interests of only one group of stakeholders should be maximised. Indeed it may be very difficult for accounting and finance students to even conceive of another way in which affairs could be ordered … even at the algebraic level, let alone the moral.'

    a Do you agree or disagree with Collison, and why?

    b If 'profit' maximization is biased towards maximizing the interests of only one stakeholder group, would you expect that over time there will be less emphasis on profits, and more emphasis on other performance indicators? Why? What might be some of the alternative measures of performance?

    c Would Collison's comments provide a justification for moves towards profit measures that incorporate 'full costs' (that is, that consider the externalities of business)?

9.12 If a particular social or environmental incident occurs which involves an organization and which generates negative media attention, then how would you expect the organization to react from a disclosure perspective?

9.13 How would the following theories (which are addressed in Chapters 7 and 8) explain corporate social responsibility reporting?

    a Positive Accounting Theory

    b legitimacy theory

    c stakeholder theory

    d institutional theory.

9.14 In publicly released reports a number of organizations are referring to their 'public licence to operate'. What do you think they mean by this, and is there a theoretical perspective that can explain what this term means?

9.15 What is 'enlightened self-interest'?

9.16 Some people argue that fixating on maximizing corporate profits and increasing shareholder value will ultimately lead to benefits for all people within society (perhaps through a 'trickle down effect'). Evaluate this view.

9.17 Consider how the concept of sustainable development, as it applies to business entities, compares to the accountant's notion of a 'going concern'. Do you believe that they are similar, or are they quite different?

9.18 If a major European mining company reports record profits is this profit figure misleading if the same company has polluted various river systems and has emitted various toxic substances into the air, but has not placed a cost on these externalities?

9.19 Read Accounting Headline 9.6 which discusses the health effects caused by highly processed food products, and then:

a Explain how or why processed food companies can report accounting profits even though the consequences of their activities are believed to be causing significant social and economic impacts within society.

b Suggest an approach to accounting that would require food producers to internalize the social and economic impacts that their products create for society. Your suggestion can represent a departure from existing or traditional accounting practices.

Accounting Headline 9.6

Accounting profits ignore social impacts of corporation's products

Free choice isn't healthy for the food industry's menu

By Felicity Lawrence

… The National Institute for Health and Clinical Excellence (Nice) has concluded that the government could save 40,000 lives and many millions of pounds each year by tackling our junk food industry … Nice, which has the unenviable job of giving guidance on NHS spending priorities, is merely highlighting what has been obvious for years: that the state could make huge savings if it prevented the cancers, heart disease, strokes, diabetes and obesity caused by poor diet rather than waiting to treat them, just as health experts did with tobacco. But its recommendations have already been overtaken by events.

New brooms at the Department of Health have thanked Nice for its pains by suggesting it has overreached itself, and by reverting to the tired old mantra that eating healthily is a matter of individual responsibility and choice.

Traffic-light labelling was voted down in Europe only last week, scuppered by food industry lobbying of breathtaking determination and expense. European consumer watchdogs say €1bn was spent by multi-nationals bombarding MEPs with emails and meetings ahead of the vote. Instead an industry-sponsored scheme of nutrition labelling that serves only to confuse has won the day.

… This is not a world in which individuals make free, fully informed choices about food. It is a world in which children are targeted by junk-food manufacturers from the youngest age. We live in a culture in which adult appetites are shaped by marketing that preys on our insecurities and emotional needs. It is an environment in which understanding the labels on our food practically requires a PhD in food chemistry.

… Food manufacturers operate in a market system that puts no monetary value on health or social costs. They cannot make the same return from good, plain food that they can from the industrialised packaging of cheap commodity ingredients – fats, starches and sugars.

City analysts at JP Morgan expressed the quandary neatly in a report in 2006 on how the industry was responding to the obesity crisis. Categories of food that are healthy – fresh fruits, wholegrains, pulses – only give manufacturers and processors below-average margins of 3% to 6%. Relatively simple processed foods, like cheese or plain yoghurt, give 9% to

> 12% margins. Highly processed cereals, snacks, biscuits, soft drinks and confectionery give brand manufacturers more than 15% margins.
>
> They have to stay up the 'value chain'. But the problem for the rest of us is that what they call added value is not nutritional value. Nutritional value is generally stripped away in inverse proportion to the shareholder value added, which is why governments and Nice have to intervene.
>
> Source: *Guardian,* 23 June 2010, p. 32
> ©Guardian News and Media Limited 2010

9.20 Read Accounting Headline 9.6 and then answer these questions.

    a How would a food company account for the social costs created by obesity?

    b Should a food company account for the social costs created by obesity?

9.21 An article appearing in *The Independent* newspaper (UK, 18 April 2005, p. 20) entitled 'The ethical revolution sweeping through the world's sweatshops' identified how organizations such as Nike and Gap had put in place various mechanisms to help ensure improvement in the conditions of factory workers. In relation to the responses of Nike and Gap:

    a Why do you think that companies like Nike and Gap responded to the community concerns?

    b Is this a case of enlightened self-interest or a case of a company embracing a form of responsibility to the stakeholders affected by its operations?

References

Accounting Standards Steering Committee (1975) *The Corporate Report,* London: Institute of Chartered Accountants in England & Wales.

Adams, C.A. (2002) 'Internal organizational factors influencing corporate social and ethical reporting', *Accounting, Auditing & Accountability Journal,* **15** (2), 223–50.

Adams, C.A. (2004) 'The ethical, social and environmental reporting-performance portrayal gap', *Accounting, Auditing & Accountability Journal,* **17** (5), 731–57.

Adams, C. & Frost, G. (2004) *The Development of Corporate Web-sites and Implications for Ethical, Social and Environmental Reporting through these Media,* Edinburgh: Institute of Chartered Accountants in Scotland.

Adams, C.A. & Harte, G. (1998) 'The changing portrayal of the employment of women in British banks' and retail companies' corporate annual reports', *Accounting, Organizations & Society,* **23** (8), 781–812.

Anderson, J.C. & Frankle, A.W. (1980) 'Voluntary social reporting: An Iso-beta portfolio analysis', *The Accounting Review,* **55** (3), 467–79.

Bebbington, J. & Gray, R. (2001) 'An account of sustainability: Failure, success and a reconceptualisation', *Critical Perspectives on Accounting*, **12** (5), 557–87.

Bebbington, J. & Larrinaga-Gonzalez, C. (2008) 'Carbon trading: Accounting and reporting issues', *European Accounting Review*, **17** (4), 697–717.

Beck, U. (1992) *Risk Society: Towards a New Modernity*, London: SAGE.

Beck, U. (1999) *World Risk Society*, Cambridge: Polity Press.

Belkaoui, A.R. (1976) 'The impact of the disclosure of environmental effects of organizational behavior on the market', *Financial Management* (Winter), 26–31.

Benston, G.J. (1982) 'Accounting and corporate accountability', *Accounting Organizations and Society*, **6** (2), 87–105.

Bhimani, A. & Soonawalla, K. (2010) 'Sustainability and organizational connectivity at HSBC', in: Hopwood, A.G., Unerman, J. & Fries, J. (eds.) *Accounting for Sustainability: Practical Insights*, London: Earthscan, 173–90.

Blacconiere, W.G. & Patten, D.M. (1994) 'Environmental disclosures, regulatory costs and changes in firm value', *Journal of Accounting and Economics*, **18**, 357–77.

Brady, A. (2003) *Forecasting the Impact of Sustainability Issues on the Reputation of Large Multinational Corporations*, Cambridge: Judge Institute of Management, University of Cambridge.

Brigham, M., Kiosse, P.V. & Otley, D. (2010) '"One Aviva, twice the value": connecting sustainability at Aviva plc', in: Hopwood, A.G., Unerman, J. & Fries, J. (eds.) *Accounting for Sustainability: Practical Insights*, London: Earthscan, 191–214.

Buhr, N. (1998) 'Environmental performance, legislation and annual report disclosure: The case of acid rain and Falconbridge', *Accounting, Auditing and Accountability Journal*, **11** (2), 163–90.

Buhr, N. (2007) 'Histories and rationales for sustainability reporting', in: Unerman, J., Bebbington, J. & O'Dwyer, B. (eds.) *Sustainability Accounting and Accountability*. Abingdon: Routledge, 57–69.

Campbell, D. J. (2000) 'Legitimacy theory or managerial construction? Corporate social disclosure in Marks and Spencer Plc corporate reports, 1969–1997', *Accounting Forum*, **24** (1), 80–100.

Ceres (2010) *The 21st Century Corporation: The Ceres Roadmap for Sustainability*, Boston, MA: Ceres.

Clarkson, M. (1995) 'A stakeholder framework for analyzing and evaluating corporate social performance', *Academy of Management Review*, **20** (1), 92–118.

Collison, D. J. (2003) 'Corporate propaganda: Its implications for accounting and accountability', *Accounting, Auditing & Accountability Journal*, **16** (5), 853–86.

Commission of European Communities (2001) *Promoting a European Framework for Corporate Social Responsibility*, Brussels: Green Paper: Commission of European Communities.

Coulson, A. (2007) 'Environmental and social assessment in sustainable finance', in: Unerman, J., Bebbington, J. & O'Dwyer, B. (eds.) *Sustainability Accounting and Accountability*. Abingdon: Routledge, 266–81.

Deegan, C. (1996) 'A review of mandated environmental reporting requirements for Australian corporations together with an analysis of contemporary Australian and overseas environmental reporting practices', *Environmental and Planning Law Journal*, **13** (2), 120–32.

Deegan, C. (2005) *Australian Financial Accounting*, Sydney: McGraw-Hill.

Deegan, C.M. & Rankin, M. (1997) 'The materiality of environmental information to users of accounting reports', *Accounting, Auditing and Accountability Journal*, **10** (4), 562–83.

Dey, C. & Burns, J. (2010) 'Integrated reporting at Novo Nordisk', in: Hopwood, A.G., Unerman, J. & Fries, J. (eds.) *Accounting for Sustainability: Practical Insights*. London: Earthscan, 215–32.

Dillard, J.F., Brown, D. & Marshall, R.S. (2005) 'An environmentally enlightened accounting', *Accounting Forum*, **29** (1), 77–101.

Donaldson, T. (1982) *Corporations and Morality*, Englewood Cliffs, NJ: Prentice-Hall.

Elkington, J. (1997) *Cannibals with Forks: The Triple Bottom Line of 21st Century Business*, Oxford: Capstone.

Engels, A. (2009) 'The European Emissions Trading Scheme: An exploratory study of how companies learn to account for carbon', *Accounting, Organizations and Society*, **34** (3–4), 488–98.

Environmental Accounting and Auditing Reporter (2000) 'First standard for building corporate accountability and trust', Vol. 5, No. 1.

European Commission (1992) *Towards Sustainability: A Community Programme of Policy and Action in Relation to the Environment and Sustainable Development*, Brussels: European Commission.

Freedman, M. & Patten, D.M. (2004) 'Evidence on the pernicious effect of financial report environmental disclosure', *Accounting Forum*, **28** (1), 27–41.

Freedman, M. & Stagliano, A.J. (2008) 'Accountability and emissions allowance trading: Lessons learned from the U.S. electric utility industry', *Social and Environmental Accountability Journal*, **28** (2), 62–77.

Freeman, R. (1984) *Strategic Management: A Stakeholder Approach*, Marshall, MA: Pitman.

Friedman, M. (1962) *Capitalism and Freedom*, Chicago: University of Chicago Press.

Georgakopoulos, G. & Thomson, I. (2005) 'Organic salmon farming: Risk perceptions, decision heuristics and the absence of environmental accounting', *Accounting Forum*, **29** (1), 49–75.

Gray, R. (1992) 'Accounting and environmentalism: An exploration of the challenge of gently accounting for accountability, transparency and sustainability', *Accounting Organizations and Society*, **17** (5), 399–426.

Gray, R. (2005) 'Social, environmental and sustainability reporting and organisational value creation? Whose value? Whose creation?', in: European Accounting Association annual congress – Symposium on New Models of Business Reporting, 18–20 May 2005, Gothenburg.

Gray, R. (2010) 'Is accounting for sustainability actually accounting for sustainability … and how would we know? An exploration of narratives of organizations and the planet', *Accounting, Organizations and Society*, **35** (1), 47–62.

Gray, R. & Bebbington, J. (1992) 'Can the grey men go green?', Discussion Paper, Centre for Social and Environmental Accounting Research, University of Dundee.

Gray, R. & Bebbington, J. (2001) *Accounting for the Environment*, London: Sage.

Gray, R., Bebbington, J., Collison, D., Kouhy, R., Lyon, B., Reid, C., Russell, A. & Stevenson, L. (1998) *The Valuation* *of Assets and Liabilities: Environmental Law and the Impact of the Environmental Agenda for Business*, Edinburgh: Institute of Chartered Accountants in Scotland.

Gray, R., Dey, C., Owen, D., Evans, R. & Zadek, S. (1997) 'Struggling with the praxis of social accounting: Stakeholders, accountability, audits and procedures', *Accounting, Auditing and Accountability Journal*, **10** (3), 325–64.

Gray, R., Owen, D. & Adams, C. (1996) *Accounting and Accountability: Changes and Challenges in Corporate Social and Environmental Reporting*, London: Prentice-Hall.

Gray, R., Owen, D. & Maunders, K.T. (1991) 'Accountability, corporate social reporting and the external social audits', *Advances in Public Interest Accounting*, **4**, 1–21.

GRI (2006) *Sustainability Reporting Guidelines, Version 3.0*, Amsterdam: Global Reporting Initiative.

Guthrie, J. & Parker, L.D. (1989) 'Corporate social reporting: a rebuttal of legitimacy theory', *Accounting & Business Research*, **19** (76), 343–52.

Habermas, J. (1992) *Moral Consciousness and Communicative Action*, Cambridge: Polity Press.

Hopwood, A.G., Unerman, J. & Fries, J. (eds.) (2010) *Accounting for Sustainability: Practical Insights*, London: Earthscan.

Hutton, W. (1996) *The State We're In*, London: Vintage.

Ingram, R.W. (1978) 'Investigation of the information content of certain social responsibility disclosures', *Journal of Accounting Research*, **16** (2), 270–85.

ISEA (2005) *Accountability: AA1000 Series* [online]. Available at: http://www.accountability.org.uk/aa1000/default.asp [accessed 8 June 2005].

Jaggi, B. & Freedman, M. (1982) 'An analysis of the information content of pollution disclosures'. *Financial Review*, **19** (5), 142–52.

Lewis, L. & Unerman, J. (1999) 'Ethical relativism: A reason for differences in corporate social reporting?', *Critical Perspectives on Accounting*, **10** (4), 521–47.

Lohmann, L. (2009) 'Toward a different debate in environmental accounting: The cases of carbon and cost-benefit', *Accounting, Organizations and Society*, **34** (3–4), 499–534.

Lorraine, N.H.J., Collison, D.J. & Power, D.M. (2004) 'An analysis of the stock market impact of environmental performance information', *Accounting Forum*, **28** (1), 7–26.

Lovell, H., Aguiar, T., Bebbington, J. & Larrinaga-Gonzalez, C. (2010) *Accounting for Carbon, ACCA Research Report 122*. London: Association of Chartered Certified Accountants and International Emissions Trading Association.

Mathews, M.R. (1993) *Socially Responsible Accounting*, London: Chapman and Hall.

Meadows, D.H., Randers, J. & Meadows, D.L. (2004) *Limits to Growth: The 30 Year Update*, London: Earthscan.

Neimark, M.K. (1992) *The Hidden Dimensions of Annual Reports: Sixty Years of Social Conflict at General Motors*, New York: Markus Wiener.

O'Dwyer, B. (2005) 'The construction of a social account: A case study in an overseas aid agency', *Accounting, Organizations and Society*, **30** (3), 279–96.

Owen, D., Shaw, K. & Cooper, S. (2005) *The Operating and Financial Review: A Catalyst for Improved Corporate Social and Environmental Disclosure?*, London: ACCA.

Rinaldi, L. & Unerman, J. (2009) 'Stakeholder engagement and dialogue initiatives of UK FTSE100 companies over the Internet: An empirical analysis', *Interdisciplinary Perspectives on Accounting Conference*, Innsbruck.

Shane, P. & Spicer, B. (1983) 'Market response to environmental information produced outside the firm', *The Accounting Review*, **58** (3), 521–38.

Solomon, A. & Lewis, L. (2002) 'Incentives and disincentives for corporate environmental disclosure', *Business Strategy and the Environment*, **11** (3), 154–69.

Stern, N. (2007) *The Economics of Climate Change: The Stern Review*, Cambridge: Cambridge University Press.

Stern, N. (2009) *Managing Climate Change and Overcoming Poverty: Facing the Realities and Building a Global Agreement*, London: Grantham Research Institute on Climate Change and the Environment, London School of Economics and Political Science.

Tinker, A. & Neimark, M. (1987) 'The role of annual reports in gender and class contradictions at General Motors: 1917–1976', *Accounting, Organizations and Society*, **12** (1), 71–88.

Tinker, A. & Neimark, M. (1988) 'The struggle over meaning in accounting and corporate research: A comparative evaluation of conservative and critical historiography', *Accounting, Auditing & Accountability Journal*, **1** (1), 55–74.

Unerman, J. (2000a) 'An investigation into the development of accounting for social, environmental and ethical accountability: A century of corporate social disclosures at Shell', Unpublished PhD thesis, University of Sheffield.

Unerman, J. (2000b) 'Reflections on quantification in corporate social reporting content analysis', *Accounting, Auditing & Accountability Journal*, **13** (5), 667–80.

Unerman, J. (2007) 'Stakeholder engagement and dialogue', in: Unerman, J., Bebbington, J. & O'Dwyer, B. (eds.) *Sustainability Accounting and Accountability.* Abingdon: Routledge, 86–103.

Unerman, J. & Bennett, M. (2004) 'Increased stakeholder dialogue and the internet: towards greater corporate accountability or reinforcing capitalist hegemony?', *Accounting, Organizations and Society*, **29** (7), 685–707.

Unerman, J. & O'Dwyer, B. (2010) 'Evolution of risk, opportunity and the business case in embedding connected reporting at BT', in: Hopwood, A.G., Unerman, J. & Fries, J. (eds.) *Accounting for Sustainability: Practical Insights.* London: Earthscan, 149–72.

Venetoulis, J., Chazan, D. & Gaudet, C. (2004) *Ecological Footprint of Nations*, Oakland, CA: Redefining Progress.

World Commission on Environment and Development (1987) *Our Common Future (the Brundtland Report)*, Oxford: Oxford University Press.

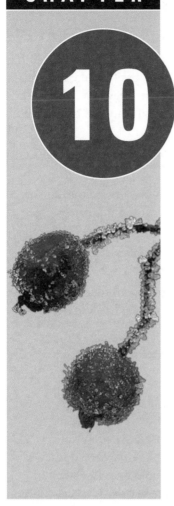

10

Reactions of Capital Markets to Financial Reporting

❖ LEARNING OBJECTIVES

Upon completing this chapter readers should:

❖ understand the role of capital market research in assessing the information content of accounting disclosures;

❖ understand the assumptions of market efficiency typically adopted in capital market research;

❖ understand the difference between capital market research that looks at the information content of accounting disclosures, and capital market research that uses share price data as a benchmark for evaluating accounting disclosures;

❖ be able to explain why unexpected accounting earnings and abnormal share price returns are expected to be related;

❖ be able to outline the major results of capital market research into financial accounting and disclosure.

Opening issues

Assume that there are five companies from the same industry with the same accounting year-end date, 31 December. All five companies are to make earnings announcements for the financial year (the announcements being made in February), but the earnings announcements are spread over two weeks, with no two companies announcing their earnings on the same date.

- Would you expect the earnings announcements made by each company to impact on their share prices and, if so, why?
- If it is found that the share prices of some entities change more around the date of the earnings announcement than others, what might have caused this price–effect differential?
- Would you expect the share prices of larger companies, or smaller companies, to be relatively more affected by an earnings announcement?
- Once the first company in the sample of five makes its earnings announcement, would you expect this announcement to impact on the prices of shares in the other four companies? Why?

10.1 Introduction

In some of the previous chapters we have considered various normative prescriptions pertaining to how accounting *should* be undertaken. For example, Chapter 5 discussed theories that had been developed to prescribe how accounting should be undertaken in times of rising prices and changing asset values (for example, general price level accounting, current cost accounting, continuously contemporary accounting and fair value accounting). Chapter 6 considered the role of conceptual frameworks in providing prescription (such frameworks can tell us what the objective of accounting is; what qualitative characteristics accounting information should possess; how elements of accounting should be defined and recognized; and how assets and liabilities should be measured). Chapter 9 provided an insight into various approaches adopted to disclose information about an organization's social and environmental performance (which has indeed become an area of accounting research that has grown rapidly in recent years).

While the above-mentioned chapters provided a great deal of prescription, they tended not to provide any theoretical arguments as to the *motivations* for managers to make the disclosures. This void was filled by Chapters 7 and 8 which provided different theoretical perspectives about what drives management to make the disclosures. Chapter 7 discussed Positive Accounting Theory and it indicated that, where management had a choice in selecting a particular approach to accounting, both efficiency arguments and opportunistic arguments could be advanced to explain and predict management's accounting choices. Chapter 8 provided alternative explanations of management's behaviour. It showed that the choice of a particular accounting method might be made to restore the legitimacy of an organization (from legitimacy theory), or because such disclosure was necessary to retain the support of powerful stakeholders (from stakeholder theory), or because the accounting method had been adopted by other organizations (from institutional theory).

While the above material provided a perspective of what motivates managers to provide particular accounting information, the material did not consider the further issue of how individuals, or groups of individuals in aggregate, react to accounting disclosures. This chapter and Chapter 11 provide material that addresses this issue. That is, we have changed our focus to research and theories that describe how individuals, or groups of individuals, react to accounting disclosures rather than focusing on what motivated preparers to make the disclosures.

This chapter and Chapter 11 examine the impact of financial accounting and disclosure decisions on the users of financial reports. Specifically, we look at research that focuses on the impact of alternative accounting and disclosure choices on the investment decisions of financial statement users such as share market investors, financial analysts, bank lending officers and auditors.

Reported profit depends on many financial accounting decisions. Managers have much scope in selecting between alternative accounting methods and accounting assumptions. For example, they will choose between expensing or capitalizing particular costs; they will choose between alternative accounting methods such as straight-line or reducing-balance depreciation; they will exercise discretion in relation to accounting estimates such as the useful life of assets to be depreciated; and so on. Further, decisions must be made in relation to how much information to disclose, the medium for disclosure, and, in some circumstances, whether to recognize particular items in the financial statements or merely disclose them in the footnotes to the financial statements.

Financial reporting decisions impact on the information subsequently provided to the users of financial reports. This in turn may have implications for the decisions that users make. There are two ways to assess the impacts of financial reporting decisions: (1) determine the impact of the information on the decisions of individual information users (behavioural research), and (2) determine what impact the release of information has on share price (capital market research). In this chapter we consider capital market research (which considers reactions at an *aggregate* or *market* level). In Chapter 11 we review behavioural research undertaken at the *individual* level.

10.2 An overview of capital market research

Capital market research explores the role of accounting and other financial information in equity markets. That is, it investigates how the disclosure of particular information influences the aggregate trading activities taken by individuals participating within capital markets. According to Kothari (2001, p. 108):

> A large fraction of published research in leading academic accounting journals examines the relation between financial statement information and capital markets, referred to as capital markets research.

Capital market research often involves examining statistical relations between financial information and share prices or returns. Reactions of investors are evidenced by their capital market transactions. Favourable reactions to information are presumed to be evidenced by a price increase in the particular security, whereas unfavourable reactions to information are evidenced by a price decrease. No price change around the time of the release of information implies no reaction to the information (the information release does not provide anything that is new).

Conclusions about the market's reaction to particular information releases or events are generally based on evidence from a large number of companies, with data sometimes spanning several years. This type of research is often used to examine equity market reactions to announcements of company information, and to assess the relevance of alternative accounting and disclosure choices for investors. If security prices change around the time of the release of particular information, and assuming that the information and not some other event caused the price change, then it is considered that the information was relevant and useful for investment decision-making. That is, investors reacted to the information.

In contrast to behavioural research (considered in Chapter 11), which analyses individual responses to financial reporting, capital market research assesses the aggregate effect of financial reporting, particularly the reporting of accounting earnings, on investors.[1] By analysing share price reactions to financial information releases, the sum of individual investor decisions is captured in aggregate. But when considering such research, a possible question that comes to mind is why have so many research studies been undertaken that focus on the market's response to accounting earnings announcements? Brown (1994, p. 24) provides one answer to this issue. He argues:

> Four reasons are that, according to the Financial Accounting Standards Board, information about earnings and its components is the primary purpose of financial reporting; earnings are oriented towards the interests of shareholders who are an important group of financial statement users; earnings is the number most analysed and forecast by security analysts; and reliable data on earnings were readily available.

Another important difference between capital market and behavioural research is that capital market research considers only investors, while behavioural research is often used to examine decision-making by other types of financial statement users such as bank managers, loan officers or auditors.

Capital market research relies on the underlying assumption that equity markets are efficient. Market efficiency is defined in accordance with the efficient market hypothesis (EMH) as a market that adjusts rapidly to impound fully information into share prices when the information is released (Fama *et al.*, 1969). Capital market research in accounting typically assumes that equity markets are *semi-strong-form efficient*. That is, that all publicly available information, including that available in financial statements and other financial disclosures, is rapidly and fully impounded into share prices in an unbiased manner as it

---

[1] Capital markets research is also used to investigate the response of investors to other types of information other than financial accounting information. For example, capital markets research could be used to investigate how share prices react to particular government announcements, or how share prices react to companies winning particular awards. Nevertheless, a great deal of capital markets research focuses on share price reaction to the disclosure of financial information and this will be the main focus of this chapter.

is released. Relevant information is not ignored by the market. But why does the capital market react so quickly to information? According to Lee (2001, p. 236):

> Why do we believe markets are efficient? The answer boils down to a visceral faith in the mechanism of arbitrage. We believe markets are efficient because we believe arbitrage forces are constantly at work. If a particular piece of value-relevant information is not incorporated in price, there will be powerful economic incentives to uncover it, and to trade on it. As a result of these arbitrage forces, price will adjust until it fully reflects the information. Individual agents within the economy may behave irrationally, but we expect arbitrage forces to keep prices in line. Faith in the efficacy of this mechanism is a cornerstone of modern financial economics.[2]

Semi-strong-form efficiency is the most relevant for capital market research in accounting, since it relates to the use of *publicly available* information. Again, predictions based on the assumption that markets are 'semi strong form' efficient are based on the view that markets respond rapidly to publicly available information. Other hypotheses about market efficiency are the *weak-form efficiency* perspective, and the *strong-form efficiency* perspective. The weak form of market efficiency assumes that existing security prices simply reflect information about past prices and trading volumes. The strong form of market efficiency assumes that security prices, on average, reflect all information known to anyone at that point in time (including information not publicly available). According to Watts and Zimmerman (1986, p. 19) the available evidence is generally consistent with the semi-strong form of the EMH.[3] That is, the share market reacts rapidly to impound within the share prices publicly available information which is considered to be relevant for determining the value of such shares.

The view that markets are efficient does not imply that share prices will always provide an accurate prediction of the value of future cash flows. Market predictions are sometimes proved in hindsight to be wrong, thus necessitating subsequent adjustments. As Hendriksen and Van Breda (1992, p. 177) state:

> It needs to be stressed that market efficiency does not imply clairvoyance on the part of the market. All it implies is that the market reflects the best guesses of all its participants, based on the knowledge available at the time. New information appears all the time that proves the market was incorrect. In fact, by definition, the market will not react until it learns something that it did not know the day before. One cannot prove the market inefficient, therefore, by looking back, using the benefits of hindsight and pointing to places where the market was incorrect. Market efficiency simply asserts that prices are appropriately set based on current knowledge; practical evidence shows that with hindsight the market is always incorrect.

---

[2] The Macquarie Dictionary defines arbitrage as 'the simultaneous purchase and sale of the same securities, commodities, or moneys in different markets to profit from unequal prices'.

[3] Brown (1994, p. 14) notes that 'few if any investors would seriously accept the strong form, although many would accept the semi-strong form as their working hypothesis'.

The assumption of market efficiency is central to capital market research.[4] But why is the assumption of information efficiency so important for capital market research in accounting? Simply put, unless such an assumption of efficiency is accepted, it is hard to justify efforts to link security price movements to information releases. A great deal of capital market research considers the relationship between share prices and information releases. The reason for looking at this relationship is that share prices in an efficient market are deemed to be based on expectations about future earnings. If particular information leads to a price change, then the assumption is that the information was *useful* and caused investors to revise their expectations about the future earnings of the organization in question. That is, share prices and returns are used as benchmarks against which the usefulness of financial information is assessed. If we do not assume market efficiency, then there is an inability to explain how or why share prices change around the date of information releases. If share markets are not semi-strong-form efficient, they do not provide accurate benchmarks against which to assess alternative financial reporting choices. Overall, market inefficiency would render capital market research results to be at best less convincing, and at worst extremely unreliable, depending on the extent of inefficiency present.

Assumptions about market efficiency in turn have implications for accounting. If markets are efficient, they will use information from various sources when predicting future earnings, and hence when determining current share prices. If accounting information does not impact on share prices then, assuming semi-strong-form efficiency, it would be deemed not to provide any information over and above that currently available. At the extreme, accounting's survival would be threatened.[5]

While the acceptance of market efficiencies is central to much capital market research, there is some research that suggests that markets might not impound information as quickly as many researchers have assumed (see Frankel and Lee, 1998). Nevertheless, most researchers working within the capital markets research area still assume that relevant information is impounded very quickly into share prices.[6] We will consider issues related to potential market inefficiencies towards the end of the chapter.

Within an 'efficient market', share prices will react to new information to the extent that the information has implications for reassessing the future cash flows of an organization. While we will be focusing on the market's reaction to financial accounting information, information of a non-financial data is also of relevance to capital markets if that information has implications for expectations about a firm's future cash flows. For example,

---

[4] Given this is a central assumption of the research, if particular researchers did not accept this central assumption about market efficiency then they would be inclined to disregard many of the results being generated by capital markets research. As we have emphasized throughout this book, and from a logical perspective, before we are prepared to accept particular theories or particular research we must consider and evaluate the assumptions being made within the research.

[5] Once we relax notions of efficiency, and once we consider broader issues about corporate accountability to stakeholders other than investors, threats to accounting's survival tend to dissipate.

[6] According to Kothari (2001, p. 109), the view that markets do not react rapidly has had the effect of 'spurring research on fundamental analysis'. According to Kothari, 'fundamental analysis entails the use of information in current and past financial statements, in conjunction with industry and macroeconomic data to arrive at a firm's intrinsic value. A difference between the current price and the intrinsic value is an indication of the expected rewards for investing in the security'. Rewards from fundamental analysis would diminish in an efficient market.

Accounting Headline 10.1

New information of a non-accounting nature and its implications for share prices

BP sends Tony Hayward to Siberia to appease US

By Terry Macalister and Andrew Clark

BP is poised to stun the City tomorrow by nominating Tony Hayward to the board of its Russian business as a consolation prize for being axed as chief executive.

Following its board meeting in London, the oil group will formally announce tomorrow when it unveils second-quarter results that Hayward is standing down from the company's top job in October. It will use his departure to appease public opinion over the Gulf oil spill in the US where Hayward has been dubbed public enemy number one for his gaffe-ridden response to the crisis.

... Hayward's expected departure was thought to be the ideal way for BP to draw a line under the Deepwater Horizon oil spill – the worst in American history – after it succeeded in capping the gushing well earlier this month.

... It is thought that his departure from the frontline will help restore relations with Washington where the White House and Congress members have been hugely critical of Hayward's handling of the Deepwater Horizon disaster.

City investors signalled their approval of reports of Hayward's exit by sending BP shares up 5% to 417p.

Source: *Guardian*, 27 July 2010, p. 21
©Guardian News and Media Limited 2010

---

consider Accounting Headline 10.1 which provides an extract from a newspaper article that discussed how a senior executive resigned and how this appeared to have an immediate impact in creating an increase in the company's share price. Share price changes often are reported to occur around the time of departure or appointment of a senior executive. What do you, the reader, think the market is indicating if share prices increase when an executive's resignation is announced?

As indicated above, share prices are predicted to react to various types of information, some of which will be of an accounting nature, while some will relate to other corporate matters. Various capital market researchers investigate how the capital market reacts to different events and different types of information. Again, an efficient capital market is predicted to respond to all types of information to the extent that it is of relevance in predicting future cash flows associated with a firm's securities. As one such example, Clarkson *et al.* (2006) investigate whether takeover rumours on a particular Internet discussion site created a share price reaction.[7] Clarkson *et al.* identify the time when takeover rumours were posted to a popular business and finance Internet discussion site and then they investigate whether there appeared to be an associated share price change. In looking for a market reaction they look at intraday return and trading volume data ('intraday' data

---

[7] For the purposes of their research, any information not capable of objective verification is classified as a rumour.

means that data is collected at various points of time within a particular day). Clarkson *et al.* review 10-minute trading intervals surrounding the time of the posting of the rumours. In justifying the use of narrow 10-minute observation periods the authors state:

> By examining intraday return and trading volume data, we are better able to isolate the effects of the rumour posting, if any. Although an analysis of daily return and trading volume data surrounding the rumour posting day has the potential to provide insights into the market reaction to the posting, competing explanations also exist. For example, the market reaction might simply be to information released through other media that could not reasonably be screened during the sample construction process. Alternatively, if posters are merely reacting to increases in share price and/or trading volume, the observed market activity, although correlated with the IDS rumour, would not be in response to its posting. It is far less likely that reactions observed in the 10 min posting interval would be vulnerable to these or other competing explanations.

According to Clarkson *et al.* (2006), their results indicate a price increase and increased trading volume around the time takeover rumours are posted. This is deemed to indicate that such information is of relevance to investors, and is being used despite the fact that it is based on rumour. As we have already indicated, the basis of capital markets research is that the market is expected to quickly respond to relevant information from various sources. In discussing the implications of their finding, Clarkson *et al.* refer to concerns held by regulators that some individuals ('posters') have been posting information to particular internet sites to 'pump up' share prices before they subsequently sell the shares at a profit. Clarkson *et al.* state (p. 33):

> Litigation by the Australian Securities and Investment Commission (ASIC) and the US Securities and Exchange Commission (SEC) of posters deemed to have inappropriately used Internet Discussion Sites, including 'pump and dump' strategies, indicates a belief by regulatory bodies that rumour posted on these sites affects firm value. Our findings provide formal support for the regulators' view of Internet Discussion Sites as a source of information for the market.

Reflective of the concerns of regulators in relation to rumours and, in particular, the spreading of 'false rumours', Accounting Headline 10.2 provides some extracts from a newspaper article that appeared in the *New York Times* on 14 July 2008. It examined investigations being undertaken by the Securities Exchange Commission in the US in relation to the spreading of rumours and its impacts on share prices.[8]

Following the above theme that an efficient market will react to various types of relevant information, then we might also anticipate that any concerns raised by external auditors as a result of undertaking their audit work also has the potential to create share price changes. This would particularly be the case if the audit opinion signals to investors that there are uncertainties about the future profitability, and hence, about the future cash flows of an organization. In this regard Herbohn *et al.* (2007) considered the share price reaction of a

---

[8] The extract refers to 'short sellers' – these are individuals or organizations who sell a security before they actually own it. They can gain by selling at a particular price and then acquiring it at a lower price. They then transfer the security to the new owner and make a gain in the overall transaction.

Accounting Headline 10.2

Concerns about the impacts of rumours on share prices

S.E.C. warns Wall Street: Stop spreading the false rumors

By Stephanie Clifford and Jenny Anderson

The Securities and Exchange Commission announced on Sunday that it and other regulators would begin examining rumor-spreading intended to manipulate securities prices.

The timing of the announcement, made before the markets opened in Asia, was meant to warn broker-dealers, hedge funds and investment advisers to quell any spreading of rumors before trading started Monday ... The examinations are expected to begin Monday and will focus on what policies firms have in place to prevent the passing of false information. The intent is to stop malicious rumors without hampering the natural exchange of information in the marketplace.

Since the almost overnight collapse of Bear Sterns earlier this year, top-level Wall Street executives have been pleading with regulators to investigate what they see as efforts by short sellers to plant false information and profit from it.

Lehman Brothers, for example, faced rumors last week that two major clients had stopped doing business with the firm. Lehman's stock dived almost 20 percent before recovering somewhat as both clients denied the rumors.

number of Australian companies around the time the companies received a going concern modification (GCM) of their audit report. A GCM in the form of a qualification is issued when the auditor is satisfied that it is highly improbable that the entity will continue as a going concern. According to the authors, a GCM of an audit report is a significantly unambiguous 'bad news' event for stock market participants and an adverse stock market reaction is to be expected (p. 465). The authors studied share price movements in the 12 months leading to, and the 12 months following, a company receiving its first GCM. They also studied share price reactions around the event date, which is defined to be the day of the release of the annual report that includes the audit qualification. The authors find no evidence of a market reaction to a first-time GCM announcement around the event date. The lack of a share price reaction to the audit report is explained by the authors on the basis that in an efficient market, investors would have been preconditioned to expect that the organizations to receive the GCMs were suffering financial difficulties. The audit report would act to confirm market expectations, rather than to cause a revision to expectations (a revision to market expectations about future cash flows would have caused a price change). In explaining their results, the authors state (p. 489):

> The underlying research question of this paper is what is the value added from the audit report. Prima facie, our results that show a significant negative market reaction in the pre-event period rather than the post-event period are consistent with the audit report fulfilling an attestation function rather than signalling

additional information to the market. Additionally, in the 12 months prior to the GCM announcement, the sample of GCM firms underperforms a matched sample of firms in similar financial distress that have unmodified audit opinions for the same period. We contend that these results are consistent with investors viewing a GCM as having information content because it confirms a deteriorating financial condition. That is, a GCM is an independent confirmation by an auditor that, at the very least, there is significant uncertainty that a firm is able to pay its debts as and when they fall due. Furthermore, once issued a GCM increases the financial pressures on a firm through bank credit freezes, possible debt defaults and worsening relations with suppliers. Therefore, receipt of a GCM confirms the likelihood of tightening of debt constraints for the firm.

A question raised by our results is why does the negative market reaction for GCM firms occur in the 12 months prior to the GCM announcement and not persist in the 12 months post-announcement as documented on the LSE by Taffler *et al.* (2004)? One explanation is that the Australian market is well informed because of the continuous disclosure regime in place. The announcement of a GCM is not an isolated or sudden event. Rather, it is a culmination of multiple events over time. The majority of these events are likely to be price-sensitive and, therefore, are required to be disclosed immediately to the market under the continuous disclosure regime of the Australian Stock Exchange. Therefore, it seems likely that the underperformance of our sample firms in the 12 months pre-GCM announcement is a result of a conditioning of market expectations from the price-sensitive disclosures made to the ASX. Because the market is fully informed at the time of the GCM announcement, there is no significant adverse market reaction that persists in the 12 months post-GCM.

Hence, Herbohn *et al.* (2007) were able to use assumptions about the efficiency of the market to explain how the market would have anticipated the news provided by the auditor (as a result of the 'continuous disclosure regime' in Australia), and hence as the audit report was in accordance with expectations, then no significant share price movement would occur.

While some of the above events relate to specific firms (for example, a particular firm receiving a particular form of audit report), share prices will also react to market-wide events. For example, within the United States the introduction of the Sarbanes–Oxley Act of 2002 had potential cash flow implications for a very large number of organizations.[9] Zhang (2007) used capital markets research to investigate reactions to the introduction of the Act. In considering the implications of the Act, Zhang (p. 75) stated:

> By requiring more oversight, imposing greater penalties for managerial misconduct, and dealing with potential conflicts of interest, the Act aims to prevent

---

[9] US Congress passed the Sarbanes–Oxley Act in July 2002 in response to a number of high-profile corporate scandals that came to light in 2001, most notably, scandals associated with the major US company, Enron. The Act was named after two people who were largely involved in its development, these being Senator Paul Sarbanes and Congressman Michael Oxley. The Act imposed additional disclosure requirements as well as requiring significant changes in corporate governance policies.

deceptive accounting and management misbehaviour. However, despite the claimed benefits of this Act, the business community has expressed substantial concerns about its costs. Whereas the out-of-pocket compliance costs are generally considered significant (Solomon and Bryan-Low, 2004), they are likely swamped by the opportunity costs SOX imposed on business. Executives complain that complying with the rules diverts their attention from doing business (Solomon and Bryan-Low, 2004). Furthermore, the Act exposes managers and directors to greater litigation risks and stiffer penalties. CEOs allegedly will take less risky actions, consequently changing their business strategies and potentially reducing firm value (Ribstein, 2002).

While US corporations had to comply with the Act, non-US companies that traded their securities within the US did not have to comply with the Act. Zhang (2007) examined the abnormal returns earned on the shares of US companies around significant Sarbanes–Oxley (SOX) legislative events relative to returns earned on the shares of foreign firms listed in the US. Zhang found that the introduction of the Act appeared to be associated with negative share price reactions for US firms relative to foreign firms that did not comply with the Act. While the negative share price reaction could be interpreted as a negative consequence of introducing the Act, Zhang does note that focusing on share price reactions alone does not take into consideration various social benefits that might arise as a result of introducing the Act – benefits that would be shared by individuals who are not investors. As Zhang (2007, p. 77) states:

> This study does not explore the social welfare implication of the Act. An investigation of changes in security prices provides evidence for the private benefits and costs of regulations, but social benefits and costs may not be fully reflected in stock prices.

What the preceding discussion has highlighted is the variety of events than can influence share prices. It also reflects the variety of issues or events that capital markets researchers explore as part of their research. As we have emphasized, a share price reaction to the release of financial information or other information is taken to indicate that the announcement has 'information content'. The absence of a share price movement indicates that the information is either irrelevant, or that it confirms market expectations. In relation to accounting information, a high association between financial information and share prices or returns over an extended period of time indicates that the information provided by the accounting system reflects information that is being used by the capital market (and this information will come from a multitude of sources). Each of these roles for accounting information in equity markets is explored in the following sections. While the 'information content' of many types of financial information can be assessed using capital market research, the bulk of this work has focused on earnings as the primary measure of the financial accounting system. For example, one issue that has been the subject of many research papers is whether corporate earnings announcements cause a movement in share price. This focus is reflected in the following discussion.

10.3 The information content of earnings

Many research papers have investigated capital market reactions to corporate earnings announcements. That is, when a company announces its earnings for the year (or half-year or quarterly earnings), what is the impact, if any, on its share price? Such studies, that look at the changes in share prices around a particular event, such as the release of accounting information, are often referred to as 'events studies'.[10] According to Kothari (2001, p. 116):

> In an event study, one infers whether an event, such as an earnings announcement, conveys new information to market participants as reflected in changes in the level or variability of security prices or trading volume over a short time period around the event (see Watts and Zimmerman, 1986, Chapter 3, Collins and Kothari, 1989, p. 144). If the level or variability of prices changes around the event date, then the conclusion is that the accounting event conveys new information about the amount, timing, and/or uncertainty of future cash flows that revised the market's previous expectations. The degree of confidence in this conclusion critically hinges on whether the events are dispersed in calendar time and whether there are any confounding events (e.g., a simultaneous dividend and earnings announcement which in themselves could have been responsible for causing revised estimates about the firm's future cash flows thereby creating revisions in share prices) co-occurring with the event of interest to the researcher. As noted earlier, the maintained hypothesis in an event study is that capital markets are informationally efficient in the sense that security prices are quick to reflect the newly arrived information. Because event studies test for the arrival of information through an accounting event, they are also referred to as tests of information content in the capital markets literature in accounting.

Assuming that capital markets are semi-strong-form efficient (they react swiftly and in an unbiased manner to publicly available information), a movement in share price is considered to indicate that the new information in the public earnings announcement has been incorporated into the security's price through the activities of investors in the market. The information was useful in reassessing the future cash flows of the entity.

A number of studies have shown information about earnings to be linked to changes in the price of securities. But, why would we expect accounting earnings and share prices to be related? Modern finance theory proposes that a share price can be determined as the sum of expected future cash flows from dividends, discounted to their present value using a rate of return commensurate with the company's level of risk. Further, dividends are a function of accounting earnings, since they can generally only be paid out of past and current earnings. It follows therefore that if cash flows are related to (a function of) accounting earnings, then the price of a share in company i, which we can denote as (P_i), can be viewed as the

---

[10] The studies considered earlier, such as the study by Clarkson *et al.* (on Internet discussion sites) and by Zhang (on the Sarbanes–Oxley Act) would also be considered to be 'event studies' because they investigated share price reactions around particular events.

sum of expected future earnings per share ($\bar{E}$), discounted to their present value using a risk-adjusted discount rate (k_i).[11] That is, for company i today:

$$P_i = \sum_{t=1}^{\infty} \bar{E}_t / (1 + k_i)^t \qquad (10.1)$$

Equation 10.1 shows that a relation exists between share price and expected future earnings. In general, after adjusting for risk, companies with higher expected future earnings will have higher share prices. These expectations are formed, at least in part, on the basis of historical earnings for the company. However, all currently available information (for example, media releases, analysts' reports, production statistics, market surveys, market rumours, impending legislation) is considered when predicting future earnings. Any revisions to expectations about future earnings per share, including those resulting from new information contained in announcements of current earnings, will be reflected in a change in share price.

Revisions to expectations about future earnings per share will result only from *new* information, since under the maintained assumption of a semi-strong-form-efficient market, price is assumed to reflect already all *publicly known* information, including expectations about current earnings. Therefore, only the unexpected component of current earnings announcements constitutes new information. That is, unexpected earnings, rather than total earnings, are expected to be associated with a change in share price. For example, if CMR Company announces annual earnings of €11 million when only €10.5 million was expected, unexpected earnings are equal to €0.5 million. Any share price reaction will be to these unexpected earnings rather than to total annual earnings of €11 million, since investors already anticipated most of this. Accounting Headlines 10.3 through to 10.5 provide extracts of articles that discussed unexpected profit results and how these unexpected results impacted share prices. Again, it is emphasized that if reported profits were in accord with market expectations then we would not expect share prices to adjust.

A change in share price results in a return to investors (R_{it}), since returns are a function of capital gains or losses, in addition to dividends received (D_{it}). Thus, for an investment in firm i for one holding period ($t - 1$ to t) the return would be:[12]

$$R_{it} = \frac{(P_{it} - P_{it-1}) + D_{it}}{P_{it-1}} \qquad (10.2)$$

The length of time over which returns are calculated (the return period) depends on the particular research focus, but is generally not less than one day (although shorter intraday returns could be used) or longer than one year. In return periods where no dividend is paid, returns can simply be calculated as a percentage change in share price. This is generally the case when returns are calculated on a daily (or shorter) basis.

---

[11] The risk-adjusted discount rate chosen should be commensurate with the level of uncertainty associated with the expected earnings stream.

[12] Where price at the end of the holding period (P_{it}) is adjusted for any capitalization changes such as rights issues or bonus issues.

Accounting Headline 10.3

Market response to unexpected profit announcement

Millennium & Copthorne Hotels shine on new year optimism, London success

By Katie Allen

Millennium and Copthorne Hotels has shot up more than 10% to the top of the midcap gainers board this morning after it managed to shake off travel industry gloom and post 2009 profits above expectations.

Reporting just days after InterContinental Hotels sent shares throughout the sector lower with a cautious outlook, M&C said the final months of 2009 exceeded its expectations.

The shares are up 42.7p, or 11.3%, at 419.2p in mid-morning trading, the biggest risers in a FTSE 250 down 21.7 points at 9363.5.

For 2009, pre-tax profits fell 20.3% to £81.9m as revenues were hit hard in many of its markets, notably New York and Singapore, in the first half of 2009 as the recession dented travel. But the profits were still ahead of City forecasts. Analysts in a Reuters poll gave a consensus forecast of £77m.

Source: *Guardian,* 19 February 2010, 'Market Forces Live' blog
©Guardian News and Media Limited 2010

Accounting Headline 10.4

Another example of a market response to an unexpected profit announcement

GE reports unexpected profit drop, shares tumble

General Electric Co posted an unexpected 6% drop in first-quarter profit on Friday, as the slumping US economy and credit crunch drove down profits at its financial, industrial and health care units.

Shares of the second-largest US company by market capitalization fell almost 10%, dragging down global markets. Due to the size and variety of its operations, GE is regarded as a bellwether of the US economy.

'It's confirmation that we're in a recession,' said Jerome Heppelmann, portfolio manager at Liberty Ridge Capital in Berwyn, Pennsylvania. The company also lowered its earnings forecast for the year, reflecting a slower economy and challenging capital markets.

'These results confirm that the slowdown is widespread and beginning to impact capex (capital expenditures) and longer-cycle businesses,' said Stephen Surpless, senior analyst at Cantor Fitzgerald in London.

Source: *Guardian,* 11 April 2008, online edition
©Guardian News and Media Limited 2010

For example, if CMR Company's share price moved from €5.42 to €5.56 during the day when earnings were announced, the daily return (R_{CMR}) is equal to (€5.56 – €5.42)/€5.42, or 2.6 per cent.

Given that returns are a function of changes in share prices (from Equation 10.2), and share price can be expressed as a function of expected future earnings (from Equation 10.1), returns are related to changes in expected future earnings. This relation is often referred to as the earnings/return relation. For CMR Company, the unexpected announcement of an additional €0.5 million of earnings has resulted in a return to investors of approximately 2.6 per cent, as indicated in the above calculation. This positive return indicates that investors expect future earnings to be higher than originally expected.

Of course, not all share returns are due to investors trading on information about individual companies. Share prices tend to change on a daily basis due to things that affect the whole market, or sectors of it. We can call these 'systematic changes'. For example, the publication of new (and unexpected) statistics about factors likely to affect the whole economy to some extent – such as rates of inflation, new legislation which will impact the activities of investors or companies, levels of unemployment, or the general level of consumer or business confidence – and daily returns for individual companies largely reflect this.

The market model (see Fama, 1976, for details about its early development), which is derived from the capital asset pricing model (CAPM), is used to separate out firm-specific share price movements from market-wide movements.[13] The CAPM explains how a market should decide the appropriate return on a share, given its riskiness. It predicts a linear relationship between expected returns and systematic risk, where systematic risk is the riskiness of an asset when it is held as part of a thoroughly diversified portfolio. Systematic risk is the non-diversifiable or unavoidable risk that investors are compensated for through increased returns. The market model is expressed as:

$$R_{it} = \alpha_{it} + \beta_{it} R_{mt} + \mu_{it} \tag{10.3}$$

where R_{it} is the return for company i during period t, calculated in accordance with Equation 10.2; R_{mt} is the return for the entire market during period t (as would be approximated by the average return generated from a very large diversified portfolio of securities); and β_{it} is company i's level of systematic risk, which indicates how sensitive the returns of firm i's securities are relative to market-wide (systematic) movements.[14] Again, market-wide movements will potentially account for a significant proportion of the change in a company's share prices. α_{it} is a constant specific to firm i, while μ_{it} is an error term that provides an indication of how the return on a security relates or moves with respect to specific events, such as the release of new accounting information. It is μ_{it} that capital market researchers are typically interested in identifying as it is considered to reflect the reaction of the company's shares to the new information being disclosed. It reflects the difference between what the market return was expected to be (based on the model) and what it actually was following a particular event, such as the release of accounting earnings data.

For the market model it is assumed that the variations in returns on individual securities are largely due to market-wide factors. As a portfolio of investments increases in diversity, the non-systematic risk of the diversified portfolio (measured by $\alpha_{it} + \mu_{it}$) tends to disappear, thereby leaving only returns that are due to market-wide movements (that is, $\beta_{it} R_{mt}$). The market model makes a number of assumptions, including that investors are risk averse and that investors have homogeneous expectations (they think alike).

Equation 10.3 shows that total or actual returns can be divided into normal (or expected) returns, given market-wide price movements ($\alpha_{it} + \beta_{it} R_{mt}$), and abnormal (or unexpected) returns due to firm-specific share price movements (μ_{it}).[15] Normal returns are expected to vary from company to company, depending on their level of systematic risk in relation to the market, while abnormal returns are expected to vary from company to company depending on whether there is new information about the company that causes investors to revise expectations about future earnings. According to Kothari (2001, p. 115):

> The risk-related variation in returns is generally not of interest to researchers who focus on firm-specific accounting information and its relation to the

---

[13] For further information on the development of the CAPM reference can be made to Sharpe (1964) or Lintner (1965).

[14] For example, if the returns of firm i's securities are expected to fluctuate in period t at the same rate as a very large diversified portfolio of securities, then beta (β_{it}) would be approximately 1. If the returns of the individual are twice as sensitive or volatile as general market movements (indicating that the returns on the undiversified security are more risky than the returns on a very large diversified portfolio) then beta would be approximately 2, and so on.

[15] Normal returns can also be thought of as the level of return to investors that is expected simply as a reward for investing and bearing risk. Abnormal returns are the realized rate of return, less the expected normal rate of return (calculated by reference to the market model).

firm-specific component of the stock return. Therefore, the Capital Asset Pricing Model (CAPM), along with the efficient market hypothesis, greatly facilitated the estimation of the firm-specific return component. The use of the firm-specific component alone enhances the power of the tests of information content of accounting reports (Brown and Warner, 1980, 1985).

The market model is used to control for share price movements due to market-wide events, allowing the researcher to focus on share price movements due to firm-specific news. For example, part of the 2.6 per cent return earned by CMR Company upon announcing its annual earnings may be due to an overall rise in the market on the announcement day. A researcher analysing the impact of the earnings announcement would control for the impact of this rise in the market by deducting it from CMR Company's return. Assuming $\alpha_{CMR} = 0$, $\beta_{CMR} = 1$ and $R_m = 1$ per cent, this calculation would leave an abnormal return (μ_{CMR}) of 1.6 per cent.[16] It is abnormal returns, or firm-specific share price movements, that are analysed by researchers to determine the information effects of company announcements.

Capital market research into the earnings/return relation analyses firm-specific price movements (abnormal returns) at the time of earnings announcements. These abnormal returns are used as an indicator of the information content of the announcement. That is, how much, if any, new information has been released to the capital markets. If there is no share price reaction, it is assumed that the announcement contained no new information. That is, the information was already known or anticipated by market participants, or alternatively, was deemed to be irrelevant.

10.4 Results of capital market research into financial reporting

Capital market research has been a major focus of financial accounting research over the past 40 years. The research has investigated the information content of corporate earnings announcements as well as many other accounting and disclosure items. Results of this research are useful for both practising accountants and finance professionals such as security analysts. Knowledge of these results is considered to be particularly useful in relation to making financial reporting decisions. It is often argued that more informed choices between accounting and disclosure alternatives can be made if the expected impacts on share prices are anticipated when making financial reporting decisions. A summary comprising some of the more important capital market research results follows.

Historical cost income is used by investors

Ball and Brown (1968), in the first major capital market research publication in accounting, investigated the usefulness of accounting earnings under a historical cost model. Prior to their research, there was a widely held view that historical cost accounting methods resulted in 'meaningless' information that was not useful for investors and other users of financial statements.[17] Ball and Brown saw the need for empirical evidence about whether

---

[16] When returns are calculated on a daily basis, the assumption that $\alpha = 0$ and $\beta_{it} = 1$ is not unrealistic.

[17] For example, see Chambers (1965) and Sterling (1975).

accounting earnings, calculated using historical cost accounting principles, provide useful information to investors. They state (p. 159):

> If, as the evidence indicates, security prices do in fact adjust rapidly to new information as it becomes available, then changes in security prices will reflect the flow of information to the market. An observed revision of stock prices associated with the release of the income report would thus provide evidence that the information reflected in income numbers is useful.[18]

Using data for 261 US companies, they tested whether firms with unexpected increases in accounting earnings had positive abnormal returns, and firms with unexpected decreases in accounting earnings had negative abnormal returns (on average). Unexpected earnings were calculated (quite simplistically) as the difference between current earnings and the previous year's earnings. That is, they assumed that this year's earnings were expected to be the same as last year's earnings. Monthly share price data were used, with the market model being used to calculate abnormal returns for each company. Cumulative abnormal returns (CARs) were then calculated for each of (1) the full sample of companies, (2) firms with unexpected increases in earnings (favourable announcements), and (3) firms with unexpected decreases in earnings (unfavourable announcements), by summing the average abnormal returns for each of these groups over time.

They found evidence to suggest that the information contained in the annual report is used in investment decision-making, despite the limitations of the historical cost accounting system. This result is evidenced by the CARs during the month of the earnings announcements (month 0). As can be seen from Figure 10.1, firms with unexpected increases in earnings (favourable announcements), represented by the top line in the chart, had positive abnormal returns, while firms with unexpected decreases in earnings (unfavourable announcements), represented by the bottom line in the chart, had negative abnormal returns during the announcement month (on average). Since Ball and Brown's early study, this research has been replicated many times using more sophisticated data and research methods. The results appear to confirm the usefulness of historical cost income to investors. This is not to say that the historical cost accounting system is the 'most useful', since a present value or current cost accounting system may be more useful, but it gives some credence to the continued use of historical costs.

Prior to an earnings release, investors obtain much of the information they need from other sources

In addition to confirming the usefulness of the historical cost accounting model, Ball and Brown (1968) found that most of the information contained in earnings announcements (85–90 per cent) is anticipated by investors. The gradual slope in the lines (which represent the cumulative abnormal returns) prior to the earnings announcements (which were made at time 0) in Figure 10.1 provide evidence of this. Anticipation of earnings changes by

---

[18] However, just because the market reacts to information, which might reflect that the information was used to revise expectations about future cash flows (that is, the information was useful and led to changes in share prices), this does not necessarily mean other forms of accounting not based on historical costs might not have been more useful for revising expectations about future cash flows.

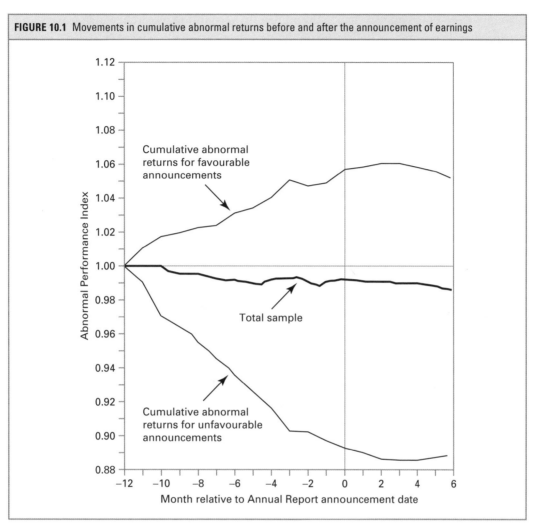

FIGURE 10.1 Movements in cumulative abnormal returns before and after the announcement of earnings

Source: Ball and Brown (1968).

investors indicates that investors obtain much of the information useful for investment decision-making from sources other than annual earnings announcements (perhaps from media releases, analysts' releases, information about the industry's production and sales trends and so on). This is not surprising given that alternative sources of information such as conference calls to analysts and press releases are generally more timely than the annual report, which tends to be issued several weeks after year end (the reporting date) and less frequently than many alternative sources of information. Therefore, we can never expect to produce accounting statements that will tell investors everything they may want to know. That is, provision of all relevant information to investors is not a good basis for regulation or practice. When making financial reporting decisions, it is important to remember that, while accounting appears to be an important source of information for the stock market, it is not the only source of information.

In finishing our brief discussion of Ball and Brown (1968) it is perhaps worth noting that their paper is generally accepted as the most cited academic accounting article. It certainly represented quite a change from previous accounting research, which was predominantly normative. Reflecting on the significance of Ball and Brown (1968), Brown (1994, p. 24) states:

> A number of reasons have been given to explain the paper's major impact on the accounting literature since 1968:
>
> - It was cast in the mould of a traditional experiment: hypothesis, data collection, data analysis, conclusion.
> - It expressed a view that ran counter to the critics of GAAP (these critics arguing that historical cost accounting information was meaningless and useless).
> - It was an early plea for 'empirical research'.
> - It emphasised the use of data to test a belief.
> - It adopted an information perspective.
> - It contained the basic elements of a research design that became a model for future research: the semi-strong form of the EMH was a maintained hypothesis, so the focus was on market behaviour around an announcement date; earnings predictions were modelled to identify the news in, or what was new about, the earnings report; GAAP earnings were compared with a primary version of operating cash flows; and abnormal returns were measured by the Market Model and the CAPM.
> - It was a particularly robust experiment, in the sense that it has been replicated for firms with different fiscal years, in different countries, and at different times.
> - It gave rise to many papers in related areas.

As Chapter 7 indicates, Watts and Zimmerman (1986) credit the development of Positive Accounting Theory, at least in part, to the early experimental approach adopted by Ball and Brown (1968).

Studies of markets' reactions to particular accounting disclosures – such as Ball and Brown's – have been used to make recommendations to accounting standard-setters. Relying upon the maintained assumption that capital markets are efficient, researchers have been known to argue against standard-setters requiring particular information if research has shown that share prices did not react when the particular information was disclosed. As Kothari (2001, p. 119) states:

> The early evidence of earnings' association with security returns and evidence of capital market efficiency in finance and economics led some accounting researchers to draw standard-setting implications. For example, Beaver (1972) in the Report of the American Accounting Association Committee on Research Methodology in Accounting, suggests that the association of accounting numbers with security returns can be used to rank order alternative accounting methods as a means of determining the accounting method that should become a standard. The report states that the 'method which is more highly associated with security prices ought to be the method reported in the financial statements' (p. 428), subject to considerations of competing sources of information and costs.

The information content of earnings announcements depends on the extent of alternative sources of information

Research indicates that the information content of earnings varies between countries and between companies within a country. For example, Brown (1970) found that when compared to US markets, the Australian market has slower share price adjustments during the year, with larger adjustments at the earnings announcement date. This result implies that annual reports were a more important source of information for the Australian capital markets than they were for US capital markets because there were fewer alternative sources of information for Australian companies. This difference in the extent of alternative sources of information is partly due to Australian regulations that required only semi-annual rather than quarterly reporting, and is also a function of differences in average firm sizes between the two countries. Smaller firms tend to have fewer alternative sources of information than larger firms, and are less likely to be followed by security analysts. This difference in the extent of alternative sources of information between smaller and larger firms causes differences in the usefulness of earnings announcements, with these being more useful for smaller than larger Australian firms.

Therefore, the extent of alternative sources of information should be considered when making financial reporting decisions. (We return to the issue of size later in this chapter.)

The capital market impact of unexpected changes in earnings depends on whether the change is expected to be permanent or temporary

Following Ball and Brown's finding that the direction of unexpected earnings changes is positively related to the direction of abnormal share price returns, further research was conducted into the relation between the magnitude of the unexpected change in earnings, or earnings per share, and the magnitude of the abnormal returns. This relationship is often referred to as the earnings response coefficient. The results show that this is not a one-to-one relationship. Indeed, some research has shown that the average abnormal return associated with a 1 per cent unexpected change in earnings is only 0.1 to 0.15 per cent (Beaver *et al.*, 1980). This relationship varies, depending on whether the change in earnings is expected to be permanent or temporary. Permanent increases are expected to result in increased dividends, and therefore increased future cash flows, and this implies a change in the value of the company. On the other hand, temporary increases are discounted or ignored, since they are not expected to have the same impact on expected future dividends (Easton and Zmijewski, 1989). While some earnings changes such as those due to one-off restructuring charges are obviously temporary, it is more difficult to determine whether other earnings changes are likely to persist.

Earnings persistence depends on the relative magnitudes of cash and accruals components of current earnings

The accrual system of accounting differs from the cash basis of accounting owing to differences in when cash flows are recognized in the financial statements. Under the accrual system, some items are recognized before the cash flows are received or paid (for example, credit sales and purchases), while others are recognized on a periodic basis (for example, the cost of a fixed asset is recognized over its useful life through periodic depreciation charges). Therefore, the accrual process involves adjusting the timing of when the cash inflows and outflows of a firm are recognized to achieve a matching of revenues and expenses. Earnings, the summary performance measure of the accrual system, has fewer timing and mismatching problems than performance measures based on unadjusted cash flows (for example, cash flows from operations). However, application of the accrual system can be a subjective rather than an objective process and, depending upon the choices made, many different earnings figures can be achieved. For example, if the reducing-balance method of depreciation is chosen over the straight-line method, reported profits will initially be lower, owing to a greater depreciation expense. However, reported earnings will be higher in the later years of the asset's life due to lower depreciation expense. Sloan (1996) undertook a study to see if share prices behave as if investors simply 'fixate' on reported earnings without considering how those numbers have actually been determined (that is, what methods of accounting have been employed). According to Sloan (1996, p. 291):

> A meaningful test of whether stock prices fully reflect available information requires the specification of an alternative 'naïve' expectation model, against which to test the null of market efficiency. The naïve model employed in this study is that investors 'fixate' on earnings and fail to distinguish between the accrual and cash flow component of current earnings. This naïve earnings expectation model is consistent with the functional fixation hypothesis, which has received empirical support in capital market, behavioral and experimental research.[19]

Sloan provides evidence that firms with large accruals relative to their actual cash flows are unlikely to have persistently high earnings, since the accruals reverse over time, reducing future earnings. However, share prices are found to act as if investors simply 'fixate' on reported earnings, thereby failing to take account of the relative magnitudes of the cash and accrual components of current earnings (fixation implying a degree of market inefficiency). In concluding his paper, Sloan (1996, p. 314) states:

> This paper investigates whether stock prices reflect information about future earnings contained in the accrual and cash flow components of current earnings. The persistence of earnings performance is shown to depend on the relative magnitudes of the cash and accrual components of earnings. However, stock prices act as if investors fail to identify correctly the different properties of these two components of earnings.

Hence, while earnings can be managed up through various discretionary accruals, this cannot be done indefinitely, and earnings will eventually be lower as the accruals subsequently reverse. Likewise, while it may be possible to increase share price through reporting higher earnings, this effect will be reversed when lower earnings are reported in the future. Although the lower earnings are due to the reversal of accruals, evidence

---

[19] According to Watts and Zimmerman (1986, p. 160), 'the hypothesis of functional fixation maintains that individual investors interpret earnings numbers in the same way, regardless of the accounting procedures used to calculate them. If all investors acted in this way, there would be a mechanical relation between earnings and stock prices, and the stock market would not discriminate between efficient and less efficient firms.'

indicates that the market fixates on the lower reported earnings, and share prices therefore fall as the accruals subsequently reverse. Notions questioning market efficiency, such as the functional fixation perspective, have been hotly contested in the accounting literature.

The earnings announcements of other firms in the same industry have information content

When a company announces its annual earnings, this generally results in abnormal returns not only for the company concerned, but also for other companies in the same industry (Foster, 1981). That is, there is information content for similar firms as well as for the announcing firm. This phenomenon, known as 'information transfer', reduces the surprise (unknown) element in earnings announcements of other firms in the industry that choose to announce their earnings later. The direction of the capital market reaction is related to whether the news contained in the announcement reflects a change in conditions for the entire industry, or changes in relative market share within the industry. Because information is gained from the announcements of similar firms, information releases about sales and earnings changes result in price reactions for other firms in an industry, as well as the firm making the announcement (Freeman and Tse, 1992). Therefore, in forming expectations about how information releases, such as earnings announcements, might affect share prices, it is important to consider the timing of information releases relative to those of similar firms, since information about a company can be gained from the information releases of similar companies.

Firth (1976) investigated the 'information transfer' issue. He sought to 'investigate the impact of a company's results being publicly announced have on the share price behaviour of competing firms' (p. 298). His results indicated that when 'good news' was released about accounting earnings, the share prices of the non-announcing firms in the same industry reacted quickly (the same day) by showing a statistically significant increase. Interestingly, there seemed to be no abnormal returns in the days before the announcement (limited anticipation) or the days after the announcement. That is, most of the adjustment appeared to occur fairly immediately. Similar results were found with respect to 'bad news' earnings announcements. The share prices of non-disclosing firms in the industry tended to fall on the day of the 'bad news' earnings announcement.

If the announcement of earnings by one company impacts on the share prices of other companies in the same industry, there would be an expectation that if a number of companies are about to release earnings information then, all other things being equal, the largest share price reactions might be generated by the entity that makes the first release. By the time the last entity releases its earnings announcements for a particular year end, it could be expected that a great deal of this information would already have been impounded in share prices and hence the last announcement would have relatively little impact on share prices. This expectation was confirmed by Clinch and Sinclair (1987). In summarizing their findings they state (p. 105):

> The directional association between daily price changes for announcing and non-announcing firms and the magnitude of the price change diminishes for subsequent announcing firms in the same industry over the reporting period.

We can relate the view that announcements by one company can impact on share prices of another company to a newspaper article relating to consumer product companies. Accounting Headline 10.6 shows that when two large consumer product companies released profit warnings, this seemed to cause share price reactions in the shares of other companies in the sector. This is consistent with the results reported above.

Accounting Headline 10.6

An illustration of the 'information transfer' effect

Colgate, Unilever warn on profits: Consumer products sector hit as household names highlight pressure to cut costs and keep sales

By Lauren Foster and Adam Jones

Unilever and Colgate-Palmolive yesterday delivered profit warnings that knocked shares across the consumer products sector and highlighted the intense competition in an industry trying to please price-conscious retailers and consumers.

Unilever, the maker of Dove soap and Knorr soup, saw its shares fall five per cent to 459 1/2p after it said that it would not report the promised double-digit growth in underlying earnings per share this year. It now expects only low single-digit growth.

Colgate shares fell more than 10 per cent after it warned third- and fourth-quarter earnings would be lower than expected as increased marketing spending outweighed growth in volumes and market share and higher raw material costs offset its cost-cutting programme.

As well as competition from rival manufacturers, consumer goods multinationals have also had to cope with pricing pressure from powerful retail customers such as Wal-Mart, as well as a reluctance among many consumers to pay extra for brands.

Unilever's profit warning was a blow for Niall FitzGerald, its co-chairman, who steps down at the end of this month after 37 years with the company.

It is also another failure for the company's ambitious Path to Growth restructuring, which is coming to the end of its five-year life. The Path to Growth leading brands'

sales target of 5–6 per cent annual growth had already been abandoned.

Unilever said that the poor summer weather in northern Europe had hit sales of ice cream and 'ready-to-drink' tea.

The market for toiletries and cleaning products became tougher in western Europe, with many consumers reluctant to pay extra for branded goods. Sales of its leading brands are expected to fall in the third quarter.

Patrick Cescau, Mr FitzGerald's successor, said he did not see a need for radical structural change, such as splitting the company into a stand-alone food business and another business selling toiletries.

He said: 'The challenge we are facing at the moment is one of underperformance and operation'.

Unilever also pledged to increase the amount of money it spent on marketing its brands. Last month the *Financial Times* reported that some investors feared the company was endangering its brands by spending too little on advertising and promotions to avoid a profit warning.

Reuben Mark, Colgate chairman and chief executive, also highlighted the need for high marketing budgets.

He said: 'We are confident that we are taking the right measures to accelerate our growth and profitability for 2005 and beyond.

'It is vital that we maintain the aggressive commercial spending to build market share and blunt competitive efforts'.

He said Colgate expected earnings of 57–59 cents a share for the third and fourth quarters – well below consensus forecasts.

Analysts expected earnings of 67 cents a share for the third quarter, and 68 cents a share for the fourth quarter, according to Thomson First Call.

Colgate is locked in a fierce battle with Procter & Gamble for leadership of the US toothpaste and tooth-whitening markets. Its shares were down 11.4 per cent at $48.15 in late afternoon trade.

Source: *Financial Times*, 21 September 2004, p. 1
©The Financial Times Limited 2010

While the above discussion has discussed the industry implications of corporate earnings or profit announcements, other studies have also shown that there can be industry share price implications that flow from other events that impact on specific organizations within the industry. Blacconiere and Patten (1994) examined the market reaction to Union Carbide's chemical leak in India in 1984. In December 1984, methyl isocyanate (MIC) gas leaked from the Union Carbide India Limited (UCIL) plant in Bhopal killing approximately 3,800 people and causing several thousand other individuals to experience permanent or partial disabilities. Using a sample of 47 US firms, Blacconiere and Patten observed a significant impact on the share prices of Union Carbide directly following the disaster (as might be expected). They also found a significant intra-industry market reaction to the event. However, firms with more extensive environmental disclosures in their annual reports before the disaster (with the disclosures covering such issues as emergency response policies) experienced a smaller negative share price reaction than those with less extensive disclosures.

Earnings forecasts have information content

Announcements of earnings forecasts by both management and security analysts are associated with share returns. That is, not only do announcements of actual earnings appear to cause share prices to change, but announcements of expected earnings also appear to cause price changes. Similar to earnings announcements, earnings forecasts are associated with market returns in terms of both direction and magnitude (Imhoff and Lobo, 1984; Penman, 1980). These results are not surprising since earnings forecasts are expected to contain new information that can be used in the prediction of future earnings. Forecasts of expected future earnings appear to be an effective way of communicating information to the share market. Also, bad news forecasts about lower than anticipated future earnings may be useful for avoiding potential shareholder lawsuits (Skinner, 1997).

Earnings forecasts have also been explored in terms of the 'information transfer' phenomenon discussed above. Baginski (1987) generated results that showed that the share prices of firms within the same industry that did not provide an earnings forecast were positively correlated with the change in earnings expectation indicated by earnings forecasts released by managers of other firms within the same industry.

Accounting Headline 10.7 provides an example of where it appears that a profit forecast led to a decrease in share price, consistent with some of the research results reported above. (It also further illustrates the 'information transfer' effect discussed in the previous

---

Accounting Headline 10.7

Profit forecasts and their potential influence on share price

Icap shares plunge knocks £80m off Tory treasurer's wealth

By Jill Treanor

Almost £80m was wiped off the personal wealth of Michael Spencer, the Conservative party treasurer, today after the Icap money-broker he runs issued a surprise profit warning, knocking 20% off the company's share price.

... The company's cut in pre-tax profit forecast for the year to end-March to £295m–£315m from as much as £350m in November rattled the markets and helped to knock confidence in Tullett Prebon, run by rival Terry Smith, which fell 10%.

... Through the trust and the shares held in his own name, Spencer continues to control 17.4% of Icap which he has developed into the world's largest interdealer broker through a series of acquisitions since creating Intercapital in 1986. The value of those shares fell by almost £80m today.

Icap has been hit by factors including Barack Obama's surprise pledge to crack down on banks' proprietary trading through the Volcker rule. While Icap estimates that little more than 5% of its revenue is generated from banks using their own money to trade, market activity had slowed since the US president's plan was announced in January.

The company had also found that some of its newer businesses, such as equities, were not making profits as quickly as its investments in new countries such as Brazil and other parts of Latin America.

The company has invested £400m in new businesses over the past three years, including £300m in acquisitions.

Source: *Guardian*, 5 February 2010, online edition
©Guardian News and Media Limited 2010

---

subsection.) However, what must be remembered in research that looks at market reactions around particular events is that it is possible that share prices might actually be reacting to other unknown (by the researcher) contemporaneous events.

There are benefits associated with the voluntary disclosure of information

The disclosure of additional information, over and above that required by accounting regulations, has benefits in the capital markets. Voluntary disclosures include those contained within the annual report, as well as those made via other media such as press releases and conference calls to security analysts. For example, Lang and Lundholm (1996) show that firms with more informative disclosure policies have a larger analyst following and more accurate analyst earnings forecasts. They suggest that potential benefits to disclosure include increased investor following and reduced information asymmetry. Further, Botosan (1997) shows that increased voluntary disclosure within the annual report is associated with reduced costs of equity capital, particularly for firms with low analyst following. For these low-analyst firms, disclosure of forecast information and key non-financial statistics is particularly important, while for firms with a high analyst following, disclosure of historical summary information is beneficial. Therefore, the potential benefits of increased disclosure should perhaps not be ignored when deciding the extent of voluntary disclosure.

Recognition is perceived differently to mere footnote disclosure

Recognizing an item by recording it in the financial statements and including its numerical amount in the financial statement's totals is perceived differently to merely disclosing the amount in footnotes to the financial statements. For example, Aboody (1996) finds that where firms in the US oil and gas industry recognize a write-down in their financial statements the negative pricing effect is significant, whereas when firms in the same industry merely disclose such a write-down in footnotes the pricing effect is not significant. In other words, the market perceives recognized write-downs to be more indicative of a value decrement than disclosed write-downs. Further, Cotter and Zimmer (1999) show that mere disclosure of current values of land and buildings indicates that the amount is less certain when compared to current values that are recognized in the statement of financial position via an asset revaluation. These results indicate that investors place greater reliance on recognized amounts than on disclosed amounts. Therefore, while it is not necessary to recognize information in the statement of financial position for it to be useful, since merely disclosing the information in the footnotes conveys the information to investors, disclosed information is perceived to be less reliable than recognized information.

Size

There is evidence that the relationship between earnings announcements and share price movements is inversely related to the size of an entity. That is, earnings announcements have been found generally to have a greater impact on the share prices of smaller firms relative to larger firms. This is explained on the basis that with larger firms there is generally more information available in the marketplace and therefore greater likelihood that projections about earnings have already been impounded in the share price. The earnings announcement for larger firms would have a relatively limited unexpected component. For example, research has shown that the relationship between the information content in earnings announcements and changes in share prices tends to be more significant for smaller firms. That is, in general, larger firms' earnings announcements have relatively less information content (for example, Collins *et al.*, 1987; Freeman, 1987). This is consistent with the EMH and is explained by the fact that larger firms tend to have more information being circulated about them as well as attracting more attention from such parties as security analysts. Hence, on average, earnings announcements for larger firms tend to be more anticipated, provide less surprise, and hence already impounded in the share price prior to the earnings announcement.

Grant (1980) also explored this issue. He investigated the information content of earnings announcements of securities traded on the New York Stock Exchange, as well as securities traded on what is known as the Over The Counter Market (OTC). Firms traded on the OTC are typically smaller than firms traded on the New York Stock Exchange. Consistent with the perceived size effect, the prices of securities traded on the OTC were more responsive to earnings announcements than were the prices of securities traded on the New York Stock Exchange.

Unexpected changes in accounting earnings created by unexpected increases in revenues rather than unexpected reductions in expenses

Where there is an unexpected increase in earnings (profits) this could be due to either an increase in revenues, a reduction in expenses, or a combination of both. In this regard, would it make a difference to the share price reaction if an unexpected increase in earnings was due to a revenue increase rather than a reduction in expenses, or vice versa? Jegadeesh and Livnat (2006) explored this issue. They state (p. 148):

> We examine the incremental information conveyed by revenues reported during preliminary earnings announcements. Several factors motivate our analysis of the information content of revenues. Earnings by definition, is revenues minus aggregate expenses. If earnings surprises are accompanied by revenue surprises of similar magnitude in the same direction, then the earnings surprises are driven by revenue growth rather than by a reduction in expenses. We expect earnings growth driven by revenue growth to exhibit a different level of persistence compared with earnings growth driven by expense reduction.

Jegadeesh and Livnat's results indicate that the market does tend to react more to unexpected earnings when these 'surprises' are due to increases in revenues. These results are generally consistent with those provided by Ertimur *et al.* (2003) who found that market prices react significantly to unexpected revenue increases on earnings announcement dates after controlling for unexpected earnings announcements.

10.5 Do current share prices anticipate future accounting earnings announcements?

The previous discussion in this chapter has provided evidence that accounting earnings announcements, because of their potential information content, can have some impact on share prices. That is, prices change in relation to information as it becomes available. However, the impact of 'new' information seems to be more significant for smaller firms. As we saw, this is explained on the basis that there tends to be more information available for larger firms (for example, through analysts paying particular attention to the larger firms). Hence, as firm size increases, the general perspective taken is that share prices incorporate information from a wider number of sources (including, perhaps, numerous forecasts of the larger entity's earnings) and therefore there is relatively less unexpected information when earnings are ultimately announced. Therefore, for larger firms, we might actually be able to argue that share prices anticipate future earnings announcements with some degree of accuracy. As Brown (1994, p. 105) states, if we take the perspective that share prices anticipate earnings announcements, then we are effectively 'looking back the other way' from traditional perspectives that assume that earnings or profit announcements actually drive share price changes.

A more recent focus in capital market research investigates how well accounting information, such as annual profits, captures information that is relevant to investors. This is a different focus from research considered previously in this chapter. Rather than determining whether earnings/profit announcements provide information to investors, this alternative form of research seeks to determine whether earnings announcements reflect information that has already been used by investors in decision-making. That is, this research views market prices, and hence returns, as leading accounting earnings, while 'information content' research (the previous focus of this chapter) views earnings as leading (or driving) market returns. Both perspectives have merit, since the earnings announcement is likely to contain some information about a firm's activities that was not previously known to investors, as well as information that investors have already determined (or anticipated) from alternative sources.

In considering why share prices convey information about future accounting earnings, Brown (1994, p. 106) argues:

> In a world of rational expectations, events that affect future distributions to shareholders will be reflected in today's share price, whereas accounting stand-ards often require that the recognition of those events be deferred until some future accounting period.

Share prices and returns ('returns' being changes in share prices plus dividends) are considered by some researchers to provide useful benchmarks for determining whether accounting information is relevant for investor decision-making. Share prices are deemed to represent a benchmark measure of firm value (per share), while share returns represent a benchmark measure of firm performance (per share). These benchmarks are in turn used to compare the usefulness of alternative accounting and disclosure methods. For example, this methodology is used to answer questions such as: are cash flows from operations a better measure of a firm's performance than earnings calculated using the accruals system? Each of these accounting measures of performance is compared to the market benchmark measure of performance (returns) to determine which accounting measure best reflects the market's assessment of company performance. This type of capital market research also assumes that the market is efficient, and acknowledges that financial statements are not the only source of information available to the markets, such that security prices reflect information that is generally available from a multitude of sources. In particular, it assumes that investors and financial analysts actively seek out relevant information when making investment decisions or recommendations, rather than awaiting the release of the annual report. Further, this area of the research allows researchers to consider questions about balance sheet (statement of financial position) measures. For example, are disclosures about current values of assets value-relevant? That is, are they associated with, or linked to, the current market value of the company? Again, there is an assumption that market values reflect all publicly available information, including, but not limited to, information contained in financial statements.

This area of the research is based on a theoretical framework that is derived from the premise that market values and book values are both measures of a firm's value (stock of wealth), even though book value measures wealth with some error. That is, at any point in time, the market value of a company's equity (MV_{it}) is equal to the book value of shareholders' equity (BV_{it}) plus some error (ε_{it}):

$$MV_{it} = BV_{it} + \varepsilon_{it} \tag{10.4}$$

This error is due to the conservative nature of the accounting system. Book value is generally expected to be lower than market value for a number of reasons. First, not all assets and liabilities are recognized in the financial statements. For example, human resources, customer satisfaction levels and internally generated intangible assets including goodwill are not recognized in the balance sheet, nor are their values amortized to the profit and loss account (income statement). Nevertheless, while such assets are not recognized for accounting purposes, the expectation is that an efficient market will consider such assets when determining the appropriate market price for the firm's securities.[20] Second, some assets are recognized at less than their full value. For example, fixed assets that have not been revalued to fair value and inventory are generally recorded at less than their expected sale prices.

If markets are assumed to be efficient, market value provides a benchmark measure against which alternative measures of book value can be assessed. As we see shortly, there is a great deal of research that evaluates the output of the accounting system on the basis of how the accounting information relates or compares to current market prices of the firm's securities.[21]

If market value (based on the number of securities issued and their respective market values) and book value of a company are considered as 'stocks' of wealth, then changes in each of these measures of wealth between two points in time can be considered as 'flows' of wealth. Just as market and book measures of stocks of wealth equate with error, market and book measures of flows of wealth (changes in value) can be equated, albeit with some degree of error:

$$\Delta MV_{it} = \Delta BV_{it} + \varepsilon'_{it} \tag{10.5}$$

Change in market value (ΔMV_{it}) is simply the difference in the market capitalization of a company between two points in time ($t-1$ to t). On a 'per share' basis, it can be expressed as the change in the price of one share.

$$\Delta MV_{it}/\text{no. of shares} = P_{it} - P_{it-1} \tag{10.6}$$

Change in book value (ΔBV_{it}) is the difference between opening and closing total shareholders' equity. However, if we assume that there have been no additional capital

---

[20] As another example, the appointment of a very reputable managing director would be value-relevant because it is an action that could be expected to lead to improved company performance, cash flows, and hence share value. However, such an appointment would not generally be reflected in the financial statements themselves. The disparity between the value of net assets as represented in the statement of financial position, and the market value of the firm's securities, will tend to be greater for those organizations with operations that are more dependent upon intangible assets (such as human capital) relative to those organizations that rely more heavily upon tangible assets (such as property and equipment).

[21] This research assumes, perhaps somewhat simplistically, that the market has it 'right' in its determination of the firm's value. Thereafter, accounting figures are compared with the market's 'benchmark'. Clearly, the benchmark figure of valuation might overvalue or undervalue the entity relative to the value that would be placed on it if all private and public information was known and 'appropriately' used. As noted earlier in this chapter, market predictions are sometimes, in hindsight, proved to be wrong, thus necessitating subsequent adjustments.

contributions during the period, ΔBV_{it} can also be measured by considering the change in retained earnings for the period. On a per share basis, this is measured as earnings per share (E_{it}) less dividends paid per share (D_{it}):

$$\Delta BV_{it} / \text{no. of shares} = E_{it} - D_{it} \tag{10.7}$$

This formula is based on the concept of 'clean surplus' earnings, which assumes that all increases in book value pass through the income statement. Clean surplus earnings does not always hold in practice, since items such as asset revaluation increments are credited directly to owners' equity (through a credit to revaluation reserve). However, the assumption of clean surplus is useful for simplifying our analysis. Substituting Equations 10.6 and 10.7 into Equation 10.5 gives:

$$P_{it} - P_{it-1} = E_{it} - D_{it} + \varepsilon'_{it} \tag{10.8}$$

That is, there is a theoretical relationship between change in price and change in retained earnings for the period. With a small amount of manipulation, this equation can be expressed to relate returns to earnings (the return/earnings relation). First, adding dividends to both sides of the equation, and dividing through by beginning of period price, gives:

$$\frac{(P_{it} - P_{it-1}) + D_{it}}{P_{it} - 1} = E_{it} / P_{it-1} + \varepsilon''_{it} \tag{10.9}$$

Since the left-hand side of the equation, $((P_{it} - P_{it-1}) + D_{it}) / P_{it-1}$, is equal to returns (Equation 10.2), we are left with an equation relating returns to earnings:

$$R_{it} = E_{it} / P_{it-1} + \varepsilon''_{it} \tag{10.10}$$

Equation 10.10 shows that we should expect returns (R_{it}) and earnings per share divided by beginning of period price (E_{it} / P_{it-1}) to be related.

In short, this perspective says that if market value is related to book value, returns should be related to accounting earnings per share, divided by price at the beginning of the accounting period. This analysis provides an underlying reason why we should expect returns to be related to earnings over time. However, it is interesting to note that it is total earnings per share rather than unexpected earnings per share that this theoretical framework proposes should be associated with returns. This is in contrast to research that assesses the 'information content' of earnings announcements by analysing the association between unexpected earnings per share and abnormal returns at the time of the announcement. We will see that there has been a number of studies that evaluate reported earnings (which is an accounting number) on the basis of how closely the movements in reported earnings (or earnings per share) relate to changes in share prices.[22]

Beaver *et al.* (1980) was an early paper that sought to investigate how efficiently data about share prices enable a researcher to estimate future accounting earnings. Accepting that share price is the capitalized value of future earnings, they regressed the annual percentage change in share price on the percentage change in annual earnings per share.

[22] Again, this research assumes, perhaps somewhat simplistically, that the market has determined the 'right' valuation of the organization.

Consistent with Equation 10.10, they found that share prices and related returns were related to accounting earnings, but they also found that share prices in year t were positively associated with accounting earnings in year $t+1$ (share prices led accounting earnings). It was accepted that share price movements provided an indication of future movements in accounting earnings. Because of various information sources, prices appeared to anticipate future accounting earnings. These findings were also supported in a later study by Beaver *et al.* (1987), who regressed changes in security prices on the percentage changes in earnings.

In previous discussion we showed that research indicates that share prices of larger firms do not adjust as much to earnings announcements as do the share prices of smaller firms. This was explained on the basis that there is more information available and analysed in relation to larger firms, and hence information about earnings is already impounded in the share price. That is, 'for larger firms, there is a broader and richer information set, and there are more market traders and more analysts seeking information' (Brown, 1994, p. 110).

Now if we adopt the position taken in this section of the chapter that share prices can actually anticipate earnings announcements ('looking back the other way'), as indicated in Beaver *et al.* (1980 and 1987), then perhaps share prices anticipate accounting earnings more efficiently in the case of larger firms. Collins *et al.* (1987) found evidence to support this view – size does matter, with the share prices being a better indicator of future earnings in larger companies.

As noted above, there have been a number of studies using stock market valuations as a basis for evaluating accounting information. In Equation 10.10 we indicated that, theoretically, market returns should be related to earnings. Dechow (1994) investigates how well accounting earnings reflect market returns. She also considers whether another measure of performance, based on cash flows, relates better to returns than earnings based on the accrual accounting system. According to Dechow (1994, p. 12):

> This paper assumes that stock markets are efficient in the sense that stock prices unbiasedly reflect all publicly available information concerning firms' expected future cash flows. Therefore, stock price performance is used as a benchmark to assess whether earnings or realised cash flows better summarise this information.

According to Dechow, earnings are predicted to be a more useful measure of firm performance than cash flows because they are predicted to have fewer timing and matching problems. In her conclusions, she states (p. 35):

> This paper hypothesizes that one role of accounting accruals is to provide a measure of short-term performance that more closely reflects expected cash flows than do realized cash flows. The results are consistent with this prediction. First, over short measurement intervals earnings are more strongly associated with stock returns than realized cash flows. In addition, the ability of realized cash flows to measure firm performance improves relative to earnings as the measurement interval is lengthened. Second, earnings have a higher association with stock returns than do realized cash flows in firms experiencing large changes in their working capital requirements and their investment and financing activities. Under these conditions, realized cash flows

have more severe timing and matching problems and are less able to reflect firm performance.

Using the market value of a firm's securities as a benchmark, a number of studies have also attempted to determine which asset valuation approaches provide accounting figures that best reflect the valuation the market places on the firm. The perspective taken is that book values that relate more closely to market values (determined through a review of share prices) provide more relevant information than other accounting valuation approaches. Barth *et al.* (1996) undertook a study that investigated whether fair value estimates of a bank's financial instruments (as required in the USA at the time) seem to provide a better explanation of bank share prices relative to values determined on the basis of historical cost accounting. Their findings indicate that the disclosures required by the US accounting standard SFAS No. 107 'provide significant explanatory power for bank share prices beyond that provided by book values' (p. 535), thereby providing evidence that such values are the values that are relevant to investors.

Easton *et al.* (1993) investigate whether revaluations of assets result in an alignment between information reflected in annual reports and information implicit in share prices and returns. Again, share price data are used as the 'benchmark' against which accounting data are assessed. According to Easton *et al.* (1993, p. 16):

> Prices are used to assess the extent to which the financial statements, including asset revaluations, reflect the state of the firm at a point in time, while returns are used to assess the summary of change in financial state that is provided in the financial statements.

They found that the revaluation of assets generally resulted in better alignment of market and book values. In concluding their paper, they state (p. 36):

> Our analyses support the conclusion that book values including asset revaluation reserves are more aligned with the market value of the firm than book values excluding asset revaluation. That is, asset revaluation reserves as reported under Australian GAAP help to provide a better summary of the current state of the firm. Thus, allowing or requiring firms to revalue assets upward should be carefully considered by organizations such as the UK Accounting Standards Board, the Japanese Ministry of Finance, and the International Accounting Standards Committee as they debate the merits of various proposed changes in asset revaluation practice.

Consistent with a view that market prices already seem to reflect the current values of an entity's assets, as indicated in the research discussed above, it is interesting to note that asset revaluations do not appear to provide information to investors over and above historical cost accounting information. That is, some studies have indicated that the provision of current cost data in financial statements does not have information content (Brown and Finn, 1980). These results suggest that investors are able to estimate current value information prior to it being disclosed in the financial statements. Therefore, while the provision of current value information does not provide new information to investors, it appears to reflect the information used by investors in making their investment decisions.

10.6 Relaxing assumptions about market efficiency

The research discussed so far in this chapter has relied upon a fundamental assumption that capital markets are efficient – which basically means that relevant publicly available information is quickly (or instantaneously) impounded within share prices. According to Kothari (2001, p. 114):

> Building on past theoretical and empirical work, Fama (1965) introduced, and subsequently made major contributions to the conceptual refinement and empirical testing of the efficient markets hypothesis. Fama (1965, p. 4) notes 'In an efficient market, on the average, competition' among rational, profit maximizing participants 'will cause the full effects of new information on intrinsic values to be reflected "instantaneously" in actual prices'. The maintained hypothesis of market efficiency opened the doors for positive capital markets research in accounting. Ball and Brown (1968, p. 160) assert that capital market efficiency provides 'justification for selecting the behaviour of security prices as an operational test of usefulness' of information in financial statements. Beaver (1968) offers a similar argument. Unlike previous normative research on accounting theories and optimal accounting policies, positive capital markets research began using changes in security prices as an objective, external outcome to infer whether information in accounting reports is useful to market participants.

However, in recent years there has been some research which has questioned assumptions of market efficiency. As Kothari (2001, p. 107) states:

> The mounting evidence of apparent market inefficiency documented in the financial economics and accounting literature has fuelled accounting researchers' interest in fundamental analysis, valuation, and tests of market efficiency. Evidence of market inefficiency has created an entirely new area of research examining long-horizon stock-price performance following accounting events. This is in sharp contrast to the boom in short window event studies and studies of economic consequences of standard setting of the 1970s and 1980s. Future work on tests of market efficiency with respect to accounting information will be fruitful if it recognizes that (i) deficient research design choices can create the false appearance of market inefficiency; and (ii) advocates of market inefficiency should propose robust hypotheses and tests to differentiate their behavioral-finance theories from the efficient market hypothesis that does not rely on irrational behavior.

Much of the research that challenges market efficiencies does so on the basis that it appears that the capital market's response to information appears to be longer than previously believed. As we have already indicated, much previous research was predicated on the view that capital markets react – through changes in share prices – almost instantaneously to relevant information. According to Kothari (2001, p. 130):

> If the market fails to correctly appreciate the implications of a current earnings surprise in revising its expectations of future earnings, the price change associated with earnings change will be too small. There is a large body of evidence that suggests that the stock market under-reacts to earnings information and recognizes the full impact of the earnings information only gradually over

time. Smaller-than-predicted values of earnings response coefficients are consistent with capital market inefficiency.

Where share prices are found to take time to react to particular information – such as corporate earnings announcement – this is referred to in the literature as 'drift'. As Kothari (2001, p. 193) states:

> Post-earnings-announcement drift is the predictability of abnormal returns following earnings announcements. Since the drift is of the same sign as the earnings change, it suggests the market under-reacts to information in earnings announcements. Ball and Brown (1968) first observe the drift. It has been more precisely documented in many subsequent studies. The drift lasts up to a year and the magnitude is both statistically and economically significant for the extreme good and bad earnings news portfolios. A disproportionate fraction of the drift is concentrated in the three-day periods surrounding future quarterly earnings announcements, as opposed to exhibiting a gradually drifting abnormal return behavior. Because of this characteristic and because almost all of the drift appears within one year, I characterize the drift as a short-window phenomenon, rather than a long-horizon performance anomaly. The profession has subjected the drift anomaly to a battery of tests, but a rational, economic explanation for the drift remains elusive.

If we relax assumptions about the speed with which the capital market reacts to information (that is, if we accept that the market does not react instantaneously and there is 'drift') then this leads to opportunities for some capital market participants to make gains in periods when share prices do not fully reflect the available information. Lee (2001, p. 238) states:

> Is it possible for mispricing to exist in equilibrium? Certainly. In fact, it strikes me as self-evident that arbitrage cannot exist in the absence of mispricing. Arbitrageurs are creatures of the very gap created by mispricing. Therefore, either both exist in equilibrium, or neither will. Arbitrage cannot take place without some amount of mispricing. If by some mystical force prices always adjust instantly to the right value, we would have no arbitrageurs. Therefore, if we believe that arbitrage is an equilibrium phenomenon, we must necessarily believe that some amount of mispricing is also an equilibrium phenomenon.

If further evidence continues to surface that capital markets do not always behave in accordance with the EMH, then should we reject the research that has embraced the EMH as a fundamental assumption? In this regard we can return to earlier chapters of this book in which we emphasized that theories are abstractions of reality. Capital markets are made of individuals and as such it would not (or perhaps, should not) be surprising to find that the market does not always act in the same predictable manner. Nevertheless, the EMH has helped provide some useful predictions and no doubt will continue to be relied upon by many researchers for a considerable period of time. As Lee (2001, p. 238) states:

> A common assertion is that even if the EMH is not strictly true, it is sufficient to serve as a starting point for research purposes. Like Newtonian physics, it is more than good enough for everyday usage. Unfortunately, it is becoming increasingly more difficult to accommodate what we know about the behavior of prices and returns within this traditional framework.

However, as we noted in Chapter 7, in light of market failures surrounding the sub-prime banking crisis, the credit crunch and the global financial crisis that came to light from 2007 onwards, several commentators have argued that some of the fundamental assumptions underlying much modern economic theory (including the efficiency of markets) have been shown to be unrealistic in practice (McSweeney, 2009).

At the present time there is some research into capital markets that does not rely upon market efficiencies. The consideration of 'other forces' that shape share prices and returns might eventually lead to a revolution in thought (Kuhn, 1962) – but it will arguably take a long time. As we stated in Chapter 1, Kuhn (1962) explained how knowledge, or science, develops: scientific progress is not evolutionary but, rather, revolutionary. His view is that knowledge advances when one theory is replaced by another as particular researchers attack the credibility of an existing paradigm and advance an alternative, promoted as being superior, thereby potentially bringing the existing paradigm into 'crisis'. As knowledge develops, the new paradigm may be replaced by a further research perspective, or a prior paradigm may be resurrected. In discussing the process of how researchers switch from one research perspective (or paradigm) to another, Kuhn likens it to one of 'religious conversion'.[23] Whether the EMH will ever be abandoned in favour of a different perspective is an interesting issue to consider.

Chapter summary

In concluding our discussion on capital market research we can see that this research has investigated a number of issues. Central to the research are assumptions about the efficiency of the capital market. In the 'information content' studies considered in the earlier part of this chapter we saw that researchers investigated share market reactions to the releases of information, often specifically the release of accounting information. The view taken was that the accounting disclosures often revealed new information, and in a market that was deemed to be informationally efficient with regard to acting upon new information, share prices react to this information.

In the latter part of this chapter we considered studies that investigated whether accounting disclosures reflected, or perhaps confirmed, information already impounded in share prices. The perspective taken was that in an informationally efficient capital market, market prices of shares will reflect information from a multitude of sources. If the accounting information did not reflect the information already impounded in share prices, then some researchers would argue that accounting data that do not relate to share prices, and changes therein, are somewhat deficient. The idea is that market prices reflect information from many sources and if the accumulated data provide a particular signal, the accounting disclosures should also provide similar signals. As we noted, this approach

---

[23] Kuhn's 'revolutionary' perspective about the development of knowledge is in itself a theory about how knowledge develops, and, as with financial accounting theories, there are alternative views of how knowledge develops and advances. Although a review of the various perspectives of the development of science is beyond the scope of this book, interested readers are referred to Chalmers (1982), Feyerabend (1975), Lakatos and Musgrove (1974) and Popper (1959).

implies that the market has it 'right' when determining share prices, and hence returns. In practice, the market cannot be expected always to get it 'right'.

Because much knowledge about the performance of an entity will be gained from sources other than accounting, it is perhaps reasonable to expect that accounting information should relate (not perfectly) to expectations held by capital market participants, as reflected in share prices. However, because there will arguably always be some unexpected information released when accounting results are made public, we might expect that not all accounting disclosures will be of a confirmatory nature. Some information in the accounting releases will be new and, in a market that is assumed to be informationally efficient, some share price revisions are to be expected.

Many share price studies have investigated the market's reaction to particular disclosures. Often, if no reaction is found, it is deemed that the information is not useful and therefore entities should not go to the trouble and expense involved in making such disclosures. This form of argument has been used to criticize accounting regulators for mandating particular disclosure requirements. What must be recognized, however, is that capital market research investigates the aggregate reaction of one group of stakeholders, the investors. While the share market is an important user of accounting information, provision of information to the share market is not the only function of the accounting system. Accounting information is also used for monitoring purposes (Jensen and Meckling, 1976; Watts and Zimmerman, 1990), and hence financial statements play an important role in relation to the contracting process (see Chapter 7). Financial statements provide a relatively low cost way of measuring managers' performance and monitoring compliance with contract terms, thereby helping to reduce agency costs. Further, financial statement information can be used to satisfy people's 'rights to know', that is, to fulfil the duty of accountability (see Chapter 8 for an overview of the notion of accountability). Therefore, while investors are important users of financial statements, it would be foolish to focus solely on the investor-information role of financial reporting, to the exclusion of considerations about the monitoring/accountability role. Arguably organizations have an accountability to a broader group of stakeholders other than just shareholders.

Questions

10.1 What is the role of capital market research?

10.2 What assumptions about market efficiency are typically adopted in capital market research? What do we mean by market efficiency?

10.3 If some research is undertaken that provides evidence that capital markets do not always behave in accordance with the efficient markets hypothesis, then does this invalidate research that adopts an assumption that capital markets are efficient?

10.4 What would be the implications for capital market research if it was generally accepted that capital markets were not efficient in assimilating information?

10.5 If an organization releases its earnings figures for the year and there is no share price reaction, how would capital market researchers possibly explain this finding?

10.6 How would a researcher undertaking capital market research typically justify that a particular item of information has 'value' to investors?

10.7 Evaluate the following statement: If an item of accounting information is released by a corporation and there is no apparent change in the share price of the company, then the information is not relevant to the market and therefore there is no point disclosing such information again.

10.8 What, if any, effect would the size of an entity have on the likelihood that the capital market will react to the disclosure of accounting information?

10.9 If an organization's operations rely heavily upon the specialized expertise of its management team then would you expect there to be a higher or lower correspondence between the net assets recognized in the balance sheet, and the total market value of the organization's securities, relative to an organization that relies more upon tangible assets (for example, commonly used plant and machinery) to generate its income? Why would you expect this?

10.10 Would you expect an earnings announcement by one firm within an industry to impact on the share prices of other firms in the industry? Why?

10.11 The following comments appeared in a newspaper blog posting entitled 'Severn Trent rises 2% as cost cutting helps lift profit' (by Nick Fletcher in the *Guardian*, 'Market Forces Live' blog on 28 May 2010):

> Severn Trent has become the latest water company to reveal a hefty rise in profits, with its figures helped by cost cutting.
>
> The company said underlying profits jumped 23.7% to £338.4m, with its efficiency programme delivering higher than expected savings, including the loss of 275 back office staff. Despite the cost cutting, chief executive Tony Wray also said Severn Trent had improved its performance to customers, receiving the maximum score for customer service in a recent Ofwat survey. On the other hand, only 9 out of its 20 performance targets were in the top quartile. It admitted there were areas where it needed to do more:
>
> > *For example, on unplanned interruptions, we have not fully addressed issues such as poor network condition and incident response. We have an action plan in place focused on improving network monitoring and resilience, and how we deal with incidents causing supply interruptions.*
>
> The company's shares have climbed 23p to £11.82 on the news.

Required:
Relying upon material provided in this chapter, provide an explanation as to why the capital market responded as positively as it did to Severn Trent's profit announcement.

10.12 Researchers such as Chambers and Sterling have made numerous claims that historical cost information is meaningless and useless. Are the results of capital market research consistent with this perspective?

10.13 Some recent capital market research investigates whether accounting information reflects the valuations that have already been made by the market (as reflected in share prices). In a sense, it assumes that the market has it 'right' and that a 'good' accounting approach is one that provides accounting numbers that relate to, or confirm, the market prices/returns. If we assume that the market has it 'right', then what exactly is the role of financial accounting?

10.14 Review Accounting Headline 10.6 (newspaper article entitled 'Colgate, Unilever warn on profits: Consumer products sector hit as household names highlight pressure to cut costs and keep sales') and explain the reason for the change in the prices of Unilever's and Colgate-Palmolive's shares. Also, what might have caused the price changes in the shares in the other consumer product companies?

10.15 In this chapter we have emphasized that the capital market appears to respond to information from many sources, including, but not limited to, accounting. As an illustration of how non-accounting information appears to impact on share prices, consider Accounting Headline 10.8. Why do you think the market reacted the way it did to the announcement, and do you think that the announcement implies market efficiency or inefficiency?

Accounting Headline 10.8

An illustration of how non-accounting information may impact upon share price

Appearance by new chief lifts Swiss Aviation

By Haig Simonian

The first public appearance by Christoph Franz as the new chief executive of Swiss International Airlines was marked yesterday by a 10 per cent rally in its share price.

Mr Franz, a former board member of the Deutsche Bahn railways group, gave no indication of his plans for Swiss, which is struggling to regain profitability.

The rise in the price of the illiquid stock came in spite of the fact that Mr Franz was pushed out of Deutsche Bahn last year after a public outcry over a controversial new fare system.

In a brief news conference at Zurich airport, the surprise successor to Andre Dose, the Swiss boss who stepped down unexpectedly last month, said he would spend his first two months getting to know the company and its staff. Although he will join Swiss at the beginning of next month, Mr Franz will not formally take up the chief executive role until July 1.

The appointment of Mr Franz, who played a part in the restructuring of Lufthansa, the German airline, in the early 1990s, came far sooner than expected. It was made possible by the fact that, since leaving Deutsche Bahn, he has been working as an independent transport industry 'adviser'.

Analysts said his quick appointment would help to build confidence in Swiss, in spite of continuing uncertainties about its viability.

Pieter Bouw, the Swiss chairman who took on the additional jobs of chief executive following Mr Dose's departure, said Mr Franz's selection had been a unanimous decision by the airline's four-member nomination committee. An initial list of 12 candidates had been whittled down to a shortlist of six, the company said.

Mr Franz, a 43-year-old German, has had extensive transport industry experience. As an additional advantage in multilingual Switzerland, he yesterday displayed fluent French alongside his native German.

Source: *Financial Times*, 21 April 2004, p. 32
©The Financial Times Limited 2010

10.16 Review Accounting Headline 10.7 earlier in this chapter (newspaper article entitled 'Icap shares plunge knocks £80m off Tory treasurer's wealth). In an efficient capital market, why would a profit forecast lead to a revision in Icap's share price?

10.17 Read Accounting Headline 10.9 and, relying upon some of the capital market studies we have considered in this chapter, explain why the share prices of the pharmaceutical companies might have reacted in the way they did.

Accounting Headline 10.9

Market reactions to drug marketing ruling

Market reactions to drug marketing ruling

By Rachel Stevenson

Shares in the pharmaceutical sector received a shot in the arm yesterday after an American drug authority panel ruled that controversial painkillers could stay on sale.

AstraZeneca, GlaxoSmithKline and Shire Pharmaceuticals all saw their share prices soar following a Food and Drug Administration (FDA) advisory panel recommendation on Friday that Vioxx, Merck's controversial painkiller, can return to shelves and drugs of the same class can stay on sale.

The FDA said Vioxx, which was pulled from the market in September on concerns it doubled the risk of heart attacks and strokes, was safe to market, albeit with heightened safety warnings, because the benefits of the drug outweighed the risks. Pfizer's rival painkillers, Celebrex and Bextra, which have also been under threat because of elevated risks of heart problems, were also given clearance to stay on sale.

GlaxoSmithKline, which is developing a painkiller in the same class as Vioxx, saw its shares rise 4.4 per cent, closing 54p up at 1,295p. It is due to meet with FDA officials to discuss developments on its drug shortly.

AstraZeneca also rose more than 4 per cent to close at 2,162 and Shire bounced up 3.4 per cent to 581p. Shire saw its shares tumble 16 per cent last week after its key hyperactivity and attention deficit disorder drug was withdrawn in Canada after fears for its safety. The three companies were yesterday's highest risers in the FTSE 100.

There had been fears that the FDA would introduce much tighter safety regulations, causing many more drug withdrawals and a slower rate of approvals on new treatments. Adrian Howd, an analyst at ABN Amro, said: 'This was a relief rally after the FDA showed some common sense with regard to drug safety. All drugs carry risks and some side effects will always be found ... but the FDA appears to have seen the balance between safety and the rewards from drugs.'

The panel found that the key component of the drugs, called Cox-2 inhibitors, did increase risks of heart problems and should carry the strongest possible warnings, but the drugs would help patients who have struggled to find other treatments that work.

Source: *The Independent,* 22 February 2005, p. 34
©The Independent Newspaper

10.18 Read Accounting Headline 10.10 which provides an extract from a newspaper article that appeared in the *Wall Street Journal* on 12 July 2008. You are to read the extract and then explain how a capital markets researcher would differentiate between the component of the share price change of UAL that related to market-wide movements, and the component that related to the write-down of the organization's intangible assets.

Accounting Headline 10.10

Market reactions to an accounting write-down
Corporate News: UAL to Record Up to $2.7 Billion in Charges

By Susan Carey

Shares of United Airlines parent UAL Corp. fell 13% Friday to hit a 52-week low after the carrier said it plans to take second-quarter noncash charges of as much as $2.7 billion, mostly to reflect a write-down to zero of the value of its intangible assets, or goodwill.

Its stock slump came as the larger market plummeted on oil and mortgage worries.

Chicago-based UAL, the second-largest U.S. airline by traffic after AMR Corp.'s American Airlines, said the write-down is the result of record-high fuel prices hammering its financial results and its market capitalization.

As of Friday, UAL, which generates about $20 billion in annual revenue, had an equity value of $433 million, less than the retail price of two jumbo jets. Its stock has plunged 93% in the past year, more than most of its big U.S. rivals, although the entire sector has been rocked by the rapid run-up in fuel prices.

UAL shares fell 54 cents to $3.63 in 4 p.m. composite trading on the Nasdaq Stock Market, hitting a 52-week low of $3.47 in intraday trading.

Source: *Wall Street Journal,* 12 July 2008, p. B5

References

Aboody, D. (1996) 'Recognition versus disclosure in the oil and gas industry', *Journal of Accounting Research* (Supplement), 21–32.

Baginski, S.P. (1987) 'Intra-industry information transfers associated with management forecasts of earnings', *Journal of Accounting Research*, **25** (2), 196–216.

Ball, R. & Brown, P. (1968) 'An empirical evaluation of accounting income numbers', *Journal of Accounting Research*, **6** (2), 159–78.

Barth, M., Beaver, W. & Landsman, W. (1996) 'Value-relevance of banks fair value disclosures under SFAS 107', *The Accounting Review*, **71** (4), 513–37.

Beaver, W. (1968) 'The information content of annual earnings announcements', *Journal of Accounting research*, **6** (Supplement), 67–92.

Beaver, W. (1972) 'The behavior of security prices and its implications for accounting research (methods), in the "Report of the Committee on Research Methodology in Accounting"', *The Accounting Review*, **47** (Supplement), 407–37.

Beaver, W.H., Lambert, R. & Morse, D. (1980) 'The information content of security prices', *Journal of Accounting and Economics*, **2** (1), 3–38.

Beaver, W.H., Lambert, R.A. & Ryan, S.G. (1987) 'The information content of security prices: A second look', *Journal of Accounting and Economics*, **9** (2), 139–57.

Blacconiere, W.G. & Patten, D.M. (1994) 'Environmental disclosures, regulatory costs and changes in firm value', *Journal of Accounting and Economics*, **18**, 357–77.

Botosan, C.A. (1997) 'Disclosure level and the cost of equity capital', *The Accounting Review*, **72** (3), 323–50.

Brown, P. (1970) 'The impact of the annual net profit report on the stock market', *Australian Accountant* (July), 273–83.

Brown, P. (1994) 'Capital markets-based research in accounting: An introduction', *Coopers and Lybrand Research Methodology Monograph No. 2*, Melbourne: Coopers and Lybrand.

Brown, P. & Finn, F. (1980) 'Asset revaluations and stock prices: Alternative explanations of a study by Sharpe and Walker', in: Ball, R. (ed.) *Share Markets and Portfolio Theory*, St Lucia: University of Queensland Press, 349–54.

Brown, S.J. & Warner, J.B. (1980) 'Measuring security price performance', *Journal of Financial Economics*, **8** (3), 205–58.

Brown, S.J. & Warner, J.B. (1985) 'Using daily stock returns: The case of event studies', *Journal of Financial Economics*, **14** (1), 3–31.

Chalmers, A.F. (1982) *What Is this Thing Called Science?*, Brisbane, Australia: University of Queensland Press.

Chambers, R. (1965) 'Why bother with postulates?', *Journal of Accounting Research*, **1** (1), 3–15.

Clarkson, P.M., Joyce, D. & Tutticci, I. (2006) 'Market reaction to takeover rumour in Internet discussion sites', *Accounting & Finance*, **46** (1), 31–52.

Clinch, G.J. & Sinclair, N.A. (1987) 'Intra-industry information releases: A recursive systems approach', *Journal of Accounting and Economics*, **9** (1), 89–106.

Collins, D., Kothari, S. & Rayburn, J. (1987) 'Firm size and information content of prices with respect to earnings', *Journal of Accounting and Economics*, **9** (2), 111–38.

Collins, D.W. & Kothari, S.P. (1989) 'An analysis of intertemporal and cross-sectional determinants of earnings response coefficients', *Journal of Accounting and Economics*, **11** (2–3), 143–81.

Cotter, J. & Zimmer, I. (1999) 'Why do some firms recognize whereas others merely disclose asset revaluations?', Unpublished working paper, Universities of Queensland and Southern Queensland.

Dechow, P. (1994) 'Accounting earnings and cash flows as measures of firm performance: The role of accounting accruals', *Journal of Accounting and Economics*, **18**, 3–24.

Easton, P.D., Eddey, P. & Harris, T.S. (1993) 'An investigation of revaluations of tangible long-lived assets', *Journal of Accounting Research*, **31** (Supplement), 1–38.

Easton, P.D. & Zmijewski, M.E. (1989) 'Cross-sectional variation in the stock market response to accounting earnings announcements', *Journal of Accounting and Economics*, **11** (2), 117–41.

Ertimur, Y., Livnat, J. & Martikainen, M. (2003) 'Differential market reactions to revenue and expense surprises', *Review of Accounting Studies*, **8** (2), 185–211.

Fama, E. (1965) 'The behavior of stock market prices', *Journal of Business*, **38**, 34–105.

Fama, E.F. (1976) *Foundations of Finance*, New York: Basic Books.

Fama, E.F., Fisher, L., Jensen, M.C. & Roll, R. (1969) 'The adjustment of stock prices to new information', *International Economic Review*, **10** (1), 1–21.

Feyerabend, P. (1975) *Against Method: Outline of an Anarchic Theory of Knowledge*, London: New Left Books.

Firth, M. (1976) 'The impact of earnings announcements on the share price behavior of similar type firms', *Economic Journal*, **96**, 296–306.

Foster, G.J. (1981) 'Intra-industry information transfers associated with earnings releases', *Journal of Accounting and Economics*, **3** (4), 201–32.

Frankel, R. & Lee, C.M.C. (1998) 'Accounting valuation, market expectation, and cross-sectional stock returns', *Journal of Accounting and Economics*, **25** (3), 283–319.

Freeman, R. (1987) 'The association between accounting earnings and security returns for large and small firms', *Journal of Accounting and Economics*, **9**, 195–228.

Freeman, R. & Tse, S. (1992) 'Intercompany information transfers', *Journal of Accounting and Economics* (June/September), 509–23.

Grant, E.B. (1980) 'Market implications of differential amounts of interim information', *Journal of Accounting Research*, **18** (1), 255–68.

Hendriksen, E.S. & Van Breda, M.F. (1992) *Accounting Theory*, Homewood, IL: Irwin.

Herbohn, K., Ragunathan, V. & Garsden, R. (2007) 'The horse has bolted: Revisiting the market reaction to going concern modifications of audit reports', *Accounting & Finance*, **47** (3), 473–93.

Imhoff, E.A. & Lobo, G.J. (1984) 'Information content of analysts forecast revisions', *Journal of Accounting Research*, **22** (2), 541–54.

Jegadeesh, N. & Livnat, J. (2006) 'Revenue surprises and stock returns', *Journal of Accounting and Economics*, **41** (1–2), 147–71.

Jensen, M.C. & Meckling, W.H. (1976) 'Theory of the firm: Managerial behavior, agency costs and ownership structure', *Journal of Financial Economics*, **3** (October), 305–60.

Kothari, S.P. (2001) 'Capital markets research in accounting', *Journal of Accounting and Economics*, **31** (1–3), 105–231.

Kuhn, T.S. (1962) *The Structure of Scientific Revolutions*, Chicago: University of Chicago Press.

Lakatos, I. & Musgrove, A. (1974) *Criticism and the Growth of Knowledge*, Cambridge: Cambridge University Press.

Lang, M.H. & Lundholm, R.J. (1996) 'Corporate disclosure policy and analyst behavior', *The Accounting Review*, **71** (4), 467–92.

Lee, C.M.C. (2001) 'Market efficiency and accounting research: A discussion of "Capital market research in accounting" by S.P. Kothari', *Journal of Accounting and Economics*, **31** (1–3), 233–53.

Lintner, J. (1965) 'The valuation of risk assets and the selection of risky investments in stock portfolios and capital budgets', *Review of Economics and Statistics*, **47**, 13–37.

McSweeney, B. (2009) 'The roles of financial asset market failure denial and the economic crisis: Reflections on accounting and financial theories and practices', *Accounting, Organizations and Society*, **34** (6–7), 835–48.

Penman, S.H. (1980) 'An empirical investigation of the voluntary disclosure of corporate earnings forecasts', *Journal of Accounting Research*, **18** (1), 132–60.

Popper, K.R. (1959) *The Logic of Scientific Discovery*, London: Hutchinson.

Ribstein, L.E. (2002) 'Market vs. regulatory responses to corporate fraud: A critique of the Sarbanes-Oxley Act of 2002', *Journal of Corporation Law*, **28** (1), 1.

Sharpe, W.F. (1964) 'Capital asset prices: A review of market equilibrium under conditions of risk', *Journal of Finance*, **19**, 425–42.

Skinner, D.J. (1997) 'Earnings disclosures and stockholder lawsuits', *Journal of Accounting and Economics*, **23**, 249–82.

Sloan, R.G. (1996) 'Do stock prices fully reflect information in accruals and cash flows about future earnings?', *The Accounting Review*, **71** (3), 289–316.

Solomon, D. & Bryan-Low, C. (2004) 'Companies complain about cost of corporate-governance rules', *Wall Street Journal*, 10 February.

Sterling, R. (1975) 'Towards a science of accounting', *Financial Analysts Journal*.

Taffler, R.J., Lu, J. & Kausar, A. (2004) 'In denial? Stock market underreaction to going-concern audit report disclosures', *Journal of Accounting and Economics*, **38**, 263–96.

Watts, R.L. & Zimmerman, J.L. (1986) *Positive Accounting Theory*, Englewood Cliffs, NJ: Prentice-Hall.

Watts, R.L. & Zimmerman, J.L. (1990) 'Positive accounting theory: A ten year perspective', *The Accounting Review*, **65** (1), 131–56.

Zhang, I.X. (2007) 'Economic consequences of the Sarbanes-Oxley Act of 2002', *Journal of Accounting and Economics*, **44** (1–2), 74–115.

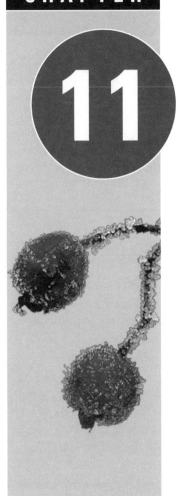

11

Reactions of Individuals to Financial Reporting: An Examination of Behavioural Research

Upon completing this chapter readers should understand:

❖ how behavioural research differs from capital market research;

❖ how different accounting-related variables can be manipulated in behavioural research;

❖ how the results of behavioural research can be of relevance to

corporations and the accounting profession for anticipating individual reactions to accounting disclosures;

❖ how the results of behavioural research can form the basis for developing ways to use accounting-related data more efficiently;

❖ the limitations of behavioural research.

Opening issues

The accounting profession often considers introducing new regulations relating to the disclosure of new items of information, or specifically requiring information to be disclosed in a particular format. A concern that often arises is how or whether various categories of financial statement users will react to the new disclosures which are potentially going to be mandated, particularly given that new disclosure requirements typically impose costs on those entities required to make the disclosures. How can behavioural research be used to assist the concerns of accounting regulators about financial statement users' reactions to the proposed requirements?

11.1 Introduction

In Chapter 10 we considered capital market research. Capital market research considers the *aggregate behaviour* of investors in the capital market. This aggregate behaviour is typically observed by looking at movements in share prices around the time of particular events, such as when earnings announcements are made. Capital markets research does not consider how items of information are actually processed or used by the market participants – it simply looks for a share price reaction.

In this chapter we consider decision-making at the *individual level*. The research, which we refer to as behavioural research, involves performing studies to see how a variety of financial statement user groups (not just investors, as is the case in capital market research) react to a variety of accounting information, often presented in different forms and in different contexts. According to Birnberg and Shields (1989, p. 24):

> Behavioural Accounting Research applies theories and methodologies from the behavioural sciences to examine the interface between accounting information and processes and human (including organizational) behaviour.

In previous chapters, theories that seek to explain or predict particular actions, such as the manager's choice of accounting methods, were discussed. For example, in Chapter 7 we discussed Positive Accounting Theory and agency theory. Economics-based theories such as these make assumptions about what motivates human actions (for example, a quest to maximize personal wealth), and such motivations are attributed across all individuals. By contrast, behavioural research studies individuals' actions and choices and typically does not make broad-based assumptions about how all individuals behave, or about their motivations. Further, behavioural research is typically grounded in organizational theory, and theories from psychology and sociology rather than from economics. However, like theories such as Positive Accounting Theory, legitimacy theory, institutional theory (discussed in Chapter 8), behavioural research can be considered as 'positive research' because it seeks to explain particular actions or behaviours (in contrast to 'normative research' which prescribes how certain activities *should* be undertaken).

By generating knowledge about how different categories of financial statement users (for example, investors, research analysts, auditors, bankers, loan officers and so on) react to particular accounting disclosures, corporations, the accounting profession and regulators (such as the International Accounting Standards Board) will be better placed to *anticipate* how different individuals will react to particular information.

Apart from the anticipatory implications associated with behavioural research, results of analysis of the decision-making processes of individuals can also provide the basis for developing procedures to improve future decision-making.

The field of behavioural research can be subdivided into a number of different 'schools'. According to Birnberg and Shields (1989), behavioural research in accounting can be classified into five main branches (or 'schools'), these being:

1 Managerial control. This research considers such issues as the roles of budgets in affecting the level of managerial performance and behaviour; the impacts of leadership style on managerial performance; the role of feedback on managerial performance; the impact of different incentives on managerial performance.

2 Accounting information processing. This research considers how users of financial reports process accounting information – often referred to as the human information processing (HIP) branch of behavioural research. This research frequently involves the use of the 'lens model' – something that we discuss within this chapter. The lens model allows the researcher to assess the effects of multiple cues (items of information, for example) on decisions without the need for a prohibitively large number of subjects in a between subjects design.

3 Accounting information system design. This branch of research relates behavioural issues to the design of information systems.

4 Auditing process research. This branch of research often uses the lens model. It delves into the decision-making processes of auditors and would cover such issues as what cues an auditor would utilize in formulating an opinion about financial statements.

5 Organizational sociology. This branch of research investigates changes which may occur in an organization's accounting system over time, and links changes in accounting systems to particular events.

Within this chapter we will not consider all of the above branches of behavioural accounting research. Rather, we will tend to concentrate on those areas that are related to individual behaviour with respect to financial accounting (not managerial accounting) information. As such, we will tend to concentrate on accounting information processing (human information processing) and auditing process research.

11.2 An overview of behavioural research

In Chapter 10 we considered research that investigated the aggregate reaction of the capital market to various accounting disclosures. In this chapter we turn to a different approach to research that considers how *individuals* react to various accounting disclosures. Research that considers how individuals react or behave when provided with particular items of information can be classified as *behavioural research*. According to Libby (1975, p. 2), research that attempts to describe individual behaviour is often grounded in a branch of psychology called *behavioural decision theory,* which has its roots in cognitive psychology, economics and statistics. According to Libby (1975, p. 2):

> The goal of much of this work is to describe actual decision behavior, evaluate its quality, and develop and test theories of the underlying psychological processes which produce the behavior. In addition, these descriptions reveal flaws in the behavior and often suggest remedies for these deficiencies.

Behavioural research was first embraced by accounting researchers in the 1960s (Maines, 1995) but became particularly popular in the 1970s when embraced by researchers such as Ashton and Libby. In reflecting on the evolution of behavioural research, Dyckman (1998, p. 1) states:

> While research in behavior is anything but new, it was not until the 20th century that researchers investigated the behavior of individuals in business organizations. Research into the behavioral impact of what occurs in accounting is an even more recent phenomenon, traceable perhaps back to the early sixties although the groundwork for much of the early efforts had been laid earlier.

Behavioural research has been used to investigate a variety of decision-making processes such as the valuation of market shares by individual analysts, the lending decisions of loan officers, the assessment of bankruptcy by bankers or auditors, and the assessment of risk by auditors. According to Birnberg and Shields (1989, p. 25):

> The method of systematic observation in behavioural accounting research usually involves the systematic observation of people either in the laboratory or field as opposed to archival data on human behaviour or computer simulation of behaviour.[1] The theories which are used to identify important variables for a study or to explain the behaviours observed are drawn from the behavioural sciences. Thus, behavioural studies can be differentiated from Efficient Markets Research because the latter relies exclusively on archival data and focuses on market forces not individual or group behaviour.

Some of the various published behavioural accounting research studies have been undertaken in a laboratory setting where a group of individuals are assigned a number of simple or complex tasks (which may or may not be reflective of 'real-life' decisions), while other research has been conducted in the individual's own workplace.[2] Behavioural research can have a number of aims. Some research has been undertaken to *understand* underlying decision-making processes, while other research has been conducted to *improve* decision-making. Some research manipulates the amount and types of information provided to particular subjects to assess how such differences impact on any final decisions, while other research provides all subjects with the same information and attempts to derive a model to

---

[1] Where data is generated by the researcher, perhaps through an experiment, then the data is often labelled as 'primary data'. Data that is already available independent of the researcher from sources such as publicly accessible archives is referred to as 'secondary data'. Share price data, the subject of Chapter 10, is secondary data.

[2] A laboratory setting would constitute a setting different from where the subjects would normally undertake their work and where the researcher is relatively more able to control certain variables relating to the decision-making task than would otherwise be possible.

explain how decisions by a particular category of decision-maker appear to be made (for example, decisions by auditors, stockbrokers, bankers or lending officers).

11.3 The Brunswik Lens Model

In explaining behavioural research a number of researchers have found it useful to relate their work to a model developed by Brunswik, this being the Brunswik Lens Model (Brunswik, 1952). Libby (1981, p. 6) provides a simplistic representation of the Lens Model. See Figure 11.1.

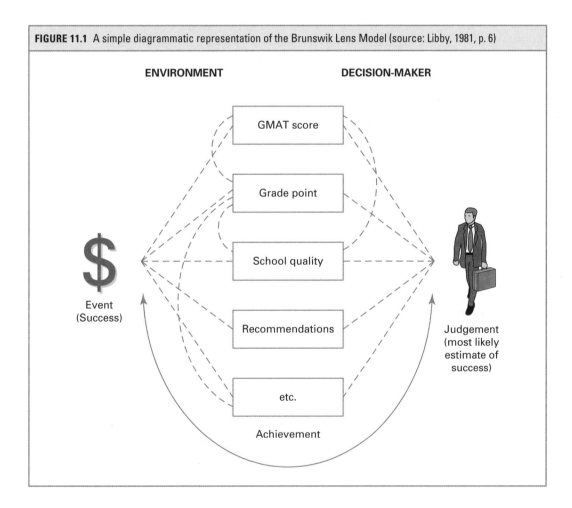

FIGURE 11.1 A simple diagrammatic representation of the Brunswik Lens Model (source: Libby, 1981, p. 6)

According to Birnberg and Shields (1989, p. 45):

> The suggestion that the lens model be adapted to behavioural accounting research from the psychological literature was outlined in the report of the Committee on Accounting Valuation Basis (1972) in a section initially authored by Nick Gonedes. Ashton (1974) discussed the lens model and asked what kinds of phenomena could be examined by the lens model. Libby (1975) was the first to utilise the lens model to look at a user oriented issue, the prediction of

corporate failure by loan officers. He developed a model of loan officers' behaviour and examined both the predictability and the stability of their judgements. Libby (1975) served to demonstrate the richness of the lens model and to demonstrate the greater insight into user behaviour available using the lens model compared to the earlier stimulus-response studies. As one might expect, Libby's study led to a series of subsequent studies using the lens model to examine the use of accounting data. The lens model made it possible for the experimenter to examine the patterns of cue utilization by the subjects and in that way begin to investigate what previously had been viewed as a 'black box'.

Libby (1981, p. 5) illustrates the application of the Brunswik Lens Model to the decision by graduate schools to admit students. As indicated in Figure 11.1, the criterion event is the students' future success, denoted by $ (on the left-hand side of the model). Given that this event will take place in the future, the decisions made by admissions officers within particular schools must be based on a number of factors or environmental 'cues' (pieces of information), which can be probabilistically related to the particular event under consideration (in this case, student success). A number of cues (in this case, items of information) can be used, for example GMAT scores, grade point averages in prior studies, quality of the undergraduate school attended, recommendations or references from various people, whether the individual participates in extracurricular activities and answers to particular subjective questions.[3] As Libby indicates, none of these individual cues, or combinations of cues, can be expected to provide a perfect indication of the future success of the student, but some may be linked, with some degree of probability, to success. As Libby explains, in effect, perspectives about the environment (the issue in question in this case being student success) are generated (observed) through a 'lens' of imperfect cues. The relationships between these imperfect cues and the judgement about success are represented by broken lines.[4]

There would also be an expectation that some of the cues will be interrelated. For example, the GMAT score might be expected to be correlated with grade point averages, as well as quality of school attended. Such interrelationships are represented by the broken lines linking the various cues, as indicated in Figure 11.1. To determine the weighting (or importance) of the various cues (independent variables) to the criterion event of success (the dependent variable which could simplistically be categorized as either success or failure in this case), as well as the correlations between the cues, various advanced statistical modelling approaches are applied. One model might be developed that provides a linear representation of the assessors' weightings of the various cues. This then provides a model of how the assessors actually went about their job of assessing applications. Knowledge of this model may be useful to a number of parties. For example, intending students would know what factors (cues) are particularly important to the assessors and hence the students may then know what factors to concentrate on. From the assessors' perspective it might be interesting for them to see how as a group they appear to be making their judgements. This might not be obvious until such a model is developed.

---

[3] As we show later, in an accounting study such as the prediction of bankruptcy the 'cues' might be information about various accounting ratios.

[4] Libby (1981, p. 5) notes also that relative reliance on various cues is likely to change over time as a result of fatigue, special circumstances, learning, and so on.

A model could also be developed that looks at the relationship between the actual outcome (student success or failure) and the various items of information available. That is, a model could also be developed by looking in the reverse direction from the event (the left-hand side) back to the cues (that is, not involving individuals making judgements). Obviously, such analysis could only be undertaken when a measure of actual success or failure can be obtained.

Libby (1981) provides an insight into the general applicability of the Lens Model to various decision-making scenarios. As he states (p. 6):

> This structure is very general and can be applied to almost any decision-making scheme. Again, consider a simplified commercial lending decision in which the principal task of the loan officer is to predict loan default. Loan default–non default is mainly a function of the future cash flows which will be available to the customer to service the debt. The customer provides a number of cues, some of which are probabilistically related to future cash flows. These include indicators of liquidity, leverage, and profitability drawn from financial statements, management evaluations resulting from interviews, plant visits, discussions with other knowledgeable parties, and outside credit ratings. No individual cue or combinations of cues is a perfect predictor of future cash flows, and there is overlap in the information (e.g., credit ratings are closely associated with profitability and liquidity measures). In making this judgement, the loan officer combines these cues into a prediction of future cash flows. Even if the banker's judgemental policy is highly stable over time, some inconsistencies are likely to arise, which will result in a probabilistic relationship between the cues and the final judgement. At the end of the term of each loan, the officer's prediction of cash flows can be compared with the actual event, and any resulting losses can be computed to measure achievement. While this example is highly simplified, it illustrates the generality of the framework and its importance for accountants. The model's principal concern with information-processing achievements in an uncertain world coincides with accountants' interest in improving the decisions made by users of accounting information and their more recent attention to the quality of their own decisions.

In applying the Lens Model it is common for researchers to model mathematically both the left-hand and right-hand sides of the lens. For example, on the right-hand side of the model we are interested in providing a model (typically linear) of how the individual uses cues to make an ultimate decision about the issue under investigation. This is often the major goal of much behavioural research. This can be undertaken by considering how each particular cue individually relates to the ultimate decision (univariate analysis), or how the entire set of cues relates to the ultimate decision or judgement (multivariate analysis). If statistical regression is undertaken as part of the multivariate analysis, the decision-maker's response might be summarized or modelled as follows:[5]

$$\hat{Y}_s = a_s + B_{1s}X_1 + B_{2s}X_2 + \dots B_{ks}X_k \tag{11.1}$$

---

[5] We have elected to provide only a brief overview of this modelling. For further insight, interested readers are referred to Libby (1981, pp. 19–21) and Trotman (1996, pp. 33–36).

where:

$\hat{Y}_s$ is the model's prediction of the judgement (for example, that the student succeeds or fails) based on the individual's judgements or predictions;

$X_1, X_2, \ldots X_k$ represent the set of cues (for example, the GMAT score, grade point average, etc.) for cue number 1 through to cue number k;

$B_1, B_2, \ldots B_k$ represent the weighting in the model given to each of the cues, based on the responses of the subjects.

If a cue contributes nothing to the prediction, it will be given a zero weighting. Conversely, if a particular item of information (cue) is relatively important in making a particular decision or judgement then it will have a greater weighting. Because the model will need to be generated from many observations and because models such as the above assume that individual cues contribute to the decision in a linear manner, it is clear that the model will not explain or predict with total accuracy the actual judgements made by particular individuals – but as we would appreciate, it is not expected to – it is a model of individual behaviour. As Libby states (1981, p. 22):

It is important to note that the algebraic models resulting from these studies simply indicate the functional relationship between the cues and the judgement. These, like all models, are abstractions and do not purport to represent 'real' mental processes.

Some researchers also model the left-hand side of the Lens Model (often referred to as the environmental side) which looks at the relationship between the *actual phenomenon* under consideration and the particular *cues* provided. Without relying on judgements provided by individuals, this equation can be used to predict a particular environmental event.[6] The model can be represented as follows:

$$\hat{Y}_e = a_e + B_{1e}X_1 + B_{2e}X_2 + \ldots B_{ke}X_k \tag{11.2}$$

where:

$\hat{Y}_e$ is the model's prediction of the environmental event under consideration (for example, student succeeds or fails);

$X_1, X_2, \ldots X_k$ represent the set of cues (for example, the GMAT score, grade point average for cue number 1 through to cue number k;

$B_1, B_2, \ldots, B_k$ represent the weighting in the model given to each of the cues, based on the modelling of the relationship between the actual event and the available cues.

Researchers often compare the results of the model derived from studying the decision-making processes of individuals (Equation 11.1) with the results of the model provided

---

[6] For example, Altman (1968) developed a bankruptcy prediction model by forming equations that related a particular environmental event (bankruptcy) with particular financial variables (derived from financial statements). Representative of modelling the left-hand side of the 'lens', no use was made of decisions of individual judges or experts.

by considering the relationship of the actual environmental event and the various cues (Equation 11.2). As we will see below, other issues focused on by researchers include how different individuals or groups weight particular cues, the consistency (or stability) of the weighting, what issues associated with the presentation format of the cues might influence factor usage and weighting, and so on.

Because the Lens Model generates an explanation which is in the form of an equation (see above), there is an implicit assumption that all relevant factors are considered simultaneously, rather than sequentially. In reality, individuals might not consider information simultaneously, but would consider particular information cues before moving on to other items of information.[7]

We can use the Lens Model to categorize a great deal of the behavioural research that has been undertaken over the last 20 to 30 years. The Lens Model explicitly considers *inputs* (uses of various cues), the *decision process* and *outputs* (ultimate decisions). Libby (1981, p. 8) provides a summary of the type of issues that can be considered when undertaking research about how individuals process information when making a decision. These issues include:

At the *input* level (that is, issues pertaining to the cues):

- scaling characteristics of individual cues (for example, whether the presentation of the cues as nominal, ordinal, discrete, continuous, deterministic or probabilistic influences whether the cues are used in making a decision);
- method of presentation (for example, does the presentational format appear to impact on the use of the cue(s));
- context (for example, do perceived rewards, social setting and so on seem to impact on the use of the various cues).

At the level of *processing* the information:

- characteristics of the person making the judgement (for example, whether the demographics, attitudes of the judge or the level of prior experience or interest impact on the decision that is made);
- characteristics of the decision rule (for example, how the individuals weight the cues; whether the judgements are stable over time; whether the judges use any simplifying heuristics when presented with potentially complex data).

At the *output* or decision level:

- qualities of the judgement (whether the response is accurate, quick, reliable; whether it incorporates particular biases; whether the judgements are consistent over time; whether there is consensus between the various judges);
- self-insight (whether the judge is aware of how they appear to weight various factors, etc.). The results of the research may provide the individual with insights about their own decision-making processes that they were previously unaware of.

---

[7] Later in this chapter we will consider protocol analysis which requires subjects of an experiment to 'think aloud' about how they make decisions. This research method would help to identify the sequence of how individuals process information.

11.4 The use of particular information items and the implications of different forms of presentation

At the *input* level, the issue of how and whether particular cues (information items) are used in decision-making is particularly relevant to the accounting profession. If it is shown that users of financial statements do not use particular information items (cues), it could be deemed that such information is not *material* and hence does not require disclosure or associated disclosure regulation. Alternatively, it could indicate that users of financial statements do not know how to use particular information, which might indicate some needs for education. The accounting profession would also be particularly interested in whether form of disclosure (for example, whether an item is provided in the statement of financial position, in a supplementary financial statement or in a footnote) impacts on users' decisions. We now consider a limited number of papers that have considered such issues.[8]

In relation to the use of particular items of accounting information, Pankoff and Virgil (1970) investigated financial analysts' predictions of financial returns on particular shares. They found that the analysts acquired earnings and sales information (often through purchasing such information) more often than other types of information. In another study of financial analysts' information demands (cue usage) Mear and Firth (1987) also found that analysts believed that sales growth and profitability were particularly important for estimating returns on particular securities.

From time to time accounting professions throughout the world consider whether they should require reporting entities to provide additional information as a supplement to existing financial information. One particular instance of this was the accounting profession's move in the 1980s to require supplementary current cost (inflation-adjusted) financial information to be disclosed in corporate annual reports. Clearly, research can be useful in providing an insight into how and whether current cost information would actually be used by readers of annual reports.[9] Such research includes that undertaken by Heintz (1973) and McIntyre (1973). These studies examined how three forms of disclosure impacted on investment decisions. Subjects were provided with either historical cost information (only); current cost information (only); or both current cost and historical cost information. The results generally questioned the provision of current cost information, as the subjects did not appear to alter their decisions as a result of being provided with current cost information. Such results

---

[8] The overview of research provided in this chapter is certainly not comprehensive. Rather, the intention is to provide an insight into some of the different research that has been undertaken in this area. For those readers desiring a more comprehensive insight, reference could be made to Ashton (1982), Ashton and Ashton (1995), Libby (1981), and Trotman (1996).

[9] Also, behavioural research relating to reactions to particular disclosures can be done in advance of an accounting requirement being introduced. On the basis of the behavioural research findings, accounting regulators might determine that there is no point in progressing a particular issue past its initial stages of development. This can be contrasted with capital market research which relies on historical share price data; data which capture how the market actually reacted to the implementation or formal proposal of the particular requirement.

obviously challenged the accounting profession's move to require supplementary current cost information.[10]

Behavioural research has also been undertaken in human resource accounting, an area that has been typically neglected by the accounting profession. In related research, both Elias (1972) and Hendricks (1976) found that the disclosure of information on costs incurred in relation to recruiting, training and personnel development had an impact on subjects' decisions about acquiring shares in particular sample companies. We could imagine that such results, particularly if replicated across a number of studies, would potentially act as a stimulus for the accounting profession to put such issues on their agenda for consideration. In the absence of this type of research, the accounting profession might be ignorant of the fact that people would actually use such information if it were provided.

In relation to the *format of presentation* some studies have found that different presentation formats seem to impact on users' decisions. For example, some researchers have investigated how the presentation of particular graphics, such as the inclusion of bar charts, line graphs, pie charts and tables, impact on the decisions of different user groups (Davis, 1989; DeSanctis and Jarvenpaa, 1989). In a famous piece of research, Moriarity (1979) examined whether the accuracy of subjects' (students and accounting practitioners) judgements pertaining to potential bankruptcy of merchandising firms was affected by whether they were given a number of financial ratios, or whether they were provided with a series of schematic faces (referred to as Chernoff faces, see Chernoff and Rizvi, 1975), where the faces themselves were constructed on the basis of the various ratios. Depending on the ratios, different facial features were provided (for example, mouth shape, angle of the eyebrow, nose length, represented changes in ratios). The findings of the research indicated that the students and accountants using the faces outperformed those using ratios in predicting bankruptcy. Further, the subjects using the faces were able to outperform models of bankruptcy that had been developed by other researchers (for example, Altman, 1968). The potential implications of this research are interesting. On the basis of the results, companies perhaps should provide numerous cartoon-like faces in their annual reports if they want to assist people in their decision-making processes (perhaps the accounting profession might release an accounting standard on drawing faces?). However, to date, the disclosure of faces in annual reports is not an approach adopted by corporate management.

Another disclosure issue that has been addressed is whether subjects will make different decisions depending upon whether particular information is incorporated within the financial statements themselves or included in footnotes only. One study that investigated this issue was Wilkins and Zimmer (1983). They studied the decisions of bank lending officers and how their decisions were influenced by whether information about leases was incorporated in the financial statements or simply provided in the footnotes. They

---

[10] In Chapter 7 we discussed research that investigated the incentives for managers to lobby in support of and/or potentially to adopt general price level accounting (which, like current cost accounting, adjusts historical cost accounting information to take account of rising prices). Specifically, we considered Watts and Zimmerman (1978). This research applied economic-based theory to explain lobbying positions of individuals. It did not directly involve any human subjects in the experimentation. Other research has considered how capital markets react to current cost information by investigating share price changes around the time of the information disclosure (for example, Lobo and Song, 1989). What is being emphasized here is that there is a variety of approaches that can be taken to investigate particular phenomena.

found that from the loan officers' perspective the format of disclosure did not impact on their assessment of the entity's ability to repay a debt. Again, such evidence should be of potential interest to the accounting profession when deciding whether to mandate adoption of particular accounting methods within the financial statements or simply within the footnotes to those accounts.[11]

Research has also investigated whether the disclosure of segmental information will impact on the decisions of particular individuals. For example, Stallman (1969) found that providing information about industry segments reduced the subjects' reliance on past share prices when making choices to select particular securities. Doupnik and Rolfe (1989) found that subjects were more confident in making assessments about future prices of an entity's shares when they were also provided with information about geographical performance.

Another issue often addressed in behavioural research is the issue of 'information overload'. It has been found that increasing the amount of information (cues) provided to individuals can improve the quality of decision-making to a point, beyond which the introduction of additional cues can actually lead to a reduction in the quality of the decisions being made (Snowball, 1980).

In Chapter 9 we addressed an area of reporting that is attracting growing attention, this being sustainability (social and environmental) reporting. Because of the growing importance of information about the social and environmental performance of organizations we would anticipate that accounting researchers will explore how various information cues influence environmentally and socially related activities. In this regard we can consider research undertaken by Wood and Ross (2006). They explored how particular 'environmental social controls' can impact managers' capital investment decisions with respect to investing in less-polluting plant and equipment. The environmental social controls that were examined for their impact on capital investment decisions were:

- mandatory disclosure, meaning environmental disclosure required by law and accounting standards;
- regulatory costs, meaning direct payments on pollutant emissions, clean-up costs, and/or regulatory compliance;
- subsidization, meaning depreciation allowances that provide higher tax benefits; and
- stakeholder opinion, meaning how the investment will be approved by various non-government stakeholder groups such as shareholders, creditors, and customers.

In their experiment, which was undertaken with the use of corporate financial managers, the four 'environmental social controls' (namely, mandatory disclosure, regulatory costs, depreciation allowances and stakeholder opinion) were varied to gauge their influence on the managers' capital investment in less polluting plant and machinery. The results of the study indicated that stakeholder opinion was the most influential factor influencing

---

[11] Consistent with a great deal of behavioural research, the results of Wilkins and Zimmer were contradicted by other research. For example, Sami and Schwartz (1992) provided evidence that loan officers' judgements about an entity's ability to repay a debt were influenced by whether information about pension liabilities was included in the financial statements or in the footnotes. However, because this research relates to pension liabilities, it is not clear whether the results contradict a general notion that users can equate information provided by way of footnote disclosure with information provided by financial statement disclosure, or whether the differences in the respective studies' results were due to the fact that one study considered pension liabilities, while the other study considered lease liabilities.

investment decisions, followed by subsidization. Regulatory costs ranked third, while mandatory disclosure was quite lowly rated and was ranked fourth. In discussing the results, Wood and Ross (2006, p. 691) state:

> Stakeholder opinion is a very important social control, with approximately 40 per cent of the combined weight of the environmental social controls. This suggests that managers are much more responsive to stakeholder opinion than they are to regulatory costs, subsidy or mandatory disclosure.

In considering the implications of their study for government action, Wood and Ross (2006, p. 692) state:

> Subsidisation, the 'carrot' among social controls, was found to be an influential factor, with a weighting of 27 per cent. This was second only to stakeholder opinion. The relatively high level responsiveness of managers to change in the level of subsidy suggests that managers would be very responsive to increased subsidisation. This finding adds support to the suggestion in the published literature ... that subsidies can be very effective as an incentive for environmental improvement. The experiment adds support to the conclusion that there is room for increased use of subsidisation. Some (or all) of the cost to government might be offset by increased tax receipts from higher profits made by firms, savings in the cost of 'policing' of small firms, and reduction in environmental damage.

While the above examples of behavioural research only provide a very small snapshot of the total research that is available, it nevertheless provides an insight into how researchers can manipulate various items (or cues) to see how this impacts particular decisions. Such results provide valuable insights for understanding and potentially improving particular decision-making processes.

11.5 Decision-making processes and the use of heuristics

In relation to research that considers the *processes* involved in making a judgement (the middle part of the Lens Model), a number of studies have considered issues associated with how the various cues (information items) are weighted. As an example of such research Schultz and Gustavson (1978) used actuaries as subjects (who were deemed to be experts) to develop a model to measure the litigation risk of accounting firms. They found that cues deemed to be important (relatively more weighted) were the number of accountants employed within the firm, the extent to which the work of the accountants was rotated among themselves, the size and financial condition of the clients and the percentage of 'write-up' work performed.[12]

---

[12] Another approach to gathering such information would simply be to send out questionnaires asking respondents to rank the importance of various items of information in terms of the various decisions they make. Of course, this would be much simpler than a process involving the actual modelling of decision-making which typically occurs in Lens Model-type research.

Another issue that has been considered is *consistency*. For example, do the individuals make the same judgements over time? Ashton (1974) investigated this issue. Ashton used 63 practising auditors in a study that required the auditors to assess the internal control system associated with an organization's payroll. In undertaking the assessment the subjects were required to do the task twice, the second time being between 6 and 13 weeks after the first time. The findings indicated that the subjects were very consistent in their weightings over time and that the weightings between the various subjects were quite consistent. Further, the cue that was weighted the most was 'separation of duties'.

When considering how individuals make decisions, researchers have also found evidence that decision-makers often appear to employ simplifying heuristics when making a decision.[13] Tversky and Kahneman (1974) identified three main heuristics often employed in decision-making: representativeness, anchoring and adjustment, and availability. We can briefly consider them.

According to Maines (1995, p. 83), individuals who use the *representativeness heuristic* assess the likelihood of items belonging to a category by considering how similar the item is to the typical member of this category. For example, the probability that a certain person is an accountant would be assessed by how closely he or she resembles the image of a typical accountant. The fact that there may be few or many accountants is ignored. An implication of this bias is that individuals typically ignore the base rate of the population in question. In some cases this bias has the effect of overstating the number of cases placed within a particular category. For example, in bankruptcy prediction studies, this bias may lead to an overstatement in the prediction of bankrupt firms as the base rate of real bankrupt firms is typically quite low.

The *anchoring and adjustment* heuristic indicates that individuals often make an initial judgement or estimate (perhaps based on past experience or through partial computation of the various factors involved) and then only partially adjust their view as a result of access to additional information. That is, they 'anchor' on a particular view and then will not move sufficiently in the light of additional information or changing circumstances. Joyce and Biddle (1981) undertook research that sought to provide evidence of this heuristic being used by auditors when they assess internal control systems. They found that new information (obtained through various substantive testing) was used by auditors to revise their assessments about the quality of internal controls, and that no evidence could be found of anchoring and adjustment. However, results of anchoring and adjustment were found when Kinney and Ueker (1982) investigated similar tasks. Other research to support the use of this heuristic is provided in Biggs and Wild (1985) and Butler (1986).

The *availability heuristic* relates to whether recollections of related occurrence and events can easily come to mind. That is, the probability judgements regarding the occurrence of an event are influenced by the ease with which the particular type of event can be recalled (Maines, 1995, p. 100). For example, in assessing the likelihood of a plane crash, a subject might overstate the probability as a result of remembering a number of highly publicized crashes. The actual base rates of such an occurrence are ignored. In a

---

[13] A heuristic can be defined as a simplifying 'rule of thumb'. That is, rather than fully considering all the potentially relevant factors, a simplifying rule may be employed which takes a lot less time but nevertheless generates a fairly acceptable (and cost-effective) prediction or solution.

study of this heuristic, Moser (1989) found that when subjects were required to make an assessment about whether the earnings of a company would increase, their assessments were influenced by the order of the information provided to them.

We have briefly considered a number of heuristics, or rules of thumb, that might be employed in decision-making. But, *so what*? Why would it be useful to know about such heuristics? First, if the heuristic results in inappropriate decisions being made (for example, lending funds to organizations that are not creditworthy, or accepting that internal controls are functioning soundly when they are not) then this behavioural tendency should be highlighted so that remedial action (perhaps training) can be undertaken.[14] Second, perhaps the heuristic employed by particular experts are efficient relative to costly data gathering and processing. If this is the case then perhaps novices should be encouraged to adopt the rule of thumb.

Just as decision-making undertaken by individuals within an organization might show particular biases, such as those described above, so might the decision-making of investors. As one particular example, investors might have tendencies to hold loss-making shares for too long when things are not going well, or they may have tendencies to sell 'winning' shares too early and thereby miss out on larger gains. Behavioural research could be used to investigate such investor tendencies (and many others). For example, Krishnan and Booker (2002) investigate the existence of a 'disposition effect' in relation to investor choices.[15] They state (p. 130):

> Prior research in finance and economics has documented the presence of a 'disposition effect,' that is, the tendency for investors to sell winning stock too early and hold losing stocks too long. The disposition effect is an application of prospect theory (Kahneman and Tversky, 1979) to investments and predicts that investors are risk-averse in gains and risk-seeking in losses. Hence, they will sell a winning stock so as to cash in on their sure gains and hold on to a losing stock in order to avoid a sure loss. Empirical support for the disposition effect has been found in financial markets … and experimental markets … We examine if executive subjects commit the disposition error and then examine whether the availability of an analyst summary recommendation report reduces the occurrence of the disposition error. We also examine if the reduction in the disposition error is a function of the strength of supporting arguments in the analysts' summary recommendation report.

For the purposes of their research an 'analysts' summary recommendation' is a report that contains the average recommendation of several analysts to either buy (if the future prospects seem favourable), hold (if the future prospects seem marginally favourable), or sell (if the future prospects seem unfavourable), and some supporting arguments. The

---

[14] For example, Kida (1984) provides evidence that auditors when undertaking particular tasks often initially formulate a hypothesis to explain a certain event (for example, the reduction in bad debt write-offs) and then seek information to confirm this hypothesis (hypothesis-confirming strategies). Clearly, such information gathering is not objective and could expose the auditors to certain risks. Knowledge of this behavioural tendency would therefore be useful.

[15] In their study they actually used MBA students as surrogates for investors. They justified using MBA students as the subjects of their experiment because the MBA students were deemed likely to have had prior investing experience and would have read analyst reports.

investor evaluates the report and decides to buy, hold, or sell the stock. The researchers vary the strength of the recommendations given to different subjects and the researchers predict that the strength of the supporting arguments provided with the analysts' report will mitigate the disposition effect by motivating investors to act in a manner consistent with the analysts' recommendations (i.e., to sell losing stocks and hold winning stocks). In explaining how they conducted their behavioural experiment, Krishnan and Booker (2002, p. 136) state:

> In the first experiment, we examine subjects' likelihood to sell or hold a stock on which they have a paper gain or loss position, when presented with a simple favorable or unfavorable future scenario in the absence of analysts' recommendations. This experiment provides a benchmark to measure the extent of the disposition error. In the second experiment, we present information about a stock with expected values identical to the stock in Experiment 1, in the form of a summary analyst recommendation report. One-half of the subjects in Experiment 2 receive a 'weak' form of analysts' recommendations, i.e., with no supporting information, while the second half of the subjects receive a 'strong' form of analysts' recommendations, i.e., with supporting information.[16] The second experiment allows us to examine whether the presence of an analysts' summary recommendation report has any influence on subjects' decisions. It also allows us to examine whether the strength of the analysts' summary recommendation report has any effect on subjects' decisions.

In relation to the results of their study, Krishnan and Booker (2002, p. 131) state:

> Our results indicate that information presented in the form of a summary report of analysts' recommendations reduces the disposition error for winning stocks. That is, when subjects receive information about the future prospects of a stock, and the information is not presented in the form of a summary analyst recommendation report, subjects commit the disposition error and sell winning stocks too early and hold losers too long. However, when information about a stock with identical expected values is presented in the form of a summary analyst report, the disposition error is reduced for the winning stocks but not for losing stocks. Our findings also suggest that the strength of information disclosed in analysts' recommendations affects the tendency for subjects to sell winners too soon and hold losers too long. A strong form of the summary analyst report (i.e., with supporting information used by the analysts to arrive at the stock judgment) further reduced the disposition error for winning stocks. For losing stocks, a weak-summary recommendation report did not reduce the dispositional tendency to hold. However, a strong summary recommendation report significantly reduced the tendency to hold. It appears that individuals have a much greater desire to avoid losses and that this 'loss aversion' is adequately mitigated only by a strong analyst summary recommendation report. Our study demonstrates that summary analysts' reports are not only

---

[16] Strength of the recommendation was manipulated via an additional paragraph that either provided supporting information for the recommendation (strong) or provided no details for the recommendation (weak).

valuable for their information content, but also as instruments that reduce judgment errors and that this error-reduction property is enhanced by greater detail and strength of arguments in the summary analysts' report.

In reflecting upon the implications of their study, Krishnan and Booker (2002, p. 150) state:

> This study contributes to the literature on investors' use of analyst recommendations in several ways. First, it shows that subjects' acting in the absence of summary analyst recommendations expressed likelihood to sell winning stocks too early and hold losing stock for too long. These 'noise traders' with common judgmental biases can affect stock prices … Second, it finds that the mere presence of summary analyst recommendations reduces the level of the disposition error for winning stocks. Thus, even the use of a weak analyst recommendation may reduce the irrational behavior of selling winning stocks too early. Third, we show that subjects pay attention to and appeared persuaded by supporting arguments to the analyst recommendation. Thus, the availability of strong analyst recommendations with supplementary information reduces the likelihood to sell winning stock too early and hold losers too long. The implications of our findings may extend beyond the current setting to error reduction properties of accounting disclosures in general.

Accounting Headline 11.1 provides a newspaper article that discusses some of the ways people act in relation to buying and selling securities. The information in the newspaper article discusses investment strategies informed by the findings of behavioural research. The article also refers to heuristics such as 'anchoring' and how this can distort our decision-making processes.

Accounting Headline 11.1

Newspaper coverage of behavioural research

Sell! Sell! Sell!

By Mark Jones

That's the roar from the ranks of panicking financial market traders, caught up in the madness of the crowd. But they would be better off stepping outside the herd, taking a leaf out of Ronan Keating's songbook, and saying 'nothing at all'.

If personal happiness is all about being in control, then we live in very unhappy times. Anyone whose prosperity and livelihood is locked up in the money markets watches helplessly as those markets plunge and bounce and our nest eggs are flung around in the chaos. Even if our money is not invested in equities, we can't help but feel the market will get us in the end. Budgets will freeze, consumer spending will dry up. At work you suddenly see the HR chief around a lot and the finance director is urgently searching for that book on downsizing he hasn't looked at since the early Nineties.

It's a bad, bad feeling. Remember how we felt when we read about that Devon couple who came back from holiday to find that their lovely house had been trashed by a party of gatecrashing teenagers? We are that couple, and that is what's happening to our money: it has been taken over by teenagers. The market is a creature of hormones and wild mood swings, destructive, euphoric, depressive. One day it's going baseball cap in hand to the central banks and moaning that it's not fair that it has a hangover and broke a bank or two. The next it seems plain evil, spreading false rumours, destroying institutions and people for the hell of it.

As for the banks and the finance ministers, they are like ultra-liberal parents who are suddenly asked to enforce some discipline. There's little they can do but spend lots of money clearing up the mess.

The teenager analogy isn't original. It comes up a lot at times like these. So does the tendency to anthropomorphise and psychoanalyse the market. When profits are strong, house prices buoyant and the FTSE never makes the front page, investing is a stable science. We consult league tables, examine risk indices, trust the computer models. When the bad times come we start seeing the financial world in cartoon terms.

So what can you do to evict the teenagers from your house and wrest control again? Like many people, I'm an averagely stupid investor who is now more than averagely confused and uncertain about what to do. I listened to last week's reports and kicked myself that I didn't see the various rallies coming; then kicked myself I didn't get out when the going was bad.

Of all the reports, one stuck with me. On Radio 4, the BBC's economics editor, Evan Davis, who sounded audibly tired of trying to explain and second-guess what turn the credit crunch would take next, began talking instead about market movements in behavioural terms. His thrust was this. In good times, traders' optimism is easily fuelled: they are listening out for data that will support their decision to pile into those shares or support that flotation or rights issue. Bubbles and booms

are the consequence. When bulls turn to bears, they suddenly see the world in shades of blue and only hear music in the minor key. The people making decisions on investments are tuned in exclusively to the bad news channel. Sentiment and psychology are more important than stats.

… So what do we trust: psychology or economics? In its early days, the latter was a branch of the humanities. Adam Smith's first major work was not *The Wealth of Nations* but *The Theory of Moral Sentiments*. One of the Victorian era's most influential works on economics was written by a Scottish songwriter and poet called Charles Mackay. His *Extraordinary Popular Delusions and the Madness of Crowds* sought to explain the reasons for the South Sea Bubble and Dutch tulip mania; it is still cited by investors today.

Yet in the century that followed, economics became redefined as a science as the statisticians and model-theorists took the high ground: until 2002 when something strange and rather unexpected happened. The Nobel Prize for Economics went to a writer who had never studied the subject. Daniel Kahneman was a research psychologist and his studies showed (this is a crude summary) how humans make errors when they think they are being at their most analytical and objective.

Here's a typical Kahneman experiment. He asked an audience to give him the last four digits of their social security numbers, then estimate the number of physicians in New York. The two sets of numbers had nothing to do with each other, of course; yet the correlation between the answers people gave was well beyond what might be expected by chance. The process is known as anchoring. We are highly influenced by the numbers and facts we're given, even if they are guesswork or wildly inaccurate. So we could all have a bet on the number of runs England are going to score in the second innings of the current test match. I'll go first and say 420. You might think that number is ridiculously high based on what you know about the England team and the record of teams batting last. Yet the chances are you will err on the high side when you make your own estimates; I've influenced you.

… So back to the matter of feeling in control. Here's how some investors do it. They are called contrarians; they exploit the foibles and group-think of the supposedly objective analysts, economists and company managers. Their unofficial leader is David Dreman, investment house owner and a columnist in *Forbes* magazine. The contrarians trace their lineage back to Mackay and are often known for their pessimism – they are 'perma-bears', sellers rather than buyers. But they are just as likely to be very busy snapping up stocks in times like these. They seek out otherwise sound companies who are just in the wrong sector at the wrong time; or less sound companies whose prospects are not quite as bleak as the herd thinks. One Wall Street group which specialises in the field calls itself 'the Dogs of the Dow'. A leading British exponent of the behavioural finance school puts it like this: 'I buy other people's anxiety'.

So you should buy, not sell. Fine if you're Warren Buffett (who many think of as the most successful contrarian of the lot); or if, as a City friend puts it, 'you've got balls of steel'. But we are not all the richest man in the world and our cojones are made of flesh and blood. If the market keeps on falling, banks keep imploding, you can't help but think the rational thing to do is bail out. After all, people who bought stocks before the Wall Street Crash would have waited until the 1950s for their investments to return to par.

The behavioural finance experts have one last piece of advice. Take it easy this weekend. Enjoy the spring. Forget about the stock market. Don't listen to your broker, listen to Ronan Keating. Ronan may not have been thinking about long-term investment stratagems when he crooned, 'You say it best when you say nothing at all'; but the advice could be very useful all the same.

Jonathan Harbottle, marketing director of Liontrust, a fund management company specialising in behavioural finance, puts it like this: 'Market timing is a mug's game. Two-thirds of people who think they can spot the bottom of the market get it wrong. Long term, investing in equities is proven to be the route to real wealth.'

Harbottle makes a further argument for inactivity, also beloved by the Dogs of the Dow and their friends, which goes like this. While you're waiting for your rubbish shares to recover, they are paying you for the privilege. Dividends are calculated on the share prices; the share price is low – you get a better dividend. So sit tight.

That may just be the hardest thing of all. James Montier of Société Générale, who has been described as 'one of the truly great minds on the psychology of investing', uses the example of a goalkeeper facing a penalty. The ball goes down the middle 28.7 per cent of the time (apparently). But goalies always dive left or right. Montier believes it's because we feel better – more in control – if we're seen to be doing something. You could take the analogy further. Investment experts, like goalkeepers, trust in their ability to read what's going to happen – which way the market/ball is going to go. But they don't know; the stats don't change.

So as an averagely stupid investor, I'm plumping for inactivity. After all, isn't that the best way to treat teenagers? Ignore them. They're only after your attention.

Source: *The Independent*, 23 March 2008
©The Independent Newspaper

11.6 Issues of decision accuracy

When looking at the actual *output* of the decision-making process (the decision or judgement) some research has considered how *accurate* the predictions are relative to the actual environmental outcomes. For example, Libby (1975) investigated the accuracy with which loan officers predict business failure. The results showed that loan officers were able to predict bankruptcies fairly regularly, with their various answers also being relatively consistent.

In a similar study, Zimmer (1980) investigated how accurate bankers and accounting students were in predicting bankruptcy when provided with a number of accounting-related cues. The results showed that bankruptcies were typically correctly predicted. Also, a composite model of bankruptcy prediction generated from pooling all the bankers' responses typically outperformed the judgements of individuals.[17] A particularly interesting finding was that the students with limited experience performed nearly as well as the bankers.

Research has also considered the potential improvements to decision-making that might result from combining the decisions of multiple decision-makers. As noted above, Zimmer (1980) found that the composite model developed by combining the judgements of the different subjects was able to outperform judgements and models derived from individual subjects. Such findings are also presented in Libby (1976). Further, evidence indicates that decision-makers working together in an interactive team can also outperform individuals working alone. Chalos (1985) found this result when reviewing the bankruptcy predictions of interacting loan officers relative to predictions provided by loan officers working independently. Such results were subsequently explained by Chalos and Pickard (1985) as being due to the greater consistency in decision-making that happens when groups, as opposed to individuals, are involved in making decisions. Again, these findings have implications for how organizations might make decisions in practice. Perhaps when major loans are being made, and assuming that these results are perceived as being reliable, banks should consider requiring approvals to be based on committee decisions.

11.7 Protocol analysis

Another approach to researching the decision-making processes at the individual level that we can also briefly consider now is research undertaken using *verbal protocol analysis*. This form of analysis usually requires subjects to think aloud (that is, to verbalize their thought processes) while they are making decisions or judgements. The subjects' comments are taped and then transcribed for further coding and analysis.[18] This form of research has tended to be more popular in auditing than in other financial accounting areas. One of the

---

[17] As the composite model out-predicted the individuals, there could be a case to make the model available to the lending officers, particularly the inexperienced bankers. The model could provide a low-cost approach to screening loan applications at the initial stages of the application.

[18] This form of data collection can sometimes lead to many hundreds of pages of typed quotes which can tend to become quite unmanageable. There are a number of computer packages available to organize transcribed data into a more manageable form. One such package is NVivo, which is not an acronym, but is based around the word 'in vivo' which means it is done in real life.

first studies using this method was Biggs and Mock (1983) who reviewed judgements being made by auditors when assessing internal controls. Other auditing-based studies to use verbal protocol analysis include Biggs *et al.* (1989) and Bedard and Biggs (1991).

According to Trotman (1996) there are a number of advantages and disadvantages in the use of protocol analysis. In relation to some possible advantages he states (p. 56):

> One of the main advantages of verbal protocol analysis is the ability to examine the process by which judgements are made. Understanding how judgements are made is an important start in improving those judgements. Second, verbal protocols are particularly useful in examining information search. The sequence in which information is obtained can be traced and the amount of time a subject devotes to particular cues can be determined. Third, verbal protocol can be useful in theory development. For example, Biggs, Mock and Watkins (1989) suggest the need to 'begin gathering data about how auditors make analytical review judgements in realistic settings and attempt to build a new theory from the results' (p. 16).

In relation to some of the potential disadvantages or limitations that arise from using verbal protocol analysis, Trotman states (p. 56):

> Consistent with all other methods of studying auditor judgements, verbal protocol studies have a number of limitations. First, it has been noted that the process of verbalising can have an effect on the auditors' decision process (Boritz, 1986). Second there is an incompleteness argument (Klersy and Mock, 1989) which suggests that a considerable portion of the information utilised by the subjects may not be verbalised. Third, some have described the process as epiphenomenal, that is, subjects provide verbalisations which parallel but are independent of the actual thought process. Fourth, there has been some criticism of the coding methods. For example, Libby (1981) notes that the choice of coding categories, the choice of phrases that serve as the unit of analysis, and the assignment of each phrase to categories are highly subjective. Libby suggests the need for comparisons using competing coding schemes. Finally, there are significant difficulties in communicating the results to the reader, given the large quantity of data and possibly large individual variations in decision processes.

Trotman has provided a number of limitations in relation to protocol analysis which, as he indicates, can also be applied to behavioural research in general. In concluding our discussion on behavioural research, we consider some of these limitations further (following a brief consideration of 'culture').

11.8 The relevance of differences in culture

We considered the issue of 'culture' in Chapter 4 and in that chapter we discussed how culture can influence the accounting information being demanded and produced in different countries. We argued in Chapter 4 that efforts to standardize financial accounting internationally ignores research that suggests that different cultures have different financial information demands and expectations. Some cultures, for example, are considered to be more secretive than others; some cultures seek greater uncertainty avoidance than others; and so forth. These differences at a national level were then related back to the international differences in accounting practices that existed prior to the international adoption of International Financial Reporting Standards issued by the IASB (Gray, 1988). Culture has also been suggested as a factor in influencing organizational structures, legal systems and so forth. Given a view that differences in culture influence the cognitive functioning of individuals (Triandis *et al.*, 1971), it is reasonable to argue that an individual's use of particular cues (information items) will in part be dependent upon the cultural background of the individual. Hence, while we have not previously considered issues of culture in this chapter, it is very reasonable to expect that studies which investigate decision-making processes in particular countries will not be generalizable to other countries – particularly if the respective countries have significantly different cultural attributes. Determining the validity of a particular decision-making model across different cultures would be an important area for future accounting research. At this point in time there is very little behavioural accounting research which explores how the usage of cues in particular decisions is affected by specific cultural attributes.

11.9 Limitations of behavioural research

First, as we have already seen in some of the material presented in this chapter, many of the studies that review similar issues generate conflicting results. This clearly has implications for whether the research can confidently provide guidance in particular areas. Unfortunately, it is often difficult or impossible to determine what causes the inconsistencies in the various results because typically a number of variables differ between the studies (for example, the issue of concern, the realism of the setting, the experience and background of the subjects, the incentives provided and so on). Further, within studies, differences in judgements between the subjects are frequently not explored to any extent, meaning that some unknown but potentially important decision-making factor remains unknown.

Another perceived limitation relates to the settings in which the research is undertaken. These settings are quite often very different from real-world settings, with obvious implications for the generalizability of the findings. In the 'real world' there would typically be real incentives and ongoing implications from making particular decisions – this usually cannot be replicated in a laboratory setting.[19] Further, there will be no real accountability for the decisions being made.

---

[19] Interestingly, at one meeting of professional accountants held in Sydney some time ago (attended by one of the authors of this text) some researchers made use of the assembled attendees to undertake an experiment related to interactive judgements and their impact on bankruptcy prediction tasks. In an attempt to provide an 'incentive' (perhaps in an effort to increase the 'realism' of the task) at the commencement of the task the subjects were told that each member of the 'winning team' was to be provided with a bottle of fine Scotch whisky. Clearly this is an imperfect incentive and might actually introduce other unwanted factors into the analysis. For example, people with a 'drinking problem' might find this a tremendous incentive and really try hard to win. Others might be fairly indifferent, whereas others, perhaps with a religious objection to alcohol, might actually make judgements that guarantee that they and their team mates will not 'win'. What this indicates is that when offering incentives to increase the realism of a task, great care needs to be taken in selecting appropriate incentives.

Related to the above point is the realism of the cues provided to the subjects. It is very difficult to replicate the various cues that would typically be available in the workplace. Also knowing that the results on a particular judgement are being carefully scrutinized could clearly be expected to have an effect on the decision-making processes being employed.

A number of studies also use students as surrogates for auditors, investors, lending officers and so on. This has also been seen as a limitation because such people perhaps have limited training in the area and have not had the same background experiences as the parties for whom they are acting as proxies (there has been some research that shows that students do make judgements comparable to those of particular experts; however, such findings are not universal).

A final criticism that we can raise is the typically small number of subjects used in experiments and, again, whether results based on relatively small samples can be expected to apply to the larger population.

What still appears to be lacking in this area of research is a theory as to why people rely upon particular items of information, adopt simplifying heuristics in some situations, and so on. For example, much of the research tells us that some decision-makers were consistent in their judgements while others were not, or that particular groups seemed to adopt a particular heuristic. But we are still not sure *why* they did this. Perhaps theory will develop in this area. It is perhaps not surprising that behavioural accounting research is not grounded in a particular underlying theory. Unlike capital markets researchers (Chapter 10) and Positive Accounting Theorists (Chapter 7) who have theory that is generated from particular fields of economics, behavioural accounting researchers embrace a variety of theoretical backgrounds from psychology, sociology, and so on.

Chapter summary

In this chapter we considered how individuals use information to make decisions. More specifically we considered how individuals use accounting information to make a variety of judgements. Research pertaining to individual decision-making (behavioural research) has shed a great deal of light on how various groups of individuals such as auditors, lending officers and bankers make decisions. We found that financial statement users often employ simplifying heuristics when making particular judgements. The perspective taken is that if we know how individuals appear to make decisions, we can *anticipate* how they will react to particular accounting disclosures and forms of disclosures. This could be particularly relevant to the accounting profession when contemplating the introduction of a new accounting requirement. Knowledge of how financial statement users make decisions could also provide the basis for making suggestions about how decision-making can be improved (for example, it might be found that a certain category of financial statement users is inappropriately adopting particular heuristics, possibly unknowingly, that could lead to potentially costly implications).

Questions

11.1   Contrast behavioural research with capital market research.

11.2   How and why would the accounting profession use the results of behavioural research in accounting?

11.3   How and why would the management of individual reporting entities be interested in the results of behavioural research in accounting?

11.4   Briefly explain the Brunswik Lens Model and its relevance to explaining the various facets of the decision-making process.

11.5   What is a 'heuristic' and why could it be beneficial for a group of financial statement users to be informed that they are applying a particular heuristic?

11.6   What is the point of modelling the decision-making processes of different financial statement user groups (that is, for example, identifying how they appear to weight particular cues when making judgements)?

11.7   If the results of behavioural research indicate that a particular accounting-related information item (cue) is not used by individuals when making decisions, should this be grounds for the accounting profession to conclude that such information is not material and therefore does not warrant the related development of mandatory disclosure requirements? Explain your answer.

11.8   There have been a number of behavioural studies in financial accounting and auditing that have generated conflicting results. What are some possible reasons for the disparity in results?

11.9   What is 'protocol analysis' and what are some of its strengths and weaknesses?

11.10 What are some general strengths and limitations of behavioural research?

11.11 How 'generalizable' are the results derived from behavioural accounting research?

11.12 During 2006 the International Accounting Standards Board (IASB) in conjunction with the Financial Accounting Standards Board (FASB) were going through a process of revising the conceptual framework (*The Framework for the Preparation and Presentation of Financial Statements*). This process is expected to take a number of years to complete. As part of that work they were addressing 'measurement' issues. Could the IASB and the FASB utilize techniques from behavioural accounting research in revising the conceptual framework and, if so, how?

References

Altman, E.I. (1968) 'Financial ratios, discriminant analysis and the prediction of corporate bankruptcy', *Journal of Finance*, **23** (4), 589–609.

Ashton, A.H. & Ashton, R.H. (eds.) (1995) *Judgement and Decision-making Research in Accounting and Auditing*, Cambridge: Cambridge University Press.

Ashton, R.H. (1974) 'An experimental study of internal control judgements', *Journal of Accounting Research*, **12**, 143–57.

Ashton, R.H. (1982) *Human Information Processing in Accounting*, American Accounting Association Studies in Accounting Research No. 17, Sarasota, FL: American Accounting Association.

Bedard, J.C. & Biggs, S.F. (1991) 'Pattern recognition, hypothesis generation, and auditor performance in an analytical review task', *The Accounting Review*, **66** (3), 622–42.

Biggs, S.F. & Mock, T.J. (1983) 'An investigation of auditor decision processes in the evaluation of internal controls and audit scope decisions', *Journal of Accounting Research*, **21** (1), 234–55.

Biggs, S.F., Mock, T.J. & Watkins, P.R. (1989) 'Analytical review procedures and processes in auditing', *Audit Research Monograph No. 14*, The Canadian Certified Accountants' Research Foundation.

Biggs, S.F. & Wild, J.J. (1985) 'An investigation of auditor judgement in analytical review', *The Accounting Review*, **60** (4), 607–33.

Birnberg, J. & Shields, J. (1989) 'Three decades of behavioural accounting research: A search for order', *Behavioural Research in Accounting*, **1** (1), 23–74.

Boritz, J.E. (1986) 'The effect of research on audit planning and review judgements', *Journal of Accounting Research*, **24** (2), 335–48.

Brunswik, E. (1952) *The Conceptual Framework of Psychology*, Chicago: University of Chicago Press.

Butler, S. (1986) 'Anchoring in the judgmental evaluation of audit samples', *The Accounting Review*, **61** (1), 101–11.

Chalos, P. (1985) 'Financial distress: A comparative study of individual, model and committee assessments', *Journal of Accounting Research*, **23**, 527–43.

Chalos, P. & Pickard, S. (1985) 'Information choice and cue use: an experiment in group information processing', *Journal of Applied Psychology*, **70**, 634–41.

Chernoff, H. & Rizvi, M. (1975) 'Effect of classification error on random permutations of features in representing multivariate data by faces', *Journal of the American Statistical Association*, **70**, 548–54.

Committee on Accounting Valuation Bases (1972) 'Report of Committee on Accounting Valuation Bases', *The Accounting Review*, **47** (4), 534–73.

Davis, L. (1989) 'Report format and the decision makers task: An experimental investigation', *Accounting, Organizations and Society*, **14**, 495–508.

DeSanctis, G. & Jarvenpaa, S. (1989) 'Graphical presentation of accounting data for financial forecasting: An experimental investigation', *Accounting, Organizations and Society*, **14**, 509–25.

Doupnik, T. & Rolfe, R. (1989) 'The relevance of aggregation of geographic area data in the assessment of foreign investment risk', *Advances in Accounting*, Vol. 7, Greenwich CT: JAI Press, 51–65.

Dyckman, T.R. (1998) 'The ascendancy of the behavioral paradigm in accounting: The last 20 years', *Behavioural Research in Accounting*, **10**, 1–10.

Elias, N. (1972) 'The effects of human asset statements on the investment decision: An experiment', *Journal of Accounting Research*, **10**, 215–33.

Gray, S.J. (1988) 'Towards a theory of cultural influence on the development of accounting systems internationally', *ABACUS*, **24** (1), 1–15.

Heintz, J.A. (1973) 'Price-level restated financial statements and investment decision making'. *The Accounting Review*, **48**, 679–89.

Hendricks, J. (1976) 'The impact of human resource accounting information on stock investment decisions: An empirical study', *The Accounting Review*, **51**, 292–305.

Joyce, E.J. & Biddle, G.C. (1981) 'Anchoring and adjustment in probabilistic inference in auditing', *Journal of Accounting Research*, **19**, 120–45.

Kahneman, D. & Tversky, A. (1979) 'Prospect theory: An analysis of decision under risk', *Econometrica*, **47** (2), 263–92.

Kida, T. (1984) 'The impact of hypothesis testing strategies on auditors use of judgement data', *Journal of Accounting Research*, **22**, 332–40.

Kinney, W.R. & Ueker, W.C. (1982) 'Mitigating the consequences of anchoring in auditor judgements', *The Accounting Review*, **57**, 55–69.

Klersy, G.F. & Mock, T.J. (1989) 'Verbal protocol research in auditing', *Accounting Organizations and Society*, **14** (2), 133–51.

Krishnan, R. & Booker, D. (2002) 'Investors' use of analysts' recommendation', *Behavioural Research in Accounting*, **14**, 130–56.

Libby, R. (1975) 'Accounting ratios and the prediction of failure: Some behavioral evidence', *Journal of Accounting Research*, **13** (1), 150–61.

Libby, R. (1976) 'Man versus model of man: The need for a non-linear model', *Organizational Behavior and Human Performance*, **16**, 13–26.

Libby, R. (1981) *Accounting and Human Information Processing: Theory and Applications*, Englewood Cliffs, NJ: Prentice-Hall.

Lobo, G. & Song, I. (1989) 'The incremental information in SFAS 33 income disclosures over historical cost income and its cash and accrual components', *The Accounting Review*, **64** (2), 329–43.

Maines, L.A. (1995) 'Judgment and decision-making research in financial accounting: A review and analysis', in: Ashton, R.H. & Ashton, A.H. (eds.) *Judgment and Decision-making Research in Accounting and Auditing*. Cambridge: Cambridge University Press.

McIntyre, E. (1973) 'Current cost financial statements and common stock investment decisions', *The Accounting Review*, **48**, 575–85.

Mear, R. & Firth, M. (1987) 'Assessing the accuracy of financial analyst security return predictions', *Accounting, Organizations and Society*, **12**, 331–40.

Moriarity, S. (1979) 'Communicating financial information through multidimensional graphics', *Journal of Accounting Research*, **17**, 205–24.

Moser, D. (1989) 'The effects of output interference, availability, and accounting information on investors predictive judgements', *The Accounting Review*, **64** (3), 433–44.

Pankoff, L. & Virgil, R. (1970) 'Some preliminary findings from a laboratory experiment on the usefulness of financial accounting information to security analysts', *Journal of Accounting Research*, **8**, 1–48.

Sami, H. & Schwartz, B. (1992) 'Alternative pension liability disclosure and the effect on credit evaluation: An experiment', *Behavioral Research in Accounting*, **4**, 49–62.

Schultz, J.J. & Gustavson, S.G. (1978) 'Actuaries perceptions of variables affecting the independent auditors legal liability', *The Accounting Review*, **53**, 626–41.

Snowball, D. (1980) 'Some effects of accounting expertise and information load: An empirical study', *Accounting, Organizations and Society*, **5** (3), 323–38.

Stallman, J. (1969) 'Toward experimental criteria for judging disclosure improvements', *Journal of Accounting Research*, **7**, 29–43.

Triandis, H., Malpass, R. & Davidson, A. (1971) 'Cross-cultural psychology', in: Siegel, B.J. (ed.) *Biennial Review of Anthropology 1971*. Stanford, CA: Stanford University Press.

Trotman, K.T. (1996) 'Research methods for judgement and decision making studies in auditing', *Coopers and Lybrand Research Methodology Monograph No. 3*, Melbourne: Coopers and Lybrand.

Tversky, A. & Kahneman, D. (1974) 'Judgment under uncertainty: Heuristics and biases', *Science*, **185**, 1124–31.

Watts, R.L. & Zimmerman, J.L. (1978) 'Towards a positive theory of the determination of accounting standards', *The Accounting Review*, **53** (1), 112–34.

Wilkins, T. & Zimmer, I. (1983) 'The effect of leasing and different methods of accounting for leases on credit evaluation', *The Accounting Review*, **63**, 747–64.

Wood, D. & Ross, D.G. (2006) 'Environmental social controls and capital investments: Australian evidence', *Accounting & Finance*, **46** (4), 677–95.

Zimmer, I. (1980) 'A lens study of the prediction of corporate failure by bank loan officers', *Journal of Accounting Research*, **18** (2), 629–36.

12

Critical Perspectives of Accounting

Upon completing this chapter readers should:

❖ have gained an insight into particular perspectives that challenge conventional opinions about the role of accounting within society;

❖ understand the basis of arguments that suggest that financial accounting tends to support the positions of individuals who hold power, wealth and social status, while undermining the positions of others;

❖ understand that the disclosure (or non-disclosure) of information can be construed to be an important strategy to promote and legitimize particular social orders, and maintain the power and wealth of elites.

Opening issues

As we saw in Chapter 6, conceptual framework projects promote approaches to financial accounting that are built on qualitative characteristics such as *neutrality* and *representational faithfulness*. How do arguments regarding the unequal distribution of power between different social groups challenge assumptions of the *neutrality* and *objectivity* of financial reports?

12.1 Introduction

In previous chapters we explored numerous issues, including how accounting may be used to assist in decision-making (Chapters 5 and 6); reduce agency and political costs (Chapter 7); maintain or assist in bringing legitimacy to an organization (Chapter 8); and satisfy the information demands of particular stakeholders (Chapter 8). We also considered how the practice of accounting could be modified to take into account some social and environmental aspects of an organization's operations (Chapter 9), as well as considering how accounting disclosures might impact on share prices (Chapter 10). In this chapter we provide an overview of an alternative perspective about the role of accounting. This perspective, which is often called the *critical perspective*, explicitly considers how the practice of accounting tends to support particular economic and social structures, and reinforces unequal distributions of power and wealth across society. In doing so, this form of accounting research rejects the view that accounting simply provides an objective and unbiased account of particular transaction and events.

The view promoted by researchers operating from a *critical perspective* is that accounting, far from being a practice that provides a *neutral* or *unbiased* representation of underlying economic facts, actually provides the means of maintaining the powerful positions of some sectors of the community (those currently in *power*, and with *wealth*) while holding back the position and interests of those without wealth. These theorists challenge any perspectives which suggest that various *rights* and *privileges* are spread throughout society[1] – instead they argue that most rights, opportunities and associated power reside in a small (but perhaps well-defined) group, often referred to as an 'elite'.

This chapter considers various (critical) arguments about the role of the state (government), the role of accounting research and the role of accounting practice in sustaining particular social orders that are already in place – social orders that some researchers argue function on the basis of inequities, where some individuals (with capital or wealth) prosper at the expense of those without capital and where accounting is therefore regarded as one of the tools used by those with (more) capital to help subjugate (undermine) those without (or with considerably less) capital. We will see that researchers adopting a critical perspective often do not provide direct solutions to particular inequities, but rather seek to highlight the inequities which they perceive to exist in society, and the

---

[1] The assumption that there is a spread of rights and privileges across different groups within society is commonly referred to as pluralism.

role which they argue accounting plays in sustaining and legitimizing those perceived inequities. Because the theoretical perspectives investigated in this chapter make calls for changes that will have broad impacts across society, the perspectives are quite different to the other theories addressed in other chapters of this book.

12.2 The critical perspective defined

Under the heading (or umbrella) of *critical accounting theory*, there are several different specific perspectives on critical accounting. Therefore, a single critical perspective is not easy to define. In broad terms, critical accounting theory is used to refer to an approach to accounting research that goes beyond questioning whether particular methods of accounting should be employed, and instead, critical theorists tend to focus on the role of accounting in sustaining the privileged positions of those in control of particular resources (capital) while undermining or restraining the voice of those without capital. According to Roslender (2006, p. 250):

> Critical Theory is intimately wedded to change. More specifically it is con-cerned with the promotion of a better society, one in which the prevailing social arrangements serve the interests of the mass of people, whose 'potenti-alities' are perceived to be constrained by those arrangements already in place … Critical Theory seeks to provide a form of knowledge that is questioning of the prevailing social arrangements, i.e. an alternative knowledge. More than this, however, the resulting knowledge will serve as an input into a process of reflection by society's members on the nature of their involvement within the prevailing social arrangements and how this might be changed, for their ben-efit. Critical Theory is not concerned with the provision of insights for their own sake but for the purpose of informing the transformation of 'what is' into what those who experience it wish it to be, through a process of interaction and reflection. Or put another way, Critical Theory aims to promote self-awareness of both 'what is' and 'what might be', and how the former might be transformed to install the latter.

Roslender (2006, p. 264) further states that from a critical perspective:

> Simply interpreting or understanding what we chose to study is not enough. The purpose of the exercise is to turn this learning to the advantage of society, i.e. the promotion of a better society. The presupposition is that there are many things about the existing social arrangements that merit changing. 'Traditional' theory does not subscribe to this axiom. It is this quality that distinguishes 'criti-cal' theory from traditional theory. This is not to imply that all of those scholars who elect to embrace other ways of seeing are committed to the reproduction of the existing social arrangements, rather that they do not avail themselves of a way of seeing, Critical Theory, that explicitly links understanding and change to the enactment of the philosophy of praxis (a philosophy in which 'theory' informs 'practice' and vice versa). Viewed in a slightly different way, Critical Theory makes no pretence of being objective. Those who embrace a Critical Theory perspective do so because they recognise and value its partiality.

Tinker (2005, p. 101) has also offered a definition of critical accounting research which is useful. He sees critical accounting as encompassing:

> all forms of social praxis that are evaluative, and aim to engender progressive change within the conceptual, institutional, practical, and political territories of accounting.

A key element of this definition is the notion of 'social praxis', as distinct from the investigation (for example, in other branches of accounting theory and research) of social (accounting) practice.[2] *Praxis* within critical accounting research envisages a broad understanding of both 'theory' and 'practice' and is generally understood to refer to the assumption that there is a two-way (and possibly circular) relationship between theories and practices, whereby theory influences social practices (that is, the theoretical views and assumptions we have about practice actually impacts practice) while social practices also influence theory. That is, theory informs (or provides a foundation for) existing practice and also existing practice informs theory.[3] One implication of this relationship between theory and practice is that when social conditions (and practices) change, theories based on these conditions need also to change. This should not be a new concept to you, as in many parts of this book we have discussed accounting theories which evolved to suit (or reflect) business practices.

The other key implication of the two-way relationship between theory and practice embodied in the term *praxis*, and possibly the more important implication from the perspective of critical accounting, is that development of different theoretical perspectives can bring about (needed) changes in social practices and structures (such as the distribution of wealth and power). For example, if we develop theories that question the wealth distribution impacts of unregulated markets, or question the operations of capital markets in terms of providing sustainable outcomes, and if our arguments gain acceptance with various parties within society, then this might have implications for how such markets are regulated. Our theories will impact practice. Similarly, if we have well-developed theories which question the objectivity of financial accounting, and if we are able to generate sufficient support for the theory then ultimately this could create the necessary impetus for changes in the way financial accounting is practised. For example, perhaps the compelling nature of our newly developed theories might act to reduce society's focus on corporate financial performance (which critical theorists believe particularly promotes the interests of investors and senior managers), and instead our new theory might encourage a new business philosophy in which measures of corporate performance reflect efforts made

---

[2] The *Oxford English Dictionary* (2nd edn, 1989) contains several definitions of the word 'praxis', including 'The practice or exercise of a technical subject or art, as distinct from the theory of it' and 'Habitual action, accepted practice, custom'. However, as will become clear from the discussion in the next few paragraphs, the word 'praxis' in most critical accounting research is used in a very specific manner which accords with the following definition from the *Oxford English Dictionary*: 'A term used ... to denote the willed action by which a theory or philosophy (esp. a Marxist one) becomes a social actuality'.

[3] For example, if we believe in, and promote, a theory of economics that says that markets operate most efficiently when left unregulated then this will influence market-based practices. Regulators may use the research to further support efforts to reduce market regulation. Conversely, if we observe markets and find that those markets that operate efficiently are unregulated then this will influence the theories we develop. Hence, theories might impact practice, or existing practice might impact theories.

towards benefiting a diverse group of stakeholders and the environment – that is, the theory could ultimately lead to reforms in how business and society operates (which again links to the notion of 'social praxis' in which theory informs practice, and vice versa).

What is different about the relationship between theory and practice as embodied in the term *praxis* (as used in critical accounting research) is the explicit notion of a two-way relationship. Each of the theoretical perspectives we studied earlier in this book tend to rely on a one-way relationship whereby either theory determines practice *or* practice determines theory.

What is also different is the focal point of changes in practice implied in the term *praxis*. While the normative theories we examined earlier in this book sought to develop and then implement specific accounting practices which particular normative researchers argued were (in some way) superior to existing practices, the focus of the changes in practice embodied in the term praxis are usually at the broader level of society rather than specific technical accounting practices within that society. More specifically, a critical accounting understanding and use of the term praxis is usually informed by a Marxist-inspired approach 'whose central concern [is] to study and influence the role of free creative activity in changing and shaping ethical, social, political, and economic life along humanistic socialist lines' (De George, 1995, p. 713), and this is why we argue that the role of theory in changing social practices is probably more important to many critical accounting scholars than the role of changed social practices in altering theories. Tinker (2005, p. 101) argues that this approach to critical accounting both 'promises a rich synthesis of new forms of praxis', and requires that critical accounting scholars 'who participate [in critical accounting research] must do so from committed, partisan, passionate, and sometimes militant positions'.

Insights into the partisan nature of accounting

While we have argued earlier in this book that all research is likely to be influenced to some extent by the (possibly subconscious) biases of the researchers involved, this explicit promotion of partisan research in critical accounting studies might upset and worry researchers who adopt other approaches.[4] However, it could be considered simply more honest in that it is making explicit that all research in social sciences relies on the subjective (and therefore biased) interpretations of the researchers involved. Within critical accounting research, these explicit biases usually range from moderate socialism to more extreme anti-capitalist positions, which could be regarded as threatening by those accounting researchers (and students and practitioners) who have prospered under the capitalist system. We return to this point later in the chapter.

Researchers within the critical accounting area, who we call *critical accounting theorists*, therefore seek to highlight, through critical analysis, the key role of accounting in society. The perspective they provide challenges the view that accounting can be construed as being objective or neutral, and these researchers often seek to provide evidence to support

---

[4] According to the *Oxford English Dictionary*, a partisan approach is one taken 'by an adherent or supporter of a person, party, or cause'. Therefore, if a critical theorist had a particular view (or theory) about how society should function to achieve certain ends or causes then, in accord with a partisan approach, this will impact the practices they support or oppose.

this view. Accounting is seen as a means of constructing or legitimizing particular social structures. As Hopper *et al.* (1995, p. 528) state:

> in communicating reality accountants simultaneously construct it (Hines, 1988) and accounting is a social practice within political struggles and not merely a market practice guided by equilibrium in an efficient market.

This view is supported by Baker and Bettner (1997, p. 305). They state:

> Critical researchers have convincingly and repeatedly argued that accounting does not produce an objective representation of economic 'reality', but rather provides a highly contested and partisan representation of the economic and social world. As such, the underlying substance of accounting cannot be obtained through an ever more sophisticated elaboration of quantitative methods. Accounting's essence can be best captured through an understanding of its impacts on individuals, organizations and societies. Hence it is important for accounting research to adopt a critical perspective.

As noted at the beginning of this section, the term 'critical accounting' is a very broad term that captures a variety of different perspectives about accounting. However, what these perspectives have in common is that they seek to highlight, oppose and change the perceived role of accounting in supporting the privileged positions of some people in society. As Hopper *et al.* (1995, p. 535) state:

> Critical theory is an umbrella term for a wide variety of theoretical approaches perhaps more united in what they oppose than what they agree upon.

Consistent with the above perspective of critical theory, Reiter (1995, p. 53) states:

> In the critical world, there is no single established theory or approach, and little consensus on how to proceed, aside from an absolute horror of modernity and neo-classical economics.

A Marxist critique of accounting

One of the main branches, and probably the founding branch, of critical accounting theory is (as indicated above in discussing the term 'social praxis') grounded in a Marxist-informed critique of capitalism. Within this Marxist critique, owners of capital are regarded as having (unfairly) accumulated their wealth by the historical exploitation and expropriation (over several centuries) of the value created by workers (or labour); workers are seen as feeling alienated both from society and from the products they produce, as their lives are largely controlled by external and impersonal markets rather than by their own free choices;[5] and capitalism is also regarded as fundamentally structurally flawed. To give an example of one such fundamental structural flaw, a key Marxist argument is that one effective way for individual businesses to increase profits (or economic returns to capital) over a long period

---

[5] In this Marxist perspective on workers' feelings of alienation, 'the market-place … purports to be a sphere of individual freedom, but is in fact a sphere of collective slavery to inhuman and destructive forces' (Wood, 1995, p. 525).

of history has been to increase the level of mechanization in a factory or office process, and thereby replace the productive capacity of some workers (labour) – who have to be paid and cannot work 24 hours per day – with the productive capacity of additional machinery (capital – which ultimately has been paid for by accumulating the value created by labour and expropriated over the years by capital). The costs of usage of this machinery (such as depreciation, repairs and the opportunity cost of capital invested in the machinery) were historically often considerably lower than the cost of the labour displaced by the machinery, and the machinery could also be 'worked' for long periods with minimal stoppage (rest) periods. While such mechanization might have been in the economic interests of the owners of one business, Marxists argued that there was a fundamental contradiction in the drive of all owners of all businesses to increase the returns to capital through ever greater mechanization. This fundamental flaw in the structure of the capitalist system is that for capital to earn returns, not only do costs need to be minimized but also revenues need to be maximized. While the actions of one or two factory owners in replacing some labour with capital might not affect the market for their goods, and therefore makes economic sense for these business owners individually, Marxists historically argued that if all business owners acted in this way then, as the total amount paid to labour overall would decline, total buying capacity in the consumer markets overall would decline. At some point, the reduction in resources available to consumers to purchase the end-products of the production process would, it was argued, be greater than the increase in productive capacity from mechanization and would therefore lead to a reduction (or collapse) in demand, and thereby threaten the overall prosperity of capital.

Marxist theorists argue that as the capitalist system operates in a manner which alienates workers (and the working class), and is riddled with inherent structural contradictions (such as the one discussed in the last paragraph), it is fundamentally unstable. This inherent instability will, it is argued, manifest itself in different symptoms in different eras, such as unemployment, inflation, economic depression. While action might be taken by governments and businesses to address the negative symptoms (or outcomes) of the instability of capitalism that manifest themselves in a particular era, Marxists regard this as treating a symptom (such as policies against unemployment in one era, anti-inflation policies in another era) rather than addressing the common cause of all these symptoms – the structural instability of the capitalist system itself. Furthermore, 'successfully' treating the current negative symptom of the inherent instability of capitalism will not, it is argued, prevent the inevitability of new symptoms (whose precise nature is unforeseen and largely unforeseeable) arising in future periods – perhaps the sub-prime banking crisis and ensuing global financial crisis could be regarded as simply the latest of these symptoms. Policies to address these symptoms are therefore regarded as acting at a relatively superficial level and, rather like pharmaceutical products that treat the symptoms rather than the underlying causes of a disease, will do little in the long term to cure what Marxists regard as the deeper malaise of capitalism.

Many of these symptoms, and/or the social unrest caused by these symptoms, are regarded by Marxist scholars as threatening to undermine the power and wealth of capital (to quote Marx: 'capitalism produces its own gravediggers' – Marx and Engels, 1967, p. 94, as cited in Tinker, 2005, p. 122). Therefore, the privileges, power and wealth of capital are regarded by Marxists as being unstable, and owners of capital will take action to defend their privileges, power and wealth.

Critical accounting theorists regard accounting as a powerful tool in both enhancing the power and wealth of capital, and in helping to protect this power and wealth from threats arising from the structural instability of capitalism. As, following Tinker's (2005) arguments outlined earlier in this chapter, many critical accounting researchers tend to be opponents of many aspects of the capitalist system and of accounting, they seek to expose the role of accounting in supporting unequal distributions of power and wealth across society, and some seek to subvert this role of accounting. This aim also tends to be shared by several of the critical accounting researchers who do not adopt a pure Marxist perspective.

As Gray *et al.* (1996, p. 63) state, a major concern of the critical (or 'radical' theorists) is that:

> the very way in which society is ordered, the distribution of wealth, the power of corporations, the language of economics and business and so on, are so fundamentally flawed that nothing less than radical structural change has any hope of emancipating human and non-human life. The social, economic and political systems are seen as being fundamentally inimical.

Given that the practice of accounting is in the hands of reporting entities, such as large corporations, and accounting regulation is in the hands of government and associated regulatory bodies (which are viewed as being linked to, or under substantial influence from, large corporations and therefore as having a vested interest in maintaining the *status quo*), accounting information will, it is argued, never act to do anything but support our current social system, complete with all its perceived problems and inequities. Moore (1991) also suggests that the low level of consideration, or use of, critical accounting theory by US accounting academics could be due to the universities' reliance on business funding – funding which does not tend to support research of a 'critical' nature.

12.3 Critical accounting research versus social and environmental accounting research

One of the key areas in which our current social system is perceived by large numbers of people (and not just Marxist scholars) to produce many problems and inequities is in the area of the social and environmental impact of business. We discussed many issues in this area, and their relationship to accounting theory and practice, in Chapters 8 and 9. In this section of this chapter on critical accounting theory, we consider how critical accounting research differs from and/or complements social and environmental accounting research, as it might be considered that both are seeking substantial changes in social practices.

The critical perspective adopted by many critical accounting researchers is grounded in political economy theory, which we also considered in Chapter 8. More specifically, critical accounting research tends to be grounded in 'classical' political economy theory. As Chapter 8 indicates, the 'political economy' has been defined by Gray *et al.* (1996, p. 47) as the 'social, political and economic framework within which human life takes place'. The view is that *society*, *politics* and *economics* are inseparable, and economic issues cannot meaningfully be investigated in the absence of considerations about the political, social and institutional framework in which economic activity takes place. Relating these arguments specifically to accounting, Guthrie and Parker (1990, p. 166) state:

> The political economy perspective perceives accounting reports as social, political, and economic documents. They serve as a tool for constructing, sustaining and legitimising economic and political arrangements, institutions and ideological themes which contribute to the organisation's private interests.

As Chapter 8 also indicates, political economy theory has been divided into two broad streams that Gray, *et al.* (1996, p. 47) and others have classified as 'classical' and 'bourgeois' political economy. The 'bourgeois' political economy perspective does not explore structural inequities, sectional interests, class struggles and the like.[6] It accepts the way society is currently structured as 'a given'. Many critical theorists consider that research which simply accepts the existing nature and structure of society without challenge effectively supports that (undesirable) society (Hopper and Powell, 1985). By accepting a pluralist conception of society it thereby tends to ignore struggles and inequities within society (Puxty, 1991). Critical accounting researchers have therefore often considered it necessary to challenge the works of researchers who they regard as researching within the bourgeois stream of political economy, including those who have for many years been promoting the need for organizations to be more accountable for their social and environmental performance (that is, to provide more information in relation to whether the corporations are meeting community expectations in their social and environmental performance). As Gray *et al.* (1996, p. 63) state, critical theorists believe that:

> Corporate social reporting (CSR) will be controlled by the reporting corporations and a State which has a vested interest in keeping things more or less as they are, CSR has little radical content. Furthermore, CSR may do more harm than good because it gives the impression of concern and change but, in fact, will do no more than allow the system to 'capture' the radical elements of, for example, socialism, environmentalism or feminism and thus emasculate them.

Critical theorists argue that any such emasculation (undermining or weakening) of these movements, which seek to protect and advance the interests of groups or entities often regarded as negatively affected by capitalism, will have the effect of protecting the capitalist system from the 'threats' these movements pose to the power and wealth of capital.[7]

Thus, while to many of us calls for greater disclosure of social responsibility information would seem to be a move in the right direction, some critical theorists argue that such efforts are wasted unless they are accompanied by fundamental changes in how society is structured. They would tend to argue that the disclosure of corporate social responsibility information only acts to legitimize, and not challenge, those providing the information. Cooper and Sherer (1984), for example, argue that attempts to resolve technical issues (such as how to account for environmental externalities) without consideration of inequities in

---

[6] Legitimacy theory and stakeholder theory, which were both examined in Chapter 8, are embedded within a 'bourgeois' political economy perspective.

[7] Included in the *Oxford English Dictionary*'s (2nd edn, 1989) definition of *emasculation* is: 'The depriving of force, vigour ...; making weak'.

the existing social and political environment may result in an imperfect and incomplete resolution, owing to the acceptance of current institutions and practices – which are seen to be part of the problem itself.

Reflecting on some of the views of critical theorists about the deficiencies of social and environmental accounting research, Owen *et al.* (1997, p. 181) note:

> Early radical critique of the social accounting movement emanated from a socialist, largely Marxist, perspective. For writers such as Tinker *et al.* (1991) and Puxty (1986, 1991) society is characterised by social conflict. In Tinker et al.'s (1991) analysis, the social accounting movement, particularly as represented in the work of Gray et al. (1987, 1988), fails to examine the basic contradictions and antinomies of the social system under investigation and is therefore, at best, irrelevant, and, at worst, malign, in implicitly adopting a stance of 'political quietism' that simply benefits the already powerful (i.e. the capitalist class). Thus, for example, Puxty writing in 1986 suggested the irrelevance of social accounting, in noting that 'more radical critics of capitalist society have been more concerned with the broader issues of accountancy and accountants within that society than particular (almost parochial) issues such as social accounting which appears to be … rearranging the deck chairs on the Titanic' (p. 107).

> However, by 1991, Puxty had taken his critique a stage further in arguing that by leaving basic social structures intact, social accounting can even lead to legitimation 'since the powerful can point to their existence as evidence of their openness in listening to criticism, it paves the way for … the extension of power' (p. 37).

According to this perspective, as accounting is deemed to sustain particular social structures, the introduction of new forms of accounting (for example, experimental methods relating to accounting for social costs) will only help sustain that social system. Reflecting on the critical theorists' perception of the ongoing research being undertaken to explore how to account for the social and environmental implications of business, Gray *et al.* (1996, p. 63) state that some critical theorists consider that by undertaking such research:

> one is using the very process (current economics and accounting) that caused the problem (environmental crisis) to try to solve the problem. This is known as the process of 'juridification' and it is well established that one is unlikely to solve a problem by applying more of the thing which caused the problem.

Although the above discussion indicates substantial disagreements (or even antagonisms) from some critical accounting researchers towards social and environmental accounting research, in recent years several social and environmental accounting researchers have made attempts to address some of the concerns expressed by these critical accounting researchers. However, there does not seem to have been much of a reciprocal movement by some critical accounting researchers towards recognizing the potential impact that some social and environmental accounting research may have had in reducing a variety of negative social and environmental externalities of some businesses. This lack of movement by some critical accounting researchers is implied, for example, in a statement by Tinker (2005, p. 124, n. 18) that in selecting areas of accounting research for one of his critiques based on a Marxist approach to critical accounting 'Environmental research is another candidate, however as far as "the canon" is concerned I have little to add to the 1991 critique (Tinker *et al.*, 1991)'.

Therefore, while many critical accounting scholars believe that social and environmental accounting scholars are wrong to seek to *alter* existing practices, as this simply perpetuates and perhaps strengthens the existing inequitable social and political system, rather than seeking to overturn it, many social and environmental accounting scholars who recognize the inequities in the existing system take what they regard as a more pragmatic approach. They do not think that the demise of the capitalism system is likely in the short to medium term. Rather, they recognize that seeking to reform some of the 'worst' inequities in capitalism by engaging with, and winning the support of, key players in the business and political worlds is more likely to be successful in reducing some of the most damaging outcomes of business practices in the short and medium term.

Unlike critical accounting scholars who appear to approach social change in dichotomous terms – either the existing system has to be overthrown or else no change is worthwhile – many social and environmental accounting scholars therefore see the possibility for reform in terms of a spectrum ranging from no reform through to the critical scholars' desire for fundamental change (Unerman and Bennett, 2004). Although some social and environmental accounting scholars do not appear to call for much, if any, reform to the existing role of business (these are often referred to as *managerialist* approaches as they often simply seek to develop social and environmental accounting practices that will help managers further the existing aims of their businesses), others draw on many insights provided by critical accounting researchers to help develop practices that reduce, as far as possible, some of the inequities and dysfunctionalities of the existing social, political and capital system. These researchers would argue that it is better to engage with businesses to seek to improve – through development of new accounting practices – their social and environmental performance rather than simply critiquing the capitalist system while putting forward few (if any) practical proposals for how to improve the system. For example, Bailey, Harte and Sugden (2000), Boyce (2000), Lehman (1999, 2001), O'Dwyer (2005) and Unerman and Bennett (2004) are just some of the social and environmental accounting research studies that have touched upon issues and implications of differential power between organizations and different groups of stakeholders in accountability relationships.

At a different (and less explicit) level, in the introductory chapter of a book of social and environmental accounting case studies, aimed primarily at a readership of managers and practitioners, Hopwood, *et al.* (2010, pp. 17–18) included the following argument that is informed by some ideas drawn from critical accounting perspectives:

> without explicit connection within an organization's reporting between finan-
> cial and wider economic, social and environmental impacts, including an indi-
> cation of the materiality of these impacts, it is easy for a company to convey a
> false sense of meaningful action on sustainability. Without this explicit connec-
> tion, its sustainability reporting may focus on incremental changes in socially

or environmentally immaterial impacts … There is a real difference between an organization genuinely striving to become sustainable and a company merely employing the rhetoric of sustainability in its external reports without much substance underlying this rhetoric … The latter type of company is unlikely to have information that would enable it to meaningfully report on its sustainability in a connected manner and may be using its external reporting as a form of greenwash.

Much more clearly drawing on core notions underlying critical accounting theory, the prominent and highly respected social and environmental accounting scholar Rob Gray has in recent years published papers that theorize and/or analyse social and environmental reporting practices, at least in part, from a critical perspective (Tinker and Gray, 2003). For example, he argues that it is inappropriate and inaccurate for business organizations to describe their practices using the terms 'sustainability' or 'sustainable development' as these businesses and their practices are inherently socially and environmentally unsustainable (Gray, 2010). He argues that the terms 'sustainability' and 'sustainable development' have been captured and used by the powerful business sector to make their unsustainable practices appear safe, thereby protecting and enhancing the wealth of the owners of these corporations. Gray (2010, pp. 57–58) states:

> In the line-up of potential villains who might be charged with, if not causing, then significantly contributing to (un)sustainability, we have already seen modernity and to this we need to add modernity's greatest spawn – capitalism. International financial capitalism has been identified as a principal component in (particularly) ecological destruction for much of the modern environmental movement's history, (see, for example, Zimmerman, 1984, p. 153). Kovel (2002) offers a more strident critique of capitalism as the principal source of ecological destruction placing the nature of capitalism as ensuring that social justice and ecological destruction are inevitable. Capitalism and its destructive tendencies are manifest through its greatest creation – the corporation (see, for example, Bakan, 2004) The corporation is placed at the heart of concern for three broad reasons. First, the nature of the publicly held corporation is such that its room for discretion is slight compared to the pressures upon it to deliver short-term financial return at virtually any price. Second, the corporation achieves this return through becoming a waste generating machine that thrives upon the ever expanding but increasingly fatuous consumption of wastefulness. Finally, the lobbying and legitimising powers of the corporation are turned towards civil society and the state to ensure that any tendencies to rein in or hold corporations to account is, at best muted (Bakan, 2004, Beder, 2006).

> Thus we can place the organisation at the heart of our concerns about how sustainability is threatened, represented and manifested. As we see above, the increasingly seductive claims of the corporation to a state of sustainability are the natural deployment of simple discourse mechanisms to permit the organisation to pursue its psychopathic drives within capitalism.

Having briefly explored the relationship between critical accounting research and social and environmental accounting research, we now turn to an examination of the impact of critical accounting research on accounting and business practices and on so-called 'mainstream' accounting research, including a discussion of some possible reasons for the marginalization that many critical accounting scholars believe they experience.

12.4 Possible impact of critical accounting research on social practice

As previously stated, the critical perspective tends to be grounded in a 'classical' political economy perspective, and as such explicitly considers structural conflict, inequity and the role of the state at the heart of the analysis.

By adopting a research (and arguably, ideological) perspective that is grounded in classical political economy theory, critical accounting researchers can highlight particular issues that might not otherwise be addressed. According to Cooper and Sherer (1984, p. 208):

> Social welfare is likely to be improved if accounting practices are recognised as being consistently partial; that the strategic outcomes of accounting practices consistently (if not invariably) favour specific interests in society and disadvantage others. Therefore, we are arguing that there already exists an established, if implicit, conceptual framework for accounting practice. A political economy of accounting emphasises the infrastructure, the fundamental relations between classes in society. It recognises the institutional environment which supports the existing system of corporate reporting and subjects to critical scrutiny those issues (such as assumed importance of shareholders and securities markets) that are frequently taken for granted in current accounting research.

While a substantial amount of critical research is informed by the work of philosophers such as Karl Marx, not all critical accounting research is based on a pure Marxist critique of capitalism. For example, reference is made by Owen *et al.* (1997) to critical researchers who are identified as 'deep ecologists' and 'radical feminists'. The 'deep ecologists' question the trade-off between economic performance and ecological damage – they question the morality of systems that justify the extinction of species on the basis of associated 'economic benefits'. According to Gray *et al.* (1996, p. 61):

> The essence of these views is that the very foundation – even the existence – of our economic (and social) system is an anathema. Put at its simplest, our economic system can, and does, contemplate trade-offs between, for example, the habitat of threatened species and economic imperatives. To a deep ecologist it is inconceivable that a trade-off could have any form of moral justification. Such a view therefore challenges virtually every aspect of taken for granted ways of human existence, especially in the developed Western nations.

The 'radical feminists', on the other hand, believe that accounting maintains and reinforces masculine traits such as the need for success and competition, and that accounting acts to reduce the relevance of issues such as cooperation, respect, compassion and so forth. The masculine versus feminine dichotomy was also discussed in Chapter 4 of this book when we considered various societal values in the context of international accounting, and how a country's ranking in terms of 'masculinity' or 'femininity' in turn influenced the national accounting practices being adopted. According to Hofstede (1984):

> Masculinity stands for a preference in society for achievement, heroism, assertiveness, and material success. Its opposite, Femininity, stands for a preference for relationships, modesty, caring for the weak, and the quality of life.

Researchers working with the feminist literature argue for the need for accounting to be less 'masculine' and more 'feminine' in orientation. According to Reiter (1995, p. 35):

> Feminist theory has many voices, and the considerable volume of feminist criticism published to date represents many different viewpoints. In the late 1980s, accounting scholars began exploring the idea that feminist theory could be used to critique accounting.

In relation to economic theory, upon which much accounting theory is developed, Reiter (1995, p. 40) states:

> Economic theories tend to value the characteristics associated with masculine stereotypes such as abstraction, mind, efficiency, equilibrium, rationality, pursuit of self-interest, and autonomy. The opposite characteristics of concretism, body, randomness, humanity, mutuality and connectedness, which are associated with feminine stereotypes, are missing from economic theory.

In explaining how the incorporation of feminist values in economic theory could potentially lead to a more promising theory, Reiter (1995, p. 47) states:

> Folbre and Hartmann (1988) explain that 'a growing body of interdisciplinary feminist research complements the efforts many economists are making to develop a more complete theory of economic interests, one that can encompass concepts like cooperation, loyalty and reciprocity' (p. 197). Nelson (1992) suggests that incorporation of positive feminine qualities such as flexibility, intuition, humanism and connectedness of individuals and the concept that individual choice is influenced by societal and cultural factors would lead to increased richness and applicability of economic theory. She also argues that the exclusive focus of neo-classical economics on problems of exchange is also a denial of the feminine quality of need ... The view of economic behaviour incorporated in financial economic theories such as agency theory concentrated on conflict and discipline rather than on productive activity and mutuality of interests. A single goal (profit maximisation) benefiting a single group (shareholders) is promoted rather than a multiplicity of goals benefiting all parties. Suppose in contrast that we concerned ourselves with modes of co-operation between shareholders and managers to promote development of quality products and services and the skills to thrive in the complex international markets of the twenty-first century? A different set of concepts and metaphors would be appropriate, and a different view of the roles of capital markets and accounting information would be needed.

In adopting positions, and/or pursuing outcomes, which are at variance with the dominant capitalist ideology (whether motivated by a pure Marxist position or, as is the case with many critical accounting researchers, motivated by other philosophical positions such as the deep ecologists or the radical feminists) critical theorists provide arguments which are often driven by a desire to create a climate for change in social structures. By arguing for a change in the *status quo* it has been argued that 'critical researchers' are often marginalized to a greater extent than researchers adopting other theoretical or ideological perspectives (Baker and Bettner, 1997). Another possible basis of some of this 'marginalization' is that critical theorists often do not provide solutions to what they see as perceived problems (Sikka and Willmott, 2005). That is, they are often 'critical' without providing direct guidance on how the perceived problems can be solved.[8] For example, Owen *et al.* (1997) argue that critical analysis alone is perhaps not enough. As they state (p. 183):

> Restricting one's activities to critique, rather than actively seeking to reform practice, we would suggest, poses a minimal threat to current orthodoxy. Thus Neu and Cooper (1997) are led to observe that: 'while critical accounting scholars have illuminated the partisan functioning of accounting, we have been less successful in transforming accounting (and social) practices' (p. 1).

Further, Sikka and Willmott (2005, p. 142) state that:

> Marxist traditions must continuously be renewed through lived experiences and opposition to institutions of oppression and exploitation in an effort to enable human beings to live less brutalised and destructive lives. But how are the agents of such change to be galvanized? While there is a role for scholarship and related forms of rarefied intellectual engagement with radical ideas, this activity should not displace principled involvement in the mundane world of practical affairs.

As accountants, we are often trained to provide information to solve particular (predominantly economic) problems, hence 'culturally' many of us might be conditioned against criticism that does not provide a *solution*. Reflecting on the 'attitudes and orientations' of accountants, Cooper and Sherer (1984, p. 222) state:

> A critical approach to accounting, however, starts from the premise that problems in accounting are potentially reflections of problems in and of society and accordingly that the latter should be critically analysed. Thus if a major problem in accounting is identified, say as its overwhelming orientation to investors, then a critical perspective would suggest that this problem is a reflection of society's orientation and to change accounting practice requires both social

---

[8] From a research perspective it has also been argued that critical theorists have been marginalized because they do not tend to use mathematical modelling and statistical analysis – both of which have become (to many researchers, as well as to a number of editors of accounting journals) part of accepted accounting research. As Hopper *et al.* (1995, p. 532) state: 'Critical researchers emphasise the social embeddedness of accounting practice, consequently, they tend to neglect mathematical modelling, preferring detailed historical and ethnological studies of structures and processes which help identify societal linkages to show that accounting is not merely a technically rational service activity but plays a vital role in effecting wealth transfers at micro-organisational and macro-societal levels (Chua, 1986).'

awareness (e.g. identification of alternative 'accounts' and the roles of accounting in society) and ultimately social change.

Whether critical theory can in practice be applied to accounting research depends on whether researchers can free themselves from the attitudes and orientations which result from their social and educational training and which are reinforced by the beliefs of the accounting profession and the business community. For this socialisation process has produced accounting researchers who may exhibit subconscious bias in the definition of the problem set of accounting and the choice of theories to analyse and solve these problems. The criterion of critical awareness involves recognising the contested nature of the problem set and theories and demystifying the ideological character of those theories.

Critical theorists are often strong in their condemnation of accountants, and this in itself could also provide a basis for some of the marginalization that many believe they experience. Consider the statement of Tinker *et al.* (1991, p. 37):

The enduring nature of this 'Radical Critique' is attributable to the persistence of the underlying social antagonisms, to which it attempts to speak, and the complicity of accountants, which it seeks to elucidate.

More specifically, Sikka and Willmott (2005, p. 138) explain that some of the critical accounting studies in which they have been involved have:

shown that [some accountancy professional associations] have a long history of opposing reforms which arguably would have advanced the accountability of major corporations (Puxty et al., 1994); that accounting technologies play a major part in the exploitation of workers (Sikka et al., 1999); and that the accountancy industry is engaged in a ruthless exploitation of citizens (Cousins et al., 2000). We have also sought to mobilise opinion by holding a mirror to the accountancy trade associations and argue that their claims of ethics, integrity etc are little more than rhetorical garnishes, and that neither their policies nor their actions come anywhere near their self-representations (Willmott, 1990, Mitchell et al., 1994, Puxty et al., 1994, Cousins et al., 2000).

In considering the above quote from Sikka and Willmott, we are being informed by the critical theorists that we, as accountants, are complicit in relation to 'social antagonisms', 'exploitation of workers' or 'a ruthless exploitation of citizens'. This is not something that is likely to be seen in a favourable light by many accountants and accounting researchers. It is confronting. However, although we might elect not to agree necessarily with what a number of the critical theorists are telling us (perhaps because of some profound ideological differences), it is nevertheless useful, perhaps, to put ourselves under scrutiny from a broader societal perspective. The critical theorists (both Marxists and non-Marxists) encourage such scrutiny.

A critical perspective on Positive Accounting Theory

A review of the academic literature will show that a number of critical theorists have been vocal critics of research that has adopted Positive Accounting Theory as its theoretical basis, as well as being critical of related capital market research (we look more closely at this issue later in this chapter). Positive Accounting Theory focuses on conflicts between what might be construed as 'powerful' groupings within society (for example, owners, managers, debtholders) and does not consider conflicts between these powerful groups and parties that have less ability to impact on the wealth of such powerful parties. Many critical theorists have also been particularly critical of the anti-regulation stance often advocated by Positive Accounting theorists because such a stance further advances the interests of those with power or wealth (for example, owners of corporations, because lack of regulation enables the power and wealth of capital to be exercised largely unhindered by anything other than market forces – which operate to the benefit of many powerful businesses) while undermining the interests of those who might need some form of regulatory protection. Critical theorists would also argue that in assessing the usefulness of accounting information we really need to look beyond capital market (share price) reactions. The capital market response is driven (obviously) by those with capital. Capital market studies ignore 'other voices'.

We now turn from an examination of the role and possible impact of critical accounting theorists to a consideration, informed by critical accounting theory, of perspectives about the role of the state, accounting research and, ultimately, accounting practice in supporting current social structures (and inequalities). Again, as has been emphasized throughout this book, the views that are presented below are those of a subset of the research community. There will, as we would expect, be other 'subsets' of the research community that challenge such views.

12.5 The role of the state in supporting existing social structures

Researchers working within the critical perspective typically see the state (government) as being a vehicle of support for the holders of capital (for example, shareholders), as well as for the capitalist system as a whole. Under this perspective the government will undertake various actions from time to time to enhance the legitimacy of the social system, and thereby protect and advance the power and wealth of those who own capital, even though it might appear (to less critical eyes) that the government was acting in the interests of particular disadvantaged groups. For instance, a government might impose mandatory disclosure requirements for corporations in terms of the disclosure of information about how the corporations attend to the needs of certain minorities or the disabled. Arnold (1990) would argue, however, that such disclosures (which, on average, really do not cause excessive inconvenience for companies) are really implemented to pacify the challenges, for example by and/or on behalf of particular minorities, that may be made against the capitalist system in which corporations are given many rights and powers. Relating this perspective to the development of various Securities Acts throughout the world, Merino and Neimark (1982, p. 49) contend that 'the Securities Acts were designed to maintain the ideological, social, and economic status quo while restoring confidence in the existing system and its institutions'.

It is generally accepted that to make informed decisions an individual or groups of individuals must have access to information. Restricting the flow of information, or the availability of specific types of information, can restrict the ability of other parties to make informed choices. Hence, restricting available information is one strategy that can be employed to assist in the maintenance of particular organizations and social structures. Puxty (1986, p. 87) promotes this view by arguing that:

> financial information is legislated by the governing body of society (the state) which is closely linked to the interests of the dominant power group in society (Miliband, 1969, Offe and Ronge, 1978, Miliband, 1983) and regulated either by agencies of that state or by institutions such as exist within societies like the United Kingdom, United States, and Australia that are linked to the needs of the dominant power group in partnership with the state apparatus (albeit a partnership that is potentially fraught with conflict).

Hence we are left with a view that government does not operate in the public interest, but in the interests of those groups that are already *well off* and *powerful*.[9]

Apart from the state and the accounting profession, researchers and research institutions have also been implicated as assisting in the promotion of particular (inequitable) social structures. We now consider some of the arguments that have been advanced to support this view.

12.6 The role of accounting research in supporting existing social structures

Rather than thinking of accounting researchers as being relatively *inert* with respect to their impact on parties outside their discipline, numerous critical theorists see many accounting researchers as providing research results and perspectives that help to legitimize and maintain particular political ideologies. Again, this is a different perspective from what most of us would be used to.

Accounting research and support for deregulation of accounting

As an example, in the late 1970s and in the 1980s there were moves by particular governments around the world towards deregulation. This was particularly the case in the United States and the United Kingdom. Around this time, researchers working within the Positive Accounting framework, and researchers who embraced the efficient market hypothesis, came to prominence.[10] These researchers typically took an anti-regulation stance, a stance that matched the views of the government of the time. Coincidentally

---

[9] Contrast this with the view provided by public interest theory – a theory of regulation described in Chapter 3 and in which it is argued that government puts in place rules and regulations for the benefit of society generally.

[10] According to Tinker *et al.* (1982), researchers within the Positive Accounting and efficient markets paradigm adopted 'a neoconservative ideological bias that encourages us to take the "free" market and implicit institutional apparatus as given'. We discussed PAT and the efficient markets hypothesis in Chapters 7 and 10 respectively.

[11] Consistent with this perspective, in 1979 Milton Friedman, a leading advocate of deregulation, became a senior adviser to US President Reagan.

perhaps, such research, which supported calls for deregulation, tended to attract considerable government-sourced research funding.[11] As Hopper *et al.* (1995, p. 518) state:

> Academic debates do not exist in a vacuum. It is not enough for a paradigm to be intellectually convincing for its acceptance, it must also be congruent with prevailing powerful beliefs within society more generally. The history of ideas is littered with research that was mocked but which subsequently became the dominant paradigm when other social concerns, ideologies and beliefs became prevalent. The story of PAT can be told in such terms. Its rise was not just due to its addressal of academic threats and concerns at the time of its inception but it was also in tandem with and connected to the right wing political ideologies dominant in the 1980s.

Mouck (1992) also adopts a position that argues that the rise of Positive Accounting Theory was made possible because it was consistent with the political views of those in power (that is, the state). He argues that:

> the credibility of Watts and Zimmerman's rhetoric of revolt against government regulation of corporate accountability was conditioned, to a large extent, by the widespread, ultra-conservative movement toward deregulation that was taking place in society at large ... I would argue that accountants have been willing to accept the PAT story, which is built on Chicago's version of laissez faire economics, because the rhetoric of the story was very much attuned to the Reagan era revolt against government interference in economic affairs.

Consistent with the development of PAT, in the late 1970s a great deal of accounting research sought to highlight the economic consequences of new accounting regulation. This perspective (which we considered in Chapters 2 and 3) argues that the implementation of new accounting regulations can have many unwanted economic implications and, hence, before a new requirement such as an accounting standard is mandated, careful consideration is warranted. Economic consequences analysis often provided a rationale for not implementing accounting regulation. Critical researchers have argued that it was the economic implications for shareholders (for example, through changes in share prices) and managers (for example, through reductions in salary or loss of employment) that were the focus of attention by those who researched the economic consequences of accounting regulation. As Cooper and Sherer (1984, pp. 215, 217) argue:

> It seems unfortunate, however, that the 'rise of economic consequences' (Zeff, 1978) seems to have been motivated, at least in the United States, by a desire of large corporations to counter attempts to change the existing reporting systems and levels of disclosure. To date, it would seem that accounting researchers have generally reiterated the complaints of investors and businessmen about the consequences of changes in required accounting practice. Studies using ECA (economic consequences analysis) have almost invariably evaluated the consequences of accounting reports solely in terms of the behaviors and interest of the shareholder and/or corporate manager class (Selto and Neumann, 1981).
>
> More fundamentally, studies adopting the ECA approach have focused their attention on a very limited subset of the total economy, namely, the impact on the shareholder or manager class. The effects of accounting reports directly

on other users, e.g., governments and unions, and indirectly on 'non-users', e.g. consumers, employees, and taxpayers, have been ignored. The basis of such a decision can, at best, be that any such effects are either secondary and/or lacking in economic significance. Thus, these studies have made an implicit value statement that the needs of the shareholder and manager class are of primary importance and the concentration on those needs is sufficient for an understanding of the role of accounting reports in society. Unless the insignificance of the effects on other users and 'non-users' is demonstrated rather than merely assumed, the conclusion from this research cannot be generalised for the economy as a whole and these studies are insufficient for making accounting prescriptions intended to improve overall social welfare.

Apart from indicating that economic consequences research focused predominantly on the economic implications for managers and shareholders, Cooper and Sherer (1984) also note that major studies that adopted this paradigm were funded by the US Securities Exchange Commission and the US Financial Accounting Standards Board. It was considered that the interests of these bodies were aligned with the 'shareholder and manager class', rather than society as a whole.

In a similar vein, Thompson (1978) and Burchell *et al.* (1980) suggest that the research efforts into inflation accounting in the 1960s and 1970s were not actually motivated by the rate of inflation *per se*. Instead, they argue that the research had been motivated by a desire to alleviate the shifts in real wealth away from owners (in the form of lower real profits and dividends) and towards higher wages.

If research gains prominence because it supports particular political beliefs of those in power, then we might assume that as the views of those in 'power' change, so will the focus of research. During the 1990s many governments around the world tended to move away from deregulation. Reflecting on this, Hopper *et al.* (1995, p. 540) noted:

> The environment is continually being reconstituted within changing economic, political conditions. Accordingly, the ability of PAT to resonate with the prevailing discursive climate may be subject to challenge … Following the removal of the Republican government in the USA, this particular period and form of conservative reform may have ended. In the USA President Clinton is [was] adopting a more interventionist strategy and in the UK, the Major regime claims [claimed] to espouse an alternative 'caring society', albeit with market forces, in contrast to the harsher face of Thatcherism. In the 1990s a new set of values may be emerging which do not emphasise so greatly the efficiency and effectiveness of unregulated markets, for example, ecology, health care in the USA, gender issues. The ability of PAT to resonate with this changed environment may be brought into question, for example, the consecutive failure of some business enterprises and the stock market crash of 1987 augmented the call for more regulation.

A critical accounting interpretation of increased accounting regulation post-Enron

Despite the election of what many consider to be a highly pro-business and anti-regulation Republican president (George W. Bush) and government in the USA at the beginning of the twenty-first century, and the re-election of this president and government at the end of 2004, few governments (including the US government) have reversed this 1990s trend against deregulation of accounting. Although the Bush government initially made moves towards greater deregulation of accounting, this policy direction was reversed following public revelations about the large-scale accounting failures (or abuses) at Enron, WorldCom and several other large US corporations in 2001 and 2002, and the apparent complicity of Enron's auditor (Andersen) in some of these failed and damaging accounting practices. Despite any existing governmental desire there may have been to empower large corporations further by deregulating accounting practices, Unerman and O'Dwyer (2004) argue that these highly publicized accounting failures led to a considerable reduction of trust placed by many investors and workers in both accounting practices and, more importantly, in the reliability of capital markets as a medium for investment. One reaction of many governments throughout the world to these corporate and accounting failures was to increase regulation of accounting and corporate governance, in an attempt to rebuild trust in the reliability of both accounting information and in the capital markets, which are supposedly dependent on the claimed reliability of this accounting information. From a critical perspective, this increase in regulation would be regarded as serving the needs of large corporations (rather than protecting investors) as it was aimed at sustaining investor trust in the capital markets upon which large corporations rely.

The damaging impact of accounting failures at Enron, followed by highly publicized accounting failures over a relatively short period of time at several other large corporations – both in North America and in Europe and elsewhere (for example, Parmalat in Italy, Ahold in the Netherlands, Addeco in Switzerland and Fyffes in Ireland) could be regarded by critical accounting scholars as just another symptom of the inherent instability of the capitalist system (as discussed earlier in this chapter). Failures of banks following the sub-prime banking crisis from 2007 were also partially blamed by some on the outcomes from fair value accounting requirements for some financial instruments, and these failures could also be regarded from a critical perspective as yet another symptom of the instability of the capitalist system. These critical accounting researchers would tend to argue that any actions taken to prevent a reoccurrence of these latest symptoms of the structural conflicts inherent in capitalism (accounting and banking failures) misses the point that it is the capitalist system itself which is flawed, and the only way to prevent other (different) failures emerging in the future is to replace the capitalist system with a different system in which the weak (employees, the environment, many sections of society) are not exploited by the powerful (large corporations and the governments they support). Several researchers have indeed examined the early twenty-first century accounting failures at Enron (and other large corporations), and/or the regulatory reaction to these failures, from a variety of critical perspectives (see, for example, Arnold and de Lange, 2004; Baker, 2003; Briloff, 2004; Craig and Amernic, 2004; Froud *et al.*, 2004; Fuerman, 2004; O'Connell, 2004; Williams, 2004).

A critical accounting view on the active role of academic and non-academic discourse in protecting capitalism

In another area, some critical theorists have implicated the editors of accounting journals in ensuring that accounting research does not challenge the interests of dominant groups in society, arguing that these editors will reject research that does not have 'complementarity with themes prevailing in the social milieu' (Mouck, 1992). In relation to the role of accounting journals, Tinker *et al.* (1991, p. 44) state:

> Accounting literature represents the world in a manner conducive to the changing needs of capital accumulation. Journals such as Accounting Review, adjudicate in secondary conflicts by filtering research, scholarship (and untenured scholars) in a manner conducive to this primary purpose. The hostility of this journal to even the tamest 'deviants' is well known.[12]

Other research in critical accounting demonstrates that it is not just academic discourse which is biased in a manner designed to support the interests of capitalism. For example, Collison (2003) characterizes as propaganda many of the justifications which are given by organizations operating in the corporate sector in support of existing business and accounting practices, where subjective values (biased in the direction of furthering the power and wealth of capital) are portrayed as objective facts. He argues (p. 853) that:

> The effect of this use of propaganda … is to buttress the hegemony of discourse … in which the contestable values that are often implicit in the practices and terminology of accounting and finance are treated as though they are uncontentious … [and that propaganda is] a tool that can be used by powerful interests, often covertly, to support and proselytise a prevailing ideology.

Developing this theme of accounting being used as a tool to 'objectify' subjective views, we now move our analysis to the critical theorists' perceptions of the role of accounting practice in supporting existing social structures.

12.7 The role of accounting practice in supporting existing social structures

As we know, the qualitative attributes of *objectivity*, *neutrality* and *representational faithfulness* are promoted in various conceptual framework projects throughout the world as being 'ideals' to which external financial accounts should aspire. There is a view promoted by the profession that accounting can and should provide an objective representation of the underlying economic facts.[13]

However, a number of critical theorists see a different role for conceptual frameworks: a role that involves legitimizing the accounting profession, as well as the financial reports produced by reporting entities. Hines (1991, p. 328) states:

---

[12] In recent years, however, it does appear that more research of a critical nature is being published within some leading accounting journals. One highly regarded journal that has been in existence for a number of years and which publishes various 'critical' papers is *Critical Perspectives on Accounting*. The journal's aims are 'to provide a forum for a growing number of accounting researchers and practitioners who realize that conventional theory and practice is ill-suited to the challenges of the modern environment, and that accounting practices and corporate behaviour are inextricably connected with many allocative, social and ecological problems of our era. From such concerns, a new literature is emerging that seeks to reformulate corporate, social and political activity, and the theoretical and practical means by which we apprehend and affect that activity.'

[13] This is consistent with the argument provided by Solomons (1978) that to increase the usefulness of accounting reports they should be as objective as cartography. That is, just as an area can be objectively 'mapped', so can the financial position and performance of an organization.

Conceptual Frameworks (CFs) presume, legitimise and reproduce the assumptions of an objective world and as such they play a part in constituting the social world ... CFs provide social legitimacy to the accounting profession. Since the objectivity assumption is the central premise of our society ... a fundamental form of social power accrues to those who are able to trade on the objectivity assumption. Legitimacy is achieved by tapping into this central proposition because accounts generated around this proposition are perceived as 'normal'. It is perhaps not surprising or anomalous then that CF projects continue to be undertaken which rely on information qualities such as 'representational faithfulness', 'neutrality', 'reliability', etc., which presume a concrete, objective world, even though past CFs have not succeeded in generating Accounting Standards which achieve these qualities. The very talk, predicated on the assumption of an objective world to which accountants have privileged access via their 'measurement expertise', serves to construct a perceived legitimacy for the profession's power and autonomy.

The role of accounting statements in creating a selective 'reality'

Hines (1988) argues that accountants impose their own views about which performance characteristics are important and thereby require emphasis (for example, 'profits'). Accountants also decide which attributes of organization performance are not important, and therefore are not worthy of measurement or disclosure. Through the practice of accounting, attention will be directed to the particular measures that the (apparently objective) accountant has emphasized and, in turn, these measures will become a means of differentiating 'good' organizations from 'bad' organizations. For example, if 'profits' are promoted as an objective measure of organizational performance, then people will focus on profits as calculated by the accountant and a profitable company will be deemed to be a 'good' company whereas a loss-making company will be deemed to be a 'bad' company. This is despite the fact that 'profits', as determined by the accountant, will ignore many social and environmental externalities caused by the business – as we discussed in Chapter 9. Further, because the accountant ignores many social and environmental externalities (for example, if the organization emits pollution but there are no costs or fines attached to the emissions), then no costs will be recognized despite the damage to the environment and society that is potentially being caused by the emissions.

Hines (1988) argues that in *communicating reality*, accountants simultaneously *construct reality*. Hence, for example, the failure to account for the effects of pollution emissions means that to many people, such emissions are non-existent. They do not appear in the accounts of the company's performance. If the accountant perhaps put a cost on such emissions then they would become 'real', and the organization would become accountable. Accounting provides a selective visibility for particular issues within an organization that dictates which financial issues are 'significant' (Carpenter and Feroz, 1992). Cooper *et al.* (1981, p. 182) also adopt this perspective in stating:

> Accounting systems encourage imitation and coercion by defining the problematic (by choosing which variables are measured and reported) and they help to fashion solutions (by choosing which variables are to be treated as

controllable). Of course, the way accounting systems are used is highly significant, but nevertheless the structure and elements of accounting systems help to create the appropriate and acceptable ways of acting, organising and talking about issues in organisations. Accounting systems are a significant component of the power system in an organization.

In exploring the role of accounting reports in 'constructing' particular 'realities', Macintosh and Baker (2002) and Macintosh (2001) draw on developments in literary theory, and argue that accounting reports can be viewed as a form of literary texts/documents. They demonstrate that in literary theory the 'expressive realism' notion that a text is an objective reflection of an underlying reality (that a novel, for example, 'acts like a mirror to reflect reality' (Macintosh and Baker, 2002, p. 189)) has long been regarded as highly problematic, and they draw on these criticisms from literary theory to demonstrate how similar assumptions of accounting reports objectively reflecting an external economic reality are equally problematic (p. 192):

> the common-sense view of accounting assumes that the financial reality of an enterprise is 'out-there' prior to its capture in accounting reports. The proper way of ascertaining this reality is thought to be with objective and verifiable measurement processes. This realist correspondence view of the accounting assumes the financial reality of a corporation exists independently of accountants, auditors, and accounting reports. Yet accounting runs up against the same problem that undermined expressive realism [in literary theory]. Different equally qualified professional accountants come up with different financial statements for identical transactions and events. (Macintosh and Baker, 2002, p. 192)

Macintosh (2001) and Macintosh and Baker (2002) then use different paradigms in literary theory to analyse and explain the subjectivity of accounting reports, and the partial views of reality constructed by these reports. They argue that any accounting report will tend to present selective and biased information in a manner designed to lead to the construction of a single view of the underlying reality, with this view being the one that most favours management and providers of capital. These academics then argue, based on poststructuralist literary theory, for accounting reports to change so they contain a sufficient variety of information to enable different users of accounts to see a variety of sometimes contradictory views of the reality underlying the business, rather than accounting information being selectively presented in an objectified manner to 'force' a single partisan view of the business.

The power of accountants through a false image of neutrality

For those people who have not previously considered accountants in the same light as do the critical theorists, there may be some form of bewilderment. How can accountants have so much power? In part, some arguments for this issue have been provided in the discussion above. The accounting profession is portrayed (through such vehicles as conceptual frameworks) as being objective and neutral – that is, free from any form of bias. Such characteristics (if true) are apparently beyond reproach. In fact, accountants are perceived as so *objective* and *neutral* that they have a reputation for being very *dull*. But if we are to believe the critical theorists, this 'dullness' is a façade that perhaps hides a great deal of social power.[14] As Carpenter and Feroz (1992, p. 618) state:

> accounting may be viewed as a means of legitimising the current social and political structure of the organisation. Hopwood (1983) further suggests that the legitimising force of accounting derives in part from the apparently dull, unobtrusive, and routine nature of accounting procedures, which generate an aura of objectivity and legitimacy in the eyes of financial statement users. Far from being dull and routine, accounting and accountants can and do take sides in social conflicts.

Tinker *et al.* (1982, p. 184), argue:

> This image of the accountant – often as a disinterested, innocuous 'historian' – stems from a desire to deny the responsibility that accountants bear for shaping subjective expectations which, in turn, affect decisions about resource allocation and the distribution of income between and within social classes. The attachment to historical facts provides a veneer of pseudo-objectivity that allows accountants to claim that they merely record – not partake in – social conflicts.

Earlier in this chapter (as well as in Chapter 3) we considered research that investigated the economic consequences of accounting requirements. Once a profession starts considering the economic consequences of particular accounting standards, it is difficult to perceive that the accounting standards, and therefore accounting, can really be considered as truly objective and neutral.

A critical accounting perspective of accounting and legitimation

Moving onto another aspect of how critical accounting researchers believe that accounting practices 'silently' and 'stealthily' reinforce capitalist power, among the other theoretical perspectives we considered earlier in this book is legitimacy theory (which we discussed in Chapter 8). We explained how organizations often use documents, such as annual reports, to legitimize the ongoing existence of the entity. While these disclosures were explained in terms of a desire by the corporation to appear to be acting in terms of the 'social contract' (which may or may not be the case), some critical theorists see the legitimation motive as potentially quite harmful, particularly if it legitimizes activities that are not in the interests of particular classes within society. As Puxty (1991, p. 39) states:

> I do not accept that I see legitimation as innocuous. It seems to me that the legitimation can be very harmful indeed, insofar as it acts as a barrier to enlightenment and hence progress.

In considering the use of social and environmental disclosures to legitimize corporate behaviour, Deegan *et al.* (2002, p. 334) state:

---

[14] We are again back to the position that we introduced in Chapter 2 – accountants are indeed very powerful individuals.

Legitimising disclosures mean that the organisation is responding to particular concerns that have arisen in relation to their operations. The implication is that unless concerns are aroused (and importantly, the managers *perceive* the existence of such concerns) then unregulated disclosures could be quite minimal. Disclosure decisions driven by the desire to be legitimate are not the same as disclosure policies driven by a management view that the community has a *right-to-know* about certain aspects of an organisation's operations. One motivation relates to survival, whereas the other motivation relates to responsibility.

Deegan *et al.* (2002, p. 335) further state:

Legitimising disclosures are linked to corporate survival. In jurisdictions where there are limited regulatory requirements to provide social and environmental information, management appear to provide information when they are coerced into doing so. Conversely, where there is limited concern, there will be limited disclosures. The evidence suggests that higher levels of disclosure will only occur when community concerns are aroused, or alternatively, until such time that specific regulation is introduced to eliminate managements' disclosure discretion. However, if corporate legitimising activities are successful then perhaps public pressure for government to introduce disclosure legislation will be low and managers will be able to retain control of their social and environmental reporting practices.

Consistent with the above discussion, according to Guthrie and Parker (1990, p. 166), the political economy perspective adopted by critical theorists emphasizes the role of accounting reports in maintaining (or legitimizing) particular social arrangements. As they state:

The political economy perspective perceives accounting reports as social, political, and economic documents. They serve as a tool for constructing, sustaining, and legitimising economic and political arrangements, institutions, and ideological themes which contribute to the corporation's private interests.

The role of accounting in legitimizing the capitalist system

Given the role of accounting reports in 'constructing, sustaining, and legitimising economic and political arrangements, institutions, and ideological themes which contribute to the corporation's private interests' (Guthrie and Parker, 1990, p. 166), the classical political economy perspective views one of the key roles of accounting reports as being to legitimize the capitalist system as a whole, and protect this system from threats arising as a result of the outcomes of the structural conflict inherent in the capitalist system (as discussed earlier in the chapter). This, for example, is part of the reason why many critical accounting scholars are opposed to much research into corporate social and environmental reporting practices, as we highlighted earlier in this chapter.

A major critical accounting empirical study, examining the role which disclosures in annual reports were argued to have played in protecting (and legitimizing) the capitalist system as a whole from the outcomes of social conflict, analysed the annual reports of the US-based car multinational General Motors over the period 1917 to 1976. This empirical material was analysed in a series of papers (Neimark, 1983; Neimark and Tinker, 1986; Tinker and Neimark, 1987, 1988; Tinker *et al.*, 1991), which demonstrated that the focus of voluntary, discursive material in the annual reports tended to change across different periods of time to address the changing challenges to capitalism arising from the structural instability of capitalism. For example, in times when the (claimed) symptoms of this structural instability were weaknesses in overall consumer demand, the annual reports focused on giving the impression that increased consumption – such as regularly buying a new car – was an ideal social norm. At other times, when a main symptom of the structural instability of capitalism was labour militancy, the focus of the core messages in the annual report switched to a demonstration that workers were better off if they acted in cooperation rather than in conflict with managers.

The argument in these studies seems to be that while successful articulation of these management viewpoints might benefit General Motors economically, through maintaining the support of economically powerful stakeholders, they also benefited the capitalist system as a whole. This was because, for example, developing a norm of consumption in times of weakened overall economic demand should result in greater demand for the products of many businesses. If many other businesses also used their annual reports, in conjunction with messages in many other media, such as advertising and newspaper articles, at this point in history to help reinforce a consistent message about the social desirability of consumption, this would help protect and advance the power and wealth of many businesses by increasing overall consumer demand. As Tinker *et al.* (1991, p. 39) state:

> The General Motors studies (Neimark, 1983, Neimark and Tinker, 1986, Tinker and Neimark, 1987, Tinker and Neimark, 1988) focus on the various ways the company uses its annual reports as an ideological weapon, and the social circumstances that govern one use rather than another … [they uncover] the conflictual and antagonistic situations that embroiled GM over that period, and the way the firm's reports were used to modify and ameliorate these conflicts … This is not to argue that annual reports have a dramatic impact on business and political decision-making. Rather, like other ideological materials (party political statements, advertising, public relations 'fluff', religious dogma) it is the repetition of the mundane and particularly the censoring of other points of view that make these reports most effective.

Chapter summary

This chapter provides an overview of research that has been undertaken by people who have been classified as working within the critical perspective of accounting. These researchers are very critical of current accounting practices. They argue that existing financial accounting practices support the current economic and social structures – structures that unfairly benefit some people at the expense of others. The view that financial accounting practices are neutral and objective (as promoted in various conceptual framework projects) is challenged.

The critical perspective of accounting covers many different specific perspectives, of which we have only had space to explore a few of the major ones in this chapter. However, at a broad level, much critical accounting research is grounded in classical political economy theory in which conflict, inequity and the role of the state are central to the analysis. While the research positions of many critical accounting scholars are informed by a Marxist critique of capitalism, there are many other critical accounting researchers whose critiques of the role of accounting in sustaining inequities in society are not based on Marxist philosophy. A common theme among most Marxist (and some non-Marxist) critical accounting theorists are calls for fundamental changes in how society is structured as, without this restructuring, they believe that any changes or modifications to accounting practices will have no effect in making society more equitable for all. Critical theorists also argue that governments (the state) tend to put in place mechanisms and regulations to support existing social structures. Many accounting researchers are also believed to be supporters of particular political ideologies with the results of their research being influential in supporting those people with privileged access to scarce capital.

Although this chapter is relatively brief, the aim has been to provide an insight into a point of view that traditionally has not received a great deal of attention in accounting education or in accounting journals. Perhaps, as the critical theorists would argue, this lack of attention is due to the fact that this branch of the accounting literature challenges so many of the views and values held not only by accountants but by many others within society. The literature can indeed be quite confronting. It does, however, provide a different perspective on the role of accountants, and one that we should not immediately dismiss. If the literature causes us to be critical of our own position as accountants within society, well and good. As a concluding quote, we can reflect on the following statement by Baker and Bettner (1997, p. 293):

> Accounting's capacity to create and control social reality translates into empowerment for those who use it. Such power resides in organisations and institutions, where it is used to instill values, sustain legitimizing myths, mask conflict and promote self-perpetuating social orders. Throughout society, the influence of accounting permeates fundamental issues concerning wealth distribution, social justice, political ideology and environmental degradation. Contrary to public opinion, accounting is not a static reflection of economic reality, but rather is a highly partisan activity.

Questions

12.1   What is a *critical perspective* of accounting?

12.2   What are some of the fundamental differences between the research undertaken by *critical theorists*, relative to the work undertaken by other accounting researchers?

12.3   From a critical perspective, what is the role of a conceptual framework project?

12.4   From a critical perspective, can financial reports ever be considered objective or neutral? Explain your answer.

12.5   If it is accepted that there are many inequities within society, would critical theorists argue that introducing more accounting, or *improved* methods of accounting, would or could help, or would they argue that such a strategy will only compound existing problems? Explain your answer. Do you agree with the position taken by the critical theorists? Why?

12.6 Critical theorists would challenge the work of authors whose work is grounded within Positive Accounting Theory. What is the basis of their opposition?

12.7 Critical theorists would challenge the work of authors whose work is grounded within legitimacy theory. What is the basis of their opposition?

12.8 If accounting is deemed to be complicit in sustaining social inequities, how would critical theorists argue that accounting can be 'fixed'?

12.9 Tinker *et al.* (1982) argue that 'the social allegiances and biases of accounting are rarely apparent; usually, they are 'masked' pretensions of objectivity and independence'. Explain the basis of this argument.

12.10 Cooper and Sherer (1984) argue that 'accounting researchers should be explicit about the normative elements of any framework adopted by them. All research is normative in the sense that it contains the researcher's value judgements about how society should be organised. However, very few accounting researchers make their value judgements explicit'. Do you agree or disagree with this claim? Why?

12.11 Explain the importance in critical accounting theory of assumptions regarding the distribution of power in society. How do these assumptions differ from those adopted in other theoretical perspectives?

12.12 Why might critical theorists be opposed to academic research that attempts to assist corporations to put a cost on their social and environmental impacts?

References

Arnold, B. & de Lange, P. (2004) 'Enron: An examination of agency problems', *Critical Perspectives on Accounting*, **15** (6–7), 751–65.

Arnold, P. (1990) 'The state and political theory in corporate social disclosure research: A response to Guthrie and Parker', *Advances in Public Interest Accounting*, **3**, 177–81.

Bailey, D., Harte, G. & Sugden, R. (2000) 'Corporate disclosure and the deregulation of international investment', *Accounting, Auditing and Accountability Journal*, **13** (2), 197–218.

Bakan, J. (2004) *The Corporation: The Pathological Pursuit of Profit and Power*, London: Constable and Robinson.

Baker, C. & Bettner, M. (1997) 'Interpretive and critical research in accounting: A commentary on its absence from mainstream accounting research', *Critical Perspectives on Accounting*, **8** (1), 293–310.

Baker, R.C. (2003) 'Investigating Enron as a public private partnership', *Accounting, Auditing and Accountability Journal*, **16** (3), 446–66.

Beder, S. (2006) *Suiting Themselves: How Corporations Drive the Global Agenda*, London: Earthscan.

Boyce, G. (2000) 'Public discourse and decision making: Exploring possibilities for financial, social and environmental accounting', *Accounting, Auditing and Accountability Journal*, **13** (1), 27–64.

Briloff, A. (2004) 'Accounting scholars in the groves of academe In Pari Delicto', *Critical Perspectives on Accounting*, **15** (6–7), 787–96.

Burchell, S., Clubb, C., Hopwood, A., Hughes, J. & Naphapiet, J. (1980) 'The roles of accounting in organizations and society', *Accounting, Organization and Society*, **5** (1), 5–28.

Carpenter, V. & Feroz, E. (1992) 'GAAP as a symbol of legitimacy: New York State's decision to adopt generally accepted accounting principles', *Accounting, Organizations and Society*, **17** (7), 613–43.

Chua, W.F. (1986) 'Radical developments in accounting thought', *The Accounting Review*, **61** (4), 601–32.

Collison, D.J. (2003) 'Corporate propaganda: Its implications for accounting and accountability', *Accounting, Auditing and Accountability Journal*, **16** (5), 853–86.

Cooper, D., Hayes, D. & Wolf, F. (1981) 'Accounting in organized anarchies', *Accounting, Organizations and Society*, **6**, 175–91.

Cooper, D.J. & Sherer, M.J. (1984) 'The value of corporate accounting reports-arguments for a political economy of accounting', *Accounting, Organizations and Society*, **9** (3/4), 207–32.

Cousins, J., Mitchell, A., Sikka, P., Cooper, C. & Arnold, P. (2000) *Insolvent Abuse: Regulating the Insolvency Industry*, Basildon: Association for Accountancy and Business Affairs.

Craig, R.J. & Amernic, J.H. (2004) 'Enron discourse: The rhetoric of a resilient capitalism', *Critical Perspectives on Accounting*, **15** (6–7), 813–52.

De George, R. (1995) 'Praxis', in: Honderich, T. (ed.) *The Oxford Companion to Philosophy*, Oxford: Oxford University Press, 713.

Deegan, C., Rankin, M. & Tobin, J. (2002) 'An examination of the corporate social and environmental disclosures of BHP from 1983–1997', *Accounting, Auditing and Accountability Journal*, **15** (3), 312–43.

Folbre, N. & Hartmann, H. (1988) 'The rhetoric of self-interest: Ideology of gender in economic theory', in: Klamer, A., McCloskey, D.N. & Solow, R.M. (eds.) *The Consequences of Economic Rhetoric*, New York: Cambridge University Press, 184–203.

Froud, J., Johal, S., Papazian, V. & Williams, K. (2004) 'The temptation of Houston: A case study for financialisation', *Critical Perspectives on Accounting*, **15** (6–7), 885–909.

Fuerman, R.D. (2004) 'Accountable accountants', *Critical Perspectives on Accounting*, **15** (6–7), 911–26.

Gray, R. (2010) 'Is accounting for sustainability actually accounting for sustainability … and how would we know? An exploration of narratives of organizations and the planet', *Accounting, Organizations and Society*, **35** (1), 47–62.

Gray, R., Owen, D. & Adams, C. (1996) *Accounting and Accountability: Changes and Challenges in Corporate Social and Environmental Reporting*, London: Prentice-Hall.

Gray, R., Owen, D. & Maunders, K. (1988) 'Corporate social reporting: Emerging trends in accountability and the social contract', *Accounting, Auditing and Accountability Journal*, **1** (1), 6–20.

Gray, R., Owen, D. & Maunders, K.T. (1987) *Corporate Social Reporting: Accounting and Accountability*, Hemel Hempstead: Prentice-Hall.

Guthrie, J. & Parker, L. (1990) 'Corporate social disclosure practice: A comparative international analysis', *Advances in Public Interest Accounting*, **3**, 159–75.

Hines, R. (1988) 'Financial accounting: In communicating reality, we construct reality', *Accounting Organizations and Society*, **13** (3), 251–62.

Hines, R. (1991) 'The FASBs conceptual framework, financial accounting and the maintenance of the social world', *Accounting Organizations and Society*, **16** (4), 313–51.

Hofstede, G. (1984) 'Cultural dimensions in management and planning', *Asia Pacific Journal of Management*, **1** (2), 81–99.

Hopper, T., Annisette, M., Dastoor, N., Uddin, S. & Wickramasinghe, D. (1995) 'Some challenges and alternatives to positive accounting research', in: Jones, S., Romano, C. & Ratnatunga, J. (eds.) *Accounting Theory: A Contemporary Review*. Sydney: Harcourt Brace.

Hopper, T. & Powell, A. (1985) 'Making sense of research into the organizational and social aspects of management accounting: A review of its underlying assumptions', *Journal of Management Studies*, **22** (5), 429–65.

Hopwood, A.G. (1983) 'On trying to study accounting in the context in which it operates', *Accounting, Organizations and Society*, **8** (2/3), 287–305.

Hopwood, A.G., Unerman, J. & Fries, J. (eds.) (2010) *Accounting for Sustainability: Practical Insights*, London: Earthscan.

Kovel, J. (2002) *The Enemy of Nature: The End of Capitalism or the End of the World?*, London: Zed Books.

Lehman, G. (1999) 'Disclosing new worlds: A role for social and environmental accounting and auditing', *Accounting, Organizations and Society*, **24** (3), 217–42.

Lehman, G. (2001) 'Reclaiming the public sphere: Problems and prospects for corporate social and environmental accounting', *Critical Perspectives on Accounting*, **12**, 713–33.

Macintosh, N.B. (2001) *Accounting, Accountants and Accountability*, London: Routledge.

Macintosh, N.B. & Baker, R.C. (2002) 'A literary theory perspective on accounting: Towards heteroglossic accounting reports', *Accounting, Auditing and Accountability Journal*, **15** (2), 184–222.

Marx, K. & Engels, F. (1967) *The Communist Manifesto*, Harmondsworth: Penguin.

Merino, B. & Neimark, M. (1982) 'Disclosure regulation and public policy: A socio-historical appraisal', *Journal of Accounting and Public Policy*, **1**, 33–57.

Miliband, E. (1969) *The State in Capitalist Society*, London: Weidenfeld & Nicholson.

Miliband, E. (1983) 'State power and class interest', *New Left Review* (March), 57–68.

Mitchell, A., Puxty, A., Sikka, P. & Willmott, H. (1994) 'Ethical statements as smokescreens for sectional interests: The case of the UK accountancy profession', *Journal of Business Ethics*, **13** (1), 39–51.

Moore, D.C. (1991) 'Accounting on trial: The critical legal studies movement and its lessons for radical accounting', *Accounting, Organizations and Society*, **16** (8), 763–91.

Mouck, T. (1992) 'The rhetoric of science and the rhetoric of revolt in the story of positive accounting theory', *Accounting, Auditing and Accountability Journal*, **5**, 35–56.

Neimark, M. (1983) *The Social Constructions of Annual Reports: A Radical Approach to Corporate Control*, unpublished PhD thesis, New York University.

Neimark, M. & Tinker, A. (1986) 'The social construction of management control systems', *Accounting, Organization and Society*, **11** (3), 369–96.

Nelson, J.A. (1992) 'Gender, metaphor, and the definition of economics', *Economics and Philosophy*, **8** (01), 103–25.

Neu, D. & Cooper, D. (1997) 'Accounting interventions', in: *Fifth Interdisciplinary Perspectives on Accounting Conference*, University of Manchester.

O'Connell, B.T. (2004) 'Enron. Con: "He that filches from me my good name … makes me poor indeed"', *Critical Perspectives on Accounting*, **15** (6–7), 733–49.

O'Dwyer, B. (2005) 'The construction of a social account: A case study in an overseas aid agency', *Accounting, Organizations and Society*, **30** (3), 279–96.

Offe, C. & Ronge, V. (1978) 'Theses on the theory of the state', in: Giddens, A. & Held, D. (eds.) *Class, Power and Conflict*, London: Edward Arnold, 32–39.

Owen, D., Gray, R. & Bebbington, J. (1997) 'Green accounting: Cosmetic irrelevance or radical agenda for change?', *Asia-Pacific Journal of Accounting*, **4** (2), 175–98.

Puxty, A. (1986) 'Social accounting as immanent legitimation: A critique of a technist ideology', *Advances in Public Interest Accounting*, **4**, 95–112.

Puxty, A. (1991) 'Social accountability and universal pragmatics', *Advances in Public Interest Accounting*, **4**, 35–46.

Puxty, A., Sikka, P. & Willmott, H. (1994) '(Re)Forming the circle: Education, ethics and accountancy practices', *Accounting Education*, **3** (1), 77–92.

Reiter, S. (1995) 'Theory and politics: lessons from feminist economics', *Accounting, Auditing and Accountability Journal*, **8** (3), 34–59.

Roslender, R. (2006) 'Critical theory', in: Hoque, Z. (ed.) *Methodological Issues in Accounting Research: Theories and Method*, London: Spiramus Press, 247–70.

Selto, F. & Neumann, B. (1981) 'A further guide to research on the economic consequences of accounting information', *Accounting and Business Research*, **11** (44), 317–22.

Sikka, P., Wearing, B. & Nayak, A. (1999) *No Accounting for Exploitation*, Basildon: Association for Accountancy and Business Affairs.

Sikka, P. & Willmott, H. (2005) 'The withering of tolerance and communication in interdisciplinary accounting studies', *Accounting, Auditing and Accountability Journal*, **18** (1), 136–46.

Solomons, D. (1978) 'The politicization of accounting', *Journal of Accountancy*, **146** (5), 65–72.

Thompson, G. (1978) 'Capitalist profit calculation and inflation accounting', *Economy and Society*, 395–429.

Tinker, A. & Gray, R. (2003) 'Beyond a critique of pure reason: From policy to politics and praxis in environmental and social research', *Accounting, Auditing and Accountability Journal*, **16** (5), 727–61.

Tinker, A., Lehman, C. & Neimark, M. (1991) 'Falling down the hole in the middle of the road: Political quietism in corporate social reporting', *Accounting, Auditing and Accountability Journal*, **4** (1), 28–54.

Tinker, A. & Neimark, M. (1987) 'The role of annual reports in gender and class contradictions at General Motors: 1917–1976', *Accounting, Organizations and Society*, **12** (1), 71–88.

Tinker, A. & Neimark, M. (1988) 'The struggle over meaning in accounting and corporate research: A comparative evaluation of conservative and critical historiography', *Accounting, Auditing and Accountability Journal*, **1** (1), 55–74.

Tinker, A.M., Merino, B.D. & Neimark, M.D. (1982) 'The normative origins of positive theories: Ideology and accounting thought', *Accounting Organizations and Society*, **7** (2), 167–200.

Tinker, T. (2005) 'The withering of criticism: A review of professional, Foucauldian, ethnographic, and epistemic studies in accounting', *Accounting, Auditing and Accountability Journal*, **18** (1), 100–35.

Unerman, J. & Bennett, M. (2004) 'Increased stakeholder dialogue and the internet: towards greater corporate accountability or reinforcing capitalist hegemony?', *Accounting, Organizations and Society*, **29** (7), 685–707.

Unerman, J. & O'Dwyer, B. (2004) 'Enron, WorldCom, Andersen *et al*: A challenge to modernity', *Critical Perspectives on Accounting*, **15** (6–7), 971–93.

Williams, P. F. (2004) 'You reap what you sow: The ethical discourse of professional accounting', *Critical Perspectives on Accounting*, **15** (6–7), 995–1001.

Willmott, H. (1990) 'Serving the public interest', in: Cooper, D.J. & Hopper, T.M. (eds.) *Critical Accounts*, London: Macmillan.

Wood, A. (1995) 'Marx, Karl Heinrich', in: Honderich, T. (ed.) *The Oxford Companion to Philosophy*, Oxford: Oxford University Press, 523–26.

Zeff, S.A. (1978) 'The rise of economic consequences', *Journal of Accountancy*, **146** (6), 56–63.

Zimmerman, M.E. (1984) *Contesting Earth's Future: Radical Ecology and Postmodernity*, London: University of California Press.

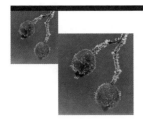

Index